Frommer's®

Paris 2002

This dazzling rose window illuminates the interior of Notre Dame. See chapter 7.
© John Elk III Photography.

Paris's flowers are a feast for the eyes and the nose. The biggest market is on the Ile de la Cité, along the Seine—see chapter 9. © Robert Holmes Photography.

Paris glows by night. See chapter 7 for details on enjoying the view from a bateau-mouche cruise along the Seine. © Malcolm/Image Bank.

Basilique du Sacré-Coeur looms high above Montmartre, offering one of the best views of Paris. See chapters 7 & 8. © John Elk III Photography.

Cliché or not, the Jardin des Tuileries has long been a favorite spot for lovers. See chapter 7.
© Bryan F. Peterson/The Stock Market.

The ever controversial, inside-out Pompidou Centre is known locally as Beaubourg. See chapter 7 for a description of this museum of modern art. © Matthew Weinreb/Image Bank.

The Hôtel de Ville is not a hotel at all, but Paris's City Hall. See chapter 7 for the gruesome history of the building's site. © Catherine Karnow Photography.

If Paris had nothing else to offer, many would still flock here for the food. See chapter 6 for our favorite bakeries, and chapter 9 for our favorite places to buy fresh produce, chocolate, and other foodstuffs. Top © Steven Rothfeld/Tony Stone Images; bottom © Bill Gallery/Viesti Associates, Inc.; opposite © Robert Holmes Photography.

Notre Dame is at the very center of
Paris, geographically and historically. See chapter 7 for the story of
the city's most famous church.
Opposite © Kevin Galvin Photography;
left © Harald Sund/Image Bank;
below © Herbert Hartmann/Image Bank.

Even subway stations can be works of art in Paris. This Art-Nouveau subway entrance is at Port Dauphine. See chapter 2 for details on the city's art and architecture.
© Stephen Studd/Tony Stone Images.

Even if you don't buy anything, Galeries Lafayette department store is worth visiting for its grandiose turn-of-the-century architecture. See chapter 9. © Romilly Lockyer/Image Bank.

The Louvre, with the controversial glass pyramid in its courtyard, lives up to its reputation as one of the world's greatest museums. See chapter 7. Opposite © Kevin Galvin Photography; above © Dave Bartruff Photography.

The Picasso Museum offers a more intimate museum experience. See chapter 7. © Catherine Karnow Photography.

The Château of Versailles is a tribute to the folly and opulence of France's grand century. Its Hall of Mirrors (bottom photo) was the setting for the treaty that ended World War I. See chapter 11. *Both photos © Robert Holmes Photography.*

Giverny, home of Impressionist painter Claude Monet, makes for a lovely and inspiring getaway from the city. See chapter 11. *Above © Robert Holmes Photography; left © James Martin/Tony Stone Images.*

The Eiffel Tower casts a romantic glow over the City of Light. See chapter 7 for details on the famous tower and its nightly light shows. © *Hollenbeck Photography.*

When should I travel to get the best airfare?
Where do I go for answers to my travel questions?
What's the best and easiest way to plan and book my trip?

frommers.travelocity.com

Frommer's, the travel guide leader, has teamed up with **Travelocity.com,** the leader in online travel, to bring you an in-depth, easy-to-use resource designed to help you plan and book your trip online.

At **frommers.travelocity.com**, you'll find free online updates about your destination from the experts at Frommer's plus the outstanding travel planning and purchasing features of Travelocity.com. Travelocity.com provides reservations capabilities for 95 percent of all airline seats sold, more than 47,000 hotels, and over 50 car rental companies. In addition, Travelocity.com offers more than 2,000 exciting vacation and cruise packages. Travelocity.com puts you in complete control of your travel planning with these and other great features:

Expert travel guidance from Frommer's - over 150 writers reporting from around the world!

Best Fare Finder - an interactive calendar tells you when to travel to get the best airfare

Fare Watcher - we'll track airfare changes to your favorite destinations

Dream Maps - a mapping feature that suggests travel opportunities based on your budget

Shop Safe Guarantee - 24 hours a day / 7 days a week live customer service, and more!

Whether traveling on a tight budget, looking for a quick weekend getaway, or planning the trip of a lifetime, Frommer's guides and Travelocity.com will make your travel dreams a reality. You've bought the book, now book the trip!

A New Star-Rating System & Other Exciting News from Frommer's!

In our continuing effort to publish the savviest, most up-to-date, and most appealing travel guides available, we've added some great new features.

Frommer's guides now include a new **star-rating system.** Every hotel, restaurant, and attraction is rated from 0 to 3 stars to help you set priorities and organize your time.

We've also added **seven brand-new features** that point you to the great deals, in-the-know advice, and unique experiences that separate travelers from tourists. Throughout the guide look for:

Finds	Special finds—those places only insiders know about
Fun Fact	Fun facts—details that make travelers more informed and their trips more fun
Kids	Best bets for kids—advice for the whole family
Moments	Special moments—those experiences that memories are made of
Overrated	Places or experiences not worth your time or money
Tips	Insider tips—some great ways to save time and money
Value	Great values—where to get the best deals

We've also added a **"What's New"** section in every guide—a timely crash course in what's hot and what's not in every destination we cover.

Other Great Guides for Your Trip:

Frommer's Paris from $80 a Day

Frommer's Irreverent Guide to Paris

Paris For Dummies

Unofficial Guide to Paris

Frommer's Memorable Walks in Paris

Frommer's Born to Shop Paris

Frommer's France

France For Dummies

Hanging Out in France

Frommer's Food Lover's Companion to France

Frommer's France's Best Bed & Breakfasts & Country Inns

Frommer's Europe

Frommer's Europe from $70 a Day

Paris

2002

by Darwin Porter & Danforth Prince

Here's what the critics say about Frommer's:

"Amazingly easy to use. Very portable, very complete."

—*Booklist*

"The only mainstream guide to list specific prices. The Walter Cronkite of guidebooks—with all that implies."

—*Travel & Leisure*

"Complete, concise, and filled with useful information."

—*New York Daily News*

"Hotel information is close to encyclopedic."

—*Des Moines Sunday Register*

Best-Selling Books • Digital Downloads • e-Books • Answer Networks
e-Newsletters • Branded Web Sites • e-Learning
New York, NY • Cleveland, OH • Indianapolis, IN

About the Author

Veteran travel writers **Darwin Porter** and **Danforth Prince** have written numerous best-selling Frommer's guides, notably to France, Italy, England, and Germany. Porter, who was bureau chief for the *Miami Herald* when he was 21, has lived in Paris periodically and written about the city for many years. For several years, Prince lived in the city as a member of the Paris bureau of the *New York Times*.

Published by:

Hungry Minds, Inc.

909 Third Ave.
New York, NY 10022

ISBN 0-7645-6481-1
ISSN 0899-3203

Editor: Lisa Torrance
Production Editor: Christina Van Camp
Cartographer: Nicholas Trotter
Photo Editor: Richard Fox
Chapter 2 illustrations by Rashell Smith and Karl Brandt
Production by Hungry Minds Indianapolis Production Services

Front cover photo: © Chad Ehlers/Tony Stone Images
Back cover photo: © Adina Tovy/Photo 20-20

Special Sales

For general information on Hungry Minds' products and services please contact our Customer Care department; within the U.S. at 800-762-2974, outside the U.S. at 317-572-3993 or fax 317-572-4002. For sales inquiries and reseller information, including discounts, bulk sales, customized editions, and premium sales, please contact our Customer Care department at 800-434-3422.

Manufactured in the United States of America

5   4   3   2   1

Contents

List of Maps

An Invitation to the Reader

In researching this book, we discovered many wonderful places—hotels, restaurants, shops, and more. We're sure you'll find others. Please tell us about them, so we can share the information with your fellow travelers in upcoming editions. If you were disappointed with a recommendation, we'd love to know that, too. Please write to:

Frommer's Paris 2002
Hungry Minds, Inc. • 909 Third Avenue • New York, NY 10022

An Additional Note

Please be advised that travel information is subject to change at any time—and this is especially true of prices. We therefore suggest that you write or call ahead for confirmation when making your travel plans. The authors, editors, and publisher cannot be held responsible for the experiences of readers while traveling. Your safety is important to us, however, so we encourage you to stay alert and be aware of your surroundings. Keep a close eye on cameras, purses, and wallets, all favorite targets of thieves and pickpockets.

New! Frommer's Star Ratings & Icons

Every hotel, restaurant and attraction listing in this guide has been ranked for quality, value, service, amenities, and special features using a star-rating scale. In country, state, and regional guides, we also rate towns and regions to help you narrow down your choices and budget your time accordingly. Hotels and restaurants in the Very Expensive and Expensive categories are rated on a scale of one (highly recommended) to three stars (exceptional). Those in the Moderate and Inexpensive categories rate from zero (recommended) to two stars (very highly recommended). Attractions, towns, and regions are rated according to the following scale: zero stars (recommended), one star (highly recommended), two stars (very highly recommended), and three stars (must-see).

In addition to the rating system, we also use seven icons to highlight insider information, useful tips, special bargains, hidden gems, memorable experiences, kid-friendly venues, places to avoid, and other useful information:

| Finds | Fun Fact | Kids | Moments | Overrated | Tips | Value |

The following abbreviations are used for credit cards:

| AE | American Express | DC | Diners Club | V | Visa |
| DISC | Discover | MC | MasterCard | | |

FROMMERS.COM

Now that you have the guidebook to a great trip, visit our website at **www.frommers.com** for travel information on nearly 2,000 destinations. With features updated regularly, we give you instant access to the most current trip-planning information available. At Frommers.com, you'll also find the best prices on air fares, accommodations, and car rentals—and you can even book travel online through our travel booking partners. At Frommers.com you'll also find the following:

• Daily Newsletter highlighting the best travel deals
• Hot Spot of the Month/Vacation Sweepstakes & Travel Photo Contest
• More than 200 Travel Message Boards
• Outspoken Newsletters and Feature Articles on travel bargains, vacation ideas, tips & resources, and more!

What's New in Paris

Paris continues to reinvent itself. We visit anew for the memories and the evocative cityscapes, but we are forever searching for what is cutting edge. As has often been noted, Paris is a city of contradiction—one that remains the same, one that is eternal, but one that is forever changing.

PLANNING YOUR TRIP TO PARIS **American Airlines** now flies into Roissy-Charles de Gaulle instead of Orly Airport. Facilities at its new terminal, 2A, include a deluxe Admirals Club, plus a mammoth Arrivals Lounge complete with 10 showers for those on long flights across continents. For more on not only American but all other major airlines flying into Paris, see chapter 3.

GETTING TO KNOW THE CITY OF LIGHT A century old, the **Paris Métro** will soon become one of the most modern and efficient in the world. At its centenary in the summer of 2000, the Métro announced a gigantic overhaul program that will refurbish some 200 of the system's nearly 300 stations by 2003. As central Paris grows more expensive, artists are flocking to the **11th arrondissement,** which is becoming "blue collar chic," as galleries, hip bars, and trendy restaurants move in. For more about the developments of Paris, refer to chapter 4.

WHERE TO STAY The restoration of two of the most famous French *luxe* hotels in the world are attracting the well-heeled to Paris. **Four Seasons Hôtel George V,** 31 Ave. George V

(② **800/332-3442**), opened in 1928 but had grown into a lovely relic of fading grandeur until a prince of the Saudi Arabian royal family, its owner, closed it for 2 years for a major renovation. He ordered that the rooms and suites be reduced from 300 to 245, which virtually eliminated any small units. The merely rich are also flocking to the **Hôtel Meurice,** 228 rue de Rivoli, 1st arr. (② **01-44-58-10-10**), which also benefited from an ambitious 2-year renovation. Immediately after its opening, the new Meurice has been hailed as a success—from its Art Nouveau–style glass roof (covered back in the '60s and now aglow once again) to its even larger apartment-style guest rooms (it too reduced the size of the room count to make for more generous living space). Just when Parisians thought that no one could come up with another town-house hotel to rival existing competition, along came **Hôtel Sofitel Trocadéro Dokhan,** 117 rue de Lauriston, 16th arr. (② **01-53-65-66-88**). There is no place in Paris that feels more like a family *pied-à-terre.* Even the lobby's ecru toile curtains were hand sewn with the care of an haute-couture gown. On the ground floor, you find the only champagne bar in Paris. For more information about these hotels and all other new arrivals, see chapter 5, "Where to Stay."

WHERE TO DINE Parisians are flocking to the latest restaurant craze, dining at **Georges,** the utterly fashionable new Paris restaurant atop the

Centre Pompidou, 4th arr. (© **01-44-78-47-99**). This chic rendezvous commands miles of space, including a trio of gigantic aluminum "pods" shielding the kitchen. At tables made from sandblasted glass, diners feed on an elegantly refined cuisine that mixes both the French and Italian kitchens and also turns to Asia for inspiration. The only five-star Michelin chef in Paris, Alain Ducasse, has installed himself as the culinary guru at **Restaurant Plaza Athénée,** 25 Ave. Montaigne, 8th arr. (© **01-53-67-65-00**), and the well-heeled foodies of Paris are flocking to his new precincts in this *luxe* hotel. Ducasse is a far bigger sensation in Paris than he is in New York. Those gourmets who find Ducasse old hat secure a reservation at **Les Elysées du Vernet,** in the Hôtel Vernet, 25 rue Vernet, 8th arr. (© **01-44-31-98-98**). Here a fast-rising gastronomic wonder is the Montpellier-born chef, Alan Solivérès. He is currently the hot dining ticket for *tout Paris.* For news about these developments, and many others, refer to chapter 6, "Where to Dine."

EXPLORING PARIS   Everyone knows about the views from the Eiffel Tower and Sacré-Coeur. Savvy travelers are learning of another great panoramic view. Take the elevator and some stairs to the 11th floor at the top of the **Samaritaine** department store (No. 2) at 19 rue de la Monnaie, 1st arr. (© **01-40-41-20-20**). At 245 feet, a 360-degree panorama sweeps across Paris, taking in the bridge, pont Neuf, and absorbing the dome of Invalides, before sweeping over to the cathedral at Notre Dame. Just inaugurated is a new garden that's a return to the Middle Ages at the Left Bank **Musée National du Moyen Age** at 6 place Paul-Painlevé, 5th arr. (© **01-53-73-78-00**). The garden was inspired by the luxuriant detail of the museum's most fabled treasure, the 15th century tapestry of *The Lady of the Unicorn.*

It's small but richly planted and rests under chestnuts and sycamores. The incandescent **Eiffel Tower** stole the millennium show as the best act in Europe, and the good news is that it's here to stay for years to come. The tower, dressed in diamond-like sparkles, will continue its special 10-minute light show every hour. For these and other developments, refer to "Exploring Paris," chapter 7.

SHOPPING   In the late summer of 2000, **Paris Art Market** emerged as "the place to go" on a Sunday. The Art Market at the foot of Montparnasse Tower is like an open-air gallery and has done much to restore the reputation of Montparnasse as a *quartier* for artists. Parisians continue their love affair with pastry. **Fauchon,** 26 Place de la Madeleine, 8th arr. (© **01-47-42-90-10**), the greatest food emporium in Paris, has opened a new tea salon, which showcases the talents of that greatest of pâtissiers, Sébastien Gaudard. For more details, refer to chapter 9, "Shopping."

PARIS AFTER DARK   The creators of Buddha Bar, currently the hottest table reservation in Paris, now have a place to invite you after your dinner. It's the **Barrio Latino,** 46 rue de Faubourg St-Antoine, 4th arr. (© **01-55-78-84-75**), spread over four levels of a gutted Eiffel building near Place de la Bastille.

SIDE TRIPS FROM PARIS   The gardeners of **Versailles** claim (in French, of course) that it's an ill wind that doesn't blow someone some good. Before a crippling storm at Christmas in 1999, many of their trees were too tall, weak, aged, and diseased. The storms took care of that, uprooting such classics as Marie Antoinette's much loved Virginia tulip tree planted in 1783. With $40 million in funds allocated, the park is being restored to the way it was in the heyday of the Sun King, Louis XIV.

The Best of Paris

The discovery of the City of Light and the experience of making it your own is and always has been the most compelling reason to visit. If you're a first-timer, everything in Paris, of course, will be new to you. If you've been away for a while, expect changes: Taxi drivers may no longer correct your fractured French but address you in English—and that's tantamount to a revolution. More Parisians have a rudimentary knowledge of English, and the country, at least at first glance, seems less hysterically xenophobic than in past years—spending your much-needed francs or euros, you likely won't be looked at as an "ugly American" anymore. Part of this derives from Parisians' interest in music, videos, and films from foreign countries, and part is caused by France's growing awareness of its role within a united Europe.

Yet France has never been more concerned about the loss of its identity, as it continues to attract an increasing number of immigrants from its former colonies. Many have expressed concern that the country will lose the battle to keep its language strong, distinct, and unadulterated by foreign (particularly American) slang or catchwords (*le weekend,* for example). In fact, the rancor of France's collective xenophobia has been increasingly redirected toward the many immigrants seeking better lives in Paris, where the infrastructure has nearly been stretched to its limits.

Though Paris is in flux culturally and socially, it lures travelers for the same reasons it always has. You'll still find grand old sights like the Tour Eiffel, Notre-Dame, the Arc de Triomphe, Sacré-Coeur, and all those atmospheric cafes, as well as trendy new projects like the Grand Arche de La Défense, the Cité des Sciences et de l'Industrie, the Cité de la Musique, and the Bibliothéque François-Mitterrand. And don't forget the parks, gardens, and squares; the Champs-Elysées and other grand boulevards; and the river Seine and its quays. Paris's beauty is still overwhelming, especially in the illumination of night, when it certainly is the City of Light.

1 Frommer's Favorite Paris Experiences

- **Whiling Away an Afternoon in a Parisian Cafe:** The cafe is where passionate meetings of writers, artists, philosophers, thinkers, and revolutionaries once took place (perhaps still do). Parisians stop by their favorite cafes to meet current lovers and friends, to make new ones, or to sit in solitude with a newspaper or book. Whether you order a small coffee or the most expensive cognac in the house, nobody will hurry you from your invaluable viewpoint on Paris life. For our recommendations, see "The Top Cafes" in chapter 6.

- **Taking Afternoon Tea à la Française:** Drinking tea in London has its charm, but the Parisian *salon de thé* is unique. Skip over those cucumber-and-watercress sandwiches and delve into a luscious dessert like the Mont Blanc, a creamy purée of sweetened chestnuts and meringue once beloved by the Aga Khan. The grandest Parisian tea salon is **Angélina,** but you might also want to stop by **Berthillon,** especially if you want to try one of its scrumptious ice creams, or the **Café/Restaurant/Salon de Thé Bernardaud,** especially if you want your tea served on gorgeous Bernardaud porcelain. See chapter 6 for details on all three.

- **Strolling Along the Seine:** Such painters as Sisley, Turner, and Monet have fallen under the Seine's spell. On its banks, lovers still walk hand in hand, anglers still cast their lines, and *bouquinistes* still peddle their mix of postcards, 100-year-old pornography, and tattered histories of Indochina. Clochards still seek a home for the night under its bridges, and the Bateaux-Mouches still ply its waters. For a spectacular view of the Louvre, cross the city's first iron bridge, the pont des Arts, one of only four pedestrian bridges. Paris's oldest and most famous bridge is the ironically named pont-Neuf (New Bridge), from where you have an excellent view of the Palais de Justice and Sainte-Chapelle on Ile de la Cité. For more details about the sights and moments of Paris, refer to chapter 7.

- **Spending a Day at the Races:** Paris boasts eight tracks for horse racing. The most famous and the classiest is **Longchamp,** in the Bois de Boulogne, the site of the Prix de l'Arc de Triomphe and Grand Prix (see chapter 7). These and other top races are major social events, so you'll have to dress up (buy your outfit on rue du Faubourg St-Honoré—see

entry below). Take the Métro to Porte d'Auteuil, then a special bus from there to the track. The racing newspaper *Paris Turf* and weekly entertainment magazines have details about race times.

- **Calling on the Dead:** You don't have to be a ghoul to be thrilled by a visit to Europe's most famous cemetery: **Père-Lachaise.** You can pay your respects to the likes of Jim Morrison, Gertrude Stein and Alice B. Toklas, Oscar Wilde, Yves Montand and Simone Signoret, Edith Piaf, Isadora Duncan, Abélard and Héloïse, Frédéric Chopin, Marcel Proust, Eugène Delacroix, and more. And the residents aren't the only fascination—the tomb designs are intriguing and often eerie. Laid out in 1803 on a hill in Ménilmontant, the cemetery offers a surprise a minute with its bizarre monuments, unexpected views, and ornate sculpture. See chapter 7 for details.

- **Discovering Hidden Montmartre:** This is Paris's most touristy area. However, far removed from the area's top draw, Sacré-Coeur awaits the neighborhood of the true Montmartrois. Wander the back streets away from the souvenir shops. Arm yourself with a good map and seek out such streets as rue Lepic (refresh yourself at the Lux Bar at no. 12), rue Constance, rue Tholozé (with its view over the Paris rooftops), rue des Abbesses, and rue Germain-Pilon. None of these is famous, but each boasts buildings whose detailing shows the pride and care permeating Paris's architecture. Flank out from these and discover dozens of other streets on your own. At dusk, sit on Sacré-Coeur's top steps and watch as Paris turns into the City of Light. For a walking tour of Montmartre, see chapter 8.

- **Checking Out the Marchés:** A daily Parisian ritual is ambling through one of the open-air markets to buy fresh food—perhaps a properly creamy Camembert or a pumpkin-gold cantaloupe—to be eaten before sundown. You can take part in this time-honored tradition by purchasing the makings for a picnic in a park or even in your room. Like artists, the vendors arrange their wares into a mosaic of vibrant colors: Sanguine, an Italian citrus with juice the color of a brilliant orange sunset; ruby-red peppers; and golden-yellow bananas from Martinique—all dazzle the eye. Our favorite market is on rue Montorgeuil, beginning at rue Rambuteau, 1st arr. (Métro: Les Halles). On mornings at this grubby little cluster of food stalls, we've spotted some of France's finest chefs stocking up for the day. For more details on shops and shopping, refer to chapter 9.

- **Window-Shopping in the Faubourg St-Honoré:** In the 1700s, the wealthiest of Parisians resided in the faubourg St-Honoré; today the quarter is home to stores catering to the rich, particularly on rue du faubourg St-Honoré and avenue Montaigne. Even if you don't buy anything, it's great to window-shop big names like Hermès, Dior, Laroche, Courrèges, Cardin, and Saint-Laurent. If you want to browse in the stores, be sure to dress the part. See chapter 9 for the lowdown on these boutiques.

- **Exploring Ile de la Cité's Flower Market:** A fine finish to any Monday to Saturday spent meandering along the Seine is a stroll through the **Marché aux Fleurs,** place Louis-Lépine (see chapter 9). Here you can buy rare flowers, the gems of the French Riviera, bouquets that have inspired artists throughout the centuries. Even the most basic hotel room will feel like a luxury suite once you fill it with bunches of carnations, lavender, roses, tulips, and the like. On Sunday, the area is transformed into the famed **Marché aux Oiseaux,** where you can admire rare birds from around the world.

- **Going Gourmet at Fauchon:** An exotic world of food, **Fauchon** (see chapter 9) offers more than 20,000 products from around the globe. Everything you never knew you were missing is in aisle after aisle of coffees, spices, pastries, fruits, vegetables, rare Armagnacs, and much more. Take your pick: Tonganese mangoes, Scottish smoked salmon, preserved cocks' combs, Romanian rose-petal jelly, blue-red Indian pomegranates, golden Tunisian dates (only from the most famous oasis), larks stuffed with foie gras, dark morels from France's rich soil, Finnish reindeer's tongue, century-old eggs from China, and a Creole punch from Martinique reputed to be the best anywhere.

- **Attending a Free Concert:** Summer brings one of the joys of Paris: free concerts in parks and churches all over the city. Pick up an entertainment weekly for details. Some of the best concerts are held at the **American Church in Paris,** 65 quai d'Orsay, 7th arr. (© **01-40-62-05-00;** Métro: Alma-Marceau; RER: Pont de l'Alma). **Sainte-Chapelle** is known for its splendid concerts several times a week; call the box office at 4 bd. du Palais, 1st arr. (© **01-53-73-78-50;** Métro: Cité). For more concerts, refer to chapter 10.

- **Attending a Ballet or an Opera:** In 1989, the **Opéra Bastille** was inaugurated to compete with the grande dame of the music scene, the **Opéra Garnier,** which then was reserved for dance only and soon closed for renovations. The Garnier reopened a few years ago, and opera has joined dance in the rococo splendor created by Charles Garnier, beneath a controversial ceiling by Chagall. The modern Bastille, France's largest opera house, with curtains by designer Issey Miyake, features opera and symphony performances in four concert halls (its main hall seats 2,700). Whether for a performance of Bizet or Tharp, dress with pomp and circumstance. See chapter 10 for details on both houses.

• **Watching the Show at the Folies-Bergère:** Often denounced, the campy showcase at the **Folies-Bergère** (see chapter 10) has been pleasing audiences since 1868, even though classic acts like Maurice Chevalier, Mistinguett, and Josephine Baker (who performed her famous banana dance here) vanished long ago. True, the Tour Eiffel cancan is a bit corny and the show has become less daring, but those ladies in their sequins, feathers, and pom-poms still evoke an older Paris, immortalized on a Manet canvas. The show, tacky or not, seems to go on forever. See chapter 10 for details.

• **Sipping Cocktails at Willi's:** Back in the early 1970s, the first-timer to Paris might have arrived with a copy of Hemingway's *A Moveable Feast* and, taking the author's endorsement to heart, headed for Harry's Bar at "Sank roo doe Noo." Harry's is still around but now draws an older, conservative clientele. Today's chic younger expats head for **Willi's Wine Bar** (see chapter 10), where the long-haired young bartenders are mostly English, as are the waitresses, dressed in Laura Ashley garb. The place is like an informal club for Brits, Australians, and Yanks, especially in the afternoon. Some 300 wines await your selection.

2 Best Hotel Bets

For full details on the following hotels, turn to chapter 5.

• **Best Newcomer:** A hotel that has been around as long as the **Hôtel Meurice,** 228 rue Rivoli, 1st arr. (✆ **01-44-58-10-10**), isn't exactly a newborn infant. Yet it is. Emerging after a spectacular 2-year renovation, this landmark faces the 21st century reborn, and it's better than ever. Media darlings check in for a touch of Right Bank elegance and glamour—and so can you.

• **Best for Business Travelers:** Corporate types from all over the world converge at the **Hôtel Balzac,** 6 rue Balzac, 8th arr. (✆ **01-44-35-18-00**), a Belle-Époque town house with a good business center 2 blocks from many of the business offices along the Champs-Elysées. Its restaurant serves some of the best food in town and is suitable for entertaining clients.

• **Best for Families:** An affordable Left Bank choice is the **Hôtel de Fleurie,** 32–34 rue Grègoire-de-Tours, 6th arr. (✆ **01-53-73-70-00**), in the heart of St-Germain-des-Prés. The accommodations are thoughtfully appointed, and many connecting rooms with two large beds are perfect for families. Children under 12 stay free with their parents.

• **Best Value:** Not far from the Champs-Elysées, the **Résidence Lord Byron,** 5 rue de

Chateaubriand, 8th arr. (☎ 01-43-59-89-98), is a classy little getaway that's far from opulent but is clean and comfortable and worth every franc. Another good choice is the **Hôtel de Lutèce,** 65 rue St-Louis-en-l'Ile, 4th arr. (☎ 01-43-26-23-52). The hotel resembles a Breton country house and has flourished despite forever refusing to raise its rates. Its rooms, with antiques and fine reproductions, provide an affordable elegance.

- **Best Location:** Lying only a 2-minute walk from Paris's most historic and most beautiful square, **Hôtel de la Place des Vosges,** 12 rue de Birague, 4th arr. (☎ 01-42-72-60-46), is a little charmer. In a building 350 years old, it is small scale and inviting, with some decorative touches that evoke the era of Louis XIII.

- **Best View:** Of the 32 rooms at the **Hôtel du Quai-Voltaire,** 19 quai Voltaire, 7th arr. (☎ 01-42-61-50-91), 28 open onto views of the Seine. If you stay here, you'll be following in the footsteps of Wilde, Baudelaire, and Wagner. This 17th-century abbey was transformed into a hotel back in 1856 and ever since has been welcoming guests who appreciate its tattered charms.

- **Best for Nostalgia:** If you yearn for a Left Bank "literary" address, make it the **Odéon-Hôtel,** 3 rue de l'Odéon, 6th arr. (☎ 01-43-25-90-67), in the heart of the 6th arrondissement, filled with the ghosts of Gide, Hemingway, Fitzgerald, Joyce, and Stein and Toklas. Evoking a Norman country inn, this hotel of considerable charm lures guests with its high, crooked ceilings, exposed beams, and memories of yesterday.

- **Best for Stargazing:** The tycoons, hot stars, and hotter mistresses of yesterday—Douglas Fairbanks and Mary Pickford, William Randolph Hearst and Marion Davies—knew where to stay back then. Tom Cruise and his ilk know *the* address in Paris is still the **Hôtel de Crillon,** 10 place de la Concorde, 8th arr. (☎ 01-44-71-15-00), once the palace of the duc de Crillon. If you want its grandest suite and have a discriminating taste for the macabre, ask for the Marie Antoinette Apartment—it exhibits Antoinette-style elegance, and its namesake was beheaded practically at the doorstep of this deluxe citadel.

- **Best for Opulence:** Now owned by Mohammed al-Fayed, the **Hôtel Ritz,** 15 place Vendôme, 1st arr. (☎ 01-43-16-30-30), has dripped with wealth, luxury, and decadence since César Ritz opened it in 1898. Barbara Hutton, Coco Chanel, and Marcel Proust are just a few names inscribed in its glorious guest book; if you're into romantic tragedy, remember this was where Princess Diana and Dodi al-Fayed had their last meal. By staying here you can join the parade of Saudi oil princes, Milanese divas, and movie legends—if you have big bucks.

- **Best-Kept Secret:** Built in 1913 and long in a seedy state, the fully restored **Terrass Hôtel,** 12–14 rue Joseph-de-Maistre, 18th arr. (☎ 01-46-06-72-85), is now the only four-star choice in Montmartre, an area not known for luxury accommodations. Its rooms take in far-ranging views of the Tour Eiffel, Arc de Triomphe, and Opéra Garnier.

- **Best Historic Hotel:** Inaugurated by Napoléon III in 1855, the **Hôtel du Louvre,** place André-Malraux, 1st arr. (☎ 01-44-58-38-38), was once described by a

French journalist as "a palace of the people, rising adjacent to the palace of kings." Today, the hotel offers luxurious accommodations and panoramic views down avenue de l'Opéra.

- **Best for Romance:** Until the 1970s, **L'Hôtel,** 13 rue des Beaux-Arts, 6th arr. (℅ **01-44-41-99-00**), was a fleabag filled with drunks and addicts (in 1900, Oscar Wilde died here penniless). Millions of francs of renovations later, the rooms that were once cramped and claustrophobic are now ravishingly romantic, wrought like small jewel boxes.

- **Most Trendy Hotel:** A converted town house, the **Hôtel Costes,** 239 rue St-Honoré, 1st arr. (℅ **01-42-44-50-50**), evokes the imperial heyday of Napoléon III. Fashion headliners especially like it—Costes is the choice of many a lanky model, as the Paris offices of *Harper's Bazaar* are close at hand. If you're into heavy swags, patterned fabrics, jewel-tone colors, and lavish accessories, this can be your gilded-age address.

- **Best Service:** Though you can't fault the flawless decor of the **Hôtel Plaza Athénée,** 25 av. Montaigne, 8th arr. (℅ **01-53-67-66-65**), the billionaires check in because they get the royal treatment from the jaded but indulgent and ever-so-polite staff. In an upscale neighborhood between the Seine and the Champs-Elysées, the Plaza Athénée offers service that's impeccable.

3 Best Dining Bets

For full details on the following restaurants, turn to chapter 6.

- **Best Chef:** Can there be any doubt? Proud owner of five Michelin stars, **Alain Ducasse,** 25 avenue Montaigne, 8th arr. (℅ **01-53-67-65-00**), has taken Paris by storm, assuming the throne of semi-retired Joël Robuchon now that he splits his time between his restaurant here and his one in Monte Carlo. He artfully combines produce from every French region in a cuisine that's contemporary but not quite new, embracing the Mediterranean without abandoning France.

- **Best All-Around Restaurant:** Named for a 14th-century chef who wrote one of the oldest known books on French cookery, **Taillevent,** 15 rue Lamennais, 8th arr. (℅ **01-44-95-15-01**), occupies a grand 19th-century town house off the Champs-Elysées. Though its owner likes to keep about 60% of the crowd French, we suggest you try for a reservation at Paris's most outstanding all-around restaurant.

- **Best Newcomer:** Now that Michelin has bestowed a coveted two stars, **Les Elysées du Vernet,** 25 rue Vernet, 8th arr. (℅ **01-44-31-98-98**), is hosting *tout Paris* and the media. Montpelliere-born chef, Alain Solivérès, is emerging as one of the greatest in Paris, challenging some big-name chefs. His Provençal cookery is the freshest and among the best in the whole country.

- **Best Old-Fashioned Bistro:** Established back in 1931 and bouncing back from a period of decline, **Allard,** 41 rue St-André-des-Arts, 6th arr. (℅ **01-43-26-48-23**), is better than ever from its zinc bar to its repertoire of the classics we associate with traditional French cuisine—escargots, frogs' legs, foie gras, *boeuf à la mode,* and cassoulet. This is a good bet for a real Left Bank bistro ambience.

- **Best Underappreciated Restaurant:** Henri Faugeron may no longer be the media darling he once was, but his **Relais Gourmand Faugeron,** 52 rue de Longchamp, 16th arr. (✆ **01-47-04-24-53**), is just as stunning as ever, though the dishes may not be as "revolutionary" as he proclaims. The food is outstanding and uses only the freshest of ingredients, handled with skill by a stellar kitchen staff.

- **Best Decor:** Declared a French national treasure, the Belle-Époque **Le Train Bleu** in the Gare de Lyon, 12th arr. (✆ **01-43-43-09-06**), evokes the heyday of the gilded age. Completely restored, the restaurant boasts heavy purple velvet hangings, boxes sprinkled with green plants, Napoléon III antiques, gleaming brass, and lighting fixtures made of bronze and Bohemia opaline-shaped glass cups. Incidentally, we said this restaurant had the best decor in Paris—not the finest cuisine.

- **Best View:** A penthouse restaurant, **La Tour d'Argent,** 15–17 quai de la Tournelle, 5th arr. (✆ **01-43-54-23-31**), is owned by shrewd ex-playboy Claude Terrail, who pays part of Notre-Dame's electric bill to illuminate the cathedral at night for his diners' pleasure. Dining here is a theatrical event.

- **Best for Stargazing:** No, it's not Taillevent or even Alain Ducasse. On the see-and-be-seen circuit, the star is the **Buddha Bar,** 8 rue Boissy d'Anglas, 8th arr. (✆ **01-53-05-90-00**). The crowd doesn't actually come for the cuisine, though its fusion of French and Pacific Rim is exceedingly well-executed. If you don't want to dine, stop by the hip lacquered bar across from the dining room.

- **Best-Unkept Secret:** In the heart of the Latin Quarter, **Perraudin,** 157 rue St-Jacques, 5th arr. (✆ **01-46-33-15-75**), duplicates the allure of an early-1900s bistro. You get the feeling Emile Zola could walk in the door at any minute. It offers great food and great value, with old-fashioned dining that's too rapidly disappearing from the city.

- **Best Brasserie:** Head for the Left Bank and the **Brasserie Balzar,** 49 rue des Ecoles, 5th arr. (✆ **01-43-54-13-67**), opened in 1898. If you dine on the familiar French food here, you'll be following in the footsteps of Sartre and Camus and countless others. You can even have a complete dinner in the middle of the afternoon.

- **Best Baby Bistro:** A few years ago, several great French chefs realized the average visitor can't afford the haute cuisine served at their restaurants, so they created "baby bistros" to serve superb food at affordable prices. The best of these is a sideshow created by one of the grandest chefs, Jacques Cagna: **La Rôtisserie d'Armaillé,** 6 rue d'Armaillé, 17th arr. (✆ **01-42-27-19-20**), near place de Etoile.

- **Best Seafood:** The fattest lobsters and prawns in the Rungis market emerge on platters at **Goumard,** 9 rue Duphot, 1st arr. (✆ **01-42-60-36-07**), so chic that even the toilets are classified as historic monuments. Nothing is allowed to interfere with the taste of the sea: You'll have to fly to the Riviera to find a better bouillabaisse.

- **Best *Cuisine Bourgeoise* (Comfort Food):** If, today, Joyce, Verlaine, Valéry, and Hemingway rose from the grave and strode into the **Crémerie-Restaurant Polidor,** 41 rue Monsieur-le-Prince, 6th arr. (✆ **01-43-26-95-34**), they wouldn't notice any difference, not even on the menu, but would calmly ask for their napkins locked in a cabinet in back with their names on them.

- **Best Atmosphere:** A favorite of Colette and Cocteau, the world-famous **Le Grand Véfour,** 17 rue de Beaujolais, 1st arr. (✆ **01-42-96-56-27**), at the Palais-Royal, has an interior classified as a historic monument. Incidentally, it serves some of the most refined cuisine in Paris.

- **Best for Opulence:** Belle-Époque Paris lives on at **Lucas-Carton (Alain Senderens),** 9 place de le Madeleine, 8th arr. (✆ **01-42-65-22-90**), one of Paris's temples of haute gastronomy. Lose yourself in a world of glittering mirrors, polished brass, wood paneling, and fresh flowers. The cuisine? It ranks at the very top in Paris.

- **Best Lyonnais Cuisine:** Lyon is hailed as France's gastronomic capital, and the best place in Paris to introduce yourself to this regional cuisine is at **Aux Lyonnais,** 32 rue St-Marc, 2nd arr. (✆ **01-42-96-65-04**). This fin-de-siècle bistro turns out all the dishes for which Lyon is famous, from perfectly prepared pike dumplings to large Lyonnais sausages—all washed down, of course, with Beaujolais.

- **Best Kosher Food:** If corned beef, pastrami, herring, and dill pickles thrill you, head to **rue des Rosiers** in the 4th arrondissement (Métro: St-Paul). John Russel wrote that rue des Rosiers is the "last sanctuary of certain ways of life; what you see there in miniature is Warsaw before the ghetto was razed." North African overtones reflect the long-ago arrival of Jews from Morocco, Tunisia, and Algeria. The best time to go is Sunday

morning: You can wander the streets eating as you go—apple strudel, Jewish rye bread, pickled lemons, smoked salmon, and *merguez,* a spicy smoked sausage from Algeria. Many spots offer sit-down meals, like **Chez Jo Goldenberg,** 7 rue des Rosiers, 4th arr. (✆ **01-48-87-20-16**), where the *carpe farcie* (stuffed carp) is outstanding and the beef goulash a fine runner-up.

- **Best American Cuisine:** A Yankee outpost in Les Halles, **Joe Allen,** 30 rue Pierre-Lescot, 1st arr. (✆ **01-42-36-70-13**), serves the finest burgers in the city. Desserts include real New York cheesecake, pecan pie with fresh pecans imported from the United States, and the inspired cultural fusion of American brownies made with French chocolate.

- **Best Pizza:** The **Chicago Pizza Pie Factory,** 5 rue de Berri, 8th arr. (✆ **01-45-62-50-23**), is devoted to the almighty pizza pie, with the chef creating endless delicious variations on eight themes.

- **Best Vegetarian Cuisine:** One of the best-known veggie restaurants in the Marais is **Aquarius,** 54 rue Ste-Croix-de-la-Bretonnerie, 4th arr. (✆ **01-48-87-48-71**). Choose from the array of soups and salads or have a mushroom tart or a galette of wheat with raw vegetables. In this rustic 17th-century setting you can expect flavorful, wholesome, and generous meals.

- **Best Wine Cellar:** At the elegant **Lasserre,** 17 av. Franklin-D. Roosevelt, 8th arr. (✆ **01-43-59-53-43**), you'll find not only wonderful food but also one of the great wine cellars of France, with some 180,000 bottles.

- **Best for Cheese:** Cheese is king at **Androuët,** 49 rue Saint Roch, 1st arr. (✆ **01-42-97-57-39**). Many cheese lovers opt for a bottle of wine, a green salad, and all-you-can-eat choices from the most sophisticated *dégustation de fromages* in the world.

- **Best on the Champs-Elysées:** The specialties of Denmark are served with flair at the **Restaurant Copenhague/Flora Danica,** 142 av. des Champs-Elysées, 8th arr. (*©* **01-44-13-86-26**). In summer you can dine on the terrace of this "Maison du Danemark."

- **Best Late-Night Dining:** Nowhere else in Paris can you be more assured of getting a good meal at 3am than at **Au Pied de Cochon,** 6 rue Coquillière, 1st arr. (*©* **01-40-13-77-00**). Though everyone lauds its grilled pig's feet with béarnaise sauce, few have noticed you can also find some of the freshest oysters in town here.

- **Best for Tea:** Try **Angélina,** 226 rue de Rivoli, 1st arr. (*©* **01-42-60-82-00**), for a view of haute couture's lionesses having their tea. The house specialty is the Mont Blanc, a combination of chestnut cream and meringue. If you're looking for luscious ice cream along with your tea,

try **Berthillon,** 31 rue St-Louis-en-l'Ile, 4th arr. (*©* **01-43-54-31-61**).

- **Best for Picnic Fare:** For the most elegant picnic fixings in town, go to **Fauchon,** 26 place de la Madeleine, 8th arr. (*©* **01-47-42-60-11**), where you'll find a complete charcuterie and famous pastry shop. It's said to offer 20,000 kinds of imported fruits, vegetables, and other exotic delicacies, snacks, salads, and canapés, all packed to take out. For details, see chapter 9.

- **Best Champagne Julep:** While you wait for a table at **Closerie des Lilas,** 171 bd. du Montparnasse, 6th arr. (*©* **01-40-51-34-50**), savor the best champagne julep in the world at the bar.

- **Best People Watching:** Spend an afternoon on the terrace of the **Café de la Paix,** place de l'Opéra, 9th arr. (*©* **01-40-07-30-20**), and watch the world go by. See and be seen or settle into anonymity while enjoying the vast variety of faces in this international mingling joint.

4 The Best Cafes

For full details on the following cafes, turn to chapter 6.

- **Most Evocative Left Bank Cafe:** The old bohemia still lives at this old-fashioned Parisian cafe, **La Palette,** 43 rue de Seine, 6th arr. (*©* **01-43-26-68-15**), where patrons still down the same drinks, Ricard and Pernod, that they did back in the 1930s. It's a battered but artistic *Quartier Latin* cafe.

- **Most Historical Cafe:** Ardent fans of French history still flock to **Le Procope,** 13 rue de l'Ancienne-Comedie, 6th arr. (*©* **01-40-46-79-00**), where Voltaire, Oscar Wilde, and even Napoléon

used to hang out. The ground-floor room is outfitted like an antique library.

- **Most Legendary Hangout:** Once a gathering place for French intellectuals, **Les Deux Magots,** 6 place St-Germain-des-Prés, 6th arr. (*©* **01-45-48-55-25**), is still going strong, even though tourists have replaced Gore Vidal and James Baldwin at the tables. See chapter 6.

- **Most Chic Cafe of Today:** Today's equivalent of La Couple or even the Deux Magots is **Café Cosmos,** 101 bd. Du Montparnasse 6th arr. (*©* **01-43-26-74-36**), where today's hip media

Tips   The Best Websites for Paris

Here are some of the best websites for information on the City of Light:

- **Bonjour Paris, www.bparis.com**, is one of the most comprehensive and fun sites about life in Paris, written from an American expatriate point of view.
- **Paris Digest, www.parisdigest.com**, is an independent site containing articles that link to restaurants, some hotels, museums, monuments, parks, and activities. It includes history about the city and tips for getting around.
- **Paris France Guide, www.parisfranceguide.com**, is produced by the publishers of such magazines as *Living in France, Study in France*, and *What's On in France*. This site has lots of useful information about Paris, such as current articles and listings on nightlife, restaurants, events, theater, and music.
- **Paris Free Voice, www.parisvoice.com**, is the online version of the monthly *Paris Voice*, a hip and opinionated guide for "English-speaking Parisians." The calendar of events includes music, movies, and performance-art listings. There are also restaurant reviews and guides like "Where to Kiss in Paris."
- **Paris Pages, www.paris.org**, offers a wealth of information on Paris for a widespread audience. The lodging reviews are organized by area and the monuments that stand nearby. The city guide includes an event calendar, shop listings, a map of attractions with details about each, and photo tours.
- **Paris Tourist Office, www.paris-touristoffice.com**, offers information on city events arranged by week, month, favorites, and year, plus the closest Métro stops for museums, lodgings, resturants, and nightlife. You can tour parks and gardens and discover Paris's trendy districts.

crowd gathers. Because "no one writes novels any more," today's generation consists of those in film, photography, modeling, or whatever.

- **Most Quintessential Paris Left Bank Cafe:** Vying with Deux Magots (see above), **Café de Flore,** 172 bd. St-Germain, 6th arr. (© **01-45-48-55-26**) still basks in its memories of its famous visitors, which included Camus, Picasso, and Apollinaire. Even if tourists have taken their table, Café de Flore still pulls off a left Bank aura.

A Traveler's Guide to Paris's Art & Architecture

by Reid Bramblett

Paris is arguably the premier artistic capital of Europe. For centuries, the city has produced, and been home to, countless artists and artistic movements. This chapter will help you find the best examples of each period in the city's museums and architecture.

1 Art 101

GOTHIC (1100–1400)

Almost all artistic expression in medieval France was church-related. Paris retains no art to speak of from the Classical or Romanesque eras, but much remains from the medieval Gothic era when artists cranked out sculpture and stained glass for churches.

Because Mass was recited in Latin, images were used to communicate the Bible's most important lessons to the illiterate masses. *Bas reliefs* (sculpture that projects slightly from a flat surface) were used to illustrate key tales that inspired faith in God and fear of sin (*Last Judgements* were favorites). These reliefs were wrapped around column capitals, festooned onto facades, and fitted into the *tympanum* (the arched spaces above doorways; the complete door, tympanum, arch, and supporting pillars assemblage is the **portal**).

The French were also becoming masters of **stained glass.** Many painterly conventions began in this era on windowpanes, or as elaborate doodles in the margins of **illuminated manuscripts,** which developed into altarpieces of the colorful **International Gothic** style.

In both Gothic painting and sculpture, figures tend to be highly stylized, flowing, and rhythmic. The figures' features and gestures are exaggerated for symbolic or emotional emphasis.

Outstanding examples and artists include:

- **Cathédrale de Chartres** (1194–1220). A day trip from Paris, Cathédrale de Chartres boasts magnificent sculpture and some of the best stained glass in Europe.
- **Cathédrale de Notre-Dame** (1163–1250). The Gothic highpoints of this famous cathedral are the sculpture on the facade, an interior choir screen lined with deep-relief carvings, and three rose windows filled with stained glass.
- **Sainte-Chapelle** (1240–50). The finest stained glass in the world adorns this tiny chapel.

- **Unicorn Tapestries** (1499–1514). These famed tapestries shine brightly as a final statement of medieval sensibilities while borrowing some burgeoning Renaissance conventions. Find them in the **Musée de Cluny.**

THE RENAISSANCE (1400–1600)

Renaissance means "rebirth," in this case of Classical ideals originating in Greece and Rome. Humanist thinkers rediscovered the wisdom of the ancients, while artists strove for greater naturalism, using newly developed techniques such as linear perspective to achieve new heights of realism. Famous practitioners of the style include **Michelangelo** (1475–1564) and **Leonardo da Vinci** (1452–1519). **Mannerism,** the late 16th-century branch of the High Renaissance, took Michelangelo's bright color palate and twisting figures to extremes and exhausted the movement.

Aside from collecting Italian art, the French had little to do with the Renaissance, which started in Italy and was quickly picked up in Germany and the Low Countries. France owes many of its early Renaissance treasures to **François I,** who imported art (paintings by Raphael and Titian) and artists (he brought Leonardo da Vinci to his court). Henri II's Florentine wife, **Catherine de Médici,** also collected 16th-century Italian masterpieces.

Significant artists and examples to look for in Paris include:

- **Italian Artists.** Many works by Italy's finest reside in the **Louvre,** including paintings by **Giotto, Fra' Angelico,** and **Veronese;** sculptures by **Michelangelo;** and a handful of works by **Leonardo da Vinci,** who moved to a Loire Valley château for the last 3 years of his life and whose *Mona Lisa* (1503–05), perhaps the world's most famous painting, hangs here.
- **The School of Fontainebleau.** This group of artists working on the **Palais de Fontainebleau** outside Paris from 1530 to 1560 were actually imported Italian Mannerists who combined painting, stucco, sculpture, and woodwork to decorate the château's Galerie Francois I. They included **Niccolò dell'Abbate, Benvenuto Cellini, Primaticcio,** and **Rosso Fiorentino.** (If you don't make it out to Fontainebleau, check out Cellini's sculpture *Diana of Fontainebleau* [1543–44] in the Louvre.)

THE BAROQUE (1600–1800)

The 17th-century **Baroque** is hard to pin down. In some ways it was a result of the Catholic Counter-Reformation, reaffirming spirituality in a simplified, monumental, and religious version of Renaissance ideals. In other ways, it delved even deeper into Classical modes and a kind of super-realism based on using peasants as models and the exaggerated *chiaroscuro* (interplay or contrast of light and dark) of Italian painter Caravaggio.

Some view those two movements as mere extensions of Renaissance experiments, and find the true Baroque in later complex compositions—all explosions of dynamic fury, movement, color, and figures—that are well-balanced, but in such cluttered abundance as to appear untamed. **Rococo** is this later Baroque art gone awry, frothy, and chaotic.

Significant practitioners of the Baroque with examples in the **Louvre** include:

- **Poussin** (1594–1665). The most Classical French painter, Poussin created mythological scenes that presaged the Romantic movement. His balance and predilection to paint from nature influenced French Impressionists such as Cézanne.

- **Watteau** (1684–1721). Watteau indulged in the wild, untamed complexity of the Rococo. Cruise the Louvre for his colorful, theatrical works. He began the short-lived *fête galante* style that featured china-doll figures against stylized landscapes of woodlands or ballrooms.
- **Boucher** (1703–70). Louis XV's Rococo court painter, Boucher studied Watteau and produced lots of decorative landscapes and genre works.
- **Fragonard** (1732–1806). Boucher's student and the master of Rococo, pastel scenes, Fragonard painted an overindulgence of pink-cheeked, wispy genteel lovers frolicking against billowing treescapes. The Louvre hangs his famous *The Bathers.*

NEOCLASSICAL & ROMANTIC (1770–1890)

As the Baroque got excessive, the Rococo got cute, and the somber Counter-Reformation got serious about the limits on religious art, several artists looked for relief to the ancients. Viewing new excavations of Greek and Roman sites (Pompeii and Paestum) and statuary became integral parts of the Grand Tour through Italy, while the Enlightenment (and growing Revolutionary) interest in Greek democracy beat an intellectual path to the distant past. This gave rise to a **neoclassical** artistic style that emphasized symmetry, austerity, clean lines, and Classical themes, such as depictions of events from history or mythology.

The **Romantics,** on the other hand, felt both the ancients and the Renaissance had gotten it wrong and that the Middle Ages was the place to be. They idealized Romantic tales of chivalry and held a deep respect for nature, human rights, and the nobility of peasantry, and a suspicion of progress. Their paintings were heroic, historic, (melo)dramatic, and quested for beauty.

The greatest artists and movements of the era, all with examples in the **Louvre,** include:

- **David** (1744–1825). David dropped the Baroque after a year of study in Rome exposed him to Neoclassicism, which he brought back to Paris and displayed in such paintings as *The Oath of the Horatii* (1784) and *Coronation of Napoléon and Josephine* (1805–08).
- **Ingres** (1780–1867). Trained with David, Ingres become a defender of the Neoclassicists and the Royal French Academy, and opposed the Romantics. His *Grand Odalisque* (1814) hangs in the Louvre.
- **Géricault** (1791–1824). One of the great early Romantics, Géricault painted the large, dramatic history painting, *The Raft of the Medusa* (1819), which served as a model for the movement.
- **Delacroix** (1798–1863). His *Liberty Leading the People* (1830) was painted in the Romantic style, but the artist was also experimenting with color and brushstroke.
- **The Barbizon School.** This school of landscape painters, founded in the 1830s by **Théodore Rousseau** (1812–67), painted directly from nature at Barbizon near Paris. **Millet** (1814–75) preferred classical scenes and local peasants; his works are at the **Musée d'Orsay. Corot** (1796–1875), the third Barbizon great, was a sort of idealistic Proto-Impressionist.

IMPRESSIONISM (1870–1920)

Formal, rigid Neoclassicism and idealized Romanticism rankled some late–19th century artists interested in painting directly from nature. Seeking to capture the fleeting *impression* light made when reflecting off objects, they adopted a free, open style; deceptively loose compositions; swift, visible brushwork; and ofte light colors. For subject matter, they turned away from the Classical themes of previous styles to landscapes and scenes of modern life. Unless otherwise specified below, you'll find some of the best examples of their works in the **Musée d'Orsay.**

Impressionist greats include:

- **Manet** (1832–83). His groundbreaking *Picnic on the Grass* (1863) and naked *Olympia* (1863) weren't Impressionism proper, but they helped inspire the movement with their harsh realism, visible brushstrokes, and thick outlines.
- **Monet** (1840–1926). The Impressionist movement officially began with an 1874 exhibition in which Monet exhibited his loose, Turner-inspired *Impression, Sunrise* (1874), now in the **Musée Marmottan,** which one critic picked to lambaste the whole exhibition, deriding it all as "Impressionist." Far from being insulted, the anti-establishment artists in the show adopted the word for their exhibits, held through the 1880s.
- **Renoir** (1841–1919). Originally Renoir was a porcelain painter, which helps explain his figures' ivory skin and chubby pink cheeks.
- **Degas** (1834–1917). Degas was an accomplished painter, sculptor, and draughtsman—his pastels of dancers and bathers are particularly memorable.
- **Rodin** (1840–1917). The greatest Impressionist-era sculptor, Rodin crafted remarkably expressive bronzes, refusing to idealize the human figure as had his Neoclassical predecessors. The **Musée Rodin,** his former Paris studio, contains, among other works, his *Burghers of Calais* (1886), *The Kiss* (1886–98), and *The Thinker* (1880).

POST-IMPRESSIONISM (1880–1930)

Few experimental French artists of the late 19th century were technically Impressionists, though many were friends with those in the movement. The smaller movements or individual styles are usually lumped together as "Post-Impressionist."

Again, you'll find the best examples of their works at the **Musée d'Orsay,** though you'll find pieces by Matisse, Chagall, and the Cubists, including Picasso, in the **Centre Pompidou.** Important Post-Impressionists include:

- **Cézanne** (1839–1906). He adopted the short brushstrokes, love of landscape, and light color palate of his Impressionist friends, but Cézanne was more formal and deliberate in his style. He sought to give his art monumentality and permanence, even if the subjects were simple still-lifes, portraits, or landscapes.
- **Gauguin** (1848–1903). Gauguin could never settle himself or his work, trying Brittany first, where he developed **Synthetism** (black outlines around solid colors), and later hopping around the South Pacific, where he was inspired by local styles and colors.
- **Seurat** (1859–91), **Signac** (1863–1935), and **Pissaro** (1830–1903). Together these artists developed **Divisionism** and its more formal cousin **pointillism.** Rather than mixing, say, yellow and blue paint together to make green, they applied tiny dots of yellow and blue right next to each other so that the viewer's eye mixes them together to make green.
- **Toulouse-Lautrec** (1864–1901). Most famous for his work with thinned-down oils, Toulouse-Lautrec created paintings and posters of wispy, fluid lines anticipating Art Nouveau and often depicting the Bohemian life of

Paris's dance halls and cafes. In Montmartre you can still visit the **Moulin Rouge,** the cabaret he immortalized on canvas.

- **Van Gogh** (1853–90). Though Dutch, he spent most of his tortured artistic career in France. He combined Divisionism, Synthetism, and a touch of Japanese influence, and painted with thick, short strokes. Never particularly accepted by any artistic circle, he is the most popular painter in the world today (his paintings fetch record sums at auction, and he sells more postcards and posters than any other artist), even though he sold only one painting in his short life.

- **Matisse** (1869–1954). He took a hint from Synthetism and added wild colors and strong patterns to create **Fauvism** (a critic described those who used the style as *fauves,* meaning "wild beasts"). Matisse continued exploring these themes even when most artists were turning to Cubism. When his health failed later in life, he began assembling brightly colored collages of paper cutouts.

- **Picasso** (1881–1973). Along with **Braque** (1882–1963), this Barcelona-born artist painted objects from all points of view at once, rather than use optical tricks like perspective to fool viewers into seeing three dimensions. The fractured result was **Cubism** and was expanded upon by the likes of **Léger** (1881–1955) and the Spaniard **Gris** (1887–1927), while Picasso moved on to other styles. You can see all of his periods at the **Musée Picasso** in the Marais.

2 Architecture 101

While each architectural era has its own distinctive features, there are some elements, general floor plans, and terms common to many.

From the Romanesque period on, most **churches** consist either of a single wide **aisle,** or a wide central **nave** flanked by two narrow aisles. A row of **columns,** or square stacks of masonry called **piers,** connected by **arches,** separates the aisles from the nave.

This main nave/aisle assemblage is usually crossed by a perpendicular corridor called a **transept** near the far, east end of the church so that the floor plan looks like a Latin cross (shaped like a lowercase "t"). At the east end sits the holy **altar.** This is usually on a raised dais and in the entrance to—or, especially later, just in front of—the large **chapel** formed by the shorter, far end of the cross. If this large, main chapel is rounded off on the end, it is called an **apse;** it is often elongated and filled with the stalls of the **choir.** Some churches, especially after the Renaissance when mathematical proportion became important, were built on a Greek Cross plan, each axis the same length like a giant "+."

It's worth pointing out that very few buildings (especially churches) were built in

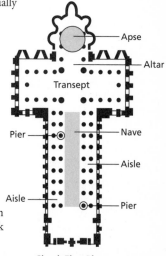

Church Floor Plan

one particular style. These massive, expensive structures often took centuries to complete, during which time tastes would change and plans would be altered.

ANCIENT ROMAN (BC 125–450 AD)

France was Rome's first transalpine conquest, and the legions of Julius Caesar quickly subdued the Celtic tribes across France, converting it into Roman Gaul and importing Roman building concepts.

IDENTIFIABLE FEATURES
- The **load-bearing arch.**
- The use of **concrete and brick.**

BEST EXAMPLES
- **Parvis Archeological Excavations.** The Romanized village of Lutèce, later renamed after its native *Parisii* tribe of Celtic Gauls, is partially excavated under place du Parvis in front of Nôtre-Dame.
- **Musée de Cluny.** This medieval monastery was built on top of a **Roman baths complex,** remnants of which are still visible on the grounds outside and in the huge preserved *frigidarium* (the cold water bath) that is now a room of the museum. The museum itself also contains an ancient statuary.

ROMANESQUE (800–1100)

Romanesque architects concentrated on building large churches with wide aisles to accommodate the masses who came to hear Mass and worship at the altars of various saints. The Romanesque took its inspiration from ancient Rome (hence the name). Early Christians in Italy had adapted the basilica (ancient Roman law court buildings) to become churches. Few examples of the Romanesque remain in Paris, however, with most churches having been rebuilt in later eras.

IDENTIFIABLE FEATURES
- **Rounded arches.** These load-bearing architectural devices allowed the architects to open up wide naves and spaces, channeling all that weight of the stone walls and ceiling across the curve of the arch and down into the ground via the columns or pilasters.
- **Thick walls, infrequent and small windows, and huge piers.** These were necessary to support the weight of all that masonry, giving Romanesque churches a dark, somber, mysterious, and often oppressive feeling.
- **Apse.** This rounded space behind the altar in many Romanesque churches opens up the holiest, east end of the church.
- **Radiating chapels.** These smaller chapels began to sprout off the east end of the church, especially later in the Romanesque period, often in the form of a fan of minichapels radiating off the **apse** (see above).
- **Ambulatory.** This curving corridor separates the altar and choir area from the ring of smaller, **radiating chapels** (see above). This, too, was a convention of the later Romanesque and carried into the Gothic.

BEST EXAMPLES
- **St-Germain-des-Prés.** The overall building is Romanesque, including the fine sculpted column capitals near the entrance of the left aisle; only the far left corner is original, the others are copies. By the time builders got to creating the choir, the early Gothic was on—note the pointy arches. Over the (early Renaissance) portal is a Romanesque carving of the *Last Judgement.*
- **St-Julien-le-Pauvre.** This small church has a general Romanesque plan overwritten by later Gothic embellishments, including the facade.

GOTHIC (1100–1500)

By the 12th century, engineering developments freed church architecture from the heavy, thick walls of Romanesque structures and allowed ceilings to soar, walls to thin, and windows to proliferate.

Instead of dark, somber, relatively unadorned Romanesque interiors that forced the eyes of the faithful toward the altar, where the priest stood droning on in unintelligible Latin, the Gothic interior enticed the churchgoers' gaze upward to high ceilings filled with light. The priests still conducted Mass in Latin, but now peasants could "read" the Gothic comic books of stained glass windows.

The squat, brooding exteriors of the Romanesque fortresses of God were replaced by graceful buttresses and soaring spires, which rose from town centers like beacons of religion.

IDENTIFIABLE FEATURES

- **Pointed arches.** The most significant development of the Gothic era was the discovery that pointed arches could carry far more weight than rounded ones.
- **Cross vaults.** Instead of being flat, the square patch of ceiling between four columns arches up to a point in the center, creating four sail shapes, sort of like the underside of a pyramid. The "X" separating these four sails is often reinforced with ridges called **ribbing.** As the Gothic progressed, four-sided cross vaults became six- or eight-sided as architects played with the angles.

Cross Vault

- **Flying buttresses.** These free-standing exterior pillars connected by graceful, thin arms of stone help channel the weight of the building and its roof out and down into the ground. To help counter the cross forces involved in this engineering sleight of hand, the piers of buttresses were often topped by heavy pinnacles, which took the form of minispires or statues.
- **Spires.** These pinnacles of masonry seem to defy gravity and reach toward heaven itself.
- **Gargoyles.** Disguised as wide-mouthed creatures, gargoyles are actually drain spouts.
- **Tracery.** These lacy spider webs of carved stone grace the pointy ends of windows and sometimes the spans of ceiling vaults.
- **Stained glass.** Because pointy arches can carry more weight than rounded ones, windows could be larger and more numerous. They were often filled with Bible stories and symbolism writ in the colorful patterns of stained glass.
- **Rose windows.** Huge circular windows filled with elegant **tracery** (see above) and "petals"

Flying Buttress

Cross Section of Gothic Church

of stained glass, rose windows often appear as the centerpiece of facades and, in some larger churches, at the ends of transepts as well.

- **Ambulatory.** The Gothic made much greater use of this corridor of space wrapping behind the apse and often around a **choir** (the boxed-off area, usually behind the altar, where the choir sat and sang).
- **Choir screen.** Serving as the inner wall of the ambulatory and the outer wall of the choir section, choir screens are often decorated with carvings or tombs.

BEST EXAMPLES

- **Basilique St-Denis** (1140–1144). Today you'll find the world's first Gothic cathedral in a Paris suburb.
- **Cathédrale de Chartres** (1194–1220). This Gothic masterpiece boasts good statuary, a soaring spire, and some 150 glorious stained glass windows.
- **Cathédrale de Nôtre-Dame** (1163–1250). This famous cathedral possesses pinnacled flying buttresses, a trio of France's best rose windows, good portal carvings, a choir screen of deeply carved reliefs, and spiffy gargoyles (though many of those are actually 19th-century Neo-Gothic).

Cathédrale de Chartres

RENAISSANCE (1500–1630)

In architecture, as in painting, the Renaissance came from Italy and was only slowly Frenchified. And, as in painting, its rules stressed proportion, order, Classical inspiration, and mathematical precision to create unified, balanced structures.

IDENTIFIABLE FEATURES

- **Proportion and symmetry.** Other than a close eye to these Renaissance ideals, little specifically identifies buildings of this period.
- **Steeply pitched roofs.** Many roofs are of pale stone with dark gray tiles. This feature is really a throwback to medieval sensibilities, but because almost no medieval mansions survive in Paris, the buildings that *do* sport steep roofs tend to be Renaissance.
- **Dormer windows.** These tend to be tall and made of stone, which differentiates them from the lower, less extravagant, wooden ones of later periods.

BEST EXAMPLES

- **Hôtel Carnavalet** (1544). Another prime example of a Renaissance mansion, this is the only 16th-century hotel left in Paris. It now contains the **Musée Carnavalet,** a museum devoted to the history of Paris and the French Revolution.
- **Place des Vosges.** This square is lined by Renaissance mansions rising above a lovely arcaded corridor that wraps all the way around.

CLASSICISM & ROCOCO (1630–1800)

While Italy and Germany embraced the opulent Baroque, France took the fundamentals of Renaissance **Classicism** even further, becoming more imitative of ancient models—this represents a change from the Renaissance preference to find inspiration in the Classic era.

During the reign of Louis XIV, art and architecture were subservient to political ends. Buildings were grandiose and severely ordered on the Versailles model. Opulence was saved for interior decoration, which increasingly (especially from 1715 to 1750, after the death of Louis XIV) became an excessively detailed and self-indulgent **Rococo** (*rocaille* in French). Externally, this later style is only noticeable by a greater elegance and delicacy.

Rococo tastes didn't last long, though, and soon a **neoclassical** movement was raising structures, such as Paris's **Panthéon** (1758), even more strictly based on ancient models than the earlier Classicism was.

IDENTIFIABLE FEATURES

- **Symmetrical, rectangular structures.** French Classicism concentrated on horizontal and vertical lines and simple proportions.
- **Classical throwbacks.** Classicism was favored for the very fact that it brought back such elements as Classical orders (Doric, Ionic, and Corinthian) and projecting central sections topped by triangular pediments.

Classical Orders

- **Mansard roofs.** A defining feature and true French trademark developed by **François Mansart** (1598–1666) in the early 15th century, a mansard roof has a double slope, the lower being longer and steeper than the upper.
- **Dormer windows.** Unlike the larger Renaissance ones flanked by showy stone scrolls, later dormers tended to be lower, less extravagant, and wooden.
- ***Oeil-de-bouef* windows.** These small, round "ox-eye" windows poke out of the roof's slope.

Mansard Roof

- **Excessive detail.** Rococo interior decoration is often asymmetrical and abstract with shell-like forms and many C- and S-curves. Naturalistic flowers and trees are sometimes playfully introduced.

BEST EXAMPLES

- **Palais du Louvre** (1650–1670). A collaborative Classical masterpiece, the Louvre was designed as a palace. **Le Vau** (1612–70) was its chief architect, along with collaborators **François Mansarts,** the interior decorator **Le Brun** (1619–90), and the unparalleled landscape gardener **Le Nôtre** (1613–1700). The structure subsequently had several purposes (see chapter 7 for the complete history) before becoming a museum.
- **Versailles** (1669–1685). Versailles is France's—indeed, Europe's—grandest palace, the Divine Monarchy writ as a massive statement of fussily decorative, politically charged Classical architecture, though the interior was later redecorated in more flamboyant styles. The chief architects of its complete overhaul under Louis XIV were the oft-used team (see Palais du Louvre, above) of Le Vau, Mansarts, Le Brun, and Le Nôtre. Mansart's grandnephew (and Louis XIV's chief architect) **Jules Hardouin-Mansart** (1646–1708) took over after Le Vau's death, changing much of the exterior look. The **Clock Room** is a good example of Rococo interior decoration.

Versailles

- **Panthéon** (1758). This left-bank monument is a perfect example of the strict neoclassical style.

THE 19TH CENTURY

Architectural styles in 19th-century Paris were eclectic, beginning in a severe Classical mode and ending with an identity crisis torn between Industrial-Age technology and Art Nouveau organic. The "Identifiable Features" section explores the main facets of competing styles during this turbulent century.

IDENTIFIABLE FEATURES

- **First Empire.** Elegant, Neoclassical furnishings—distinguished by strong lines often accented with a simple curve—became the rage during Napoléon's reign.
- **Second Empire.** Napoléon III's reign saw the eclectic Second Empire reinterpret Classicism in an ornate, dramatic mode. Urban planning was the architectural rage, and Paris became a city of wide boulevards courtesy of **Baron Haussmann** (1809–91), commissioned by Napoléon III in 1852 to redesign the city. Paris owes much of its remarkably unified look to Haussmann, who drew his beloved thoroughfares directly across the city, tearing down existing structures along the way. He lined the boulevards with elegantly simple, six-story apartment blocks, sort of like elongated

18th-century town houses with a continuous balcony wrapping around the third and sixth floors and mansard roofs with dormer windows.

- **Third Republic.** Expositions in 1878, 1889, and 1900 were the catalysts for constructing huge glass-and-steel structures that showed off modern techniques and the engineering prowess of the Industrial Revolution. This produced such enduring Parisian monuments as the Tour Eiffel and Sacré-Coeur.
- **Art nouveau.** These architects and decorators rebelled against the Third-Republic era of mass production by stressing the uniqueness of craft. They created asymmetrical, curvaceous designs based on organic inspiration (plants and flowers) in such mediums as wrought iron, stained glass, tile, and hand-painted wallpaper.

BEST EXAMPLES

- **Palais de Fontainebleau.** Napoléon spent his Imperial decade (1804–14) refurbishing his quarters in this palace in First-Empire style.
- **Arc de Triomphe** (1836). Napoléon's oversize imitation of a Roman triumphal arch is the ultimate paean to the Classical era. The arch presides over **L'Etoile,** an intersection of 12, wide boulevards laid out by Baron Haussman in the Second Empire.
- **Tour Eiffel** (1889). In 1889, under the Third Republic, the French wanted to show how far they had come in the 100 years since the Revolution. They hired **Gustave Eiffel** (1832–1923) to slap together the world's tallest structure, a temporary 1,051-foot tower made of ultramodern riveted steel girders. Everyone agreed it was tall; most thought it was ugly and completely lacking in aesthetics. Its usefulness as a radio transmitter saved Eiffel's tower from being torn down.
- **Métro station entrances.** Art Nouveau was less an architectural mode than a decorative movement. You can still find some of the original Art-Nouveau Métro entrances designed by **Hector Guimard** (1867–1942). (A recently renovated entrance is at the Porte Dauphine station on the number 2 line.)

THE 20TH CENTURY

France commissioned some ambitious modern architectural projects in the last century, most of them the *grand projets* of the late François Mitterand. The majority were considered controversial, outrageous, or even offensive when completed. Only slowly have structures such as the Centre Pompidou or Louvre's glass pyramids become accepted. Over time, a lucky few may even become as beloved as the once-despised Tour Eiffel.

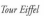

Tour Eiffel

IDENTIFIABLE FEATURES

Other than a concerted effort to be unique, break convention, and look stunningly modern, nothing communally identifies France's recent architecture.

BEST EXAMPLES

- **Centre Pompidou** (1977). Brit Richard Rogers (b. 1933) and Italian Renzo Piano (b. 1937) turned architecture inside out—literally—to craft Paris's eye-popping modern art museum. Exposed pipes, steel supports, and plastic-tube escalators wrap around the exterior.

Centre Pompidou

- **Louvre's glass pyramids** (1989). Chinese-American architect I. M. Pei (b. 1917) was called in to cap the Louvre's new underground entrance with these pyramids smack in the center of the Palais du Louvre's 17th-century courtyard.
- **Opera Bastille** (1989). In 1989, Paris's opera company moved into this curvaceous, dark glass mound of space designed by Canadian Carlos Ott. (Unfortunately, the acoustics have been lambasted.)

3

Planning Your Trip to Paris

This chapter provides the nuts-and-bolts details you need before setting off for Paris—everything from information sources to money matters to the major airlines and how to save money on your flight.

1 Visitor Information

TOURIST OFFICES

Your best source of information is the **French Government Tourist Office,** which you can reach at the following addresses:

IN THE UNITED STATES 444 Madison Ave., 16th Floor, New York, NY 10022 (℃ **212/838-7800**); 676 N. Michigan Ave., Suite 3360, Chicago, IL 60611 (℃ **312/751-7800**); 9454 Wilshire Blvd., Suite 715, Beverly Hills, CA 90212 (℃ **310/271-6665;** fax 310/276-2835). To request information at any of these offices, call the **France on Call** hot line at ℃ **410/286-8310.**

IN CANADA Maison de la France/French Government Tourist Office, 1981 av. McGill College, Suite 490, Montréal, PQ H3A 2W9 (℃ **514/288-4264;** fax 514/845-4868); 30 St. Patrick St., Suite 700, Toronto, ON M5T 3A3 (℃ **416/491-7622;** fax 416/979-7587).

IN THE UNITED KINGDOM Maison de la France/French Government Tourist Office, 178 Piccadilly, London, W1V 0AL (℃ **090/6824-4123;** fax 020/7943-6594).

IN IRELAND Maison de la France/French Government Tourist Office, 10 Suffolk St., Dublin 2, Ireland (℃ **01/679-0813;** fax 01/880-7772).

IN AUSTRALIA French Tourist Bureau, 25 Bligh St., Sydney, NSW 2000 (℃ **02/9231-5244;** fax 02/9221-8682).

WEBSITES

You can contact the French Government Tourist Office through its website at www.francetourism.com.

For general information, see "Planning Your Trip Online," later in this chapter. For more Paris-related websites, see "The Best Websites for Paris" box in chapter 1.

2 Entry Requirements & Customs Regulations

PASSPORT & VISAS

All non-French nationals need a **valid passport** to enter France (check its expiration date). The French government no longer requires visas for **U.S. citizens,** providing they're staying less than 90 days. For longer stays, they must apply for a long-term visa, residence card, or temporary-stay visa.

Each requires proof of income or a viable means of support in France and a legitimate purpose for remaining in the country. Applications are available from the **Consulate Section of the French Embassy,** 4101 Reservoir Rd. NW, Washington, DC 20007 (℃ **202/944-6000**), or from the **Visa Section of the French Consulate,** 10 E. 74th

St., New York, NY 10021 (© **212/ 606-3689**). Visas are required for students planning to study in France even if the stay is less than 90 days.

At the moment, citizens of Australia, Canada, New Zealand, Switzerland, Japan, and European Union countries do not need visas.

If your passport is lost or stolen, head to your consulate as soon as possible for a replacement.

Passport applications are downloadable from the Internet at the following sites: http://travel.state. gov (U.S.); www.dfait-maeci.gc.ca/ passport (Canada); www.open.gov.uk/ ukpass/ukpass.htm (U.K.); www. irlgov.ie/iveagh/foreignaffairs/services (Ireland); www.dfat.gov.au/passports (Australia).

CUSTOMS REGULATIONS
WHAT YOU CAN BRING INTO FRANCE　Customs restrictions differ for citizens of European Union (EU) countries and citizens of non-EU countries.

For Non-EU Nationals　You can bring in, duty-free, 200 cigarettes, 100 cigarillos, 50 cigars, or 250 grams of smoking tobacco. This amount is doubled if you live outside Europe. You can also bring in 2 liters of wine and either 1 liter of alcohol over 22 proof or 2 liters of wine under 22 proof. In addition, you can bring in 50 grams (1.75 ounces) of perfume, a quarter liter (250ml) of eau de toilette, 500 grams (1 pound) of coffee, and 200 grams (half pound) of tea. Visitors 15 and over may also bring in other goods totaling 1,200F (182.40€, $174); the allowance for those 14 and under is 600F (91.20€, $87). (Customs officials tend to be lenient about general merchandise, realizing the limits are unrealistically low.)

For EU Citizens　Visitors from fellow European Union countries can bring into France any amount of goods as long as it's intended for their personal use—not for resale.

WHAT YOU CAN BRING HOME FROM FRANCE　For U.S. Citizens　If you've been out of the country for 48 hours or more, you can bring back into the States $400 worth of goods (per person) without paying a duty. On the first $1,000 worth of goods over $400 you pay a flat 10%. Beyond that, it works on an item-by-item basis. There are a few restrictions on amount: 1 liter of alcohol (you must be over 21), 200 cigarettes, and 100 cigars. Antiques over 100 years old and works of art are exempt from the $400 limit, as is anything you mail home. Once per day, you can mail yourself $200 worth of goods duty-free; mark the package "For Personal Use." You can also mail to other people up to $100 worth of goods per person per day; label each package "Unsolicited Gift." Any package must state on the exterior a description of the contents and their values. You can't mail alcohol, perfume (it contains alcohol), or tobacco products.

For more details on regulations, check out the **U.S. Customs Service** website at www.customs.ustreas.gov or contact the office at P.O. Box 7407, Washington, DC 20044 (© **202/ 927-6724;** www.customs.ustreas.gov), to request the free "Know Before You Go" pamphlet.

To prevent the spread of diseases, you can't bring in any plants, fruits, vegetables, meats, or other foodstuffs. This includes even cured meats like salami. You may bring in the following: bakery goods, all but the softest cheeses (the rule is vague, but if the cheese is at all spreadable, don't risk confiscation), candies, roasted coffee beans and dried tea, fish (packaged salmon is okay), seeds for veggies and flowers (but not for trees), and mushrooms. Check out the USDA's website at www.aphis.usda.gov/oa/travel.html for more details.

For Canadian Citizens For a clear summary of Canadian rules, write for the booklet "I Declare," issued by **Revenue Canada,** 2265 St. Laurent Blvd., Ottawa K1G 4KE (© **506/ 636-5064**), or check out the website www.ccra-adrc.gc.ca. Canada allows its citizens a $750 exemption if you're gone for 7 days or longer (only $200 if you're gone between 48 hours and 7 days), and you're allowed to bring back, duty-free, 200 cigarettes, 50 cigars, and 1.5 liters of wine *or* 1.14 liters of liquor *or* 8.5 liters of beer or ale. In addition, you're allowed to mail gifts to Canada at the rate of $60 a day, provided they're unsolicited and aren't alcohol or tobacco (write on the package "Unsolicited Gift, Under $60 Value").

For U.K. Citizens You'll go through a separate Customs exit (the "Blue Exit") especially for EU travelers. You can bring home almost as much as you like of any goods from any EU country (theoretical limits run along the lines of "90 litres of wine"). If you're returning home from a non-EU country, you're allowed to bring home 200 cigarettes, 2 liters of table wine plus 1 liter of spirits or 2 liters of fortified or sparkling wine, 60 ml/cc of perfume, 250 ml/cc of toilet water, and a total of £145 in other goods. For more information, get in touch with **Her Majesty's Customs and Excise Office,** Berkeley House, 304 Regents Park Rd., Finchley, London N3 2JY

(© **020/7202-4131** in central London; call 020/7202-4227 for other locations), or check out its website at www.hmce.gov.uk.

For Australian Citizens The duty-free allowance in Australia is A$400 or, for those under 18, A$200. Upon returning to Australia, citizens can bring in 250 cigarettes or 250 grams of loose tobacco and 1.125 liters of alcohol. A helpful brochure, available from Australian consulates or Customs offices, is "Know Before You Go." For more information, contact **Australian Customs Services,** GPO Box 8, Sydney NSW 2001 (© **02/ 921-32-000** within Australia; 02/ 6275-6666; www.customs.gov.au from overseas).

For New Zealand Citizens The duty-free allowance for New Zealand is NZ$700. Citizens over 17 can bring back 200 cigarettes or 50 cigars or 250 grams of tobacco (or a mix of all three if their combined weight does not exceed 250 grams); plus 4.5 liters of wine *or* beer, plus 1.125 liters of liquor. Most questions are answered in the free "Advice to Travelers" pamphlet available at New Zealand consulates and Customs offices. For more information, contact the **New Zealand Customshouse,** 17–21 Whitmore St., Box 2218, Wellington (© **800/428-786** or 04-473-6099), or check out its website at www. customs.govt.nz.

3 Money

CURRENCY

During part of the life of this edition, France will have two currencies—the old French franc and the new euro adopted by 11 nations of the European Union. French currency is based on the **franc (F),** which consists of 100 **centimes (c).** Coins come in units of 5c, 10c, 20c, and 50c and 1F, 2F, 5F, and 10F. Notes come in

denominations of 20F, 50F, 100F, 200F, 500F, and 1,000F. The front of the 200F note honors Gustave Eiffel, creator of the Eiffel Tower, father of experimental aerodynamics, and part-designer of New York's Statue of Liberty.

The franc will remain France's currency only until March 1, 2002. Then the **euro,** which has already been

The Euro & You

The **euro (E or EUR)**, the new single European currency, became the official currency of France and 10 other countries on January 1, 1999. You'll likely see prices in restaurants, shops, and so on listed in both French francs and euros. However, the franc will remain the only currency for cash transactions until December 21, 2001 (you can use it in non-cash transactions, as with checks and credit cards). At that time, euro banknotes and coins will be introduced, and franc banknotes and coins will be withdrawn from circulation during a maximum 2-month transition period. On March 1, 2002, the euro will become the only currency.

For more details on the euro, check out the website www.europa.eu.int/euro.

introduced, will take over completely. See "The Euro & You" above.

All banks are equipped for foreign exchange, and you'll find exchange offices at the airports and airline terminals. Banks are open Monday to Friday, from 9am to noon and 2 to 4pm. Major bank branches also open their exchange departments on Saturday, from 9am to noon.

When converting your home currency into French francs or euros, be aware that rates vary. Your hotel will probably offer the worst exchange rate. In general, banks offer the best rate, but even banks charge a commission for the service, often $5, depending on the transaction. Whenever you can, stick to the big Paris banks, like Crédit Lyonnais, which usually offer the best exchange rates and charge the least commission.

ATMS

Using ATMs is the fastest, easiest, and least expensive way to change money. You take advantage of the bank's bulk exchange rate (better than anything you'll get on your own exchanging cash or traveler's checks) and, unless your home bank charges you for using a non-proprietary ATM, you won't have to pay a commission.

Both the **Cirrus** (②**800/424-7787;** www.mastercard.com) and the **PLUS** (② **800/843-7587;** www.visa.com) networks have automated ATM locators listing the banks in Paris that will accept your card. Or just search out any machine with your network's symbol emblazoned on it. Be sure to check the daily withdrawal limit before you depart and ask whether you need a new PIN (see the "A PIN Alert" box in this chapter).

CREDIT CARDS

Credit cards are invaluable when traveling. They're a safe way to carry money, they provide a convenient record of all your expenses, and you can withdraw cash advances from your credit cards at any bank (though you'll start paying hefty interest on the advance the moment you receive the cash and won't receive frequent-flyer miles on an airline credit card). At most banks, you don't even need to go to a teller; you can get a cash advance at the ATM with your PIN (see the "A PIN Alert" box in this chapter).

Almost every credit-card company has an emergency toll-free number you can call if your wallet or purse is stolen. The company may be able to wire you a cash advance off your credit

The French Franc, the U.S. Dollar, the British Pound & the Euro

Because exchange rates fluctuate, this table should be used only as a general guide.

For the best exchange rate, cash your traveler's checks at banks or foreign-exchange offices, not at shops and hotels. The French franc (F) is divided into 100 centimes. There are coins of 5, 10, 20, and 50 centimes (the latter is usually referred to as a half-franc coin); and 1, 2, 5, 10, and 20 francs. Bills come in 20, 50, 100, 200, and 500-franc denominations, although the 20-franc bill is increasingly rare, as it's being gradually withdrawn from circulation.

At this writing, $1 U.S. = about 6.89F (or 1F = 14.5¢); this was the rate of exchange used to calculate the dollar values, both in the rest of this guidebook and in the table below. At this writing, one British pound = about 10.34F (or 1F = 9.7 pence). As a rough guideline, subject to multiple revisions as Europe's newest currency increases in usage, 1 Euro = about 91 U.S. cents, 6.57 French francs, or 63 U.K. pence.

FF	U.S.$	UK£	Euro	FF	U.S.$	UK£	Euro
1	0.15	0.97	0.15	75	10.88	72.75	11.4
2	0.29	1.94	0.30	100	14.50	97.00	15.20
3	0.44	2.91	0.46	125	18.13	121.25	19.00
4	0.58	3.88	0.61	150	21.75	145.50	22.80
5	0.73	4.85	0.76	175	25.38	169.75	26.60
6	0.87	5.82	0.91	200	29.00	194.00	30.40
7	1.02	6.79	1.06	225	32.63	218.25	34.20
8	1.16	7.76	1.22	250	36.25	242.50	38.00
9	1.31	8.73	1.37	275	39.88	266.75	41.80
10	1.45	9.70	1.52	300	43.50	291.00	45.60
15	2.18	14.55	2.28	350	50.75	339.50	53.20
20	2.90	19.40	3.04	400	58.00	388.00	60.80
25	3.63	24.25	3.80	500	72.50	485.00	76.00
50	7.25	48.50	7.60	1000	145.00	970.00	152.00

card immediately and, in many places, can deliver an emergency card in a day or two. The issuing bank's toll-free number is usually on the back of the credit card—though that doesn't help you if the card was stolen. Citicorp Visa's U.S. emergency number is ⓒ **800/336-8472** or 410/581-3836. American Express cardholders and traveler's check holders should call ⓒ **800/233-5439** for all money emergencies. MasterCard holders should call ⓒ **800/307-7309.**

TRAVELER'S CHECKS

These days, traveler's checks seem less necessary than they used to because most cities have 24-hour ATMs allowing you to withdraw small amounts of cash as needed. Many banks, however, impose a fee every time a card is used at an ATM in a different city or bank. If you're withdrawing money every day, you may be better off with traveler's checks—provided you don't mind showing ID every time you want to cash a check.

Tips A PIN Alert

Make sure the PINs on your bankcards and credit cards will work in Paris. You usually need a four-digit code (six digits often won't work). Also keep in mind that you're usually able to access only your checking account, not savings, from ATMs abroad.

American Express (℡ 800/221-7282; www.americanexpress.com) is one of the largest issuers, and its checks are the most commonly accepted. It'll also sell checks to holders of certain types of American Express cards at no commission. **Thomas Cook** (℡ **800/223-7373** in the U.S. and Canada, 0800/622-101 in the U.K., or 44-1733/294-451 collect from other parts of the world; www.thomascook.com) issues Master-Card traveler's checks. **Citicorp** (℡ **800/645-6556** in the U.S. and Canada, or 813/623-1709 collect from anywhere else in the world; www.citicorp.com) and many other banks issue checks under their own name or under MasterCard or Visa.

4 When to Go

In August, Parisians traditionally leave town for their annual holiday and put the city on a skeleton staff to serve visitors. July has also become a popular vacation month, with many a restaurateur shuttering up for a month-long respite.

Hotels, especially first-class and deluxe, are easy to come by in July and August. Budget hotels, on the other hand, are likely to be full during these months of student invasion. You might also try to avoid the first 2 weeks in October, when the annual auto show attracts thousands of enthusiasts.

THE WEATHER: APRIL IN PARIS?

Balmy weather in Paris has prompted more popular songs and love ballads than weather conditions in any other city. But the weather here is actually quite fickle. Rain is much more common than snow throughout the winter, prompting many longtime residents to complain about the occasional bone-chilling dampness.

In recent years, Paris has had only about 15 snow days a year, and there are only a few oppressively hot days (over 86°F) in midsummer. What will most likely chill a Parisian heart, however, are blasts of rapidly moving air— wind tunnels sweep along the city's long boulevards, channeled by bordering buildings of uniform height. Other than the occasional winds and rain (which add an undeniable drama to many of the city's panoramas), Paris offers some of the most pleasant weather of any capital in Europe, with a highly tolerable average temperature of 53°F.

HOLIDAYS

Holidays in France are known as *jours feriés.* Shops and banks are closed, as well as many (but not all) restaurants and museums. Major holidays include January 1, Easter, Ascension Day (40 days after Easter), Pentecost (seventh Sunday after Easter), May 1, May 8 (VE Day), July 14 (Bastille Day), August 15 (Assumption of the Virgin Mary), November 1 (All Saints' Day), November 11 (Armistice Day), and December 25 (Christmas).

PARIS CALENDAR OF EVENTS

Check the Paris Tourist Office website at **www.paris-touristoffice.com** and other websites listed in chapter 1 for up-to-the-minute details on these and other events.

January

International Ready-to-Wear Fashion Shows (Salon International de Prêt-à-Porter), Parc des Expositions, 15th arr. Hundreds of designers, from the giants to the virtually unknown, unveil their visions (hallucinations?) about what you should be wearing 6 months down the road. The event in the massive Porte de Versailles convention facilities is geared to wholesalers, retailers, buyers, journalists, and industry professionals, but for the 130F ($20.80) entrance fee, the rules are usually bent for the merely fashion conscious. Much more exclusive are the *défilés* (fashion shows) held around the same time at the headquarters of individual houses like Lagerfeld, Lanvin, Courrèges, and Valentino. For details, call ℂ **01-44-94-70-00.** Mid-January to mid-February.

February

Special Exhibitions, Special Concerts: During Paris's grayest month, look for a splash of temporary expositions and concerts designed to perk up the city. Concerts and theaters spring up at such diverse sites as the **Salle Pleyel,** 252 rue du faubourg St-Honoré, 8th arr. (ℂ **01-45-61-53-00;** Métro: Ternes); the **Théâtre des Champs-Elysées,** 15 av. Montaigne, 8th arr. (ℂ **01-49-52-50-50;** Métro: Alma-Marceau); and the **Maison Radio-France,** 116 av. du Président-Kennedy, 16th arr. (ℂ **01-42-30-15-16;** Métro: Passy-Ranelagh). Also look for openings of new operas at the **Opéra Bastille,** 2 place de la Bastille, 4th arr.

(ℂ **08-36-69-78-68;** Métro: Bastille), operas and dance at the **Opéra Garnier,** place de l'Opéra, 9th arr. (ℂ **01-40-01-17-89**), and concerts beneath Europe's most famous glass pyramid, the **Pyramide du Louvre,** 1st arr. (ℂ **01-40-20-52-29;** Métro: Musée du Louvre) and the **Salle Cortot,** 78 rue Cardinet, 17th arr. (ℂ **01-47-63-85-72;** Métro: Malesherbes). A copy of *Pariscope* or *L'Officiel des Spectacles* is the best info source.

March

Foire du Trône, Bois de Vincennes, 12th arr. A mammoth amusement park that its fans promote as France's largest country fair, the Foire du Trône boasts origins dating from the year 957, when merchants met with farmers on a nearby site to exchange grain and wine. This high-tech continuation of that tradition, held on the lawns of the Pelouse de Reuilly, incorporates a Ferris wheel, carousels, acrobats, jugglers, fire eaters, and amusements and diversions that seem like a Gallic Coney Island. It's open Sunday to Thursday from 2pm to midnight and Friday and Saturday from 2pm to 1am. For details, call ℂ **01-46-27-52-29.** Late March to late May.

April

Fête de Jazz de Paris, citywide. Some of the world's best-known jazz artists descend on Paris for this 14-day jazz fest, followed by their aficionados. Clubs both high- and lowbrow throw open their doors. The atmosphere is dark and smoky, the crowds hip. For details, call ℂ **01-47-83-33-58.** Late April to mid-May.

International Marathon of Paris. Beginning on the Champs-Elysées at 9am, runners take over many of Paris's boulevards in a televised race that draws competitors from around the world. Depending on their speed and endurance, participants arrive at the finishing point on avenue Foch, 16e, beginning about 2½ hours later. If you haven't felt like jogging lately, this event might inspire you. For details, call ℂ **01-41-33-15-68.** First weekend in April.

Les Grandes Eaux Musicales, Versailles. These musical events are intended to re-create the atmosphere of the ancient regime. On these rare occasions, the fountains of the parks around the palace are turned on, with special emphasis on the Neptune Fountain, which sits squarely in front of the best view of the château. You can promenade in the garden and listen to the drifting music of French composers (Couperin, Charpentier, and Lully) and others (Mozart or Haydn) whose careers thrived during the years of the palace's construction. The music is generally recorded, but concerts take place every Sunday from 11:15am to 5:30pm. For details, call ℂ **01-39-24-88-88.** April to early October.

May

VE Day, citywide. The celebration commemorating the capitulation of the Nazis on May 7, 1945, lasts 4 days in Paris, with a parade along the Champs-Elysées and additional ceremonies in Reims. Pro-American sentiments are probably higher during this festival than at any other time of year. May 5 to 8.

Grand Steeplechase de Paris, Auteuil and Longchamp racetracks, Bois de Boulogne. This is a counterpoint to the horse races conducted at Chantilly (below). For details, call ℂ **01-49-10-20-30.** May 27.

French Open Tennis Championship, Stade Roland-Garros, 16th arr. The Open features 10 days of Grand Slam men's and women's tennis, with European and South American players traditionally dominating on the hot, dusty red courts. For details, call ℂ **01-47-43-48-00.** Late May to mid-June.

June

Prix du Jockey Club (June 6 at 2pm) **& Prix Diane-Hermès** (June 8 at 2pm), Hippodrome de Chantilly. Thoroughbreds from as far away as Kentucky and Brunei, as well as mounts sponsored by Europe's old and new fortunes, compete in a very civil competition broadcast around France and talked about in horsey circles around the world. On race days, as many as 30 trains depart from Paris's Gare du Nord for Chantilly, where they're met by free shuttle buses to the track. Alternatively, buses depart on race days from place de la République and Porte de St-Cloud, on a schedule that coincides with the beginning and end of the races. For details on this and all other equine events in this calendar, call ℂ **01-49-10-20-30.**

Fête de St-Denis, St-Denis. This series presents 4 days of artfully contrived music in the burial place of the French kings, a grim early Gothic monument in this industrialized northern suburb. For details, call ℂ **01-48-13-06-07.** June 13 to July 3.

Paris Air Show, Le Bourget. This is where France's military-industrial complex shows off enough high-tech hardware to make anyone think twice about invading La Patrie. Fans, competitors, and industrial spies mob the airport's exhibition halls for a taste of what Gallic technocrats have wrought. For details, call ℂ **01-53-23-33-33.** June 14 to 18 (in odd-numbered years only).

Fête Chopin, Orangerie du Parc de Bagatelle, Versailles. Hear all you ever wanted to hear at these piano recitals from the Polish exile who lived most of his life in Paris. For details, call ✆ **01-45-00-22-19.** June 19 to July 14.

Festival du Marais, the Marais. A major event for the arts, this festival offers the finest in classical music, traditional and modern dance, and plays in the historic *hôtels* (mansions) and churches of this district in the 4th arrondissement. For details, call ✆ **01-48-87-60-08.** Mid-June to mid-July.

Fête de la Musique, citywide. This celebration at the summer solstice is the one day that noise laws don't apply in Paris. Musicians and wannabes pour out into the streets, where you can make music with anything, even if it means banging two garbage cans together or driving around blowing your car horn (illegal otherwise). You might hear anything from newly arrived Russians on the balalaikas to Cubans playing salsa rhythms. There are musical parties in virtually all the open spaces, with more organized concerts at place de la Bastille and place de la République and in La Villette and the Latin Quarter. For details, call ✆ **01-40-03-94-70.** June 21.

Festival Musique en l'Ile. A series of concerts, most including dignified masses composed from the 17th to the late 19th centuries, are presented at the Church Saint Louis en'Ile and the Church Saint-Germain-des-Prés. For more information, call La Toison d'Art at ✆ **01-44-62-00-55.** June 26 to September 3.

Gay Pride Parade, place de l'Odéon to place de la Bastille. A week of expositions and parties climaxes in a massive parade patterned after those in New York and San Francisco. It's followed by a dance at the Palais de Bercy, a major convention hall/sports arena. For details, see www.gaypride.fr. June 23.

La Course des Garçons de Café, throughout the city. There's no more amusing race in Paris. Balancing heavily loaded trays, the *garçons* (both waiters and waitresses) line up in front of the Hôtel de Ville in the 4th arrondissement and then race for 5 miles through the streets, ending back at the Hôtel de Ville. Some obviously don't make it. A Sunday in the last week of June or the first week of July.

La Villette Jazz Festival, La Villette. This dynamic homage to the art of jazz incorporates 50 concerts in churches, auditoriums, and concert halls in all neighborhoods of this Paris suburb. Past festivals have included Herbie Hancock, Shirley Horn, Michel Portal, and other artists from around the world. For details, call ✆ **08-03-30-63-06.** Late June to the first week in July.

July

Tour de France. This is Europe's most visible, most highly contested, and most overabundantly televised bicycle race. Crews of wind-tunnel-tested athletes speed along an itinerary tracing the six sides of the French "hexagon" and detouring deep into the Massif Central and across the Swiss Alps. The race is decided at a finish line drawn across the Champs-Elysées. For details, call ✆ **01-41-33-15-00.** July 3 to 21.

Bastille Day, citywide. This celebration of the 1789 storming of the Bastille is the accepted birth date of modern France, and festivities reach their peak in Paris with street fairs, pageants, fireworks, and feasts. The day begins with a parade down the Champs-Elysées and ends with fireworks in Montmartre. Wherever you are, before the end of the day you'll hear Piaf warbling "La Foule" ("The Crowd"), the song that celebrated her passion for the stranger she met and later lost in a crowd on Bastille Day, and lots of people singing "La Marseillaise." July 14.

Paris Quartier d'Eté, Latin Quarter. For 4 weeks, the Arènes de Lutèce or the Sorbonne's Cour d'Honneur host pop orchestral concerts. The dozen or so concerts are usually grander than the outdoor setting would imply and include performances by the Orchestre de Paris, Orchestre National de France, and Baroque Orchestra of the European Union. On the fringes you can find plays, jazz concerts, and parades in the Tuileries. For details, call ✆ **01-44-94-98-00** or fax 01-44-94-98-01. July 15 to August 15.

September

Biennale des Antiquaires, Cour Carrée at the Louvre or the Grand Palais. Antiques dealers and lovers from all over the world gather at this gilded event in even-numbered years. Precious furnishings and objets d'art are displayed in the underground exhibit halls linked to the Louvre or perhaps in the Grand Palais once it's restored. For details, call ✆ **01-44-51-74-74;** www.antiquaries-sna.com. Usually first week in September.

Fête d'Automne (Autumn Festival), citywide. Paris welcomes the return of its residents from their August holidays with an ongoing and eclectic festival of modern music, ballet, theater, and modern art. Venues include art galleries, churches, concert halls, auditoriums, and parks throughout Paris. There's a great emphasis on experimental works, which the festival's promoters scatter judiciously between more traditional productions. Depending on the

event, tickets cost from 200 to 600F (30.40–91.20€, $29–$87). For details, contact the **Festival d'Automne,** 156 rue de Rivoli, 75001 Paris (✆ **01-53-45-17-00;** fax 01-53-45-17-01). Late September to mid-December.

International Ready-to-Wear Fashion Shows (Salon International de Prêt-à-Porter), Parc des Expositions, 15th arr. More of what took place at the fashion shows in January (above), with a stress on what le beau monde will be wearing next spring. Early September.

October

Paris Auto Show, Parc des Expositions, 15th arr. Glitzy attendees and lots of hype attend this showcase for European car design. The auto show takes place near the Porte de Versailles in western Paris. In addition, a permanent exhibit on French auto design at the Cité des Sciences et de l'Industrie is upgraded and enriched during October. For details, call ✆ **01-56-88-22-40.** Fifteen days in early October in even-numbered years.

Prix de l'Arc de Triomphe, Hippodrome de Longchamp, 16th arr. France's answer to England's Ascot is the country's most prestigious horse race, culminating the equine season in Europe. For details, call ✆ **01-49-10-20-30.** Early October.

November

Armistice Day, citywide. The signing of the controversial document that ended World War I is celebrated with a military parade from the Arc de Triomphe to the Hôtel des Invalides. November 11.

Fête d'Art Sacré (Festival of Sacred Art). A dignified series of classical concerts is held in five of the oldest and most recognizable churches of Paris. For details, call ✆ **01-44-70-64-10.** Mid-November to mid-December.

Release of the Beaujolais Nouveau, citywide. Parisians eagerly await the yearly release of the first of the new Beaujolais, that fruity wine from Burgundy. Signs are posted in bistros, wine bars, and cafes—these places report their heaviest patronage of the year during this celebration from the vineyards. Third Thursday in November.

December

Paris Boat Show (Salon International de la Navigation de Plaisance), Parc des Expositions, 15th arr. This is Europe's most visible exposition of what's afloat and of interest to wholesalers, retailers, individual boat owners (or wannabes), and anyone involved in the business of waterborne holiday-making. For details, call ✆ **01-41-90-47-10,** fax 01-41-90-47-00, or check on the Web at www.salonnautiqueparis.com. Eight days in early December.

Fête de St-Sylvestre (New Year's Eve), citywide. It's most boisterously celebrated in the Latin Quarter around the Sorbonne. At midnight, the city explodes. Strangers kiss strangers, and boulevard St-Michel and the Champs-Elysées become virtual pedestrian malls. December 31.

5 Health & Insurance

STAYING HEALTHY

If you're worried about getting sick away from home, you may want to consider **medical travel insurance** (see below). In most cases, however, your existing health plan will provide all the coverage you need. Be sure to carry your ID card in your wallet. If you suffer from a chronic illness, consult your doctor before your departure. For conditions like epilepsy, diabetes, or heart problems, wear a **Medic Alert Identification Tag** (✆ **800/825-3785;** www.medicalert.org), which will immediately alert doctors to your condition and give them access to your records through Medic Alert's 24-hour hot line. Membership is $35, plus a $15 annual fee.

Pack prescription medications in your carry-on luggage. Carry written prescriptions in generic, not brand-name, form, and dispense all prescription medications from their original labeled vials. Also bring along copies of your prescriptions in case you lose your pills or run out.

The **International Association for Medical Assistance to Travelers (IAMAT)** (✆ **716/754-4883** or 416/652-0137; www.sentedx.net/~iamat), offers tips on travel and health concerns in Europe and lists many local English-speaking doctors.

INSURANCE

There are three kinds of travel insurance: trip cancellation, medical, and stolen/lost luggage. **Trip-cancellation insurance** is a good idea if you've paid a large portion of your vacation expenses up front. This type of insurance covers two emergencies—one if your trip is cancelled and two if a death or sickness prevents you from going. The other two types, however, don't make sense for most travelers. *Note:* Check your existing policies before you buy any additional coverage.

Your existing health insurance should cover you if you get sick while on vacation (though if you belong to an HMO, you should check to see whether you're fully covered when away from home). If you need hospital treatment, most health insurance plans and HMOs will cover out-of-country hospital visits and procedures, at least to some extent. However, most make you pay the bills up front at the time of care, and you get a refund after you've returned and filed all the paperwork. Members of **Blue Cross/ Blue Shield** can now use their cards at select hospitals in most major cities worldwide (© **800/810-BLUE;** www. bluecares.com). For independent travel health-insurance providers, see below, although insurance packages, covering such items as health and luggage, are usually available through your travel agent.

The differences between travel assistance and insurance are often blurred, but in general, the former offers on-the-spot assistance and 24-hour hot lines (mostly oriented toward medical problems), while the latter reimburses you for travel problems (medical, travel, or otherwise) after you've filed the paperwork. The coverage you should consider will depend on how much protection is already contained in your existing health insurance or other policies. Some credit-card companies may insure you against travel accidents if you buy plane, train, or bus tickets with their cards. Before buying additional insurance, read your policies and agreements carefully. Some credit cards offer automatic flight insurance against death or dismemberment in case of an airplane crash. Call your

insurers or credit-card companies if you have any questions.

If you do require extra insurance, try one of these reputable issuers: **Access America,** 6600 W. Broad St., Richmond, VA 23230 (© **800/ 284-8300;** www.accessamerica.com); **Travel Guard International,** 1145 Clark St., Stevens Point, WI 54481 (© **800/826-1300;** www.noelgroup. com); **Travel Insured International, Inc.,** P.O. Box 280568, East Hartford, CT 06128 (© **800/243-3174;** www. travelinsured.com); **Columbus Travel Insurance Ltd.,** 279 High St., Croydon CR0 1QH (© **020/7375-0011** in London; www2.columbusdirect. net); **Travelex Insurance Services,** P.O. Box 9408, Garden City, NY 11530-9408 (© **800/228-9792;** www.travelex-insurance.com).

Companies specializing in accident and medical care include **MEDEX International,** P.O. Box 5375, Timonium, MD 21094-5375 (© **888/ MEDEX-00** or 410/453-6300; fax 410/453-6301; www.medexassist. com), and **Travel Assistance International,** 9200 Keystone Crossing, 300, Washington, DC 20005 (© **800/ 821-2828** or 202/828-5894; fax 202/ 828-5896; www.specialtyrisk.com/tai).

6 Tips for Travelers with Special Needs

FOR TRAVELERS WITH DISABILITIES
A disability shouldn't stop anyone from traveling, and there are more resources than ever before. Facilities in Paris for travelers with disabilities are certainly better than you'll find in most cities. Every year the French government does more and more to help ease life for these individuals. Nearly all modern hotels in France now have rooms designed especially for persons with disabilities. Older hotels, unless renovated, may not provide important features like elevators, special toilet facilities, or ramps for wheelchair accessibility. Depending on your

needs, it's best to contact each hotel directly and make your special needs known before you arrive.

Most high-speed trains in France can deal with wheelchairs, and guide dogs ride free. Older trains have special compartments built for wheelchair boarding. On the Paris Métro, persons with disabilities can sit in wider seats provided for their comfort. Some stations don't have escalators or elevators, however, and this may present problems.

A World of Options, a 658-page book of resources for persons with disabilities, covers everything from biking trips to scuba outfitters. It costs

$35 ($30 for members) and is available from **Mobility International USA,** P.O. Box 10767, Eugene, OR 97440 (© **541/343-1284;** www.miusa.org). Annual membership is $35, which includes the quarterly newsletter *Over the Rainbow.* In addition, **Twin Peaks Press,** P.O. Box 129, Vancouver, WA 98666 (© **360/694-2462**), publishes travel-related books for people with disabilities.

To gain access to its vast network of connections in the travel industry, you can join the **Society for the Advancement of Travel for the Handicapped (SATH),** 347 Fifth Ave., Suite 610, New York, NY 10016 (© **212/447-7284;** fax 212/725-8253; www.sath. org), for $45 annually, $30 for seniors/students. It provides info sheets on destinations and referrals to tour operators specializing in traveling with individuals with disabilities. Its quarterly magazine, *Open World for Disability and Mature Travel,* is full of good information and resources; a year's subscription is $18 ($35 outside the U.S.).

You can obtain a copy of *Air Transportation of Handicapped Persons* by writing to Free Advisory Circular No. AC12032, Distribution Unit, U.S. Department of Transportation, Publications Division, M-4332, Washington, DC 20590.

Travelers with vision impairments should contact the **American Foundation for the Blind,** 11 Penn Plaza, Suite 300, New York, NY 10001 (© **800/232-5463** or 212/502-7600; www.afb.org), for information on traveling with Seeing Eye dogs.

A non-profit French organization equipped to answer your questions is the **APF Evasion** (Association des Paralysés de France), 17 bd. Auguste-Blanqui, 75013 Paris (© **01-40-78-69-00**). Occasionally, they organize tours through France (sometimes farther afield) for small groups; if you show an interest in participating,

they'll make special efforts to hire English-speaking guides and monitors. If you don't want to travel as part of a group, it'll try to put you in contact with a fully enabled paid escort.

FOR GAYS & LESBIANS

France is one of the world's most tolerant countries toward gays and lesbians, and no special laws discriminate against them. "Gay Paree" boasts a large gay population, with dozens of gay clubs, restaurants, organizations, and services. Before leaving home, you may want to pick up a copy of *Frommer's Gay & Lesbian Europe,* with chapters on Paris and Nice and the Côte d'Azur.

The **International Gay & Lesbian Travel Association (IGLTA),** 4331 N. Federal Hwy., Suite 304, Ft. Lauderdale, FL 33308 (© **800/448-8550;** fax 954/776-3303; www.iglta.com), is a great general resource. Members ($100 to join, plus $150 a year) get a newsletter and membership directory, but even non-members can get advice on specialist travel agencies (or search for local ones on the website). A general gay/lesbian travel agency is **Kennedy Travels,** 314 Jericho Turnpike, Floral Park, NY 11001 (© **800/988-1181;** www.kennedytravel.com).

The magazine *Our World,* 1104 North Nova Rd., Suite 251, Daytona beach, FL 32117 (© **904/441-5367;** www.ourworldmag.com), covers options and bargains for gay and lesbian travel worldwide. It costs $35 for 10 issues. *Out and About,* 657 Harrison St., San Francisco, CA 94107 (© **800/929-2268;** 415/229-1793; www.outandabout.com), has been hailed for its "straight" reporting about gay travel. It profiles the best gay or gay-friendly hotels, gyms, clubs, and other places at destinations throughout the world. It costs $49 for 10 information-packed issues. **SOS Ecoute Gay** at © **01-44-93-01-02** is a gay hot line designed to creatively counsel persons with gay-related problems. The phone is answered by volunteers, some of whom are more helpful than others. A phone counselor responds to calls Monday and Wednesday from 8 to 10pm and Tuesday, Thursday, and Friday from 6 to 8pm. Also helpful is **La Maison des Femmes,** 163 rue de Charenton, 12e (© **01-43-43-41-13;** Métro: Reuilly-Diderot), offering information about Paris for lesbians and bisexual women, and sometimes sponsoring informal dinners and get-togethers. Call anytime for a recorded announcement that gives the hours that someone will be available for that particular week.

Gai Pied's publication *Guide Gai* (revised annually) is the best source of information on gay and lesbian clubs, hotels, restaurants, organizations, and services in the capital. Lesbian or bisexual women might also like to pick up a copy of *Lesbia,* if only to check out the ads. These and other publications are available at Paris's largest gay bookstore, **Les Mots à la Bouche,** 6 rue Ste-Croix-de-la-Bretonnerie, 4th arr. (© **01-42-78-88-30**). Hours are Monday to Saturday from 11am to 11pm and Sunday from 2 to 8pm. Both French- and English-language publications are available.

FOR SENIORS

Don't be shy about asking for discounts, but always carry some kind of ID, like a driver's license, showing your date of birth. And mention the fact that you're a senior when you first make your travel reservations. For example, many hotels offer senior discounts. In most cities, people over 60 qualify for reduced admission to theaters, museums, and other attractions, and discounted fares on public transportation.

Members of the **American Association of Retired Persons (AARP),** 601 E St. NW, Washington, DC 20049 (© **800/424-3410** or 202/434-AARP; www.aarp.org), get discounts not only on hotels but also on airfares and car rentals. AARP offers members a wide range of special benefits, including *Modern Maturity* magazine and a monthly newsletter.

The non-profit **National Council of Senior Citizens,** 8403 Colesville Rd., Suite 1200, Silver Spring, MD 20910 (© **301/578-8800;** www.ncscinc.org), offers a newsletter six times a year (partly devoted to travel tips) and discounts on hotel and auto rentals; annual dues are $13 per person or couple. **Travel Companion Exchange,** P.O. Box 5249, Reno, NV 89513 (© **800/392-1256** or 631/454-0880; www.whytravelalone.com), helps travelers, 45-plus find compatible companions through a personal voice-mail service. Contact them for details.

Mature Traveler, a monthly 12-page newsletter on senior travel, is a valuable resource, available by subscription ($30 a year) from GEM Publishing Group, Box 50400, Reno, NV 89513-0400. Another helpful publication is *101 Tips for the Mature Traveler,* available from Grand Circle Travel, 347 Congress St., Suite 3A, Boston, MA 02210 (© **800/221-2610** or 617/350-7500; fax 617/346-6700).

Grand Circle Travel, 347 Congress St., Suite 3A, Boston, MA 02210 (© **800/221-2610** or 617/350-7500; www.gct.com), is also one of the hundreds of travel agencies specializing in vacations for seniors. Many of these packages, however, are of the tour-bus variety, with free trips thrown in for those who organize groups of 10 or more. Seniors seeking more independent travel should probably consult a regular travel agent. **SAGA International Holidays,** 222 Berkeley St., Boston, MA 02116 (© **800/343-0273;** www.sagaholidays.com), offers inclusive tours and cruises for those 50 and older. SAGA also sponsors the more substantial **Road Scholar Tours** (© 800/621-2151).

A variation on the same theme, **Elderhostel** provides educational travel for seniors. On these escorted tours, the days are packed with seminars, lectures, and field trips, and the sightseeing is led by academic experts. **Elderhostel,** 75 Federal St., Boston, MA 02110-1941 (© 877/426-8056; www.elderhostel.org), arranges study programs for those 55 and over (and a spouse or companion of any age) in the United States and in 77 countries around the world, including France. Most courses last about 3 weeks and many include airfare, accommodations in student dorms or modest inns, meals, and tuition. Write or call for a free catalog that lists upcoming courses and destinations.

FOR STUDENTS

Paris offers student discounts on nearly everything, from museums to movies. The best resource for students is the **Council on International Educational Exchange (CIEE);** © 212/822-2700. It can set you up with an ID card (see below), and its travel branch, **Council Travel Service** (© 888/COUNCIL; www.ciee.org), is the biggest student travel agency operation in the world. It can get you discounts on plane tickets, rail passes, and the like.

From CIEE you can obtain the student traveler's best friend, the $18 **International Student Identity Card (ISIC).** It's the only officially acceptable form of student ID, good for cut rates on rail passes, plane tickets, and other discounts. It also provides you with basic health and life insurance and a 24-hour help line. If you're no longer a student but are still under 26, you can get from the same people a **GO 25 card,** which will get you the insurance and some of the discounts.

In Canada, **Travel CUTS,** 200 Ronson St., Ste. 320, Toronto, ONT M9W 5Z9 (© 800/667-2887 or 416/614-2887; www.travelcuts.com), offers similar services. **USIT Campus,** 52 Grosvenor Gardens, London SW1W 0AG (© 0870/240-1010; www.usitcampus.co.uk), opposite Victoria Station, is Britain's leading specialist in student and youth travel.

7 Getting There

BY PLANE
THE MAJOR AIRLINES
FROM NORTH AMERICA One of the best choices for travelers in the southeastern United States and the Midwest is **Delta Airlines** (© 800/241-4141; www.delta.com). From cities like New Orleans, Phoenix, Columbia (South Carolina), and Nashville, Delta flies to Atlanta, connecting every evening with a non-stop flight to Paris. Delta also operates daily non-stop flights to Paris from Cincinnati and New York.

Another excellent choice is **United Airlines** (© 800/538-2929; www.ual.com), with non-stop flights from Chicago, Washington, D.C., and San Francisco to Paris. United also offers discounted fares in the low and shoulder seasons to London from five major North American hubs. From London, it's an easy train and Hovercraft or Chunnel connection to Paris, a fact that tempts many passengers to spend a weekend in London either before or after their visit to Paris.

Another good option is **Continental Airlines** (© 800/231-0856; www.flycontinental.com), serving the Northeast and much of the Southwest through its busy hubs in Newark and Houston. From both of those cities, Continental provides non-stop flights to Paris.

TWA (© 800/221-2000; www.twa.com), operates daily non-stop service to Paris from New York and in

Sample Flying Times

The flying time to Paris from New York is about 7 hours; from Chicago, 9 hours; from Los Angeles, 11 hours; from Atlanta, about 8 hours; from Washington, D.C., about 7½ hours; from London, about 1 hour; from Edinburgh, 2 hours; from Dublin, 2 hours; from Sydney, 21½ hours; from Auckland, 23¼ hours.

summer several flights a week from Boston and Washington, D.C. In summer, TWA also flies to Paris from St. Louis several times a week non-stop and from Los Angeles three times a week, with connections in St. Louis or New York. In winter, flights from Los Angeles and Washington, D.C. are suspended and flights from St. Louis are routed with brief touch-downs en route to Paris in New York or Boston.

The French flag carrier, **Air France** (© 800/237-2747; www.airfrance. com), offers daily or several-times-a-week flights to Paris from Newark; Washington, D.C.; Miami; Chicago; New York; Houston; San Francisco; Los Angeles; Boston; Cincinnati; Atlanta; Montréal; Toronto; and Mexico City.

American Airlines (© 800/433-7300; www.aa.com), provides daily non-stop flights to Paris from Dallas/Fort Worth, Chicago, Miami, Boston, and New York. American Airlines now flies into Roissy-Charles de Gaulle instead of Orly Airport. Facilities at its new terminal 2A include a deluxe Admirals Club, plus a mammoth Arrivals Lounge complete with 10 showers. And **USAirways** (© 800/428-4322; www.usairways.com) offers daily non-stop service from Philadelphia to Paris.

If you'd like to see London before traveling on to Paris, there are dozens of **British Airways** (© 800/247-9297; www.british-airways.com) flights from North America and Canadian cities to London. You can fly first from, say, New York to London, then take the BA shuttle flight to Paris following a holiday in England.

Canadians usually choose **Air Canada** (© 888/247-2262 from the U.S. and Canada; www.aircanada.ca) for flights to Paris from Toronto and Montréal. Non-stop flights from Montréal and Toronto depart every evening. Two of the non-stop flights from Toronto are shared with Air France and feature Air France aircraft.

FROM THE UNITED KINGDOM From London, **Air France** (© 0845/084-5111; www.airfrance.com) and **British Airways** (© 0345/222-111 in the U.K.; www.british-airways. com) fly frequently to Paris, offering up to 17 flights daily from Heathrow. **Aer Lingus** (© 800/223-6537 in the U.S., or 01-886-31-54; www. aerlingus.ie) has frequent direct flights from Dublin to Paris throughout the day. Many commercial travelers also use regular flights from the London City Airport in the Docklands. There are also direct flights to Paris from major cities such as Manchester, Edinburgh, and Southampton. For more information, contact Air France, British Airways, or **British Midland** (© 0870/607-0555; www.flybritish-midland.com).

FROM AUSTRALIA Getting to Paris from Australia is rather difficult, because **Air France** (© 08-20-82-08-20; www.airfrance.fr) has discontinued all direct flights to and from that country, requiring transfers through, among others, Singapore, with ongoing service to Sydney provided by Qantas. Consequently, on virtually any route, and with any airline you take, you have to change planes at least once (and sometimes twice) en route. **British Airways** (℡ **08-25-82-54-00;** www.british-airways.com) flies daily from both Sydney and Melbourne to London in time for any of several connecting flights to Paris. **Qantas** (℡ **08-03-84-68-46;** www.qantas.com) can route passengers from Australia into London, where plentiful connections exist for the hop across the Channel. Qantas also flies into Sydney from Auckland, where you can catch a flight to London. Another valid option is **Swissair** (℡ **08-02-30-04-00;** www.swissair.com), which flies to Paris from Sydney, albeit with two transfers (Zurich and Bangkok, with the segment between Bangkok and Sydney serviced by Qantas) en route.

PARIS AIRPORTS

Paris has two major international airports: **Orly** (℡ **01-49-75-15-15**), 14 kilometers (8½ miles) south of the city, and **Charles de Gaulle (Roissy)** (℡ **01-48-62-22-80**), 23 kilometers (14¼ miles) northeast. An 80F (12.15€, $11.60) Air France shuttle operates between the two airports about every 30 minutes, taking 50 to 75 minutes.

CHARLES DE GAULLE AIRPORT (ROISSY)

At Charles de Gaulle, foreign carriers use Aérogare 1 and Air France uses Aérogare 2. From Aérogare 1, you take a moving walkway to the passport checkpoint and the Customs area. The two terminals are linked by a **shuttle bus** (*navette*).

The free shuttle bus connecting Aérogare 1 with Aérogare 2 also transports passengers to the Roissy rail station, from which fast **RER trains** leave every 15 minutes for such Métro stations as Gare du Nord, Châtelet, Luxembourg, Port Royal, and Denfert-Rochereau. The train fare from Roissy to any point in central Paris is 69F (10.50€, $10) in first class or 49F (7.45€, $7.10) in second. You can also take an **Air France shuttle bus** to central Paris for 75F (11.40€, $10.90). It stops at the Palais des Congrès (Porte Maillot), then continues on to place Charles de Gaulle–Etoile, where underground lines can carry you farther along to any other point. Depending on traffic, the ride takes between 45 and 55 minutes. The shuttle departs about every 12 minutes between 5:40am and 11pm.

Another option, the **Roissybus** (℡ **01-48-04-18-24**), departs from a point near the corner of the rue Scribe and place de l'Opéra every 15 minutes from 5:45am to 11pm. The cost for the 50-minute ride is 48F (7.30€, $6.95).

Taxis from Roissy into the city run about 350F (53.20€, $50.75) on the meter. At night (8pm to 7am), fares are about 40% higher. Long queues of both taxis and passengers form outside each of the airport's terminals in a surprisingly orderly fashion.

ORLY AIRPORT   Orly has two terminals: Orly Sud (south) for international flights and Orly Ouest (west) for domestic flights. A free shuttle bus links them together.

Air France buses leave from exit E of Orly Ouest and from exit F, Platform 5 of Orly Sud every 12 minutes from 5:45am to 11pm, heading for Gare des Invalides in central Paris at a cost of 45F (6.85€, $6.55) one-way. Other buses depart for place Denfert-Rochereau in the south of Paris at a cost of 35F (5.30€, $5.10).

An alternative method for reaching central Paris involves taking a free shuttle bus that leaves both of Orly's terminals at intervals of about every 15 minutes for the nearby **RER train station** (Pont de Rungis/Aéroport d'Orly), from which RER trains take 30 minutes to reach the city center. A trip to Les Invalides, for example, costs 47F (7.15€, $6.80).

Tips **Flying for Less: Tips for Getting the Best Airfares**

Passengers in the same airplane cabin rarely pay the same fare for their seats. Business travelers who need to buy tickets at the last minute, change their itinerary at a moment's notice, or get home before the weekend, pay the full fare. Passengers who can book their tickets long in advance, who don't mind staying over Saturday night, or who are willing to travel on a Tuesday, Wednesday, or Thursday after 7pm will pay a fraction of that fare.

Here are some great ways to save money so you can splurge on that gourmet meal at Taillevent or that classic suit at Chanel:

- **Take advantage of APEX fares.** Advance-purchase booking or APEX fares are often the key to getting the lowest fare. You generally must be willing to make your plans and buy your tickets as far ahead as possible: The **21-day APEX** is seconded only by the **14-day APEX**. Because the number of seats allocated to APEX fares is sometimes less than 25 percent of plane capacity, the early bird gets the low-cost seat. There's often a surcharge for flying on a weekend, and cancellation and refund policies can be strict.

- **Watch for sales.** You'll almost never see them during July and August or the Thanksgiving or Christmas seasons, but at other times you can get great deals. If you already hold a ticket when a sale breaks, it may even pay to exchange it, which usually incurs a $50 to $75 charge. If your schedule is flexible, ask if you can secure a cheaper fare by **staying an extra day** or by **flying midweek.** (Many airlines won't volunteer this information.)

- **Find a low fare with a consolidator** (a.k.a. a bucket shop). A consolidator buys seats in bulk from airlines and sells them to the public at prices below even the airlines' discounted rates. Their small-boxed ads usually run in the Sunday travel section. **Council Travel** (�C 888/ COUNCIL; www.counciltravel.com) and **STA Travel** (�C 800/781-4040; www.sta.travel.com) cater especially to young travelers, but their bargain prices are available to all ages. **1-800-AIRFARE** (℃ 800/AIR-FARE; www.1800airfare.com) now offers the deepest discounts on many other airlines, with a 4-day advance purchase. Other consolidators

A **taxi** from Orly to the center of Paris costs about 200F (30.40€, $29) and is higher at night and on weekends. Returning to the airport, **buses** to Orly leave from the Invalides terminal to either Orly Sud or Orly Ouest every 15 minutes, taking about 30 minutes.

Caution: Don't take a meterless taxi from Orly Sud or Orly Ouest—it's much safer (and usually cheaper) to hire a metered cab from the taxi queues, which are under the scrutiny of a police officer.

BY TRAIN

If you're already in Europe, you might decide to travel to Paris by train, especially if you have a Eurailpass. For example, a one-way first-class fare between Paris and London is $279 ($199 in second). Rail passes or individual rail tickets within Europe are available at most travel agencies, at are **1-800-FLY-CHEAP** (www.1800flycheap.com); **TFI Tours International** (© 800/745-8000 or 212/736-1140), a clearinghouse for unused seats; and "rebators" like **Travel Avenue** (© 800/333-3335 or 312/876-1116), which rebate part of their commissions to you.

- **Book a seat on a charter flight.** Most charter operators advertise and sell their seats through travel agents. Before deciding to take a charter, however, check the ticket restrictions: You may be asked to buy a tour package, pay in advance, be amenable if the departure day is changed, pay a service charge, fly on an airline you're not familiar with (unusual), and pay harsh penalties if you cancel—but be understanding if the charter doesn't fill up and is canceled up to 10 days before departure. Summer charters fill up more quickly than others and are almost sure to fly, but if you decide on a charter, seriously consider cancellation and baggage insurance.

- **Look into courier flights.** Companies that hire couriers use your luggage allowance for their business baggage; in return, you get a deeply discounted ticket. Flights are often offered at the last minute, and you may have to arrange a pre-trip interview to make sure you're right for the job. One reliable courier service is **Now Voyager** (© 212/431-1616; www.nowvoyager.com), open Monday to Friday from 10am to 5:30pm and Saturday from noon to 4:30pm. It also offers non-courier discounted fares, so call the company even if you don't want to fly as a courier.

- **Join a travel club.** Both **Moment's Notice** (© 718/234-6295; www.moments-notice.com) and **Sears Discount Travel Club** (© 800/433-9383; www.travelersadvantage.com) supply unsold tickets at discounted prices. You pay an annual membership fee to get the club's hot-line number. Of course, you're limited to what's available and have to be flexible.

- **Search for deals on the Web.** It's possible to get some great deals on airfare, hotels, and car rentals via the Internet. For details on getting the most from the Web, see "Planning Your Trip Online" at the end of this chapter.

any office of **Rail Europe** (© 800/848-7245 in the U.S., 800/361-RAIL in Canada; www.raileurope.com), or at **Eurostar** (© 800/EUROSTAR in the U.S., 0990/300-003 in London, 01-44-51-06-02 in Paris; www.eurostar.com).

There are six major train stations in Paris: **Gare d'Austerlitz,** 55 quai d'Austerlitz, 13th arr. (serving the southwest, with trains from the Loire Valley, the Bordeaux country, and the Pyrénées); **Gare de l'Est,** place du 11 Novembre 1918, 10th arr. (serving the east, with trains from Strasbourg, Nancy, Reims, and beyond to Zurich, Basel, Luxembourg, and Austria); **Gare de Lyon,** 20 bd. Diderot, 12th arr. (serving the southeast with trains from the Côte d'Azur, Provence, and beyond to Geneva, Lausanne, and Italy); **Gare Montparnasse,** 17 bd. Vaugirard, 15th arr. (serving the west, with trains from Brittany); **Gare du**

Tips The New Airport Shuttle

Cheaper than a taxi for one or two people but more expensive than airport buses and trains, the new **Airport Shuttle,** 2 av. Général-Leclerc, 14th arr. (© **01-43-21-06-78;** fax 01-43-21-35-67; www.paris-anglo.com/clients/ashuttle.html), will pick you up in a minivan at Charles de Gaulle or Orly and take you to your hotel for 120F (18.25€, $17.40) for one person or 89F (13.55€, $12.90) per person for parties of two or more. It'll take you out to the airports from your hotel for the same price. The **Paris Airport Service,** BP 41, CEDEX 94431 Chennevières (© **01-49-62-78-78;** fax 01-49-62-78-79), offers a similar service costing 145F (22.05€, $21.05) for one person or 180F (27.35€, $26.10) for two or more persons from Charles de Gaulle, and 115F (17.50€, $16.70) for one person or 135F (20.50€, $19.60) for two or more persons from Orly. Both companies accept Visa and MasterCard, with 1-day advance reservations required.

Nord, 18 rue de Dunkerque, 15th arr. (serving the north, with trains from Holland, Denmark, Belgium, and northern Germany); and **Gare St-Lazare,** 13 rue d'Amsterdam, 8th arr. (serving the northwest, with trains from Normandy).

For general train information and to make reservations, call © **08-36-35-35-35** daily from 7am to 8pm. Buses operate between rail stations. Each of these stations has a Métro stop, making the whole city easily accessible. Taxis are also available at designated stands at every station. Look for the sign that says TÊTE DE STATION. Be alert in train stations, especially at night.

BY BUS

Bus travel to Paris is available from London and many other cities on the Continent. In the early 1990s, the French government established strong incentives for long-haul buses not to drive into the center of Paris, so the arrival/departure point for Europe's largest bus operators, **Eurolines France,** is a 35-minute Métro ride from central Paris, at the terminus of Métro line 3 (Gallieni), in the eastern suburb of Bagnolet. Despite this inconvenience, many people prefer bus travel. Eurolines France is at 28 av. du Général-de-Gaulle, 93541 Bagnolet (© **08-36-69-52-52**).

Long-haul buses are equipped with toilets, and they stop at mealtimes for rest and refreshment. The price of a round-trip ticket between Paris and London (a 7-hour trip) is 470 to 520F (71.45–79.05€, $68.15–$75.40) for passengers 26 or over and 430F (65.35€, $62.35) for passengers under 26.

Because Eurolines doesn't have a U.S.-based sales agent, most people wait until they reach Europe to buy their tickets. Any European travel agent can arrange these purchases. If you're traveling to Paris from London, contact **Eurolines (U.K.) Ltd.,** 52 Grosvenor Gardens, Victoria, London SW1 (© **0990/143219**), for information or credit-card sales.

BY CAR

Driving in Paris is definitely not recommended. Parking is difficult, traffic is dense, and networks of one-way streets make navigation, even with the best of maps, a problem. If you do drive, remember that Paris is encircled by a ring road called the *périphérique.* Always obtain detailed directions to your destination, including the name of the exit on the périphérique you're looking for (exits aren't numbered). Avoid rush hours. Few hotels, except the luxury ones, have garages, but the staff will usually be able to direct you to one nearby.

The **major highways** into Paris are A1 from the north (Great Britain and Benelux); A13 from Rouen, Normandy, and other points of northwest France; A10 from Bordeaux, the Pyrénées, France's southwest, and Spain; A6 from Lyon, the French Alps, the Riviera, and Italy; and A4 from Metz, Nancy, and Strasbourg in eastern France.

BY FERRY FROM ENGLAND

Despite competition from the Chunnel, services aboard ferries and hydrofoils operate day and night in all seasons, with the exception of last-minute cancellations during fierce storms. Many channel crossings are carefully timed to coincide with the arrival/departure of major trains (especially those between London and Paris); trains let you off a short walk from the piers. Most ferries carry cars, trucks, and massive amounts of freight, but some hydrofoils take passengers only. The major routes include at least 12 trips a day between Dover or Folkestone and Calais or Boulogne. Hovercraft and hydrofoils make the trip from Dover to Calais, the shortest distance across the Channel, in just 40 minutes during good weather; the slower-moving ferries might take several hours, depending on weather conditions and tides. If you're bringing a car, it's important to make reservations, as space below decks is usually crowded. Timetables can vary depending on weather conditions and many other factors.

The leading operator of ferries across the Channel is **P&O Stena Lines** (call BritRail for reservations at ⓒ **800/677-8585** in North America or 087/0600-0600 in England). It operates car and passenger ferries between Portsmouth, England, and Cherbourg, France (three departures a day; 4¼ hours each way during daylight hours, 7 hours each way at night); between Portsmouth and Le Havre, France (three a day; 5½ hours each way). Most popular are the routes it operates between Dover and Calais, France (25 sailings a day; 75 minutes each way), costing £25 ($37.50) one-way adults or £12 ($18) children.

The shortest and by far the most popular route is between Calais and Dover. **Hoverspeed** operates at least 12 hovercraft crossings daily; the trip takes 35 minutes. It also runs a SeaCat (a catamaran propelled by jet engines) that takes slightly longer to make the crossing between Boulogne and Folkestone; the SeaCats depart about four times a day on the 55-minute voyage. For reservations and information, call Hoverspeed (ⓒ **800/677-8585** for reservations in North America or 0870/5240241 in England). Typical one-way fares are £25 ($37.50) per person.

If you plan to transport a rental car between England and France, check in advance with the rental company about license and insurance requirements and additional drop-off charges. And be aware that many car-rental companies, for insurance reasons, forbid transport of one of their vehicles over the water between England and France. Transport of a car each way begins at £109 ($113.50).

UNDER THE CHANNEL

One of the great engineering feats of our time, the $15-billion Channel Tunnel (Chunnel) opened in 1994, and the **Eurostar Express** now has daily service from London to both Paris and Brussels. The 31-mile journey takes 35 minutes, though the actual time spent in the Chunnel is only 19 minutes. Stores selling duty-free goods, restaurants, service stations, and bilingual staffs are available to travelers on both sides of the Channel.

Eurostar tickets are available through **Rail Europe** (ⓒ **800/4-EURAIL;**

A Weekend Trip to London

For a look at package deals with the Chunnel, turn to "A Weekend in London" in chapter 11.

www.raileurope.com). In Great Britain, make reservations for Eurostar at © 0345/484950; in the United States, call © 800/EUROSTAR. Chunnel train traffic is roughly competitive with air travel, if you calculate door-to-door travel time. Trains leave from London's Waterloo Station and arrive in Paris at the Gare du Nord.

The tunnel also accommodates passenger cars, charter buses, taxis, and motorcycles, transporting them under the Channel from Folkestone, England, to Calais, France. It operates 24 hours a day, running every 15 minutes during peak travel times and at least once an hour at night. You can buy tickets at the tollbooth at the tunnel's entrance. With Le Shuttle (© 0990/353-535; www.eurodrive.co.uk), gone are the days of weather-related delays, seasickness, and advance reservations.

Before boarding Le Shuttle, motorists stop at a tollbooth and pass through British and French immigration services at the same time. They then drive onto a half-mile-long train and travel through the tunnel. During the ride, motorists stay in bright air-conditioned carriages, remaining inside their cars or stepping outside to stretch their legs. When the trip is completed, they simply drive off. Total travel time is about an hour. Once on French soil, British drivers must remember to drive on the right-hand side of the road.

BY PACKAGE TOUR

Package tours aren't the same thing as escorted tours. They're simply a way to buy airfare and accommodations at the same time. For popular destinations like Paris, they're a smart way to go because they save you a lot of money. In many cases, a package that includes airfare, hotel, and transportation to and from the airport will cost you less than just the hotel alone would have, had you booked it yourself. That's because packages are sold in bulk to tour operators, who resell them to the public at a cost that drastically undercuts standard rates.

Packages, however, vary widely. Some offer a better class of hotels than others. Some offer the same hotels for lower prices. Some offer flights on scheduled airlines, while others book charters. In some packages, your choice of accommodations and travel days may be limited. Some packages let you choose between escorted vacations and independent vacations; others will allow you to add on just a few excursions or escorted day trips (also at lower prices than you could locate on your own) without booking an entirely escorted tour. Each destination usually has one or two packagers that are cheaper than the rest because they buy in even greater bulk. If you spend the time to shop around, you'll save in the long run.

FINDING A GENERAL PACKAGE

The best place to start your search is the travel section of your local Sunday newspaper. Also check the ads in the back of national travel magazines such as *Travel & Leisure, National Geographic Traveler,* and *Condé Nast Traveler.*

Liberty Travel (© 888/271-1584 to be connected with the agent closest to you; www.libertytravel.com), one of the biggest packagers in the Northeast, often runs a full-page ad in the Sunday papers. You won't get much in the way of service, but you will get a good deal.

American Express Travel (© 800/446-6234; www.americanexpress.com) is another option. Check out its **Last Minute Travel Bargains** site, offered in conjunction with **Continental Airlines** (www.american express.com), with deeply discounted vacation packages and reduced airline fares that differ from the E-savers bargains Continental e-mails weekly to subscribers. **Northwest Airlines** (www.nwa.com) offers a similar service. Posted on Northwest's website every Wednesday, its **Cyber Saver Bargain Alerts** offer special hotel rates, package deals, and discounted airline fares.

Another good resource is the airlines themselves, which often package their flights together with accommodations. Among the airline packagers, your options are **American Airlines Vacations** (© 800/321-2121; www.aavacations.com), **Delta Vacations** (© 800/872-7786; www.deltavacations.com), and **US Airways Vacations** (© 800/455-0123; www.usairwaysvacations.com). Delta Dream Vacations offers a full package called Jolie France, lasting 10 nights and costing $3,850 to $4,280 for two, taking in not only Paris but also some of France's regional highlights, like Tours, Bordeaux, Carcassonne, Nice, Nìmes, and Dijon. All hotels, tours, and breakfasts are included, plus four dinners.

The **French Experience,** 370 Lexington Ave., Room 812, New York, NY 10017 (© 212/986-1115; fax 212/986-3808; www.frenchexperience.com), offers inexpensive tickets to Paris on most scheduled airlines and arranges tours and stays in various types and categories of country inns, hotels, private châteaus, and B&Bs. In addition, it takes reservations for about 30 small hotels in Paris and arranges short-term apartment rentals in the city or farmhouse rentals in the countryside and offers all-inclusive packages in Paris

as well as prearranged package tours of various regions of France. Any tour can be adapted to suit individual needs.

FINDING A SPECIALTY PACKAGE What about special-interest tours? For a city as diverse and popular as Paris, there are only a few specialty tours.

One outfit that expertly coordinates hotel stays with major musical events, usually within at least one (and often both) of the city's opera houses, is **Dailey-Thrope Travel,** 330 West 58th Street, Suite 610, New York, NY 10019 (© **800/998-4677;** www.operatravel.com). Sojourns in Paris tend to last between 3 and 7 days and, in many cases, are tied into opera performances in other cities (usually London, Berlin, or Milan) as well. Expect accommodations in well-respected deluxe hotels such as the Grand, the Louvre, or the Scribe, and a staff that has made arrangements for all the nuts-and-bolts of your arrival in, and artistic exposure to, Paris.

Die-hard tennis fans set their calendars by the events that transpire every year within Paris' Roland-Garros stadium at the French Open. You can always compile your hotel bookings and tickets to the event on your own, but if you're unsure about how to match the dates of your visit with tennis tournaments that will be watched around the world, consider handing the problem to a California-based company that specializes in this issue: **Advantage Tennis Tours,** 33 White Sail Drive, Suite 100, Laguna Niguel, CA 92677 (© **800/341-8687;** www.advantagetennistours.com). Packages usually include either 5 or 6 nights of hotel accommodations in Paris, 2 or 3 days on Center Court, the organizational skills of a bilingual hostess, and a chance to meet and mingle, at any of at least one catered lunch, with tennis fans of many different nationalities. There will even be an opportunity to grab a racquet and play some tennis on your own, in between bouts of sightseeing. Rates, per person, without airfare, begin at $2,600, double occupancy, depending on your choice of hotel and the duration of your visit.

8 Planning Your Trip Online

With a mouse, a modem, and a certain do-it-yourself determination, Internet users can tap into the same travel-planning databases that were once accessible only to travel agents. Sites such as **Travelocity, Expedia,** and **Orbitz** allow consumers to comparison shop for airfares, book flights, learn of last-minute bargains, and reserve hotel rooms and rental cars.

But don't fire your travel agent just yet. Although online booking sites offer tips and hard data to help you bargain shop, they cannot endow you with the hard-earned experience that makes a seasoned, reliable travel agent an invaluable resource, even in the Internet age. And for consumers with a complex itinerary, a trusty travel agent is still the best way to arrange the most direct flights to and from the best airports.

Still, there's no denying the Internet's emergence as a powerful tool in researching and plotting travel time. The benefits of researching your trip online can be well worth the effort:

- **Last-minute specials,** known as "E-savers," such as weekend deals or Internet-only fares, are offered by airlines to fill empty seats. Most of these are announced on Tuesday or Wednesday and must be purchased online. They are only valid for travel that weekend, but some can be booked weeks or months in advance. Sign up for weekly e-mail alerts at airline websites (see "Getting There," earlier in this chapter) or check megasites that compile comprehensive lists of E-savers, such as Smarter Living (www.smarterliving.com) or WebFlyer (www.webflyer.com).
- Some sites will send you **e-mail notification** when a cheap fare becomes available to your favorite destination. Some will also tell you when fares to a particular destination are lowest.
- The best of the travel planning sites are now **highly personalized;** they track your frequent-flier miles, and store your seating and meal preferences, tentative itineraries, and credit-card information, letting you plan trips or check agendas quickly.
- All major airlines offer **incentives**—bonus frequent-flier miles, Internet-only discounts, sometimes even free cellphone rentals—when you purchase online or buy an e-ticket.
- Advances in mobile technology provide business travelers and other frequent travelers with the ability to check flight status, change plans, or get specific directions from handheld computing devices, mobile phones, and pagers. Some sites will e-mail or page a passenger if a flight is delayed.

TRAVEL PLANNING & BOOKING SITES

The best travel planning and booking sites cast a wide net, offering domestic and international flights, hotel and rental-car bookings, plus news, destination information, and deals on cruises and vacation packages. Keep in mind that free (one-time) registration is often required for booking. Because several airlines are no longer willing to pay commissions on tickets sold by online travel agencies, be aware that these online agencies will either charge a $10 surcharge if you book a ticket on that carrier—or neglect to offer those air carriers' offerings.

Frommers.com: The Complete Travel Resource

For an excellent travel planning resource, we highly recommend **Arthur Frommer's Budget Travel Online** (www.frommers.com). We're a little biased, of course, but we guarantee you'll find the travel tips, reviews, monthly vacation giveaways, and online-booking capabilities thoroughly indispensable. Among the special features are: **"Ask the Expert"** bulletin boards, where Frommer's authors answer your questions via online postings; **Arthur Frommer's Daily Newsletter,** for the latest travel bargains and inside travel secrets; and Frommer's **Destinations archive,** where you get expert travel tips, hotel and dining recommendations, and advice on the sights to see for more than 200 destinations around the globe. Once your research is done, the **Online Reservation System** (www.frommers.com/booktravelnow) takes you to Frommer's favorite sites for booking your vacation at affordable prices.

The sites in this section are not intended to be a comprehensive list, but rather a discriminating selection to get you started. Recognition is given to sites based on their content value and ease of use and is not paid for—unlike some website rankings, which are based on payment. *Remember:* This is a press-time snapshot of leading websites—some undoubtedly will have evolved or moved by the time you read this.

- **Travelocity** (www.travelocity.com or www.frommers.travelocity.com) and **Expedia** (www.expedia.com) are the most longstanding and reputable sites, each offering excellent selections and searches for complete vacation packages. Travelers search by destination and dates coupled with how much they are willing to spend.
- The latest buzz in the online travel world is about **Orbitz** (www.orbitz.com), a site launched by United, Delta, Northwest, American, and Continental airlines. It shows all possible fares for your desired trip, offering fares lower than those available through travel agents. (Stay tuned: At press time, travel-agency associations were waging an antitrust battle against this site.)
- **Qixo** (www.qixo.com) is another powerful search engine that allows you to search for flights and hotel rooms on 20 other travel-planning sites (such as Travelocity) at once. Qixo sorts results by price, after which you can book your travel directly through the site.

SMART E-SHOPPING

The savvy traveler is one armed with good information. Here are a few tips to help you navigate the Internet successfully and safely.

- **Know when sales start.** Last-minute deals may vanish in minutes. If you have a favorite booking site or airline, find out when last-minute deals are released to the public. (For example, Southwest's specials are posted every Tuesday at 12:01am central time.)
- **Shop around.** Compare results from different sites and airlines—and against a travel agent's best fare, if you can. If possible, try a range of times and alternate airports before you make a purchase.

- **Follow the rules of the trade.** Book in advance, and choose an off-peak time and date if possible. Some sites will tell you when fares to a particular destination tend to be cheapest.
- **Stay secure.** Book only through secure sites (some airline sites are not secure). Look for a key icon (Netscape) or a padlock (Internet Explorer) at the bottom of your web browser before you enter credit card information or other personal data.
- **Avoid online auctions.** Sites that auction airline tickets and frequent-flier miles are the number-one perpetrators of Internet fraud, according to the National Consumers League.
- **Maintain a paper trail.** If you book an e-ticket, print out a confirmation, or write down your confirmation number, and keep it safe and accessible—or your trip could be a virtual one!

ONLINE TRAVELER'S TOOLBOX

Veteran travelers usually carry some essential items to make their trips easier. Following is a selection of online tools to bookmark and use.

- **Visa ATM Locator** (www.visa.com/pd/atm) or **MasterCard ATM Locator** (www.mastercard.com/atm). Find ATMs in hundreds of cities in the U.S. and around the world.

- **Foreign Languages for Travelers** (www.travlang.com). Learn basic terms in more than 70 languages and click on any underlined phrase to hear what it sounds like. *Note:* Free audio software and speakers are required.
- **Intellicast** (www.intellicast.com). Weather forecasts for all 50 states and cities around the world. *Note:* Temperatures are in Celsius for many international destinations.
- **Mapquest** (www.mapquest.com). The best of the mapping sites, Mapquest lets you choose a specific address or destination, and in seconds, it returns a map and detailed directions.
- **Cybercafes.com** (www.cybercafes.com) or **Net Café Guide** (www.netcafeguide.com/mapindex.htm). Locate Internet cafes at hundreds of locations around the globe. Catch up on your e-mail and log onto the Web for a few dollars per hour.
- **Universal Currency Converter** (www.xe.net/currency). See what your dollar or pound is worth in more than 100 other countries.
- **U.S. State Department Travel Warnings** (www.travel.state.gov/travel_warnings.html). Reports on places where health concerns or unrest might threaten U.S. travelers. It also lists the locations of U.S. embassies around the world.

4

Getting to Know the City of Light

Ernest Hemingway called the many splendors of Paris a "moveable feast" and wrote, "There is never any ending to Paris, and the memory of each person who has lived in it differs from that of any other." It's this aura of personal discovery that has always been the most compelling reason to come to Paris. And perhaps that's why France has been called *le deuxième pays de tout le monde*—"everybody's second country."

The Seine not only divides Paris into the Right Bank and the Left Bank but also seems to split the city into two vastly different sections and ways of life. Depending on your time, interest, and budget, you may quickly decide which section of Paris suits you best.

In the very heart of Paris, the old clichés about the Left Bank being for poor, struggling artists, and the Right Bank being for the well-heeled have long ago broken down. The very heart of the Left Bank, including the areas around Odéon and St-Germain-des-Prés, are just as chic as anything on the Right Bank—and just as expensive.

The history of Paris repeats itself. In the old days, Montmartre was the artists' quarter until prices and massive tourism drove these "bohemians" to newly emerging and less expensive *quartiers* such as Montparnasse. But Montparnasse long ago became gold-plated real estate.

So where does the poor struggling artist go today? Not to the central core of the Right or Left Bank. He or she must move farther afield. First, it was the seedy Marais until that district, too, saw rents spiral and the average visitor on its streets carrying a gold American Express card. Now, it's farther east, into the 11th, a blue-collar neighborhood sandwiched between the Marais, Ménilmontant, and République. The heartbeat of this area is rue Oberkampf. If you'd like to see this newly gentrified area before it, too, changes forever, refer to the box, "A Bar Crawl in Trendy Ménilmontant," in chapter 10.

1 Essentials

VISITOR INFORMATION

At the airports are small **info offices,** which, for a fee, will help you make a hotel reservation. But the prime source is the **Office de Tourisme de Paris,** 127 av. des Champs-Elysées, 8th arr. (© **08-36-68-31-12;** fax 01-49-52-53-00; www.paris-touristoffice.com; Métro: Charles de Gaulle–Etoile or George V), where you can obtain info about both Paris and the provinces. It's open April to October daily from 9am to 8pm. From November to March hours are Monday to Saturday from 9am to 8pm and Sunday from 11am to 7pm. The staff will make an accommodations reservation for you on the same day you want a room: 8F (1.20€, $1.15) for hostels and *foyers* ("homes"), 20F (3.05€, $2.90) one-star hotels, 25F (3.80€, $3.65) two-star hotels, and 40F (6.10€, $5.80) three-star

---

Impressions

If you are lucky enough to have lived in Paris as a young man, then wherever you go for the rest of your life, it stays with you, for Paris is a moveable feast.

—Ernest Hemingway, *A Moveable Feast* (1964)

---

hotels. (Stars refer to government ratings, rather than those used in this book.) It's often very busy in summer, so you'll probably have to wait in line.

There is a tourist office, **Bureau Gare de Lyon,** at the major rail terminus, Gare de Lyon, 12th arr. (© **0143-43-33-24**), serving rail passengers arriving by train. It is open Monday to Saturday from 8am to 8pm. Métro: Gare de Lyon.

There are **other branches** in the base of the Eiffel Tower (open May to September, daily from 11am to 6pm) and in the arrivals hall of the Gare de Lyon (open year-round Monday to Saturday from 8am to 8pm). All these offices will give you free copies of the English-language *Time Out* and *Paris User's Guide.*

CITY LAYOUT

Paris is surprisingly compact. Occupying 1,119 sq. kilometers (432 sq. miles), it's home to more than 10 million people. The city is divided into 20 municipal wards called *arrondissements,* each with its own mayor, city hall, police station, and central post office. Some even have remnants of market squares.

The river Seine divides Paris into the **Right Bank** (Rive Droite) to the north and the **Left Bank** (Rive Gauche) to the south. These designations make sense when you stand on a bridge and face downstream; watching the water flow out toward the sea, to your right is the north bank, to your left the south. Thirty-two bridges link the banks of the Seine, some providing access to the two small islands at the heart of the city, **Ile de la Cité,** the city's birthplace and site of Notre-Dame, and **Ile St-Louis,** a moat-guarded oasis of sober 17th-century mansions. These islands can cause some confusion to walkers who think they've just crossed a bridge from one bank to the other, only to find themselves caught up in an almost medieval maze of narrow streets and old buildings.

As part of Napoléon III's massive urban redevelopment project, Baron Georges-Eugène Haussmann forever changed the look of Paris between 1860 and 1870 by creating the **legendary boulevards:** St-Michel, St-Germain, Haussmann, Malesherbes, Sébastopol, Magenta, Voltaire, and Strasbourg.

The "main street" on the Right Bank is, of course, the **Champs-Elysées,** beginning at the Arc de Triomphe and running to place de la Concorde. Haussmann also created avenue de l'Opéra (as well as the Opéra), and the 12 avenues that radiate star-like from the Arc de Triomphe, giving it its original name, place de l'Etoile (*étoile* means "star"); it was renamed place Charles de Gaulle following the general's death and is often referred to as **place Charles de Gaulle–Etoile.**

Haussmann also cleared Ile de la Cité of its medieval buildings, transforming it into a showcase for Notre-Dame. Finally, he laid out the two elegant parks on the western and southeastern fringes of the city: the **Bois de Boulogne** and the **Bois de Vincennes.**

FINDING AN ADDRESS

The key to finding any address in Paris is looking for the arrondissement number, rendered either as a number followed by "e" or "er" (1er, 2e, and so on) or more formally as part of the postal code (the last two digits indicate the

---

Tips **Country & City Telephone Codes**

The country code for France is 33. The city code for Paris (as well as for all cities in the Ile de France region) is 1; use this code if you're calling from outside France. If you're calling Paris from within Paris or from anywhere else in France, use 01, which is now built into all phone numbers in the Ile de France, making them 10 digits long.

---

arrondissement—75007 indicates the 7th arrondissement, 75017 the 17th). Numbers on buildings running parallel to the Seine usually follow the course of the river—east to west. On north-south streets, numbering begins at the river.

If you're staying more than 2 or 3 days, buy an inexpensive pocket-size book that includes the *plan de Paris* by arrondissement, available at all major newsstands and bookshops. If you can find it, the little forest-green *Paris Classique l'Indispensable* is a thorough, well-indexed, and accurate guide to the city and its suburbs. Most map guides provide you with a Métro map, a foldout map of the city, and indexed maps of each arrondissement, with all streets listed and keyed. We've given you a head start by including a **free full-color foldout map** at the back of this guide.

THE ARRONDISSEMENTS IN BRIEF

Each of Paris's 20 arrondissements possesses a unique style and flavor. You'll want to decide which district appeals most to you and then try to find accommodations there. Later on, try to visit as many areas as you can so you get the full taste of Paris.

1ST ARR. (MUSÉE DU LOUVRE/LES HALLES)   "I never knew what a palace was until I had a glimpse of the Louvre," wrote Nathaniel Hawthorne. Perhaps the world's greatest art museum, the **Louvre,** a former royal residence, still lures all visitors to Paris to the 1st arrondissement. Walk through the **Jardin des Tuileries,** Paris's most formal garden (originally laid out by Le Nôtre, gardener to Louis XIV). Pause to take in the classic beauty of **place Vendôme,** the opulent home of the Hôtel Ritz. Zola's "belly of Paris" (Les Halles) is no longer the food-and-meat market of Paris (traders moved to the new, more accessible suburb of Rungis); today the **Forum des Halles** is a center of shopping, entertainment, and culture.

2ND ARR. (LA BOURSE)   Home to the **Bourse** (stock exchange), this Right Bank district lies mainly between the Grands Boulevards and rue Etienne-Marcel. From Monday to Friday, brokers play the market until it's time to break for lunch, when the movers and shakers of French capitalism channel their hysteria into the area restaurants. Much of the eastern end of the arrondissement (**Le Sentier**) is devoted to wholesale outlets of the Paris garment district, where thousands of garments are sold (usually in bulk) to buyers from clothing stores throughout Europe. "Everything that exists elsewhere exists in Paris," wrote Victor Hugo in *Les Misérables,* and this district provides ample evidence of that.

3RD ARR. (LE MARAIS)   This district embraces much of *Le Marais* (the swamp), one of the best loved of the old Right Bank neighborhoods. (It extends into the 4th as well.) After decades of seedy decay, Le Marais recently made a comeback, though it may never again enjoy the prosperity of its 17th-century aristocratic heyday; today it contains Paris's **gay neighborhood,** with lots of gay/lesbian restaurants, bars, and stores, as well as the remains of the old Jewish

Paris Arrondissements

quarter, centered on **rue des Rosiers.** Two of the district's chief attractions are the **Musée Picasso,** a kind of pirate's ransom of painting and sculpture the Picasso estate had to turn over to the French government in lieu of the artist's astronomical death duties, and the **Musée Carnavalet,** which brings to life the history of Paris from prehistoric times to the present.

4TH ARR. (ILE DE LA CITÉ/ILE ST-LOUIS & BEAUBOURG)   At times it seems as if the 4th has it all: not only Notre-Dame on Ile de la Cité, but Ile St-Louis and its aristocratic town houses, courtyards, and antiques shops. **Ile St-Louis,** a former cow pasture and dueling ground, is home to dozens of 17th-century mansions and 6,000 lucky Louisiens, its permanent residents. Seek out **Ile de la Cité's** two glorious Gothic churches, **Sainte-Chapelle** and **Notre-Dame,** a majestic structure that, according to poet E. E. Cummings, doesn't budge an inch for all the idiocies of this world. You'll find France's finest bird and flower markets along with the nation's law courts, which Balzac described as a "cathedral of chicanery." It was here that Marie Antoinette was sentenced to death in 1793. The 4th is also home to the freshly renovated **Centre Pompidou,** one of the top three attractions in France. After all this pomp and glory, you can retreat to **place des Vosges,** a square of perfect harmony and beauty where Victor Hugo lived from 1832 to 1848 and penned many of his famous master-pieces. (His house is now a museum—see chapter 7.)

5TH ARR. (LATIN QUARTER)   The Quartier Latin is the intellectual heart and soul of Paris. Bookstores, schools, churches, smoky jazz clubs, student dives, Roman ruins, publishing houses, and expensive and chic boutiques characterize the district. Discussions of Artaud or Molière over long cups of coffee may be rarer than in the past, but they aren't at all out of place here. Beginning with the founding of the **Sorbonne** in 1253, the quarter was called Latin because all stu-dents and professors spoke the scholarly language. You'll follow in the footsteps of Descartes, Verlaine, Camus, Sartre, James Thurber, Elliot Paul, and Heming-way as you explore this historic area. Changing times have brought Greek, Moroccan, and Vietnamese immigrants, among others, hustling everything from couscous to fiery-hot spring rolls and souvlaki. The 5th borders the Seine, and you'll want to stroll along quai de Montebello, inspecting the inventories of the *bouquinistes,* who sell everything from antique Daumier prints to yellowing copies of Balzac's *Père Goriot* in the shadow of Notre-Dame. The 5th also has the **Panthéon,** built by a grateful Louis XV after he recovered from the gout and wanted to do something nice for Ste-Geneviève, Paris's patron saint. It's the rest-ing place of Rousseau, Gambetta, Zola, Braille, Hugo, Voltaire, and Jean Moulin, the World War II Resistance leader whom the Gestapo tortured to death.

6TH ARR. (ST-GERMAIN/LUXEMBOURG)   This is the heartland of Paris publishing and, for some, the most colorful Left Bank quarter, where waves of earnest young artists still emerge from the famous Ecole des Beaux-Arts. The secret of the district lies in discovering its narrow streets, hidden squares, and magnificent gardens. To be really authentic, stroll with an unwrapped loaf of sourdough bread from the wood-fired ovens of **Poilâne** at 8 rue du Cherche-Midi. Everywhere you turn in the area, you'll encounter famous historic and lit-erary associations, none more so than on **rue Jacob.** At no. 7, Racine lived with his uncle as a teenager; Richard Wagner resided at no. 14 from 1841 to 1842; Ingres once lived at no. 27 (now it's the office of the French publishing house Editions du Seuil); and Hemingway once occupied a tiny upstairs room at no.

44. The 6th takes in the **Jardin du Luxembourg,** a 60-acre playground where Isadora Duncan went dancing in the predawn hours and a destitute Ernest Hemingway went looking for pigeons for lunch, carrying them in a baby carriage back to his humble flat for cooking.

7TH ARR. (EIFFEL TOWER/MUSÉE D'ORSAY) Paris's most famous symbol, the **Tour Eiffel,** dominates Paris and especially the 7th, a Left Bank district of respectable residences and government offices. The tower is now one of the most recognizable landmarks in the world, despite the fact that many Parisians (especially its nearest neighbors) hated it when it was unveiled in 1889. Many of Paris's most imposing monuments are in the 7th, like the **Hôtel des Invalides,** which contains Napoléon's Tomb and the Musée de l'Armée, and the **Musée d'Orsay,** the world's premier showcase of 19th-century French art and culture, housed in the old Gare d'Orsay. But there's much hidden charm here as well. **Rue du Bac** was home to the swashbuckling heroes of Dumas's *The Three Musketeers* and to James McNeill Whistler, who moved to no. 110 after selling *Mother*. Auguste Rodin lived at what's now the **Musée Rodin,** 77 rue de Varenne, until his death in 1917.

8TH ARR. (CHAMPS-ELYSÉES/MADELEINE) The prime showcase of the 8th is the **Champs-Elysées,** stretching grandly from the **Arc de Triomphe** to the purloined Egyptian obelisk on **place de la Concorde.** By the 1980s, the Champs-Elysées had become a garish strip, with too much traffic, too many fast-food joints, and too many panhandlers. In the 1990s, Jacques Chirac, then the Gaullist mayor, launched a massive cleanup, broadening the sidewalks and planting new rows of trees. Now you'll find fashion houses, elegant hotels, and expensive restaurants and shops. Everything in the 8th is the city's "best, grandest, and most impressive": It has the best restaurant (**Taillevent**); the sexiest strip joint (**Crazy Horse Saloon**); the most splendid square (**place de la Concorde**); the best rooftop cafe (**La Samaritaine**); the grandest hotel (the **Crillon**); the most impressive triumphal arch (**Arc de Triomphe**); the most expensive residential street (**avenue Montaigne**); the world's oldest subway station (**Franklin D. Roosevelt**); and the most ancient monument (the 3,300-year-old **Obelisk of Luxor**).

9TH ARR. (OPÉRA GARNIER/PIGALLE) From the Quartier de l'Opéra to the strip joints of Pigalle (the infamous "Pig Alley" for World War II GIs), the 9th endures, even if fickle fashion prefers other addresses. Over the decades, the 9th has been celebrated in literature and song for the music halls that brought gaiety to the city. No. 17 bd. de la Madeleine was the death site of Marie Duplessis, who gained fame as the heroine Marguerite Gautier in Alexandre Dumas the younger's *La Dame aux camélias*. (Greta Garbo later redoubled Marie's legend by playing her in the film *Camille*.) At **place Pigalle,** gone is the cafe La Nouvelle Athènes, where Degas, Pissarro, and Manet used to meet. Today, you're more likely to encounter nightclubs in the area. Other major attractions include the **Folies Bergère,** where cancan dancers have been high-kicking it since 1868. More than anything, it was the Rococo **Opéra Garnier** (home of the notorious Phantom) that made the 9th the last hurrah of Second Empire opulence. Renoir hated it, but several generations later, Chagall did the ceilings. Pavlova danced *Swan Lake* here, and Nijinsky took the night off to go cruising.

10TH ARR. (GARE DU NORD/GARE DE L'EST) The **Gare du Nord** and **Gare de l'Est,** along with porno houses and dreary commercial zones, make the 10th one of the least desirable arrondissements for living, dining, or sightseeing.

Impressions

In Paris they simply stared when I spoke to them in French; I never did
succeed in making those idiots understand their language.
                    —Mark Twain, *Wisdom and Ignorance* (1869).

We always try to avoid it, except for two longtime favorite restaurants (see chapter 6): **Brasserie Flo,** 7 cour des Petites-Ecuries, best known for its formidable choucroute, a heap of sauerkraut garnished with everything; and **Julien,** 16 rue du faubourg St-Denis, called the poor man's Maxim's for its Belle-Époque interiors and moderate prices.

11TH ARR. (OPÉRA BASTILLE)   For many years, this quarter seemed to sink lower and lower into poverty and decay, overcrowded by working-class immigrants from the far reaches of the former Empire. The opening of the **Opéra Bastille,** however, has given the 11th new hope and new life. The facility, called the "people's opera house," stands on the landmark place de la Bastille, where on July 14, 1789, 633 Parisians stormed the fortress and seized the ammunition depot, as the French Revolution swept across the city. Over the years, the prison held Voltaire, the Marquis de Sade, and the mysterious "Man in the Iron Mask." The area sandwiched between the Marais, Ménilmontant, and République is now being called "blue-collar chic," as the *artistes* of Paris have been driven from the costlier sections of the Marais and can now be found walking the gritty sidewalks of rue Oberkamf. Hip Parisians in search of a more cutting-edge experience are now found living and working among the decaying 19th-century apartments and the 1960s public housing with graffiti-splattered walls.

12TH ARR. (BOIS DE VINCENNES/GARE DE LYON)   Very few out-of-towners came here until a French chef opened a restaurant called **Au Trou Gascon** (see chapter 6). The 12th's major attraction remains the **Bois de Vincennes,** sprawling on the eastern periphery of Paris. This park has been a longtime favorite of French families, who enjoy its zoos and museums, its royal château and boating lakes, and most definitely its **Parc Floral de Paris,** a celebrated flower garden boasting springtime rhododendrons and autumn dahlias. Venture into the dreary **Gare de Lyon** for **Le Train Bleu,** a restaurant whose ceiling frescoes and Art-Nouveau decor are classified as national artistic treasures; the food's good, too (see chapter 6). The 12th, once a depressing urban wasteland, has been singled out for budgetary resuscitation and is beginning to sport new housing, shops, gardens, and restaurants. Many of these will occupy the site of the former Reuilly rail tracks.

13TH ARR. (GARE D'AUSTERLITZ)   Centered around the grimy **Gare d'Austerlitz,** the 13th might have its devotees, but we've yet to meet one. British snobs who flitted in and out of the train station were among the first of the district's foreign visitors and in essence wrote the 13th off as a dreary working-class counterpart of London's East End. The 13th is also home to Paris's **Chinatown,** stretching for 13 square blocks around the Tolbiac Métro stop. It emerged out of the refugee crisis at the end of the Vietnam War, taking over a neighborhood that had held mostly Arab-speaking peoples. Today, recognizing the overcrowding that's now endemic in the district, the Paris civic authorities are imposing new, not particularly welcome, restrictions on population densities.

14TH ARR. (MONTPARNASSE)   The northern end of this large arrondissement is devoted to **Montparnasse,** home of the "lost generation" and former
stamping ground of Stein, Toklas, Hemingway, and other American expats of
the 1920s. After World War II, it ceased to be the center of intellectual life, but
the memory lingers in its cafes. One of the monuments that sets the tone of the
neighborhood is **Rodin's statue of Balzac** at the junction of boulevard Montparnasse and boulevard Raspail. At this corner are some of the world's most
famous **literary cafes,** including La Rotonde, Le Select, La Dôme, and La
Coupole. Though Gertrude Stein avoided them (she loathed cafes), all the other
American expatriates, including Hemingway and Fitzgerald, had no qualms
about enjoying a drink here (or quite a few of them, for that matter). Stein
stayed at home (27 rue de Fleurus) with Alice B. Toklas, collecting paintings,
including those of Picasso, and entertaining the likes of Max Jacob, Apollinaire,
T. S. Eliot, and Matisse.

15TH ARR. (GARE MONTPARNASSE/INSTITUT PASTEUR)   A mostly
residential district beginning at **Gare Montparnasse,** the 15th stretches all the
way to the Seine. In size and population, it's the largest quarter of Paris but
attracts few tourists and has few attractions, except for the **Parc des Expositions,** the **Cimetière du Montparnasse,** and the **Institut Pasteur.** In the early
20th century, many artists—like Chagall, Léger, and Modigliani—lived in this
arrondissement in a shared atelier known as "The Beehive."

16TH ARR. (TROCADÉRO/BOIS DE BOULOGNE)   Originally the village of Passy, where Benjamin Franklin lived during most of his time in Paris,
this district is still reminiscent of Proust's world. Highlights include the **Bois de
Boulogne;** the **Jardin du Trocadéro;** the **Maison de Balzac;** the **Musée
Guimet** (famous for its Asian collections); and the **Cimetière de Passy,** resting
place of Manet, Talleyrand, Giraudoux, and Debussy. One of the largest of the
city's arrondissements, it's known today for its well-heeled bourgeoisie, its
upscale rents, and some rather posh (and, according to its critics, rather smug)
residential boulevards. The arrondissement also has the best vantage of the Eiffel
Tower, **place du Trocadéro.**

17TH ARR. (PARC MONCEAU/PLACE CLICHY)   Flanking the northern
periphery of Paris, the 17th incorporates neighborhoods of conservative bourgeois respectability (in its western end) and less affluent neighborhoods in its
eastern end. It boasts two of the greatest restaurants of Paris, **Guy Savoy** and
Michel Rostang (see chapter 6).

18TH ARR. (MONTMARTRE)   The 18th is the most famous outer quarter
of Paris, containing **Montmartre,** the **Moulin Rouge, Sacré-Coeur,** and ultra-
touristy **place du Tertre.** Utrillo was its native son, Renoir lived here, and
Toulouse-Lautrec adopted the area as his own. The most famous enclave of
artists in Paris's history, the **Bateau-Lavoir,** of Picasso fame, gathered here. Max
Jacob, Matisse, and Braque were all frequent visitors. Today, place Blanche is
known for its prostitutes, and Montmartre is filled with honky-tonks, too many
souvenir shops, and terrible restaurants. You can still find pockets of quiet
beauty, though. The city's most famous flea market, the **Marché aux Puces de
Clignancourt,** is another landmark.

19TH ARR. (LA VILLETTE)   Today, visitors come to what was once the village of La Villette to see the much-publicized angular **Cité des Sciences et de
l'Industrie,** a spectacular science museum and park built on a site that for years

was devoted to the city's slaughterhouses. Mostly residential, and not at all upscale, the district is one of the most ethnically diverse in Paris, the home of people from all parts of the former Empire. A highlight is **Les Buttes Chaumont,** a park where kids can enjoy puppet shows and donkey rides.

20TH ARR. (PÈRE-LACHAISE CEMETERY)   The 20th's greatest landmark is **Père-Lachaise Cemetery,** the resting place of Jim Morrison, Edith Piaf, Marcel Proust, Oscar Wilde, Isadora Duncan, Sarah Bernhardt, Gertrude Stein and Alice B. Toklas, Colette, and many, many others. Otherwise, the 20th arrondissement is a dreary and sometimes volatile melting pot comprising residents from France's former colonies. Though nostalgia buffs sometimes head here to visit Piaf's former neighborhood, **Ménilmontant-Belleville,** it has been almost totally bulldozed and rebuilt since the bad old days when she grew up here.

2 Getting Around

Paris is a city for strollers whose greatest joy in life is rambling through unexpected alleyways and squares. Only when you're dead tired and can't walk another step or have to go all the way across town in a hurry, should you consider using the swift and dull means of urban transport.

For information on the city's public transportation, call ℂ **08-36-68-77-14.**

BY MÉTRO & RER

A century old, the **Paris Métro** will soon become one of the most modern and efficient in the world. At its centenary in the summer of 2000, the Métro announced a gigantic overhaul program that will refurbish some 200 of the system's nearly 300 stations by 2003. The **Métro** (ℂ **08-36-68-77-14**) is the easiest and most efficient way to get around Paris. Most stations display a map of the system at the entrance. Within Paris, you can transfer between the subway and the RER regional trains for no additional cost. To make sure you catch the right train, find your destination, then visually follow the line it's on to the end of the route and note its name. This is the sign you look for in the stations and the name you'll see on the train. Transfer stations are known as *correspondances.* (Note that some require long walks—Châtelet–Les Halles is the most notorious.)

Few trips will require more than one transfer. Some stations have maps with push-button indicators that'll help you plot your route by lighting up when you press the button for your destination. A ride on the urban lines costs 8F (1.20€, $1.15) to any point within the 20 arrondissements of Paris, as well as to many of its near suburbs. A bulk purchase of 10 tickets (which are bound together into what the French refer to as a *carnet*) costs 58F (8.80€, $8.40). Métro fares to outlying suburbs on the Sceaux, the Noisy–St-Léger, and St-Germain-en-Laye lines cost more and are sold on an individual basis depending on the distance you travel. At the entrance to the Métro station, insert your ticket into the turnstile and pass through. Take the ticket back, because it may be checked by uniformed police officers when you leave the subway. There are also occasional ticket checks on the trains, platforms, and passageways. If you're changing trains, get out and determine which direction (final destination) on the next line you

---

A Métro Map Note
See the inside front cover of this guide for a full-color Paris Métro map.

Discount Passes

You can buy a **Paris Visite pass,** valid for 1, 3, or 5 days on the public transport system, including the Métro, the city buses, the RER (regional express) trains within Paris city limits, and even the funicular to the top of Montmartre. (The RER has both first- and second-class compartments, and the pass lets you travel in first class.) The cost is 60F (9.10€, $8.70) for 1 day, 95F (14.45€, $13.83) for 2 days, 130F (19.75€, $18.85) for 3 days, or 185F (28.10€, $26.85) for 5 days. The card is available at the **Services Touristiques de la Régie Autonome des Transports Parisiens (RATP),** with offices at place de la Madeleine, 8th arr. (© **08-36-68-77-14** or 01-40-06-71-45; Métro: Madeleine; www.ratp.fr), and 54 quai de la Rapée, 12th arr. (© **01-44-68-20-20** or 08-36-63-77-14; Métro: Gare de Lyon); the tourist offices (see above); or the main Métro stations.

Another more economical pass available to visitors is **Carte Mobilis,** allowing unlimited travel on all bus, Métro, and RER lines in Paris during a 1-day period for 32 to 74F (4.85–11.25€, $4.65–$10.75), depending on the zone. You will need to provide a passport-size photo of yourself. You can buy the pass at any Métro station.

Most economical of all, for anyone who happens to arrive in Paris early (Monday, Tuesday, or even Wednesday) of any given week, is a **Carte Orange.** Sold at any large Métro station, it allows 1 full week of unlimited Métro or bus transit within central Paris (the 20 arrondissements and the nearby suburbs) for 85F (12.90€, $12.35). To get one, you'll have to submit a passport-size photo. They're valid from any Monday to the following Sunday, and they're sold only on Monday, Tuesday, or Wednesday of any given week.

want, then follow the bright orange CORRESPONDANCE signs until you reach the proper platform. Don't follow a SORTIE sign, which means "exit." If you exit, you'll have to pay another fare to resume your journey.

The Paris Métro runs daily from 5:30am to around 1:15am, at which time all underground trains reach their final terminus at the end of each of their respective lines. Be alert that the last train may pass through central Paris as much as an hour before that time. The subways are reasonably safe at any hour, but beware of pickpockets.

BY BUS

Bus travel is much slower than the subway. Most buses run from 7am to 8:30pm (a few operate to 12:30am, and 10 operate during the early-morning hours). Service is limited on Sundays and holidays. Bus and Métro fares are the same and you can use the same *carnet* tickets on both. At certain stops, signs list the destinations and numbers of the buses serving that point. Destinations are usually listed north to south and east to west. Most stops along the way are also posted on the sides of the buses. To catch a bus, wait in line at the bus stop. Signal the driver to stop the bus and board.

Most bus rides (including any that begin and end within Paris's 20 arrondissements and nearby suburbs) require one ticket (the same that's used within the

Métro). For bus travel to some of the city's more distant suburbs, an additional ticket might be required. If you intend to use the buses a lot, pick up an **RATP bus map** at its offices on place de la Madeleine and quai de la Rapée (see the "Discount Passes" box) or at any tourist office. For details on bus and Métro routes, call © **08-36-68-41-14.**

The same entity that maintains Paris's network of Métros and buses, the **RATP** (© **08-36-68-77-14**) has initiated a motorized mode of transport designed exclusively as a means of appreciating the city's visual grandeur. Known as the **Balabus,** it's a fleet of big-windowed orange-and-white motor coaches whose most visible drawback is their limited hours—they run only on Sunday and national holidays from noon to 9pm, April 15 to October 30. The coaches journey in both directions between the Gare de Lyon and the Grande Arche de La Défense, encompassing some of the city's most monumental vistas and making regular stops. Presentation of two Métro tickets 16F (2.45€, $2.30), a valid Carte Mobilis (see box), or a valid Paris Visite pass (see the "Discount Passes" box) will carry you along the entire route. You'll recognize the bus and the route it follows by the "Bb" symbol emblazoned on each bus's side and on signs posted beside the route it follows.

BY CAR

Again, don't even think about driving in Paris. The streets are narrow, with confusing one-way designations, and parking is next to impossible. Besides, most visitors don't have the ruthlessness required to survive in Parisian traffic. Think about renting a car only if you plan to explore the Ile de France and beyond.

You can rent cars from locally based agencies like **Autorent,** 92 rue de la Convention, 15th arr. (© **01-45-54-22-45;** Métro: Boucicaut), or from competitors like **Rent-a-Car,** 62 bd. Malesherbes, 8th arr. (© **01-45-22-28-28;** Métro: Gare St. Lazare) and **Inter Touring Service,** 117 bd. Auguste-Blanqui, 13th arr. (© **01-45-88-52-37;** Metro: Glacière). **Budget** (© **800/472-3325** in the U.S. and Canada; www.budgetrentacar.com) maintains about 30 locations in Paris, with its largest branch at 81 av. Kléber, 16th arr. (© **01-47-55-61-00;** Métro: Trocadéro). **Hertz** (© **800/654-3001** in the U.S. and Canada; www.hertz.com) maintains about 15 locations in Paris, including offices at the airports and the main office at 27 rue St-Ferdinand, 17th arr. (© **01-45-74-97-39;** Métro: Argentine). Be sure to ask about any promotional discounts. **Avis** (© **800/331-2112** in the U.S. and Canada; www.avis.com) has offices at both airports, as well as a headquarters at 5 rue Bixio, 7th arr. (© **01-44-18-10-50;** Métro: Ecole Militaire), near the Eiffel Tower. **National** (© **800/227-3876** in the U.S. and Canada; www.nationalcar.com) is represented in Paris by **Europcar,** whose largest office is at 165 bis rue de Vaugirard (© **01-44-38-61-61;** Métro: St-Sulpice). It has offices at both airports as well.

BY TAXI

Taxi drivers are organized into an effective lobby to keep their number limited to around 15,000, and it's nearly impossible to get one at rush hour. You can hail regular cabs on the street when their signs read *libre.* Taxis are easier to find at the many stands near Métro stations.

The flag drops at 13F (2.03€, $1.94), and you pay 3.87F (.60€, 55¢) per kilometer. At night, expect to pay 6.32F (.95€, 90¢) per kilometer. On airport trips, you're not required to pay for the driver's empty return ride. You're allowed several small pieces of luggage free if they're transported inside and don't weigh more than 5kg (11 pounds). Heavier suitcases carried in the trunk cost 6F

Tips **A Taxi Warning**

Always check the taxi's meter to make sure you're not paying the previous passenger's fare. Beware of cabs without meters, which often try to snare tipsy patrons outside nightclubs—always settle the tab in advance.

(.90€, 85¢) apiece. Tip 12% to 15%—the latter usually elicits a *merci.* To radio cabs, call ✆ **01-44-52-23-86** or 01-44-52-23-58; you'll be charged from the point where the taxi begins the drive to pick you up.

BY BICYCLE

To bike through the streets and parks of Paris, perhaps with a baguette tucked under your arm, might've been a fantasy of yours since you saw your first Maurice Chevalier film. In recent years, the city has added many miles of right-hand lanes designated for cyclists as well as hundreds of bike racks. (When these aren't available, many Parisians simply chain their bikes to fences or lampposts.) Cycling is especially popular in the larger parks and gardens.

Paris-Vélos, 2 rue du Fer-à-Moulin, 5th arr. (✆ **01-43-37-59-22;** Métro: Censier-Daubenton), rents by the day, weekend, or week, charging 90 to 160F (13.73–24.30€, $13.05–$23.20) per weekday, 160 to 220F (24.30–33.45€, $23.20–$31.90) Saturday and Sunday, and 450 to 600F (68.40–91.20€, $65.25–$87) per week. You must leave a 2,000F (304€, $290) deposit. It's open Monday to Saturday from 10am to 12:30pm and 2 to 7pm.

BY BOAT

In April and mid-October, the **Batobus** (✆ **01-44-11-33-44**), a series of 150-passenger ferries with big windows for viewing the riverfronts, operates at 25-minute intervals daily from 10am to 7pm. Boats chug along between the quays at the base of the Eiffel Tower and the quays at the base of the Louvre, stopping at the Musée d'Orsay, St-Germain-des-Prés, Notre-Dame, the Hôtel-de-Ville, the Louvre, and what the organizers of this affair refer to as the Champs-Elysées, but which is actually a stop at the base of the Pont Alexandre-III. Transit between any two stops costs 20F (3.05€, $2.90) for children and adults, and 10F (1.50€, $1.45) for transit between any additional stops, although passengers who intend to use the boat as a sightseeing opportunity usually opt to pay a flat rate (good all day) of 65F (9.90€, $9.45) for adults and 35F (5.30€, $5.13) for children under 19, and then settle back and watch the monuments. Photo ops are countless aboard this leisurely but intensely panoramic "floating observation platform."

  ***FAST FACTS:* Paris**

American Express From its administrative headquarters in the Paris suburb of Reuil-Malmaison, at 4 rue de Louis-Blériot, 92561 Rueil-Malmaison CEDEX, the largest travel service in the world operates a 24-hour hot line at ✆ **01-47-77-70-00.** Day-to-day services, like tours and money exchange, are available at 11 rue Scribe, 9th arr., 75009 Paris (✆ **01-47-77-77-07;** Métro: Opéra), or the smaller branch at 38 av. Wagram, 8th arr., 75008 Paris (✆ **01-42-27-58-80;** Métro: Ternes). Both are open Monday to Friday from 9am to 6:30pm, with money-changing services ending at 4:45pm. The rue Scribe office is open Saturday from 10am to 5pm (no mail pickup).

Banks American Express may be able to meet most of your banking needs. If not, banks in Paris are open Monday to Friday from 9am to 5pm. A few are open on Saturday. Ask at your hotel for the location of the bank nearest you. Shops and most hotels will cash your traveler's checks, but not at the advantageous rate a bank or foreign-exchange office will give you, so make sure you've allowed enough funds for "le weekend."

Business Hours Opening hours in France are erratic, as befits a nation of individualists. Most museums close 1 day a week (often Tuesday) and national holidays; hours tend to be from 9:30am to 5pm. Some museums, particularly the smaller ones, close for lunch from noon to 2pm. Most French museums are open Saturday, but many close Sunday morning and reopen in the afternoon. (See chapter 7 for specific times.) Generally, **offices** are open Monday to Friday from 9am to 5pm, but don't count on it. Always call first. **Large stores** and **chain stores** are open from 9 or 9:30am (often 10am) to 6 or 7pm without a break for lunch. Some **shops**, particularly those operated by foreigners, open at 8am and close at 8 or 9pm. In some **small stores**, the lunch break can last 3 hours, beginning at 1pm.

Dentists For emergency dental service, call **S.O.S. Dentaire,** 87 bd. Du Port-Royal, 13th arr. (✆ **01-43-37-51-00**; Métro: Port-Royal), Monday to Friday from 8pm to midnight and Saturday and Sunday from 9:30am to midnight. You can also call or visit the **American Hospital,** 63 bd. Victor-Hugo, Neuilly (✆ **01-46-41-25-25**; Métro: Pont de Levallois or Pont de Neuilly; Bus: 82). A 24-hour English/French dental clinic is on the premises.

Doctors See "Hospitals," below.

Drugstores After regular hours, ask at your hotel where the nearest 24-hour *pharmacie* is. You'll also find the address posted on the doors or windows of other drugstores in the neighborhood. One all-night drugstore is the **Pharmacy Derhy,** in La Galerie Les Champs, 84 av. des Champs-Elysées, 8th arr. (✆ **01-45-62-02-41**; Métro: George V).

Electricity In general, expect 200 volts AC (60 cycles), though you'll encounter 110 and 115 volts in some older establishments. Adapters are needed to fit sockets. Many hotels have two-pin (in some cases, three-pin) sockets for electric razors. It's best to ask at your hotel before plugging in any electrical appliance.

Embassies/Consulates If you have a passport, immigration, legal, or other problem, contact your consulate. Call before you go, as they often keep strange hours and observe both French and home-country holidays.

The Embassy of the **United States,** at 2 av. Gabriel, 8th arr. (✆ **01-43-12-22-22**; Métro: Concorde), is open Monday to Friday from 9am to 6pm. Passports are issued at its consulate at 2 rue St-Florentin (✆ **01-43-12-22-22**; Métro: Concorde). Getting a passport replaced costs $55. The Embassy of **Canada** is at 35 av. Montaigne, 8th arr. (✆ **01-44-43-29-00**; Métro: F. D. Roosevelt or Alma-Marceau), open Monday to Friday from 9am to noon and 2 to 4pm. The Canadian consulate is at the embassy. The Embassy of the **United Kingdom** is at 35 rue du faubourg St-Honoré, 8th arr. (✆ **01-44-51-31-00**; Métro: Concorde or Madeleine), open Monday to Friday from 9:30am to 12:30pm and 2:30 to 5pm. The consulate is at 16 rue d'Anjou, 8th arr. (✆ **01-44-51-31-00**; Métro: Consulate), open Monday to Friday from 9:30am to 12:30pm and 2:30 to 5pm. The Embassy of **Australia** is at 4 rue Jean-Rey, 15th arr. (© **01-40-59-33-00**; Métro: Bir Hakeim), open Monday to Friday from 9:15am to noon and 2:30 to 4:30pm. The Embassy of **New Zealand** is at 7 ter rue Léonard-de-Vinci, 16th arr. (© **01-45-00-24-11**; Métro: Victor Hugo), open Monday to Friday from 9am to 1pm and 2:30 to 6pm. The Embassy of **Ireland** is at 4 rue Rude, 16th arr. (© **01-44-17-67-00**; Métro: Etoile), open Monday to Friday from 9:30am to noon.

Emergencies For the police, call © **17**; to report a fire, call © **18**. For an ambulance, call the fire department at © **01-45-78-74-52**; a fire vehicle rushes patients to the nearest emergency room. For **S.A.M.U.**, an independently operated, privately owned ambulance company, call © **15**. For less urgent matters, you can reach the police at 9 bd. du Palais, 4th arr. (© **01-53-73-53-71** or 01-53-73-53-73; Métro: Cité).

Hospitals Open Monday to Saturday from 8am to 7pm, **Central Médical Europe**, 44 rue d'Amsterdam, 9th arr. (© **01-42-81-93-33**; Métro: Liège), maintains contacts with medical and dental practitioners in all fields. Appointments are recommended. Another choice is the **American Hospital of Paris**, 63 bd. Victor-Hugo, Neuilly (© **01-46-41-25-25**; Métro: Pont de Levallois or Pont de Neuilly; Bus: 82), which operates 24-hour medical and dental service. An additional clinic is the **Centre Figuier**, 2 rue du Figuier (© **01-49-96-62-70**; Métro: St-Paul). Call before visiting.

Internet Access To surf the Net or check your e-mail, try the **Cybercafé Latino**, 13 rue de l'Ecole Polytechnique, 5th arr. (© **01-40-51-86-94**; www.cybercafelatino.com; Métro: Maubert-Mutualité), open Monday to Saturday from 11:30am to 2am; Sunday from 3 to 9pm, or **Le Rendez-vous Toyota**, 79 av. des Champs-Elysées (© **01-56-89-29-79**; http://www.lerendez-voustoyota.com/; Métro: George V), open Monday to Thursday from 10:30am to 9pm and Friday and Saturday from 10:30am to midnight. See also **Le Web Bar** in chapter 10.

Liquor Laws You'll find it easier to buy wine, beer, or spirits in France than in England or other countries. Supermarkets, smaller grocery stores, and cafes all sell alcoholic beverages. The legal drinking age is 16, but persons under that age can be served an alcoholic drink in a bar or restaurant if accompanied by a parent or legal guardian. Wine and liquor are sold every day of the week, year-round. Hours of cafes vary. Some open at 6am, serving drinks to 3am; others are open 24 hours. Bars and nightclubs may stay open as late as they wish.

The Breathalyzer test is in use in France, and a motorist is considered "legally intoxicated" with 0.5 grams of alcohol per liter of blood (the more liberal U.S. law is 1 gram per liter). If convicted, a motorist faces a stiff fine and a possible prison term of 2 months to 2 years. If bodily injury results, sentences can range from 2 years to life.

Mail/Post Offices Most post offices in Paris are open Monday to Friday from 8am to 7pm and Saturday from 8am to noon. The **main post office (PTT)** for Paris is at 52 rue du Louvre, 75001 Paris (© **01-40-28-76-00**; Métro: Louvre). It's open 24 hours a day for the sale of stamps, phone calls, and sending faxes and telegrams, with limited hours (Monday to Friday from 8am to 5pm and Saturday from 8am to noon) for more esoteric financial services like the sale of money orders. Stamps can also usually be purchased at your hotel reception desk and at cafes with red TABAC signs. You can send faxes at the main post office in each arrondissement.

Airmail letters within Europe cost 3F (.45€, 45¢); to the United States and Canada, 4.40F (.65€, 65¢); and to Australia and New Zealand, 5.10F (.83€, 75¢). You can have mail sent to you *poste restante* (general delivery) at the main post office for a small fee. Take an ID, such as a passport, if you plan to pick up mail. American Express (see above) also offers a *poste restante* service, but you may be asked to show an American Express card or traveler's checks.

Newspapers/Magazines English-language newspapers are available at nearly every kiosk. Published Monday to Saturday, the *International Herald-Tribune* is the most popular paper with visiting Americans and Canadians; the *Guardian* provides a British point of view. For those who read in French, the leading domestic newspapers are *Le Monde, Le Figaro,* and *Libération;* the top magazines are *L'Express, Le Point,* and *Le Nouvel Observateur.* Kiosks are generally open daily from 8am to 9pm.

Pets If you have certificates from a vet and proof of rabies vaccination, you can bring most house pets into France.

Police Call ℂ **17** for emergencies. The principal Préfecture is at 9 bd. du Palais, 4th arr. (ℂ **01-53-71-53-71**; Métro: Cité).

Rest Rooms If you're in dire need, duck into a cafe or brasserie to use the lavatory. It's customary to make some small purchase if you do so. In the street, the domed self-cleaning lavatories are a decent option if you have small change; Métro stations and underground garages usually have public lavatories, but the degree of cleanliness varies.

Safety In Paris, be especially aware of child pickpockets. They roam the capital, preying on tourists around attractions like the Louvre, Eiffel Tower, and Notre-Dame, and they also often strike in the Métro, sometimes blocking a victim from the escalator. A band of these young thieves can clean your pockets even while you try to fend them off. Their method is to get very close to a target, ask for a handout (sometimes), and deftly help themselves to your money or passport.

Although public safety is not as much a problem in Paris as it is in large American cities, concerns are growing. Robbery at gun- or knifepoint is uncommon here, but not unknown. Be careful.

Taxes See chapter 9 for an explanation of the value-added tax refund.

Telephone Public phones are found in cafes, restaurants, Métro stations, post offices, airports, and train stations, and occasionally on the streets. Finding a coin-operated telephone in France is an arduous task. A simpler and more widely accepted method of payment is the *télécarte,* a prepaid calling card available at kiosks, post offices, and Métro stations and costing 49 to 97.50F (7.45–14.80€, $7.10–$14.15) for 50 and 120 units, respectively. A local call costs 1 unit, which provides you with 6 to 18 minutes of conversation, depending on the rate. Avoid making calls from your hotel, which might double or triple the charges.

To call **long distance within France,** dial the 10-digit number (9-digit in some cases outside Paris) of the person or place you're calling. To make a **direct international call,** first dial 00, listen for the tone, then slowly dial the country code, the area code, and the local number. The country code for the **USA** and **Canada** is 1; **Great Britain,** 44; **Ireland,** 353; **Australia,** 61; **New Zealand,** 64; **South Africa,** 27.

An easy and relatively inexpensive way to call home is **USA Direct/AT&T World Connect.** From within France, dial any of the following numbers: (✆ **0800/99-0011,** -1011, -1111, or -1211). Then follow the prompt, which will ask you to punch in the number of either your AT&T credit card or a MasterCard or Visa. Along with the United States, the countries participating in the system—referred to as World Connect—include **Canada,** the **United Kingdom, Ireland, Australia,** and **New Zealand.** By punching in the number of the party you want in any of these countries, you'll avoid the surcharges imposed by the hotel operator. An AT&T operator will be available to help you with complications arising during the process.

Time France is usually 6 hours ahead of eastern standard time in the United States. French daylight saving time lasts from around April to September, when clocks are set 1 hour ahead of the standard time.

Tipping By law, all bills show *service compris,* which means the tip is included; additional gratuities are customarily given as follows: For **hotel staff,** tip the porter 6 to 10F (.90–1.50€, 85¢–$1.45) per item of baggage and 10F (1.50€, $1.45) per day for the chambermaid. You're not obligated to tip the concierge, doorman, or anyone else unless you use his or her services. In **cafes** and **restaurants,** waiter service is usually included, though you can leave a couple of francs. Tip **taxi drivers** 12% to 15% of the amount on the meter. In **theaters** and **restaurants,** give cloakroom attendants at least 5F (.75€, 75¢) per item. Give **restroom attendants** in nightclubs and such places about 2F (.30€, 34¢). Give **cinema** and **theater ushers** about 2F (.30€, 34¢). Tip the **hairdresser** about 15%, and don't forget to tip the person who gives you a shampoo or a manicure 10F (1.50€, $1.45). For **guides** for group visits to museums and monuments, 5 to 10F (.75–1.50€, 75¢–$1.45) is a reasonable tip.

Water Drinking water is generally safe, though it has been known to cause diarrhea in some unaccustomed stomachs. If you ask for water in a restaurant, it'll be bottled water (for which you'll pay), unless you specifically request tap water (*l'eau du robinet*).

5

Where to Stay

Paris boasts some 2,000 hotels—with about 80,000 rooms—spread across its 20 arrondissements. They range from the Ritz and the Crillon to dives so repellent even George Orwell, author of *Down and Out in Paris and London,* wouldn't have considered checking in. (Of course, you won't find any of those in this guide!) We've included deluxe places for those who can afford to live like the Sultan of Brunei as well as a wide range of moderate and inexpensive choices for the rest of us.

Most visitors, at least those from North America, come to Paris in July and August. Many French are on vacation then, and trade fairs and conventions come to a halt, so there are usually plenty of rooms, even though these months have traditionally been the peak season for European travel. In most hotels, February is just as busy as April or September because of the volume of business travelers and the increasing number of tourists who've learned to take advantage of off-season discount airfares.

Because hot weather rarely lasts long in Paris, few hotels, except the deluxe ones, provide air-conditioning. If you're trapped in a garret on a hot summer night, you'll have to sweat it out. You can open your window to get some cooler air, but open windows admit the nuisance of noise pollution. To avoid this, you can request a room in back when reserving.

READING THE GOVERNMENT RATINGS

The French government grades hotels with a star system, ranging from one star for a simple inn to four stars for a deluxe hotel. Moderately priced hotels usually get two or three stars. This system is based on a complicated formula of room sizes, facilities, plumbing, elevators, dining options, renovations, and so on. In one-star hotels, the bathrooms are often shared and the facilities extremely limited (such as no elevator), and the rooms may not have phones or TVs; breakfast is often the only meal served. In two- or three-star hotels, there are usually elevators, and rooms will likely have baths, phones, and TVs. In four-star hotels, you'll get the works, with all the amenities plus facilities and services such as room service, 24-hour concierges, elevators, and perhaps even health clubs.

However, the system is a bit misleading. For tax reasons, a four-star hotel might deliberately elect to have a three-star rating, which, with the hotel's permission, is granted by the government. The government won't add a star where it's not merited, but will remove a star with the hotel's request.

WHICH BANK IS FOR YOU?

The river dividing Paris geographically and culturally demands you make a choice. Are you more **Left Bank,** wanting a room in the heart of St-Germain, perhaps where Jean-Paul Sartre and Simone de Beauvoir once spent the night?

A Room in Paris

If you seek something other than a hotel, **Alcôve & Agapes,** 8 bis rue Coysevox, 750198 Paris (✆ **01-44-85-06-05;** fax 01-44-85-06-14; info@paris-bedandbreakfast.com), acts as an intermediary between travelers who seek rooms in private homes and Parisians who wish to welcome B&B visitors. Hosts range in age between 25 and 65, and most of them speak English. Rates for rooms with a shared bathroom range from 290 to 350F (44.10 to 53.20€, $42.05 to $50.75), going up to 350 to 450F (53.20 to 68.40€, $50.75 to $65.25) with a private bath. These tariffs are per room for one or two guests. Another agency promoting upmarket B&B accommodations is **European B&B,** 437 J Street, Suite 210, San Diego, CA 92101 (✆ **800/872-2632** in the U.S. or fax 619/531-1686; www.parisbandb.com). All the B&B properties are in private family homes or else unhosted apartments in upscale neighborhoods.

Or are you more **Right Bank,** preferring sumptuous quarters like those at the Crillon, perhaps where Tom Cruise once slept? Would you rather look for that special old curio in a dusty shop on the Left Bank's rue Jacob or inspect the latest Lagerfeld or Dior couture on the Right Bank's avenue Montaigne? Each of Paris's neighborhoods has its own flavor, and your experiences and memories of Paris will likely be formed by where you choose to stay.

If you desire chic surroundings, choose a Right Bank hotel. That puts you near the most elegant shops and within walking distance of major sights like the Arc de Triomphe, place de la Concorde, the Jardin des Tuileries, the Opéra Garnier, and the Louvre. The best Right Bank hotels are near the Arc de Triomphe in the 8th arrondissement, though many first-class lodgings cluster near the Trocadéro and Bois du Boulogne in the 16th or near the Palais des Congrès in the 17th. If you'd like to be near place Vendôme, try for a hotel in the 1st. Also popular are the increasingly fashionable Marais and Bastille areas in the 3rd and 4th arrondissements and Les Halles/Beaubourg, home of the Centre Pompidou and Les Halles shopping mall, in the 3rd.

If you want less formality and tiny bohemian streets, head for the Left Bank, where prices are traditionally lower. Hotels that cater to students are found in the 5th and 6th arrondissements, the 5th known as the Latin Quarter. These areas, with their literary overtones, boast the Sorbonne, the Panthéon, the Jardin du Luxembourg, cafe life, bookstores, and publishing houses. The 7th arrondissement provides a touch of avant-garde St-Germain.

BEST HOTEL BETS

See chapter 1 for a list of our hotel favorites—the best newcomer, the best view, and more.

1 On the Right Bank

We'll begin with the most centrally located arrondissements on the Right Bank, then work our way through the more outlying neighborhoods and to the area around the Arc de Triomphe.

> *Tips*   **Cafe and a Croissant?**
>
> Hotel breakfasts are fairly uniform and include your choice of coffee, tea, or hot chocolate; a freshly baked croissant and roll; and limited quantities of butter and jam or jelly. It can be at your door moments after you call for it and is served at almost any hour. (When we mention breakfast charges in our listings, we refer to continental breakfasts only.) Breakfasts with eggs, bacon, ham, or other items must be ordered from the à la carte menu. For a charge, larger hotels serve the full or "English" breakfast, but smaller hotels typically serve only the continental variety.

1ST ARRONDISSEMENT
VERY EXPENSIVE

Hôtel Costes ★★★   Grand style and a location close to the headquarters of some of Paris's most upscale shops, as well as the offices of *Harper's Bazaar,* attract lots of high-style fashion types. Don't expect the Ritz, but other than that, this is one of the shining stars of Paris hostelries. The town-house-style premise was a *maison bourgeoise* for many generations, presenting a severely dignified facade. In 1996, it was richly adorned with jewel-toned colors, heavy swagged curtains, and lavish Napoléon III accessories. Today, everything about it evokes the rich days of the Gilded Age, especially the guest rooms. Some are small, but they're cozy and ornate, with one or two large beds, CD players, and fax machines. The best units are called Grande Chambre and they contain sitting areas. For the ultimate luxury, ask for one of the duplex units with split-level layouts.

239 rue St-Honoré, 75001 Paris. ⓒ **01-42-44-50-50.** Fax 01-42-44-50-01. 83 units. 3,000–3,500F (456–532€, $435–$507.50) double; from 7,500F (1,140€, $1,087.50) suite. AE, DC, MC, V. Métro: Tuileries or Concorde. **Amenities:** Restaurant (French); bar; indoor pool; health club; car-rental desk; room service; massage; baby-sitting; laundry/dry cleaning. *In room:* A/C, TV, minibar, hair dryer.

Hôtel de Vendôme ★★   For a time the Embassy of Texas (when that state was a nation), this jewel box opened in 1998 at one of the world's most prestigious addresses. It is comparable and almost as good as Costes. Though the guest rooms are only moderate in size, you live in opulent comfort. Most of the rooms are in classic Second Empire style with luxurious beds, tasteful fabrics, and well-upholstered, hand-carved furnishings. The security is fantastic, with TV intercoms. This new version of the hotel replaces a lackluster one that stood here for a century, and its facade and roof are classified as historic monuments by the French government.

1 place Vendôme, 75001 Paris. ⓒ **01-55-04-55-00.** Fax 01-49-27-97-89. reservations@ hoteldevendome.com. 29 units. 2,800–3,200F (425.60–486.40€, $406–$464) double; 4,500–5,500F (684–836€, $652.50–$797.50) suite. AE, DC, MC, V. Métro: Concorde or Opéra. **Amenities:** Restaurant (French); bar; room service; laundry. *In room:* A/C, TV, minibar, hair dryer.

Hôtel du Louvre ★★   After a massive overhaul, the hotel is now in a neck-and-neck race with the Regina for neighborhood supremacy. When Napoléon III inaugurated the hotel in 1855, French journalists described it as "a palace of the people, rising adjacent to the palace of kings." In 1897, Camille Pissarro moved into a room with a view that inspired many of his landscapes. Between the Louvre and the Palais Royal, the hotel has a decor of marble, bronze, and gilt. The guest rooms are quintessentially Parisian, filled with souvenirs of the Belle Époque. Most were renovated between 1996 and 1998. Some are small, but most are medium-size to spacious—with elegant fabrics and upholstery, excellent carpeting, double-glazed windows, comfortable beds, and traditional wood furniture.

Place André-Malraux, 75001 Paris. ✆ **800/888-4747** in the U.S. and Canada, or ✆ **01-44-58-38-38**. Fax 01-44-58-38-01. www.hoteldulouvre.com. 195 units. 2,350–5,280F (357.20–802.55€, $340.75–$765.60) double; from 6,000F (912€, $870) suite. Ask about midwinter discounts. AE, DC, MC, V. Parking 120F (18.25€, $17.40). Métro: Palais Royal or Louvre-Rivoli. **Amenities:** 2 restaurants (both French); 2 bars; health club; room service; massage; laundry/dry cleaning. In room: A/C, TV, minibar, hair dryer, safe.

Hôtel Regina 🏵   Restored to its old-fashioned grandeur, it is adjacent to rue de Rivoli's equestrian statue of Joan of Arc opposite the Louvre. The management has poured millions into the renovation, retaining the patina of the Art-Nouveau interior and making historically appropriate improvements. The guest rooms are richly decorated and spacious; those overlooking the Tuileries enjoy panoramic views as far away as the Eiffel Tower. The mid-size to large bathrooms are very appealing, even with stained glass or windows in most cases. The public areas contain every period of Louis furniture imaginable, Oriental carpets, 18th-century paintings, and bowls of flowers. Fountains play in a flagstone-covered courtyard. There are more grace notes in this hotel than at its closest competitor, Hotel du Louvre.

2 place des Pyramides, 75001 Paris. ✆ **01-42-60-31-10**. Fax 01-40-15-95-16. www.regina-hotel.com. 120 units. 2,070–2,900F (314.65–440.80€, $300.15–$420.50) double; from 3,000F (456€, $435) suite. AE, DC, MC, V. Parking 150F (22.80€, $21.75). Métro: Pyramides or Tuileries. **Amenities:** 2 restaurants (both French); bar; room service; massage; baby-sitting; laundry/dry cleaning. In room: A/C, TV, minibar, hair dryer, safe.

Hôtel Ritz 🏵🏵🏵   The Ritz is Europe's greatest hotel, an enduring symbol of elegance on one of Paris's most beautiful and historic squares. César Ritz, the "little shepherd boy from Niederwald," converted the private Hôtel de Lazun into a luxury hotel that he opened in 1898. With the help of the culinary master Escoffier, he made the Ritz a miracle of luxury living.

In 1979, the Ritz family sold the hotel to Egyptian businessman Mohammed al Fayed, who refurbished it and added a cooking school. (You may remember that his son, Dodi al Fayed, and Princess Diana dined here before they set out on their fateful drive.) Two town houses were annexed, joined by a long arcade lined with miniature display cases representing 125 of Paris's leading boutiques. The public salons are furnished with museum-caliber antiques. Each guest room is uniquely decorated, most often with Louis XIV or XV reproductions; all have fine rugs, marble fireplaces, tapestries, brass beds, and more. The spacious marble bathrooms are the city's most luxurious, filled with deluxe toiletries, scales, private phones, cords to summon maids and valets, robes, full-length and

---

⸜Fun Fact A Hotel Tale

During Paris's occupation, on August 25, 1944, Ernest Hemingway "liberated" the Ritz. Armed with machine guns, "Papa" and a group of Allied soldiers pulled up to the hotel in a Jeep, intent on capturing Nazis and freeing, if only symbolically, the landmark. After a sweep from the cellars to the roof, the group discovered the Nazis had already fled. Hemingway led his team to the Ritz bar to order a round of dry martinis. In commemoration of the 50th anniversary of the liberation, the renovated Bar Hemingway reopened on August 25, 1994.

Hotels in 1st–4th, 9th–12th & 18th Arrondissements

Hôtel Britannique **19**
Hôtel Burgundy **6**
Hôtel Caron de
Beaumarchais **22**
Hôtel Central **21**
Hôtel Concorde St-Lazare **4**
Hôtel Costes **11**

Hôtel de la Place des Vosges **31**
Hôtel de la Tour
d'Auvergne **2**
Hôtel de Lutéce **24**
Hôtel des Chevaliers **30**
Hôtel des Deux-Îles **25**
Hôtel des Tuileries **12**

Hôtel de Vendôme **10**
Hôtel du Jeu de Paume **26**
Hôtel du Louvre **14**
Hôtel du 7e Art **27**
Hôtel Ermitage **1**
Hôtel Henri IV **18**
Hôtel Mansart **8**

Métro Stop Ⓜ
RER Stop Ⓡ
Railway ----

Hôtel Pavillon Bastille **33**
Hôtel Regina **13**
Hôtel Ritz **7**
Hôtel Saint Merry **20**
Hôtel St-Louis **23**
Hôtel Victoires Opéra **16**
Hôtel Williams Opéra **3**

Le Stendhal **9**
Libertel Croix de Malte **29**
Nouvel Hôtel **32**
Relais du Louvre **17**
Résidence Alhambra **28**
Terrass Hôtel **1**
Timhôtel Le Louvre **15**
Tulip Inn de Noailles **5**

makeup mirrors, and dual basins. Ever since Edward VII got stuck in a too-narrow bathtub with his lover of the evening, the tubs at the Ritz have been deep and big.

15 place Vendôme, 75001 Paris. ✆ **800/223-6800** in the U.S. and Canada, or ✆ **01-43-16-30-30.** Fax 01-43-16-31-78. www.ritzparis.com. 175 units. 4,000–4,560F (608–693.10€, $580–$661.20) double; from 5,415F (823.13€, $785.23) suite. AE, DC, MC, V. Parking 230F (34.95€, $33.35). Métro: Opéra, Concorde, or Madeleine. **Amenities:** 2 restaurants (both French); 2 bars; indoor pool; health club; shopping arcade; room service; massage; laundry/dry cleaning. *In room:* A/C, TV, minibar, hair dryer, safe.

EXPENSIVE

Hôtel des Tuileries ✿   On a quiet narrow street, this hotel occupies a 17th-century town house Marie Antoinette used when she left Versailles for unofficial Paris visits. Don't expect mementos of the queen, as all the frippery of her era was long ago stripped away. But in honor of its royal antecedents, the hotel's public areas and guest rooms are filled with copies of Louis XV furniture—a bit dowdy, but still dignified and very comfortable. In 2001, major improvements were made to the building structure, including the elevators. Each unit has a full tub and shower bath.

10 rue St-Hyacinthe, 75001 Paris. ✆ **01-42-61-04-17.** Fax 01-49-27-91-56. www.hotel-des-tuileries.com. 26 units. 1,090–1,400F (165.70–212.80€, $158.05–$203) double. AE, DC, MC, V. Parking 110F (16.70€, $15.95). Métro: Tuileries or Pyramides. **Amenities:** Room service (7am–10pm only); baby-sitting; laundry. *In room:* A/C, TV with cable, minibar, hair dryer, safe.

MODERATE

Hôtel Britannique *(Value)*   Conservatively modern and plush, this is a much-renovated 19th-century hotel near Les Halles, the Pompidou, and Notre-Dame. It was re-rated with three government stars after a complete renovation in the mid-1980s. The place not only is British in name but also seems to have culti-vated an English style of graciousness. The guest rooms may be small, but they're immaculate and soundproof, with comfortable beds. A satellite receiver gets U.S. and U.K. television shows. The reading room is a cozy retreat.

20 av. Victoria, 75001 Paris. ✆ **01-42-33-74-59.** Fax 01-42-33-82-65. www.hotel-britannic.com. 40 units. 820–1,130F (124.65–171.75€, $118.90–$163.85) double. AE, DC, MC, V. Parking 100F (15.20€, $14.50). Métro: Châtelet. **Amenities:** Room service. *In room:* TV, minibar, hair dryer, safe.

Hôtel Burgundy ✿ *(Value)*   The Burgundy is one of this outrageously expensive area's best values. The frequently renovated building began as two adjacent town houses in the 1830s, one a pension where Baudelaire wrote some of his eerie poetry in the 1860s and the other a bordello. They were linked by British-born managers, who insisted on using the English name. Radically renovated in 1992, with continued improvements in 2001, the hotel hosts many North and South Americans and features conservatively decorated rooms and comfortable beds, each with a full tub and shower in the bathroom. The Charles Baudelaire restau-rant and its bar are open for lunch and dinner Monday to Friday.

8 rue Duphot, 75001 Paris. ✆ **01-42-60-34-12.** Fax 01-47-03-95-20. 89 units. 1,000–1,150F (152–174.80€, $145–$166.75) double; 1,600–1,900F (243.20–288.80€, $232–$275.50) suite. AE, DC, MC, V. Métro: Madeleine or Concorde. **Amenities:** Restaurant (French); bar; room service (breakfast); baby-sitting. *In room:* A/C, TV, minibar, hair dryer.

Hôtel Mansart *(Value)*   After operating as a glorious wreck for many decades, this hotel—designed by its namesake—was fully renovated in 1991 and offers some of the lowest rates in this pricey area. The public rooms contain Louis reproductions and startling floor-to-ceiling geometric designs inspired by the inlaid marble floors (or formal gardens) of the French Renaissance. The small-to medium-size guest rooms are subtly formal and comfortable, though only half a dozen of the suites and most expensive rooms actually overlook the famous square. Twenty rooms are air-conditioned, and all come with a tub and shower in the bathroom. Breakfast is the only meal served.

5 rue des Capucines, 75001 Paris. © 01-42-61-50-28. Fax 01-49-27-97-44. www.hotelinformation.com. 57 units. 650–1,100F (99–167€, $93–$160) double; 1,500–1800F (228–274€, $218–$261) suite. AE, DC, MC, V. Métro: Opéra or Madeleine. **Amenities:** Bar; room service (drinks); baby-sitting; laundry/dry cleaning. *In room:* TV, minibar, safe.

Relais du Louvre   One of the neighborhood's most up-to-date hotels, it opened in 1991, midway between the wings at the eastern end of the Louvre. Between 1800 and 1941, its upper floors contained the printing presses that recorded the goings-on in Paris's House of Representatives. Its street level held the Café Momus, favored by Voltaire, Hugo, and intellectuals of the day and where Puccini set one of the pivotal scenes of *La Bohème*. The guest rooms are boldly colored, with modern conveniences, soundproof windows, reproduction furniture, and grace notes like French doors opening in some cases onto tiny balconies. Many rooms are a bit small, but others contain roomy sitting areas, and 16 units come with complete tubs and showers in their bathrooms.

19 rue des Prêtres-St-Germain-l'Auxxerrois, 75001 Paris. © **01-40-41-96-42.** Fax 01-40-41-96-44. 31 units. 920–1,050F (139.85–159.60€, $133.40–$152.25) double; 1,300–2,500F (197.60–380€, $188.50–$362.50) suite. AE, DC, MC, V. Parking 80F (12.15€, $11.60). Métro: Louvre or Pont Neuf. **Amenities:** Room service (drinks); laundry/dry cleaning; baby-sitting. *In room:* TV, minibar, hair dryer, safe.

INEXPENSIVE

Hôtel Henri IV   This is our funky, fun selection. Four hundred years ago, this decrepit narrow building housed the printing presses used for the edicts of Henri IV. Today one of the most famous and most consistently crowded budget hotels in Europe sits in a dramatic location at the westernmost tip of Ile de la Cité, beside a formal park. The crowd is mostly bargain-conscious academics, journalists, and Francophiles, many of whom reserve rooms as much as 2 months in advance. The low-ceilinged lobby, a flight above street level, is cramped and bleak; the creaky stairway leading to the guest rooms is almost impossibly narrow. The rooms are considered romantically threadbare by many and run-down and substandard by others. Each contains a sink, but not even the five rooms with showers have toilets.

25 place Dauphine, 75001 Paris. © **01-43-54-44-53.** 21 units, 5 with shower only. 190–220F (28.90–33.45€, $27.55–$31.90) double without shower; 250–290F (38–44.10€, $36.25–$42.05) double with shower. Rates include breakfast. No credit cards. Métro: Pont Neuf. *In room:* No phone.

Timhôtel Le Louvre *Kids*   This hotel and its sibling, the Timhôtel Palais-Royal, are mirror images of each other, at least inside; they're part of a new breed of government-rated two-star family-friendly hotels cropping up around France. These Timhôtels share the same manager and the same temperament, and though the rooms at the Palais-Royal branch are a bit larger than the ones here, this branch is so close to the Louvre as to be almost irresistible. The ambience is standardized modern, with monochromatic guest rooms and wall-to-wall carpeting that was upgraded in 1998. Each bedroom comes with a full tub and shower in the bathroom.

The **Timhôtel Palais-Royal** is at 3 rue de la Banque, 75002 Paris (© **01-42-61-53-90;** fax 01-42-60-05-39; Métro: Bourse).

Splish, Splash . . . Taking a Bath

Throughout the hotels in this chapter, expect the bathrooms in very expensive and expensive hotels to be a bit larger than normal, with fine toiletries, plush towels, and perhaps bathrobes. The bathrooms in moderate and inexpensive hotels tend to be cramped but still acceptable, with towels that are perhaps a bit less plush than those at expensive places.

Be aware that some hotels offer tub/shower combinations, some offer shower stalls, and some offer a mix. If this is important to you, request your preference when reserving. Also be aware that almost all hotels, except the inexpensive ones, include hair dryers in the bathrooms.

4 rue Croix des Petits-Champs, 75001 Paris. ℂ **01-42-60-34-86.** Fax 01-42-60-10-39. Louvre@timhotel.fr. 56 units. 750–850F (114.16–129.38€, $108.85–$123.37) double. AE, DC, MC, V. Métro: Palais Royal. **Amenities:** Baby-sitting; laundry/dry cleaning. *In room:* A/C, TV.

2ND ARRONDISSEMENT
EXPENSIVE

Hôtel Victoires Opéra ⊛   Head to this little charmer if you want a reasonably priced place convenient to Les Halles and the Pompidou as well as to the Marais, with its shops and gay and straight restaurants. It's a classically decorated hotel, evoking the era of Louis Philippe. Recent renovations include the addition of a private bathroom for every room. Because a junior suite is priced about the same as a double, request a double suite—you'll enjoy the extra space. Most of the rooms are alike— comfortable, but a bit tiny. They're reached by elevator from the second floor. Twenty of its units come with a tub-shower combination; the others with a shower. Skip the hotel breakfast (which costs extra) and cross the street to Stohrer at no. 51, one of Paris's most historic pâtissèries, founded in 1730 by the pâtissier to Louis XV.

56 rue Montorgueil, 75002 Paris. ℂ **01-42-36-41-08.** Fax 01-45-08-08-79. www.hotelvictoiresopera.com. 26 units. 1,400F (212.80€, $203) double; 1,800F (273.60€, $261) junior suite. AE, DC, MC, V. Parking 120F (18.25€, $17.40). Métro: Les Halles. **Amenities:** 24-hour room service; baby-sitting; laundry/dry cleaning. *In room:* A/C, TV, minibar, iron/ironing board.

Le Stendhal ⊛   Opened in 1992, this hotel mixes a young hip style with a sense of tradition. Its location, close to the glamorous place Vendôme jewelry stores, couldn't be grander. Overall, the effect is that of a boutique-style *hôtel de luxe* that seems like a Parisian version of an upscale English B&B. The rooms, accessible via a tiny elevator, have vivid color schemes. Most are small but not without their charm, and each bathroom comes with a full tub and shower combo. The red-and-black Stendhal Suite pays homage to the author, who made this his private home for many years and died here in 1842.

22 rue Danielle-Casanova, 75002 Paris. ℂ **01-44-58-52-52.** Fax 01-44-58-52-00. h1610@accor-hotels.com. 20 units. 1,480F (224.95€, $214.60) double; from 1,900F (288.80€, $275.50) suite. AE, DC, MC, V. Parking 100F (15.20€, $14.50). Métro: Opéra. **Amenities:** Room service (breakfast and drinks); baby-sitting. *In room:* A/C, TV, minibar, hair dryer, safe.

MODERATE

Tulip Inn de Noailles   If you're looking for a postmodern hotel in the style of Putman and Starck, book in here. Proprietor Martine Falck has turned this old-fashioned place in a great location into a refined Art-Deco choice with bold colors and cutting-edge style. Yet the prices remain reasonable. The guest rooms come in various shapes and sizes, but all are comfortable; half are air-conditioned, and all but five come with a shower only. A favorite is no. 601 with its own terrace.

9 rue de la Michodière, 75002 Paris. © 800/344-1212 in the U.S., or © 01-47-42-92-90. Fax 01-49-24-92-71. www.hoteldenoailles.com. 61 units. 1,200F (182.40€, $174) double; 1,400F (212.80€, $203) suite. Rates include breakfast if you book directly with the hotel. AE, DC, V. Parking 100F (15.20€, $14.50). Métro: 4 Septembre or Opéra. **Amenities:** Bar; health club; sauna; room service; massage; baby-sitting; laundry/dry cleaning. *In room:* A/C, hair dryer.

3RD ARRONDISSEMENT
MODERATE
Hôtel des Chevaliers   Half a block from the northwestern edge of place des Vosges, this renovated hotel occupies a dramatic corner building whose 17th-century vestiges have been elevated into high art. These include the remnants of a stone-sided well in the cellar, a sweeping stone barrel vault covering the breakfast area, half-timbering artfully exposed in the stairwell, and Louis XIII accessories that'll remind you of the hotel's origins. Each guest room is comfortable and well-maintained, and all units come with a complete tub and shower in the bathroom. Rooms on the top floor have artfully exposed ceiling beams.

30 rue de Turenne, 75003 Paris. © **01-42-72-73-47**. Fax 01-42-72-54-10. 24 units. 680–820F (103.35–124.65€, $98.60–$118.90) double; 895–995F (136.05–151.25€, $129.80–$144.30) triple. Parking 60F (9.10€, $8.70). Métro: Chemin Vert or St-Paul. *In room:* TV, minibar, hair dryer, safe.

4TH ARRONDISSEMENT
EXPENSIVE
Hôtel du Jeu de Paume ⭐   It's small-scale and charming, with a layout that includes an interconnected pair of 17th-century town houses accessed via a timbered passageway from the street outside. This hotel has rooms that are a bit larger than those within some of its nearby competitors on the Ile St-Louis. It originated as a "clubhouse" that was used by members of the court of Louis XIII who amused themselves with *Les jeux de paume* (an early form of tennis) on a vacant lot nearby. Bedrooms are outfitted in a simple and unfrilly version of Art Deco. In terms of mentality and aesthetics, here you'll feel more closely aligned with the pervasive ethic of the Marais than within the *Quartier Latin* to the south. There's an elevator on the premises, and scads of charm from the well-meaning staff.

54 rue St-Louis en l'Isle, 75004 Paris. © **01-43-26-14-18**. Fax 01-40-46-02-76. www.jeudepaumehotel.com. 30 units. 1,365–1,650F (207.50–250.80€, $197.95–$239.25) double; 2,500–2,750F (380–418€, $362.50–$398.75) suite. AE, DC, MC, V. Parking: 120F (18.25€, $17.40). Métro: Pont-Marie. **Amenities:** Exercise room; sauna; baby-sitting; laundry/dry cleaning. *In room:* TV, minibar, hair dryer, safe.

MODERATE
Hôtel Caron de Beaumarchais *(Value)*   Built in the 18th century and gracefully upgraded in 1998, this good-value choice features floors of artfully worn gray stone, antique reproductions, and elaborate fabrics based on antique patterns. Hotelier Alain Bigeard likes his primrose-colored guest rooms to evoke the taste of the French gentry in the 18th century when the Marais was the scene of high-society dances or even duels. Most rooms retain their original ceiling beams. The smallest units overlook the interior courtyard, and the top-floor rooms are tiny but have panoramic balcony views across the Right Bank. Each of the bedrooms comes with a tub-shower combination.

> ### Kids Family-Friendly Hotels
>
> **Hôtel de Fleurie** (*see p. 94*) In the heart of St-Germain-des-Prés, this has long been a Left Bank family favorite. The hotel is known for its *chambres familiales*—two connecting rooms with a pair of large beds in each room. Children under 12 stay free with their parents.
>
> **Hôtel du Ministère** (*see p. 86*) For the family on a budget that doesn't mind cramped quarters, the Ministère is one of the best bets in this expensive area near the Champs-Elysées.
>
> **Résidence Lord Byron** (*see p. 86*) The Byron is not only a good value and an unusually family-oriented place for the swanky 8th arrondissement, but also is only a 10-minute walk from many of the city's major monuments.
>
> **Timhôtel Le Louvre** (*see p. 75*) This is an especially convenient choice because it offers some rooms with four beds for the price of a double. And the location near the Louvre is irresistible.

---

12 rue Vieille-du-Temple, 75004 Paris. ✆ **01-42-72-34-12.** Fax 01-42-72-34-63. www.carondebeaumarchais. com. 19 units. 790–870F (120.10–132.25€, $114.55–$126.15) double. AE, DC, MC, V. Métro: St-Paul or Hôtel de Ville. **Amenities:** Baby-sitting; laundry/dry cleaning. *In room:* A/C, TV, minibar, hair dryer.

Hôtel de Lutèce 🏆🏆 *Value* This hotel feels like a country house in Brittany. The lounge, with its old fireplace, is graciously furnished with antiques and contemporary paintings. Ranging in size from small to medium, each of the individualized guest rooms boasts antiques, adding to a refined atmosphere that attracts celebrities like the duke and duchess of Bedford. Many were renovated in 1998, and each unit comes either with a tub or shower. The hotel is comparable in style and amenities to the Deux-Iles (see below), under the same ownership.

65 rue St-Louis-en-l'Ile, 75004 Paris. ✆ **01-43-26-23-52.** Fax 01-43-29-60-25. www.hotel-ile-saintlouis. com. 23 units. 920F (140.03€, $133.53) double; 1,100F (167.20€, $159.50) triple. AE, MC, V. Métro: Pont Marie or Cité. **Amenities:** Room service; laundry/dry cleaning. *In room:* A/C, TV, hair dryer.

Hôtel des Deux-Iles 🏆 This is a much-restored 18th-century town house. It was an inexpensive hotel until 1976, when an elaborate decor with lots of bamboo and reed furniture and French provincial touches was added. The result is an unpretentious but charming hotel with a great location. The guest rooms are on the small side, however. A garden of plants and flowers off the lobby leads to a basement breakfast room with a fireplace.

59 rue St-Louis-en-l'Ile, 75004 Paris. ✆ **01-43-26-13-35.** Fax 01-43-29-60-25. hotel2iles@free.fr. 17 units. 910F (138.51€, $132.08) double. AE, MC, V. Métro: Pont Marie. **Amenities:** Garden; room service; laundry/dry cleaning. *In room:* A/C, TV, hair dryer.

Hôtel Saint-Louis *Value* Proprietors Guy and Andrée Record maintain a charming family atmosphere at this small, antique-filled hotel in a 17th-century town house. Despite a full renovation completed in 1998, it represents an incredible value considering its prime location on Ile St-Louis. Expect cozy, slightly cramped rooms. With mansard roofs and old-fashioned moldings, the top-floor rooms sport tiny balconies with sweeping rooftop views. The breakfast room is in the cellar, with 17th-century stone vaulting.

75 rue St-Louis-en-l'Ile, 75004 Paris. © **01-46-34-04-80.** Fax 01-46-34-02-13. www.hotel-paris-saintlouis. com. 21 units. 815–1,300F (123.90–197.60€, $118.20–$188.50) double. MC, V. Métro: Pont Marie. **Amenities:** Room service; baby-sitting; laundry. *In room:* TV, hair dryer, safe.

Hotel Saint-Merry *(Finds)*   The rebirth of this once-notorious brothel as a charming, upscale hotel is yet another example of how the Marais has been gentrified. It contains only a dozen rooms, each of them relatively small, but charmingly accented with exposed stone, 18th-century ceiling beams, and lots of quirky architectural details, all carefully preserved by a team of architects and decorators. Expect a clientele here that's estimated by the staff as about 50 percent gay and male, the other half straight and involved in the arts scene that flourishes in the surrounding neighborhood. Before it became a bordello, incidentally, this place was conceived as the presbytery of the nearby Church of Saint-Merry.

78 rue de la Verrerie. 75004 Paris. © **01-42-78-14-15.** Fax 01-40-29-06-82. 12 units. 900–1,300F (136.80–197.60€, $130.50–$188.50) double; 1,900F (288.80€, $275.50) suite. Metro: Hôtel de Ville or Châtelet. *In room:* TV.

INEXPENSIVE

Hôtel de la Place des Vosges *(★★) (Value)*   Built about 350 years ago, during the same era as the majestic square it's named after, and which lies less than a 2-minute walk away, this is a well-managed, small-scale property with reasonable prices and lots of charm. Many of the bedrooms have beamed ceilings, relatively small dimensions, tiled bathrooms (with tub or shower), small TV sets hanging from chains in the ceiling, and a sense of cozy, well-ordered efficiency. There are patches of chiseled stone at various parts of the hotel, a decorative touch that helps evoke the era of Louis XIII.

12 rue de Birague, 75004 Paris. © **01-42-72-60-46.** Fax 01-42-72-02-64. hotel.place.des.vosges@ gofernet.com. 16 units. 660–690F (100.30–104.90€, $95.70–$100.05) double. MC, V. Métro: Bastille. *In room:* TV, hair dryer.

Hôtel du 7e Art   The building that contains this place is one of many 17th-century buildings in this neighborhood classified as historic monuments. Don't expect grand luxury: Rooms are cramped but clean, and outfitted with the simplest of furniture, relieved by 1950s-era posters promoting the glories of old Hollywood. Each has white walls, and some—including those under the sloping mansard-style roof on the uppermost floor—have exposed ceiling beams. All have small-size shower-only bathrooms. There's a bar in the lobby and a breakfast room, but be warned in advance that there's no elevator for access to any of this place's five stories (*4 étages*). The hotel is named after the "7th Art," a French reference to filmmaking.

20 rue St-Paul, 75004 Paris. © **01-44-54-85-00.** Fax 01-42-77-69-10. 23 units. 460–592F (69.90–90€, $66.70–$85.85) double; 789F (119.95€, $114.40) suite. AE, DC, MC, V. Parking: 100F (15.20€, $14.50). Métro: St-Paul. *In room:* TV.

9TH ARRONDISSEMENT
EXPENSIVE

Hôtel Concorde St-Lazare *(★)*   Across from the St-Lazare rail station, this hotel—the area's best—first greeted visitors flocking to the Universal Exposition of 1889. During the late 1990s, each of the guest rooms was elevated to modern standards of comfort and redecorated. Many rooms (medium-size to quite large) have high ceilings, especially those on the lower floors, which also have double-glazed windows to cut down on the noise. The beds are plush and comfortable.

> **Tips   Good, Clean Rooms for Under $50 a Night?
> C'est possible!**
>
> Largely unnoticed by U.S. visitors—as of yet—a new French Revolution is
> taking place, but quietly. Some two dozen modern and amenity-packed
> hotels have sprouted up in Paris under the Ibis Hotel banner. These cookie-
> cutter properties have become the McDonald's of French budget lodgings.
> Operated by Accor Hotels (© **800/221-4542**), they have attractive but tiny
> rooms and lie near Métro stops a 5-minute ride from the Seine. If you stay
> at Motel 6 and Red Roof Inns in the United States and don't mind the chain
> experience, you can book a room at an Ibis for the price of two martinis at
> the George V. Call the toll-free number above to arrange bookings.

108 rue St-Lazare, 75008 Paris. © **800/888-4747** in the U.S. outside New York State and Canada, © **212/
752-3900** in New York State, © **0171/630-1704** in London, or © **01-40-08-44-44**. Fax 01-42-93-01-20.
www.concordestlazare-paris.com. 300 units. 1,600–3,200F (243.20–486.40€, $232–$464) double; from
4,500F (684€, $652.50) suite. AE, DC, MC, V. Parking 150F (22.80€, $21.75). Métro: St-Lazare. **Amenities:**
Restaurant (French); bar; cafe; room service; baby-sitting; laundry. *In room:* A/C, TV, minibar, hair dryer.

INEXPENSIVE

Hôtel de la Tour d'Auvergne   Here's a good, safe bet for those who want to
be near the Opera or the Gare du Nord. This building was erected before Baron
Haussmann reconfigured Paris's avenues around 1870. Later, Modigliani rented
a room here for 6 months, and the staff will tell you Victor Hugo and Auguste
Rodin briefly lived on this street. The interior was long ago modernized into a
glossy internationalism. The guest rooms are meticulously coordinated, yet the
small decorative canopies over the headboards make them feel cluttered. Though
the views over the back courtyard are uninspired, even gloomy, some guests
request rear rooms for their relative quiet. Every year, five rooms are renovated,
so the comfort level is kept at a high standard, and all units come with a tub-
shower combination.

10 rue de la Tour d'Auvergne, 75009 Paris. © **01-48-78-61-60**. Fax 01-49-95-99-00. 24 units. 550–750F
(83.60–114€, $79.75–$108.75) double. AE, DC, MC, V. Métro: Cadet or Anvers. **Amenities:** Room service;
baby-sitting. *In room:* TV, minibar, hair dryer.

Hôtel Williams Opéra   Even now, this hotel remains relatively unknown.
Behind the dignified facade of a 19th-century building, entrepreneurs installed
a little hotel in 1992. The guest rooms are clean and uncomplicated, though the
decor is a bit cold. Each is soundproof, thanks to double-glazing, and has a safe.
The front rooms overlook one of the area's largest public gardens, a verdant oasis
in an otherwise congested commercial neighborhood; fifth- and second-floor
rooms offer small wrought-iron balconies. About half of the accommodations
have tub baths, the rest contain showers.

3 rue Mayran, 75009 Paris. © **01-48-78-68-35**. Fax 01-45-26-08-70. www.ewh.com. 30 units. 650F
(98.80€, $94.25) double. AE, MC, V. Parking 70F (10.65€, $10.15). Métro: Cadet. *In room:* TV.

11TH ARRONDISSEMENT
INEXPENSIVE

Libertel Croix de Malte   A member of a nationwide chain of mostly
government-rated two-star hotels, this is a well-maintained choice. Business

increased thanks to a radical 1992 overhaul and its proximity to the Opéra Bastille and the Marais. The hotel consists of buildings of two and three floors, one of which is accessible through a shared breakfast room. There's a landscaped courtyard in back with access to a lobby bar. The cozy guest rooms contain brightly painted modern furniture accented with vivid green, blue, and pink patterns that flash back to the 1960s. About half of the units contain tubs, the rest are equipped with showers.

5 rue de Malte, 75011 Paris. ℂ **01-48-05-09-36.** Fax 01-43-57-02-54. www.all-hotels-in-paris.com. 29 units. 685F (104.10€, $99.35) double. AE, MC, V. Métro: Oberkampf. **Amenities:** Room service (breakfast); baby-sitting. *In room:* TV, hair dryer.

Résidence Alhambra   Named for the famous cabaret/vaudeville theater that once stood nearby, the Alhambra dates from the 1800s. A radical renovation in 1989 plus upgrades in 2000 gave the hotel its fine contemporary format. In the rear garden, its two-story chalet offers eight additional guest rooms. The rather small accommodations are bland but comfortable, each in a monochromatic pastel scheme that includes white and ocher. The private bathrooms are equally divided between tubs and showers.

13 rue de Malte, 75011 Paris. ℂ **01-47-00-35-52.** Fax 01-43-57-98-75. www.hotelalhambra.fr. 58 units. 370–420F (56.25–63.85€, $53.65–$60.90) double; 450–530F (68.40–80.55€, $65.25–$76.85) triple. AE, DC, MC, V. Parking 100F (15.20€, $14.50). Métro: Oberkampf. **Amenities:** Garden; baby-sitting. *In room:* TV.

12TH ARRONDISSEMENT
MODERATE
Hôtel Pavillon Bastille   Hardly your cozy little backstreet dig, this is a bold, brassy, innovative hotel in a 1991 town house across from the Opéra Bastille and a block south of place de la Bastille. A 17th-century fountain graces the courtyard between the hotel and the street. The guest rooms have twin or double beds, partially mirrored walls, and contemporary built-in furniture. If you're looking for a bargain, note that the cheapest rooms have the same size and configuration as the more expensive *chambres privilegées* (the extra cost gets you amenities like slippers, better cosmetics, fruit baskets, and a complimentary bottle of wine—not worth it). Each unit comes with a tub-shower combo.

65 rue de Lyon, 75012 Paris. ℂ **01-43-43-65-65.** Fax 01-43-43-96-52. www.france-paris.com. 25 units. 840–955F (127.70–145.15€, $121.80–$138.50) double; 1,375F (209€, $199.40) suite. AE, DC, MC, V. Parking 75F (11.40€, $10.90). Métro: Bastille. **Amenities:** Laundry/dry cleaning. *In room:* A/C, TV, minibar, hair dryer, iron/ironing board, safe.

INEXPENSIVE
Nouvel Hôtel   This hotel evokes the French provinces far more than urban Paris. Surrounded by greenery in a neighborhood rarely visited by tourists, the Nouvel conjures a calmer day, when parts of Paris still seemed like small country towns. The beauty of the place is most visible from the inside courtyard, site of warm-weather breakfasts, the only meal served. Winding halls lead to small guest rooms overlooking either the courtyard or, less appealingly, the street. Each contains flowered fabrics and old-fashioned furniture, but only three have tub baths, the rest are equipped with showers.

24 av. du Bel-Air, 75012 Paris. ℂ **01-43-43-01-81.** Fax 01-43-44-64-13. www.nouvel-hotel-paris.com. 28 units. 436–594F (66.25–90.30€, $63.20–$86.15) double. Rates include breakfast. AE, DC, MC, V. Métro: Nation. *In room:* TV.

18TH ARRONDISSEMENT
EXPENSIVE

Terrass Hôtel ★★ *(finds)*   Built in 1913 and richly renovated into a plush but traditional style in 1991, this is the only government-rated four-star hotel on the Butte Montmartre. In an area filled with some of Paris's seediest hotels, this place is easily in a class of its own. Its main advantage is its location amid Montmartre's bohemian atmosphere (or what's left of it). Staffed by English-speaking employees, it has a large marble-floored lobby ringed with blond oak paneling and accented with 18th-century antiques and even older tapestries. The guest rooms are high-ceilinged and well-upholstered, often featuring views. All the bathrooms are well-maintained, each with a shower and about half with both a shower and tub.

12–14 rue Joseph-de-Maistre, 75018 Paris. © **01-46-06-72-85.** Fax 01-42-52-29-11. www.terrass-hotel. com. 100 units. 1,430–1,580F (217.35–240.15€, $207.35–$229.10) double; 1,920F (291.85€, $278.40) suite. Rates include breakfast. AE, DC, MC, V. Parking 100F (15.20€, $14.50). Métro: Place de Clichy or Blanche. **Amenities:** 2 restaurants (both French); bar; laundry/dry cleaning; room service; baby-sitting. *In room:* A/C, TV, minibar, hair dryer.

INEXPENSIVE

Hôtel Ermitage   Built in 1870 of chiseled limestone in the Napoléon III style, this hotel's facade evokes a perfectly proportioned small villa. It's set in a calm area, a brief uphill stroll from Sacré-Coeur. Views extend out over Paris, and there's a verdant garden in the back courtyard. The small guest rooms are like those in a countryside auberge with exposed ceiling beams, flowered wallpaper, and casement windows opening onto the garden or a street seemingly airlifted from the provinces. Half of the bedrooms come with tubs, the rest with showers.

24 rue Lamarck, 75018 Paris. © **01-42-64-79-22.** Fax 01-42-64-10-33. 12 units. 530F (80.55€, $76.85) double. No credit cards. Parking 60F (9.10€, $8.70). Métro: Lamarck-Caulaincourt. **Amenities:** Garden; baby-sitting. *In room:* hair dryer.

8TH ARRONDISSEMENT
VERY EXPENSIVE

Four Seasons Hôtel George V ★★★   Even in its latest reincarnation, with all its glitz and glamour, this hotel is for the merely rich. Both the Bristol and Plaza Athénée accurately claim they have more class. Its history is as gilt-edged as they come: Opened in 1928 in honor of George V (father of the present Queen of England) and noted for grandeur that managed to stylishly survive the Depression and two world wars, it was soon-after designated as an official branch of the now-defunct League of Nations. During the liberation of Paris, it housed Dwight D. Eisenhower and his war machine. After its acquisition by Saudi Prince Al Waleed, and a 2-year shutdown for renovations, it was re-opened late in 1999 under the banner of Toronto-based Four Seasons. Rooms are about as close as you'll come to residency within a supremely well-upholstered private home. The renovation reduced the number of units from 300 to 245, which now come in three sizes. The largest are supremely magnificent, the smallest are, in the words of a spokesperson, *"très agreeable."* Security is tight here—a fact appreciated by sometimes notorious guests.

31 Ave. George V, 75008 Paris. © **800/332-3442** in the U.S. or Canada, or © **01-53-53-28-00.** Fax 01-49-52-70-20. www.fourseasons.com. 245 units. 4,264–5,706F (648.15–867.30€, $618.30–$827.35) double; from 8,200F (1,246.40€, $1,189) suite. Parking 263F (40€, $38.15). AE, DC, MC, V. Métro: George V. **Amenities:** 2 restaurants (both French); bar; indoor pool; health club; room service. *In room:* A/C, TV, minibar, hair dryer, safe.

Hotels in the 8th & 16th–17th Arrondissements

Au Palais de Chaillot Hôtel **3**
Four Seasons Hôtel George V **14**
Galileo Hôtel **13**
Hôtel Balzac **12**
Hôtel Bristol **10**
Hôtel de Crillon **17**
Hôtel du Ministère **18**
Hôtel Eber **9**
Hôtel Flaubert **8**
Hôtel Les Hauts de Passy **1**
Hôtel Meurice **16**
Hôtel Opal **19**
Hôtel Plaza Athénée **15**
Hôtel Queen Mary **20**
Hôtel Regent's Garden **7**
Hôtel St-James Paris **4**
Hôtel Sofitel Trocadéro Dokhan's **2**
Les Trois Couronnes **6**
Marmotel Etoile **5**
Résidence Lord Byron **11**

Hôtel Balzac ★★★   If the Crillon and the Ritz are Rolls-Royces, then the Balzac is a Bentley, boasting a well-trained formal staff. Elegant and discreet, it opened in 1986 in a Belle-Époque mansion, then was redecorated in 1994 by English designer Nina Campbell. Most of the guest rooms are medium to spacious in size, with modern furniture, double-glazing, mirrored closets, and king-size beds.

6 rue Balzac, 75008 Paris. © 800/457-4000 in the U.S. and Canada, or ©] 01-44-35-18-00. Fax 01-44-35-18-05. hbalzac@cybercable.fr. 70 units. 2,200F (334.40€, $319) double; from 3,300F (501.60€, $478.50) suite. AE, DC, MC, V. Parking 150F (22.80€, $21.75). Métro: George V. **Amenities:** Restaurant (French); bar; room service; baby-sitting; laundry/dry cleaning. *In room:* A/C, TV, minibar, hair dryer.

Hôtel Bristol ★★★   This palace is near the Palais d'Elysée (home of the French president), on the shopping street running parallel to the Champs-Elysées. In terms of style and glamour, here's how the line-up reads in Paris: (1) Ritz, (2) Plaza Athénée, and (3) Bristol. The classic 18th-century Parisian facade has a glass-and-wrought-iron entryway, where you're greeted by uniformed English-speaking attendants. Hippolyte Jammet founded the Bristol in 1924, installing many valuable antiques and Louis XV and XVI furnishings. The guest rooms are opulent, with either antiques or well-made reproductions, inlaid wood, bronze, crystal, Oriental carpets, and original oil paintings. Each room is freshened every 3 years. Personalized old-world service is rigidly maintained here—some guests find it forbidding, others absolutely adore it.

112 rue du Faubourg St-Honoré, 75008 Paris. © 01-53-43-43-00. Fax 01-53-43-43-26. www.hotel bristol.com. 175 units. 3,800–4,400F (577.60–668.80€, $551–$638) double; from 6,700F (1,018.40€, $971.50) suite. AE, DC, MC, V. Free parking. Métro: Miromesnil. **Amenities:** Restaurant (French); bar; indoor pool; spa; room service; baby-sitting; laundry/dry cleaning. *In room:* A/C, TV, minibar, hair dryer, safe.

Hôtel de Crillon ★★★   One of Europe's grand hotels, the Crillon sits across from the U.S. Embassy. Although some international CEOs and diplomats treat it as a shrine, those seeking less pomposity might prefer the Plaza Athénée or the Ritz. The 200-plus-year-old building, once the palace of the duc de Crillon, has been a hotel since the early 1900s and is now owned by Jean Taittinger of the champagne family. The public salons boast 17th- and 18th-century tapestries, gilt-and-brocade furniture, chandeliers, fine sculpture, and Louis XVI chests and chairs. The guest rooms are large and luxurious. Some are spectacular, like the Leonard Bernstein Suite, which has one of the maestro's pianos and one of the grandest views of any hotel room in Paris. The marble bathrooms are sumptuous as well, with deluxe toiletries, dual sinks, robes, and (in some) thermal taps.

10 place de la Concorde, 75008 Paris. © 800/223-6800 in the U.S. and Canada, or © 01-44-71-15-00. Fax 01-44-71-15-02. www.crillon.com. 160 units. 3,950–4,650F (600.40–706.80€, $572.75–$674.25) double; from 6,800F (1,033.60€, $986) suite. AE, DC, MC, V. Free parking. Métro: Concorde. **Amenities:** 2 restaurants (both French); bar; tea room; exercise room; room service; laundry/dry cleaning. *In room:* A/C, TV, minibar, hair dryer, safe.

Hôtel Meurice ★★★   After a spectacular 2-year renovation, the landmark Meurice, which reopened in mid-2000, is better than ever. The hotel is now more media hip and style conscious, in addition to being better located, than the also restored George V, its closest rival. Since the early 1800s it has been welcoming the royal, the rich, and even the radical: The deposed king of Spain, Alfonso XIII, once occupied suite 108; and the mad genius Salvador Dalí made the Meurice his headquarters, as did General von Cholritz, the Nazi who ruled Paris during the occupation. The mosaic floors, elaborate plaster ceilings, hand-carved moldings, and Art-Nouveau glass roof atop the Winter Garden look like new. Each guest room is individually decorated with period pieces, fine carpets, Italian and French fabrics, rare marbles, and modern features such as fax and Internet access. Louis XVI and Empire styles predominate. Our favorites and the least expensive are the sixth-floor dormer rooms. Some rooms have painted ceilings of puffy clouds and blue skies along with canopied beds. Each unit comes with a full state-of-the-art bathroom.

228 rue de Rivoli, Paris 75001. ℭ **01-44-58-10-10.** Fax 01-44-58-10-15. www.meuricehotel.com. 160 units. 4,300–4,600F (653.60–699.20€, $623.50–$667) double; from 5,900F (896.80€, $855.50) suite. Métro: Tuileries or Concorde. Parking 120F (18.25€, $17.40). **Amenities:** 2 restaurants (both French); bar; exercise room; full-service spa; room service; baby-sitting; laundry/dry cleaning. *In room:* A/C, TV, minibar, hair dryer, safe.

Hôtel Plaza Athénée ⭐⭐⭐   The Plaza Athénée, an 1889 Art-Nouveau marvel, is a landmark of discretion and style. In the 8th, only the Bristol can tackle it. Its nearest competitor is George V. (What's the difference? An international CEO tells us that he goes to George V for discrete visits and here for more public ones.) About half the celebrities visiting Paris have been pampered here; in the old days, Mata Hari used to frequent the place. The finest public room is the Montaigne Salon, paneled in grained wood and dominated by a marble fireplace. The quietest guest rooms overlook a courtyard with awnings and parasol-shaded tables; they have ample closet space, and their large tiled bathrooms contain double basins. Some rooms overlooking avenue Montaigne have views of the Eiffel Tower. In 1999, the hotel completed a radical overhaul, creating larger rooms out of some of the smaller, less desirable ones.

25 av. Montaigne, 75008 Paris. ℭ **866/732-1106** in the U.S. and Canada, or ℭ **01-53-67-66-65.** Fax 01-53-67-66-66. www.plaza-athenee-paris.com. 185 units. 3,850–4,400F (585.20–668.80€, $558.25–$638) double; from 4,950F (752.40€, $717.75) suite. AE, DC, MC, V. Parking 120F (18.25€, $17.40). Métro: F. D. Roosevelt or Alma-Marceau. **Amenities:** 2 restaurants (both French); bar; health club; salon; room service; massage; baby-sitting; laundry/dry cleaning. *In room:* A/C, TV, minibar, hair dryer, safe.

MODERATE

Galileo Hôtel ⭐ *Finds*   This is one of the 8th's most charming boutique hotels. It's the invasion of Roland and Elisabeth Buffat, who have won friends from around the world with their Hotel des Deux-Iles and Hotel de Lutèce on St-Louis-en-l'Ile (earlier in this chapter). A short walk from the Champ-Elysées, the town-house hotel is the epitome of French elegance and charm. The guest rooms are medium in size for the most part and a study in understated taste, decorated in various shades of cocoa and beige. The most spacious are nos. 501 and 502, with a glass-covered veranda you can use even in winter. For such a tiny neighborhood, the prices are moderate.

54 rue Galilée, 75008 Paris. ℭ **01-47-20-66-06.** Fax 01-47-20-67-17. 27 units. 950F (144.40€, $137.75) double. AE, DC, MC, V. Parking 150F (22.80€, $21.75). Métro: Charles de Gaulle–Etoile or George V. **Amenities:** Room service (drinks and snacks); baby-sitting; laundry/dry cleaning. *In room:* A/C, TV, minibar, hair dryer, safe.

Hôtel Queen Mary ⭐   Meticulously renovated inside and out, this early-1900s hotel is graced with an iron-and-glass canopy, ornate wrought iron, and the kind of detailing normally reserved for more expensive hotels. The public rooms have touches of greenery and reproductions of mid-19th-century antiques; each guest room has an upholstered headboard, comfortable beds, and mahogany furnishings, plus a carafe of sherry. All the rooms, ranging from small to medium, were fully renovated in 1998, and 31 come with a tub and shower combination, except five shower-only accommodations.

9 rue Greffulhe, 75008 Paris. ℭ **01-42-66-40-50**. Fax 01-42-66-94-92. www.hotelqueenmary.com. 36 units. 780–995F (118.55–151.25€), $113.10–$144.30) double; 1,400F (212.80€, $203) suite. AE, DC, MC, V. Parking 100F (15.20€, $14.50). Métro: Madeleine or Havre-Caumartin. **Amenities:** Bar; business center; room service; baby-sitting. *In room:* A/C, TV, minibar, hair dryer, safe.

INEXPENSIVE

Hôtel du Ministère 😊*Kids*   The Ministère is a winning choice near the Champs-Elysées and the American Embassy, though it's far from Paris's cheapest budget hotel. Long a family hotel, it received new owners in 1999 who began a program of refurbishing, making the hotel better than ever. The guest rooms are on the small side, but each is comfortably appointed and well-maintained; many have oak beams and furnishings that, though worn, are still serviceable. Try to avoid a room on the very top floor, as you'll be too cramped. Each accommodation is equipped with a tub-shower combo.

31 rue de Surène, 75008 Paris. ℭ **01-42-66-21-43**. Fax 01-42-66-96-04. www.argia.fr/hotel-ministere. 28 units. 890–990F (135.30–150.50€, $129.05–$143.55) double; from 1,090F (165.70€, $158.05) junior suite. AE, MC, V. Parking 110F (16.70€, $15.95). Métro: Madeleine or Miromesnil. **Amenities:** Bar; room service; laundry/dry cleaning. *In room:* A/C, TV, minibar, hair dryer, safe.

Hôtel Opal *Finds*   This rejuvenated hotel is a real find behind La Madeleine church and near the Opéra Garnier. The guest rooms are somewhat tight but very clean and comfortable, and many of them are air-conditioned. Those on the top floor are reached by a narrow staircase; some have skylights. Most rooms have twin brass beds, and all of them come with a tub and shower combo. Reception will make arrangements for parking at a nearby garage.

19 rue Tronchet, 75008 Paris. ℭ **01-42-65-77-97**. Fax 01-49-24-06-58. www.hotels.fr/opal. 36 units. 950–1,100F (144.40–167.20€, $137.75–$159.50) double. Extra bed 100F (15.20€, $14.50). AE, DC, V. Parking 130F ($20.80) nearby. Métro: Madeleine. **Amenities:** Room service (breakfast); baby-sitting; laundry/dry cleaning. *In room:* A/C, TV, minibar, hair dryer, safe.

Résidence Lord Byron 😊😊*Kids* *Value*   Off the Champs-Elysées on a curving street of handsome buildings, the Lord Byron may not be as grand as other hotels in the neighborhood, but it's more affordable. Unassuming and a bit staid, it's exactly what repeat guests want: a sense of luxury, solitude, and understatement, a fine choice for families. The guest rooms are small to medium in size. You can eat breakfast in the dining room or in a shaded inner garden.

5 rue de Chateaubriand, 75008 Paris. ℭ **01-43-59-89-98**. Fax 01-42-89-46-04. www.paris.org. 31 units. 910–1,015F (138.30–154.30€, $131.95–$147.20) double; 1,430–1,730F (217.35–262.95€, $207.35–$250.85) suite. AE, DC, MC, V. Parking 75F (11.40€, $10.90). Métro: George V. RER: Etoile. **Amenities:** Garden; room service; baby-sitting; dry cleaning. *In room:* A/C, TV, minibar, hair dryer, safe.

16TH ARRONDISSEMENT
VERY EXPENSIVE

Hôtel Saint-James Paris 😊😊😊   In an 1892 stone building inspired by a château in the French countryside, the Saint-James is as grand as any of the very expensive hotels in the more visible (and central) neighborhoods of Paris. It's set among the staid yet luxurious residences of the 16th arrondissement, and staying here gives you access to the private restaurant, bar, and fitness center reserved for aristocratic Parisian members. You'll find it intimate and warm, even if exclusivity and snobbery are part of its image. The guest rooms are spacious, the older ones featuring Art Deco detailing, the more newly renovated ones with sleek contemporary styling.

43 av. Bugeaud, 75016 Paris. ℭ **800/525-4800** in the U.S. and Canada, or ℭ **01-44-05-81-81**. Fax 01-44-05-81-82. www.travel-in-paris.com. 48 units. 2,650F (402.80€, $384.25) double; from 2,950F (448.40€,

$427.75) suite. AE, DC, MC, V. Free parking. Métro: Porte Dauphine. RER: Av. Foch. **Amenities:** Restaurant (French); bar; health club; Jacuzzi; sauna; room service; massage; baby-sitting; laundry/dry cleaning. *In room:* A/C, TV, kitchenette (in some units), minibar, hair dryer, safe.

Hotel Sofitel Trocadéro Dokhan S ✦✦   Except for the fact that porters tend to walk through its public areas carrying luggage, you might suspect that this well-accessorized hotel was a private home. It's housed within a stately looking 19th-century building that was vaguely inspired by Palladio, and it contains the kind of accessories that would look appropriate on the set of a Viennese operetta. This includes antique paneling, lacquered Regency-era armchairs, gilded bronze chandeliers, and a pervasive sense of good, upper-bourgeois taste. Like many a large private home, the bedrooms come in a wide range of sizes from small to spacious, as do the beautifully maintained bathrooms. Bedrooms each benefit from a different decorative style, and each has antiques or good reproductions, ornamental swags and curtains above the headboards, lots of personalized touches, and triple-glazed windows to seal away noises from the neighborhood outside. Each contains a CD player and a personal fax machine. Well-respected decorator Frédéric Méchiche designed and decorated all aspects of this decor.

117 rue Lauriston, 75116 Paris. ℂ **01-53-65-66-99.** hotel.trocadero.dokhans@wanadoo.fr. 45 units. 2,300–2,700F (349.60–410.40€, $333.50–$391.50) double; 5,000F (760€, $725) suite. AE, DC, MC, V. Parking 90F (13.70€, $13.05). Metro: Trocadéro. **Amenities:** Restaurant (French, lunch only); champagne bar. *In room:* A/C, TV, minibar, hair dryer.

INEXPENSIVE
Au Palais de Chaillot Hôtel   When Thierry and Cyrille Pien, brothers trained in the States, opened this excellent hotel in 1997, budgeters came running. Between the Champ-Elysées and Trocadéro, the town house was restored from top to bottom and the result is a contemporary yet informal style of Parisian chic. The guest rooms come in various shapes and sizes, and are furnished with a light touch, with bright colors and wicker. Nos. 61, 62, and 63 afford partial views of the Eiffel Tower. Each unit comes with a neatly tiled shower-only bathroom.

35 av. Raymond-Poincaré, 75016 Paris. ℂ **01-53-70-09-09.** Fax 01-53-70-09-08. www.chaillotel.com. 28 units. 625F (95€, $90.65) double; 755F (114.75€, $109.50) triple. AE, DC, MC, V. Parking 90F (13.70€, $13.05). Métro: Victor Hugo or Trocadéro. **Amenities:** Room service (breakfast and drinks); laundry/dry cleaning. *In room:* TV, hair dryer.

Hôtel Les Hauts de Passy   Across the river from the Eiffel Tower in a chic residential neighborhood, this coming hotel sits on a pedestrian-only street where an outdoor market takes place every day except Monday. All the rooms were recently renovated and are inviting, with new mattresses, large pillows, and double-glazed windows. The baths, though small, are squeaky clean, with a tub in only a few units. Just outside the front door is a wonderful *boulangerie* where you can have breakfast while watching the market bustle. Be patient with the hotel staff, as their English is minimal.

37 rue de l'Annonciation, 75016 Paris. ℂ **01-42-88-47-28.** Fax 01-42-88-99-09. 31 units. 550–600F (83.60–91.20€, $79.75–$87) double. MC, V. Parking 95F (14.45€, $13.80). Métro: La Muette or Passy. *In room:* TV, minibar, hair dryer.

17TH ARRONDISSEMENT
MODERATE
Best Western Hôtel Regent's Garden ✦   Near the convention center (Palais des Congrés) and the Arc de Triomphe, the Regent's Garden boasts a

proud heritage: Napoléon III built this stately château for his physician. The interior resembles a classically decorated country house. Fluted columns mark the entryway, which leads to a casual mix of furniture in the lobby. The guest rooms have flower prints on the walls, traditional French furniture, and tall soundproof windows, plus neatly organized private bathrooms with both a tub and shower. There's a garden with ivy-covered walls and umbrella-shaded tables—a perfect place to meet other guests.

6 rue Pierre-Demours, 75017 Paris. ℂ **01-45-74-07-30.** Fax 01-40-55-01-42. www.bestwestern.com. 39 units. 812–1,506F (123.40–228.90€, $117.75–$218.35) double. AE, DC, MC, V. Parking 60F (9.10€, $8.70). Métro: Ternes or Charles de Gaulle–Etoile. **Amenities:** Garden; room service (drinks); baby-sitting. *In room:* A/C, TV, minibar, hair dryer.

Hôtel Eber   Hidden on a quiet side street, this early-1900s government-rated three-star hotel is comfortably rustic, with exposed stone and wood paneling, paneled ceilings, and a Renaissance-style fireplace. The guest rooms are quite pleasant, and most have armchairs for reading. Every accommodation has a well-maintained private bathroom—half with a tub, half with a shower. The courtyard provides a quiet oasis for breakfast and afternoon tea.

18 rue Léon-Jost, 75017 Paris. ℂ **01-46-22-60-70.** Fax 01-47-63-01-01. 18 units. 710–880F (107.90–133.75€, $102.95–$127.60) double; 1,300–1,500F (197.60–228€, $188.50–$217.50) suite. AE, DC, MC, V. Parking 100F (15.20€, $14.50). Métro: Courcelles. **Amenities:** Bar; room service (snacks and drinks); baby-sitting; laundry/dry cleaning. *In room:* A/C, TV, minibar, hair dryer.

INEXPENSIVE

Hôtel Flaubert   If you want an inexpensive retreat in the 17th, this is as good as it gets. The staff here long ago became accustomed to handling all the problems their international guests might have. Terra-cotta tiles and bentwood furniture in the public areas make for an efficient if not lushly comfortable setting for breakfast. Though the lush climbing plants in the courtyard overshadow the guest rooms, they're nonetheless appealing and (particularly those beneath the mansard's eaves) cozy, as well as small to medium in size. In 2000, management added about a dozen new rooms, thanks to the acquisition and refurbishment of a building next door. Throughout, accommodations are modern, relatively small-scale, and comfortable. About half of the private bathrooms contain tubs, the others showers.

19 rue Rennequin, 75017 Paris. ℂ **01-46-22-44-35.** Fax 01-43-80-32-34. 49 units. 620F (94.25€, $89.90) double. AE, DC, MC, V. Métro: Ternes or Charles de Gaulle–Etoile. **Amenities:** Garden; room service (breakfast). *In room:* TV, minibar, hair dryer.

Les Trois Couronnes   This prestigious older hotel in Paris's business hub is within easy access of the Métro and many of the city's attractions. With its blend of Art Deco and Art Nouveau, it was radically redecorated and upgraded in 1995 and is under new management. The cheerful guest rooms, small and old-fashioned but pleasant, take in the surrounding area. Bathrooms are neatly kept and tiled. All contain a private shower, some a tub-shower combo.

30 rue de l'Arc-de-Triomphe, 75017 Paris. ℂ **01-43-80-46-81.** Fax 01-46-22-53-96. www.3couronnes.com. 20 units. 495–695F (75.25–105.65€, $71.80–$100.80) double. AE, DC, MC, V. Parking 100F (15.20€, $14.50). Métro: Charles de Gaulle–Etoile. **Amenities:** Room service (breakfast). *In room:* TV, minibar, hair dryer, safe.

Marmotel Etoile   This hotel is on an inconvenient side of place Charles de Gaulle–Etoile, and you have to ford a roaring river of traffic to get to the nearby Champs-Elysées. The guest rooms are simple and small but comfortable. The ones overlooking the carefully landscaped flagstone-covered courtyard benefit from an unexpected oasis of calm; those fronting the avenue's traffic are less peaceful. Bedrooms are equally divided between those that have a shower only or those with a tub-shower combo.

34 av. de la Grande Armée, 75017 Paris. ✆ **01-47-63-57-26.** Fax 01-45-74-25-27. 23 units. 470–490F (71.45–74.50€, $68.15–$71.05) double. AE, DC, MC, V. Métro: Argentine. **Amenities:** Room service; dry cleaning. *In room:* TV, minibar, safe.

2 On the Left Bank

We'll begin with the most centrally located arrondissements on the Left Bank, then work our way through the more outlying neighborhoods and to the area near the Eiffel Tower.

5TH ARRONDISSEMENT
MODERATE

Grand Hôtel St-Michel   Built in the 19th century, this hotel is larger and more business-like than many of the town-house-style inns nearby. It basks in the reflected glow of Brazilian dissident Georges Amado, whose memoirs (released in 1996) recorded his 2-year literary sojourn in one of the rooms. The public rooms are tasteful, with oil portraits and rich upholsteries. In 1997, the hotel completed a renovation and moved from a government rating of two- to three-star status. All but four of the units now have a tub-shower combination. The changes enlarged some rooms, lowering their ceilings and adding modern amenities like minibars, but retained old-fashioned touches such as wrought-iron balconies (fifth floor only). Sixth-floor rooms offer interesting views over the rooftops.

19 rue Cujas, 75005 Paris. ✆ **01-46-33-33-02.** Fax 01-40-46-96-33. 46 units. 890F (135.30€, $129.05) double; 1,290F (196.10€, $187.05) triple. AE, DC, MC, V. Métro: Cluny–La Sorbonne. RER: Luxembourg or St-Michel. **Amenities:** Bar; baby-sitting; laundry/dry cleaning. *In room:* TV, minibar, hair dryer, safe.

Hôtel Abbatial St-Germain   The origins of this hotel run deep: Interior renovations have revealed such 17th-century touches as dovecotes and massive oak beams. In the early 1990s, a radical restoration made the public areas especially appealing and brought the small rooms, furnished in faux Louis XVI, up to modern standards. All windows are double-glazed, and the fifth- and sixth-floor rooms enjoy views over Notre-Dame. The small bathrooms are neatly kept and equipped with showers, or else a tub and shower.

46 bd. St-Germain, 75005 Paris. ✆ **01-46-34-02-12.** Fax 01-43-25-47-73. www.abbatial.com. 43 units. 780–920F (118.70–140.05€, $113.20–$113.50) double. AE, MC, V. Parking 110F (16.70€, $15.95). Métro: Maubert-Mutualité. **Amenities:** Baby-sitting; laundry/dry cleaning. *In room:* A/C, TV, minibar, hair dryer, safe.

Hôtel Agora St-Germain   One of the best of the neighborhood's moderately priced choices, this hotel occupies a building constructed in the early 1600s, probably to house a group of guardsmen protecting the brother of the king at his lodgings nearby. It's in the heart of the artistic/historic Paris and offers compact soundproof guest rooms, each not particularly fashionably furnished. All but seven of the bedrooms have a tub-shower combo, the rest only a shower.

42 rue des Bernardins, 75005 Paris. ✆ **01-46-34-13-00.** Fax 01-46-34-75-05. agorastg@hotellerie.net. 39 units. 800–880F (121.60–133.75€, $116–$127.60) double. AE, DC, MC, V. Parking 130F (19.75€, $18.85). Métro: Maubert-Mutualité. *In room:* A/C, TV, minibar, hair dryer, safe.

Hôtel des Arènes   In a 19th-century building whose chiseled stone facade evokes fine old traditions, this hotel offers well-maintained modern guest rooms. Many in back overlook the tree-dotted ruins of Paris's ancient Roman arena,

Hotels in the 5th–6th & 13th–14th Arrondissements

unearthed in 1865. Rooms in back are very quiet, almost like living in the country. Although the gardens of the ancient arena do not belong to the hotel, guests have direct access to them.

51 rue Monge, 75005 Paris. ✆ **01-43-25-09-26.** Fax 01-43-25-79-56. 52 units. 550–695F (83.60–105.65€, $79.75–$100.80) double. AE, MC, V. Parking 100F (15.20€, $14.50). Métro: Monge or Cardinal Lemoine. **Amenities:** Room service (breakfast). *In room:* TV, minibar, hair dryer, safe.

Hôtel des Grands Hommes Built in the 18th century and renovated in the early 1990s, this hotel offers direct profile views (from many rooms) of the

Panthéon. All but a handful of the accommodations have exposed ceiling beams and pleasantly old-fashioned furnishings that sometimes include brass beds. Fifth- and sixth-floor rooms have small balconies and also the best views. Those with the most space are on the ground floor. In 2000, the bedrooms were renovated, and now each comes with a complete tub and shower combo.

17 place du Panthéon, 75005 Paris. (C) **01-46-34-19-60.** Fax 01-43-26-67-32. 32 units. 850–1,100F (129.20–167.20€, $123.25–$159.50) double; 1,200–2,000F (182.40–304€, $174–$290) suite. AE, DC, MC, V. Parking 90F (13.70€, $13.05). Métro: Cardinal Lemoine or Luxembourg. **Amenities:** Baby-sitting; laundry/dry cleaning. *In room:* A/C, TV, minibar, hair dryer.

Hôtel des Jardins du Luxembourg   Built during Baron Haussmann's 19th-century overhaul of Paris, this hotel boasts an imposing facade of honey-colored stone accented with ornate iron balconies. The interior is outfitted in strong, clean lines, often with groupings of Art-Deco furnishings. The high-ceilinged guest rooms, some with Provençal tiles and ornate moldings, are well-maintained, the size ranging from small to medium. Best of all, they overlook a quiet dead-end alley, ensuring relatively peaceful nights. Some have balconies overlooking the rooftops. In 2000, all the carpeting was replaced in all the bedrooms. Each unit comes with a neat, tidily arranged bathroom with a combined tub and shower.

5 impasse Royer-Collard, 75005 Paris. ℂ **01-40-46-08-88.** Fax 01-40-46-02-28. www.travel-in-paris.com. 26 units. 825–890F (125.40–135.30€, $119.65–$129.05) double. AE, DC, MC, V. Parking 100F (15.20€, $14.50). Métro: Cluny–La Sorbonne. RER: Luxembourg. **Amenities:** Baby-sitting; laundry/dry cleaning. In room: A/C, TV, minibar, hair dryer, safe.

Hôtel Moderne St-Germain   In the heart of the Latin Quarter, the Grand Hôtel Moderne is better than ever since it ended the 20th century with a complete overhaul. Its charming owner, Mme Gibon, welcomes guests warmly to her spotless rooms. In the rooms fronting rue des Ecoles, double-glazed aluminum windows hush the traffic. Though the rooms are small, this is still one of the neighborhood's better government-rated three-star hotels. All the bathrooms contain a shower, and about half of them also have a tub. Guests enjoy access to the sauna and Jacuzzi at the Hôtel Sully next door.

33 rue des Ecoles, 75005 Paris. ℂ **01-43-54-37-78.** Fax 01-43-29-91-31. www.tulipinn.com. 45 units. 650–950F (98.80–144.40€, $94.25–$137.75) double; 1,200F (182.40€, $174) triple. AE, DC, MC, V. Parking 150F (22.80€, $21.75). Métro: Maubert-Mutualité. **Amenities:** Use of sauna and Jacuzzi next door; laundry/dry cleaning. In room: A/C, TV, minibar, hair dryer.

Hôtel Observatoire-Luxembourg   The hotel's simple Art-Nouveau facade is something of an architectural oddity in this neighborhood. Many of its rooms, especially those on the fifth and sixth floors, overlook either the Jardin du Luxembourg across the street or the nearby St-Jacques church. (Room 507, though not the largest, boasts the best view, encompassing both trees and medieval architecture.) The mattresses are a bit older than you might hope for but nonetheless comfortable. A successful renovation in 2001 upgraded the public areas; they're streamlined and angular but softened by bright colors. All the bedrooms have a private shower; half of the units also come with tubs.

107 bd. St-Michel, 75005 Paris. ℂ **01-46-34-10-12.** Fax 01-46-33-73-86. fa.sol@wanadoo.fr. 37 units. 792–947F (120.40–143.95€, $114.85–$137.30) double. AE, DC, MC, V. Métro: Saint-Michel. RER: Luxembourg. **Amenities:** Room service; baby-sitting; laundry/dry cleaning. In room: A/C, TV, hair dryer, safe.

Hôtel-Résidence Saint-Christophe   This hotel, in one of the Latin Quarter's undiscovered but charming areas, offers a gracious English-speaking staff. It was created in 1987 when a derelict hotel was connected to a butcher shop. All the small- to medium-size rooms were successfully renovated in 1998, with Louis XV–style furniture, wall-to-wall carpeting, and firm mattresses. All the bedrooms have private showers and half of the units also have a tub.

17 rue Lacépède, 75005 Paris. ℂ **01-43-31-81-54.** Fax 01-43-31-12-54. hotelstchristophe@compuserve.com. 31 units. 700F (106.40€, $101.50) double. AE, DC, MC, V. Parking 100F (15.20€, $14.50). Métro: Place Monge. **Amenities:** Laundry/dry cleaning. In room: TV, minibar, hair dryer.

INEXPENSIVE

Familia-Hôtel   As the name implies, this is a hotel that has been family-run for decades. Many personal touches make the place unique, and it was lavishly renovated in 1998. As in many Paris hotels, rooms are quite small and cozy but still comfortable. The walls of 14 rooms are graced with finely executed, sepia-colored frescoes of Parisian scenes. Eight rooms have restored stonewalls, and seven have balconies with delightful views over the Latin Quarter. All units have showers, and half of the rooms also come with tubs.

11 rue des Ecoles, 75005 Paris. ☎ **01-43-54-55-27**. Fax 01-43-29-61-77. 30 units. 550–665F (83.60–101.10€, $79.75–$96.45) double. Rates include breakfast. AE, DC, MC, V. Métro: Jussieu or Maubert-Mutualité. *In room:* TV, minibar, hair dryer.

Hôtel des Grandes Ecoles *Value*

Few other hotels in the neighborhood offer so much low-key charm at such reasonable prices. It's composed of a trio of high-ceilinged buildings, interconnected via a sheltered courtyard where in warm weather singing birds provide a worthy substitute for the TVs deliberately missing from the rooms. Accommodations, as reflected by the price, range from snug, cozy doubles to more spacious chambers. Each is comfortable, but with a lot of luggage the very smallest would be cramped. The room decor is artfully old-fashioned, with feminine touches such as Laura Ashley–inspired flowered upholsteries and ruffles. Many offer views of a garden whose trellises and flowerbeds evoke the countryside.

75 rue de Cardinal-Lemoine, 75005 Paris. ☎ **01-43-26-79-23**. Fax 01-43-25-28-15. www.hotel-grandes-ecoles.com. 51 units. 550–720F (83.60–109.45€, $79.75–$104.40) double. MC, V. Parking 100F (15.20€, $14.50). Métro: Cardinal Lemoine or Monge. *In room:* Hair dryer.

Hôtel Le Home Latin *Value*

This is one of Paris's most famous budget hotels, known since the 1970s for its simple lodgings. The blandly functional rooms were renovated in 1999; some have small balconies overlooking the street. Those facing the courtyard are quieter than those fronting the street. The elevator doesn't reach beyond the fifth floor, but to make up for the stair climb, the sixth floor's *chambres mansardées* offer a romantic location under the eaves and panoramic rooftop views. Forty-seven units come only with a shower, the rest contain a tub and shower combo.

15–17 rue du Sommerard, 75005 Paris. ☎ **01-43-26-25-21**. Fax 01-43-29-87-04. www.homelatinhotel.com. 54 units. 595–650F (90.45–98.80€, $86.30–$94.25) double; 750F (114€, $108.75) triple; 860F (130.70€, $124.70) quad. AE, DC, MC, V. Parking 85F (12.90€, $12.35). Métro: St-Michel or Maubert-Mutualité. *In room:* Hair dryers; no phone.

Hotel Minerve

This is a well-managed, well-located, government-rated two-star hotel in the heart of the Latin Quarter, with snug but comfortable rooms and a staff with a sense of humor. Bedrooms have contemporary-looking wooden furniture, compact dimensions, comfortable mattresses, and color schemes that come in a medley of tones. Depending on your room assignment, bathrooms range in dimension from cramped to mid-size. If there's no space at the Minerve, a staff member will arrange an equivalent (and equivalently priced) lodging in its sibling, the Familia, 11 rue des Ecoles (☎ 01-43-54-55-27).

12 rue des Ecoles, 75005 Paris. ☎ **01-43-26-26-04**. Fax 01-44-07-01-96. www.hotel-paris-minerve.com. 54 units. 480–680F (72.95–103.35€, $69.60–$98.60) double. AE, MC, V. Metro: Cardinal Lemoine. *In room:* TV.

Timhôtel Jardin des Plantes

Opened in 1986 and renovated in 1997, the government-rated two-star Timhôtel lies across from the Jardin des Plantes, the botanical gardens created by order of Louis XIII's doctors in 1626 (there are still some 15,000 medicinal herbs in the gardens). Some of the small but well-equipped guest rooms open onto flowered terraces. About half of the bathrooms have tubs, the others have showers. Each was renovated in 2001. The hotel has a small roof terrace and a vaulted basement lounge.

5 rue Linné, 75005 Paris. ℂ **01-47-07-06-20.** Fax 01-47-07-62-74. www.timhotel.com. 33 units. 700F (106.40€, $101.50) double. AE, DC, MC, V. Parking 80F (12.15€, $11.60). Métro: Jussieu. Bus: 67 or 89. **Amenities:** Sauna; room service; baby-sitting; laundry/dry cleaning. *In room:* A/C, TV, hair dryer.

6TH ARRONDISSEMENT
VERY EXPENSIVE

Relais Christine 🌟🌟 The Relais Christine welcomes you into what was a 16th-century Augustinian cloister. You enter from a narrow cobblestone street into first a symmetrical courtyard and then an elegant reception area with baroque sculpture and Renaissance antiques. Each guest room is uniquely decorated with wooden beams and Louis XIII–style furnishings; the rooms come in a wide range of styles and shapes, and some are among the Left Bank's largest, with extras like mirrored closets, plush carpets, thermostats, and even balconies facing the outer courtyard. The least attractive, smallest, and dimmest rooms are those in the interior. Each comes with a complete tub and shower bathroom.

3 rue Christine, 75006 Paris. ℂ **800/525-5800** in the U.S., or ℂ **01-40-51-60-80.** Fax 01-40-51-60-81. www.relais-christine.com. 51 units. 2,000–2,600F (304–395.20€, $290–$377) double; 3,200–4,500F (486.40–684€, $464–$652.50) duplex or suite. AE, DC, MC, V. Free parking. Métro: Odéon. **Amenities:** Honor bar in lobby; room service; baby-sitting; laundry/dry cleaning. *In room:* A/C, TV, minibar, hair dryer, safe.

EXPENSIVE

Hôtel de Fleurie 🌟🌟 *(Kids)* Off boulevard St-Germain on a colorful little street, the Fleurie is one of the best of the "new" old hotels, with its statuary-studded facade recapturing a 17th-century elegance. The stone walls have been exposed in the reception salon, where you check in at a refectory desk. About half the guest rooms and tub and shower bathrooms were renovated in 1999, and many have elaborate curtains and antique reproductions. This hotel has long been a family favorite—interconnecting doors in certain pairs of rooms create safe havens the hotel refers to as *chambres familiales.*

32–34 rue Grégoire-de-Tours, 75006 Paris. ℂ **01-53-73-70-00.** Fax 01-53-73-70-20. www.hotel-de-fleurie.tm.fr. 29 units. 1,700–1,800F (258.40–273.60€, $246.50–$261) double; 1,700–1,800F (258.40–273.60€, $246.50–$261) family room. Children 12 and under stay free in parents' room. AE, DC, MC, V. Métro: Odéon or St-Germain-des-Prés. **Amenities:** Bar; car-rental desk; room service; baby-sitting; laundry/dry cleaning. *In room:* A/C, TV, minibar, hair dryer, trouser press.

Hôtel de l'Abbaye St-Germain 🌟 This is one of the district's most charming boutique hotels, having been a convent in the early 18th century. Its brightly colored rooms have traditional furniture like you'd find in a private club, plus touches of sophisticated flair. The more expensive units are quite spacious, but the cheaper ones are small but efficiently organized and still quite comfortable. In front is a small garden and in back a verdant courtyard with a fountain, raised flowerbeds, and masses of ivy and climbing vines. If you don't mind the expense, one of the most charming rooms has a terrace overlooking the upper floors of neighboring buildings. Bedrooms come with neatly tiled and complete bathrooms.

10 rue Cassette, 75006 Paris. ℂ **01-45-44-38-11.** Fax 01-45-48-07-86. www.Hotel-Abbaye.com. 46 units. 1,260–1,860F (191.50–282.70€, $182.70–$269.70) double; 2,440–2,540F (370.90–386.10€, $353.80–$368.30) suite. Rates include breakfast. AE, MC, V. Métro: St-Sulpice. **Amenities:** Garden; room service; baby-sitting; laundry/dry cleaning. *In room:* A/C, TV, hair dryer, safe.

La Villa 🌟 This hotel's facade resembles those of many of the other buildings in the neighborhood. Inside, however, the decor is a minimalist ultramodern creation thoroughly rejecting all traditional French aesthetics. The public areas and guest rooms contain Bauhaus-like furniture; the lobby's angular lines are somewhat softened with bouquets of leaves and flowers. Most unusual are the baths, whose shimmering stainless steel; pink, black, or beige marble; and chrome surfaces are either post-Sputnik or postmodern, depending on your frame of reference. Everything was renovated in 2000, and all but three units contain a complete tub and shower.

29 rue Jacob, 75006 Paris. ✆ **01-43-26-60-00**. Fax 01-46-34-63-63. www.villa-saintgermain.com. 31 units. 1,250–1,600F (190–243.20€, $181.25–$232) double; 1,700–2,500F (258.40–380€, $246.50–$362.50) suite. AE, MC, V. Métro: St-Germain-des-Prés. **Amenities:** Bar; room service (drinks); baby-sitting. *In room:* A/C, TV, minibar, hair dryer, safe.

L'Hôtel 🏵🏵   Ranking just a notch below the Relais Christine, this is one of the Left Bank's most charming boutique hotels. It was once a 19th-century fleabag called the Alsace, whose major distinction was that Oscar Wilde died there, broke and in despair. But today's guests aren't anywhere near poverty row: This was the sophisticated creation of late French actor Guy-Louis Duboucheron, and show business and fashion celebrities love it. The guest rooms vary in size, style, and price, from quite small to deluxe, but all have non-working fireplaces and fabric-covered walls. An eclectic collection of antiques pops up here and there: One spacious room contains the original furnishings and memorabilia of stage star Mistinguette, a frequent performer with Maurice Chevalier and his on-again/off-again lover. Her pedestal bed is set in the middle of the room, surrounded by mirrors, as she liked to see how she looked or "performed" at all times. About half the bathrooms are small, tubless nooks.

13 rue des Beaux-Arts, 75006 Paris. ✆ **01-44-41-99-00**. Fax 01-43-25-64-81. www.l-hotel.com. 27 units. 2,500–4,800F (380–729.60€, $362.50–$696) double; from 5,000F (760€, $725) suite. AE, DC, MC, V. Métro: St-Germain-des-Prés or Mabillon. **Amenities:** Room service; baby-sitting; laundry/dry cleaning. *In room:* A/C, TV, minibar, hair dryer.

Odéon-Hôtel 🏵🏵   Reminiscent of a modernized Norman country inn, the Odéon offers charming rustic touches such as exposed beams, rough stone walls, high crooked ceilings, and tapestries mixed with contemporary fabrics, mirrored ceilings, and black leather furnishings. Conveniently located near both the Théâtre de l'Odéon and boulevard St-Germain, the Odéon stands on the first street in Paris to have pavements (1779) and gutters. By the turn of the 20th century, this area, which had drawn the original Shakespeare & Co. bookshop to no. 12 rue de l'Odéon, began attracting such writers as Gertrude Stein and her coterie. The guest rooms are small to medium in size but charming, and each comes with a combo tub and shower.

3 rue de l'Odéon, 75006 Paris. ✆ **01-43-25-90-67**. Fax 01-43-25-55-98. www.odeonhotel.fr. 33 units. 950–1,400F (144.40–212.80€, $137.75–$203) double; 1,500F (228€, $217.50) suite. AE, DC, MC, V. Parking 100F (15.20€, $14.50). Métro: Odéon. **Amenities:** Room service (drinks); baby-sitting. *In room:* A/C, TV, hair dryer, safe.

Relais St-Germain 🏵   Adapted from a 17th-century building, the St-Germain is an oasis of charm and comfort. It's comparable to the Relais Chris-tine, its nearest competitor, but with a more accommodating staff. The decor is a medley of traditional and modern, evoking a charming provincial house. All the necessary amenities have been tucked in under the beams, including sound-proofing and full bathrooms. Bathrooms range from mid-size to roomy, each with a combination tub and shower. Four rooms feature kitchenettes, and two of the suites come with terraces.

9 carrefour de l'Odéon, 75006 Paris. ✆ **01-43-29-12-05**. Fax 01-46-33-45-30. 22 units. 1,600–1,850F (243.20–281.20€, $232–$268.25) double; 2,100F (319.20€, $304.50) suite. Rates include breakfast. AE, DC, MC, V. Métro: Odéon. **Amenities:** Restaurant (French); room service; massage; baby-sitting; laundry/dry cleaning. *In room:* A/C, TV, minibar, hair dryer, safe.

MODERATE

Grand Hôtel de l'Univers   In the 1400s, this was home to a family of the emergent bourgeoisie, and the hotel exudes charm and tranquility. The pleasantly renovated guest rooms are cramped but well-maintained and some provide panoramic views over the crooked rooftops. A renovation in 2000 added English-inspired decor to each of the bedrooms. All the private bathrooms contain a tub-shower combo.

6 rue Grégoire-de-Tours, 75006 Paris. ℰ **01-43-29-37-00.** Fax 01-40-51-06-45. grandhotelunivers@ wanadoo.fr. 34 units. 1,000–1,200F (152–182.40€, $145–$174) double. AE, DC, MC, V. Métro: Odéon. **Amenities:** Room service (breakfast); baby-sitting; laundry/dry cleaning. In room: A/C, TV, minibar, hair dryer, safe.

Hôtel Aviatic   Completely remodeled, this is a bit of old Paris in an interesting section of Montparnasse, with a modest inner courtyard and a vine-covered wall lattice, surrounded by cafes popular with artists, writers, and jazz musicians. It has been a family-run hotel for a century and has an English-speaking staff. The reception lounge boasts marble columns, brass chandeliers, antiques, and a petite salon. The guest rooms, which are mid-size and fairly standard throughout, were renovated in stages throughout the 1990s, and each comes with a shower or tub and shower combo.

105 rue de Vaugirard, 75006 Paris. ℰ **01-53-63-25-50.** Fax 01-53-63-25-55. www.aviatic.fr. 43 units. 950F (144.40€, $137.75) double. AE, DC, MC, V. Parking 120F (18.25€, $17.40). Métro: Montparnasse-Bienvenue or Saint-Placide. **Amenities:** Room service; baby-sitting; laundry/dry cleaning. In room: A/C, TV, minibar, hair dryer.

Hôtel des Deux Continents   Built from three interconnected historic buildings, each between three and six stories high, this hotel is a reliable choice with a sense of Latin Quarter style. The carefully coordinated guest rooms, renovated between 1992 and 1998, range from small to medium and include reproductions of antique furnishings and soundproof upholstered walls. Each is equipped with a neatly tiled shower bathroom.

25 rue Jacob, 75006 Paris. ℰ **01-43-26-72-46.** Fax 01-43-25-67-80. www.2continents-hotel.com. 41 units. 865–915F (131.55–139.15€, $125.45–$132.75); 1,120F (170.25€, $162.40) triple. MC, V. Métro: St-Germain-des-Prés. In room: TV.

Hôtel des Saints-Pères   This hotel off boulevard St-Germain is comparable to the Odéon, and there's no better recommendation than the long list of guests who return again and again (the late Edna St. Vincent Millay loved the camellia-trimmed garden). The hotel, designed by Louis XIV's architect, Jacques-Ange Gabriel, is decorated in part with antique paintings, tapestries, and mirrors. Many of the guest rooms face a quiet courtyard. Most sought after is the *chambre à la fresque,* with a 17th-century painted ceiling. The hotel has installed new plumbing and replastered and repainted the rooms.

65 rue des Sts-Pères, 75006 Paris. ℰ **01-45-44-50-00.** Fax 01-45-44-90-83. hotelsts.peres@wanadoo.fr. 39 units. 850–1,250F (129.20–190€, $123.25–$181.25) double; 1,750F (266€, $253.75) suite. AE, MC, V. Métro: St-Germain-des-Prés or Sèvres-Babylone. **Amenities:** Garden. In-room: TV, minibar.

Hôtel du Pas-de-Calais   The Pas-de-Calais goes back to the 17th century. Its elegant facade, with massive wooden doors, has been retained. Romantic novelist Chateaubriand lived here from 1811 to 1814, but its most famous guest was Jean-Paul Sartre, who struggled with the play *Les Mains Sales* (Dirty Hands) in room 41. The hotel is a bit weak on style, but as one longtime guest confided, despite the updates, "we still stay here for the memories." The modern guest rooms were extensively renovated in 2000; inner rooms surround a modest courtyard with two garden tables and several trellises. The inner rooms are the smallest and cheapest; the other rooms range in dimension from mid-size to spacious. Each bedroom comes with a tub and shower.

59 rue des Sts-Pères, 75006 Paris. ☏ **01-45-48-78-74.** Fax 01-45-44-94-57. 40 units. 850–920F (129.20–139.85€, $123.25–$133.40) double. AE, DC, MC, V. Parking 110F (16.70€, $15.95). Métro: St-Germain-des-Prés or Sèvres-Babylone. **Amenities:** Room service (drinks and snacks); baby-sitting; laundry/dry cleaning. In room: A/C, TV, hair dryer, safe.

Hôtel Le Clos Médicis

The location of this hotel across from the Jardin du Luxembourg is a major advantage. You'll find a verdant garden with lattices and exposed stone walls, a lobby with modern spotlights and simple furniture, and a multilingual staff. The warmly colored guest rooms, small to medium in size, are comfortable, and each comes with a neatly tiled shower and tub bathroom.

56 rue Monsieur-le-Prince, 75006 Paris. ☏ **01-43-29-10-80.** Fax 01-43-54-26-90. www.closmedicis.com. 38 units. 790–1,200F (120.10–182.40€, $114.55–$174) double; 1,400F (212.80€, $203) duplex suite. AE, DC, MC, V. Parking 150F (22.80€, $21.75). Métro: Odéon. RER: Luxembourg. **Amenities:** Garden; laundry. In room: A/C, TV, minibar, hair dryer.

Hôtel Le Ste-Beuve ⭐ (Finds)

The location of this discreet hideaway adds to its charms, on a street that's tucked into a narrow and quiet neighborhood, reeking of bourgeois respectability, near the Luxembourg Garden. The public areas are outfitted with deep leather armchairs and a midwinter fire that blazes merrily in an open hearth. Bedrooms each contain at least one antique, and each comes in a different color scheme. None is overly large, but all of them (four to a floor) face the quiet street, noises from which are muffled by double-glazing. Full bathrooms are sheathed in dark-brown marble. Overall, the aura is one of well-managed comfort and respectability.

9 rue Ste-Beuve, 75006 Paris. ☏ **01-45-48-30-07.** Fax 01-45-48-33-95. www.paris-hotel-charme.com. 22 units. 780–1,440F (118.55–218.90€, $113.10–$208.80) double; 1,700F (258.40€, $246.50) suite. Parking 90F (13.70€, $13.05). Metro: Notre-Dame-des-Champs. **Amenities:** Room service (drinks). In room: TV, minibar.

Hôtel Louis II

In an 18th-century building, this hotel offers guest rooms decorated in rustic French tones. Afternoon drinks and morning coffee are served in the reception salon, where gilt-framed mirrors, fresh flowers, and antiques radiate a provincial aura, like something out of Proust. The generally small soundproof rooms with exposed beams and lace bedding complete the impression. Many visitors ask for the romantic attic rooms. In 2000, the public rooms and bedrooms were renovated in a "hotel de charme" style. About half of the rooms contain tub baths, the rest showers.

2 rue St-Sulpice, 75006 Paris. ☏ **01-46-33-13-80.** Fax 01-46-33-17-29. www.hotel-louis2.com. 22 units. 700–1,050F (106.40–159.60€, $101.50–$152.25) double; 1,350F (205.20€, $195.75) triple. AE, DC, MC, V. Parking 120F (18.25€, $17.40). Métro: Odéon. **Amenities:** Room service (breakfast); laundry/dry cleaning. In room: TV, minibar, hair dryer, safe.

Hôtel St-Germain-des-Prés

Most of this hotel's attraction comes from its enviable location in the Latin Quarter, behind a well-known Left Bank street. Janet Flanner, the legendary 1920s *New Yorker* correspondent, lived here for a while. Renovated within the past few years, the guest rooms are small but charming, with antique ceiling beams and safes; air-conditioning is available in most. The public areas are severely elegant. Most of the bathrooms contain tubs, although all come with showers.

36 rue Bonaparte, 75006 Paris. ☏ **01-43-26-00-19.** Fax 01-40-46-83-63. www.hotel-st-ger.com. 30 units. 1,050–1,450F (159.60–220.40€, $152.25–$210.25) double; 1,500–2,000F (228–304€, $217.50–$290) suite. Rates include breakfast. AE, MC, V. Métro: St-Germain-des-Prés. **Amenities:** Room service (breakfast); baby-sitting; laundry/dry cleaning. In room: A/C, TV, minibar, hair dryer, safe.

INEXPENSIVE

Delhy's Hôtel   It's an oldie but goodie. On a narrow crooked alley in the Latin Quarter's densest part, this circa-1400 building was acquired by François I as a home for one of his mistresses. Don't expect luxury, but look for charming touches that help compensate for the lack of an elevator. The staircase is listed as a national relic, and most of the compact guest rooms still have the original, almost fossilized, timbers and beams. The rooms were for the most part renovated in the late 1990s. If you get a room without a bath, you'll have to go down to the ground floor for access to the public facilities.

22 rue de l'Hirondelle, 75006 Paris. ℂ **01-43-26-58-25.** Fax 01-43-26-51-06. 21 units, 7 with bathroom. 376F (57.15€, $54.50) double without bathroom; 466F (70.85€, $67.55) double with bathroom; 636F (96.65€, $92.20) triple with bathroom. Rates include breakfast. AE, DC, MC, V. Métro: St-Michel. *In room:* TV.

Hôtel Clément   This hotel sits on a quiet narrow street, within sight of the twin towers of St-Sulpice church. From the 1700s, the building was renovated several years ago into a bright, uncomplicated design. The guest rooms are simple and small, in some cases not much bigger than the beds they contain. Most of the bathrooms contain tubs; only 2 units are shower only.

6 rue Clément, 75006 Paris. ℂ **01-43-26-53-60.** Fax 01-44-07-06-83. hclement@worldnet.fr 31 units. 590–710F (89.70–107.90€, $85.55–$102.95) double; 810F (123.10€, $117.45) suite. AE, DC, V. Métro: Mabillon. *In room:* A/C, TV, hair dryer, safe.

Hôtel Delavigne   Despite radical modernization, you still get a sense of the building's 18th-century origins. The public areas feature an attractively rustic use of chiseled stone, some of which is original. The high-ceilinged guest rooms are tasteful, sometimes with wooden furniture, often with upholstered headboards, and sometimes with Spanish-style wrought iron. Those were upgraded and renovated in 2000. All of the bathrooms have both a tub and shower.

1 rue Casimir-Delavigne, 75006 Paris. ℂ **01-43-29-31-50.** Fax 01-43-29-78-56. www.hoteldelavigne.com. 34 units. 690–790F (104.90–120.10€, $100.05–$114.55) double; 890F (135.30€, $129.05) triple. MC, V. Métro: Odéon. **Amenities:** Room service (breakfast); baby-sitting; laundry/dry cleaning. *In room:* TV, hair dryer, safe.

Hôtel du Globe   Located on an evocative street, this 17th-century building has most of its original stonework and dozens of original timbers and beams. There's no elevator (you have to lug your suitcases up a very narrow antique staircase) and no breakfast area (trays are brought to your room). Each guest room is decorated with individual old-fashioned flair. *A tip:* The rooms with tubs are almost twice as large as those with shower stalls. The largest and most desirable rooms are nos. 1, 12 (with a baldachin-style bed), 14, 15, and 16. The room without a bathroom is a single at 330F (50.15€, $47.85).

15 rue des Quatre-Vents, 75006 Paris. ℂ **01-46-33-62-69.** Fax 01-46-33-62-69. hotelglobe@post. club-internet.fr. 15 units, 5 with bathroom. 430–655F (65.35–99.55€, $62.35–$95) double. MC, V. Closed 3 weeks in Aug. Métro: Mabillon, Odéon, or St-Sulpice. **Amenities:** Room service (drinks); laundry/dry cleaning. *In room:* TV.

Hôtel du Lys   The tall casement windows and high ceilings are from the 17th century. This cozy place has functioned as a hotel since the turn of the 20th century. There's no elevator, a fact that guarantees you'll make frequent use of the historic staircase. The guest rooms have different patterns of curtains and wallpaper, and about a quarter were renovated in 1998. Only a few units are large (these rent at the higher price); others are small but cozy affairs. Don't expect attentive service; the Lys is like an upscale dorm, with guests pursuing an array of interests and activities in the area. All bathrooms come with shower, and about half of the units also contain a tub.

23 rue Serpente, 75006 Paris. ✆ **01-43-26-97-57**. Fax 01-44-07-34-90. 22 units. 580–630F (88.15–95.75€, $84.10–$91.35) double; 730F (110.95€, $105.85) triple. Rates include breakfast. MC, V. Métro: Cluny–La Sorbonne or St-Michel. *In room:* TV, hair dryer, safe.

13TH ARRONDISSEMENT

Hôtel du Vert Galant   Verdant climbing plants and shrubs make this hotel feel like an auberge deep in the French countryside. The smallish guest rooms have tiled or carpeted floors, unfussy furniture, and (in most cases) views of the garden or the public park across the street. All bathrooms have showers and nearly three-fourths of them also contain tubs. One of the place's best aspects is the Basque inn next door, the Auberge Etchegorry, sharing the same management; hotel guests receive a discount.

41 rue Croulebarbe, 75013 Paris. ✆ **01-44-08-83-50**. Fax 01-44-08-83-69. 15 units. 450–550F (68.40–83.60€, $65.25–$79.75) double. AE, DC, MC, V. Parking 40F (6.10€, $5.80). Métro: Corvisart or Gobelins. **Amenities:** Restaurant (French); bar; room service (breakfast); baby-sitting. *In room:* TV, minibar, hair dryer.

14TH ARRONDISSEMENT

Hôtel du Parc-Montsouris   The residential neighborhood is far removed from central Paris's bustle, the staff is a bit absent-minded, and the decor doesn't pretend to be stylish, but the prices are reasonable enough that this government-rated two-star hotel (a simple structure built in the 1930s) attracts loyal repeat guests; they might be parents of students studying at the nearby Cité Universitaire or provincial clothiers attending fashion shows at the nearby Porte de Versailles. The guest rooms are low-key and quiet, each renovated in the late 1990s. Singles and doubles are small, but the triples are spacious, the suites even more so. All the bathrooms contain a tub and shower.

4 rue du Parc de Montsouris, 75014 Paris. ✆ **01-45-89-09-72**. Fax 01-45-80-92-72. www.hotel-parc-montsouris.com. 35 units. 420F (63.85€, $60.90) double; 470F (71.45€, $68.15) triple; 570F (86.65€, $82.65) suite. AE, MC, V. Métro: Porte d'Orléans. RER: Cité-Universitaire. **Amenities:** Room service (breakfast); laundry/dry cleaning. *In room:* TV, hair dryer.

7TH ARRONDISSEMENT
VERY EXPENSIVE

Hôtel Montalembert ★★   Unusually elegant for the Left Bank, the Montalembert dates from 1926 when it was built in the Beaux-Arts style. It was restored between 1989 and 1992 and again in 2001 and hailed as a smashing success, borrowing sophisticated elements of Bauhaus and postmodern design in honey beiges, creams, and golds. The guest rooms are spacious, except for some standard doubles, which are quite small unless you're a very thin model. The full bathrooms are luxurious with deep tubs, chrome fixtures, Cascais marble, and tall pivoting mirrors.

3 rue de Montalembert, 75007 Paris. ✆ **800/786-6397** in the U.S. and Canada, or ✆ **01-45-49-68-68**. Fax 01-45-49-69-49. www.montalembert.com. 56 units. 2,200–2,700F (334.40–410.40€, $319–$391.50) double; 3,500F (532€, $507.50) junior suite; 4,400F (668.80€, $638) suite. AE, DC, MC, V. Parking 120F (18.25€, $17.40). Métro: Rue du Bac. **Amenities:** Restaurant (French); bar; access to nearby health club; room service; baby-sitting; laundry/dry cleaning. *In room:* A/C, TV, minibar, hair dryer, safe.

EXPENSIVE

Hôtel de l'Université ★   Long favored by well-heeled parents of North American students studying in Paris, this 300-year-old town house filled with antiques enjoys a location in a discreetly upscale neighborhood. Number 54 is a favorite room, containing a rattan bed and period pieces. Another charmer is no. 35 with a fireplace, opening onto a courtyard with a fountain. The most expensive accommodation has a small terrace overlooking the surrounding rooftops. Most of the bedrooms are mid-size or even small, as are the bathrooms. But a few rented at the higher price tag have generous space.

22 rue de l'Université, 75007 Paris. ℰ 01-42-61-09-39. Fax 01-42-60-40-84. www.hoteluniversite.com. 28 units. 850–1,300F (129.20–197.60€, $123.25–$188.50) double. AE, MC, V. Métro: St-Germain-des-Prés. **Amenities:** Baby-sitting; laundry/dry cleaning. *In room:* A/C, TV, hair dryer, safe.

L'Hotel Pont Royal 🌟 At long last this Left Bank legend is up and running again. During the mid-1990s, this hotel was locked and shuttered as part of an extensive renovation and reconfiguration of its floor space. When it reopened, Paris' literary community carefully evaluated the premises to see whether it retained the gloss that had been infused into it by such writers as Sagan, Sartre, and Styron. Regrettably, it doesn't, which is partly the result of a bar that's much smaller and more prosaic-looking than it was in the past, when editors at nearby Gallimard (one of France's top publishers) used to drop in for drinks and shop talk. What you'll find is a cozy and comfortably paneled setting that's ready, willing, and able to provide a safe and comfortable home for you in this elegant neighborhood. Bedrooms are compact—not overly large, but cozy and woodsy-looking. Views from some of the rooms on the hotel's top floor stretch all the way to Sacré Coeur. Each comes with a newly installed private bath with tub and shower combos.

5–7 rue de Montalembert. ℰ 01-42-84-70-00. Fax 01-42-84-71-00. hpr@hotel-pont-royal.com. 75 units. 1,950–2,600F (296.40–395.20€, $282.75–$377) double, 3,200–4,500F (486.40–684€, $464–$652.50) suite. AE, DC, MC, V. Metro: Rue du Bac. **Amenities:** Restaurant (French); bar; room service; baby-sitting; laundry/dry cleaning. *In room:* TV, minibar, hair dryer, safe.

Le Duc de St-Simon 🌟 On a quiet residential street, this is the only hotel in the area to pose a serious challenge to the Montalembert. Two immortal cafes, Les Deux Magots and Le Flore, are a few steps away. The small villa has a landscaped courtyard, a rear garden, and a Napoléon III (mid-18th century) decor with trompe l'oeil panels. Climbing wisteria graces the courtyard. Each guest room is unique and sure to include at least one antique; a few are somewhat cramped, but most offer adequate space. Each room has a beautifully kept private bathroom with tub and shower combo.

14 rue de St-Simon, 75007 Paris. ℰ 01-44-39-20-20. Fax 01-45-48-68-25. 34 units. 1,275–1,650F (193.80–250.80€, $184.90–$239.25) double; 2,000–2,250F (304–342€, $290–$326.25) suite. AE, MC, V. Métro: Rue du Bac. **Amenities:** Garden; bar; room service; baby-sitting; laundry/dry cleaning. *In room:* hair dryer, safe.

MODERATE

Best Western Hôtel Derby Eiffel Upgraded in the early 1990s, this hotel faces the Ecole Militaire and contains airy public areas. Our favorite is a glass-roofed conservatory in back, filled year-round with plants and used as a breakfast area. The soundproof and conservatively modern guest rooms employ thick fabrics and soothing neutral colors. Most front-facing rooms offer views of the Eiffel Tower. In 1998, enormous sums were spent upgrading the rooms and bathrooms and generally improving the hotel's interior aesthetics. All bathrooms have showers and about half of the rooms also contain tubs.

Hotels in the 7th Arrondissement

Best Western Hôtel
  Derby Eiffel **6**
Grand Hôtel l'Eveque **3**
Hôtel de l'Académie **15**
Hôtel de l'Empereur **4**
Hôtel de l'Université **14**
Hôtel de Nevers **16**
Hôtel du Champ de Mars **2**
Hôtel du Palais Bourbon **7**
Hôtel du Quai-Voltaire **12**
Hôtel Lenox **13**
Hôtel Le Tourville **5**
Hôtel Lindbergh **17**
Hôtel Montalembert **10**
Hôtel Saint-Dominique **1**
Hôtel Verneuil **11**
Le Duc de St-Simon **8**
L'Hôtel Pont Royal **9**

5 av. Duquesne, 75007 Paris. © **800/528-1234** in the U.S. and Canada, or © **01-47-05-12-05.** Fax 01-47-05-43-43. www.derbyeiffelhotel.com. 43 units. 750–950F (114–144.40€, $108.75–$137.75) double; 900–1,290F (136.80–196.10€, $130.50–$187.05) triple, 1,200–1,600F (182.40–243.20€, $174–$232) suite. AE, DC, MC, V. Métro: Ecole Militaire. **Amenities:** Room service; baby-sitting; laundry/dry cleaning. *In room:* A/C, TV, minibar, hair dryer, safe.

Hôtel de l'Académie ★★

The exterior walls and old ceiling beams are all that remain of this 17th-century residence of the duc de Rohan's private guards. In 1999, the hotel was completely renovated to include an elegant reception area. The up-to-date guest rooms have a lush Ile-de-France decor and views over the neighborhood's 18th- and 19th-century buildings. By American standards the rooms are small, but they're average for Paris. All but eight bathrooms have a full tub-shower combo.

32 rue des Sts-Pères, 75007 Paris. © **800/246-0041** in the U.S. and Canada, or © **01-45-49-80-00.** Fax 01-45-44-75-24. www.academiehotel.com. 34 units. 990–1,290F (150.50–196.10€, $143.55–$187.05) double; from 1,590F (241.70€, $230.55) suite. AE, DC, MC, V. Parking 150F (22.80€, $21.75). Métro: St-Germain-des-Prés. **Amenities:** Exercise room; massage; baby-sitting. *In room:* A/C, TV, minibar, hair dryer, safe.

Hôtel du Quai-Voltaire ★★

Built in the 1600s as an abbey, then transformed into a hotel in 1856, the Quai-Voltaire is best-known for its illustrious guests, such as Wilde, Wagner, and Baudelaire, who occupied rooms 47, 55, and 56, respectively. Camille Pissarro painted Le Pont Royal from the window of his fourth-floor room. Many guest rooms in this modest inn have been renovated, and most overlook the bookstalls and boats of the Seine. Doubles tend to be small, the triples mid-size but not spacious. Each unit comes with a small, shower-only bathroom. *Warning:* This hotel is not for everyone, although it has its diehard devotees. The front rooms enjoy one of the greatest views of Paris, but are exposed to the roar of traffic. It's also a long walk from any Métro stop.

19 quai Voltaire, 75007 Paris. © **01-42-61-50-91.** Fax 01-42-61-62-26. 33 units. 750–800F (114–121.60€, $108.75–$116) double; 870F (132.25€, $126.15) triple. AE, DC, MC, V. Parking 110F (16.70€, $15.95) nearby. Métro: Musée d'Orsay or Rue du Bac. **Amenities:** Bar; room service; laundry. *In room:* TV, hair dryer.

Hôtel Lenox

The Lenox is a favorite for those seeking reasonably priced accommodations in St-Germain-des-Prés. In 1910, T. S. Eliot spent a summer here "on the old man's money" when it was just a basic pension. Today this much-improved place offers a helpful staff and cramped but comfortable guest rooms radically and expensively upgraded in 2000. Rooms evoke the chintzes and furniture of an English country house. Many returning guests request the attic duplex with its tiny balcony and skylight. All bathrooms have a shower and half come with a tub, too.

9 rue de l'Université, 75007 Paris. © **01-42-96-10-95.** Fax 01-42-61-52-83. www.lenoxsaintgermain.com. 34 units. 750–950F (114–144.40€, $108.75–$137.75) double; 1,250–1,700F (190–258.40€, $181.25–$246.50) duplex suite. AE, DC, MC, V. Métro: Rue du Bac. **Amenities:** Bar; room service (breakfast); laundry/dry cleaning. *In room:* A/C, TV, hair dryer, safe.

Hotel Le Tourville ★

This is a well-managed, relatively personalized "hotel de charme" that occupies a desirable town house midway between the Eiffel Tower and Les Invalides. It originated in the 1930s as a hotel, and was revitalized and reconfigured during the 1990s into the stylish charmer you see today. Bedrooms each contain original artworks, an antique or an antique reproduction, and some kind of traditional wooden furniture covered in modern, sometimes bold, upholsteries. Four of the rooms, including the suite, have private terraces for soaking up the Parisian sunshine. Rooms 16 and 18 are the most desirable. About half the bathrooms are small with shower stalls, the others are more generously endowed with a tub and shower combination. Staff is particularly well-trained. Breakfast is the only meal served, but you can get a drink in the lobby.

16 av. de Tourville, 75007 Paris. ℂ **01-47-05-43-90.** Fax 01-47-05-43-90. www.hoteltourville.com. 30 units. 890–1,390F (135.30–211.30€, $129.05–$201.55) double; 1,990F (302.50€, $288.55) suite. AE, DC, MC, V. Métro: École Militaire. **Amenities:** Bar. *In room:* A/C, TV, hair dryer.

Hôtel Verneuil ★ (Finds) Small-scale and personalized, this hotel, in the words of a recent critic, "combines modernist sympathies with nostalgia for *la vieille France.*" Within what was built in the 1600s as a town house, it offers a creative and intimate jumble of charm and coziness. Expect a mixture of antique and contemporary furniture, lots of books, and in the bedrooms, trompe l'oeil ceilings, antique beams that in some cases have been painted white, quilts, and walls covered in fabric in a rainbow of colors. Bathrooms come with combo tubs and showers or shower only.

8 rue de Verneuil, 75007 Paris. ℂ **01-42-60-82-14.** Fax 01-42-61-40-38. verneuil@cybercable.fr. 26 units. 850–1,100F (129.20–167.20€, $123.25–$159.50) doubles, suites. AE, DC, MC, V. Parking 120F (18.25€, $17.40). Métro: St-Germain-des-Prés. **Amenities:** Bar; room service (drinks); baby-sitting; laundry/dry cleaning. *In room:* TV, minibar, hair dryer.

INEXPENSIVE

Grand Hôtel L'Eveque Built in the 1930s, this hotel draws lots of English-speaking guests, many of whom appreciate its proximity to the Eiffel Tower. In 2000, the interior was completely renovated and repainted with all the carpets changed. The pastel-colored guest rooms retain an Art-Deco inspiration, just enough space to be comfortable, and double-insulated windows overlooking a courtyard in back or the street in front. The small bathrooms contain showers.

29 rue Cler, 75007 Paris. ℂ **01-47-05-49-15.** Fax 01-45-50-49-36. www.hotel-leveque.com. 50 units. 400–500F (60.80–76€, $58–$72.50) double; 600F (91.20€, $87). AE, MC, V. Métro: Ecole Militaire. *In room:* TV, hair dryer, safe.

Hôtel de l'Empereur This convenient hotel was built in the early 1700s and enjoys a loyal group of repeat visitors. There's an elevator to haul you and your luggage to one of the smallish but attractively decorated guest rooms, with mostly shower only bathrooms. In 1998, the two top floors were renovated. There's no restaurant or bar, but a nearby restaurant will send up platters of food on request.

2 rue Chevert, 75007 Paris. ℂ **01-45-55-88-02.** Fax 01-45-51-88-54. www.hotelempereur.com. 38 units. 475–535F (72.20–81.43€, $68.90–$77.65) double; 660F (100.30€, $95.70) triple; 760F (115.50€, $110.20) quad. AE, DC, MC, V. Parking 110–150F (16.70–22.80€, $15.95–$21.75) across the street. Métro: Latour-Maubourg. **Amenities:** Room service; laundry/dry cleaning. *In room:* TV, fridge, hair dryer.

Hôtel de Nevers ★ This is one of the neighborhood's most historic choices—it was a convent from 1627 to 1790, when it was disbanded by the Revolution. The building is *classé*, meaning any restoration must respect the original architecture. That precludes an elevator, so you'll have to use the beautiful white staircase. The cozy and pleasant guest rooms contain a mix of antique and reproduced furniture. Rooms 10 and 11 are especially sought after for their terraces overlooking a corner of rue du Bac or a rear courtyard. In 2000, many aspects of this place were upgraded and renovated. All units have a shower, and about half have full bathrooms.

83 rue du Bac, 75007 Paris. ℂ **01-45-44-61-30.** Fax 01-42-22-29-47. 11 units. 500–540F (76–82.10€, $72.50–$78.30) double. No credit cards. Métro: Rue du Bac. *In room:* TV, minibar, hair dryer.

Hôtel du Champ de Mars   Favored by families, this hotel sits close to the park flanking the base of the Eiffel Tower. It offers clean and simple guest rooms that are frilly and pretty enough to be referred to as "coquettish" by the manager. In 1998, most of the rooms were renovated and redecorated, retaining their charm and rather cramped dimensions. Bathrooms are small but efficiently organized with a shower stall. The most memorable of the public areas is a stone-sided breakfast room, where the staff serves the hotel's only meal.

7 rue du Champ de Mars, 75007 Paris. ☎ 01-45-51-52-30. Fax 01-45-51-64-36. www.hotel-du-champ-de-mars.com. 25 units. 440–470F (66.90–71.45€, $63.80–$68.15) double. MC, V. Parking 100–150F (15.20–22.80€, $14.50–$21.75) in nearby public parking lot. Métro: Ecole Militaire. *In room:* TV.

Hôtel du Palais Bourbon   The solid stone walls of this 18th-century building aren't nearly as grand as those of the embassies and stately private homes nearby. But don't be put off by the tight entrance hall and rather dark halls: Though the guest rooms on the upper floors are larger, all the rooms are pleasantly decorated, with carefully crafted built-in furniture. Each bathroom contains both a tub and a shower.

49 rue de Bourgogne, 75007 Paris. ☎ 01-44-11-30-70. Fax 01-45-55-20-21. www.hotel-palais-bourbon.com. 32 units. 690F (104.90€, $100.05) double; 800F (121.60€, $116) triple; 870F (132.25€, $126.15) quad. Rate includes breakfast. MC, V. Métro: Varenne. **Amenities:** Room service (breakfast). *In room:* A/C, TV, mini-bar, hair dryer, safe.

Hôtel Lindbergh   About a 3-minute walk from St-Germain-des-Prés, this hotel offers streamlined and simple, medium-size guest rooms. About two-thirds of the bathrooms contain a tub, although all of them are equipped with a shower. Breakfast is the only meal served, but the staff will point out worthy restaurants nearby—an inexpensive bistro, Le Cigale, is a few buildings away.

5 rue Chomel, 75007 Paris. ☎ 01-45-48-35-53. Fax 01-45-49-31-48. www.hotellindbergh.com. 26 units. 580–660F (88.15–100.30€, $84.10–$95.70) double; 790–880F (120.10–133.75€, $114.55–$127.60) triple; 840–930F (127.70–141.35€, $121.80–$134.85) quad. AE, DC, MC, V. Parking 110F (16.70€, $15.95). Métro: Sèvres-Babylone or St-Sulpice. **Amenities:** Laundry/dry cleaning. *In room:* TV, hair dryer.

Hôtel Saint-Dominique   Part of this place's charm derives from its division into three buildings connected through an open-air courtyard. The most visible of these was an 18th-century convent—you can still see its battered ceiling beams and structural timbers in the reception area. The guest rooms aren't large, but each is warm and simply decorated; many have wallpaper in nostalgic patterns. Bathrooms are neatly laid out, each with a shower or else a complete bath in about one-third of the units.

62 rue St-Dominique, 75007 Paris. ☎ 01-47-05-51-44. Fax 01-47-05-81-28. hotel.saint.dominique@wanadoo.fr. 34 units. 700–850F (106.40–129.20€, $101.50–$123.25) double. AE, MC, V. Métro: Latour-Maubourg or Invalides. **Amenities:** Room service (breakfast). *In room:* TV, minibar, hair dryer (in some), safe.

3 Near the Airports

ORLY

EXPENSIVE

Hilton Paris Orly Airport   Boxy and bland, the Hilton at Orly remains a solid and well-maintained hotel business travelers appreciate for its convenience. Incoming planes can't penetrate the guest rooms' sound barriers, guaranteeing you a shot at a decent night's sleep. (And unlike the 24-hour Charles de Gaulle Airport, Orly is closed to arriving flights from midnight to 6am.) The rooms are standard for a chain hotel. Each was renovated in the late 1990s.

Aéroport Orly, 267 Orly Sud, 94544 Orly Aerogare Cedex. *C* **800/445-8667** in the U.S. and Canada, or *C* **01-45-12-45-12.** Fax 01-45-12-45-00. www.hilton.com. 351 units. 720–920F (109.45–139.85€, $104.40–$133.40) double; 1,200F (182.40€, $174) suite. AE, DC, MC, V. Parking 90F (13.70€, $13.05). Free shuttle bus between hotel and both Orly terminals; 40-minute taxi ride from central Paris, except during rush hours. **Amenities:** Restaurant (French); bar; health club; nearby tennis court; sauna; room service; laundry/dry cleaning. *In room:* A/C, TV, minibar, hair dryer.

INEXPENSIVE

Climat de France   Boxy and contemporary-looking, and interconnected with Orly by frequent 10-minute complimentary shuttle-bus rides, this 1990s hotel offers standardized, not-particularly imaginative bedrooms. Each is comfortable, insulated against noises from the nearby airport, and a bit larger than you might have expected. Each unit comes with a neatly tiled shower-only bathroom.

58 voie Nouvelle (near the Parc Georges Mélliès), 94544 Orly. *C* **01-41-80-75-75.** Fax 01-41-80-12-12. 72 units. 390–425F (59.30–64.60€, $56.55–$61.65) double. AE, DC, MC, V. Free parking. Transit to and from airport by complimentary shuttle-bus. **Amenities:** Restaurant (French). *In room:* TV.

CHARLES-DE-GAULLE

EXPENSIVE

Hôtel Sofitel Paris Aéroport CDG *✿*   Many travelers shuttle happily through this bustling but somewhat anonymous member of the nationwide French chain. It employs a multilingual staff that's accustomed to accommodating constantly arriving and departing international business travelers. Renovated in 1998, the conservative monochromatic guest rooms are soundproof havens against the all-night roar of jets.

Aéroport Charles de Gaulle, Zone Central, B.P. 20248, 95713 Roissy. *C* **800/221-4542** in the U.S. and Canada, or *C* **01-49-19-29-29.** Fax 01-49-19-29-00. www.accor.com. 352 units. 980–1,500F (148.95–228€, $142.10–$217.50) double; from 2,250F (342€, $326.25) suite. AE, DC, MC, V. Parking 164F (24.95€, $23.80). Free shuttle bus service to/from airport. **Amenities:** Restaurant (French); bar; pool; sauna; business center; room service. *In room:* A/C, TV, minibar, hair dryer.

INEXPENSIVE

Hotel Campanile de Roissy   Accommodations at this place tend to be less expensive than those of its nearby competitors. Its boxy-looking, cement-and-glass design is barely masked by a thin overlay of cheerful-looking and rustic artifacts, but generally, this is an efficiently decorated and not particularly stylish place to stay, with a well-meaning but overworked staff. Each unit comes with a small, shower-only bathroom.

Parc de Roissy, 95700 Val-d'Oise. *C* **01-34-29-80-40.** Fax 01-34-29-80-39. 224 units. 425–525F (64.60–79.80€, $61.65–$76.15) double. Rates include breakfast. AE, DC, MC, V. Free parking. Take free shuttle van to and from Roissy. **Amenities:** Shuttle; restaurant; room service. *In room:* TV.

4 Gay-Friendly Hotels

Though any hotel recommended in this guide is considered at least tolerant of same-sex couples, this hotel is especially welcoming. For its location on a map, see the "Hotels in 1st–4th, 9th–12th & 18th Arrondissements" map on pages 72–73. For full coverage of Paris's gay/gay-friendly hotels and restaurants, see *Frommer's Gay & Lesbian Europe.*

INEXPENSIVE

Hôtel Central   This is Paris's most famous all-out gay hotel, with rooms on the second, third, and fourth floors of an 18th-century building. If you arrive from 8:30am to 5pm, you'll find a registration staff one floor above street level;

otherwise, you'll have to retrieve your room keys and register at the street-level bar, Le Central (see chapter 10). Frankly, many visitors prefer the bar over the guest rooms, but if you want a hotel that'll put you in the middle of the gay scene, this is it. The guest rooms are simple and serviceable but show wear and tear. With a single exception, one private bathroom is shared for each two rooms. Women are welcome but rare.

33 rue Vieille-du-Temple, 75004 Paris. ✆ **01-48-87-99-33**. Fax 01-42-77-06-27. 7 units, 1 with bathroom. 535F (81.30€, $77.60) double without bathroom, 750F (114€, $108.75) double with bathroom. MC, V. Métro: Hôtel de Ville.

6

Where to Dine

Welcome to the city that prides itself on being the world's culinary capital. Only in Paris can you turn onto the nearest little crooked side street, enter the first non-descript bistro you see, sit down at a bare wobbly table, order from an illegibly hand-scrawled menu, and get a truly memorable meal.

See chapter 1 for a list of our restaurant favorites—the best chef, the best view, the best baby bistro, and more.

1 Food for Thought

WHAT'S COOKING IN FRANCE Once you arrive in Paris, you'll find that the word "French" (although in great use) to describe a cuisine isn't very helpful. "French" covers such a broad scope that it doesn't prepare you for the offerings of the specialty chefs. Even the Parisians themselves might ask, "What type of French cooking?"

Sometimes a chef will include regional specialties, classic dishes, and even nouvelle cuisine, all on one menu. In that case, such a restaurant is truly "French." Other chefs prefer a more narrow focus and feature the cooking of one region or else one style—classic or modern. Still others prefer to strike middle ground between classic and modern; they're called "creative."

Regional cuisine showcases the amazing diversity of the provinces of France, from Alsace on the German border to the Basque country at the frontier of Spain. The climate has a lot to do with this diversified offering—olive oil, garlic, and tomatoes from Provence in the south to oysters and saltwater fish from Brittany. Every region is known for special dishes—Burgundy for its fat escargots plucked off the grape vines; Périgord renowned for its truffles and foie gras; Normandy for its soft, rich cheeses, Calvados, and cream sauces; and Alsace for its sauerkraut and wines. Today, almost every region of France is represented by one or more restaurants in Paris. You can go on a complete culinary tour of the country and never leave the city's limits, although regional dishes always taste better on home turf.

Few top chefs today use the expression **"nouvelle cuisine."** This cooking style, which burst upon us in the early 70s, is now old hat (or should we say old toque?). It was a rebellion against the excessive fats, butter, and sauces of haute cuisine, and used intense reductions of foodstuff to create flavor along with vegetable purées and lighter ingredients. Portions were greatly reduced. Diners were shocked sometimes to see a piece of *boeuf* the size of an egg resting on their plate under a slice of fresh kiwi. Created in the name of innovation, many of these dishes were successful, while others, such as asparagus ice cream, were dismal failures.

From nouvelle cuisine grew *cuisine improvisée,* which is creative cookery based on the freshest ingredients available. Chefs make their selections at the morning market, then rush back to their kitchen, as the clock ticks toward noon, to create spontaneous dishes often while dictating the menu of the day to an assistant who rushes it into print.

But fans of the great chef, Escoffier, can also rest assured. Nouvelle hasn't replaced **classic cuisine,** and France is still awash in béchamel and ablaze with cognac. Haute gastronomie is alive and thriving at restaurants not only in Paris, but throughout France. This richly extravagant fare is often lethal in price, but it makes use of expensive ingredients, including fatted ducks, lobster, truffles, and plenty of butter and cream, plus sauces that consume endless time in their preparation. Breaking from Escoffier, many chefs today have forged ahead with a **"new classic cuisine,"** where they have taken classic dishes and branded them with their own distinctive style and flavor, often lightening the calories.

PARIS'S RANGE OF RESTAURANTS   Paris boasts a surplus of restaurants and cafes. Ultra-expensive **temples of gastronomy** include Alain Ducasse, L'Astor, Alain Senderens, Taillevent, Pierre Gagnaire, Lasserre, Jacques Cagna, Le Grand Véfour, and La Tour d'Argent. Savvy diners confine their trips to *luxe* places for special occasions. An array of other choices awaits, including simpler restaurants dispensing cuisines from every province of France and from former colonies like Morocco and Algeria.

> **Tips   Mystifying Menu?**
>
> If you need help distinguishing a *blanquette de veau* from a *crème brûlée,* turn to the glossary of French-language menu terms in Appendix B.

Paris has hundreds of restaurants serving exotic **international fare,** reflecting the changing complexion of Paris itself and the city's increasing appreciation for food from other cultures. Your most memorable meal in Paris may turn out to be Vietnamese or West African.

You'll also find hundreds of bistros, brasseries, and cafes to choose from. In modern times their designations and roles have become almost meaningless. Traditionally, a **bistro** was a small restaurant, often with mom at the cash register and pop in the kitchen. Menus are most often handwritten or mimeographed, and the selection of dishes tends to be small. They can be chic and elegant, sometimes heavily Mediterranean in style, and often dispensing gutsy fare, including the *pot-au-feu* the chef's grandmother prepared for him as a kid.

French for brewery, most traditional **brasseries** have an Alsatian connection, and that means lots of beer, although Alsatian wines are also featured. They are almost always brightly lit and open 24 hours. Both snacks and full meals are available. The Alsatian establishments serve sauerkraut with an array of pork products.

The **cafe** is a French institution. Not just places for an aperitif, a *café au lait,* or a croissant, many serve rib-sticking fare as well, certainly *entrecôte* with french fries but often classics like *blanquette de veau* (veal in white sauce). For more lore about this French passion, see section 5, "The Top Cafes," later in this chapter.

More attention in the late 1990s focused on the **wine bar,** a host of which we recommend in chapter 10. Originally, wine bars concentrated on their lists of wines, featuring many esoteric choices and ignoring the food except for some *charcuterie* (cold cuts) and cheeses. Today, you're likely to be offered various daily specials, from homemade foie gras to *boeuf à la mode* (marinated beef braised with red wine and served with vegetables).

Tips   Dining Savoir-Faire

- Three-star dining remains extremely expensive, with appetizers sometimes priced at $50 and dinners easily costing $200 per person in the top dining rooms of celebrated chefs. But you can get around that high price tag in many places by **dining at lunch** (when prices are always cheaper) and **ordering a prix-fixe (fixed-price) menu** at lunch or dinner.

- The **fixed-price menu** or *le menu* is a set meal that the chef prepared that day. It is most often fresh and promptly served and represents a far greater bargain than if you're dining à la carte. Of course, it's very limited, so you'll have to like the choices provided. Sometimes there are one to three menus from which to choose, beginning with the less expensive and going up for a more elaborate meal. A lot depends on your pocketbook and appetite.

- In France, **lunch** (as well as dinner) tends to be a full-course meal with meat, vegetables, salad, bread, cheese, dessert, wine, and coffee. It may be difficult to find a restaurant that serves the type of light lunch North Americans usually eat. Cafes, however, offer sandwiches, soup, and salads in a relaxed setting.

- Average visitors head for the old-fashioned family-run **bistro,** and we've ferreted out the best ones. In today's Paris, tradition and nostalgia, along with affordable prices, make these bistros busier than ever, especially because so many are being forced out of existence due to rising rents.

- **Coffee** in France is served after the meal and carries an extra charge. The French consider it barbaric to drink coffee during the meal, and, unless you specifically order it with milk *(au lait),* it'll be served black. In more conscientious places, it's prepared as the traditional *café filtre,* a slow but rewarding java draw.

- In years gone by, no man would consider dining out, even at the neighborhood bistro, without a suit and tie, and no woman would be seen without a smart dress or suit. That **dress code** is more relaxed now, except in first-class and *luxe* establishments. Relaxed doesn't mean sloppy jeans and jogging attire, however. Parisians still value style, even when dressing informally.

- Sometimes service is automatically added to your tab—usually 12% to 15%. If not, look for the words *service non compris* on your bill. That means that the cost of service was not added, and you'll be expected to leave a **tip.**

Paris prices may seem extravagant to visitors from other parts of the world, particularly those who don't live in big cities, but there has been an emergence of moderately priced **informal restaurants** here, and we recommend several.

Although they're not as fashionable as they once were, still on the scene are **baby bistros,** reasonably priced spin-offs from deluxe restaurants where you can get a taste of a famous chef's cuisine without breaking the bank. We cover the best of them.

2 Restaurants by Cuisine

ALGERIAN
Au Clair de Lune (2nd arr.,
   p. 121, $)
Wally Le Saharien (9th arr.,
   p. 129, $$)

ALSATIAN
Bofinger ✸ (4th arr., p. 125, $$)
Brasserie de l'Ile St-Louis (4th arr.,
   p. 127, $)
Brasserie Flo ✸ (10th arr.,
   p. 130, $$)

AMERICAN
Chicago Pizza Pie Factory ✸✸
   (8th arr., p. 140, $)
Joe Allen ✸✸ (1st arr., p. 119, $)

ASIAN
Blue Elephant (11th arr.,
   p. 131, $$$)
Kambodia (16th arr., p. 142, $$)

AUVERGNAT
L'Ambassade d'Auvergne ✸
   (3rd arr., p. 123, $)
Restaurant Bleu (14th arr.,
   p. 155, $)

BASQUE
Au Bascou ✸ (3rd arr., p. 123, $)
Auberge Etchegorry
   (13th arr., p. 153, $$)
Chez l'Ami Jean (7th arr.,
   p. 158, $)

BRETON
Chez Michel (10th arr., p. 130, $)

BURGUNDIAN
Chez Pauline ✸ (1st arr., p. 115,
   $$)

CAFES
Brasserie Lipp (6th arr., p. 162,
   $$$)
Café Beaubourg (4th arr., p. 163,
   $$)
Café Cosmos ✸✸ (6th arr.,
   p. 164, $)

Café de Flore ✸✸ (6th arr.,
   p. 162, $$$)
Café de la Musique (19th arr.,
   p. 164, $$)
Café de la Paix ✸✸ (9th arr.,
   p. 163, $$$)
Café de l'Industrie (11th arr.,
   p. 166, $)
Café des Hauteurs (7th arr.,
   p. 164, $$)
Café Marly (1st arr., p. 164, $$)
Café/Restaurant/Salon de Thé
   Bernardaud ✸✸ (8th arr.,
   p. 165, $$)
Fouquet's ✸ (8th arr., p. 163, $$$)
La Coupole ✸ (14th arr., p. 165,
   $$)
La Palette ✸✸ (6th arr., p. 165, $)
La Rotonde (6th arr., p. 166, $)
Le Gutenberg (1st arr., p. 167, $)
Le Procope ✸✸ (6th arr., p. 166,
   $$)
Le Rouquet ✸ (7th arr., p. 163,
   $$$)
Les Deux Magots ✸✸ (6th arr.,
   p. 166, $$$)

CAMBODIAN
Kambodia (16th arr., p. 142, $$)

CANTONESE
Chez Vong ✸ (1st arr., p. 119, $)
China Club ✸ (12th arr., p. 133,
   $$)

CENTRAL EUROPEAN
Chez Jo Goldenberg ✸✸ (4th arr.,
   p. 127, $)
La Cagouille ✸ (14th arr., p. 154,
   $$)

CHINESE
China Club ✸ (12th arr., p. 133,
   $$)
Le Canton (6th arr., p. 153, $)

CREOLE
Babylone Bis (2nd arr., p. 122, $)

DANISH

Restaurant Copenhague/Flora
Danica ★★ (8th arr., p. 138,
$$$)

FRENCH CARIBBEAN

Marais-Cage (3rd arr., p. 123, $)

FRENCH (MODERN)

Alcazar Bar & Restaurant ★
(6th arr., p. 150, $$)
Bofinger ★ (4th arr., p. 125, $$)
Buddha Bar ★★ (8th arr., p. 138,
$$$)
Café la Parisienne (4th arr.,
p. 127, $)
Carré des Feuillants ★★★
(1st arr., p. 114, $$$$)
Chez Diane (6th arr., p. 152, $)
Chez Jean ★ (9th arr., p. 128,
$$$)
Jacques Cagna ★★★ (6th arr.,
p. 149, $$$$)
Julien ★ (10th arr., p. 131, $)
L'Amazonial (1st arr., p. 167, $)
L'Ambroisie ★★★ (4th arr.,
p. 124, $$$$)
L'Arpège ★★★ (7th arr., p. 155,
$$$$)
Lasserre ★★★ (8th arr., p. 134,
$$$$)
L'Astor ★★★ (8th arr., p. 135,
$$$$)
Le Bistro d'á Côté ★(17th arr.,
p. 144, $$$)
Le Coconnas ★ (4th arr., p. 126,
$$)
Le Violon d'Ingres ★★★ (7th arr.,
p. 156, $$$)
Lucas-Carton (Alain Senderens)
★★★ (8th arr., p. 135, $$$$)
Michel Rostang ★★★ (17th arr.,
p. 144, $$$$)
Pierre Gagnaire ★★★ (8th arr.,
p. 136, $$$$)
Restaurant Plaza Athénée ★★★
(Alain Ducasse) (8th arr.,
p. 136, $$$$)
Shozan ★ (8th arr., p. 139, $$$)
Taillevent ★★★ (8th arr., p. 138,
$$$$)

FRENCH (TRADITIONAL)

Allard ★★ (6th arr., p. 151, $$)
Angélina ★★ (1st arr., p. 119, $)
À Sousceyrac (11th arr., p. 131,
$$)
Astier ★ (11th arr., p. 132, $$)
Au Clair de Lune (2nd arr., p. 121,
$)
Au Gourmet de l'Ile ★ (4th arr.,
p. 126, $)
Au Pied de Cochon ★★ (1st arr.,
p. 115, $$)
Au Pied de Fouet (7th arr.,
p. 158, $)
Aux Charpentiers (6th arr.,
p. 152, $)
Aux Lyonnais ★★ (2nd arr.,
p. 122, $)
Benoit ★ (4th arr., p. 124, $$$)
Bistro de la Grille (6th arr., p. 152,
$)
Bofinger ★ (4th arr., p. 125, $$)
Brasserie Balzar ★★ (5th arr.,
p. 146, $$)
Brasserie de l'Ile St-Louis (4th arr.,
p. 127, $)
Cave de l'Os à Moelle (15th arr.,
p. 159, $)
Chartier (9th arr., p. 129, $)
Chez André (8th arr., p. 139, $$)
Chez Diane (6th arr., p. 152, $)
Chez Georges (2nd arr., p. 121,
$$)
Chez Georges (17th arr., p. 145, $$)
Chez Gramond (6th arr., p. 151,
$$)
Chez Jean ★ (9th arr., p. 128, $$$)
Chez Pauline ★ (1st arr., p. 115,
$$)
Chez René (5th arr., p. 146, $$)
Clémentine (2nd arr., p. 122, $)
Closerie des Lilas ★★ (6th arr.,
p. 150, $$)
Crémerie-Restaurant Polidor ★★
(6th arr., p. 152, $)
Guy Savoy ★★★ (17th arr.,
p. 144, $$$$)
Jacques Cagna ★★★ (6th arr.,
p. 149, $$$$)
Jamin ★★★ (16th arr., p. 141,
$$$$)

Julien ✿ (10th arr., p. 131, $)

La Butte Chaillot ✿ (16th arr., p. 142, $$)

La Cagouille ✿ (14th arr., p. 154, $$)

Ladurée (8th arr., p. 139, $$)

La Grille (10th arr., p. 130, $$)

L'Ambassade d'Auvergne ✿ (3rd arr., p. 123, $)

L'Ambroisie ✿✿✿ (4th arr., p. 124, $$$$)

L'Ami Louis ✿ (3rd arr., p. 122, $$$)

La Petite Chaise (7th arr., p. 156, $$)

La Petite Hostellerie ✿ (5th arr., p. 147 $)

La Poule au Pot (1st arr., p. 120, $)

La Rose de France ✿ (1st arr., p. 120, $)

La Rôtisserie d'Armaillé ✿✿ (17th arr., p. 145, $$)

La Rôtisserie d'en Face ✿ (6th arr., p. 151, $$)

Lasserre ✿✿✿ (8th arr., p. 134, $$$$)

La Tour d'Argent ✿✿✿ (5th arr., p. 145, $$$$)

La Tour de Monthléry (Chez Denise) (1st arr., p. 120, $)

L'Ébauchoir ✿ (12th arr., p. 133, $)

Le Berry's (8th arr., p. 140, $)

Le Bistro d'á Côté ✿ (17th arr., p. 144, $$$)

Le Bistro de l'Étoile ✿ (16th arr., p. 143, $)

Le Café du Commerce (15th arr., p. 160, $)

Le Coconnas ✿ (4th arr., p. 126, $$)

Le Grand Véfour ✿✿✿ (1st arr., p. 114, $$$$)

Le Grand Zinc (9th arr., p. 129, $)

Le Petit Marguery (13th arr., p. 154, $$)

Lescure ✿ (1st arr., p. 120, $)

Les Gourmets des Ternes (8th arr., p. 140, $)

Le Square Trousseau (12th arr., p. 134, $)

Le Train Bleu ✿✿ (12th arr., p. 133, $$)

Le Vaudeville (2nd arr., p. 121, $$)

Le Vieux Bistro ✿ (4th arr., p. 126, $$)

Le Violon d'Ingres ✿✿✿ (7th arr., p. 156, $$$)

Marie-Louise (18th arr., p. 134, $)

Michel Rostang ✿✿✿ (17th arr., p. 144, $$$$)

Perraudin ✿✿ (5th arr., p. 147, $)

Relais Gourmand Faugeron ✿✿✿ (16th arr., p. 141, $$$$)

Restaurant Plaza Athénée (Alain Ducasse) (8th arr., p. 136, $$$$)

Taillevent ✿✿✿ (8th arr., p. 138, $$$$)

Trumilou ✿ (4th arr., p. 127, $)

GASCONY

Au Trou Gascon ✿✿✿ (12th arr., p. 132, $$$)

INDIAN

Yugaraj (6th arr., p. 151, $$)

INTERNATIONAL

Georges ✿ (4th arr., p. 125, $$)

L'Amazonial (1st arr., p. 167, $)

Le Fumoir ✿ (1st arr., p. 118, $$)

Spoon, Food & Wine ✿ (8th arr., p. 139, $$$)

ITALIAN

Il Cortile ✿✿ (1st arr., p. 115, $$)

JAPANESE

Isama (4th arr., p. 125, $$)

Shozan ✿ (8th arr., p. 139, $$$)

JEWISH

Chez Jo Goldenberg ✿✿ (4th arr., p. 127, $)

KOREAN

Shing-Jung (8th arr., p. 141, $)

LATE NIGHT

Au Pied de Cochon ✿✿ (1st arr., p. 115, $$)

Babylone Bis (2nd arr., p. 122, $)

La Poule au Pot (1st arr., p. 120, $)

La Tour de Monthléry (Chez Denise) (1st arr., p. 120, $)

Le Vaudeville (2nd arr., p. 121, $$)

LEBANESE
Al Dar (5th arr., p. 146, $)

LOIRE VALLEY (ANJOU)
Au Petit Riche (9th arr., p. 129, $$)

LYONNAIS
Aux Lyonnais ★★ (2nd arr., p. 122, $)

MEDITERRANEAN
Il Cortile ★★ (1st arr., p. 115, $$)

MOROCCAN
Mansouria (11th arr., p. 132, $)

NORTHERN FRENCH
Le Bamboche (7th arr., p. 158, $$)

ORGANIC
Le Grain de Folie (18th arr., p. 134, $)

PACIFIC RIM
Buddha Bar ★★ (8th arr., p. 138, $$$)

PIZZA
Chicago Pizza Pie Factory ★★ (8th arr., p. 140, $)

PROVENÇAL
Campagne et Provence (5th arr., p. 146, $)
Chez Janou (3rd arr., p. 123, $)
La Bastide Odéon ★ (6th arr., p. 153, $)
Les Elysées du Vernet ★★★ (8th arr., p. 135, $$$$)

PYRENÉE
La Fontaine de Mars (7th arr., p. 158, $)

SEAFOOD
Goumard ★★★ (1st arr., p. 114, $$$$)
Keryado ★ (13th arr., p. 154, $)
La Cagouille ★ (14th arr., p. 154, $$)
La Grille (10th arr., p. 130, $$)
Paul Minchelli ★ (7th arr., p. 156, $$$)

SENEGALESE
Le Manguier (11th arr., p. 132, $)
Paris-Dakar (10th arr., p. 131, $)

SEYCHELLE ISLANDS
Coco de Mer ★ (5th arr., p. 147, $)

SOUTHWESTERN FRENCH
Chez l'Ami Jean (7th arr., p. 158, $)
La Fermette du Sud-Ouest ★ (1st arr., p. 119, $)
La Fontaine de Mars (7th arr., p. 158, $)
La Régalade (14th arr., p. 155, $$)
L'Assiette (14th arr., p. 154, $$)
Restaurant du Marché (15th arr., p. 159, $$)

TEA
Angélina ★★ (1st arr., p. 119, $)

VEGETARIAN
Aquarius ★★ (4th arr., p. 126, $)
Le Grain de Folie (18th arr., p. 134, $)

VIETNAMESE
Kim Anh (15th arr., p. 159, $$)
Le Canton (6th arr., p.153, $)

Don't Leave Home Without Them

No matter how long you stay in Paris, we suggest you save up and indulge in at least one break-the-bank French meal at a fabulous restaurant. The meal will be a memory you'll likely treasure long after you've recovered from paying the tab. However, to get a table at one of these places, *you must reserve far in advance*—at least a day or two ahead, sometimes even a few weeks or a few months ahead! We suggest you look over our listings at home, and then call for reservations before you leave on your trip or at least call the minute you get into town.

3 On the Right Bank

We'll begin with the most centrally located arrondissements on the Right Bank, then work our way through the more outlying neighborhoods and to the area around the Arc de Triomphe.

1ST ARRONDISSEMENT
VERY EXPENSIVE

Carré des Feuillants ★★★ FRENCH (MODERN)   This is a bastion of perfection, an elegant enclave of haute gastronomy between the Place Vendôme and the Tuileries. When leading chef Alain Dutournier turned this 17th-century convent into a restaurant, it was an overnight success. The interior is like an early-1900s bourgeois house with several small salons opening onto a sky-lit courtyard, across from which is a glass-enclosed kitchen. You'll find a sophisticated reinterpretation of cuisine from France's southwest, using seasonally fresh ingredients and lots of know-how. Examples are roasted veal kidneys cooked in their own fat; grilled wood pigeon served with chutney and polenta; rabbit filet in bitter-chocolate sauce with quince; and roasted leg of suckling lamb from the Pyrénées with autumn vegetables. Lighter dishes are scallops wrapped in parsley-infused puff pastry served with cabbage and truffles, and mullet-studded risotto with lettuce. For dessert, try a slice of pistachio cream cake with candied tangerines.

14 rue de Castiglione (near place Vendôme and the Tuileries), 1st arr. ✆ **01-42-86-82-82.** Fax 01-42-86-07-71. Reservations required far in advance. Main courses 260–340F (39.50–51.70€, $37.70–$49.30); fixed-price lunch 360F (54.70€, $52.20); fixed-price dinner 900F (136.80E, $130.50). AE, DC, MC, V. Mon–Fri noon–2:30pm; Mon–Sat 7:30–10:00pm. Closed 1st 3 weeks in Aug. Métro: Tuileries, Concorde, Opéra, or Madeleine.

Goumard ★★★ SEAFOOD   Opened in 1872, this landmark is one of Paris's leading seafood restaurants. It's so devoted to the fine art of preparing fish that other food is strictly banned from the menu (if you happen to dislike fish, the staff will orally present a limited roster of meat dishes). Much of the seafood is flown in directly from Brittany daily. Examples are a *craquant* (crispy) of crayfish in its own herb salad, lobster soup with coconut, grilled seawolf filet with a fricassée of artichokes and Provençal pistou, a grilled turbot salad on a bed of artichokes with tarragon, and poached turbot with hollandaise sauce, served with leeks in vinaigrette. In all these dishes nothing (no excess butter, spices, or salt) is allowed to interfere with the natural flavor of the sea. Be prepared for some unusual food—the staff will help translate the menu items for you. The decor consists of an unusual collection of Lalique crystal fish displayed in artificial aquariums. Even more unusual are the men's and women's restrooms, now classified as historic monuments; the commodes were designed by the Art-Nouveau master cabinetmaker Majorelle in the early 1900s.

9 rue Duphot, 1st arr. ✆ **01-42-60-36-07.** Fax 01-42-60-04-54. Reservations required far in advance. Main courses 190–390F (28.90–59.35€, $27.55–$56.55); fixed-price lunch 250F (38€, $36.25). AE, DC, MC, V. Mon–Sat 12:30–2:30pm and 7:30–10:30pm. Closed 3 weeks in Aug. Métro: Madeleine or Concorde.

Le Grand Véfour ★★★ FRENCH (TRADITIONAL)   This is the all-time winner: a great, great chef; the most beautiful restaurant decor in Paris, and a gastronomic, history-infused citadel of classic French cuisine. This restaurant has been around since the reign of Louis XV, though not under the same name. Napoléon, Danton, Hugo, Colette, and Cocteau have dined here—as the brass plaques on the tables testify—and it's still a great gastronomic experience. Guy

Martin, chef here for the past decade, bases many dishes on recipes from the French Alps. His best dish is roast lamb in a juice of herbs. Other specialties are noisettes of lamb with star anise and Breton lobster and the unusual cabbage sorbet in dark-chocolate sauce. The desserts are often grand, like the *gourmandises au chocolat,* a richness of chocolate served with chocolate sorbet.

17 rue de Beaujolais, 1st arr. ✆ **01-42-96-56-27.** Fax 01-42-86-80-71. Reservations required far in advance. Main courses 310–390F (47.10–59.30€, $44.95–$56.55); fixed-price menu 430F (65.35€, $62.35) at lunch, 1,050F (159.60€, $152.25) at dinner. AE, DC, MC, V. Mon–Fri 12:30–2pm and Mon–Thurs 8–10pm. Métro: Louvre–Palais Royal.

MODERATE

Au Pied de Cochon 🌟🌟 FRENCH (TRADITIONAL)/LATE NIGHT   Au
Pied de Cochon's famous onion soup and namesake house specialty (grilled pig's feet with béarnaise sauce) still lure visitors, and where else in Paris can you be assured of getting a good meal at 3am? Two other specialties are the *tentation* (temptation) platter, including grilled pig's tail, pig's snout, and half a pig's foot with béarnaise and *frites,* and *andouillette* (chitterling sausages) with béarnaise. Two particularly flavorful but less unusual dishes are a *jarret* (shin) of pork, caramelized in honey and served on a bed of sauerkraut, and grilled pork ribs with sage sauce. On the street outside, you can buy some of the freshest oysters in town. The attendants will give you slices of lemon to accompany them, and you can down them on the spot.

6 rue Coquillière, 1st arr. ✆ **01-40-13-77-00.** Reservations recommended for lunch and dinner hours. Main courses 80–150F (12.15–22.80€, $11.60–$21.75). AE, DC, MC, V. Daily 24 hours. Métro: Les Halles.

Chez Pauline 🌟 *Finds* BURGUNDIAN/FRENCH (TRADITIONAL)   Fans
say this *bistrot de luxe* is a less expensive, less majestic version of Le Grand Véfour. The early-1900s setting is grand enough to impress a business client and lighthearted enough to attract an impressive roster of VIPs. You'll be ushered to a table on one of two levels, amid polished mirrors, red leather banquettes, and memorabilia of long-ago Paris. The emphasis is on the cuisine of central France, especially Burgundy, as shown by the liberal use of wines in favorites like cassoulet of Burgundian snails with bacon and tomatoes, *boeuf bourguignonne* (braised beef in red-wine sauce) with tagliatelle, terrine of parslied ham, wild duckling filet with seasonal berries, salmon steak with green peppercorns, and ragout of wild hare in Pouilly aspic. Also wonderful is the roasted Bresse chicken with dauphinois potatoes. Dessert may include a *clafoutis* (pastry) of apricots and raspberries lightly sautéed in sugar as well as caramelized rice pudding. Owner/chef André Genin is an author of children's books, some on the value and techniques of French cuisine.

5 rue Villedo, 1st arr. ✆ **01-42-96-20-70.** Reservations recommended. Main courses 190–400F (28.90–60.80€, $27.55–$58); fixed-price menu 220F (33.45€, $31.90). AE, DC, V. Mon–Fri 12:15–2:30pm and 7:30–10:30pm; Sat 7:30–10:30pm. Closed Sat–Sun May–early Sept. Métro: Palais Royal.

Il Cortile 🌟🌟 ITALIAN/MEDITERRANEAN   Flanking the verdant court-
yard of a discreet small hotel, this much-talked-about restaurant serves the best Italian food in Paris. During warm weather, tables are set up in an enclosed patio—a welcome luxury in this congested neighborhood. The cuisine is fresh, inventive, and seasonal. Dishes are from throughout Italy, with emphasis on the north, as shown by a special promotion of wines of Tuscany and the Piedmont. Look for items like *farfalle* pasta with squid ink and fresh shellfish, fettuccine with *pistou* (pasta in a soup made from various vegetables), and an award-winning version of guinea fowl (spit-roasted and served with artfully-shaped

Restaurants in the 1st–4th, 9th–12th & 18th–19th Arrondissements

Androuët 23
Angélina 22
Aquarius 39
A Souscevrac 68
Astier 52
Au Bascou 46
Au Clair de Lune 29
Au Gourmet de l'Ile 59
Au Petit Riche 7
Au Pied de Cochon 31
Au Trou Gascon 60
Aux Lyonnais 14
Babylone Bis 28
Benoit 48
Berthillon 60
Blue Elephant 66
Bofinger 65
Brasserie de
  l'Ile St-Louis 56

Brasserie Flo 11
Café Beaubourg 41
Café de la Musique 50
Café de la Paix 15
Café de l'Industrie 67
Café la Parisienne 40
Café Marly 35
Carré des Feuillants 21
Chartier 9
Chez Georges 26
Chez Janou 63
Chez Jean 5
Chez Jo Goldenberg 61
Chez Michel 1
Chez Pauline 24
Chez Vong 45
China Club 69
Clémentine 13
Dalloyau 20

Georges 42
Goumard 18
Hard Rock Café 8
Il Cortile 17
Isama 57
Joe Allen 43
Julien 12
L'Amazonial 38

L'Ambassade
  d'Auvergne 44
L'Ambroisie 62
L'Ami Louis 47
La Fermette du
  Sud-Ouest 32
La Grille 4
La Poule au Pot 33

La Rose de France **37**	Le Grand Véfour **25**	Lescure **19**
La Samaritaine **31**	Le Grand Zinc **10**	Mansouria **58**
La Tour de Monthléry	Le Gutenberg **30**	Marais-Cage **53**
(Chez Denise) **34**	Le Manguier **51**	Marie-Louise **6**
L'Ebauchoir **70**	Le Square Trousseau **68**	Paris-Dakar **49**
Le Coconnas **64**	Le Train Bleu **71**	Stohrer **27**
Le Fumoir **36**	Le Vaudeville **16**	Trumilou **54**
Le Grain de Folie **2**	Le Vieux Bistro **55**	Wally Le Saharien **3**

Moments Le Grand Fromage

Cheese is king at **Androuët** ★★ *Kids*, 49 rue Saint Roch, 1st arr. (☎ **01-42-97-57-39**; Métro: Tuileries). True, it's a novelty restaurant, but if you're devoted to cheese, there's nothing like it in Europe. Opened in 1909 by M. Androuët, who frequently asked friends over to sample cheese and wine, the place (a new branch of the original headquarters) is now an institution. Most of the dishes are concocted with a cheese base. An impressive array of wines, well-prepared green salads, and ultrafresh bread is available to accompany whatever you order. Examples are a fondue of three cheeses, beef filet with Roquefort sauce flambéed with Calvados, and *magret de canard* (duckling). Many cheese lovers, however, opt for just a bottle of wine, a green salad, and all-you-can-eat choices from the most sophisticated *dégustation des fromages* (cheese tasting) in the world. Six platters, each loaded with a different category of cheese (one with goat cheeses, another with triple crèmes, and so on), are brought to your table, allowing you to select random samples. Reservations are required. Main courses cost 45 to 180F (6.85 to 27.35€, $6.55 to $26.10); a "tasting platter" with about 15 different cheeses is available for 180F (27.35€, $26.10). The restaurant is open Monday to Friday from 11:45am to 2:30pm and 7 to 9:30pm.

Androuët maintains a second branch, something that operates more like a wine bar than a food store, called **Androuët sur le Pouce,** 23, rue des Acacias, 17e (☎ **01-40-68-00-92**; Métro: Ternes). Charging the same prices as the larger branch, it maintains the same hours except that it's closed for Saturday at lunch and all day Sunday.

slices of the bird's gizzard, heart, and liver, it comes with polenta). The service is virtually flawless: The Italian-speaking staff is diplomatic and good-humored. If you want to see what's cooking, ask for a seat with a view of the open rotisserie, where spit-roasted hens and guinea fowl slowly spin.

In the Hôtel Castille, 37 rue Cambon, 1st arr. ☎ 01-44-58-45-67. Reservations recommended. Main courses 100–150F (15.20–22.80€, $14.50–$21.75); fixed-price menu 270F (41.05€, $39.15). AE, DC, DISC, MC, V. Mon–Fri noon–2:30pm and 7:30–10:30pm. Métro: Concorde or Madeleine.

Le Fumoir ★ INTERNATIONAL   Stylish and breezy, this upscale brasserie is set in an antique building a few steps from the Louvre. Currently, it's one of the most fashionable places in Paris to be seen eating or drinking. In a high-ceilinged room of warm but somber browns and indirect lighting, you can order salads, pastries, and drinks at off-hours and platters of more substantial food at conventional mealtimes. Examples are codfish filet with onions and herbs, sliced rack of veal simmered in its own juices with tarragon, calf's liver with onions, lamb chops with grilled tuna steak, and herring in mustard-flavored cream sauce.

6 rue de l'Amiral-Coligny, 1st arr. ☎ 01-42-92-00-24. Reservations recommended. Main courses 90–120F (13.70–18.25€, $13.05–$17.40). Salads, pastries, and snacks daily 11am–2pm; complete menu daily noon–3pm and 7–11:30pm. AE, V. Métro: Louvre-Rivoli.

INEXPENSIVE

Angélina ★★ FRENCH (TRADITIONAL)/TEA   In the high-rent area near the Inter-Continental (though on a section of rue de Rivoli that's getting scuzzy), this *salon de thé* combines fashion-industry glitter and bourgeois respectability. The carpets are plush, the ceilings are high, and the gilded accessories have the right amount of patina. This place has no equal when it comes to viewing the lionesses of haute couture over tea and delicate sandwiches. The overwrought and slightly snooty waitresses bear silver trays with light platters, pastries, drinks, and tea or coffee to tiny marble-topped tables. Lunch usually offers a salad and a *plat du jour* like chicken salad, steak tartare, *sole meunière,* or poached salmon. The house specialty, designed to go well with tea, is a Mont Blanc, a combination of chestnut cream and meringue.

226 rue de Rivoli, 1st arr. ☎ **01-42-60-82-00.** Reservations accepted for lunch, not for teatime. Pot of tea for 1, 35–36F (5.30–5.45€, $5.10–$5.20); sandwiches and salads 58–98F (8.80–14.90€, $8.40–$14.20); main courses 68–150F (10.35–22.80€, $9.85–$21.75). AE, V. Mon–Fri 9am–7pm; Sat–Sun 9am–7:30pm (lunch daily 11:45am–3pm). Métro: Tuileries or Concorde.

Chez Vong ★ CANTONESE   This is the kind of Les Halles restaurant you head for when you've had your fill of grand French cuisine and grander culinary pretensions. The decor is a soothing mix of green and browns, steeped in a Chinese colonial ambience that evokes early-1900s Shanghai. Menu items eature shrimp and scallops served as spicy as you like, including a super-hot version with garlic and red peppers; "joyous beef" that mingles sliced filet with pepper sauce; chicken in puff pastry with ginger; and a tempting array of fresh fish dishes.

10 rue de la Grande-Truanderie, 1st arr. ☎ **01-40-26-09-36.** Reservations recommended. Main courses 88–200F (13.40–30.40€, $12.75–$29); fixed-price lunch Mon–Fri only, 150F (22.80€, $21.75). AE, DC, MC, V. Mon–Sat noon–2:30pm and 7pm–midnight. Métro: Etienne-Marcel or Les Halles.

Joe Allen ★★ *Kids* AMERICAN   The first American restaurant to open in Les Halles is aging well. Joe Allen long ago invaded Les Halles with his hamburger. Though the New York restaurateur admits, "it's a silly idea," it works, and it's easily Paris's best burger. While listening to the jukebox, you can order savory black-bean soup, spicy chili, juicy sirloin steak, barbecued spareribs, or apple pie. Joe Allen is getting more sophisticated, however, catering to modern tastes with dishes like grilled salmon with coconut rice and sun-dried tomatoes. His saloon is the only place in Paris serving authentic New York cheesecake and real pecan pie, and thanks to French chocolate, he feels his brownies are better than those in the States. Giving the brownies tough competition are the California chocolate-mousse pie, strawberries Romanoff, and coconut-cream pie. On a regular night, if you haven't made a reservation for dinner, expect to wait at the New York bar for at least 30 minutes.

30 rue Pierre-Lescot, 1st arr. ☎ **01-42-36-70-13.** Reservations recommended for dinner. Main courses 75–140F (11.40–21.35€, $10.95–$20.30); fixed-price menu 140F (21.30€, $20.30). AE, MC, V. Daily noon–12:30am. Métro: Etienne-Marcel.

La Fermette du Sud-Ouest ★ SOUTHWESTERN FRENCH   In the heart of one of Paris's most ancient neighborhoods, a stone's throw from Ste-Eustache church, this restaurant occupies the site of a 1500s convent. After the Revolution, the convent was converted into a coaching inn that preserved the original stonework and massive beams. La Fermette prepares rich, savory stews and confits celebrating agrarian France, serving them on the ground floor and on a mezzanine resembling a medieval choir loft. Menu items include an age-old but ever-popular magret of duckling with flap mushrooms, *andouillette* (chitterling sausages), and a sometimes startling array of *cochonailles* (pork products and by-products) you probably need to be French to appreciate. Cassoulet and *pot-au-feu* (beef simmered with vegetables) are enduring specialties.

31 rue Coquillière, 1st arr. ℂ **01-42-36-73-55.** Reservations recommended. Main courses 85–130F (12.90–19.75€, $12.35–$18.85); fixed-price menus (at lunch and before 9pm at dinner) 120–145F (18.25–22.05€, $17.40–$21.05). MC, V. Mon–Sat noon–2pm and 7:30–10:00pm. Métro: Les Halles.

La Poule au Pot FRENCH (TRADITIONAL)/LATE NIGHT This bistro welcomes late-night carousers and show-biz personalities looking for a meal after a performance. (Past aficionados have included the Rolling Stones, Prince, and Johnny Hallyday.) The decor is authentically Art Deco, the ambience nurturing. The time-tested and savory menu items include a salad of warm goat cheese on toast, onion soup, pan-fried stingray with capers, burgundy-style snails, country pâté on a bed of onion marmalade, and a succulent version of the restaurant's namesake, chicken in a pot with slices of pâté and fresh vegetables (in summer, it can be served cold, on a bed of lettuce, with vinaigrette sauce).

9 rue Vauvilliers, 1st arr. ℂ **01-42-36-32-96.** Reservations recommended. Main courses 120–150F (18.25–22.80€, $17.40–$21.75); fixed-price menu 180F (27.35€, $26.10). MC, V. Tues–Sun 5pm–5am. Métro: Louvre or Les Halles.

La Rose de France ⭐ *(Value* FRENCH (TRADITIONAL) At this restaurant on Ile de la Cité near Notre-Dame, around the corner from the Pont Neuf, you'll dine with a crowd of young Parisians who know they can expect a good meal at reasonable prices. Founded more than 30 years ago by its present owner, M. Cointepas, it can be relied on for fresh food served in a friendly atmosphere. In warm weather, the sidewalk tables overlooking the Palais de Justice are most popular. Main dishes include sweetbreads, veal chop flambéed with Calvados and served with apples, beef filet en croûte, and lamb chops seasoned with Provençal herbs and served with gratin of potatoes. For dessert, try the fruit tart of the day or the sorbet of the month.

24 place Dauphine, 1st arr. ℂ **01-43-54-10-12.** Reservations recommended. Main courses 100–110F (15.20–16.70€, $14.50–$15.95); *menu du jour* 140F (21.30€, $20.30) without wine, 180F (27.35€, $26.10) with wine. AE, V. Mon–Fri noon–2pm and 7–10pm. Closed last 3 weeks in Aug and 15 days at end of Dec. Métro: Cité or Pont Neuf.

La Tour de Monthléry (Chez Denise) FRENCH (TRADITIONAL)/LATE NIGHT This restaurant is both workaday and stylish—no small feat considering its gregarious owner, Denise Bénariac, has maintained her reign here for more than 30 years. Amid a decor that has changed little since 1900 (note the long nickel-plated bar near the entrance), you can order hearty, unfussy cuisine. The food tastes best late after a long night of carousing. Menu items include grilled pig's trotters, mutton stew, steak with peppercorns, stuffed cabbage, *pot-au-feu,* and a golden-velvety pâté of chicken livers. Wine goes with this kind of food beautifully, and the restaurant complies by recommending several worthy but unpretentious vintages.

5 rue des Prouvaires, 1st arr. ℂ **01-42-36-21-82.** Main courses 95–130F (14.45–19.75€, $13.80–$18.85). V. Open continuously Mon 7am–Sat 7am. Métro: Louvre or Les Halles.

Lescure ⭐ *(Finds* FRENCH (TRADITIONAL) This animated and appealing minibistro is a major find—one of the few reasonably priced restaurants near place de la Concorde. You'll get a lot for your franc. The tables on the sidewalk are tiny, and there isn't much room inside, but what this place does have is

Jugglers, dancers and an assortment of acrobats fill the street.

She shoots you a wide-eyed look as a seven-foot cartoon character approaches.

What brought you here was wanting the kids

to see something magical while they still believed in magic.

America Online Keyword: Travel

With 700 airlines, 50,000 hotels and over 5,000 cruise and vaca-

tion getaways, you can now go places you've always dreamed of.

Travelocity.com
A Sabre Company
Go Virtually Anywhere.

"WORLD'S LEADING TRAVEL WEB SITE. 5 YEARS IN A ROW" WORLD TRAVEL AWARDS

I HAVE TO CALL THE TRAVEL AGENCY AGAIN. DARN, OUT TO LUNCH. NOW I HAVE TO CALL THE AIRLINE. I HATE CALLING THE AIRLINES. I GOT PUT ON HOLD AGAIN. "INSTRUMENTAL TOP-40" ... LOVELY. I HATE GETTING PUT ON HOLD. TICKET PRICES ARE ALL OVER THE MAP. HOW DO I DIAL INTERNATIONALLY? OH SHOOT, FORGOT THE RENTAL CAR. I'M STILL ON HOLD. THIS MUSIC IS GIVING ME A HEADACHE. I WONDER IF SOMEONE ELSE HAS CHEAPER FLIGHTS. FORGET IT, CAN'T TAKE IT ANYMORE ... I'M HANGING UP.

YAHOO! TRAVEL
100% MUZAK-FREE

Booking your trip online at Yahoo! Travel is simple. You compare the best prices. You click. You go have fun. Tickets, hotels, rental cars, cruises & more. Sorry, no muzak.

YAHOO!
Travel
travel.yahoo.com

rustic charm. The kitchen is wide open, and the aroma of drying bay leaves, salami, and garlic pigtails hanging from the ceiling fills the room. Expect *cuisine bourgeoise*—nothing innovative, just substantial hearty fare. Perhaps begin with *pâté en croûte* (pâté in puff pastry). Main-course house specialties include *confit de canard* (duckling), beef bourguignonne, and cabbage stuffed with salmon. The chef's fruit tarts are a favorite dessert. In autumn and winter, expect a savory repertoire of game dishes like venison and pheasant.

7 rue de Mondovi, 1st arr. ✆ **01-42-60-18-91.** Reservations not accepted. Main courses 50–90F (7.60–13.70€, $7.25–$13.05); 4-course fixed-price menu 115F (17.50€, $16.70). MC, V. Mon–Fri noon–2:15pm and 7–10:30pm. Closed 3 weeks in Aug. Métro: Concorde.

2ND ARRONDISSEMENT
MODERATE
Chez Georges FRENCH (TRADITIONAL)   This bistro is something of a local landmark, opened in 1964 near La Bourse (stock exchange) and run by three generations of the same family. Naturally, at lunch it's packed with stock-exchange members. The owners serve what they call *la cuisine bourgeoise* (comfort food). Waiters bring around bowls of appetizers, like celery rémoulade, to get you started. You can follow with sweetbreads with morels, duck breast with cêpe mushrooms, classic cassoulet, or *pot-au-feu*. A delight is sole filet with a sauce made from Pouilly wine and crème fraîche. Beaujolais goes great with this hearty food.

1 rue du Mail, 2nd arr. ✆ **01-42-60-07-11.** Reservations required. Main courses 130–160F (19.75–24.30€, $18.85–$23.20). AE, MC, V. Mon–Sat noon–2:15pm and 7–9:45pm. Closed 3 weeks in Aug. Métro: Bourse.

Le Vaudeville FRENCH (TRADITIONAL)/LATE NIGHT   Adjacent to La Bourse (stock exchange), this bistro retains its marble walls and Art-Deco carvings from 1918. In summer, tables dot a terrace amid banks of geraniums. The place is boisterous and informal, often welcoming groups of six or eight diners at a time. A bar near the entrance provides a perch if your reservation is delayed. The bountiful roster of platters includes snails in garlic butter, shellfish, smoked salmon, sauerkraut, and grilled meats. Three dishes reign as enduring favorites: fresh grilled codfish with mashed potatoes and truffle juice, fresh escalope of warm foie gras with grapes, and *tête du veaux* (veal's head). The main value is the fixed-price menu.

29 rue Vivienne, 2nd arr. ✆ **01-40-20-04-62.** Reservations recommended in the evenings. Main courses 90–190F (13.70–28.90€, $13.05–$27.55); fixed-price menu 138F (21€, $20) at lunch, 189F (28.75€, $27.40) at dinner. AE, DC, MC, V. Daily noon–3pm and 7pm–1am. Métro: Bourse.

INEXPENSIVE
Au Clair de Lune ALGERIAN/FRENCH (TRADITIONAL)   This is a pocket of a long-gone French colonial ambition. This neighborhood staple has flourished in the heart of Paris's wholesale garment district since the 1930s, when Algeria was a distinct part of the French-speaking world. Today you'll dine in a long narrow room whose walls are hung with colorful Berber carpets and whose patrons are likely to include shop workers from the nearby wholesale clothiers. On the menu is always the Algerian staple of couscous, as well as an array of oft-changing daily specials such as veal stew, shoulder or rack of lamb, grilled fish, and roast chicken. The portions are so large you should take along a ravenous appetite. The wines are from throughout France and North Africa.

13 rue Française, 2nd arr. ✆ **01-42-33-59-10.** Main courses 58–80F (8.80–12.15€, $8.40–$11.60); fixed-price menu 70F (10.65€, $10.15). MC, V. Daily noon–2:30pm and 7:30–11pm. Métro: Etienne-Marcel or Les Halles.

Aux Lyonnais ✹✹ FRENCH (TRADITIONAL)/LYONNAIS A LYON LE COCHON EST ROI! proclaims the sign. Pig may be king at this fin-de-siècle bistro (with walls molded with roses and garlands, brass globe lamps, potted palms, and etched glass), just behind La Bourse, but the competent kitchen staff does everything well. After a meal here, you'll know why Lyon is called the gastro-nomic capital of France. Everything is washed down with Beaujolais. Launch your repast with one of the large Lyonnais sausages, though a favorite opener remains a chicory salad with bacon and slices of hot sausages. Poached eggs in red-wine sauce and grilled pig's feet still appear on the menu. Pike dumplings are always prepared to perfection and served classically in white-butter sauce. The upside-down apple pie with crème fraîche is the dessert of choice.

32 rue St-Marc, 2nd arr. ℭ **01-42-96-65-04.** Reservations required. Main courses 90–200F (13.70–30.40€, $13.05–$29). AE, DC, MC, V. Mon–Sat 11:30am–3pm and 6:30–11:30pm. Métro: Bourse or Richelieu-Drouot.

Babylone Bis CREOLE/LATE NIGHT This place honors the French Caribbean island of Guadeloupe with culinary specialties like *accras* (fritters) of codfish and Creole *boudin* (blood sausage), which usually preface main courses like fricassée of shrimp or chicken and *colombo* (stew) of baby goat and pan-fried slices of shark-meat. Look for African masks, touches of zebra skin, and photos of the divas and celebs (Diana Ross, Stevie Wonder, Jesse Jackson, French sports stars, and fashion models) who've dined here. Don't think of coming before dark. After 2am or so, the focus shifts away from the hearty Caribbean soul food toward reggae, jazz, and cocktails.

34 rue Tiquetonne, 2nd arr. ℭ **01-42-33-48-35.** Main courses 120–150F (18.25–22.80€, $17.40–$21.75). V. Daily 8pm–8am. Métro: Etienne-Marcel or Sentier.

Clémentine FRENCH (TRADITIONAL) In an antique building adjacent to the Musée Grévin, this well-managed bistro serves time-honored food with an occasional individualistic flair. Among early-1900s panels, polished brass, and mirrors, you can order pepper steak, codfish steak studded with lard, oven-braised veal served in its own juices, and an unusual preparation of chicken breast with goat cheese. The *fondant au chocolat* (chocolate candy) seems to be an assiduously guarded, long-cherished family recipe. There's room for barely 25 diners, so advance reservations are important.

5 rue St-Marc, 2nd arr. ℭ **01-40-41-05-65.** Reservations required. Main courses 95F (14.45€, $13.83); fixed-price menu 155F (23.55€, $22.53). AE, MC, V. Mon–Fri noon–2pm and 8–10:30pm. Métro: Bourse or Grands Boulevards.

3RD ARRONDISSEMENT
EXPENSIVE

L'Ami Louis ✹ FRENCH (TRADITIONAL) L'Ami Louis is in one of cen-tral Paris's least fashionable neighborhoods, far removed from the part of the Marais that has become chic, and its facade has seen better days. It was one of Paris's most famous brasseries in the 1930s, thanks to its excellent food served in copious portions and its old-fashioned decor. Its traditions are fervently main-tained today. Amid a "brown gravy" decor (the walls retain a smoky patina), dishes like roasted suckling lamb, pheasant, venison, confit of duckling, and endless slices of foie gras may commune on your marble-topped table. Though some whisper that the ingredients aren't as select as they were in the restaurant's heyday, its sauces are as thick as they were between the wars. Don't save room for dessert, which isn't very good.

32 rue du Vertbois, 3rd arr. ☎ **01-48-87-77-48**. Reservations required far in advance. Main courses 250–350F (38–53.20€, $36.25–$50.75). MC, V. Wed–Sun noon–2pm and 8–11pm. Closed July 19–Aug 25. Métro: Temple.

INEXPENSIVE

Au Bascou ☆ *Finds* BASQUE   The succulent cuisine of France's "deep south-west" is the specialty within this restaurant, where art objects and oil paintings celebrate the beauty of the region, and hanging clusters of pimentos add spice to the air. This restaurant serves Basque food as good as it gets. For a ray of sunshine in your life, try the *piperade basquaise*, a spicy omelet loaded with peppers and onions; pimentos stuffed with a purée of codfish; and an *axoa* of veal (shoulder of calf served with a pimento-and-pepper-based green sauce). Because all starters are priced at 55F (8.35€, $8.05), and all desserts at 40F (6.10€, $5.80), a three-course meal at this place, without wine, sells for 180F (27.35€, $26.10).

38 rue Réaumur, 3rd arr. ☎ **01-42-72-69-25**. Reservations recommended. All main courses 85F (12.90€, $12.35). AE, DC, MC, V. Tues–Fri noon–3pm, Mon–Sat 8–11pm. Closed 1 week in Aug. Métro: Arts-et-Métiers.

Chez Janou PROVENÇAL   On one of the narrow 17th-century streets behind place des Vosges, this unpretentious bistro operates from a pair of cramped but cozy dining rooms filled with memorabilia from Provence. The service is brusque and sometimes hectic. The food here is like a visit to your favorite French grandmother's kitchen where she'll regale you with her time-tested dishes like large shrimp with pastis sauce, *brouillade des pleurotes* (baked eggs with oyster mushrooms), *velouté* of frogs' legs, fondue of ratatouille, gratin of mussels, and a simple but savory *daube provençale*, sometimes compared to pot roast. There's a covered terrace.

2 rue Roger-Verlomme, 3rd arr. ☎ **01-42-72-28-41**. Reservations recommended. Main courses 68–92F (10.35–14.05€, $9.85–$13.35). No credit cards. Daily noon–3pm and 7:30pm–midnight. Métro: Chemin-Vert.

L'Ambassade d'Auvergne ☆ AUVERGNAT/FRENCH (TRADITIONAL)   You enter this rustic tavern through a busy bar with heavy oak beams, hanging hams, and ceramic plates. This favorite showcases the culinary generosity of France's most isolated region, the Auvergne, whose pork products are widely celebrated. The best examples are a chicory salad with apples and pieces of country ham; pork braised with cabbage, turnips, and white beans; grilled tripe sausages with mashed potatoes and cantal cheese (a strong, hard cheese) with garlic; and pork jowls with green lentils. The cholesterol is intense, but devotees love this type of food. Non-pork specialties are pan-fried duck liver with gingerbread, perch filets steamed in verbena tea, and roasted rack of lamb with wild mushrooms. Dessert might be a poached pear with crispy almonds and caramel sauce or a wine-flavored sorbet.

22 rue de Grenier St-Lazare, 3rd arr. ☎ **01-42-782-31-22**. Reservations recommended. Main courses 86–120F (13.05–18.25€, $12.45–$17.40); fixed-price menu 170F (25.85€, $24.65). AE, MC, V. Daily noon–2pm and 7:30–11pm. Closed 2 weeks in Aug. Métro: Rambuteau.

Marais-Cage FRENCH CARIBBEAN   This restaurant contains three separate dining rooms, each covered with blue fabric, and each with furniture that evokes a Caribbean reinvention of the Napoleonic style. The culinary venue was inspired by the French-speaking islands of the Caribbean, particularly Martinique and Guadeloupe. All the dishes that were beloved by the Empress Josephine when she lived on Martinique have emigrated to Paris to dazzle you with their spice and flair. We're talking blood sausage, stuffed crabs, and accras

---

(Moments Taking an Ice Cream Break at Berthillon

A landmark on Ile St-Louis after 3-dozen years in business, the *salon de thé* **Berthillon** ✮✮✮, 31 rue St-Louis-en-l'Ile, 4th arr. (ⓒ **01-43-54-31-61;** Métro: Pont Marie), offers mousse, rhubarb, melon, kumquat, black currant, or any exotic fresh fruit in season—more than 50 flavors to choose from and nothing artificial. Parisians have flocked to this place in such numbers that gendarmes have been called out to direct the traffic of ice cream aficionados. It's open Wednesday to Sunday from 10am to 8pm.

---

de morue (codfish fritters). You'll think some Martinique mama is in that kitchen preparing succulent curried versions of chicken and lamb curries. A particularly appealing dessert is Caribbean crêpes, stuffed with pineapple and whipped cream, and flambéed in rum.

8 rue de Beauce, 3rd arr. ⓒ **01-48-87-31-20.** Reservations recommended. Main courses 85F (12.90€, $12.35) each; fixed-price menus 155–185F (23.55–28.10€, $22.50–$26.85). AE, DC, MC, V. Mon–Sat noon–2pm and 7–10pm. Métro: République or Filles-du-Calvaire.

4TH ARRONDISSEMENT
VERY EXPENSIVE
L'Ambroisie ✮✮✮ FRENCH (MODERN & TRADITIONAL)   One of Paris's most talented chefs, Bernard Pacaud draws world attention with his vivid flavors and expert culinary skill. Expect perfection at this early–17th century town house in Le Marais, with two high-ceilinged salons whose decor vaguely recalls an Italian palazzo. In summer, there's outdoor seating as well. Pacaud's tables are nearly always filled with satisfied diners who come back again and again to see where his imagination will take him next. The dishes change seasonally and may include fricassée of Breton lobster with a civet/red-wine sauce, served with a purée of peas; turbot filet braised with celery, served with a julienne of black truffles; or one of our favorite dishes in all Paris, *poulard de Bresse demi-deuil homage à la Mère Brazier* (chicken roasted with black truffles and truffled vegetables in a style invented by a Lyonnais matron after World War II). An award-winning dessert is the *tarte fine sablée* served with bitter chocolate and vanilla-flavored ice cream.

9 place des Vosges, 4th arr. ⓒ **01-42-78-51-45.** Reservations required far in advance. Main courses 370–610F (56.25–92.70€, $53.65–$88.45). AE, MC, V. Tues–Sat noon–1:30pm and 8–9:30pm. Métro: St-Paul or Chèmin Vert.

EXPENSIVE
Benoit ✮ FRENCH (TRADITIONAL)   There's something awesomely traditional and weighty about this old-fashioned historical monument, which has served every mayor of Paris since it was founded in 1912 by the grandfather of the present owner. He's one of the last *bistrotiers* who purchases Beaujolais in casks, and bottles it in his own cellars. The setting is scarlet and theatrical, and the service can be either intensely attentive or arrogant, depending on a delicate chemistry that only longtime fans of this place really understand. Prices are higher, a lot higher, than you'd expect for bistro fare, but clients just keep coming back for more. Cuisine is rich, full of flavor, and satisfying, based on time-tested classics that rarely get modernized. Traditional crowd-pleasers include salmon that's both marinated and smoked; snails served in their shell with garlic butter; and cassoulet, a white bean and pork dish from France's

southwest that's absolutely fabulous on a cold day. A dessert that gets raved about is a *Sainte-Eve,* composed of pears layered with macaroon-flavored cream enclosed in puff pastry.

20 rue St Martin, 4th arr. ℂ **01-42-72-25-76**. Reservations required. Main courses 180–250F (27.35–38€, $26.10–$36.25); fixed-price lunch 200F (30.40€, $29). AE. Daily noon–2pm and 8–10pm. Metro: Châtelet or Hôtel-de-Ville.

MODERATE

Bofinger ⍟ ALSATIAN/FRENCH (MODERN & TRADITIONAL) Opened in the 1860s, Bofinger is the oldest Alsatian brasserie in town and certainly one of the best. It's a Belle-Époque dining palace, resplendent with shiny brass and stained glass. Weather permitting, you can dine on an outdoor terrace. Affiliated today with La Coupole, Julien, and Brasserie Flo, the restaurant has updated its menu, retaining only the most popular of its traditional dishes, like sauerkraut and a well-prepared *sole meunière.* Recent additions have included roasted leg of lamb with a fondant of artichoke hearts and a purée of parsley, grilled turbot with a *brandade* of fennel, and stingray filet with chives and burnt-butter sauce. Shellfish, including an abundance of fresh oysters and lobster, is almost always available in season.

5–7 rue de la Bastille, 4th arr. ℂ **01-42-72-87-82**. Reservations recommended. Main courses 90–160F (13.70–24.30€, $13.05–$23.20). AE, DC, MC, V. Mon–Fri noon–3pm and 6:30pm–1am; Sat–Sun noon–1am. Métro: Bastille.

Georges ⍟ INTERNATIONAL With the establishment of this restaurant, the Centre Pompidou once again thrusts itself into the public spotlight as the kind of place that artsy Paris is talking about. The venue inhabits a very large space on the top floor of Paris' most comprehensive arts complex, with views through bay windows over most of the city. The decor is minimalist and postmodern, incorporating lots of brushed aluminum and stainless steel. Tables are made from sandblasted glass, lit from below, and accessorized with hyper-modern cutlery. Menu items are mostly continental, with occasional hints of Asia. Some combinations come as a surprise—macaroni with lobster, for example. Others come as exotic, including roasted ostrich steak. Other than these original dishes, some of the best items on the menu are the roasted scallops given added zest by lemon butter and a tuna steak spiced up with coriander. There's also a luscious version of *sole meunière* featured (may that dish never go out of style). To access the place, head for the exterior elevator just to the left of the Pompidou Center's main entrance, and know in advance that unless you verify your reservation to the security guard, they might not let you up.

On the uppermost (6th) floor of the Centre Georges Pompidou, 19 rue Beaubourg, 4th arr. ℂ **01-44-78-47-99**. Reservations imperative for dinner, strongly recommended for lunch. Main courses 45–180F (6.85–27.35€, $6.55–$26.10). AE, DC, MC, V. Wed–Mon noon–6pm and 7pm–2am. Métro: Les Halles.

Isama JAPANESE Dining here is guaranteed to evoke a sense of cultural dislocation—the staff is mostly from Japan, and few speak much French or English. That, however, is part of the place's allure for its loyal customers, many of whom work in the arts. The staff is quick to tell you that only authentic Japanese versions of sushi and sashimi are served, with absolutely none of what they call California/Japanese cuisine. Begin a meal with miso soup or some pickled vegetables, as a prelude for the wide array of fish (tuna, salmon, white-fish, fluke, snapper, bluefish, oysters, clams, shrimp, and more) that forms this restaurant's backbone. Lingering isn't encouraged.

4 quai d'Orléans, 4th arr. ✆ **01-40-46-06-97.** Reservations recommended. Sushi and sashimi 10–35F (1.50–5.30€, $1.45–$5.10) per piece; meals 75–225F (11.40–34.20€, $10.90–$32.65), depending on the fish and how many pieces ordered. Tues–Sat noon–2pm and 7:30–10pm. Métro: Pont Marie.

Le Coconnas ⚜ FRENCH (MODERN & TRADITIONAL)   Chef Clause Terrail (owner of La Tour d'Argent) serves superb cuisine in this restaurant named after the legendary rake whose peccadillos scandalized place des Vosges. The restaurant features a Louis XIII decor of high-backed chairs and elegantly rustic accessories. Menu items change frequently but present a cost-conscious alternative to the grand cuisine served by other restaurants in the chain. Look for foie gras maison, baked goat's cheese dunked in white wine, roasted half-duckling with mashed potatoes, coq au vin, *la poule au pot* (stewed chicken), and desserts like *crème brûlée* with honey. None of these items sets off fireworks, but the ingredients are fresh and harmonious and the prices fair for the quality.

2 bis place des Vosges, 4th arr. ✆ **01-42-78-58-16.** Reservations required. Main dishes 90–120F (13.70–18.25€, $13.05–$17.40); fixed-price menu 140F (21.30€, $20.30). AE, DC, MC, V. Wed–Sun noon–2:30pm and 7:30–10:30pm. Métro: Bastille or St-Paul.

Le Vieux Bistro ⚜ *Finds* FRENCH (TRADITIONAL)   This is one of the last old-fashioned bistros still left in the heart of Paris. Few other restaurants offer so close-up, and so forbidding, a view of the massive walls of Paris's largest cathedral, visible through lacy curtains from the windows of the front dining room. To reach it, you'll bypass a dozen souvenir stands, then settle into one of the two old-time dining rooms for a flavorful meal of French staples. The cuisine evokes the kind you're served along a little back-road deep in the heart of France, a bit heavy perhaps, but evocative of food of long ago. You can order snails with garlic butter, filet mignon roasted in a bag and served with marrow sauce, veal filets, and a classic dessert, *tarte tatin* (studded with apples and sugar, drenched with Calvados, and capped with fresh cream).

14 rue du Cloître-Notre-Dame, 4th arr. ✆ **01-43-54-18-95.** Main courses 90–330F (13.70–50.15€, $13.05–$47.85). MC, V. Daily noon–2pm and 7:30–11pm. Métro: Cité.

INEXPENSIVE

Aquarius ⚜⚜ VEGETARIAN   In a 17th-century building whose original stonework forms part of the earthy decor, this is one of the best-known vegetarian restaurants in Le Marais. The owners serve only a limited array of (strictly organic) wine, and smoking is expressly forbidden. Their flavorful meals are healthfully prepared. Choose from an array of soups and salads; a galette of wheat served with crudités and mushroom tarts; or a country plate composed of fried mushrooms and potatoes, garlic, and goat cheese, served with a salad.

54 rue Ste-Croix-de-la-Bretonnerie, 4th arr. ✆ **01-48-87-48-71.** Main courses 45–64F (6.85–9.75€, $6.55–$9.30); fixed-price menu 95F (14.45€, $13.85). MC, V. Mon–Sat noon–10:15pm. Métro: Hôtel de Ville. RER: Châtelet–Les Halles.

Au Gourmet de l'Ile ⚜ *Value* FRENCH (TRADITIONAL)   Locals swear by the cuisine at Au Gourmet de l'Ile, whose fixed-price meals are among Paris's best bargains. The setting is beautiful, with a beamed ceiling, walls from the 1400s, and candlelit tables. In the window is a sign emblazoned with AAAAA, which, roughly translated, stands for the Amiable Association of Amateurs of the Authentic Andouillette. These chitterling sausages are soul food to the French. Popular and tasty too are *la charbonnée de l'Ile*, a savory pork with onions, and stuffed mussels in shallot butter. The fixed-price menu includes a choice of 15 appetizers, 15 main courses, salad or cheese, and 15 desserts.

42 rue St-Louis-en-l'Ile, 4th arr. ℂ **01-43-26-79-27.** Reservations required. Main courses 75–120F (11.40–18.25€, $10.90–$17.40); fixed-price menus 155–195F (23.55–29.65€, $22.50–$28.30). AE, MC, V. Wed–Sun noon–2pm and daily 7–10:30pm. Métro: Pont Marie.

Brasserie de l'Ile St-Louis ALSATIAN/FRENCH (TRADITIONAL)   This is the kind of retro-chic brasserie where the likes of Brigitte Bardot, Elizabeth Taylor, Grace Jones, and John Frankenheimer have scheduled informal meals and rendezvous. Little about the place's patina and paneled decor has changed since the 1880s, giving it an aura modern competitors can only try to imitate. The menu is conservative and well-prepared, including an always-popular version of Alsatian sauerkraut, cassoulet in the old-fashioned style of Toulouse, calf's liver, and a succulent *jarret* of pork with warm apple marmalade.

55 quai de Bourbon, 4th arr. ℂ **01-43-54-02-59.** Main courses 85–150F (12.90–22.80€, $12.35–$21.75). MC, V. Thurs–Tues noon–midnight. Closed Aug. Métro: Pont Marie or Cité.

Café la Parisienne *(Kids* FRENCH (MODERN)   Whimsical and often chaotic, this appealing restaurant shares something of the avant-garde aesthetic of its neighbor, the Centre Pompidou, and was renovated in mid-1999. It was named after the bread rations that were issued here during World War II and has an enviable location beside the medieval St-Merri church and a spinning, spitting, and animatedly bobbing fountain by Jean Tinguely and Niki de Saint-Phalle. In fair weather, tables and chairs overlook the charming fountain. You might begin with beef (or shark!) carpaccio with green salad, then follow with noisettes of lamb flavored with whiskey and fresh thyme or fricassée of poultry with morels. Finish with *glace Berthillon*, Paris's best ice cream. There's also a beautiful terrace where you can enjoy a breathtaking view.

10 rue Brise-Miche, 4th arr. ℂ **01-42-78-44-11.** Reservations recommended. Main courses 60–85F (9.10–12.90€, $8.70–$12.35). MC, V. Apr–Sept daily 8am–midnight (last order); Oct–Mar daily 10am–11pm (last order). Métro: Rambuteau, Hôtel de Ville, or Châtelet–Les Halles.

Chez Jo Goldenberg *(Finds* CENTRAL EUROPEAN/JEWISH   This is the best-known restaurant on the "Street of the Rose Bushes." Albert Goldenberg, the doyen of Jewish restaurateurs in Paris, long ago moved to choicer surroundings (69 av. de Wagram, 17e), but his brother, Joseph, has remained here. Dining is on two levels, one for non-smokers. Look for the collection of samovars, the white fantail pigeon in a wicker cage, and the interesting paintings. The *carpe farcie* (stuffed carp) is a preferred selection, but the beef goulash is also good. We like the eggplant moussaka and the pastrami. The menu also offers Israeli wines, but M. Goldenberg admits they're not as good as French wine. Live Yiddish music is presented every night beginning at 9pm, and special menus are presented during Jewish holidays—reservations are a must.

7 rue des Rosiers, 4th arr. ℂ **01-48-87-20-16.** Reservations required. Main courses 75–110F (11.40–16.70€, $10.95–$15.95). AE, DC, MC, V. Daily noon–1am. Métro: St. Paul.

Trumilou *(France)* FRENCH (TRADITIONAL)   This is one of the most popular of the restaurants surrounding Paris's Hôtel de Ville and has welcomed most of France's politicians, including George Pompidou, who came here frequently before he was elected president. ("As soon as they become president, they opt for grander restaurants," say the good-natured owners, the Drumonds.) The countrified decor includes a collection of farm implements and family memorabilia, amid a clutch of tables. Most diners remain on the street level, though additional seating is in the cellar. The menu rarely changes and doesn't need to, with

> ### *Moments*   A Parisian Pique-nique
>
> One of the best ways to save money and also to participate in Parisian life is to picnic. Go to a *fromagerie* for some cheese; to a *boulangerie* for a baguette or two; to a *charcuterie* for some pâté, sausage, or salad; and to a *pâtisserie* for some luscious pastries. Add a friendly bottle of Côtes du Rhone—it usually goes well with picnics—and you'll have the makings of a delightful and typically French meal you can take to the nearest park or along the banks of the Seine. Pretend you're in Manet's *Déjeuner sur l'herbe* and enjoy! (Don't forget the corkscrew!)
>
> The best spot for a picnic is a cozy nook along one of your favorite views of the **Seine.** Otherwise the best place for picnics (also boating, walks, and jogging) is the **Bois de Boulogne** (Métro: Porte Maillot), covering some 2,000 acres at the western edge of Paris. At night it becomes a twilight zone of sex and drugs, but it's lovely during the day. (See chapter 7 for more on the Bois de Boulogne.) Even though they're in a state of restoration, the splendid gardens of **Versailles** offer another fine picnic spot. You can also enjoy your meal on the grass on a day trip to the cathedral city of **Chartres.** Go to a bucolic spot, Parc André Gagon, only a 5-minute walk northwest of the fabled cathedral.

chicken Provençal, sweetbreads "in the style of our grandmother," duckling with plums, stuffed cabbage, and *blanquette de veau* (veal in white sauce).

84 quai de l'Hôtel-de-Ville, 4th arr. (℃) **01-42-77-63-98.** Reservations recommended Sat–Sun. Main courses 75–100F (11.40–15.20€, $10.95–$14.50); fixed-price menu 98F (14.90€, $14.20). MC, V. Daily noon–3pm and 7–11pm. Métro: Hôtel de Ville.

9TH ARRONDISSEMENT

Like its counterparts from Hong Kong to Reykjavík, the **Hard Rock Cafe** *(Kids)*, 14 bd. Montmartre, 9th (℃ **01-53-24-60-00;** Métro: Grand Boulevards or Richelieu-Drouot), offers musical memorabilia as well as musical selections from 35 years of rock. The crowd appreciates the juicy steaks, hamburgers, veggie burgers, salads, and heaping platters of informal French-inspired food. It's open daily from 11:30am to 2am.

EXPENSIVE

Chez Jean *(★)* FRENCH (MODERN & TRADITIONAL)   The crowd is young, the food is good, and the vintage brassiere aura of the 1950s makes you think that the Parisian expat novelist, James Baldwin, will arrive for his table at any minute. There has been a brasserie of some sort on this site since around 1900. Amid well-oiled pinewood panels and carefully polished copper, you can choose from some of grandmother's favorites as well as more modern dishes like risotto with lobster and squid ink, scallops with endive fricassée, lamb roasted with basil, "nougat" of oxtails with balsamic vinaigrette, and pavé of duckling with honey sauce and exotic mushroom fricassée. The changing menu attracts fans who consider the food a lot more sophisticated than that served at other brasseries (the chefs gained their experience in upscale restaurants).

8 rue St-Lazare, 9th arr. ℭ **01-48-78-62-73.** Reservations recommended far in advance. Main courses 130–245F (19.75–37.25€, $18.85–$35.55); fixed-price menu 195F (29.65€, $28.30). MC, V. Mon–Fri noon–2:30pm and 7–11pm; Sat–Sun 7–11pm. Métro: Notre-Dame de Lorette, Opéra, or Cadet.

MODERATE

Au Petit Riche LOIRE VALLEY (ANJOU)   No, that's not Flaubert or Balzac walking through the door. But should they miraculously come back, the decor of old Paris with the original gas lamps and time-mellowed paneling would make them feel right at home. When it opened in 1865, this bistro was the food outlet for the Café Riche next door; today it offers yesterday's grandeur and simple well-prepared food. You'll be ushered to one of five areas crafted for maximum intimacy, with red velour banquettes, ceilings painted with allegorical themes, and accents of brass and frosted glass. The wine list favors Loire Valley vintages that go well with such dishes as *rillettes* and *rillons* (potted fish or meat, especially pork) in Vouvray wine aspic, poached fish with buttery white-wine sauce, old-fashioned blanquette of chicken, and seasonal game dishes like civet of rabbit.

25 rue Le Peletier, 9th arr. ℭ **01-47-70-68-68.** Reservations recommended. Main courses 88–160F (13.40–24.30€, $12.75–$23.20); fixed-price menus 165F (25.15€, $23.95) at lunch, 140–180F (21.35–27.35€, $20.30–$26.10) at dinner. AE, DC, MC, V. Mon–Sat noon–2:15pm and 7pm–midnight. Métro: Le Peletier or Richelieu-Drouot.

Wally Le Saharien ALGERIAN   Head to this dining room—lined with desert photos and tribal artifacts crafted from ceramics, wood, and weavings—for an insight into the spicy, slow-cooked cuisine that fueled the colonial expansion of France into North Africa. The fixed-price dinner menu begins with a trio of starters: a spicy soup, stuffed and grilled sardines, and a savory *pastilla* of pigeon in puff pastry. This can be followed by any of several kinds of couscous or a *méchouia* (slow-cooked tart) of lamb dusted with an optional coating of sugar, according to your taste. *Merguez*, the cumin-laden spicy sausage of the North African world, factors importantly into any meal, as does homemade (usually honey-infused) pastries. End your meal with traditional mint-flavored tea.

36 rue Rodier, 9th arr. ℭ **01-42-85-51-90.** Reservations recommended. À-la-carte main courses (available only at lunch) 85–138F (12.90–21.05€, $12.35–$20); fixed-price dinner 250F (38€, $36.25). MC, V. Tues–Sat noon–2pm; Mon–Sat 7–10pm. Métro: Anvers.

INEXPENSIVE

Chartier FRENCH (TRADITIONAL)   Opened in 1896, this unpretentious fin-de-siècle restaurant, long a budget favorite, is now an official monument featuring a whimsical mural with trees, a flowering staircase, and an early depiction of an airplane; it was painted in 1929 by a penniless artist who executed his work in exchange for food. The menu follows brasserie-style traditions, including items you might not dare to eat—boiled veal's head, tripe, tongue, sweetbreads, lamb's brains, chitterling sausages—as well as some old-time tempters. The waiter will steer you through dishes like *boeuf bourguignonne, pot-au-feu* (a bestseller, combining beef, turnips, cabbage, and carrots), pavé of rump steak, and at least five kinds of fish. The prices are low, even for a three-course meal, a fact that as many as 320 diners appreciate at a time.

7 rue de faubourg Montmartre, 9th arr. ℭ **01-47-70-86-29.** Main courses 40–68F (6.10–10.35€, $5.80–$9.85). MC, V. Daily 11:30am–3pm and 6–10pm. Métro: Grands Boulevards or Rue Montmartre.

Le Grand Zinc FRENCH (TRADITIONAL)   The Paris of the 1880s lives on here. You make your way into the restaurant past baskets of *bélons* (brown-fleshed oysters) from Brittany, a year-round favorite. The specialties of the house are *coq au vin* (chicken in white wine) and old-fashioned savory staples like rack of lamb, rump steak, veal chops with morels, and even a simple form of Provençal bouillabaisse. Nothing ever changes—certainly not the time-tested recipes.

5 rue de faubourg Montmartre, 9th arr. ℂ **01-47-70-88-64.** Main courses 110–300F (16.70–45.60€, $15.95–$43.50); fixed-price menu 120F (18.25€, $17.40). AE, DC, MC, V. Mon–Sat noon–midnight. Closed August. Métro: Grands Boulevards.

10TH ARRONDISSEMENT
MODERATE

Brasserie Flo ✪ ALSATIAN   This remote restaurant is a bit hard to find, but once you arrive (after walking through passageway after passageway), you'll see that fin-de-siècle Paris lives on. The restaurant opened in 1860 and has changed its decor very little since. The house specialty is *la formidable choucroute* (a heaping mound of sauerkraut with boiled ham, bacon, and sausage) for two. The onion soup and *sole meunière* are always good, as is the warm foie gras and guinea hen with lentils. Look for the *plats du jour,* ranging from roast pigeon to veal fricassée with sorrel.

7 cour des Petites-Ecuries, 10th arr. ℂ **01-47-70-13-59.** Reservations recommended. Main courses 90–168F (13.70–25.55€, $13.05–$24.35); fixed-price menus 138–179F (21.05–27.20€, $20–$25.95) at lunch 189F (28.75€, $27.40) at dinner; fixed-price late-night supper (after 10pm) 142F (21.65€, $20.65). AE, DC, MC, V. Daily noon–3pm and 7pm–1:30am. Métro: Château d'Eau or Strasbourg–St-Denis.

La Grille ⓥⁿᵘᵉ FRENCH (TRADITIONAL)/SEAFOOD   Few other moderate restaurants are as hotly pursued by Parisians as this nine-table holdover from another age. For at least a century after the French Revolution, fishermen from coastal Dieppe used this place as a springboard for carousing and cabaret-watching after delivering their fish to Les Halles market. The holy grail at La Grille is an entire turbot prepared tableside with an emulsified white-butter sauce. If the turbot doesn't appeal to you, consider the seafood terrine, *boeuf bourguignonne,* or marinated sardine filets; the high-calorie, high-satisfaction desserts include chocolate mousse and vanilla custard. (Incidentally, the restaurant name derives not from a grill used for cooking but from the 200-year-old wrought-iron grills in front, classified as national treasures and among the best examples of their kind in Paris.)

80 rue du Faubourg-Poissonière, 10th arr. ℂ **01-47-70-89-73.** Reservations required. Main courses 100–170F (15.20–25.85€, $14.50–$24.65). AE, MC, V. Mon–Fri noon–2:30pm and 7:15–10pm. Métro: Poissonière.

INEXPENSIVE

Chez Michel BRETON   Adapting to the tastes and income level of its loyal crowd, this restaurant near the Gare du Nord serves generous portions of well-prepared Breton dishes. At least part of this food derives from the northwestern origins of owner/chef Thierry Breton. In a pair of dining rooms accented with exposed wood, you'll enjoy the fruits of the fields and seacoast, densely flavored and traditional; they include veal chops fried in butter and served with gratin of potatoes enriched with bits of calf's foot gelatin and codfish filets served on beds of tomatoes and onions and a tapenade of black olives. The appropriate conclusion to a meal is a snifter of Calvados, the apple-based brandy of the northern French coast.

10 rue de Belzunce, 10th arr. ℂ **01-44-53-06-20.** Reservations recommended. Fixed-price menu 185F (28.10€, $26.85); *menu dégustation* 350F (53.20€, $50.75). MC, V. Tues–Sat noon–2pm and 7pm–midnight. Métro: Gare du Nord.

Julien ✿ FRENCH (MODERN & TRADITIONAL) Julien offers an opportunity to dine in one of the most sumptuous Belle-Époque interiors in Paris. Of special interest are the murals representing the four seasons and the sometimes very fashionable crowd. The food is in the style of *cuisine bourgeoise,* but without the heavy sauces. The sumptuous starter courses include eggplant caviar and wild-mushroom salad. Among the main courses are Gascony cassoulet, sliced foie gras with lentils, fresh salmon with sorrel, and chateaubriand béarnaise. The wine list is extensive and reasonably priced.

16 rue du faubourg St-Denis, 10th arr. ☎ **01-47-70-12-06**. Reservations required. Main courses 90–150F (13.75–22.80€, $13.05–$21.75); fixed-price menu 189F (28.75€, $27.40). AE, DC, MC, V. Daily noon–3pm and 7pm–1:30am. Métro: Strasbourg–St-Denis.

Paris-Dakar SENEGALESE Named after the famous rally that carries vehicles across the world's toughest terrain, this restaurant celebrates the culinary traditions of France's former colonies in West Africa. After receiving a genuine welcome, you'll have the option of sampling such Senegalese dishes as *yassa* (chicken braised with limes and onions); *maffé* (beef fried with peanuts, onions, and spice); and the national dish, *thiepbkoudiene* (fish sautéed with rice, fresh vegetables, and fiery chiles). The lunch menu is attractively priced. If you're adventurous, ask for a glass of the palm wine, fermented from coconuts in a style common in West Africa.

95 rue du faubourg St-Martin, 10th arr. ☎ **01-42-08-16-64**. Reservations recommended. Main courses 73–99F (11.10–15.05€, $10.65–$14.35); fixed-price menus 59–179F (8.95–27.20€, $8.55–$25.95) at lunch, 129–179F (19.60–27.20€, $18.70–$25.95) at dinner. AE, MC, V. Tues–Sun noon–3pm and 7pm–2am. Métro: Gare de l'Est.

11TH ARRONDISSEMENT
EXPENSIVE
Blue Elephant ASIAN At this Paris branch of an international chain of stylish Thai restaurants, the decor artfully evokes the jungles of Southeast Asia, interspersed with Thai sculptures and paintings. The menu items are succulent, infused with lemongrass, curries, and the aromas that make Thai cuisine so distinctive. Examples are a salad made with *pomelo,* a Thai fruit that's larger and tarter than a grapefruit, studded with shrimp and herbs; salmon soufflé served in banana leaves; chicken in green-curry sauce; and grilled fish with passion fruit. Although most of the cuisine is Thai, there's a scattering of Szechuan and Indonesian dishes as well.

43 rue de la Roquette, 11th arr. ☎ **01-47-00-42-00**. Reservations recommended far in advance. Main courses 85–160F (12.90–24.30€, $12.35–$23.20); fixed-price dinner 285F (43.30€, $41.35). AE, DC, MC, V. Mon–Fri noon–2:30pm and 7pm–midnight; Sun noon–2:30pm and 7–11pm. Métro: Bastille.

MODERATE
À Sousceyrac FRENCH (TRADITIONAL) The name derives from a village in the Lotte region of southwestern France that has always been associated with rich cuisine, traditional values, and literature. *(Le Déjeuner de Sousceyrac* by Père Benoît was a best-selling ode to French nostalgia in the 1970s.) You can capture some of this feeling at this charmer whose decor and menu have changed very little since it was established in 1925. A writer from *Gourmet* magazine noted, "À Sousceyrac was undoubtedly intended to induce deep nostalgia in Parisians the day it opened; its southwestern-inflected menu practically reads like a roster of what Frenchmen like to call '*The Patrimony*'." Classic examples include slices of velvety foie gras; mousse of grouse; and roasted rabbit *à la royale,* cooked in a blend of red wine, a puréed medley of its innards,

and its own blood. Dishes like this absolutely demand accompaniment by a strong red wine, of which the restaurant lists many.

26 rue Faidherbe, 11th arr. ☎ 01-43-71-65-30. Reservations recommended. Main courses 120–165F (18.25–25.15€, $17.40–$23.95). DC, MC, V. Mon–Fri noon–2pm and Mon–Sat 7:30–9:45pm. Closed 1 week in Apr and all of Aug. Métro: Charonnes or Faidherbe.

Astier ★ *Finds* FRENCH (TRADITIONAL)   Nobody could accuse this place of being glamorous, understanding that well-prepared hearty food has its own allure. The mandatory set menu is a good value, with at least 10 choices for each of four courses. For some real down-home cookery, French style, order the roasted rabbit with mustard sauce, *racasse* (scorpionfish) with fresh spinach, or duckling breast with foie-gras cream sauce. There's also a superbly varied cheese platter and desserts like crème caramel and chocolate mousse.

44 rue Jean-Pierre-Timbaud, 11th arr. ☎ 01-43-57-16-35. Reservations recommended. Fixed-price menus 140–208F (21.35–31.60€, $20.30–$30.15). AE, DC, MC, V. Mon–Fri noon–2pm and 8–11pm. Métro: Oberkampf or Parmentier.

INEXPENSIVE

Le Manguier SENEGALESE   Many of the patrons who dine here don't know much about Senegalese cuisine, but thanks to a charming welcome and live music presenting African jazz at its most compelling, they tend to come back. The decor evokes a West African fishing village. You can order zesty fare like roast chicken marinated with lime and served with onions, smoked shark meat, and the national dish, *thiebkoudiene* (a delectable blend of fish, rice, and fresh vegetables). The medley is perked up with a selection of fiery sauces you apply yourself. The drinks of choice are beer, a rum-based cocktail (*Le Dakar*), and wine.

67 av. Parmentier, 11th arr. ☎ 01-48-07-03-27. Reservations recommended. Main courses 75–95F (11.40–14.45€, $10.95–$13.85). AE, MC, V. Mon–Fri noon–3pm; Mon–Sat 7pm–2am. Métro: Parmentier.

Mansouria MOROCCAN   One of Paris's most charming Moroccan restaurants occupies a much-restored building midway between place de la Bastille and place de la Nation. The minimalist decor combines futuristic architecture with bare white walls accented only with sets of antique doors and portals from the sub-Sahara. The menu items are artfully prepared. Look for six kinds of couscous, including versions with chicken, beef brochettes, or lamb, onions, and almonds. *Tagines* are succulent dishes of chicken or fish prepared with aromatic herbs and slow cooked in clay pots that are carried to your table.

11 rue Faidherbe, 11th arr. ☎ 01-43-71-00-16. Reservations recommended. Main courses 98–158F (14.90–24€, $14.20–$22.90); fixed-price menus 182–280F (27.65–42.55€, $26.45–$40.60). MC, V. Tues–Sat noon–2pm and 7:30–11pm; Mon 7:30–11pm. Métro: Faidherbe-Chaligny.

12TH ARRONDISSEMENT
EXPENSIVE

Au Trou Gascon ★★★ GASCONY   One of Paris's most acclaimed chefs, Alain Dutournier lures some of the most fashionable palates of Paris to this unchic location in the 12th arrondissement. He launched his cooking career in southwest France's Gascony region. His parents mortgaged their own inn to allow him to open this early-1900s bistro. At first he got little business, but word eventually spread of a savant in the kitchen who practiced authentic *cuisine moderne*. His wife, Nicole, is the welcoming hostess, and the wine steward has distinguished himself for his exciting cave containing several little-known wines along with a fabulous collection of Armagnacs. It's estimated the wine cellar has some 800 varieties. Start with fresh duck foie gras cooked in a terrine or Gascony cured ham cut from the bone. The best main courses include fresh tuna with braised cabbage, the best cassoulet in town, and chicken from the Chalosse region of Landes, which Dutournier roasts and serves in its own drippings.

40 rue Taine, 12th arr. ⓒ **01-43-44-34-26.** Reservations required far in advance. Main courses 145–165F (22.05–25.10€, $21.05–$23.95); fixed-price menu 200F (30.40€, $29) at lunch, 320F (48.65€, $46.40) at dinner. AE, DC, MC, V. Mon–Fri noon–2pm; Mon–Sat 7:30–10pm. Closed Aug. Métro: Daumesnil.

MODERATE

China Club ⓚ CANTONESE/CHINESE   Evoking 1930s Hong Kong, this favorite is still going strong, still laughing at upstart new Asian restaurants, and still serving some of the best Asian cuisine in Paris. It's our favorite. We always imagine we're James Bond when we dine here. The food is mainly Cantonese, prepared with flair and taste. Before dinner, you might want to enjoy a drink in the upstairs smoking lounge. Nearly everything is good, especially the sautéed shrimp and calamari, Shanghai chicken, and red rice sautéed with vegetables. The vast menu offers plenty of choices. Downstairs, the Sing Song club has live music, including something called Sino-French jazz, but only on Friday and Saturday.

50 rue de Charenton, 12th arr. ⓒ **01-43-43-82-02.** Main courses 70–190F (10.65–28.95€, $10.15–$27.55); fixed-price dinner 160F (24.30€, $23.20); fixed-price Sun dinner 115F (17.55€, $16.70). AE, MC, V. Sun–Thurs 7pm–2am; Fri–Sat 7pm–3am. Closed Aug. Métro: Bastille or Ledru-Rollin.

Le Train Bleu ⓚⓚ FRENCH (TRADITIONAL)   To reach this restaurant, climb the ornate double staircase facing the Gare de Lyon's grimy platforms. The restaurant and station were built along with the Grand Palais, Petit Palais, and pont Alexandre III for the 1900 World Exhibition. Inaugurated by the French president in 1901 and renovated and cleaned at great expense in 1992, Le Train Bleu boasts a decor classified as a national artistic treasure, with a lavishly frescoed ceiling, bronze statues, mosaics, mirrors, banquettes, and 41 Belle-Époque murals (each celebrating the distant corners of the French-speaking world, which join Paris via its rail network). The formally dressed staff is fast and efficient, in case you're about to catch a train. You can choose from well-prepared soufflé of brill, escargots in Chablis sauce, steak tartare, loin of lamb Provençal, veal kidneys in mustard sauce, rib of beef for two, and rum cake with raisins. We have to be honest—this standard brasserie fare doesn't match the decor, but we always like to go here anyway for the setting alone. And the food's not that bad.

In the Gare de Lyon, 12th arr. ⓒ **01-43-43-09-06.** Reservations recommended. Main courses 135–188F (20.50–28.65, $19.65–$27.25); fixed-price menu 260F (39.50€, $37.70), including wine. AE, DC, MC, V. Daily 11:30am–3pm and 7–11pm. Métro: Gare de Lyon.

INEXPENSIVE

L'Ébauchoir ⓚ Ⓕⁱⁿᵈˢ FRENCH (TRADITIONAL)   Tucked into a neighbor-hood rarely visited by foreigners and featuring a 1950s decor that has become fashionable again, this bistro attracts neighborhood carpenters, plumbers, and electricians, as well as an occasional journalist and screenwriter. With buffed aluminum trim and plaster-and-stucco walls tinted dark orange-yellow and blue, the place might remind you of a canteen in an auto factory. You can order surprisingly generous and well-prepared stuffed sardines, snapper filet with olive oil and garlic, crabmeat soup, fried calf's liver with coriander and honey, and rack of lamb combined with saddle of lamb.

43 rue de Cîteaux, 12th arr. ⓒ **01-43-42-49-31.** Reservations recommended for dinner. Main courses 65–110F (9.95–16.70€, $9.45–$15.95); fixed-price menus 70–90F (10.65–13.75€, $10.15–$13.05). MC, V. Mon–Sat noon–2:30pm and 8–10:30pm. Métro: Faidherbe-Chaligny.

Le Square Trousseau FRENCH (TRADITIONAL)   This is a well-recommended bistro, with solid and traditional food and a setting that evokes the best of turn-of-the century France. Within a circa-1905 decor accented with etched glass, tiles, and leathery banquettes, you'll be presented with dishes that include *pot-au-feu,* sole meuniére, sweetbreads, calf's liver, and steak au poivre. A habitué told us that she comes here for "comfort food," including the terrines and tarts her mother used to prepare for her. But she notes many delicious innovations in the menu, which she calls "winds of change." Among these are some delicious risottos.

1 rue Antoine-Vollon, 12th arr. ✆ **01-43-43-06-00.** Reservations recommended. Main courses 90–140F (13.75–21.35€, $13.05–$20.30). Tues–Sat noon–2:30pm and 8–11:30pm. Métro: Ledru-Rollin.

18TH ARRONDISSEMENT
INEXPENSIVE

Le Grain de Folie ORGANIC/VEGETARIAN   Simple and wholesome, the cuisine at this vegetarian restaurant is inspired by France, Greece, California, and India. The menu includes an array of salads, cereals, tarts, terrines, and casseroles. Dessert selections might include an old-fashioned tart or a fruit salad. The decor includes potted plants and exposed stone. You can choose one of an array of wines or a frothy glass of vegetable juice to accompany your meal. This place may be a bit difficult to find, but it's worth the search.

24 rue de la Vieuville, 18th arr. ✆ **01-42-58-15-57.** Reservations recommended. Main courses 50–70F (7.60–10.65€, $7.25–$10.15); fixed-price menu 55–100F (8.35–15.20€, $8.05–$14.50). No credit cards. Daily 12:30–2:30pm and 7:30–10:30pm. Métro: Abbesses.

Marie-Louise FRENCH (TRADITIONAL)   Opened in a decidedly unfashionable neighborhood in 1957 and named after the matriarch who first owned it, this bistro offers Paris views rarely seen by visitors who gravitate toward the Seine. The decor evokes old-time France with allusions to the establishment's birth in the age of Sputnik. Opt for a table on the busy main floor or on the quieter floor above. Again and again, longtime fans order *boeuf à la ficelle* (poached beef filet tied with string and served in its natural juices). Also popular are the sautéed monkfish with pasta, coq au vin, chicken Marie-Louise (with rice and paprika cream sauce), and grilled sirloin steak with pepper or béarnaise sauce.

52 rue Championnet, 18th arr. ✆ **01-46-06-86-55.** Reservations required. Main courses 75–110F (11.40–16.70€, $10.95–$15.95); fixed-price menus 105–155F (15.95–23.55€, $15.25–$22.55). V. Tues–Sat noon–2pm and 7:30–10pm. Closed Aug. Métro: Simplon or Porte de Clignancourt.

8TH ARRONDISSEMENT
VERY EXPENSIVE

Lasserre ✿✿✿ FRENCH (MODERN & TRADITIONAL)   This elegant restaurant was a simple bistro before World War II, but it has since become a legend attracting world gourmets. The main salon stretches two stories high, with a mezzanine on each side. Tall silk-draped arched windows frame tables set with fine porcelain, gold-edged crystal glasses, and silver candelabras. The ceiling is painted with white clouds and a cerulean sky, but in good weather the staff slides back the roof to reveal the real sky. The food is a mix of Classicism and originality; count on high drama in the presentation. The appetizers are among Paris's finest, including truffle salad, three-meat terrine, and Chablis-flavored Belon oysters. The signature main course is poached sole filets *Club de la Casserole,* in puff pastry with asparagus tips and asparagus-flavored cream sauce, but also wonderful are the veal kidneys flambé and pigeon André Malraux. Among the spectacular desserts are soufflé Grand Marnier and three fresh sorbets of the season. The wine cellar, with some 180,000 bottles, is among the city's most remarkable.

17 av. Franklin-D.-Roosevelt, 8th arr. ✆ **01-43-59-53-43.** Fax 01-45-63-72-23. Reservations required far in advance. Main courses 175–290F (26.60–44.10€, $25.45–$42.05); fixed-price menu 340F (51.70€, $49.30) at lunch, 800F (121.60€, $116) at dinner. AE, MC, V. Tues–Sat 12:15–2:00pm and 7:30–10:30pm. Closed Aug. Métro: F. D. Roosevelt.

L'Astor ★★★ FRENCH (MODERN)   What happens to a great French chef when he retires? If he's lucky enough and respected enough, he takes on the title of "culinary consultant" and attaches himself to a restaurant where he can drop in several times a week to keep an eye on things. That's what happened when guru Joël Robuchon retired from his avenue Raymond-Poincaré citadel in favor of a quieter life (his replacement there was Alain Ducasse). The chef here is respected Eric Lecerf, who knows better than anyone else how to match his master's tours de force. The setting is a tawny-colored enclave beneath an etched-glass Art-Deco ceiling, with luxurious touches inspired by the 1930s. Expect an almost religious devotion to Robuchon's specialties and less emphasis on newer dishes created by Lecerf. Examples of "classic Robuchon" are caramelized sea urchins in aspic with fennel-flavored cream sauce, eggplant-stuffed cannelloni with tuna filets and olive oil, and spit-roasted Bresse chicken with flap mushrooms. Items created by Lecerf include carpaccio of Breton lobster with olive oil and tomato confit, creamy cannelloni with eggplant, roasted and braised rack of lamb, and pigeon supreme with cabbage and foie gras.

In the Hôtel Astor, 11 rue d'Astorg, 8th arr. ✆ **01-53-05-05-20.** Fax 01-53-05-05-30. Reservations required far in advance. Main courses 150–310F (22.80–47.10€, $21.75–$44.95); fixed-price menus 325–590F (49.40–89.75€, $47.15–$85.55). AE, DC, MC, V. Mon–Fri noon–2pm and 7:30–10pm. Closed Aug. Métro: St-Augustin or Madeleine.

Les Elysées du Vernet ★★★ PROVENÇAL   This darling of *tout Paris* is fast-rising as a gastronomic wonder. Capping the restaurant is one of the neighborhood's most panoramic glass ceilings, a gray and green translucent dome designed by Gustav Eiffel who also conceived Paris' famous tower. That, plus the fact that the Montpellier-born chef, Alain Solivérès, was recently awarded two Michelin stars, keeps the crowds lined up. Menu items are focused on Provençal models, and change every 2 months, based on whatever is fresh at the season of your arrival. During our midwinter visit, award-winning examples included scallops with truffles, *tournedos Rossini* (a slab of beef layered with foie gras); and a *cocotte* (small stew-pot) of lobster. There's also a melt-in-your mouth version of apple charlotte, and even a newfangled take on black-truffle ice cream, a dish that traditionalists consider somewhat far-fetched. Candles help illuminate the place at night, and during the dinner hour there's either a harpist (Monday to Wednesday) or a pianist (Thursday to Friday), whose music reverberates pleasantly off the glass dome overhead.

In the Hotel Vernet, 25 rue Vernet, 8th arr. ✆ **01-44-31-98-98.** Reservations required. Main courses 280–670F (42.55–101.85€, $40.60–$97.15). AE, DC, MC, V. Mon–Sat 12:30–2pm and 7:30–9pm. Métro: George V.

Lucas-Carton (Alain Senderens) ★★★ FRENCH (MODERN)   This is one of the city's high temples of French gastronomy right up there with Taillevent. When Alain Senderens took over this landmark Belle-Époque restaurant, he added some welcome modern touches and a brilliant culinary repertoire. The dining rooms downstairs and private rooms upstairs boast mirrors, fragrant bouquets of flowers, and wood paneling that has been polished every week since its installation in 1900. Every dish is influenced by Senderens's creative flair. Menu items, which change seasonally, include polenta with black truffles, duckling Apicius (roasted with honey and spices), pastillade of rabbit, and sweetbreads with acidified carrot juice. The chestnuts purée is a perfect way to end a meal. Senderens is constantly experimenting—his latest sensations are lobster roasted with vanilla and *poularde demi-deuil*, a Bresse hen whose flesh has been scored with black truffles (the resulting black-and-white flesh is supposed to be "in partial mourning"); it's accompanied by saffron-flavored rice.

9 place de la Madeleine, 8th arr. ℂ **01-42-65-22-90.** Fax 01-42-65-06-23. Reservations required several days ahead for lunch and several weeks ahead for dinner. Main courses 240–700F (36.50–106.40€, $34.80–$101.50); fixed-price lunch 395F (60.05€, $57.35) fixed-price dinner 1,200F (182.40€, $174). AE, DC, MC, V. Tues–Fri noon–2:30pm; Mon–Sat 8–10:15pm. Closed 3 weeks in Aug. Métro: Madeleine.

Pierre Gagnaire ✦✦✦ FRENCH (MODERN)   Though the PR here may be the worst in Paris, if you're able to make a reservation, it's worth the effort. The menus are seasonally adjusted to take advantage of France's rich bounty; Pierre Gagnaire, the famous owner, demands perfection, and the chef has a dazzling way of blending flavors and textures. One critic wrote, "Picasso stretched the limits of painting; Gagnaire does it with cooking." Try anything from a menu that changes every 2 months: Stellar examples are freshwater crayfish cooked tempura-style with thin-sliced flash-seared vegetables and sweet-and-sour sauce as well as turbot cooked in a bag and served with fennel and Provençal lemons. Chicken with truffles is part of a two-tiered service—first the breast in a wine-based aspic, second the thighs chopped into roughly textured pieces. For dessert, try the chocolate soufflé served with a frozen parfait and Sicilian pistachios.

6 rue Balzac, 8th arr. ℂ **01-44-35-18-25.** Fax 01-44-35-18-37. Reservations are imperative and difficult to make. Main courses 310–460F (47.10–69.90€, $44.95–$66.70); fixed-price menus 520–650F (79.05–98.80€, $75.40–$94.25) at lunch, 1,250F (190€, $181.25) at dinner. AE, DC, MC, V. Mon–Fri 12:30–2:15pm and 7–10pm. Métro: George V.

Restaurant Plaza Athénée (Alain Ducasse) ✦✦✦ FRENCH (MODERN & TRADITIONAL)   Few other chefs in the history of French cuisine have been catapulted to international fame as quickly as Alain Ducasse. The most recent setting for his world-renowned cuisine is an appropriately world-renowned hotel, the Plaza Athénée. There's a lot of marketing and glitter associated with this new *marriage de convenience,* but what you'll find is a lobby-level hideaway that topnotch decorator Patrick Jouin transformed with layers of pearl-gray paint and many yards of translucent organdy. By anyone's standards, the cuisine is spectacular. This five-star Michelin chef seeds his dishes with produce from every corner of France—rare local vegetables, fish from the coasts, and dishes incorporating cardoons, turnips, celery, turbot, cuttlefish, and Bresse fowl. His French cuisine is contemporary and Mediterranean yet not new. Though many dishes are light, Ducasse isn't afraid of lard, as he proves by his thick, oozing slabs of pork grilled to a crisp. There's an occasional *homage* to the great chef, Joel Robuchon, in the form of such dishes as caviar in aspic with cauliflower cream. More individualized is crayfish drenched with caviar sauce. The wine list is superb, with some selections deriving from the best vintages of France, Germany, Switzerland, Spain, California, and Italy.

In the Hotel Plaza Athénée, 25av. Montaigne, 8th arr. ℂ **01-53-67-65-00.** Fax 01-53-67-65-12. Reservations required 8 weeks in advance. Main courses 360–558F (54.70–84.80€, $52.20–$80.90); fixed-price menus 985–1,490F (149.70–226.55€, $142.85–$216.05). AE, DC, MC, V. Thurs–Fri noon–2pm; Mon–Fri 8–10:30pm. Closed mid-July–mid-Aug and Dec. 22–30. Métro: FDR or Alma-Marceau.

Restaurants in the 8th & 16th–17th Arrondissements

Buddha Bar **24**
Café/Restaurant/Salon de Thé
    Bernardaud **25**
Chez André **18**
Chez Georges **5**
Chicago Pizza Pie Factory **14**
Guy Savoy **7**
Jamin **3**
Kamboda **16**
La Butte Chaillot **1**
La Rôtisserie d'Armaillé **6**
Lasserre **22**
L'Astor **27**
Laudurée **17**
Laudurée Royale **23**
Le Berry's **28**
Le Bistro d'à Côte **8**
Le Bistro de l'Etoile **4**
Les Elysées du Vernet **15**
Les Gourmets des Ternes **10**
Lucas-Carton
    (Alain Senderens) **26**
Michel Rostang **9**
Pierre Gagnaire **12**
Relais Gourmand Faugeron **2**
Restaurant Copenhague/
    Flora Danica **11**
Restaurant Plaza Athénée
    (Alain Ducasse) **20**
Shing-Jung **29**
Shozan **19**
Spoon Food & Wine **21**
Taillevent **13**

137

Taillevent ★★★ FRENCH (MODERN & TRADITIONAL)   This is the Parisian *ne plus ultra* of gastronomy. Taillevent opened in 1946 and has climbed steadily in excellence until today it ranks as Paris's most outstanding all-around restaurant, challenged only by Lucas-Carton and Pierre Gagnaire in this highly competitive area. The restaurant, named after famous 14th-century chef Guillaume Tirel Taillevent, who wrote one of the oldest known books on French cookery, is set in a grand 19th-century town house off the Champs-Elysées, with paneled rooms and crystal chandeliers. The place is small, as the owner wishes, so he can give personal attention to every facet of the operation and maintain a discreet club atmosphere. You might begin with a *boudin* (sausage) of Breton lobster à la Nage, cream of watercress soup with Sevruga caviar, or duck liver with spice bread and ginger. Main courses include red snapper with black olives, Scottish salmon cooked in sea salt with a sauce of olive oil and lemons, and cassolette of crayfish from Brittany. Dessert might be a *nougatine glacé* with pears. The wine list is among the best in Paris. Though owner M. Vrinat likes Americans, it isn't always easy for visitors from the States and other countries to book a table, because he prefers about 60 percent of his guests to be French.

15 rue Lamennais, 8th arr. ✆ **01-44-95-15-01.** Fax 01-42-25-95-18. Reservations required weeks, even months, in advance for lunch and dinner. Main courses 290–330F (44.15–50.15€, $42.05–$47.85). AE, DC, MC, V. Mon–Fri noon–2:30pm and 7–10pm. Closed Aug. Métro: George V.

EXPENSIVE

Buddha Bar ★★ FRENCH (MODERN)/PACIFIC RIM   This place is hot, hot, hot—and still remains as Paris's "restaurant of the moment," even though it has been around a while. A location on a chic street near the Champs-Elysées and place de la Concorde and an allegiance to a fusion of French, Asian, and Californian cuisines guarantees trendy diners devoted to the whims of fashion. The vast dining room is presided over by a giant Buddha, and the cutting-edge culinary theme combines Japanese sashimi, Vietnamese spring rolls, lacquered duck, sautéed shrimp with black-bean sauce, grilled chicken skewers with orange sauce, sweet-and-sour spareribs, and crackling squab à l'orange. There are two sittings for dinner: 7 to 9pm and 10:30pm to 12:30am. Many come here just for a drink in the carefully lacquered and very hip bar, upstairs from the street-level dining room.

8 rue Boissy d'Anglas, 8th arr. ✆ **01-53-05-90-00.** Reservations required far in advance. Main courses 115–260F (17.55–39.50€, $16.75–$37.70). AE, MC, V. Mon–Fri noon–3pm; daily 7pm–12:30am. Métro: Concorde.

Restaurant Copenhague/Flora Danica ★★ DANISH   Danish specialties are served with flair at the "Maison du Danemark," in many ways the best restaurant on the Champs-Elysées, with an outdoor terrace for midsummer dining. There are two dining areas: the street-level Flora Danica and the somewhat more formal Restaurant Copenhague upstairs. To be thoroughly Danish, order an aperitif of aquavit and ignore the wine list in favor of Carlsberg. Menu items include reindeer terrine, foie gras, smoked salmon, fresh shrimp, and elegant open-faced sandwiches. The house specialty is a platter of Scandinavian delicacies drawn from the many seafood and dairy specialties the Danes prepare exceptionally well. Our preferred dish is grilled Norwegian salmon cooked on one side only.

142 av. des Champs-Elysées, 8th arr. ✆ **01-44-13-86-26.** Reservations recommended far in advance. Main courses in Coponhague 190–290F (28.95–44.15€, $27.55–$42.05); fixed-price menu 260F (39.50€, $37.70). Main courses in Hora Danica 92–195F (14.05–29.65€, $13.35–$28.35), fixed-price menu 175F (26.60€,

$25.45). AE, DC, MC, V. Daily noon–2:30pm and 7:15–11pm. Restaurant Copenhague closed Aug and Jan 1–7. Métro: George V.

Shozan ✿ FRENCH (MODERN)/JAPANESE   East and West form a perfect synthesis in this Franco-Japanese alliance. It's not for the traditionalist, but trendy young Paris enjoys the new flavors. For example, the classic foie gras appears as foie gras sushi with sansho pepper, and the roast lamb comes with a green-tea crust. The roast tuna with buckwheat seed and the scampi concoction are delectable. A chef's specialty is lobster with white-sesame sauce spiked with sweet sake. Famous interior designer Christian Liaigre created the stunning setting, dominated by wood and leather; you sit at wooden tables without cloths.

11 rue de la Trémoille, 8th arr. ℂ 01-47-23-37-32. Reservations recommended far in advance. Main courses 165–220F (25.15–33.45€, $23.95–$31.90); fixed-price menu 195F (29.65€, $28.35) at lunch, 395F (60.05€, $57.35) at dinner. AE, DC, MC, V. Mon–Fri noon–2:30pm; Mon–Sat 7–10:30pm. Closed 15 days in Aug. Métro: Alma-Marceau.

Spoon, Food & Wine ✿ INTERNATIONAL   This hypermodern venture of *wunderkind* chef Alain Ducasse is hailed as a "restaurant for the millennium" and condemned by some Parisian food critics as surreal and a bit absurd. The claustrophobic dining room evokes stylish Paris and California, and the cuisine roams the world for inspiration, with such middlebrow offerings as American macaroni and cheese, a BLT, barbecued ribs, chicken wings, and pastrami. Other dishes evoke Italy, Latin America, Asia, and India. The steamed lobster with mango chutney is a winner. For a "vegetable garden," you can mix and match among 15 ingredients, including iceberg lettuce. Pasta comes with a selection of five sauces.

In the Hôtel Marignan-Elysée, 14 rue Marignan, 8th arr. ℂ **01-40-76-34-44.** Reservations recommended far in advance. Main courses, vegetable side dishes 135–185F (20.50–28.10€, $19.60–$26.85). AE, DC, V. Mon–Fri noon–2pm and 7–11pm. Métro: F. D. Roosevelt.

MODERATE

Chez André FRENCH (TRADITIONAL)   Chez André is one of the neighborhood's favorite bistros. Its major drawback is that you'll feel a bit left out in the cold if you're not a regular. Outside, a discreet red awning stretches over an array of shellfish on ice; inside, an Art-Nouveau decor includes etched glass and masses of flowers. This has been a landmark on rue Marbeuf since 3 years before the invasion of France in 1940. It remains the same as it was when it was founded (an agreement was made with the original owners). The old-style cuisine on the menu includes pâté of thrush, Roquefort in puff pastry, grilled veal kidneys, roast rack of lamb, and bouillabaisse, several kinds of omelets, calves' head vinaigrette, a potage du jour, and fresh shellfish, along with several reasonably priced wines. For variety, some locals opt for the *plat du jour*. The dessert choices may be rum baba, chocolate cake, or a daily pastry.

12 rue Marbeuf (at rue Clément-Marot), 8th arr. ℂ **01-47-20-59-57.** Reservations recommended. Main courses 89–150F (13.55–22.80€, $12.90–$21.75); fixed-price menu 180F (27.35€, $26.10). AE, DC, MC, V. Daily noon–1am. Métro: F. D. Roosevelt.

Ladurée FRENCH (TRADITIONAL)   Ladurée, acclaimed since 1862 as one of Paris's grand cafes (located near La Madeleine), is now installed on the Champs-Elysées, adding a touch of class to this neighborhood of fast-food places. This offshoot expanded in 1999 and caters to an international set wearing everything from Givenchy to GAP. The Belle-Époque setting is ideal for sampling Ladurée's celebrated macaroons—not the sticky coconut version familiar to Americans, but two almond meringue cookies, flavored with vanilla, coffee, strawberry, pistachio, or other flavor, stuck together with butter cream. The menu of talented young chef Philippe Dandrieux is constantly adjusted to take advantage of the freshest daily ingredients and may include a crisp and tender pork filet with potato-and-parsley purée and marinated red mullet filets on a salad of cold ratatouille. If you're looking for a mid-afternoon pick-me-up to accompany your tea and macaroons, consider a *plaisir sucré,* a chocolate confection artfully decorated with spun sugar. The service isn't always efficient.

75 av. des Champs-Elysées, 8th arr. ✆ 01-40-75-08-75. Reservations required for the restaurant, not for the cafe. Main courses 150–250F (22.80–38€, $21.75–$36.25); pastries from 28F (4.25€, $4.05). AE, DC, MC, V. Daily 7:30am–1am.

INEXPENSIVE

Chicago Pizza Pie Factory ★★ *Kids* AMERICAN/PIZZA   Off the Champs-Elysées, you'll find a busy tribute to the city of Chicago in a former garage. The bar is outfitted with anything and everything to do with Chicago: photos, sports banners, and all manner of kitsch. The dining room is as large and raucous as the Windy City itself. It serves the best pizza in Paris, prepared in endless variations on eight basic themes, as well as mud pie, cheesecake, and marvelous high-fat brownies. The management proudly refuses, except under dire circumstances, to serve burgers of any kind. No one will mind if you bypass the food in favor of a drink at the bar (happy hour in the restaurant is from 4 to 7pm and at the bar from 6 to 8pm); during these times some drinks (but not beer) are reduced in price.

5 rue de Berri, 8th arr. ✆ 01-45-62-50-23. Reservations accepted only on weekdays for groups of 8 or more. Pizza for 2, 88–149F (13.45–22.65€, $12.75–$21.60); pizza for 4, 129–195F (19.60–29.65€, $18.70–$28.30); fixed-price lunch menus 61–79F (9.25–12€, $8.85–$11.45). AE, DC, MC, V. Sun–Thurs 11:30am–1am; Fri–Sat 11:30am–5am. Métro: George V.

Le Berry's FRENCH (TRADITIONAL)   This inexpensive bistro, with a setting celebrating rugby, complements one of the area's grandest restaurants, Le Grenadin. Its platters emerge from the same kitchen and are infused with the same kind of zeal as those presented next door for three times the price. Don't expect cutting-edge fare, but do look for honest dishes from France's agrarian heartland and a refreshing lack of pretension. The dishes listed on a chalkboard include fricassée of chicken with olives and mashed potatoes, thin-sliced smoked ham from Sancerre, veal filet with red-wine sauce, raw pike with cabbage, and a traditional Berry pear tart.

46 rue de Naples, 8th arr. ✆ 01-40-75-01-56. Reservations recommended. Main courses 56–92F (8.50–14.05€, $8.10–$13.35); fixed-price menu 110F (16.70€, $15.95). MC, V. Mon–Fri noon–2:30pm; Mon–Sat 7pm–1am. Métro: Villie Tues.

Les Gourmets des Ternes *Value* FRENCH (TRADITIONAL)   Les Gourmets des Ternes caters to hordes who appreciate its affordable prices and lack of pretension. Despite the brusque service, satisfied diners have included the mayor of Atlanta, who wrote the bistro a thank-you letter, as well as hundreds of ordinary folks from this neighborhood. Thriving in this spot since 1892, the place retains an early-1900s paneled decor, with some additions from the 1950s, including bordeaux-colored banquettes, mirrors, wooden panels, touches of brass, and paper tablecloths. During clement weather, there's an outdoor terrace as well. The finely grilled signature dishes include rib steak with marrow sauce and fries; country pâtés and sausages; sole, turbot, and monkfish; and satisfying desserts like peach Melba and *baba au Rhum* (rum cake with raisins).

87 bd. de Courcelles, 8th arr. 📞 **01-42-27-43-04.** Main courses 90–145F (13.75–22.05€, $13.05–$21.05). AE, MC, V. Mon–Fri noon–2:30pm and 7–10pm. Métro: Ternes.

Shing-Jung KOREAN   Of the 30 or so Korean restaurants in Paris, Shing-Jung is the best, known for low prices. Its sashimi is comparable to Japanese versions, though the portions of the fresh tuna, salmon, or daurade tend to be more generous. A specialty is the Korean barbecue called *bulgoogi,* which seems more authentic thanks to a clever decor juxtaposing Korean chests and paintings.

7 rue Clapeyron, 8th arr. 📞 **01-45-22-21-06.** Reservations recommended for dinner. Main courses 80–110F (12.15–16.70€, $11.60–$15.95); fixed-price menus 65–75F (9.95–11.40€, $9.45–$10.95) at lunch, 100–200F (15.20–30.40€, $14.50–$29) at dinner. MC, V. Mon–Fri noon–2:30pm and 7–10:30pm; Sat–Sun 7–10:30pm. Métro: Rome.

16TH ARRONDISSEMENT
VERY EXPENSIVE

Jamin ✦✦✦ FRENCH (TRADITIONAL)   This is where Paris's great chef of the 80s, Joël Robuchon, made his sensational mark. Now in charge is Robuchon's longtime second in command, Benoit Guichard, who is clearly inspired by his master but is an imaginative chef in his own right. Guichard has chosen pale green panels and pink banquettes (referred to as "Italo–New Yorkaise") for a soothing backdrop to his brief but well-chosen menu. Lunches can be relatively simple, though each dish, like a beautifully seasoned salmon tartare, is done to perfection. Classic technique and an homage to tradition characterize the cuisine—John Dory with celery and fresh ginger; pigeon sausage with foie gras, pistachios, and mâche lettuce; and beef shoulder so tender it had obviously been braising for hours. A particularly earthy dish celebrates various parts of the sow that are usually rejected, blending the tail and cheeks on a platter with walnuts and fresh herbs. Finish with a *tarte tatin.*

32 rue de Longchamp, 16th arr. 📞 **01-45-53-00-07.** Fax 01-45-53-00-15. Reservations required far in advance. Main courses 230–330F (35–50.25€, $33.40–$47.90); fixed-price menus 310–495F (47.20–75.35€, $45–$71.85) at lunch, 495F (75.35€, $71.85) at dinner. AE, DC, MC, V. Mon–Fri 12:30–2pm and 7:45–10pm. Métro: Trocadéro.

Relais Gourmand Faugeron ✦✦✦ FRENCH (TRADITIONAL)   Henri Faugeron is an inspired chef who many years ago opened this restaurant as an elegant yet unobtrusive backdrop for his superb cuisine, which he calls "revolutionary." The interior of this early-1900s building now glitters with discreet touches of gilt and has a sun motif emblazoned on the ceiling. Even so, the food, which is inspired by the Correze Region of France, outshines its surroundings. Much of the zesty cuisine depends on the season and market, because Faugeron chooses only the freshest ingredients. In winter your taste for truffles can be indulged by one of the many dishes expertly prepared, like the *brunoise* of truffles with asparagus and olive oil and the ravioli stuffed with truffles and foie gras. Roasted leg of milk-fed veal and lamb and crispy-skinned quail are also great choices. If you want something really esoteric, consider the *vol-au-vent* of lobster, sweetbreads, and morels.

52 rue de Longchamp, 16th arr. 📞 **01-47-04-24-53.** Fax 01-55-73-11-27. Reservations required far in advance. Main courses 250–360F (38–54.70€, $36.25–$52.20); fixed-price menus 370–550F (56.25–83.60€, $53.65–$79.75) at lunch, 550–700F (83.60–106.40€, $79.75–$101.50) at dinner. AE, MC, V. Mon–Fri noon–2pm and 7–10pm (Oct–Apr dinner only, Sat 7–10pm). Closed Aug. Métro: Trocadéro or Boissière.

Kids Family-Friendly Restaurants

Meals at Paris's grand restaurants are rarely suitable for young children. Nevertheless, many parents drag their kids along, often to the annoyance of other diners. You may have to make some compromises, such as dining earlier than most Parisians. **Hotel dining rooms** can be another good choice for family dining. They usually have children's menus or at least one or two *plats du jour* cooked for children, like spaghetti with meat sauce.

If you take your child to a **moderate** or an **inexpensive restaurant,** ask if the restaurant will serve a child's plate. If not, order a *plat du jour* or *plat garni,* which will be suitable for most children, particularly if a dessert is to follow. Most **cafes** welcome children throughout the day and early evening. At a cafe, children always seem to like the sandwiches (try a *croque monsieur*), the omelets, and the *pommes frites* (crispy french fries). Though this chapter lists a number of cafes (see "The Top Cafes," later in this chapter), one that particularly appeals to children is **La Samaritaine,** 75 rue de Rivoli ℂ **01-40-41-20-20);** Métro: Pont Neuf. The snack bar down below doesn't have a panoramic view, but the fifth-floor restaurant does. You can take children to the top and order ice cream for them at teatime daily from 3:30 to 6pm. The snack bar is open daily from 9:30am to 7pm.

Les Drug Stores, 149 bd. St-Germain-des-Prés, 6e, and at Publicis Champs-Elysées, 133 av. des Champs-Elysées, 8e—like American drug stores but with sections for upscale gift items and food service—also welcome children, especially in the early evening, as do most **tearooms,** and you

MODERATE

Kambodia ASIAN/CAMBODIAN   The waiters, all dressed in black cotton tunics, will welcome you to this excellent eatery that serves some of the best and most flavor-filled Asian dishes in Paris. The basement atmosphere has been called "Zen-like," but the service is welcoming and it's a good choice for a romantic dinner not far from the Champs-Elysées. Fresh ingredients are used, the best from the Asian markets. Our favorite dish is a superb seafood *pot-au-feu.* One Cambodian dish that's a delight is ginger fish wrapped in a banana leaf.

15 rue de Bassano, 16th arr. ℂ 01-47-23-31-80. Reservations required. Main courses 98–122F (14.90–18.55€, $14.20–$17.70); fixed-price lunch 118–148F (17.95–22.50€, $17.10–$21.45). AE, MC, V. Mon–Fri noon–2:30pm, Mon–Sat 7:30–11pm. Métro: George V.

La Butte Chaillot ℛ *Value* FRENCH (TRADITIONAL)   This baby bistro showcases culinary high priest Guy Savoy and draws a busy crowd from the affluent neighborhood's many corporate headquarters. Diners congregate in posh but congested areas tinted in salmon and dark yellow. Menu items change weekly (sometimes daily) and betray a strange sense of mass production not unlike that found in a luxury cruise line's dining room. Examples are a sophisticated medley of terrines; a "low-fat" version of chunky mushroom soup; a salad of snails and herbed potatoes; succulent rack of lamb; and roasted rabbit with sage and a compote of onions, bacon, and mushrooms. A starkly contemporary stainless-steel staircase leads to extra seating in the cellar.

can tide the kids over with pastries and ice cream if dinner will be late. You could also try a **picnic** in the park or one of the many fast-food chains, like **Pizza Hut** and **McDonald's,** all over the city.

Androuët *(see p. 118)*   If your kids love cheese, they'll get the fill of a lifetime here, where cheese enters all the dishes. Especially delectable is the ravioli stuffed with goat cheese.

Café la Parisienne *(see p. 127)*   This is the ideal choice when visiting the Beaubourg, with a captivating view of the most playful fountain in Paris from its terrace.

Chicago Pizza Pie Factory *(see p. 140)*   There are no frogs' legs or snails to gross out little minds and stomachs at the Chicago Pizza Pie Factory, just the City of Light's best pizza followed by a kid-pleasing cheesecake.

Crémerie-Restaurant Polidor *(see p. 152)*   One of the most popular restaurants on the Left Bank, this reasonably priced dining room is so family friendly it calls its food *cuisine familiale.* This might be the best place to introduce your child to bistro food.

Hard Rock Cafe *(see p. 128)*   At the Paris branch of this chain, good old American burgers and more are served against a background of rock memorabilia and loud rock music.

Joe Allen *(see p. 119)*   This American restaurant in Les Halles delivers everything from chili to chocolate-mousse pie to the best hamburgers in Paris.

110 bis av. Kléber, 16th arr. ℂ **01-47-27-88-88.** Reservations recommended. Main courses 98–118F (14.90–17.95€, $14.20–$17.10); fixed-price menus 150–195F (22.80–29.65€, $21.75–$28.35). AE, DC, MC, V. Daily noon–2:30pm and 7pm–midnight. Métro: Trocadéro.

INEXPENSIVE

Le Bistro de l'Étoile 🐸 *(Value* FRENCH (TRADITIONAL)   This is the most interesting of three baby bistros, each with the same name, clustered around place Charles de Gaulle–Etoile. They serve affordable versions of the grand cuisine featured in superstar Guy Savoy's nearby two-star restaurant (see below). The setting is a warmly contemporary dining room in shades of butterscotch and caramel. Menu items include a *mijotée* (pork and sage cooked over low heat for hours, coming out extremely tender, almost mushy), codfish studded with lard and prepared with a coconut-lime sauce, and red-snapper filets with caramelized endive and exotic mushrooms. A particularly interesting sampler combines three of Savoy's creations on a platter—a cup of lentil cream soup, a fondant of celery, and a pan-fried slice of foie gras. Expect some odd terms on the dessert menu, which only a professional chef can fully describe: An example is spice bread baked in the fashion of *pain perdu* (lost bread) garnished with banana sorbet and pineapple sauce.

19 rue Lauriston, 16th arr. ℂ **01-40-67-11-16.** Reservations recommended. Main courses 97–130F (14.75–19.75€, $14.05–$18.85); fixed-price lunch 165F (25.15€, $23.95). AE, DC, MC, V. Mon–Fri noon–2:30pm, Mon–Sat 7:30pm–midnight. Métro: Kleber.

17TH ARRONDISSEMENT
VERY EXPENSIVE

Guy Savoy ★★★ FRENCH (TRADITIONAL)   Consistently named one of the five or six hottest chefs in Europe, Guy Savoy serves the kind of food he likes to eat, prepared with consummate skill. We think he has a slight edge over his nearest rival, Michel Rostang (below), though Ducasse surpasses them both. Though the food is superb and meals comprise as many as nine courses, the portions are small; you won't necessarily be satiated at the end. The menu changes with the seasons but may include a light cream soup of lentils and crayfish, duckling foie gras with aspic and gray salt, and red snapper with a liver-and-spinach sauce served with crusty potatoes. If you come in the right season, you may have a chance to order masterfully prepared game like mallard and venison. Savoy is fascinated with mushrooms and has been known to serve a dozen types, especially in autumn. An example includes a delectable pan-fried combination of mussels and wild mushrooms.

18 rue Troyon, 17th arr. 🕐 **01-43-80-40-61.** Fax 01-43-80-36-22. Reservations required 1 week in advance. Main courses 335–580F (50.90–88.15€, $48.60–$84.10); *menu dégustation* (tasting menu) 1,050F (159.60€, $152.25). AE, DC, MC, V. Mon–Fri noon–2pm; Mon–Sat 7:30–10:30pm. Métro: Charles de Gaulle–Etoile or Ternes.

Michel Rostang ★★★ FRENCH (MODERN & TRADITIONAL) Michel Rostang is one of Paris's most creative chefs, the fifth generation of a distinguished French "cooking family." His restaurant contains four dining rooms paneled in mahogany, cherry, or pearwood; some have frosted Lalique crystal panels. Changing every 2 months, the menu offers modern improvements on *cuisine bourgeoise.* Truffles are the dish of choice in midwinter, and you'll find racks of suckling lamb from the salt marshes of France's western seacoasts in spring; in game season, look for sophisticated preparations of pheasant and venison. Three year-round staples are quail eggs with a coque of sea urchins, fricassée of sole, and young Bresse chicken with crusty mushroom purée and a salad composed of the chicken's thighs.

20 rue Rennequin, 17th arr. 🕐 **01-47-63-40-77.** Fax 01-47-63-82-75. Reservations required far in advance. Main courses 198–385F (30.10–58.50€, $28.70–$55.85); fixed-price menus 385–685F (58.50–104.10€, $55.85–$99.35) at lunch, 685–880F (104.10–133.75€, $99.35–$127.60) at dinner. AE, DC, MC, V. Tues–Fri 12:30–2:30pm; Mon–Sat 8–10:30pm. Closed 3 weeks in Aug. Métro: Ternes.

EXPENSIVE

Le Bistro d' á Côté ★ (Value) FRENCH (MODERN & TRADITIONAL) This is one of the four branches of Michel Rostang's baby bistro, each of which features a pared-down version of his *haute gastronomie* (see above). We feel this branch is the most interesting because it's just next door to the source. You'll enter a nostalgically decorated dining area ringed with unusual porcelain and antique copies of Michelin guides, some from around 1900. The venue is breezy, stylishly informal, and chic, with a simple menu enhanced by daily specials written on a chalkboard. Tantalizing items include ravioli stuffed with pulverized lobster, an upscale version of macaroni laced with Serrano ham, and *rable de lievre* (rabbit stew) *en cocotte.*

10 rue Gustave Flaubert, 17th arr. 🕐 **01-42-67-05-81.** Reservations recommended far in advance. Main courses 98–152F (14.90–23.10€, $14.20–$22.05); fixed-price lunch 150F (22.80€, $21.75). AE, DC, MC, V. Daily 12:30–2pm and 7:30–11pm. Métro: Ternes.

MODERATE

Chez Georges FRENCH (TRADITIONAL)   Not to be confused with a bistro of the same name in the 2nd arrondissement, this is a worthy choice. It has flourished since 1926, despite an obscure location. The setting has changed little—cheerfully harassed waiters barge through a dining room sheathed with old-fashioned paneling and etched glass, and savory odors emerge from the hysterically busy kitchen. Two enduring specialties are leg of lamb with white kidney beans and standing rib roast with herbs (especially thyme) in its own juices and a gratin of potatoes. Preceding these might be Baltic herring in cream sauce, cheese ravioli, cabbage soup, or a wide selection of sausages and pork products that taste best when eaten with bread, butter, and sour pickles. The adventurous French love the calf's head and the braised veal trotters, both served cold in vinaigrette.

273 bd. Pereire, 17th arr. ℂ **01-45-74-31-00.** Reservations recommended. Main courses 98–190F (14.90–28.90€, $14.20–$27.55). V. Daily noon–2:30pm and 7pm–midnight. Métro: Porte Maillot.

La Rôtisserie d'Armaillé ★★ (Value) FRENCH (TRADITIONAL)   The impresario behind this attractive baby bistro is Jacques Cagna, who established his role as a gastronomic star long ago from his headquarters in the Latin Quarter (see below). The chic place is popular for business lunches and dinners, also drawing residents and shoppers from the grand neighborhood. It's ringed with light-colored wood paneling and banquettes with patterns of pink and green. At lunch, the menu includes a main course and a starter or dessert; the pricier dinner meal includes a starter, main course, and dessert. Either way, you'll have many choices in each category. Examples are wild mushroom flan with red-wine sauce, a salad of sweetbreads and crayfish, and rack of lamb with parsley and sage, with apple beignets and champagne-drenched pineapple-and-mango soup for dessert. The artwork features bucolic cows, pigs, and lambs that are likely to figure among the grilled steaks and chops featured on the menu.

6 rue d'Armaillé, 17th arr. ℂ **01-42-27-19-20.** Reservations recommended. Fixed-price menu 75F (11.40€, $10.95) at lunch, 240F (36.55€, $34.80) at dinner. AE, DC, MC, V. Mon–Fri noon–2:30pm; Mon–Sat 7:30–11pm. Métro: Charles de Gaulle–Etoile.

4 On the Left Bank

We'll begin with the most centrally located arrondissements on the Left Bank, then work our way through the more outlying neighborhoods and to the area near the Eiffel Tower.

5TH ARRONDISSEMENT
VERY EXPENSIVE

La Tour d'Argent ★★★ FRENCH (TRADITIONAL)   This penthouse restaurant, a national institution, serves up an amazing view over the Seine and the apse of Notre-Dame. Although La Tour d'Argent's long-established reputation as "the best" in Paris has been eclipsed, dining here remains an unsurpassed theatrical event. A restaurant of some sort has stood on this site since at least 1582: Mme de Sévigné refers to a cafe here in her celebrated letters, and Dumas used it as a setting for one of his novels. The fame of La Tour d'Argent spread during its ownership by Frédéric Delair, who started the practice of issuing certificates to diners who ordered the house specialty—*caneton* (pressed duckling). The birds are numbered: The first was served to Edward VII in 1890, and now they're up over 1 million! Under the sharp eye of current owner Claude

Terrail, the cooking is superb and the service impeccable. A good part of the menu is devoted to duck, but the kitchen does know how to prepare other dishes. We especially recommend you start with the pheasant consommé or the pike-perch quenelles André Terrail and follow with the ravioli with foie gras or the salmon and turbot *à la Sully.*

15–17 quai de la Tournelle, 5th arr. ✆ 01-43-54-23-31. Fax 01-44-07-12-04. Reservations required far in advance. Main courses 270–515F (41.05–78.35€, $39.15–$74.75); fixed-price lunch 390F (59.35€, $56.55). AE, DC, MC, V. Tues–Sun noon–2:30pm and 7:30–10:30pm. Métro: St-Michel or Pont Marie.

MODERATE

Brasserie Balzar 🐍🐍 FRENCH (TRADITIONAL)   Opened in 1898, Brasserie Balzar is battered but cheerful, with some of Paris's friendliest waiters. The menu makes almost no concessions to nouvelle cuisine and includes pepper steak, *sole meunière,* sauerkraut with ham and sausage, pig's feet, and fried calf's liver served without garnish. Be warned that if you want just coffee or a drink, you probably won't get a table at meal hours. But, accustomed as they are to the odd hours of their many patrons, the staff will be happy to serve you if you want a full dinner in the mid-afternoon. Former patrons have included Sartre and Camus (who often got in arguments), James Thurber, countless professors from the nearby Sorbonne, and bevies of English and American journalists

49 rue des Écoles, 5th arr. ✆ 01-43-54-13-67. Reservations strongly recommended. Main courses 75–125F (11.40–19€, $10.90–$18.15). AE, MC, V. Daily noon–midnight. Métro: Odéon or Cluny–La Sorbonne.

Chez René FRENCH (TRADITIONAL)   Restaurants like this used to be widespread, particularly on the Left Bank, but many became pizzerias. Opened in 1957, Chez René maintains its allegiance to the tenets of French cuisine. The staff is often overwhelmed and the seating cramped as only a bistro can be. The dining room isn't fancy, but its patrons return loyally for the steady and reliable stream of food and the frequently changing *plats du jour.* For an appetizer, try the wild mushrooms laced with butter and garlic or the platter of country-style sausages. You'll find such reliable old-time fare as *boeuf bourguignonne* and *blanquette de veau* (veal in white sauce). Enjoy it all with a bottle of Beaujolais.

14 bd. St-Germain, 5th arr. ✆ 01-43-54-30-23. Reservations recommended. Main courses 80–170F (12.15–25.85€, $11.60–$24.65); fixed-price lunch 175F (26.60€, $25.45); fixed-price dinner 250F (38€, $36.25). V. Tues–Sat 12:15–2:15pm and 7:45–11pm. Closed Aug and 15 days in Dec. Métro: Maubert-Mutualité.

INEXPENSIVE

Al Dar LEBANESE   This well-respected restaurant works hard to popularize the savory cuisine of Lebanon. You'll dine on dishes like *taboulé,* a refreshing combination of finely chopped parsley, mint, milk, tomatoes, onions, lemon juice, olive oil, and salt; *baba ganoush,* pulverized and seasoned eggplant; and *hummus,* pulverized chickpeas with herbs. These can be followed with savory roasted chicken; tender minced lamb prepared with mint, cumin, and Mediterranean herbs; and any of several kinds of delectable tangines and couscous.

8 rue Frédéric-Sauton, 5th arr. ✆ 01-43-25-17-15. Reservations recommended. Main courses 88–96F (13.45–14.65€, $12.75–$13.90). AE, MC, V. Daily noon–midnight. Métro: Maubert-Mutualité.

Campagne et Provence PROVENÇAL   This restaurant is across from Ile de la Cité beside a quay. Bouquets of dried flowers garnish the pale blue walls, and the upholstery hints of Provence's blue sky. The waiters are likely to speak with the modulated accents of southern France. The savory food includes a salad of

---

> ⌒ *Tips* **Can You Dine Badly in Paris?**
>
> The answer is an emphatic yes. Our mailbox fills with complaints from readers who've encountered haughty service and paid outrageous prices for what turned out to be swill. Often these complaints are about restaurants catering to tourists. Avoid them by following our suggestions or looking in non-touristy areas for new discoveries. If you ask Parisians for recommendations, be sure to specify that you're looking for restaurants where *they'd* dine, not where they think you as a tourist would dine.

---

wild Provençal mesclun garnished with Parmesan, *compôté d'oignons* (Provençal tart) flavored with onions or a combination of sardines and red mullet, and grilled fish with risotto. A particularly tasty dessert is the anise-flavored *crème brûlée*.

25 quai de la Tournelle, 5th arr. ⓒ **01-43-54-05-17.** Reservations recommended. Fixed-price lunch 120F (18.25€, $17.40); 2-course fixed-price dinner 195F (29.65€, $28.35); 3-course fixed-price dinner 230F (34.95€, $33.35). V. Tues–Fri noon–2pm; Mon–Sat 7:30–11pm. Métro: Maubert-Mutualité.

Coco de Mer ⭐ *Finds* SEYCHELLE ISLANDS   The theme of this restaurant tugs at the emotions of the thousands of Parisians who have spent their holidays on the legendary beaches of the Seychelle Islands in the Indian Ocean. It contains at least three dining rooms, one of which is outfitted like a beach, with a sand-covered floor, replicas of palm trees, and a scattering of conch shells. Menu items feature such exotic dishes as tartare of tuna flavored with ginger, olive oil, salt, and pepper; and smoked swordfish, served either as a carpaccio or in thin slices with mango mousse and a spicy sauce. Main courses focus on fish, including a species of delectable red snapper (boirzoes), which is imported from the Seychelles. Dessert might consist of a *crème de banana gratinée*.

354 bd. St-Marcel, 5th arr. ⓒ **01-47-07-06-64.** Reservations recommended. Main courses 90–110F (13.75–16.70€, $13.05–$15.95). AE, DC, MC, V. Tues–Sat noon–3pm; Mon–Sat 7:30pm–midnight. Métro: Les Gobelins or St-Marcel.

La Petite Hostellerie ⭐ *Value* FRENCH (TRADITIONAL)   This 1902 restaurant offers a ground-floor dining room that's usually crowded and a larger one (seating 100) upstairs with attractive 18th-century woodwork. People come for the cozy ambience and decor, decent French country cooking, polite service, and excellent prices. The fixed-price dinner menu might feature favorites like coq au vin, duckling á l'orange, and steak with mustard sauce. Start with onion soup or stuffed mussels, and finish with cheese or salad and peach Melba or apple tart.

35 rue de la Harpe (just east of bd. St-Michel), 5th arr. ⓒ **01-43-54-47-12.** Fixed-price menus 65–89F (9.95–13.55€, $9.45–$12.90). AE, DC, MC, V. Tues–Sat noon–2pm; Mon–Sat 6:30–11pm. Closed 2 weeks in Feb and 3 weeks in Aug. Métro: St-Michel or Cluny–La Sorbonne.

Perraudin ⭐⭐ FRENCH (TRADITIONAL)   Everything about this place— decor, cuisine, price, and service—attempts to duplicate an early-1900s bistro. This one was built in 1870 as an outlet for coal and wine (sold as remedies against the cold). Eventually, it evolved into the wood-paneled bistro you see today, where little has changed since Zola was buried nearby in the Panthéon. The walls look like they've been marinated in tea; the marble-topped tables, old mirrors, and Parisian vaudeville posters have likely been here forever.

Restaurants in the 5th–6th & 13th–14th Arrondissements

Reservations aren't made in advance: Instead, diners usually drink a glass of kir at the zinc-topped bar as they wait. (Tables turn over quickly.) The menu includes roast leg of lamb with dauphinois potatoes, navarin of lamb, *boeuf bourguignonne*, and grilled salmon with sage sauce. An onion tart, pumpkin soup, or a terrine can precede the main course.

157 rue St-Jacques, 5th arr. ✆ **01-46-33-15-75.** Main courses 59F (8.95€, $8.55); fixed-price menu 65F (9.90€, $9.45) at lunch, 150F (22.80€, $21.75) at dinner. No credit cards. Tues–Fri noon–2:15pm; Mon–Sat 7:30–10:15pm. Closed 2 weeks in Aug. Métro: Cluny–La Sorbonne. RER: Luxembourg.

St-Louis en l'Île

ÎLE DE LA CITÉ

ÎLE ST-LOUIS

pont Notre-Dame
pont d'Arcole
pont Louis Philippe
pont Marie
pont Marie
pont de Sully

quai de Bourbon
quai d'Anjou
rue St-Louis en l'Île
quai d'Orléans
quai de Béthune

CITÉ
rue de la Cité
rue de Cloître N.Dame
Notre-Dame
Petit Pont
pont au Double
pont St-Louis
pont de la Tournelle

ST-MICHEL/ NOTRE-DAME
St-Nicolas
quai de la Tournelle
rue Monge

Institut du Monde Arabe

CLUNY-LA SORBONNE
Musée de Cluny
bd. St-Germain

Universités ParisVI-Paris VII

rue des Écoles
rue St-Jacques
Sorbonne
MAUBERT MUTUALITÉ
rue Valette
St-Étienne du Mont
rue du Cardinal
rue Cujas
Panthéon
rue Souflot
rue Lhomond
rue d'Ulm

JUSSIEU
rue Jussieu
Lemoine
CARDINAL LEMOINE
Arènes de Lutèce
rue Linné
rue Monge
rue St-Hilaire
PLACE MONGE

LUXEMBOURG
bd. St-Michel
rue Gay Lussac
rue Mouffetard
rue Brossolette
CENSIER DAUBENTON
rue Monge

LUXEMBOURG
École Normale Supérieure
rue Bernard
rue St-Jacques
rue Nicole
rue Berthollet

rue du Val de Grâce
Val-de-Grâce
PORT ROYAL
bd. de Port Royal
bd. de Port Royal
bd. Arago

Al Dar **24**
Alcazar Bar & Restaurant **20**
Allard **19**
Auberge Etchegorry **33**
Aux Charpentiers **10**
Bistro de la Grille **9**
Brasserie Balzar **23**
Brasserie Lipp **12**
Café Cosmos **5**
Café de Flore **11**
Campagne et Provence **25**
Chez Diane **6**
Chez Gramond **4**
Chez René **27**
Closerie des Lilas **30**
Coco de Mer **31**
Crémerie-Restaurant Polidor **7**
Jacques Cagna **17**
Keryado **26**
L'Assiette **1**
La Bastide Odéon **8**
La Cagouille **1**
La Coupole **3**
La Palette **15**
La Petite Hostellerie **22**
La Régalade **1**
La Rôtisserie d'en Face **18**
La Rotonde **2**
La Tour d'Argent **26**
Le Canton **13**
Le Petit Marguery **32**
Le Procope **21**
Lerch **28**
Les Deux Magots **14**
Perraudin **29**
Restaurant Bleu **1**
Yugaraj **16**

6TH ARRONDISSEMENT
VERY EXPENSIVE

Jacques Cagna ✦✦✦ FRENCH (MODERN & TRADITIONAL)   St-Germain knows no finer dining than at Jacques Cagna, a sophisticated restaurant in a 17th-century town house with massive timbers, burnished paneling, and 17th-century Dutch paintings. Jacques Cagna is one of the best classically trained chefs in Paris, though he has become a half-apostle to *cuisine moderne*. This is evident in his delectable carpaccio of pearly sea bream with caviar-lavished *céleric rémoulade* (celery root in mayonnaise with capers, parsley, gherkins, spring onions, chervil, chopped tarragon, and anchovy essence). Also sublime are the rack of suckling veal with ginger-and-lime sauce, Challons duckling in burgundy sauce, and fried scallops with celery and potatoes in truffle sauce. The menu is forever changing, according to the season and Cagna's inspirations, but if you're lucky, it will include his line-caught sea bass served with caviar in a potato shell.

14 rue des Grands-Augustins, 6th arr. ℭ **01-43-26-49-39.** Fax 01-43-54-54-48. Reservations required far in advance. Main courses 180–350F (27.35–53.20€, $26.10–$50.75); fixed-price menus 260–490F (39.50–74.50€, $37.70–$71.05) at lunch, 490F (74.50€, $71.05) at dinner. AE, DC, MC, V. Tues–Fri noon–2pm; Mon–Sat 7:30–10:30pm. Closed 3 weeks in Aug. Métro: St-Michel or Odéon.

EXPENSIVE

Closerie des Lilas 🏵🏵 FRENCH (TRADITIONAL)   Opened in 1847, the Closerie was long a social and culinary magnet for the avant-garde. The famous people who have sat in the "Pleasure Garden of the Lilacs" are almost countless: Gertrude Stein and Alice B. Toklas, Ingres, Henry James, Chateaubriand, Picasso, Hemingway, Apollinaire, Lenin and Trotsky (at the chess board), Whistler, and more. Today the crowd is likely to include a sprinkling of stars and the star-struck. The place resounds with the sometimes rather loud sounds of a jazz pianist, making the interior seem even more claustrophobic than it already is. It's sometimes tough to get a seat in what's called the *bateau* (boat) section, but you can make the wait a lot more enjoyable by ordering the world's best champagne julep at the bar. It's possible to have just coffee or a drink at the bar, though the food is better than ever. Try the veal kidneys with mustard, veal ribs in cider sauce, steak tartare, or pike-perch quenelles.

171 bd. du Montparnasse, 6th arr. ℭ **01-40-51-34-50.** Reservations recommended far in advance (restaurant only). Main courses 120–220F (18.25–33.45€, $17.40–$31.90); brasserie main courses 90–180F (13.75–27.35€, $13.05–$26.10). AE, DC, V. Restaurant daily noon–3pm and 7:30–11pm. Brasserie daily 11:30am–1am. Métro: Port Royal or Vavin.

MODERATE

Alcazar Bar & Restaurant 🏵 FRENCH (MODERN)   Paris's most high-profile *brasserie de luxe* is this artfully high-tech place funded by British restaurateur/*wunderkind* Sir Terence Conran. (His chain of restaurants in London has succeeded in captivating a tough audience of jaded European foodies.) It features an all-white futuristic decor in a large street-level dining room and a busy bar a floor above. Menu examples are grilled entrecôte with béarnaise sauce and fried potatoes, Charolais duckling with honey and spices, sashimi and sushi with lime, monkfish filet with saffron in puff pastry, and a collection of shellfish and oysters from the waters of Brittany. The wines are as stylish and diverse as you'd expect, and the trendy crowd tends to wear a lot of black.

62 rue Mazarine, 6th arr. ℭ **01-53-10-19-99.** Reservations recommended. Main courses 90–170F (13.75–25.85€, $13.05–$24.65); fixed-price lunch menus 140–160F (21.35–24.30€, $20.30–$23.20). AE, DC, MC, V. Daily noon–3pm and 7pm–2am. Métro: Odéon.

(*Moments* Street Eats

You can find a large variety of street food sold everywhere from the Latin Quarter to outside the *grands magasins* on the Right Bank. Tasty sandwiches, crêpes, *frites,* and (in cold weather) delicious roasted chestnuts are just a few of the items available. The crêpes are especially good—freshly made and filled with your choice of ingredients: cheese, ham, egg (or a combination of these); chocolate and nuts; apricot jam; or some other treat.

Allard ⊛⊛ FRENCH (TRADITIONAL)   Long missing from this guide, this old-time bistro, opened in 1931, is back and as good as ever following a long decline. Once it was the leading bistro, although today the competition is too great to reclaim that reputation. In the front room is a zinc bar, a haven preferred by many celebrities over the years, including Mme Pompidou and movie actor Alain Delon. All the old Allard specialties are still offered, with quality ingredients deftly handled by the kitchen. Try the snails, foie gras, veal stew, or frogs' legs. We head here on Mondays for the *boeuf à la mode* (beef braised in red wine with carrots) and on Wednesdays for the *coq au vin*. The *cassoulet Toulousain* (casserole of white beans and goose and other meats) remains one of the Left Bank's best. For dessert, we vote for the *tarte tatin*.

41 rue St-André-des-Arts, 6th arr. ✆ **01-43-26-48-23.** Reservations required. Main courses 120–200F (18.25–30.40€, $17.40–$29); fixed-price menus 150F (22.80€, $21.75) at lunch, 150–200F (22.80–30.40€, $21.75–$29) at dinner. AE, DC, MC, V. Mon–Sat 12:30–2:30pm and 7:30–11:30pm. Métro: St-Michel or Odéon.

Chez Gramond FRENCH (TRADITIONAL)   Aficionados of the way France used to be seek out this place, and if you're looking for the kind of cuisine that used to satisfy the *grands intellectuels* of the Latin Quarter in the 1960s, you might find it appealing. It seats only 20 people, each of whom is treated to the savoir-faire of Auvergne-born Jean-Claude Gramond and his charming wife, Jeannine. Listed in purple ink that's duplicated on an old-time mimeograph machine in back, the menu items may include roasted partridge in wine sauce, suckling lamb with sorrel sauce, terrines of foie gras, seared scallops with butter sauce on a bed of leeks, and succulent lamb stew with white beans. Try the *soufflé Grand Marnier* for dessert. The wine list is carefully balanced and fairly priced.

5 rue de Fleurus, 6th arr. ✆ **01-42-22-28-89.** Reservations recommended. Main courses 138–170F (21.05–25.85€, $20–$24.65). MC, V. Mon–Sat noon–2:30pm and 7–10pm. Closed in Aug. Métro: Notre-Dame des Champs.

La Rôtisserie d'en Face ⊛ *Value* FRENCH (TRADITIONAL)   This is Paris's most frequented baby bistro, operated by Jacques Cagna, whose vastly expensive restaurant (above) is across the street. The informal place features a postmodern decor with high-tech lighting and black lacquer chairs, and the simply prepared food is very good and uses high-quality ingredients. It includes several types of ravioli, pâté of duckling *en croûte* with foie gras, *friture d'éperlans* (tiny fried freshwater fish), and smoked Scottish salmon with spinach. Monsieur Cagna has added pork cheeks, based on an old family recipe. His Barbary duckling in red-wine sauce is incomparable.

2 rue Christine, 6th arr. ✆ **01-43-26-40-98.** Reservations recommended. Fixed-price menus 145–165F (22.05–25.10€, $21.05–$23.95) at lunch, 245F (37.25€, $35.55) at dinner. AE, MC, V. Mon–Fri noon–2:30pm; Mon–Sat 7–11:30pm. Métro: Odéon.

Yugaraj INDIAN   On two floors of an old Latin Quarter building, Yugaraj serves flavor-filled food based on the recipes of northern and (to a lesser degree) southern India. In recently renovated rooms done in vivid shades of "Indian pink," with a formally dressed staff and lots of intricately carved Kashmiri panels and statues, you can sample the spicy, aromatic tandoori dishes that are all the rage in France. Seafood specialties are usually made with warm-water fish imported from the Seychelles, including thiof, capitaine, and bourgeois, prepared as they would be in Calcutta, with tomatoes, onions, cumin, coriander, ginger, and garlic. Curried lamb with coriander is a particular favorite.

14 rue Dauphine, 6th arr. ℂ **01-43-26-44-91.** Reservations recommended. Main courses 102–128F (15.50–19.45€, $14.85–$18.55); fixed-price menus 99–290F (15.05–44.15€, $14.35–$42.05) at lunch, 180–290F (27.35–44.15€, $26.10–$42.05) at dinner. AE, DC, MC, V. Tues–Sun noon–2:15pm and daily 7–11pm. Métro: Pont-Neuf.

INEXPENSIVE

Aux Charpentiers FRENCH (TRADITIONAL)   This battered old veteran bistro attracts those seeking Left Bank Paris of yesterday. This bistro, opened more than 130 years ago, was once the rendezvous of the master carpenters, whose guild was next door. Nowadays young men bring their dates here. Though the food isn't especially imaginative, it's well-prepared in the best tradition of *cuisine bourgeoise*—hearty but not refined. Appetizers include pâté of duck and rabbit terrine. Especially recommended as a main course is the roast duck with olives. The *plats du jour* recall French home cooking: salt pork with lentils, *pot-au-feu,* and stuffed cabbage. The wine list has a large selection of Bordeaux, including Château Gaussens.

10 rue Mabillon, 6th arr. ℂ **01-43-26-30-05.** Reservations required. Main courses 90–130F (13.75–19.75€, $13.05–$18.85); fixed-price menu 120F (18.25€, $17.40) at lunch, 158F (24€, $22.90) at dinner. AE, DC, MC, V. Daily noon–3pm and 7–11:30pm. Métro: St-Germain-des-Près.

Bistro de la Grille FRENCH (TRADITIONAL)   Many of your fellow diners at this arts-conscious bistro are likely to own or work in nearby boutiques. If you're alone, you might opt to dine at the bar near the entrance, surrounded by photos of film stars from the early years of the French Pathé cinema. The tables upstairs are moderately more sedate than those on the bustling street level. Menu items arrive in generous portions but are rarely daring—platters of fresh shellfish, traditional bone marrow spread over roughly textured bread, sautéed salmon with wild mushrooms, and the ever-popular (at least in France) veal's head with capers and mayonnaise and mustard sauce. Desserts include traditional favorites like *tarte tatin, mousse au chocolat,* and *gratin de fruit de saison.*

14 rue Mabillon, 6th arr. ℂ **01-43-54-16-87.** Reservations recommended. Main courses 80–120F (12.15–18.25€, $11.60–$17.40); fixed-price menu 110F (16.70€, $15.95) at lunch, 160F (24.30€, $23.20) at dinner. MC, V. Daily noon–midnight. Métro: St-Germain-des Près.

Chez Diane FRENCH (MODERN & TRADITIONAL)   Come here for fashionable restaurant food at simple bistro prices. Designed to accommodate only 40 diners, this place is illuminated with Venetian glass chandeliers and paved with old-fashioned floor tiles. The deep ochres and terra-cottas are redolent of Provence's landscapes and villas. Chez Diane's offerings change with the seasons and the owners' inspirations. Recently we enjoyed sweetbreads in flap mushroom sauce, nuggets of wild boar in honey sauce, minced salmon terrine with green peppercorns, and a light-textured modern adaptation of *hachis Parmentier,* an elegant meat loaf lightened with parsley, chopped onions, and herbs. To finish with a sweet touch, we recommend the *charlotte au fromage blanc,* a tasty cheesecake with blueberry sauce.

25 rue Servandoni, 6th arr. ℂ **01-46-33-12-06.** Reservations recommended for groups of 4 or more. Main courses 100–140F (15.20–21.35€, $14.50–$20.30); fixed-price menu 160F (24.30€, $23.20). V. Mon–Fri noon–2pm; Mon–Sat 8–11:30pm. Métro: St-Sulpice.

Crémerie-Restaurant Polidor 🟊🟊 *(Kids)* FRENCH (TRADITIONAL) Crémerie Polidor is the most traditional bistro in the Odéon area, serving *cuisine familiale.* Its name dates from the early 1900s, when it specialized in frosted cream desserts, but the restaurant itself can trace its history back to 1845.

AT&T Direct® Service

1. Just dial the AT&T Access Number for the country you are calling from.
2. Dial the phone number you're calling.
3. Dial your card number.*

AT&T Access Numbers

Anguilla▲	1-800-USA-ATT1
Antigua (hotels)▲	1-800-USA-ATT1
Aruba	800-8000
Australia	**1-800-881-011**
Austria ●	0800-200-288
Bahamas	**1-800-USA-ATT1**
Barbados▲	1-800-USA-ATT1
Belgium●	**0-800-100-10**
Bermuda▲	1-800-USA-ATT1
British V.I.▲	1-800-USA-ATT1
Canada	**1-800-CALL-ATT**
Cayman Islands ▲	1-800-USA-ATT1
China, PRC▲	10811
Cook Islands	09-111
Costa Rica	0-800-0-114-114
Czech Republic▲	**00-42-000-101**
Denmark	**8001-0010**
Dominica▲	1-800-USA-ATT1
Dominican Republic▲	**1-800-USA-ATT1**
Egypt (Cairo)●	510-0200

©2001 AT&T

WW

AT&T Direct® Service

1. Just dial the AT&T Access Number for the country you are calling from.
2. Dial the phone number you're calling.
3. Dial your card number.○

AT&T Access Numbers

Fiji●	004-890-1001
Finland●	0-8001-10015
France.	0800-99-00-11
French Antilles▲	0800-99-00-11
Germany	0-800-2255-288
Greece●	00-800-1311
Grenada▲	1-800-USA-ATT1
Hong Kong	800-96-1111
Hungary●	06-800-01111
Ireland✓	1-800-550-000
Israel●	1-800-94-94-949
Italy●	172-1011
Jamaica	1-800-USA-ATT1
Jamaica▲	872
Japan▲	005-39-111
Japan●	0066-55-111
Korea●	0072-911
Malaysia▲	1-800-80-0011
Mexico●▽	01-800-288-2872
Mexico ▽	001-800-462-4240

AT&T Direct® Service

1. Just dial the AT&T Access Number for the country you are calling from.
2. Dial the phone number you're calling.
3. Dial your card number.○

AT&T Access Numbers

Netherlands●	0800-022-9111
Neth. Antilles ★ ▲	001-800-USA-ATT1
New Zealand●	000-911
Norway	800-190-11
Portugal▲	800-800-128
Puerto Rico/U.S. V.I.	1-800-CALL-ATT
St. Kitts/Nevis▲	1-800-USA-ATT1
St. Lucia▲	1-800-USA-ATT1
St. Vincent▲	1-800-USA-ATT1
Singapore	80-0001-0001
Singapore	800-0111-111
South Africa	0-800-99-0123
Spain	900-99-00-11
Sweden.	020-799-111
Switzerland●	0-800-89001
Switzerland●	001-999-111-11
Thailand<	001-999-111-11
Trinidad & Tobago▲	1-800-USA-ATT1
Turkey●	00-800-12277
U.K.	0800-89-0011
U.K.	0500-89-0011

ALPS   ASPEN

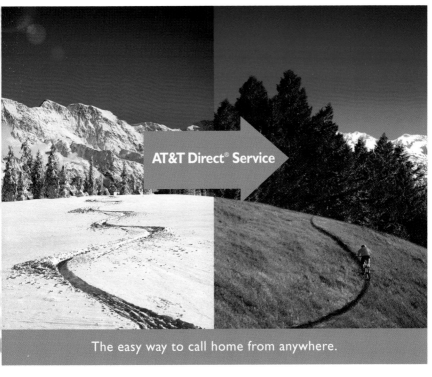

AT&T Direct® Service

The easy way to call home from anywhere.

Global   **AT&T**
connection   direct
with the AT&T   service
Network

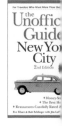

The Crémerie was André Gide's favorite, and Joyce, Hemingway, Valéry, Artaud, and Kerouac also dined here. The place is still frequented largely by students and artists, who head for the rear. Peer beyond the lace curtains and brass hat racks to see drawers where repeat customers lock up their cloth napkins. Overworked but smiling waitresses with frilly aprons and T-shirts bearing the likeness of old mère Polidor serve the 19th-century cuisine. Try the pumpkin soup followed by *boeuf bourguignonne*, Basque-style chicken, or *blanquette de veau*. For dessert, get a chocolate, raspberry, or lemon tart—the best in all Paris.

41 rue Monsieur-le-Prince, 6th arr. ✆ **01-43-26-95-34.** Main courses 40–78F (6.10–11.85€, $5.80–$11.30); fixed-price menu 55F (8.35€, $8.05) Mon–Fri only, 110F (16.70€, $15.95) at dinner. No credit cards. Daily noon–2:30pm; Mon–Sat 7pm–12:30am, Sun 7–11pm. Métro: Odéon.

La Bastide Odéon ★ *Finds* PROVENÇAL   The sunny climes of Provence come through in the pale yellow walls, heavy oaken tables, and artfully arranged bouquets of wheat and dried roses. Chef Gilles Ajuelos, formerly employed in some grand restaurants, prepares a market-based cuisine. His simplest first courses are the most satisfying, like sardines and seared sweet peppers with olive oil and pine nuts, grilled eggplant with herbs and oil, and eggplant-stuffed roasted rabbit with olive toast and balsamic vinegar. Main courses include wild duckling with pepper sauce and exotica like lamb's feet and giblets. A winning dessert is the warm almond pie with prune and Armagnac ice cream.

7 rue Corneille, 6th arr. ✆ **01-43-26-03-65.** Reservations recommended. Fixed-price menus 159–199F (24.15–30.25€, $23.05–$28.85). MC, V. Tues–Sat 12:30–2pm and 7:30–11pm. Métro: Odéon. RER: Luxembourg.

Le Canton *Finds* CHINESE/VIETNAMESE   The cuisine is exotic, especially the Vietnamese dishes, and the setting relaxing and evocative of Asia. Best of all, the food is affordable and more savory than at the nearby fast-food joints. Begin with any of the versions of *nem* (Vietnamese ravioli) stuffed with shrimp and vegetables. Delicate dim sum are available, as well as main courses like salt-and-pepper shrimp, Szechuan-style chicken, and the best-selling Yorkson shrimp quick-fried with garlic, peppers, and onions. The soups are wonderful. The chefs amply use basil, the smell of which permeates the two dining rooms.

5 rue Gozlin, 6th arr. ✆ **01-43-26-51-86.** Reservations recommended. Main courses 47–65F (7.15–9.90€, $6.80–$9.45); fixed-price menus 78–94F (11.85–14.30€, $11.30–$13.65) at lunch, 75–90F (11.40–13.75€, $10.95–$13.05) at dinner. MC, V. Mon–Sat noon–2:30pm and 7–11pm. Métro: St-Germain-des-Prés.

13TH ARRONDISSEMENT
MODERATE

Auberge Etchegorry BASQUE   Its windows overlook a verdant patch of lawn that's so green you might for a moment imagine you've entered a rustic countryside inn. Dark paneling, deep colors, hanging hams and pigtails of garlic, and lacy curtains emulate the Basque country, the corner of southwestern France adjacent to Spain. Victor Hugo and Chateaubriand ate here in centuries past. The cramped tables are a drawback, but not much of one in this rich atmosphere. The menu includes a roster of specialties like cassoulet, magret of duckling, beef filet with peppercorns, a peppery omelet known as *piperades,* cocottes of mussels, and terrines or pan-fried slices of foie gras. The comfortable three-star Hôtel du Vert Galant is associated with the restaurant (see chapter 5).

41 rue Croulebarbe, 13th arr. ✆ **01-44-08-83-51.** Reservations recommended. Main courses 75–165F (11.40–25.10€, $10.90–$23.95); fixed-price menus 190–230F (28.90–34.95€, $27.55–$33.35). AE, DC, V. Mon–Sat noon–2:30pm and 7:30–10:30pm. Métro: Gobelins or Corvisart.

Le Petit Marguery FRENCH (TRADITIONAL)   The aura of this place is that of a turn-of-the-century bistro, with antique floor tiles, banquettes, etched glass, vested waiters, and a color scheme of dark rose. Menu items are firmly based in old-fashioned French traditions, with emphasis on game dishes in autumn and fresh produce in summer. The finest examples include slices of wild duck breast, dusted with white pepper and strewn over mounds of shredded cabbage; a sauté of wild mushrooms; a *petit sale* of duckling that's served with braised cabbage and garlic-flavored cream sauce; *sole meuniére;* and an old-fashioned version of chetterling sausage (*andouillettes*) that many older French people remember from their childhoods.

9 bd. Du Port-royal, 13th arr. ✆ 01-43-31-58-59. Reservations recommended. 3-course lunch 165–215F (25.15–32.75€, $23.95–$31.25); 3-course dinner 215F (32.75€, $31.25). AE, DC, MC, V. Tues–Sat noon–2pm and 7:30–10pm. Métro: Les Gobelins.

INEXPENSIVE

Keryado ✦ *(Finds* SEAFOOD   Since it was taken over by a sophisticated management in 1992, this blue-and-white seafood bistro specializes in a dish only the most dedicated or arrogant chef would try at home: bouillabaisse. This fish stew has led to more lost reputations, crack-ups, and suicides than any other dish in the history of French cuisine. Fortunately, Keryado's version is as rich, savory, and satisfying as what you'd get in some of the best restaurants of Provence. And it's a relatively modest 140F (21.33€, $20.30) per person. If bouillabaisse isn't your cup of soup, consider other fish dishes like *chaudrée de poissons aïoli,* a stew pot of filets from six types of fish, laced with a rich garlicky broth. Slightly more experimental is a stingray with green cabbage and curry.

32 rue de Regnault, 13th arr. ✆ 01-45-83-87-58. Reservations recommended. Main courses 80–145F (12.15–22.05€, $11.60–$21.05); fixed-price menus 110–150F (16.70–22.80€, $15.95–$21.75). MC, V. Mon–Sat noon–2:30pm; Tues–Sat 7:30–10:30pm. Métro: Porte d'Ivry.

14TH ARRONDISSEMENT
MODERATE

La Cagouille ✦ *(Finds* CENTRAL EUROPEAN/FRENCH (TRADI-TIONAL)/SEAFOOD   Don't expect to find meat at this temple of seafood—burly and genteel owner Gérard Allamandou refuses to feature it on his menu. Everything about La Cagouille is a testimonial to a modern version of the culinary arts of La Charente, the flat sandy district hugging the Atlantic south of Bordeaux. In a trio of simple oak-sheathed dining rooms with marble-topped tables, you'll sample seafood prepared as simply and naturally as possible, with no fancy sauces or elaborate cooking techniques. Allamandou's preferred fish is red mullet, which might appear sautéed in a bland oil or baked in rock salt. The name of the place derives from the regional symbol of La Charente: the sea snail, whose preparation is elevated to a fine culinary art here. Look for a vast assemblage of all-French, mostly white wines and at least 150 cognacs. On place Constantine-Brancusi, during the summer, there's a partially concealed terrace for outside dining.

10–12 place Constantine-Brancusi, 14th arr. ✆ 01-43-22-09-01. Reservations recommended. Main courses 120–180F (18.25–27.35€, $17.40–$26.10); fixed-price menus 150–250F (22.80–38€, $21.75–$36.25). AE, V. Daily noon–2pm and 7:30–10:30pm. Métro: Gaîté.

L'Assiette SOUTHWESTERN FRENCH   Everything about this place appeals to a nostalgic crowd seeking down-to-earth prices and flavor-filled food. You'll recognize it by the bordeaux-colored facade and potted plants in the windows. The place was a *charcuterie* (pork butcher's shop) in the 1930s and today maintains some of its old accessories. Mitterrand used to drop in with his cronies for oysters, crayfish, sea urchins, and clams. The food is unashamedly inspired by Paris's long tradition of bistro cuisine, with a few twists. Examples are chanterelle mushroom salad; *rillettes* (a roughly textured pâté) of mackerel; roasted guinea fowl; and desserts made on the premises, including a crumbly version of apple cake with fresh North African figs. Particularly delicious is a *petit salé* (stew with vegetables) of duckling with wine from the Poitou region of west-central France.

181 rue du Château, 14th arr. ✆ **01-43-22-64-86.** Reservations recommended. Main courses 150–200F (22.80–30.40€, $21.75–$29); fixed-price menu 200F (30.40€, $29). AE, MC, V. Wed–Sun noon–2:30pm and 8–10:30pm. Closed Aug. Métro: Gaité.

La Régalade SOUTHWESTERN FRENCH   The setting is a convivial bistro with banquettes the color of aged Bordeaux wine, congenially harassed service, and unexpectedly good food. The fixed-price menu presents a choice of at least 10 starters, 10 main courses, and about a dozen freshly made desserts or selections from a cheese tray. The inspiration is Yves Camdeborde's, known for his training at the posh Hôtel de Crillon. The menu changes with the seasons but is likely to include wild boar filet with red-wine sauce, a savory mix of potatoes with blood sausage, and an always-popular platter of fried goose liver served on toasted slices of spice bread.

49 av. Jean-Moulin, 14th arr. ✆ **01-45-45-68-58.** Reservations recommended. Fixed-price menu 185F (28.10€, $26.85). V. Tues–Fri noon–2:15pm and 7pm–midnight; Sat 7pm–midnight. Closed mid-July–mid-Aug. Métro: Alésia.

INEXPENSIVE

Restaurant Bleu AUVERGNAT   Why is this restaurant named blue? The answer is no secret—it's in honor of the eyes of chef/owner Simon Christian, who has been entertaining Paris diners for the last 6 years. The decor evokes a market town's inn, with dark paneling, farm implements, paintings of barnyard animals (especially sheep), and souvenirs of long ago. The English-speaking hostess recommends a house specialty (*truffade des bergers*) to anyone who doesn't know a *saucisson* from a *saucisse*. Made with potatoes, goose fat, Auvergnat cheese, and parsley, it's a worthy opener for main courses like grilled Charolais beefsteak with a sauce made from heady Cahors red wine, grilled blood sausage, braised pork shoulder, and cassoulet of fish. Prune tarts make a flavorful ending. There are only about 40 seats, so reservations are important.

46 rue Didot, 14th arr. ✆ **01-45-43-70-56.** Reservations required. Fixed-price menu 110–175F (16.70–26.60€, $15.95–$25.45) at lunch, 140–175F (21.35–26.60€, $20.30–$25.45) at dinner. MC, V. Tues–Fri noon–2:30pm and Tues–Sat 7:30–10:15pm. Closed Aug. Métro: Alésia.

7TH ARRONDISSEMENT
VERY EXPENSIVE

L'Arpège ✹✹✹ FRENCH (MODERN)   L'Arpège is best known for Alain Passard's adventurous specialties—no restaurant in the 7th serves better food. Across from the Musée Rodin in a prosperous residential neighborhood, L'Arpège has claimed the site of what for years was the world-famous L'Archestrate, where Passard worked in the kitchens. Amid a modern decor of etched glass, burnished steel, monochromatic oil paintings, and pearwood paneling, you can enjoy innovative specialties like Breton lobster in sweet-and-sour rosemary sauce, scallops prepared with cauliflower and lime-flavored grape sauce, and pan-fried duck with juniper and lime sauce. The signature dessert is a candied tomato stuffed with 12 kinds of dried and fresh fruit and served with anise-flavored ice cream.

84 rue de Varenne, 7th arr. ℂ 01-47-05-09-06. Fax. 01-44-18-98-39. Reservations required far in advance. Main courses 320–780F (48.65–118.55€, $46.40–$113.10); *menu dégustation* (tasting menu) 1,400F (212.80€, $203). AE, DC, MC, V. Mon–Fri 12:30–2pm and 8–10pm. Métro: Varenne.

EXPENSIVE

Le Violon d'Ingres ☆☆☆ FRENCH (MODERN & TRADITIONAL)

This restaurant is Paris's pièce de résistance. Chef/owner Christian Constant is "the new Robuchon." Those who are fortunate enough to dine in the Violon's warm atmosphere of rose-colored wood, soft cream walls, and elegant chintz fabrics patterned with old English tea roses always rave about the cleverly artistic dishes. They range from a starter of pan-fried foie gras with gingerbread and spinach salad to more elegant main courses like lobster ravioli with crushed vine-ripened tomatoes, roasted veal in a light and creamy milk sauce served with tender spring vegetables, and even a selection from the rotisserie, like spit-roasted leg of lamb rubbed with fresh garlic and thyme. Chef Constant keeps a well-chosen selection of wine to accompany his meals. The service is charming and discreet.

135 rue St-Dominique, 7th arr. ℂ **01-45-55-15-05.** Fax 01-45-55-48-42. Reservations required at least 3–4 days in advance. Main courses 190–230F (28.95–34.95€, $27.55–$33.35); fixed-price *menu dégustation* 590F (89.75€, $85.55). AE, MC, V. Mon–Sat 7–11pm. Métro: Ecole Militaire.

Paul Minchelli ☆ SEAFOOD   Much of the appeal of this restaurant comes from its deliberate earthiness and refusal to indulge in gratuitous rituals. The cuisine of Marseille-born Paul Minchelli is described even by his financial backers as "marginal," rejecting Paris's culinary conventions in favor of an old-fashioned Provençal technique. He's said to have reinvented fish (or at least the way we cook it) by stripping away extra sauces and conflicting flavors to reveal the true "taste of the sea." In a dining room boasting Norwegian birchwood stained to a distinctive yellow, modern furniture, and round seascapes evocative of the portholes on a ship, you can order dishes like raw saltwater fish with only olive oil, salt, and pepper; old-fashioned merlan Colbert; grilled John Dory; sea bass filet steamed in seaweed; lobster cooked with honey and spices; and one of the best herring salads in Paris. *Be warned:* There aren't many alternatives for those who dislike fish.

54 bd. de la Tour-Maubourg, 7th arr. ℂ **01-47-05-89-86.** Reservations required far in advance. Main courses 290–630F (44.10–95.75€, $42.05–$91.35); fixed-price lunch 350F (53.20€, $50.75). MC, V. Tues–Sat noon–3pm and 8–11pm. Closed Aug. Métro: La Tour Maubourg.

MODERATE

La Petite Chaise FRENCH (TRADITIONAL)   This is Paris's oldest restaurant, opened as an inn in 1680 by the baron de la Chaise at the edge of what was a large hunting preserve. (According to popular lore, the baron used the upstairs bedrooms for afternoon dalliances, between fox and pheasant hunts.) Very Parisian, the "Little Chair" invites you into a world of cramped but attractive tables, old wood paneling, and ornate wall sconces. A vigorous chef has brought renewed taste and flavor to this longtime favorite, and the four-course set menu offers a large choice of dishes in each category. Examples are a salad with duck breast strips on a bed of fresh lettuce, seafood-and-scallop ragout with saffron, beef filet with green peppercorns, and poached fish with steamed vegetables served in a sauce of fish and vegetable stock and cream.

Restaurants in the 7th & 15th Arrondissements

Au Pied de Fouet **10**
Café des Hauteurs **6**
Café de l'Os à Moelle **13**
Chez l'Ami Jean **3**
Kim Anh **13**
La Fontaine de Mars **2**
L'Arpège **5**
La Petite Chaise **8**
Le Bamboche **9**
Le Café du Commerce **12**
Le Rouquet **7**
Le Violon d'Ingres **1**
Paul Minchelli **4**
Restaurant du Marché **11**

⊠ Post Office
✝ Church
Ⓜ Métro

36–38 rue de Grenelle, 7th arr. ✆ **01-42-22-13-35.** Reservations recommended. Fixed-price menus 160–195F (24.30–29.65€, $23.20–$28.35). AE, V. Daily noon–2pm and 7–11pm. Métro: Sèvres-Babylone or Rue du Bac.

Le Bamboche NORTHERN FRENCH   Le Bamboche charges prices that are more reasonable than you'd expect for cuisine with this degree of finesse. Meals are served in a pair of dining rooms painted in the colors of ancient Pompeii or Renaissance Tuscany (dark ochre and burnt orange), depending on your point of view. Menu items change with the season but are likely to include roasted foie gras wrapped in glazed Parma ham, served with fresh asparagus; cream of cauliflower soup with truffles and essence of lobster; sea bass braised with fresh vegetables and anise; and caramelized Corrèze veal chops with tea sauce. The desserts might include chocolate mousse served with dried fruit and herb-flavored ice cream.

15 rue de Babylone, 7th arr. ✆ **01-45-49-14-40.** Reservations recommended. Main courses 110–190F (16.70–28.90€, $15.95–$27.55); fixed-price menus 190–300F (28.95–45.60€, $27.55–$43.50). AE, MC, V. Mon–Fri noon–2:30pm and 8–11pm. Métro: Sèvres-Babylone.

INEXPENSIVE

Au Pied de Fouet FRENCH (TRADITIONAL)   Au Pied de Fouet is one of the neighborhood's smallest, oldest, and most reasonably priced restaurants. In the 1700s, it was a stopover for carriages en route to Paris from other parts of Europe, offering wine, food, and stables. Don't expect a leisurely or attentive meal: Food and drink will disappear quickly from your table, under the gaze of others waiting their turn. The dishes are solid and unpretentious and include *blanquette de veau, petit salé* (a savory family-style stew made from pork and vegetables), and *sole meunière,* a warhorse of French cuisine but always good.

45 rue de Babylone, 7th arr. ✆ **01-47-05-12-27.** Main courses 55–85F (8.35–12.90€, $8.05–$12.35). No credit cards. Mon–Sat noon–2:30pm; Mon–Fri 7–9:30pm. Closed Aug. Métro: Vaneau.

Chez l'Ami Jean BASQUE/SOUTHWESTERN FRENCH   This restaurant was opened by a Basque nationalist in 1931, and ardent fans claim its Basque cuisine and setting are the most authentic on the Left Bank. Decorative details include wood panels, memorabilia from *pelote* (a Basque game like jai alai) and soccer, and red-and-white woven tablecloths like the ones sold in Bayonne. Menu items include cured Bayonne ham; herb-laden Béarn-influenced vegetable soups; a succulent omelet with peppers, tomatoes, and onions; squid stewed in its own ink and served with tomatoes and herbs; and *poulet basquaise,* cooked with spicy sausage, onions, peppers, and very strong red wine. In springtime, look for a truly esoteric specialty rarely available elsewhere: *saumon de l'Adour* (Adour salmon) with béarnaise sauce.

27 rue Malar, 7th arr. ✆ **01-47-05-86-89.** Reservations recommended. Main courses 80–100F (12.15–15.20€, $11.60–$14.50). MC, V. Mon–Sat noon–3pm and 7–10:30pm. Métro: Invalides.

La Fontaine de Mars PYRÉNÉE/SOUTHWESTERN FRENCH   The restaurant name derives not from its location near the Champ de Mars but from the historic stone fountain on its tree-lined terrace. You'll find a sometimes boisterous dining room on the street level, plus two cozier and calmer upstairs rooms whose round tables and wooden floors make you feel like you're in a private home. An additional 70 or so seats become available by the fountain whenever weather permits. Much of the cuisine derives from the Pyrénées and southwestern France, bearing rich, heady flavors that go well with robust red wines. Examples are duckling confit with parsley potatoes, a Toulouse-inspired cassoulet, veal chops with morels, and red mullet or monkfish filets with herb-flavored butter. Our favorite dessert is a thin tart filled with a sugared purée of apples, capped with more apples, and garnished with Calvados and prunes.

129 rue St-Dominique, 7th arr. ℂ **01-47-05-46-44.** Reservations recommended. Main courses 75–165F (11.40–25.15€, $10.95–$23.95). AE, MC, V. Daily noon–2:30pm and 7:30–11pm. Métro: Ecole Militaire.

15TH ARRONDISSEMENT
MODERATE

Kim Anh VIETNAMESE   This is one of the best addresses in Paris for the savory, spicy cuisine of its former colony. It's a bit lost down in the 15th, but many Parisian foodies journey here anyway. The success of this restaurant at a smaller location a short walk away prompted a recent move into bigger, more appealing premises early in 2001. The cuisine includes the sharp, spicy, sour, and succulent flavors of Vietnam, as prepared in pork, chicken, fish, and beef dishes, many of them excellent. Waiters are very patient in explaining various dishes to newcomers. We are especially fond of the caramelized langoustines and most definitely the stuffed crabs and steamed pork ravioli.

49 av. Emile Zola, 15th arr. ℂ **01-45-79-40-96.** Reservations recommended. Main courses 100–150F (15.20–22.80€, $14.50–$21.75); fixed-price menus 220F (33.45€, $31.90). AE, DC, MC, V. Tues–Sun 7–11pm. Métro: Charles-Michels.

Restaurant du Marché SOUTHWEST FRANCE   Though little about the decor of this place has changed since the 1930s, its wood panels are waxed constantly and the bouquets of fresh flowers frequently replenished. Menu items derive from dishes popular in and around Bordeaux and include an impressive roster of that region's wines to accompany the platters of traditional foie gras, deboned hare stuffed with foie gras and braised in red wine and brandy, and hen stewed with vegetables and Armagnac. The restaurant's name derives from the fact that many of its fresh, unusual ingredients are supplied directly by producers in the Landes district, near Bordeaux.

57–59 rue de Dantzig, 15th arr. ℂ **01-48-28-31-55.** Reservations recommended. Main courses 140–170F (21.35–25.85€, $20.30–$24.65); fixed-price menu 168F (25.55€, $24.35). AE, DC, MC, V. Mon–Fri noon–2:30pm; Mon–Sat 7–11pm. Métro: Porte de Versailles.

INEXPENSIVE

Cave de l'Os à Moelle *Finds* FRENCH (TRADITIONAL)   This restaurant features family-style dining. It contains only three large tables, where guests are seated next to "potluck" strangers, who they often end up toasting with one or more glasses of wine before the end of the meal. There's only one culinary option here: a 130F (19.75€, $18.85) "grand-mère" fixed-price menu with bowls of soup and heaping platters of pâté, rilletes, and cheese. Main course and dessert selections are plunked down on a corner buffet, and guests serve themselves till their appetites are sated. Anticipate country-style beef stews, blood sausage terrine, tiny shellfish with freshly made mayonnaise, and a vast array of hail-and-hearty desserts not unfamiliar to a Norman farmer's wife. Wines are numerous and cheap—the restaurant sells glasses and bottles of wine at rates substantially less than what's available within other competitors. Overall, the experience is satisfying and jolly. Management encourages guests to come either at 7:30 or 9:30pm, as part of a carefully controlled access.

181 rue de Lourmel. 15th arr. ℂ **01-45-57-28-28.** Reservations recommended. Fixed-price menus 130F (19.75€, $18.85). MC, V. Seatings available Tues–Sun 7:30 and 9:30pm and 9:30pm to midnight. Métro: Lourmel.

In Pursuit of the Perfect Parisian Pastry

Could it be true, as rumor has it, that more eggs, sugar, cream, and butter per capita are consumed in Paris than in any other city, with the possible exception of Vienna? From a modern-day Proust sampling a buttery madeleine to a child munching a *pain au chocolat* (chocolate-filled croissant), everyone in Paris seems to be looking for two things: the perfect lover and the perfect pastry, not necessarily in that order. As a Parisian food critic once said, "A day without a pastry is a day in hell!"

Who'd think of beginning a morning in Paris without a **croissant** or two—not prepackaged ones made with lead-like dough, but freshly baked treats, flaky and light and made with real butter, preferably from Norman cows. The Greeks may have invented pastry making, but the French perfected it. Some French pastries have had a greater impact than others. The croissant and the **brioche,** a yeasty sweet breakfast bread, are baked around the world today, as is the fabled **éclair au chocolat** (chocolate éclair), a choux pastry filled with whipped cream or pastry cream and topped with chocolate. Another pastry you should sample on its home turf (you'll never get it quite right in your own kitchen) is the **Napolitain**—layers of cake flour and almonds alternating with fruit purée. (Don't confuse this term with *Neapolitan,* meaning sweets and cakes made with layers of two or more colors, each layer flavored differently.) Very much in vogue is the **millefeuille** ("thousand leaves"), made by arranging thin layers of flaky pastry one on top of the other, along with layers of cream or thick fruit purée or jam; the American version of this is the napoleon.

Here are some of our favorite pâtisseries. **Stohrer,** 51 rue Montorgueil, 2nd arr. (© **01-42-33-38-20;** Métro: Sentier or Les Halles), has been going strong ever since it was opened by Louis XV's pastry chef in 1730. With a day's notice, you can order an 18th-century specialty, **un pithivier,** a.k.a. **une galette des rois** (puff pastry made with almond paste). Available at any time is one of the most luscious desserts in Paris, **baba au rhum,** or its even richer cousin, **un Ali Baba,** which also incorporates cream-based rum-and-raisin filling. Stohrer boasts an interior decor classified as a national historic treasure, with frescoes of damsels in 18th-century costume bearing flowers and (what else?) pastries.

Le Café du Commerce FRENCH (TRADITIONAL)   Le Café is one of this area's best dining bargains. Opened in 1922, this trilevel brasserie was renovated in the late 1980s, its decor designed to hearken back to the glory days of the 1920s, with dozens of verdant plants and photos of the various writers who scribbled manuscripts on its premises. The tables are illuminated by an overhead atrium. The menu choices are old-fashioned, with no attempt at modernity or high style; examples are warm goat cheese on a bed of lettuce, *poulet sauce estragon* (chicken tarragon), duck breast with green-pepper sauce, *sole meunière, croustillant de porc au miel* (crispy baked pork with honey sauce), and escalope of salmon with sage sauce. Crème caramel or chocolate mousse makes for a satisfying dessert. This place is always crowded, but thanks to its three floors, there's usually an available table.

Opened in 1862, a few steps from La Madeleine, **Ladurée Royale,** 16 rue Royale, 8th arr. (*©* **01-42-60-21-79;** Métro: Concorde or Madeleine), is Paris's dowager tearoom. A hot young pastry chef, Pierre Hermé, is the new "star of the *macaron*," a pastry for which this place is celebrated. Karl Lagerfeld comes here and raves about them, as did the late ambassador Pamela Harriman. This macaroon isn't the sticky coconut version known to many, but two almond meringue cookies, flavored with chocolate, vanilla, pistachio, coffee, or other flavor, stuck together with buttercream. You may also want to try one of Hermé's latest creations—the *Coeur du Faubourg,* a lusciously dense chocolate cake with layers of caramel and apricots.

In business since Napoléon was in power, **Dalloyau,** 101 rue du faubourg St-Honoré, 8th arr. (*©* **01-42-99-90-00;** Métro: St-Philippe du Roule), has a name instantly recognizable throughout Paris; it supplies pastries to the Elysée Palace (the French White House) and many Rothschild mansions nearby. Its specialties are *Le Dalloyau,* praline cake filled with almond meringue that's marvelously light textured, and the famous *Mogador* (chocolate cake, chocolate mousse, and a fine layer of raspberry jam). Unlike Stohrer, Dalloyau has a tearoom (open daily from 8am to 7:30pm) one floor above street level, where ladies who lunch can drop in for a slice of pastry that Dalloyau warns is "too fragile to transport, or to mail, over long distances."

The best way to end your pastry tour of Paris is to follow Proust's lead and sample a *madeleine,* a buttery tea cake shaped like a tiny scallop shell. We head for **Lerch,** 4 rue Cardinal-Lemoine, 5th arr. (*©* **01-43-26-15-80;** Métro: Cardinal Lemoine), founded in 1971 by the Alsatian-born Lerch family. It sells goods to luminaries like Martha Stewart as well as to the Proust fans who come hoping the madeleine will "invade their senses with exquisite pleasure," as it did for the narrator of *A la recherce du temps perdu.* Ideally, the madeleine is dipped into tea, preferably the slightly lime-flavored *tilleuil.*

51 rue du Commerce, 15th arr. *©* **01-45-75-03-27.** Reservations recommended. Main courses 61–73F (9.25–11.10€, $8.85–$10.65); fixed-price menus 87–117F (13.20–17.80€, $12.60–$17). AE, DC, MC, V. Daily noon–midnight. Métro: Emile Zola, Grenelle, or La Motte–Picquet.

5 The Top Cafes

As surely everyone knows, the cafe is a Parisian institution. Parisians use them as combination club/tavern/snack bars, almost as extensions of their living rooms. They're spots where you can sit alone reading your newspaper, doing your homework, or writing your memoirs; meet a friend or lover; nibble at a hard-boiled egg; or drink yourself into oblivion. At cafes you meet your dates to go on to a show or to stay and talk. Above all, cafes are for people watching.

Their single common denominator is the encouragement of leisurely sitting. Regardless of whether you have one small coffee or the house's most expensive cognac, nobody will badger, pressure, or hurry you. If you wish to sit there until the place closes, that's your affair. Cafes keep flexible hours depending on the season, the traffic, and the part of town they're in. Nearly all stay open until 1 or 2am, and a few are open all night.

Coffee, of course, is the chief drink. It comes black in a small cup, unless you specifically order it *au lait* (with milk). Tea (*thé*, pronounced tay) is also fairly popular but is generally not of a high quality. If you prefer beer, we advise you to pay a bit more for the imported German, Dutch, or Danish brands, which are much better than the local brew. If you insist on a French beer, at least order it *á pression* (draft), which is superior. There's also a vast variety of fruit drinks, as well as Coca-Cola, which can be rather expensive. French chocolate drinks— either hot or iced—are absolutely superb and on par with the finest Dutch brands. They're made from ground chocolate, not a chemical compound.

Now just a few words on cafe etiquette. You don't pay when you get your order—only when you intend to leave. Payment indicates you've had all you want. *Service compris* means the tip is included in your bill, so it isn't necessary to tip extra; still, most people leave an extra franc or so. You'll hear the locals call for the *"garçon,"* but as a foreigner it would be more polite to say *"monsieur."* All waitresses, on the other hand, are addressed as *"mademoiselle,"* regardless of age or marital status. In the smaller cafes, you may have to share your table. In that case, even if you haven't exchanged a word with your table companion, when you leave it's customary to bid him or her *au revoir.*

For the locations of these cafes, see the corresponding arrondissement maps earlier in this chapter.

EXPENSIVE

Brasserie Lipp   This is a Left Bank institution. On the day of Paris's liberation in 1944, late owner Roger Cazes welcomed Hemingway as the first man to drop in for a drink. Then, as now, famous people often drop by for beer, wine, and conversation. Cazes's nephew, Michel-Jacques Perrochon, now runs this quintessential Parisian brasserie, where the food is secondary, yet quite good, providing you can get a seat (an hour and a half waiting time is customary if the management doesn't know you). The specialty is *choucroute garni,* Paris's best— you get not only sauerkraut but also a thick layer of ham and braised pork, which you can down with the house Riesling (an Alsatian white wine) or beer. Even if you don't go inside for a drink, you can sit at a sidewalk table to enjoy a cognac and people watch.

151 bd. St-Germain, 6th arr. ✆ **01-45-48-53-91.** Full meals average 290F (44.10€, $42.05); *café au lait* 18F (2.75€, $2.60). AE, DC, MC, V. Daily 9am–2am; restaurant service 11am–1am. Métro: St-Germain-des-Prés.

Café de Flore 👛👛👛   It's the most famous cafe in the world, still fighting to maintain the Left Bank aura in spite of massive hordes of visitors from around the world. Sartre—the granddaddy of existentialism, a key figure in the Resistance movement, and a renowned cafe-sitter—often came here during World War II. Wearing a leather jacket and beret, he sat at his table and wrote his trilogy, *Les Chemins de la Liberté* (The Roads to Freedom). Camus, Picasso, and Apollinaire also frequented the Flore. The cafe is still going strong, though the famous patrons have moved on and tourists have taken up all the tables. The menu offers omelets, salads, pavé of beef with pepper sauce, *sole meunière,* and more. The place is especially popular on Sunday mornings.

172 bd. St-Germain, 6th arr. © **01-45-48-55-26**. *Café espresso* 24F (3.65€, $3.55); glass of beer 42F (6.45€, $6.15). AE, DC, MC, V. Daily 7am–1:30am. Métro: St-Germain-des-Prés.

Café de la Paix ★★ This hub of the tourist world rules place de l'Opéra, and the legend goes that if you sit here long enough, you'll see someone you know passing by. Huge, grandiose, fashionable, and sometimes brusque and anonymous, it harbors not only Parisians but also, at one time or another, nearly every visiting American—a tradition dating from the end of World War I. Once Emile Zola sat on the terrace; later, Hemingway and Fitzgerald frequented it. The best news for tourists who stop in for a bite is that prices have recently been lowered because of stiff competition in the area. Menu items may include escalope of veal with mushrooms and cream sauce, seafood *bourride* (stew) in the style of Provence, and beef filet with red-wine/mushroom sauce.

Place de l'Opéra, 17 BD des Capucines, 9th arr. © **01-40-07-30-20**. *Café espresso* 19F (2.95€, $2.75); fixed-price menu 138F (21.05€, $20) for 2 courses, 178F (27.05€, $25.80) for 3 courses. Daily noon–midnight. Métro: Opéra.

Fouquet's ★ For people watching, this is definitely on the see-and-be-seen circuit. Fouquet's has been collecting anecdotes and a patina since it was founded in 1901. A celebrity favorite, it has attracted Chaplin, Chevalier, Dietrich, Churchill, Roosevelt, and Jackie O. The premier cafe on the Champs-Elysées sits behind a barricade of potted flowers at the edge of the sidewalk. You can choose a table in the sunshine or retreat to the glassed-in elegance of the leather banquettes and rattan furniture of the grill room. Though this is a full-fledged restaurant, with a beautiful formal dining room on the second floor, most visitors come by just for a glass of wine, coffee, or sandwich.

99 av. des Champs-Elysées, 8th arr. © **01-47-23-50-00**. Glass of wine from 36F (5.45€, $5.20); sandwiches 55F (8.35€, $8.05); main courses 160–380F (24.30–57.75€, $23.20–$55.10); fixed-price menu 300F (45.60€, $43.50). AE, MC, V. Daily 8–2am. Restaurant daily noon–3pm and 7pm–12:30am; bar 9–2am. Métro: George V.

Le Rouquet ★ *(Finds* Despite its conventional food and high prices, Le Rouquet enjoys an enviable cachet and sense of chic, partly because it competes on a less flamboyant scale with the nearby Café de Flore and Les Deux Magots and partly because the decor hasn't changed since a 1954 remodeling. Less than 60 yards from St-Germain church, you can sit for as long as you want, watching a crowd of stylish Italians and Americans performing shopping and people-watching rituals barely altered since Le Roquet's founding in 1922.

188 bd. St-Germain, 7th arr. © **01-45-48-06-93**. *Café au lait* 13–23F (2.05–3.50€, $1.95–$3.35); *plats du jour* 60F (9.10€, $8.70). MC, V. Mon–Sat 7am–9pm. Métro: St-Germain-des-Prés.

MODERATE

Café Beaubourg Located next to the all-pedestrian plaza of the Centre Pompidou, this is a trendy avant-garde cafe with soaring concrete columns and a minimalist decor. Many of the regulars work in the neighborhood's eclectic shops and galleries. You can order salads, omelets, grilled steak, chicken Cordon Bleu, pastries, and daily platters. In warm weather, tables are set up on the sprawling outdoor terrace, providing a great place to watch the young and the restless go by.

100 rue St-Martin, 4th arr. © **01-48-87-63-96**. Glass of wine 23–40F (3.50–6.10€, $3.35–$5.80); beer 27–40F (4.10–6.10€, $3.90–$5.80); American breakfast 110F (16.70€, $15.95); sandwiches and platters 40–170F (6.10–25.85€, $5.80–$24.65). AE, DC, MC, V. Sun–Thurs 8 –1am; Fri–Sat 8 –2am. Métro: Rambuteau or Hôtel de Ville.

Café Cosmos ✶✶ Does today's generation have a cafe to equal the Lost Generation's Select or Coupole? Perhaps it's the ultramodern Cosmos, where you might rub elbows with a French film star or an executive ("no one writes novels anymore"). The cafe features wooden tables, black leather chairs, and black clothing in winter—the perfect backdrop for smoked salmon with toast, rumpsteak with roquefort sauce, or grilled tuna steak.

101 bd. du Montparnasse, 6th arr. ⓒ **01-43-26-74-36.** *Café espresso* 25F (3.80€, $3.65); platters 42–85F (6.40–12.90€, $6.15–$12.35); fixed-price lunch 69F (10.55€, $10). AE, DC, MC, V. Daily 7 –2am. Métro: Vavin.

Café de la Musique This cafe's location in one of the grandest of Mitterrand's *grands travaux* guarantees a crowd passionately devoted to music; the recorded sounds that play in the background are likely to be more diverse and more eclectic than those in any other cafe in Paris. The red-and-green velour setting might remind you of a modern opera house, with windows overlooking nearby place de la Fontaine. On the menu you'll find pasta with shellfish, roast pork in cider sauce, and braised stingray in black butter sauce. Wednesdays from 10pm to 1am brings a program of live jazz and Fridays from 10pm to 1am brings live music; Saturdays a DJ entertains with disco music.

In the Cité de la Musique, Place Fontaine Aux Lions, 212 av. Jean-Jaurès, 19th arr. ⓒ **01-48-03-15-91.** *Plats du jour* 75F (11.40€, $10.95). AE, DC, MC, V. Daily 7 –2am (full menu daily 11am–midnight). Métro: Porte de Pantin.

Café des Hauteurs The designers of the Musée d'Orsay recognize the fatigue that can sometimes come with a museum visit. That's why this fifth-floor cafe is midway between a bar and a short-term rest home, where you can recuperate in front of a sweeping view stretching as far as Notre-Dame and Sacré-Coeur and looking over the glass-encased mechanism of a huge clock. In addition to the usual doses of caffeine and alcohol, you can order platters more substantial than a snack but less filling than the main course of a conventional meal. Examples are smoked salmon with shrimp salad and rye bread and a platter of assorted cheeses.

In the Musée d'Orsay, 1 rue de Bellechasse, (5th floor), 7th arr. ⓒ **01-45-49-47-03.** Salads 39–70F (5.95–10.65€, $5.65–$10.15). AE, MC, V. Tues–Wed and Fri–Sun 10am–5pm; Thurs 10am–9pm. Métro: Solférino. RER: Musée d'Orsay.

Café Marly This is for your rendezvous at the Louvre, especially if you're meeting a modern-day La Giaconda or a guy who looks like he posed for one of those Adonis statues inside the museum. In 1994, the French government gave the green light for a cafe and restaurant to open in one of the Louvre's most historic courtyards, accessible only from a point close to the famous glass pyramid that rises above the Cour Marly. It has become a favorite refuge of Parisians trying to escape the traffic roar on rue de Rivoli. Anyone is welcome to sit down for a *café au lait* daily from 8am to 2am. But more substantial fare is the norm here, served in one of three dining rooms done in tones of burgundy, black, and gilt. Menu items include club sandwiches, fresh fish, pepper steak, and an array of upscale bistro-inspired food. In summer, outdoor tables overlook the celebrated courtyard.

In the Cour Napoléon du Louvre, 93 rue de Rivoli, 1st arr. ⓒ **01-49-26-06-60.** Reservations recommended. Main courses 110–150F (16.70–22.80€, $15.95–$21.75). AE, DC, MC, V. Daily 8–2am (meals 11:30am–1am). Métro: Palais Royal or Musée du Louvre.

Café/Restaurant/Salon de Thé Bernardaud ★★ Few other Paris cafes/tearooms mingle salesmanship with culinary pizzazz as effectively as this one. The venerable Limoges-based manufacturer of porcelain Bernardaud opened it in 1995, and the staggeringly beautiful stuff is on display everywhere. Occupying some of Europe's most expensive commercial real estate, the medium-green space is upscale Art Deco in style. Lunchtime is flooded with employees of the nearby offices and shoppers, and you can opt for just a salad or something more substantial, like a medley of fresh fish in herb sauce with vegetables. Afternoon tea adds a new twist: A staff member will present a choice of five porcelain patterns in which your tea will be served, and if you finish your Earl Grey with a fixation on the pattern you've chosen, you'll be directed into the adjacent showroom to place your order.

9 rue Royale, 8th arr. ℂ **01-42-66-22-55.** Reservations recommended at lunch. Continental breakfast 55F (8.35€, $8.05); lunch main courses 90–130F (13.70–19.75€, $13.05–$18.85); afternoon tea with pastry 75F (11.40€, $10.95). MC, V. Mon–Sat 8am–7pm. Métro: Concorde.

La Coupole ★ Born in 1927 and once a leading center of artistic life, La Coupole is now the epitome of the grand Paris brasserie in Montparnasse. Former patrons included Josephine Baker, Henry Miller, Dalí, Calder, Hemingway, Fitzgerald, and Picasso. The sweeping outdoor terrace is among the finest in Paris. At one of its sidewalk tables, you can sit and watch the passing scene and order a coffee or a cognac VSOP. The food is quite good, despite the fact that the dining room resembles an enormous rail station waiting room. Try main dishes like *sole meunière,* cassoulet, fresh oysters, shellfish, and some of the best pepper steak in Paris. The waiters are as rude and inattentive as ever, and aficionados of the place wouldn't have it any other way.

102 bd. du Montparnasse, 14th arr. ℂ **01-43-20-14-20.** Breakfast buffet 90F (13.75€, $13.05); main courses 92–195F (14.05–29.65€, $13.35–$28.35) at lunch, 110–210F (16.70–31.90€, $15.95–$30.45) at dinner; fixed-price menus 138–189F (21.05–28.75€, $20–$27.40) at lunch, 189F (28.75€, $27.40) at dinner before 10:30pm, 138–189F (21.05–28.75€, $20–$27.40) after 10:30pm. AE, DC, MC, V. Daily 8:30am–1am (breakfast buffet Mon–Fri 8:30–10:30pm). Métro: Vavin.

La Palette ★★ The staff here defiantly maintains old-fashioned Parisian traditions that haven't changed much since the days of Picasso and Braque—the same drinks (Ricard and Pernod, among others) are still popular. A bustle of comings and goings makes La Palette an insider's version of a battered, artistically evocative *Quartier Latin Café.* The decor, inhabited by amiably crotchety waiters, consists of tiled murals, installed around 1935, advertising the virtues of a brand of liqueur that's no longer manufactured. If you happen to drop in during mealtime, you'll have a limited selection of salads and *croque monsieur,* plus one *plat de jour* per day, always priced at 70F (10.65€, $10.15), which may include roast beef, lamb stew, fish, and gigot of lamb. Food is well-prepared, and the dish of the day is usually announced as a kind of surprise to the joint's many devoted fans.

43 Rue de Seine, 6th arr. ℂ **01-43-26-68-15.** Sandwiches, omelets, and *plats de jour* 32–70F (4.85–10.65€, $4.65–$10.15). MC, V. Cafe and bar Mon–Sat 8am–2am; restaurant Mon–Sat 11:30am–3pm. Métro: Mabillion or St-Germain-des-Prés.

⟨ *Value* **Did You Know?**

You'll pay substantially less in a cafe if you stand at the counter rather than sit at a table, because there's no service charge.

La Rotonde Once patronized by Hemingway, the original Rotonde faded into history but is immortalized in the pages of *The Sun Also Rises,* in which Papa wrote, "No matter what cafe in Montparnasse you ask a taxi driver to bring you to from the right bank of the river, they always take you to the Rotonde." Lavishly upgraded, its reincarnation has a paneled Art-Deco elegance and shares the once-hallowed site with a motion-picture theater. The menu includes hearty fare like pepper steak with *pommes frites,* shellfish in season, and sea bass filets with herb-flavored lemon sauce.

105 bd. du Montparnasse, 6th arr. © 01-43-26-48-26. Glass of wine 23F (3.50€, $3.35); fixed-price menu 75F (11.40€, $10.95) at lunch, 200F (30.40€, $29) at dinner. AE, MC, V. Cafe daily 7am –1am; food service daily noon–2am. Métro: Vavin.

Le Procope ★★ To ardent fans of French history, this is the holy grail of Parisian cafes. Opened in 1686, it occupies a three-story town house whose architectural details are categorized as a historic monument. Inside, nine salons and dining rooms, each of whose 300-year-old walls have been carefully preserved and painted a deep red, are available for langourous afternoon coffee breaks or well-presented meals. Menu items include platters of shellfish, onion soup *au gratin, coq au vin,* duck breast in honey sauce, and grilled versions of various meats and fish. Every day between 3 and 7pm, the place makes itself available to sightseers who come to look but not necessarily eat and drink at the site that welcomed such movers and shakers as Diderot, Voltaire, Georges Sand, Victor Hugo, and Oscar Wilde. Of special charm is the ground-floor room outfitted like an antique library.

13 rue de l'Ancienne-Comédie, 6th arr. © 01-40-46-79-00. Reservations recommended. Main courses 100–150F (15.20–22.80€, $14.50–$21.75). AE, MC, V. Daily noon–midnight. Métro: Odéon.

Les Deux Magots ★★ This legendary hangout for the sophisticated residents of St-Germain-des-Prés becomes a tourist favorite in summer. Visitors monopolize the few sidewalk tables as the waiters rush about, seemingly oblivious to anyone's needs. Regulars from around the neighborhood reclaim it in the off-season. Les Deux Magots was once a gathering place of the intellectual elite, like Sartre and de Beauvoir and Giraudoux. Inside are the two large statues of Confucian wise men (*magots*) that give the cafe its name. The crystal chandeliers are too brightly lit, but the regulars seem to be accustomed to the glare. After all, some of them even read their daily newspapers here. You can order salads, pastries, ice cream, or one of the daily specials; the fresh fish is usually a good bet.

6 place St-Germain-des-Prés, 6th arr. © 01-45-48-55-25. *Café au lait* 25F (3.80€, $3.65); whiskey soda 70F (10.65€, $10.15); *plats du jour* 90–140F (13.75–21.35€, $13.05–$20.30). AE, DC, V. Daily 7:30am –1:30am. Métro: St-Germain-des-Prés.

INEXPENSIVE

Café de l'Industrie This place is so old it's new again. Founded just before the outbreak of World War II, this cafe received a vital new lease on life after the opening of the nearby Opéra Bastille. Today, its three dining rooms boast a decor evoking aspects of both the tropics and faux-baroque Europe, with green plants and lots of original oil paintings by long-term patrons. Known for decanting obscure vintages from the Touraine and the region around Beaujolais, it appeals to photographers and lesser-known characters in French-speaking show biz. If you're hungry, consider any of the generous *plats du jour.* Examples are leeks steeped in vinaigrette, *boeuf bourguignonne,* fried haddock, and tagliatelle with salmon, chives, and cream sauce.

16 rue St-Sabin, 11th arr. © **01-47-00-13-53.** Glass of wine 19–26F (2.95–3.95€, $2.75–$3.75); main courses 50–80F (7.60–12.15€, $7.25–$11.60). MC, V. Sun–Fri 10am–2am. Métro: Bastille or Breguier-Sabin.

Le Gutenberg   Behind the largest post office in France and named in honor of the printing presses that used to operate nearby, this is the most evocative and authentic of the cafes close to the Louvre. There's a zinc-top bar and two inner rooms loaded with antique mirrors and uniformed staff members. No one can agree on whether the place is 150 or 225 years old. The food runs the gamut from light broths and simple salads to roasted duck breast with orange sauce and pork tenderloin with red wine and apples.

64 rue Jean-Jacques Rousseau, 1st arr. © **01-42-36-14-90.** *Café au lait* 11F (1.65€, $1.60); sandwiches 15F (2.35€, $2.25); *plats du jour* 49F (7.45€, $7.10). No credit cards. Mon–Fri 8am–7pm; Sat noon–3:30pm. Métro: Louvre-Rivoli.

6 Gay-Friendly Restaurants

Though any restaurant recommended in this guide is at least tolerant of same-sex couples, these two restaurants are especially welcoming of gay diners. For the locations of these places, see the corresponding arrondissement maps earlier in this chapter. For full coverage of Paris's gay/gay-friendly hotels and restaurants, see *Frommer's Gay & Lesbian Europe.*

INEXPENSIVE

L'Amazonial FRENCH (MODERN)/INTERNATIONAL   One of Paris's most popular gay restaurants is in the heart of the Marais, occupying a 19th-century building with a flowered terrace extending onto the pavement. The dining room incorporates decorative elements from ancient Greece and Egypt and the Amazon basin. The menu is sometimes startling, featuring items like ostrich steak with exotic mushrooms; more conservative dishes include Barbados-style grilled prawns, *feijoada* (a Brazilian stew with beans and meat, usually pork), and *plats du jour* like flank steak with béarnaise sauce. Beware the standoffish waiters.

3 rue Ste-Opportune, 1st arr. © **01-42-33-53-13.** Reservations recommended. Main courses 65–120F (9.95–18.25€, $9.45–$17.40); fixed-price menus 105–129F (15.95–19.60€, $15.25–$18.70). AE, MC, V. Daily noon–3pm and 7pm–1:30am. Métro: Châtelet.

Exploring Paris

Paris is a city where taking in the street life—shopping, strolling, and hanging out—should claim as much of your time as sightseeing in churches or museums. Having a gourmet picnic in the Bois de Boulogne, taking a sunrise amble along the Seine, spending an afternoon bartering at a flea market—Paris bewitches you with these kinds of experiences. For all the Louvre's beauty, you'll probably remember the Latin Quarter's crooked alleyways better than the 370th oil painting of your visit.

1 Sightseeing Suggestions for the First-Timer

IF YOU HAVE 1 DAY Get up early and begin your day with some live theater by walking the streets around your hotel. Find a little cafe and order a typical Parisian breakfast of coffee and croissants. If you're a museum and monument junkie and don't dare return home without seeing the "must" sights, know that the two top museums are the **Musée du Louvre** and **Musée d'Orsay,** and the three top monuments are the **Tour Eiffel, Arc de Triomphe,** and **Notre-Dame** (which you can see later in the day). If it's a toss-up between the Louvre and the d'Orsay, we'd make it the Louvre because it holds a greater variety of works. If you need to choose among the monuments, we'd make it the Tour Eiffel just for the panoramic view of the city.

If your day is too short to visit museums or wait in line for the tower, we suggest you spend most of your time strolling the streets. The most impressive neighborhood is on **Ile St-Louis,** the most elegant place for a walk. After exploring this island and its mansions, wander at will through such Left Bank districts as **St-Germain-des-Prés** and the area around **place St-Michel,** the heart of the student quarter. As the sun sets, head for **Notre-Dame,** standing majestically along the banks of the Seine. This is a good place to watch the shadows fall over Paris as the lights come on for the night. Afterward, walk along the Seine, where vendors sell books and souvenir prints. Promise yourself a return visit and have dinner in the Left Bank bistro of your choice.

IF YOU HAVE 2 DAYS Follow the above for day 1, except now you can fit in on day 2 more of the top five sights we mention above. Day 1 covered a lot of the Left Bank, so if you want to explore the Right Bank, begin at the **Arc de Triomphe** and stroll down the **Champs-Elysées,** Paris's main boulevard, until you reach the Egyptian obelisk at **place de la Concorde,** where some of France's most notable figures lost their heads on the guillotine. Place de la Concorde affords terrific views of **La Madeleine,** the **Palais Bourbon,** the **Arc de Triomphe,** and the **Musée du Louvre.** Nearby **place Vendôme** is well worth a visit, as it represents the Right Bank at its most elegant, with the Hôtel Ritz and Paris's top jewelry stores. Now we suggest a rest stop in the **Jardin de Tuileries,** directly west and adjacent to the Louvre. After a bistro lunch, go for a walk in the **Marais** to get a total contrast to monumental Paris. Our favorite stroll is along narrow **rue des Rosiers,** at the heart of the Jewish community. And don't miss **place des Vosges.** After a rest at your hotel, select one of the restaurants down in **Montparnasse,** following in Hemingway's footsteps. This area is far livelier at night.

IF YOU HAVE 3 DAYS   Spend days 1 and 2 as above. As you've already gotten a look at the Left Bank and the Right Bank, this day should be about following your special interests. You might target the restored **Centre Pompidou** and the **Musée Carnavalet,** Paris's history museum. If you're a Monet fan, you might head for the **Musée Marmottan–Claude Monet.** Or perhaps you'd rather wander the sculpture garden of the **Musée Rodin.** If you select the **Musée Picasso,** you can use part of the morning to explore a few of the Marais's art galleries. After lunch, spend the afternoon on **Ile de la Cité,** where you'll get not only to see Notre-Dame again but also to visit the **Conciergerie,** where Marie Antoinette and others were held captive before they were beheaded. And you certainly can't miss the stunning stained glass of **Sainte-Chapelle** in the Palais de Justice. After dinner, if your energy holds, you can sample Paris's nightlife— whatever you fancy, the dancers at the **Lido** or the **Folies-Bergère** or a smoky Left Bank jazz club or a frenzied disco. If you'd like to just sit and have a drink, Paris has some of the most elegant hotel bars in the world—try the **Crillon** or the **Plaza Athénée.**

IF YOU HAVE 4 DAYS   For your first 3 days, follow the above. On day 4, head to **Versailles,** 21 kilometers (13 miles) south of Paris, the greatest attraction in the Ile de France. When Louis XIV decided to move to the suburbs, he created a spectacle unlike anything the world had ever seen. The good news is that most of the palace remains intact, in all its opulence and glitter. A full day here almost feels like too little time. After you return to Paris for the night, take a good rest and spend the evening wandering around the Left Bank's **Latin Quarter,** enjoying the student cafes and bars and selecting your bistro of choice for the evening. Two of the livelier streets for wandering are rue de la Huchette and rue Monsieur-le-Prince.

IF YOU HAVE 5 DAYS   Spend days 1 to 4 as above. On day 5, devote at least a morning to a neglected area: **Montmartre,** the community formerly known for its artists perched atop the highest of Paris's seven hills. Though the starving artists who made it the embodiment of *la vie de bohème* have long departed, there's much to enchant you, especially if you wander the back streets and avoid place du Tertre. Away from the tacky shops and sleazy clubs, you'll see the picture-postcard lanes and staircases known to Picasso, Toulouse-Lautrec, and Utrillo. Of course, it's virtually mandatory to visit **Sacré-Coeur,** for the view if nothing else. Because it's your last night in Paris, let your own interests take over. Lovers traditionally spend it clasping hands in a walk along the Seine; less goo-goo eyed visitors can still find a full agenda. We suggest a final evening at **Willi's Wine Bar** (see chapter 10), with more than 250 vintages and good food to go along with it. For a nightcap, we always head for the **Hemingway Bar** at the Ritz, where Garbo, Coward, and Fitzgerald once lifted their glasses. If that's too elegant, head for **Closerie des Lilas** in the 6th arrondissement, where you can rub shoulders with the movers and shakers of the film and fashion industries.

2 Attractions by Arrondissement

For the locations of these sights, see **The Attractions of Paris** map on pages 172–173 and the individual **arrondissement maps** that follow.

THE RIGHT BANK
1ST ARR.
Arc de Triomphe du Carrousel (p. 214)

Forum des Halles (p. 225)

Galerie Nationale du Jeu de Paume (p. 194)

Jardin des Tuileries ✦✦ (p. 213)

Jardin du Carrousel (p. 214)

Les Halles ✦ (p. 225)

Musée des Arts Décoratifs (p. 201)

Musée du Louvre ✦✦✦ (p. 187)

Musée du Parfum (p. 204)

Palais Royal ✦✦ (p. 211)

Place Vendôme (p. 168)

St-Eustache ✦✦ (p. 208)

St-Germain l'Auxerrois ✦✦ (p. 208)

3RD ARR.
Hôtel de Clisson (p. 203)

Hôtel de Rohan (p. 204)

Hôtel le Pelletier de St-Fargeau (p. 195)

Musée Carnavalet ✦ (p. 195)

Musée Cognacq-Jay ✦✦ (p. 200)

Musée de la Chasse (p. 204)

Musée de l'Histoire de France ✦ (p. 203)

Musée Picasso ✦✦✦ (p. 198)

4TH ARR.
Atelier Brancusi ✦ (p. 194)

Cathédrale de Notre-Dame ✦✦✦ (p. 183)

Centre Pompidou ✦✦✦ (p. 193)

Conciergerie ✦✦ (p. 209)

Hôtel de Lauzun (p. 224)

Hôtel de Ville ✦ (p. 210)

Hôtel Dieu (p. 224)

Hôtel Lambert (p. 225)

Maison de Victor Hugo ✦ (p. 213)

No. 9 quai d'Anjou (p. 225)

Place des Vosges (p. 169)

Pont Neuf (p. 224)

Rue des Rosiers (p. 169)

Sainte-Chapelle ✦✦✦ (p. 191)

Square du Vert Galant (p. 224)

St-Louis-en-l'Ile (p. 225)

8TH ARR.
American Cathedral of the Holy Trinity (p. 205)

Arc de Triomphe ✦✦✦ (p. 182)

Champs-Elysées (p. 168)

Grand Palais (p. 199)

La Madeleine ✦✦ (p. 206)

Musée Cernuschi ✦ (p. 200)

Musée Jacquemart-André ✦✦ (p. 195)

Musée Nissim de Camondo ✦ (p. 202)

Parc Monceau ✦ (p. 216)

Petit Palais (p. 199)

Place de la Concorde (p. 168)

9TH ARR.
Musée Grévin ✦ (p. 229)

Paristoric (p. 204)

10TH ARR.
Musée de Baccarat (p. 203)

11TH ARR.
Musée Edith Piaf (p. 201)

Villa Calte (p. 201)

12TH ARR.
Musée des Arts d'Afrique et d'Océanie (p. 200)

Parc Zoologique de Paris (p. 230)

16TH ARR.
Bois de Boulogne ✦✦ (p. 215)

Cimetière de Passy (p. 217)

Hippodrome d'Auteuil (p. 222)

Hippodrome de Longchamp ✦✦✦ (p. 222)

Jardin d'Acclimatation ✦ (p. 230)

Maison de Balzac (p. 213)

Musée d'Art Moderne de la Ville de Paris (p. 200)

The Attractions of Paris

Bibliothèque Nationale de France **7**
Cimetière du Montparnasse **4**
Cimetière du Père-Lachaise **9**
Cité des Sciences et de l'Industrie **11**
La Géode **11**
La Grande Arche de La Défense **1**
Les Catacombs **5**
Manufacture Nationale des Gobelins **6**
Musée Bourdelle **3**

Musée de la Musique **11**
Musée des Arts d'Afrique et d'Océanie **8**
Musée Edith Piaf **10**
Musée National de Céramique de Sèvres **2**
Parc de La Villette **11**
Parc Zoologique de Paris **8**
Tour Montparnasse **3**
Villa Calte **10**

See the maps that follow for the locations of each arrondissements' attractions.

Moulin
Rouge
MONTMARTRE
bd. de la Chapelle
bd. de Clichy
av. Jean Jaurès
rue Armand Carrel
place
Pigalle
bd. de Rochechouart
avenue secrétan
rue de Magenta
Gare
du Nord
St-Joseph
rue du Faubourg St-Martin
rue N.D. de Lorette
St-Georges
rue Blanche
Casino
de Paris
av. Trudaine
rue Condorcet
rue de Dunkerque
place
du Colonel
Fabien
Ste-Trinité
See "18th Arr." Map
rue de Chabrol
La Fayette
PARC DES
BUTTES-
CHAUMONT
rue La Fayette
St-Vincent
de Paul
Gare
de l'Est
Notre-Dame
de Lorette
rue de Paradis
St-Laurent
bd. de la Villette
Lazare
Folies
Bergère
rue du Faubourg Poissonnière
rue de Strasbourg
rue St-Martin
bd. Haussmann
See "9th-10th Arrs." Map
Quai de Jemmapes
Quai de Valmy
rue St-Maur
Opéra
Garnier
bd. des Italiens
bd. Montmartre
rue du Faubourg St-Denis
rue de la Grange
bd. de la Villette
See "1st Arr." Map
bd. de Bonne Nouvelle
bd. des Capucines
place
de l'Opéra
rue du 4 Septembre
rue St-Augustin
Bourse des
Valeurs
rue d'Aboukir
rue du Faubourg St-Martin
St-Joseph
bd. St-Martin
place
de la
République
rue du Faubourg du Temple
See "3rd-4th & 11th Arrs." Map
place des Petits Champs
rue de Richelieu
rue de Cléry
rue Réaumur
Conservatoire
des Arts
et Métiers
avenue de la République
place
Vendôme
St-Roch
rue du Mail
rue de Sébastopol
rue St-Martin
rue de Turbigo
bd. du Temple
Voltaire
Palais
Royal
rue du Louvre
rue de Beaubourg
rue du Temple
rue des Archives
rue de Turenne
LE
MARAIS
St-Ambroise
place A.
Malraux
bd. de Sébastopol
rue de Rivoli
Bourse du
Commerce
Forum
des Halles
rue Beaumarchais
rue du Chemin Vert
TUILERIES
place du
Carrousel
Musée
du Louvre
Archives
Nationales
St-Denis
bd. Richard-Lenoir
quai des Tuileries
St-Merri
St-Denis
rue de la Roquette
pont
Royal
quai
Voltaire
pont du Carr.
Théâtre
du Châtelet
Seine
pont au Change
Hôtel
de Ville
rue St-Antoine
place des
Vosges
Théâtre
de la Bastille
quai Malaquais
quai des Arts
pont des Arts
pont Neuf
pont N.
Dame
rue St-Martin
quai de l'Hôtel de Ville
St-Gervais
Ecole Nationale
des Beaux-Arts
quai de Conti
ILE DE LA CITÉ
St-Paul
place
de la
Bastille
rue du Faubourg St-Antoine
ST-GERMAIN-
DES-PRÉS
quai des Grands Augustins
Cloître N.Dame
pont St-Louis
ILE ST-LOUIS
Opéra
Bastille
rue de Charenton
bd. St-Germain
Notre-Dame
quai St-Michel
St-Louis
bd. Henry IV
bd. Bourdon
bd. de la Bastille
avenue Daumesnil
rue du Four
quai de la Tournelle
pont de la Tournelle
pont
de Sully
quai Henry IV
rue de Vaugirard
Palais du
Luxembourg
Sorbonne
rue des Ecoles
QUARTIER LATIN
Institut
du Monde
Arabe
quai Saint Bernard
av. L. Rollin
bd. Diderot
JARDIN DU
LUXEMBOURG
rue St-Jacques
rue d'Ulm
Panthéon
pont
de Sully
Gare
de Lyon
rue d'Assas
Université Paris VII
JARDIN DES PLANTES
pont
d'Austerlitz
quai de Bercy
bd. Raspail
Université Paris V
bd. St-Michel
rue Gay Lussac
rue Claude Bernard
St-Médard
rue Censier
Université
Paris III
Gare
d'Austerlitz
Seine
quai d'Austerlitz
quai de la Rapée
bd. du Montparnasse
rue Buffon
DU MONTPARNASSE
bd. de Port Royal
bd. Saint Marcel
rue Jeanne d'Arc
pont
de Bercy
quai de Bercy
bd. Raspail
Observatoire
de Paris
See "5th-6th Arrs." Map
bd. Arago
rue de l'Hôpital
rue Vincent d'Arc
bd. St-Jacques
place
d'Italie
rue Auriol

0   .28 Miles
0   .45 Kilometers

11
10
9
8
7
6
5

173

Attractions in the 1st Arrondissement

bd. de Sébastopol

rue St-Denis

r. Pierre Lescot

ÉTIENNE MARCEL

r. des Halles

CHÂTELET

bd. du Palais

ÎLE DE LA CITÉ

q. des Orfèvres

quai de la Mégisserie

18

17

LES HALLES

16

r. du Roule

r. Berger

r. St-Honoré

quai des Gds Augustins

q. des Grands Augustins

du Pont Neuf

rue des Bourdonnais

pont Neuf

LOUVRE RIVOLI

r. de l'Arbre

PONT NEUF

15

Seine

rue du Louvre

r. J. J. Rousseau

r. Coquillère

rue du Jour

r. du Bouloi

r. Hérold

r. Croix des Petits Champs

r. du Col. Driant

r. J. J. Rousseau

r. des Bons Enfants

rue de Rivoli

14

pont des Arts

quai du Louvre

quai Malaquais

rue de la Banque

2ᵉ

rue des Petits Champs

JARDIN DU PALAIS ROYAL

rue de Valois

13

12

MUSÉE DU LOUVRE-PALAIS ROYAL

11

10

pont du Carrousel

quai Voltaire

r. des Sts-Pères

6ᵉ

rue du Quatre Septembre

r. de Montpensier

r. de Richelieu

r. de Molière

r. de l'Échelle

9

JARDIN DU CARROUSEL

8

place du Carrousel

7

rue St-Augustin

rue de Richelieu

r. Thérèse

Casanova

av. de l'Opéra

r. de l'Échelle

PYRAMIDES

r. des Pyramides

rue St-Roch

av. Gen. Lemonnier

pont Royal

Seine

quai Anatole France

OPÉRA

rue Danielle Casanova

rue de la Sourdière

TUILERIES

rue de Rivoli

pont Solférino

place de l'Opéra

rue de la Paix

rue Daunou

rue du Mont Thabor

JARDIN DES TUILERIES

6

8ᵉ

r. des Capucines

2

place Vendôme

rue de Castiglione

rue du Mont Thabor

r. Cambon

rue St-Honoré

1

CONCORDE

MADELEINE

3

4

5

quai des Tuileries

bd. St-Germain

pont de la Concorde

rue Royale

Church
Métro

N
1/5 Mi
0.2 Km

18e 19e 20e
10e 3e 11e
9e 2e 4e 12e
17e 1e 6e 5e 13e
8e 7e
16e 14e
15e

Church
ⓜ Métro

Atelier Brancusi **5**
Cathédrale de
   Notre-Dame **1**
Centre Pompidou **5**
Conciergerie **2**
Hôtel de Clisson **7**
Hôtel de Lauzun **13**
Hôtel de Rohan **8**
Hôtel de Ville **4**
Hôtel Dieu **3**
Hôtel Lambert **15**
Hôtel le Pelletier de
   St-Fargeau **12**

Maison de Victor Hugo **17**
Musée Carnavalet **12**
Musée Cognac-Jay **11**
Musée de la Chasse **6**
Musée de l'Histoire
   de France **7**
Musée Picasso **9**
Place des Vosges **16**
Rue des Rosiers **10**
Square de Vert Galant **2**
Ste-Chapelle **2**
St-Louis en l'Ile **14**

Attractions in the 5th–6th Arrondissements

Arènes de Lutèce **16**
Institut de France **1**
Jardin des Plantes **18**
Jardin du Luxembourg **7**
Mosquée de Paris **17**
Musée National d'Histoire Naturelle **19**
Musée National du Moyen Age/
  Thermes de Cluny **11**
Musée National Eugène Delacroix **3**
Musée Zadkine **6**
Palais du Luxembourg **8**
Panthéon **13**
Roman Baths **11**
Rue de la Huchette **10**
Rue Monsieur-le-Prince **9**
Rue Visconti **2**
St-Etienne-du-Mont **14**
St-Germain-des-Prés **4**
St-Sulpice **5**
Sorbonne **12**
Val-de-Grâce **15**

Attractions in the 7th Arrondissement

Hôtel des Invalides
(Napoléon's Tomb) **5**
Les Egouts **3**
Musée d'Orsay **8**
Musée de l'Armée **4**
Musée des Plans-Reliefs **5**
Musée Rodin **6**
Palais Bourbon/
Assemblée Nationale **7**
Parc du Champ de Mars **2**
Tour Eiffel **1**

Attractions in the 8th Arrondissement

Arc de Triomphe **5**
American Cathedral of the Holy Trinity **8**
Avenue des Champs-Elysées **7**
Grand Palais **10**
La Madeleine **13**
Musée Cernuschi **1**
Musée Jacquemart-André **4**
Musée Nissim de Camondo **2**
Office de Tourisme **6**
Parc Monceau **3**
Petit Palais **11**
Place de la Concorde **12**
Place de l'Alma **9**

Attractions in the 9th–10th Arrondissements

place Pigalle

bd. de Rochechuart

av. Trudaine

bd. de Magenta

Gare du Nord

rue Blanche

rue Pigalle

rue N.D. de Lorette

rue Condorcet

rue de Dunkerque

rue de Maubeuge

rue La Fayette

rue de Châteaudun

rue La Fayette

Lazare

rue de Chabrol

Folies Bergère

rue de Paradis

④

rue Richer

bd. Haussmann

②

place de l'Opéra

①

bd. des Capucines

bd. des Italiens

bd. Montmartre

③

rue du Faubourg de Poissonnière

rue d'Hauteville

rue du Faubourg St-Denis

bd. de Strasbourg

bd. de Bonne Nouvelle

rue St-Augustin

Bourse des Valeurs

de Cléry

place Vendôme

rue des Petits Champs

rue de Richelieu

rue du Mail

rue d'Abukir

rue Réaumur

Conservatoire des Arts et Métiers

rue Montorgueil

rue St-Martin

de Turbigo

Palais Royal

place A. Malraux

rue de Valois

Banque de France

St-Eustache

rue de Sébastopol

rue St-Martin

rue Beaubourg

Tuileries

Musée des Arts Décoratifs

place du Carrousel

rue de Rivoli

rue du Louvre

Bourse du Commerce

Forum des Halles

Centre Pompidou

Musée du Louvre

St-Germain l'Auxerrois

St-Merri

pont Royal

quai des Tuileries

pont du Carr.

quai Malaquais

quai Voltaire

pont des Arts

pont Neuf

Seine

pont au Change

Théâtre du Châtelet

Tour St-Jacques

Théâtre de la Ville

Hôtel de Ville

Ecole Nationale des Beaux-Arts

Université Paris V

ST-GERMAIN-DES-PRÉS

St-Gervais

Musée de Baccarat **4**
Musée Grévin **3**
Opéra Garnier **2**
Paristoric **1**

17e 18e 19e
9e 10e
8e 2e 20e
16e 1e 3e 11e
7e 6e 4e
5e 12e
15e 14e 13e

Attractions in the 16th Arrondissement

Post Office ⊠
Church ✝
Métro Ⓜ
RER Ⓡ

Bois de Boulogne **1**
Cimetière de Passy **5**
Maison de Balzac **3**
Musée d'Art Moderne de la Ville de Paris **7**
Musée de la Marine **6**
Musée des Enfants **7**
Musée du Vin **4**
Musée Marmottan–
Claude Monet **2**
Musée National des Arts
Asiatiques–Guimet **8**

Attractions in the 18th Arrondissement

Basilique du Sacré-Coeur **8**
Cimetière de Montmartre **3**
Cimetière St-Vincent **5**
Espace Montmartre Dali **7**
Moulin de la Galette **4**
Moulin Rouge **2**
Musée de l'Erotisme **1**
Musée de Vieux Montmartre **6**

3 The Top Attractions: From the Arc de Triomphe to the Tour Eiffel

Arc de Triomphe ★★★   At the western end of the Champs-Elysées, the Arc de Triomphe suggests one of those ancient Roman arches, only it's larger. Actually, it's the biggest triumphal arch in the world, about 163 feet high and 147 feet wide. To reach it, *don't try to cross the square,* Paris's busiest traffic hub. With a dozen streets radiating from the "Star," the roundabout has been called by one writer "vehicular roulette with more balls than numbers" (death is certain!). Take the underground passage and live a little longer.

Commissioned by Napoléon in 1806 to commemorate the victories of his Grand Armée, the arch wasn't ready for the entrance of his new empress, Marie-Louise, in 1810 (he'd divorced Joséphine because she couldn't provide him an heir). It served its ceremonial purpose anyway but wasn't completed until 1836, under the reign of Louis-Philippe. Four years later, Napoléon's remains, brought from his grave on St. Helena, passed under the arch on their journey to his tomb at the Hôtel des Invalides. Since that time it has become the focal point for state funerals. It's also the site of the permanent tomb of the unknown soldier, in whose honor an eternal flame is kept burning.

The greatest state funeral was Victor Hugo's in 1885; his coffin was placed under the arch, and much of Paris turned out to pay tribute. Another notable funeral was in 1929 for Ferdinand Foch, supreme commander of the Allied forces in World War I. The arch has been the centerpiece of some of France's proudest moments and some of its most humiliating defeats, notably those of 1871 and 1940. The memory of German troops marching under the arch that had come to symbolize France's glory is still painful to the French. Who can forget the 1940 newsreel of the Frenchman standing on the Champs-Elysées weeping as the Nazi storm troopers goose-stepped through Paris? The arch's happiest moment occurred in 1944, when the liberation of Paris parade passed beneath it. That same year, Eisenhower paid a visit to the tomb of the unknown soldier, a new tradition among leaders of state and important figures. After Charles de Gaulle's death, the French government (despite protests from anti-Gaullists) voted to change the name of this site from place de l'Etoile to place Charles de Gaulle. Nowadays it's often known as place Charles de Gaulle–Etoile.

Of the sculptures on the monument, the best known is Rude's *Marseillaise,* a.k.a. *The Departure of the Volunteers.* J. P. Cortot's *Triumph of Napoléon in 1810* and Etex's *Resistance of 1814* and *Peace of 1815* also adorn the facade. The monument is engraved with the names of hundreds of generals (those underlined died in battle) who commanded French troops in Napoleonic victories.

You can take an elevator or climb the stairway to the top, where there's an exhibition hall with lithographs and photos depicting the arch throughout its history, as well as an observation deck with a fantastic view.

Place Charles de Gaulle–Etoile, 8th arr. ✆ **01-55-37-73-77.** www.monuments.fr. Admission 42F (6.40€, $6.10) adults, 26F (3.95€, $3.75) ages 18–25, children 11 and under free. Apr–Sept daily 9:30am–11pm; Oct–Mar daily 10am–10:30pm. Métro: Charles de Gaulle–Etoile.

Basilique du Sacré-Coeur ★★   Sacré-Coeur is one of Paris's most characteristic landmarks and has been the subject of much controversy. One Parisian called it "a lunatic's confectionery dream." An offended Zola declared it "the basilica of the ridiculous." Sacré-Coeur has had warm supporters as well, including poet Max Jacob and artist Maurice Utrillo. Utrillo never tired of drawing and painting it, and he and Jacob came here regularly to pray. Atop the *butte*

> (*Tips* **Best City View**
>
> From the observation deck of the Arc de Triomphe, you can see up the Champs-Elysées and such landmarks as the Louvre, the Eiffel Tower, Sacré-Coeur, and La Défense. Although we don't want to get into any arguments about this, we think the view of Paris from this perspective is the grandest in the entire city.

(hill) in Montmartre, its multiple gleaming white domes and *campanile* (bell tower) tower over Paris like a 12th-century Byzantine church. But it's not that old. After France's 1870 defeat by the Prussians, the basilica was planned as a votive offering to cure France's misfortunes. Rich and poor alike contributed money to build it. Construction began in 1876, and though the church wasn't consecrated until 1919, perpetual prayers of adoration have been made here day and night since 1885. The interior is brilliantly decorated with mosaics: Look for the striking Christ on the ceiling and the mural of his Passion at the back of the altar. The stained-glass windows were shattered during the struggle for Paris in 1944 but have been well replaced. The crypt contains a relic of what some of the devout believe is Christ's sacred heart—hence, the name of the church.

Insider's tip: Although the view from the Arc de Triomphe is the greatest panorama of Paris, we also want to endorse this stunning view from the gallery around the inner dome of Sacré-Coeur. On a clear day your eyes take in a panoramic sweep of Paris extending for 30 miles into the Ile de France. You can also walk around the inner dome, an attraction even better than the interior of Sacré-Coeur itself.

Place St-Pierre, 18th arr. (✆) **01-53-41-89-00.** Free admission to basilica; joint ticket to dome and crypt 30F (4.55€, $4.35) adults, 16F (2.45€, $2.30) students/children. Daily 9am–5:45pm; Oct–Mar daily 9am–6pm. Métro: Abbesses; then take the elevator to the surface and follow the signs to the *funiculaire*, which goes up to the church for the price of a Métro ticket.

Cathédrale de Notre-Dame ✫✫✫   Notre-Dame is the heart of Paris and even of the country itself: Distances from the city to all parts of France are calculated from a spot at the far end of place du Parvis, in front of the cathedral, where a circular bronze plaque marks **Kilomètre Zéro.**

The cathedral's setting on the banks of the Seine has always been memorable. Founded in the 12th century by Maurice de Sully, bishop of Paris, Notre-Dame has grown and grown over the years, changing as Paris has changed, often falling victim to whims of decorative taste. Its famous flying buttresses (the external side supports, giving the massive interior a sense of weightlessness) were rebuilt in 1330. Though many disagree, we feel Notre-Dame is more interesting outside than in, and you'll want to walk all around it to fully appreciate this "vast symphony of stone." Better yet, cross over the pont au Double to the Left Bank and view it from the quay.

The histories of Paris and Notre-Dame are inseparable. Many prayed here before going off to fight in the Crusades. "Our Lady of Paris" wasn't spared by the revolutionaries, who destroyed the Galerie des Rois and converted the building into a secular temple. Later, Napoléon crowned himself emperor here, yanking the crown out of Pius VII's hands and placing it on his own head before crowning his Joséphine empress (see David's *Coronation of Napoléon* in the Louvre). But carelessness, vandalism, embellishments, and wars of religion had already demolished much of the previously existing structure.

> **Tips   Exploring Ile de la Cité**
>
> After visiting Notre-Dame, try to take some time to explore Ile de la Cité and its other main attractions, the infamous **Conciergerie** (see p. 209) and the lovely **Sainte-Chapelle** (see p. 191), best seen in radiant sunlight.

The cathedral was once scheduled for demolition, but, because of the popularity of Victor Hugo's *Hunchback of Notre-Dame* and the revival of interest in the Gothic period, a movement mushroomed to restore the cathedral to its original glory. The task was completed under Viollet-le-Duc, an architectural genius. The houses of old Paris used to crowd in on Notre-Dame, but during his redesigning of the city, Baron Haussmann ordered them torn down to show the cathedral to its best advantage from the parvis. This is the best vantage for seeing the three sculpted 13th-century portals.

On the left, the **Portal of the Virgin** depicts the signs of the zodiac and the coronation of the Virgin, an association found in dozens of medieval churches. The restored central **Portal of the Last Judgment** depicts three levels: The first shows Vices and Virtues; the second, Christ and his Apostles; and above that, Christ in triumph after the Resurrection. The portal is a close illustration of the Gospel according to Matthew. Over it is the remarkable **west rose window** ⟨★★⟩, 31 feet wide, forming a showcase for a statue of the Virgin and Child. On the far right is the **Portal of St. Anne,** depicting scenes like the Virgin enthroned with Child; it's Notre-Dame's best preserved and most perfect piece of sculpture. Equally interesting (though often missed) is the **Portal of the Cloisters** (around on the left), with its dour-faced 13th-century Virgin, a survivor among the figures that originally adorned the facade. (Alas, the Child she's holding has been decapitated.) Finally, on the Seine side of Notre-Dame, the **Portal of St. Stephen** traces that saint's martyrdom.

If possible, come to see Notre-Dame at sunset. Inside, of the three giant medallions warming the austere cathedral, the **north rose window** ⟨★★⟩ in the transept, from the mid-13th century, is best. The main body of the church is typically Gothic, with slender, graceful columns. In the **choir,** a stone-carved screen from the early 14th century depicts such biblical scenes as the Last Supper. Near the altar stands the 14th-century *Virgin and Child* ⟨★⟩, highly venerated among Paris's faithful. In the **treasury** are displayed vestments and gold objects, including crowns. Exhibited are a cross presented to Haile Selassie, former emperor of Ethiopia, and a reliquary given by Napoléon. Notre-Dame is especially proud of its relic of the True Cross and the Crown of Thorns.

Finally, to visit those grimy **gargoyles** ⟨★★⟩ immortalized by Hugo, you have to scale steps leading to the twin square **towers** rising to a height of 225 feet. Once there, you can closely inspect the devils (some giving you the raspberry), hobgoblins, and birds of prey. Look carefully and you may see the hunchback Quasimodo with Esmerelda.

Approached through a garden behind Notre-Dame is the **Mémorial des Martyrs Français de la Déportation de 1945 (Deportation Memorial),** jutting out on the very tip of Ile de la Cité. Here, birds chirp and the Seine flows gently by, but the memories are far from pleasant. The memorial commemorates the French citizens who were deported to concentration camps like Auschwitz and Buchenwald during World War II. Carved into stone are these blood-red words (in French): "Forgive, but don't forget." The memorial is open Monday

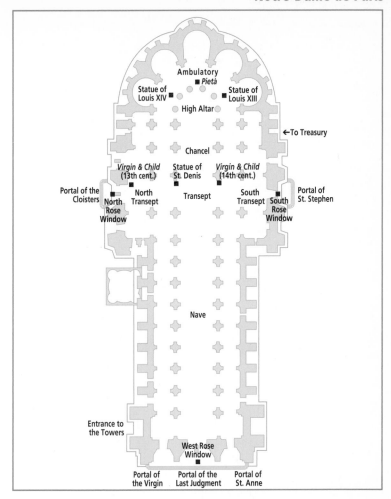

Ambulatory
■ *Pietà*
Statue of ■
Louis XIV
● ● ●
Statue of
Louis XIII
● High Altar ●

→To Treasury

● ● ●
Chancel

Virgin & Child
(13th cent.)
Statue of
St. Denis
Virgin & Child
(14th cent.)

Portal of the
Cloisters
North
Transept
Transept
South
Transept
Portal of
St. Stephen

North
Rose
Window
South
Rose
Window

Nave

Entrance to
the Towers

West Rose
Window
■

Portal of
the Virgin
Portal of the
Last Judgment
Portal of
St. Anne

to Friday from 8:30am to 9:45pm and Saturday and Sunday from 9am to
9:45pm. Admission is free.

6 place du Parvis Notre-Dame, 4th Arr. ✆ 01-42-34-56-10. www.paris.org/Monuments/NDame. Free admission to cathedral; towers 35F (5.30€, $5.10) adults, 23F (3.50€, $3.35) ages 12–25/over 60, children under 12 free; treasury 15F (2.30€, $2.20) adults, 10F (1.50€, $1.45) ages 12–25/over 60, children under 12 free. Cathedral daily 8am–6:45pm year-round. Towers and crypt Apr–Sept daily 9:30am–6pm, Oct–Mar daily 10am–5:15pm. Museum Wed and Sat–Sun 2:30–5pm. Treasury Mon–Sat 9:30–11:30am and 1–5:45pm. Métro: Cité or St-Michel. RER: St-Michel.

Hôtel des Invalides (Napoléon's Tomb) ★★★   In 1670, the Sun King
decided to build this "hotel" to house disabled soldiers. It wasn't an entirely
benevolent gesture, however, because the men had been injured, crippled, or
blinded while fighting his battles. When the building was finally completed
(Louis XIV had long been dead), a gilded dome by Jules Hardouin-Mansart
crowned it and its corridors stretched for miles. The best way to approach
the Invalides is by crossing over the Right Bank via the early-1900s pont

---

(Moments A Nighttime Walk & an "Abomination"

When Viollet-le-Duc designed the flying buttresses of the cathedral of Notre-Dame, they were denounced as "horrendous," "a blight of Paris," and an "abomination." Now they're a reason to go walking at night after a satisfying meal in a bistro. On the Ile de la Cité, wander through the garden in the rear of the cathedral. Near the Square Jean XXIII, cross the pont de l'Archevêche and walk along quai de Montebello along the Left Bank of the Seine for a wonderful perspective, especially when the *bateaux-mouches* light up the buttresses as they pass along. You'll end up at the place St-Michel where one of the cafes awaits you for your nightcap.

Alexander-III and entering the cobblestone forecourt, where a display of massive cannons makes a formidable welcome.

Before rushing on to Napoléon's Tomb, you may want to visit the world's greatest military museum, the **Musée de l'Armée.** In 1794, a French inspector started collecting weapons, uniforms, and equipment, and with the accumulation of war material over the centuries, the museum has become a horrifying documentary of man's self-destruction. Viking swords, Burgundian battle axes, 14th-century blunderbusses, Balkan khandjars, American Browning machine guns, war pitchforks, salamander-engraved Renaissance serpentines, a 1528 Griffon, musketoons, grenadiers . . . if it can kill, it's enshrined here. As a sardonic touch, there's even the wooden leg of General Daumesnil, the governor of Vincennes who lost his leg in the battle of Wagram. Oblivious to the irony of committing a crime against a place that documents man's evil nature, the Nazis looted the museum in 1940.

Among the outstanding acquisitions are suits of armor worn by the kings and dignitaries of France, including Louis XIV, the best of which are in the new Arsenal. The most famous one, the "armor suit of the lion," was made for François I. Henri II ordered his suit engraved with the monogram of his mistress, Diane de Poitiers, and (perhaps reluctantly) that of his wife, Catherine de Médicis. Particularly fine are the showcases of swords and the World War I mementos, including those of American and Canadian soldiers—seek out the Armistice Bugle, which sounded the cease-fire on November 7, 1918, before the general cease-fire on November 11, 1918. The west wing's Salle Orientale shows arms of the Eastern world, including Asia and the Mideast Muslim countries, from the 16th to the 19th century. Turkish armor (look for Bajazet's helmet) and weaponry and Chinese and Japanese armor and swords are on display.

And then there's that little Corsican who became France's greatest soldier. Here you can see the plaster death mask Antommarchi made of him, as well as an oil by Delaroche, painted at the time of Napoléon's first banishment (April 1814) and depicting him as he probably looked, paunch and all. The First Empire exhibit displays Napoléon's field bed with his tent; in the room devoted to the Restoration, the 100 Days, and Waterloo, you can see his bedroom as it was at the time of his death on St. Helena. On the more personal side, you can view stuffed Vizir, a horse he owned, as well as a saddle he used mainly for state ceremonies. The Turenne Salon contains other souvenirs, like the hat Napoléon wore at Eylau, the sword from his Austerlitz victory, and his "Flag of Farewell," which he kissed before departing for Elba.

You can gain access to the **Musée des Plans-Reliefs** through the west wing. This collection shows French towns and monuments done in scale models (the model of Strasbourg fills an entire room) as well as models of military fortifications since the days of the great Vauban.

A walk across the Cour d'Honneur (Court of Honor) delivers you to the **Eglise du Dôme,** designed by Hardouin-Mansart for Louis XIV. The great architect began work on the church in 1677, though he died before its completion. The dome is the second-tallest monument in Paris (the Tour Eiffel is the tallest, of course). The hearse used at the emperor's funeral on May 9, 1821, is in the Napoléon Chapel.

To accommodate **Napoléon's tomb** ★★★, the architect Visconti had to redesign the church's high altar in 1842. First buried on St. Helena, Napoléon's remains were exhumed and brought to Paris in 1840 on the orders of Louis-Philippe, who demanded the English return the emperor to French soil. The triumphal funeral procession passed beneath the Arc de Triomphe, down the Champs-Elysées, and to the Invalides, as snow swirled through the air. The remains were locked inside six coffins in this tomb made of red Finnish porphyry, with a green granite base. Surrounding it are a dozen amazon-like figures representing Napoléon's victories. Almost lampooning the smallness of the man, everything is done on a gargantuan scale. In his coronation robes, the statue of Napoléon stands 8½ feet high. The grave of the "King of Rome," his son by second wife Marie-Louise, lies at his feet. Napoléon's Tomb is surrounded by those of his brother Joseph Bonaparte; the great Vauban, who built many of France's fortifications; World War I Allied commander Foch; and the vicomte de Turenne, the republic's first grenadier (actually, only his heart is entombed here).

Place des Invalides, 7th Arr. ℂ **01-44-42-37-72.** Admission to Musée de l'Armée, Napoléon's Tomb, and Musée des Plans-Reliefs 40F (6.10€, $5.80) adults, 30F (4.55€, $4.35) ages 12–18, children 11 and under free. Oct–Mar daily 10am–5pm; Apr–May and Sept daily 10am–6pm; June–Aug daily 10am–7pm. Closed Jan 1, May 1, Nov 1, and Dec 25. Métro: Latour-Maubourg, Varenne, or Invalides.

Musée du Louvre ★★★   The Louvre is the world's largest palace and largest museum. As a palace, it leaves us cold, except for its old section, the **Cour Carrée.** As a museum, it's one of the greatest art collections ever. To enter, you pass through I. M. Pei's controversial 71-foot **glass pyramid** ★—a startling though effective contrast of ultramodern against the palace's classical lines. Commissioned by the late president François Mitterrand and completed in 1989, it allows sunlight to shine on an underground reception area with a complex of shops and restaurants. Automatic ticket machines help relieve the long lines of yesteryear.

People on one of those "Paris-in-a-day" tours try to break track records to get a glimpse of the Louvre's two most famous ladies: the beguiling *Mona Lisa* and the armless *Venus de Milo* ★★★. (The scene at the *Mona Lisa* is a circus—as the staff looks idly on, viewers push and shove in front of her bulletproof glass and forbidden flashbulbs pop all over. Yet still she smiles that smile, at peace among the fracas.) The herd then dashes on a 5-minute stampede in pursuit of *Winged Victory* ★★★, the headless statue discovered at Samothrace and dating from about 200 B.C. In defiance of the assembly-line theory of art, we head instead for David's *Coronation of Napoléon,* showing Napoléon poised with the crown aloft as Joséphine kneels before him, just across from his *Portrait of Madame Récamier* ★, depicting Napoléon's opponent at age 23; she reclines on her sofa agelessly in the style of classical antiquity.

Then a big question looms: Which of the rest of the 30,000 works on display would you like to see?

Between the Seine and rue de Rivoli, the Palais du Louvre suffers from an embarrassment of riches, stretching for almost half a mile. In the days of Charles V, it was a fortress, but François I, a patron of Leonardo da Vinci, had it torn down and rebuilt as a royal residence. Less than a month after Marie Antoinette's head and body parted company, the Revolutionary Committee decided the king's collection of paintings and sculpture should be opened to the public. At the lowest point in its history, in the 18th century, the Louvre was home for anybody who wanted to set up housekeeping there. Laundry hung out the windows, corners were literally pigpens, and families built fires to cook their meals during the long winters. Napoléon ended all that, chasing out the squatters and restoring the palace. In fact, he chose the Louvre as the site of his wedding to Marie-Louise.

So where did all these paintings come from? The kings of France, notably François I and Louis XIV, acquired many of them, and others were willed to or purchased by the state. Many contributed by Napoléon were taken from reluctant donors: The church was one especially heavy and unwilling giver. Much of Napoléon's plunder had to be returned, though France hasn't yet seen its way clear to giving back all the booty.

The collections are divided into seven departments: Egyptian Antiquities; Oriental Antiquities; Greek, Etruscan, and Roman Antiquities; Sculpture; Painting; Decorative Arts; and Graphic Arts. A number of galleries, devoted to Italian paintings, Roman glass and bronzes, Oriental antiquities, and Egyptian antiquities, were opened in 1997 and 1998. If you don't have to do Paris in a day, perhaps you can come here several times, concentrating on different collections or schools of painting. Those with little time should go on one of the guided tours in English.

Acquired by François I to hang above his bathtub, Leonardo's much-traveled **La Gioconda (Mona Lisa)** ✹✹✹ has been the source of legend for centuries. Note the guard and bulletproof glass: The world's most famous painting was stolen in the summer of 1911 and found in Florence in the winter of 1913. At first, both the poet Guillaume Apollinaire and Picasso were suspected, but it was discovered in the possession of a former Louvre employee, who'd apparently carried it out under his overcoat. Less well-known (but to us even more enchanting) are Leonardo's **Virgin and Child with St. Anne** ✹ and the **Virgin of the Rocks.**

After paying your respects to the "Smiling One," allow time to see some French works stretching from the Richelieu wing through the entire **Sully wing** and even overflowing into the **Denon wing.** It's all here: Watteau's **Gilles** with the mysterious boy in a clown suit staring at you; Fragonard's and Boucher's rococo renderings of the aristocracy; and the greatest masterpieces of David, including his stellar 1785 **The Oath of the Horatii** and the vast and vivid **Coronation of Napoléon.** Only Florence's Uffizi rivals the Denon wing for its Italian Renaissance collection—everything from Raphael's **Portrait of Balthazar Castiglione** to Titian's **Man with a Glove.** Veronese's gigantic **Wedding Feast at Cana** ✹, a romp of Viennese high society in the 1500s, occupies an entire wall (that's Paolo himself playing the cello).

Of the Greek and Roman antiquities, the most notable collections, aside from the *Venus de Milo* and *Winged Victory,* are fragments of a **Parthenon frieze** (in the Denon wing). In Renaissance sculpture, you'll see Michelangelo's **Esclaves**

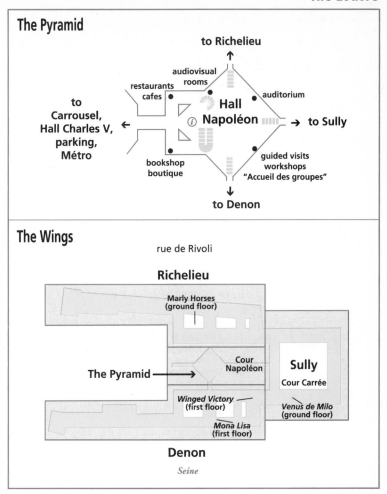

The Pyramid

to Richelieu

audiovisual rooms

restaurants cafes

auditorium

Hall Napoléon

to Carrousel, Hall Charles V, parking, Métro

(i)

to Sully

bookshop boutique

guided visits workshops "Accueil des groupes"

to Denon

The Wings

rue de Rivoli

Richelieu

Marly Horses (ground floor)

The Pyramid →

Cour Napoléon

Sully

Cour Carrée

Winged Victory (first floor)

Venus de Milo (ground floor)

Mona Lisa (first floor)

Denon

Seine

(Slaves), originally intended for the tomb of Julius II but sold into other bondage. The Denon wing houses masterpieces like Ingres's *The Turkish Bath;* the **Botticelli frescoes** from the Villa Lemmi; Raphael's *La Belle Jardinière;* and Titian's *Open Air Concert.* The Sully wing is also filled with old masters, like Boucher's *Diana Resting After Her Bath* and Fragonard's *Bathers.*

The **Richelieu wing** ★★★, reopened in 1993 after decaying empty for years, was expanded to add some 230,000 square feet of exhibition space. It houses northern European and French paintings, along with decorative arts, French sculpture, Oriental antiquities (a rich collection of Islamic art), and the Napoléon III salons. One of its galleries displays 21 works Rubens painted in a space of only 2 years for Marie de Médicis's Palais de Luxembourg. The masterpieces here include Dürer's *Self-Portrait,* Van Dyck's *Portrait of Charles I of England,* and Holbein the Younger's *Portrait of Erasmus of Rotterdam.*

When you get tired, consider a pick-me-up at **Café Marly** in the Cour Napoléon (see chapter 6). This grandiose cafe overlooks the glass pyramid and

Tips   Some Louvre Tips

Long waiting lines outside the Louvre's pyramid entrance are notorious, but there are some tricks for avoiding them.

- Order tickets by phone at ℂ **08-03-80-88-03** and have them charged to your Visa or MasterCard, then pick them up at any FNAC store (see chapter 9). This gives you direct entry through the Passage Richelieu, 93 rue de Rivoli.
- Enter via the underground shopping mall, the Carrousel du Louvre, at 99 rue de Rivoli.
- Enter directly from the Palais Royal–Musée du Louvre Métro station.
- Buy Le Pass Musée et Monuments (Museum and Monuments Pass) allowing direct entry through the priority entrance at the Passage Richelieu, 93 rue de Rivoli. For details on the pass, see "The Major Museums" later in this chapter.

offers coffees, pastries (by Paris's most legendary pastry-maker, Lenôtre), salads, sandwiches, and simple platters.

34–36 quai du Louvre, 1st Arr. Main entrance in the glass pyramid, Cour Napoléon. ℂ **01-40-20-53-17** (01-40-20-51-51 recorded message, 08-03-80-88-03 advance credit-card sales). www.louvre.fr. Admission 46F (7€, $6.65) before 3pm, 30F (4.55€, $4.35) after 3pm and on Sun, free for ages 17 and under, free 1st Sun of every month. Mon and Wed 9am–9:45pm (Mon short tour only), Thurs–Sun 9am–6pm. (Parts of the museum begin to close at 5:30pm.) 1½-hour English-language tours leave Mon and Wed–Sat various times of the day for 17F (2.60€, $2.45), children 12 and under free with museum ticket. Métro: Palais Royal–Musée du Louvre.

Musée d'Orsay ✪✪✪   Architects created one of the world's greatest museums from a defunct rail station, the neoclassical Gare d'Orsay, across the Seine from the Louvre and the Tuileries. Don't skip the Louvre, of course, but come here even if you have to miss all the other art museums in town. The Orsay boasts an astounding collection devoted to the watershed years 1848 to 1914, with a treasure trove by the big names plus all the lesser known groups (the symbolists, pointillists, nabis, realists, and late romantics). The 80 galleries also include Belle-Époque furniture, photographs, objets d'art, and architectural models. There's even a cinema showing classic films.

A monument to the Industrial Revolution, the Orsay is covered by an arching glass roof allowing in floods of light. It displays works ranging from the creations of academic and historic painters like Ingres to Romanticists like Delacroix, to neo-realists like Courbet and Daumier. The impressionists and post-impressionists, including Manet, Monet, Cézanne, van Gogh, and Renoir, share space with the fauves, Matisse, the cubists, and the expressionists in a setting once used by Orson Welles to film a nightmarish scene in *The Trial,* based on Kafka's unfinished novel. You'll find Millet's sunny wheat fields, Barbizon landscapes, Corot's mists, and parti-colored Tahitian Gauguins all in the same hall.

But it's the impressionists who keep the crowds lining up. When the nose-in-the-air Louvre chose not to display their works, a great rival was born. Led by Manet, Renoir, and Monet, the impressionists shunned ecclesiastical and mythological set pieces for a light-bathed Seine, faint figures strolling in the

Tuileries, pale-faced women in hazy bars, and even vulgar rail stations like the Gare St-Lazare. And the impressionists were the first to paint that most characteristic feature of Parisian life: the sidewalk cafe, especially in the artists' quarter of Montmartre.

The most famous painting from this era is Manet's 1863 *Déjeuner sur l'herbe (Picnic on the Grass),* whose forest setting with a nude woman and two fully clothed men sent shock waves through respectable society when it was first exhibited. Two years later, Manet's *Olympia* created another scandal by depicting a woman lounging on her bed and wearing nothing but a flower in her hair and high-heeled shoes; she's attended by an African maid in the background. Zola called Manet "a man among eunuchs."

One of Renoir's most joyous paintings is also here: the *Moulin de la Galette* (1876). Degas is represented by his paintings of racehorses and dancers; his 1876 cafe scene, *Absinthe,* remains one of his most reproduced works. Paris-born Monet was fascinated by the effect changing light had on Rouen Cathedral, and its stone bubbles to life in a series of five paintings—our favorite is *Rouen Cathedral: Full Sunlight.* Another celebrated work is by an American, Whistler's *Arrangement in Grey and Black: Portrait of the Painter's Mother,* better known as *Whistler's Mother.* It's said this painting heralded modern art, though many critics denounced it at the time as "Whistler's Dead Mother" because of its funereal overtones. Whistler was content to claim he'd made "Mummy just as nice as possible."

1 rue de Bellechasse or 62 rue de Lille, 7th Arr. ✆ **01-40-49-48-14.** www.musee-orsay.fr. Admission 40F (6.10€, $5.80) adults, 30F (4.55€, $4.35) ages 18–24/seniors, children 17 and under free. Tues–Wed and Fri–Sat 10am–6pm, Thurs 10am–9:45pm, Sun 9am–6pm (June 20–Sept 20 opens 9am). Métro: Solférino. RER: Musée d'Orsay.

Sainte-Chapelle ★★★

Countless writers have called this tiny chapel a jewel box. Yet that hardly suffices. Nor will it do to call it "a light show." Go when the sun is shining and you'll need no one else's words to describe the remarkable effects of natural light on Sainte-Chapelle. You approach the church through the Cour de la Sainte-Chapelle of the Palais de Justice. If it weren't for the chapel's 247-foot spire, the law courts here would almost swallow it up.

Begun in 1246, the bilevel chapel was built to house relics of the True Cross, including the Crown of Thorns acquired by St. Louis (the Crusader king, Louis IX) from the emperor of Constantinople. (In those days, cathedrals throughout Europe were busy acquiring relics for their treasuries, regardless of their authenticity. It was a seller's, perhaps a sucker's, market.) Louis IX is said to have paid heavily for his relics, raising the money through unscrupulous means. He died of the plague on a crusade and was canonized in 1297.

You enter through the *chapelle basse* (**lower chapel**), used by the palace servants; it's supported by flying buttresses and ornamented with fleur-de-lis designs. The king and his courtiers used the *chapelle haute* (**upper chapel**), one of the greatest achievements of Gothic art; you reach it by ascending a narrow spiral staircase. Viewed on a bright day, the 15 stained-glass windows up there seem to glow with Chartres blue and with reds that have inspired the saying "wine the color of Sainte-Chapelle's windows." The walls consist almost entirely of the glass (612 square meters of it), which had to be removed for safekeeping during the Revolution and again during both world wars. In their Old and New Testament designs are embodied the hopes and dreams (and the pretensions) of the kings who ordered their construction. The 1,134 scenes depict the Christian story from the Garden of Eden through the Apocalypse, and you read them

---

Moments The Razzle-Dazzle of Eiffel

The incandescent Eiffel Tower stole the millennium show as the best act in Europe, and the good news is that it's here to stay for years to come. The tower, dressed in diamond-like sparklers, will continue its special light show. Lights have transformed the tower into a diamond-studded "lady" every hour for about 10 minutes since January 1, 2000.

---

from bottom to top and from left to right. The great rose window depicts the Apocalypse.

Sainte-Chapelle stages **concerts** most nights in summer, with tickets from 120 to 150F (18.25 to 22.80€, $17.40 to $21.75). Call ✆ **01-42-77-65-65** for more details (daily 11am to 6pm).

Palais de Justice, 4 bd. du Palais, 4th Arr. ✆ **01-53-73-78-50.** www.monuments.fr. Admission 35F (5.30€, $5.10) adults, 23F (3.50€, $3.35) students/ages 18–25, ages 17 and under free. Apr–Sept daily 9:30am–6:30pm; Oct–Mar daily 10am–5pm. Métro: Cité, St-Michel, or Châtelet–Les Halles. RER: St-Michel.

Tour Eiffel ★★★   This is without doubt the single most recognizable structure in the world. Weighing 7,000 tons but exerting about the same pressure on the ground as an average-size person sitting in a chair, the wrought-iron tower wasn't meant to be permanent. It was built by Gustave-Alexandre Eiffel, the French engineer whose fame rested mainly on his iron bridges, to add flair to the 1889 Universal Exhibition. (Eiffel also designed the framework for the Statue of Liberty.) Praised by some and denounced by others (some called it a "giraffe," the "world's greatest lamppost," or the "iron monster"), the tower created as much controversy in the 1880s as I. M. Pei's glass pyramid at the Louvre did in the 1980s. What saved it from demolition in the early 1890s was the advent of radio—as the tallest structure in Europe at the time, it made a perfect spot to place a radio antenna (now a TV antenna).

The tower, including its 55-foot TV antenna, is 1,056 feet high. On a clear day you can see it from some 40 miles away. An open-framework construction, the tower unlocked the almost unlimited possibilities of steel construction, paving the way for the 20th century's skyscrapers. Skeptics said it couldn't be built, and Eiffel actually wanted to make it soar higher. For years it remained the tallest man-made structure on earth, until skyscrapers like the Empire State Building surpassed it.

We could fill an entire page with tower statistics. (Its plans spanned 6,000 square yards of paper, and it contains 2½ million rivets.) But forget the numbers. Just stand beneath the tower and look straight up. It's like a rocket of steel lacework shooting into the sky.

Value Tour Eiffel Bargain

The least expensive way to see the Tour Eiffel is to walk up the first two floors at a cost of 18F (2.75€, $2.60). That way you also avoid the long lines waiting for the elevator. If you dine at the tower's own **Altitude 95** (✆ **01-45-55-20-04**), an Eiffel restaurant on the first floor, management allows patrons to cut to the head of the line.

> ## *Tips*   Time Out at the Tower
>
> To see Eiffel Tower best, don't sprint—approach it gradually. We suggest taking the Métro to the Trocadéro stop and walking from the Palais de Chaillot to the Seine to get the full effect of the tower and its surroundings; then cross the pont d'Iéna and head for the base, where you'll find elevators in two of the pillars—expect long lines. (When the tower is open, you can see the 1889 lift machinery in the eastern and western pillars.) You visit the tower in three stages: The **first landing** provides a view over the rooftops as well as a cinema museum showing films, restaurants, and a bar. The **second landing** offers a panoramic look at the city. The **third landing** gives the most spectacular view; Eiffel's office has been re-created on this level, with wax figures depicting the engineer receiving Thomas Edison.
>
> Of course, it's the view most people come for, and this extends for 40 miles, theoretically (weather conditions tend to limit it). Nevertheless, it's fabulous, and the best time for visibility is about an hour before sunset.

Champ de Mars, 7th Arr. ✆ **01-44-11-23-23**. www.tour-eiffel.fr. Admission to 1st landing 24F (3.65€, $3.50), 2nd landing 45F (6.85€, $6.55), 3rd landing 62F (9.40€, $9). Stairs to 2nd floor 18F (2.75€, $2.60). Sept–May daily 9:30am–11pm; June–Aug daily 9am–midnight. Fall and winter, stairs open only to 6:30pm. Métro: Trocadéro, Ecole Militaire, or Bir-Hakeim. RER: Champ de Mars–Tour Eiffel.

4 The Major Museums

Turn to "The Top Attractions," above, for a comprehensive look at the **Musée du Louvre** and the **Musée d'Orsay.**

You can buy **Le Pass Musée et Monuments (Museum and Monuments Pass)** at any of the museums honoring it or at any branch of the Paris Tourist office (see chapter 4). It offers free entrance to the permanent collections of 65 monuments and museums in Paris and the Ile de France. A 1-day pass is 80F (12.15€, $11.60), a 3-day pass 160F (24.30€, $23.20), and a 5-day pass 240F (36.50€, $34.80). See chapter 4 for details on the **Paris Visite** pass, valid for 1 to 5 days on the public transport system, including the Métro, the city buses, the RER (regional express) trains within Paris city limits, and even the funicular to the top of Montmartre.

Centre Pompidou 🟌🟌🟌   Reopened in January 2000 in what was called in the 1970s "the most avant-garde building in the world," the restored Centre Pompidou is packing in the art-loving crowds again. The dream of former president Georges Pompidou, this center for 20th- and 21st-century art, designed by Richard Rogers and Renzo Piano, opened in 1977 and quickly became the focus of controversy. Its bold exoskeletal architecture and the brightly painted pipes and ducts crisscrossing its transparent facade (green for water, red for heat, blue for air, yellow for electricity) were jarring in the old Beaubourg neighborhood. Perhaps the detractors were right all along—within 20 years the building began to deteriorate so badly a major restoration was called for. The renovation added 5,000 square feet of exhibit space and a rooftop restaurant, a cafe, and a boutique; in addition, a series of auditoriums were created for film screenings and dance, theater, and musical performances. Access for the visitors with disabilities has also been improved.

The Centre Pompidou encompasses five attractions:

The **Musée National d'Art Moderne (National Museum of Modern Art)** ✮✮✮ offers a large collection of 20th- and 21st-century art. With some 40,000 works, this is the big attraction, though only some 850 works can be displayed at one time. If you want to view some real charmers, seek out Calder's 1926 *Josephine Baker,* one of his earlier versions of the mobile, an art form he invented. You'll also find two examples of Duchamps' series of dada-style sculptures he invented in 1936: *Boîte en Valise* (1941) and *Boîte en Valise* (1968). And every time we visit we have to see Dalí's *Hallucination partielle: Six images de Lénine sur un piano* (1931), with Lenin dancing on a piano.

> **Museum Closing Days**
>
> Generally, all museums are closed on January 1, May 1, Bastille Day (July 14), and December 25.

In the **Bibliothèque Information Publique (Public Information Library),** people have free access to a million French and foreign books, periodicals, films, records, slides, and microfilms in nearly every area of knowledge. The **Centre de Création Industriel (Center for Industrial Design)** emphasizes the contributions made in the fields of architecture, visual communications, publishing, and community planning; and the **Institut de Recherche et de Coordination Acoustique-Musique (Institute for Research and Coordination of Acoustics/Music)** brings together musicians and composers interested in furthering the cause of contemporary and traditional music. Finally, you can visit a re-creation of the jazz-age studio of Romanian sculptor Brancusi, the **Atelier Brancusi** ✮, a minimuseum slightly separate from the rest of the action.

The museum's **forecourt** is a free "entertainment center" featuring mimes, fire-eaters, would-be circus performers, and sometimes first-rate musicians. Don't miss the nearby **Stravinsky fountain,** containing mobile sculptures by Tinguely and Saint Phalle.

Place Georges-Pompidou, 4th Arr. ℂ 01-44-78-12-33. www.centrepompidou.fr. Admission 30F (4.55€, $4.35) adults, 20F (3.05€, $2.90) students, under age 13 free. Special exhibits 40F (6.10€, $5.80) adults, 30F (4.55€, $4.35) students, under age 13 free. Wed–Mon 11am–9pm. Métro: Rambuteau or Hôtel de Ville. RER: Châtelet–Les Halles.

Galerie Nationale du Jeu de Paume   For years, the Jeu de Paume was one of Paris's treasures, displaying some of the finest works of the impressionists. To the regret of many, that collection was hauled off to the Musée d'Orsay in 1986. After a $12.6-million face-lift, the Second Empire building was transformed into a state-of-the-art gallery with a video screening room. There's no permanent collection—a new show is mounted every 2 or 3 months. Sometimes the works of little-known contemporary artists are displayed; other times, exhibits feature unexplored aspects of established artists. Originally, Napoléon III built in this part of the gardens a ball court on which *jeu de paume,* an antecedent of tennis, was played—hence, the museum's name. The most infamous period in the gallery's history came during the Nazi occupation, when it served as an "evaluation center" for modern artworks: Paintings from all over France were shipped to the Jeu de Paume, and any condemned by the Nazis as "degenerate" were burned.

Tips **A Time-Saving Tip**

Museums require you to check shopping bags and book bags, and some-times lines for these can be longer than the ticket lines. If you value your time, leave your bags in your hotel room or don't go shopping before hitting the museums: Some lines can take 30 minutes. Ask if a museum has more than one check line, and, if so, go to the less frequented ones.

In the northeast corner of the Jardin des Tuileries/1 place de la Concorde, 1st Arr. ✆ **01-47-03-12-50.** Admission 45F (6.85€, $6.55) adults, 35F (5.30€, $5.10) students, age 13 and under free. Tues noon–9:30pm; Wed–Fri noon–7pm; Sat–Sun 10am–7pm. Métro: Concorde.

Musée Carnavalet ✦ If you enjoy history, but history tomes bore you, spend an hour or two here for some insight into Paris's past, which comes alive in intimate detail, right down to the chessmen Louis XVI used to distract his mind while waiting to go to the guillotine. The comprehensive and life-like exhibits are great for kids, too. The building, a renowned Renaissance palace, was built in 1544 by Pierre Lescot and Jean Goujon and later acquired by Mme de Carnavalet. The great François Mansart transformed it between 1655 and 1661.

The palace is best known because one of history's most famous letter writers, Mme de Sévigné, moved here in 1677. Fanatically devoted to her daughter (she ended up moving in with her because she couldn't bear their separation), she poured out nearly every detail of her life in her letters, virtually ignoring her son. A native of the Marais district, she died at her daughter's château in 1696. It wasn't until 1866 that the city of Paris acquired the mansion and turned it into a museum. Several salons cover the Revolution, with a bust of Marat, a portrait of Danton, and a model of the Bastille (one painting shows its demolition). Another salon tells the story of the captivity of the royal family at the Concierg-erie, including the bed in which Mme Elisabeth (the sister of Louis XVI) slept and the exercise book of the dauphin.

Exhibits continue at the **Hôtel le Pelletier de St-Fargeau,** across the courtyard. On display is furniture from the Louis XIV period to the early 20th century, including a replica of Marcel Proust's cork-lined bedroom with his actual furniture, including his brass bed.

23 rue de Sévigné, 3rd Arr. ✆ **01-44-59-58-58.** Admission 35F (5.30€, $5.10) adults, 18F (2.75€, $2.60) ages 7–26, under 7 free. Tues–Sun 10am–5:40pm. Métro: St-Paul or Chemin-Vert.

Musée Jacquemart-André ✦✦ This is the finest museum of its type in Paris, the treasure trove of a couple devoted to 18th-century French paintings and furnishings, 17th-century Dutch and Flemish paintings, and Italian Renais-sance works. Edouard André, the last scion of a family of Protestants who made a fortune in banking and industry in the 19th century, spent most of his life as an army officer stationed abroad; he eventually returned to marry a well-known portraitist of government figures and the aristocracy, Nélie Jacquemart, and they went on to compile a collection of rare decorative art and paintings in this 1850s town house.

In 1912, Mme Jacquemart willed the house and its contents to the Institut de France, which paid for an extensive renovation and enlargement. The salons drip with gilt and the ultimate in fin-de-siècle style. Works by Bellini, Carpaccio,

Uccelo, Van Dyck, Rembrandt *(The Pilgrim of Emmaus)*, Tiepolo, Rubens, Watteau, Boucher, Fragonard, and Mantegna are complemented by Houdon busts, Savonnerie carpets, Gobelin tapestries, della Robbia terra-cottas, and an awesome collection of antiques. Outstanding are the three 18th-century Tiepolo frescoes depicting spectators on balconies viewing Henri III's 1574 arrival in Venice.

Take a break from the gilded age with a cup of tea in Mme Jacquemart's high-ceilinged dining room, adorned with 18th-century tapestries. Salads, tarts, *tourtes* (round pastries filled with meat or fruit), and Viennese pastries are served during the museum's hours.

158 bd. Haussmann, 8th Arr. ✆ 01-45-62-11-59. www.musee-jacquemart-andre.com. Admission 50F (7.60€, $7.25) adults, 38F (5.80€, $5.50) ages 7–17, age 6 and under free. Daily 10am–6pm. Métro: Miromesnil or St-Philippe-du-Roule.

Musée Marmottan–Claude Monet ★★

In the past, an art historian or two would sometimes venture here to the edge of the Bois de Boulogne to see what Paul Marmottan had donated to the Académie des Beaux-Arts. Hardly anyone else did until 1966, when Claude Monet's son Michel died in a car crash, leaving a then-$10-million bequest of his father's art to the little museum. The Académie suddenly found itself with 130-plus paintings, watercolors, pastels, and drawings . . . and a passel of Monet lovers, who can now trace the evolution of the great man's work in a single museum. The collection includes more than 30 paintings of Monet's house at Giverny and many of water lilies, his everlasting fancy, plus ***Willow*** (1918), ***House of Parliament*** (1905), and a **Renoir portrait** of the 32-year-old Monet. Ironically, the museum had always owned Monet's ***Impression: Sunrise*** (1872), from which the impressionist movement got its name. Paul Marmottan's original collection includes fig-leafed nudes, First Empire antiques, assorted objets d'art, Renaissance tapestries, bucolic paintings, and crystal chandeliers. You can also see countless miniatures donated by Daniel Waldenstein.

2 rue Louis-Boilly, 16th Arr. ✆ 01-42-24-07-02. Admission 40F (6.10€, $5.80) adults, 25F (3.80€, $3.65) ages 8–24, ages 7 and under free. Tues–Sun 10am–5pm. Métro: La Muette.

Musée National du Moyen Age/Thermes de Cluny (Musée de Cluny) ★★

Along with the Hôtel de Sens in the Marais, the Hôtel de Cluny is all that remains of domestic medieval architecture in Paris. You enter through the cobblestoned Cour d'Honneur (Court of Honor), where you can admire the Flamboyant Gothic building with its clinging vines, turreted walls, gargoyles, and dormers with seashell motifs. First the Cluny was the mansion of a rich 15th-century abbot, built on top of/next to the ruins of a Roman bath (see below). By 1515, it was the residence of Mary Tudor, teenage widow of Louis XII and daughter of Henry VII and Elizabeth of York. Seized during the Revolution, the Cluny was rented in 1833 to Alexandre du Sommerard, who adorned it with his collection of medieval artworks; on his 1842 death, the building and the collection were bought back by the government.

This collection of medieval arts and crafts is superb. Most people come primarily to see the ***Unicorn Tapestries,*** the most acclaimed tapestries of their kind. A beautiful princess and her handmaiden, beasts of prey, and just plain pets—all the romance of the age of chivalry lives on in these remarkable yet mysterious tapestries discovered only a century ago in Limousin's Château de Boussac. Five seem to deal with the senses (one, for example, depicts a unicorn looking into a mirror held by a dour-faced maiden). The sixth shows a woman

---

Finds **Museum Oasis**

Just inaugurated at the Musée de Cluny is a new garden that's a return
to the Middle Ages. The garden was inspired by the luxuriant detail of
the museum's most fabled treasure, the 15th-century tapestry of *"The
Lady of the Unicorn."* The garden is small but richly planted and rests
under chestnuts and sycamores.

---

under an elaborate tent with jewels, her pet dog resting on an embroidered cush-
ion beside her, with the lovable unicorn and his friendly companion, a lion,
holding back the flaps. The background in red and green forms a rich carpet of
spring flowers, fruit-laden trees, birds, rabbits, donkeys, dogs, goats, lambs, and
monkeys.

The other exhibits range widely: Flemish retables; a 14th-century Sienese
John the Baptist and other Italian sculptures; statues from Sainte-Chapelle
(1243–48); gem-studded 12th- and 13th-century crosses; golden chalices, manuscripts, ivory carvings, vestments, leatherwork, jewelry, coins; a 13th-century
Adam; and recently discovered heads and fragments of statues from Notre-
Dame de Paris. In the fan-vaulted medieval chapel hang tapestries depicting
scenes from the life of St. Stephen.

Downstairs are the ruins of the **Roman baths,** from around A.D. 200. Of
these once-flourishing baths, the best-preserved section is seen in room X, the
frigidarium (where one bathed in cold water). Once it measured 70 by 36 feet,
rising to a height of 50 feet, with stone walls nearly 7 feet thick. The ribbed
vaulting here rests on consoles evoking ships' prows. Credit for this unusual
motif goes to the builders of the baths, Paris's boatmen. During Tiberius's reign,
a column to Jupiter was found beneath Notre-Dame's chancel and is now on
view in the court—called the "Column of the Boatmen," it's believed to be the
oldest sculpture created in Paris.

In the Hôtel de Cluny, 6 place Paul-Painlevé, 5th arr. ✆ **01-53-73-78-00.** www.musee-moyenage.fr. Admission 30F (4.55€, $4.35) adults, 20F (3.05€, $2.90) ages 18–25, age 17 and under free. Wed–Mon
9:15am–5:45pm. Métro: Cluny–La Sorbonne.

Musée National Eugène Delacroix   This museum is only for serious
Delacroix groupies, among whom we include ourselves. If you admire this artist
and want to see where he lived, worked, and died, this is worth at least an hour.
Delacroix (1798–1863) is something of an enigma to art historians. Even his
parentage is a mystery. Many believe Talleyrand had the privilege of fathering
him. One biographer saw him "as an isolated and atypical individualist—one
who respected traditional values, yet emerged as the embodiment of Romantic
revolt." Baudelaire called him "a volcanic crater artistically concealed beneath
bouquets of flowers." The museum is on one of the Left Bank's most charming
squares, with a highly romantic garden. A large arch on a stone courtyard leads
to Delacroix's studio—no poor artist's studio, but the tasteful creation of a
solidly established man. Sketches, lithographs, watercolors, and oils are hung
throughout, and a few mementos remain, like a lovely mahogany paint box. If
you want to see more of Delacroix's work, head to the Chapelle des Anges in
St-Sulpice (see "The Important Churches," later in this chapter).

6 place de Furstenberg, 6th Arr. ✆ **01-44-41-86-50.** Admission 22F (3.35€, $3.20) adults, 15F (2.30€,
$2.20) ages 18–25/over 60, age 17 and under free. Wed–Mon 9:30am–5pm. Métro: St-Germain-des-Prés.

Musée Picasso ★★★   When it opened at the beautifully restored Hôtel Salé (Salt Mansion, built by a man who made his fortune by controlling the salt distribution in 17th-century France) in the Marais, the press hailed it as a "museum for Picasso's Picassos." And that's what it is. The state acquired the world's greatest Picasso collection in lieu of $50-million in inheritance taxes: 203 paintings, 158 sculptures, 16 collages, 19 bas-reliefs, 88 ceramics, and more than 1,500 sketches and 1,600 engravings, along with 30 notebooks. These works span some 75 years of the artist's life and ever-changing style.

The range of paintings includes a remarkable 1901 self-portrait; *The Crucifixion* and *Nude in a Red Armchair;* and *Le Baiser (The Kiss), Reclining Nude,* and *Man with a Guitar,* all painted at Mougins on the Riviera in 1969 and 1970. Stroll through the handsome museum seeking your own favorite—perhaps a wicked one: *Jeune garçon à la langouste (Young Man with a Lobster),* painted in Paris in 1941. There are also several intriguing studies for *Les Demoiselles d'Avignon,* which shocked the establishment and launched cubism in 1907. Because the collection is so vast, temporary exhibits featuring items like his **studies of the Minotaur** are held twice per year. Also here is Picasso's own treasure trove of art, with works by Cézanne, Rousseau, Braque, Derain, and Miró. Picasso was fascinated with African masks, many of which are on view.

In the Hôtel Salé, 5 rue de Thorigny, 3rd Arr. © 01-42-71-25-21. www.paris.org/Musees/Picasso. Admission 30F (4.55€, $4.35) adults, 20F (3.05€, $2.90) ages 18–25/over 60, age 18 and under free. Apr–Sept Wed–Mon 9:30am–6pm; Oct–Mar Wed–Mon 9:30am–5:30pm. Métro: St-Paul, Filles du Calvaire, or Chemin Vert.

Musée Rodin ★★   Today Rodin is acclaimed as the father of modern sculpture, but in a different era his work was labeled obscene. The world's artistic taste changed, and in due course in 1911 the French government purchased Rodin's studio in this gray stone 18th-century mansion in the faubourg St-Germain. The government restored the rose gardens to their 18th-century splendor, making them a perfect setting for Rodin's most memorable works.

In the courtyard are three world-famous creations. Rodin's first major public commission, *The Burghers of Calais* commemorated the heroism of six citizens of Calais who in 1347 offered themselves as a ransom to Edward III in return for ending his siege of their port. Perhaps the single best-known work, *The Thinker,* in Rodin's own words, "thinks with every muscle of his arms, back, and legs, with his clenched fist and gripping toes." Not completed when Rodin died, *The Gate of Hell,* as he put it, is "where I lived for a whole year in Dante's *Inferno.*"

Inside the building, the sculpture, plaster casts, reproductions, originals, and sketches reveal the freshness and vitality of a remarkable artist. You can practically see many of his works emerging from marble into life. Everybody is attracted to *Le Baiser (The Kiss),* of which one critic wrote, "the passion is timeless." Upstairs are two versions of the celebrated and condemned **nude of Balzac,** his bulky torso rising from a tree trunk (Albert E. Elsen commented on the "glorious bulging" stomach). Included are many versions of his *Monument to Balzac* (a large one stands in the garden), Rodin's last major work. Other significant sculptures are the soaring *Prodigal Son, The Crouching Woman* (the "embodiment of despair"), and *The Age of Bronze,* an 1876 study of a nude man modeled after a Belgian soldier. (Rodin was falsely accused of making a cast from a living model.) Generally overlooked is a room devoted to Rodin's mistress, Camille Claudel, a towering artist in her own right. She was his pupil, model, and lover, and created such works as *Maturity, Clotho,* and the recently donated *The Waltz* and *The Gossips.*

Finds   Looking for a Quick Escape?

The little alley behind the Musée Rodin winds its way down to a pond with fountains and flowerbeds and even sandpits for children. It's one of the most idyllic hidden spots in Paris.

In the Hôtel Biron, 77 rue de Varenne, 7th Arr. ✆ **01-44-18-61-10**. www.musee-rodin.fr. Admission 28F (4.25€, $4.05) adults, 18F (2.75€, $2.60) ages 18–25, age 17 and under free. Apr–Sept Tues–Sun 9:30am–5:45pm; Oct–Mar Tues–Sun 9:30am–4:45pm. Métro: Varenne.

Petit Palais   Designed by Charles Girault, this small palace faces the **Grand Palais** (housing special exhibits; ✆ **01-44-13-17-30**); both were erected for the 1900 Universal Exhibition. The Petit Palais contains a hodgepodge of works for the serious art lover. Most people come for the temporary exhibits, not the permanent collections. Of the latter, the most prominent are the Dutuit and Tuck. In the **Dutuit Collection** are Egyptian, Greek, and Roman bronzes; rare ivory statues (the best of which is of a Roman actor); ancient Greek porcelains; enamels, sculpture, and hand-lettered and -painted manuscripts from the Middle Ages; and 17th-century Dutch and Flemish paintings, with works by Breughel the Younger *(The Wedding Pageant)*, Rubens, Hobbema, Ruysdael, and more. The **Tuck Collection,** donated by Edward Tuck in 1930, is composed mainly of 18th-century decorative artwork, including tapestries, heavily gilded furniture, wood-paneled salons, and porcelains.

A number of rooms are dedicated to 19th-century French painting, with canvases by Manet, Courbet, Daumier, Corot, Delacroix, Sisley, Cassatt *(Le Bain)*, Bonnard, Maurice Denis, and Edouard Vuillard. You'll also find works by David, Fragonard, and Greuze. The "academic school" is represented by the enormous compositions of Gustave Doré. The museum also has sculptures by Rodin, Bourdelle, Maillol, and Carpeaux and glassworks by Galle and Lalique.

Av. Winston-Churchill, 8th Arr. ✆ **01-42-65-12-73**. Admission 36F (5.45€, $5.20) adults, 23F (3.50€, $3.35) under age 25, free on Sun. Special exhibits 50F (7.60€, $7.25) adults, 25F (3.80€, $3.65) 26 and under. Tues–Sun 10am–5:40pm. Métro: Champs-Elysées.

5 Specialty Museums

Be sure to turn to "The Top Attractions" and "The Major Museums" for the cream of the crop. "Especially for Kids" includes museums parents and kids will love. The museums reviewed below represent the curious, fascinating, and sometimes arcane balance of Paris's offerings.

ART & MUSIC MUSEUMS

Musée Bourdelle ✰   Here you can see works by the star pupil of Rodin, Antoine Bourdelle (1861–1929), who became a celebrated artist in his own right. Along with changed exhibits, the museum displays the artist's drawings, paintings, and sculptures, and lets you wander through his studio, garden, and house. The original plaster casts of some of his greatest works are on display, but the most notable works are his 21 studies of Beethoven. Though some of the exhibits are badly captioned, you'll still feel the impact of Bourdelle's genius.

18 rue Antoine-Bourdelle, 15th arr. ✆ **01-49-54-73-73**. Admission 25F (3.80€, $3.65) adults, 22F (3.35€, $3.20) students, 15F (2.30€, $2.20) children. Tues–Sun 10am–5:40pm. Métro: Falguière.

Musée Cernuschi *✦*   Bordering Parc Monceau, this small museum (another mansion whose owners stuffed it with art objects, then bequeathed everything to the city) is devoted to the arts of China. The bust of Henri Cernuschi (1820–96) is a self-perpetuating memorial to a man whose interest in the East was legendary. Though the collection is no match for the Guimet's (below), the museum has a number of treasures, like a 3-ton bronze Japanese Buddha, fine Neolithic potteries, and bronzes from the 14th century B.C., the most famous being a tiger-shaped vase. The jades, ceramics, and funereal figures are exceptional. Rounding out the exhibits are some ancient paintings, the best known of which is *Horses with Grooms,* attributed to Han Kan (A.D. 8th century). The museum also houses a good collection of contemporary Chinese paintings.

7 av. Velázquez, 8th arr. ℂ **01-45-63-50-75.** Admission 22F (3.35€, $3.20) adults, 15F (2.30€, $2.20) students/seniors, age 17 and under free. Tues–Sun 10am–5:40pm. Métro: Monceau or Villiers. Bus: 30 or 94.

Musée Cognacq-Jay *✦✦*   The founders of La Samaritaine department store, Ernest Cognacq and his wife, Louise Jay, were fabled for their exquisite taste. To see what they accumulated from around the world, head for this museum in the 16th-century Hôtel Denon, with its Louis XV and Louis XVI paneled rooms. Some of the 18th century's most valuable decorative works are exhibited, ranging from ceramics and porcelain to delicate cabinets and paintings by Canaletto, Fragonard, Greuze, Chardin, Boucher, Watteau, and Tiepolo.

In the Hôtel Donon, 8 rue Elzévir, 3rd arr. ℂ **01-40-27-07-21.** Admission 30F (4.55€, $4.35) adults, 15F (2.30€, $2.20) ages 18–26, age 17 and under free. Tues–Sun 10am–5:40pm. Métro: St-Paul or Rambuteau.

Musée d'Art Moderne de la Ville de Paris & Musée des Enfants   This museum bordering the Seine has a permanent collection of paintings and sculpture owned by the city, but come here only if visits to the d'Orsay and Louvre haven't satiated you. It presents ever-changing exhibits on individual artists from all over the world or on trends in international art. You'll find works by Chagall, Matisse, Léger, Rothko, Braque, Dufy, Picasso, Utrillo, and Modigliani. Seek out Pierre Tal Coat's *Portrait of Gertrude Stein* and keep Picasso's version of this difficult subject in mind. The **Musée des Enfants** has exhibits and shows for children.

11 av. du Président-Wilson, 16th arr. ℂ **01-53-67-40-00.** Admission 45F (6.85€, $6.55) adults, 28F (4.25€, $4.05) ages 7–25, age 6 and under free. Tues–Fri 10am–5:30pm, Sat–Sun 10am–7pm. Métro: Iéna or Alma-Marceau.

Musée de la Musique   In the $120-million stone-and-glass Cité de la Musique, this museum serves as a tribute and testament to music. You can view 4,500 instruments from the 16th century to the present as well as paintings, engravings, and sculptures that relate to musical history. It's all here: cornets disguised as snakes, mandolins, lutes, zithers, antique music boxes, and even a postwar electric guitar. Models of the world's great concert halls and interactive display areas give you a chance to hear and better understand musical art and technology.

In the Cité de la Musique, 221 av. Jean-Jaurès, 19th arr. ℂ **01-44-84-44-84.** www.cite-musique.fr. Admission 40F (6.10€, $5.80) adults, 30F (4.55€, $4.35) students/age 60 and over, 15F (2.30€, $2.20) age 17 and under. Visits with commentary, 60F (9.10€, $8.70) adults, 45F (6.85€, $6.55) students/age 60 and over, 20F (3.05€, $2.90) age 17 and under. Tues–Thurs noon–6pm, Fri–Sat noon–7:30pm, Sun 10am–6pm. Métro: Porte de Pantin.

Musée des Arts d'Afrique et d'Océanie   In this Art-Deco building constructed for the 1931 French Colonial exhibition, you'll find an extensive collection of central African art that's especially rich in carved masks, carved statues, and Aboriginal bark paintings, as well as some magnificent bronzes from Benin. There are also some art objects from the Pacific islands and a limited collection of woven carpets and gold jewelry from the Magreb region of Arab-speaking North Africa. In the cellars are aquariums and terrariums containing crocodiles, iguanas, and tortoises.

293 av. Daumesnil, 12th arr. ℂ **01-44-74-84-80.** Admission 30F ($4.80) adults, under age 18 free. Fri–Wed 10am–5:30pm. Métro: Porte Dorée.

Musée des Arts Décoratifs   In the northwest wing of the Louvre's Pavillon de Marsan, this museum boasts furnishings, fabrics, wallpaper, and objets d'art from the Middle Ages to the present—but it's recommended only if you have an abiding interest in the subject. Notable on the first floor are the 1920s Art-Deco boudoir, bath, and bedroom of couturier Jeanne Lanvin by designer Rateau. Decorative art from the Middle Ages to the Renaissance is on the second floor; rich collections from the 17th, 18th, and 19th centuries occupy the third and fourth floors. The fifth has centers on wallpaper and drawings and documentary centers detailing fashion, textiles, toys, crafts, and glass trends. The newest addition is a **Musée de la Publicité (Museum of Advertising),** with advertising posters from the 18th century and film, TV, and radio commercials from the 1930s to today. Architect Jean Nouvel designed a cutting-edge interior that also displays avant-garde video techniques.

In the Union Centrale des Decoratifs, 107 rue de Rivoli, 1st arr. ℂ **01-44-55-57-50.** Admission 35F (5.30€, $5.10) adults, 25F (3.80€, $3.65) ages 18–25, age 18 and under free. Tues and Thurs–Fri 11am–6pm, Wed 11am–9pm, Sat–Sun 10am–6pm. Métro: Palais Royal or Tuileries.

Musée Edith Piaf   This privately run museum is filled with Piaf memorabilia, like photos, costumes, and personal possessions. The daughter of an acrobat, Giovanna Gassion grew up in this neighborhood and assumed the name of Piaf ("little sparrow"); her songs, like "La Vie en Rose" and "Non, je ne regrette rien," eventually were heard around the world. You must phone in advance to get the security code you'll need to buzz your way in. Nearby is the **Villa Calte,** a beautiful example of the fine architecture many locals are trying to save (ask for directions at the Piaf museum). Fronted by an intricate wrought-iron fence, the house has a pleasant garden where parts of Truffaut's *Jules et Jim* were filmed.

5 rue Crespin-du-Gast, 11th arr. ℂ **01-43-55-52-72.** Free admission but donations appreciated. Mon–Thurs 1–6pm by appointment only. Métro: Ménilmontant.

Musée National des Arts Asiatiques–Guimet ★★   This vastly expanded museum and one of the most beautiful Asian museums in the world is filled with treasures from the East. The museum was named for its founder, research chemist/industrialist Emile Guimet. The Guimet, opened in Lyon but transferred to Paris in 1889, received the Musée Indochinois du Trocadéro's collections in 1931 and the Louvre's Asian collections after World War II. The most interesting exhibits are Buddhas, serpentine monster heads, funereal figurines, and antiquities from the temple of Angkor Wat. Some galleries are devoted to Tibetan art, including fascinating scenes of the Grand Lamas entwined with serpents and demons.

6 place d'Iéna, 16th arr. ℂ **01-56-52-53-00.** Admission 35F (5.30€, $5.10) adults, free 18 and under. Wed–Mon 10am–6pm. Métro: Iéna or Alma-Marceau.

Finds **Spying on Paris as a Shopper**

Everyone knows about the views from the Eiffel Tower and Sacré-Coeur. Here's another. Shoppers can take the elevator and some stairs to the 11th floor at the top of the **Samaritaine** department store (No. 2) at 19 rue de la Monnaie, 1st arr. (© **01-40-41-20-20**; Metro: Pont Neuf or Châtelet-Les Halles). At 245 feet, a 360-degree panorama sweeps across Paris, including the bridge Pont Neuf, the dome of Invalides where Napoléon rests, and the cathedral at Notre Dame where you can imagine the gargoyles are making lascivious eyes at you. An enamel frieze on the store's roof identifies the landmarks for you.

Musée Nissim de Camondo ⭐   Visit this museum for a keen insight into the decorative arts of the 18th-century. The pre–World War I town house was donated to the Musée des Arts Décoratif by Comte Moïse de Camondo in memory of his son, Nissim, a French aviator killed in combat during World War I. The museum is like the home of an aristocrat—rich with needlepoint chairs, tapestries (many from Beauvais or Aubusson), antiques, paintings, bas-reliefs, silver, Chinese vases, crystal chandeliers, Sèvres porcelain, Savonnerie carpets, and even a Houdon bust. The Blue Salon, overlooking Parc Monceau, is most impressive.

63 rue de Monceau, 8th arr. © **01-53-89-06-50.** Admission 30F (4.55€, $4.35) adults, 20F (3.05€, $2.90) under age 18/over 60. Wed–Sun 10am–5pm. Closed Jan 1, May 1, Bastille Day (July 14), and Dec 25. Métro: Villiers.

Musée Zadkine   This museum near the Jardin du Luxembourg was once the home of sculptor Ossip Zadkine (1890–1967), and his collection has been turned over to the city for public viewing. Included are some 300 pieces of sculpture, displayed in the museum and the garden. Some drawings and tapestries are also exhibited. At these headquarters where he worked from 1928 until his death, you can see how he moved from "left wing" cubist extremism to a renewed appreciation of the classic era. You can visit his garden for free even if you don't want to go into the museum—in fact it's one of the finest places to relax in Paris on a sunny day, sitting on a bench taking in the two-faced *Woman with the Bird.*

100 bis rue d'Assas, 6th arr. © **01-43-26-91-90.** www.paris-france.org/musees. Admission 22F (3.35€, $3.20) adults, 15F (2.30€, $2.20) ages 7–26. Tues–Sun 10am–5:30pm. Métro: Notre-Dame des Champs.

CRAFT & INDUSTRY MUSEUMS
Manufacture Nationale des Gobelins ⭐   Did you know a single tapestry can take 4 years to complete, employing as many as three to five full-time weavers? The founder of this dynasty, Jehan Gobelin, came from a family of dyers and clothmakers and in the 15th century discovered a scarlet dye that made him famous. By 1601, Henry IV had become interested, and he imported from Flanders 200 weavers to make tapestries full-time. Oddly enough, until this endeavor, the Gobelin family hadn't made any tapestries. Colbert, Louis XIV's minister, eventually bought the works, and under royal patronage the craftsmen set about executing designs by Le Brun. After the Revolution, the industry was reactivated by Napoléon. Les Gobelins is still going strong, and some of the antique high-warp looms are still in use. You can visit the *ateliers*

(studios) of the weavers, who sit behind huge screens of thread, patiently inserting stitch after stitch.

42 av. des Gobelins, 13th arr. ℂ **01-44-54-19-49**. Tours in French (with English pamphlets) 50F (7.60€, $7.25) adults, 40F (6.10€, $5.80) ages 7–24/65 or older, under 7 free. Tues–Thurs 2 and 2:45pm. Métro: Les Gobelins.

Musée de Baccarat   In a Directoire building that houses Baccarat's headquarters, this museum resembles an ice palace filled with crystal of all shapes and sizes, with some of the most impressive pieces produced by the company through the years. Czars, royalty, and oil-rich sheiks have numbered among the best patrons of the prestigious company, established in 1764. At the museum entrance stands "Lady Baccarat," a chandelier in the form and size of a woman.

30 bis rue de Paradis, 10th arr. ℂ **01-47-70-64-30**. Admission 15F (2.30€, $2.20) adults, 10F (1.50€, $1.45) students, 7.50F (1.15€, $1.10) under age 17/over 60. Mon–Sat 9am–6pm. Métro: Poissonnière or Château d'Eau.

Musée National de Céramique de Sèvres ★★   Next door to the Manufacture Nationale de Sèvres (see chapter 9), this museum boasts one of the world's finest collections of faïence and porcelain, some of which belonged to Mme du Barry, Mme de Pompadour's hand-picked successor as Louis XV's mistress (Mme de Pompadour *loved* Sèvres porcelain). On view is the Pompadour rose (which the English insisted on calling the rose du Barry), a style much in vogue in the 1750s and 1760s. The painter Boucher made some of the designs used by the factory, as did the sculptor Pajou (he created the bas-reliefs for the Opéra at Versailles). The factory pioneered what became known in porcelain as the Louis Seize (Louis XVI) style—it's all here, plus lots more, including works from Sèvres's arch rival, Meissen.

Place de la Manufacture, Sèvres, 15th arr. ℂ **01-41-14-04-20**. Admission 22F (3.35€, $3.20) adults, 15F (2.30€, $2.20) ages 18–25, age 17 and under free. Wed–Mon 10am–5pm. Métro: Pont de Sèvres, then walk across the Seine to the Left Bank.

HISTORY MUSEUMS

Musée de l'Histoire de France ★   This palace has been steeped in French history since it was first built in 1371. The graceful baroque facade dates from 1705, when the building's exterior was redesigned by the much-underrated architect Delamair for the prince and princesse de Soubise. In the early 1800s, Napoléon designated the building as the official repository for his archives, and it has served that function ever since. You enter through the colonnaded Cour d'Honneur (Court of Honor). But before going inside, walk around the corner to 58 rue des Archives to the medieval turreted gateway of the **Hôtel de Clisson**. (This mansion gave way to the palace of the ducs de Guise, who owned the property until it was bought by the Soubise family. The princesse de Soubise was once the mistress of Louis XIV, and apparently the Sun King was very generous, giving her the funds to remodel and redesign the palace.)

The archives contain documents that go back even further than Charlemagne. The letter collection is highly valued, exhibiting the penmanship of Marie Antoinette (a farewell letter), Louis XVI (his will), Danton, Robespierre, Napoléon I, and Joan of Arc (the museum has the only known sketch of her completed during her life). Even the jailer's keys to the old Bastille are here. One of the showcased rooms is the **Salon de la Princesse** (a.k.a the **Salon Ovale**), a richly decorated circular room one floor above street level. Sweeping expanses of gilt and crystal offset a series of ceiling frescoes by Van Loo, Boucher, and

Natoire. Sometimes, the **Hôtel de Rohan,** around the corner on rue Vieille-du-Temple, contains some of the overflow from this place, but only in the form of temporary exhibits.

In the Hôtel de Soubise, 60 rue des Francs-Bourgeois, 3rd arr. ✆ **01-40-27-60-96.** Admission 20F (3.05€, $2.90) adults, 15F (2.30€, $2.20) children/seniors. Wed–Mon 2–6pm. Métro: Hôtel de Ville or Rambuteau.

Paristoric   This unique 45-minute multimedia show retraces the city's history in a state-of-the-art theater. The 2,000 years since Paris's birth unroll chronologically to the music of such varied musicians as Wagner and Piaf. Maps, portraits, and scenes from dramatic times are projected on the large screen as a running commentary (heard through headphones in one of 10 languages) gives details about art, architecture, and events. Many visitors come here first for a preview of what they want to see; others stop for a more in-depth look at what they've already visited.

11 bis rue Scribe, 9th arr. ✆ **01-42-66-62-06.** www.paris-story.com. Admission 53F (8.05€, $7.70) adults, 33F (5€, $4.80) students/under age 18. Daily 9am–6pm (to 9pm Apr–Oct). Shows begin every hour on the hour. Métro: Opéra. RER: Auber.

THE OFFBEAT

Musée de la Chasse (Hunting Museum)   Near the Musée Carnavalet, this mansion was also designed by Mansart, and its museum is for the specialist who, like Hemingway, hunts for sport. Mounted heads are plentiful, from the antelope to the elephant, from the bushbuck to the waterbuck to the bush pig. You'll find a Rembrandt sketch of a lion, a number of Desportes wild-animal portraits, and rifles (many from the 17th century) inlaid with pearls or engraved with ivory. The outstanding hunt tapestries are often perversely amusing—one a cannibalistic romp, another showing a helmeted man standing eye to eye with a bear he's stabbing to death. The collection of paintings includes works by Rubens, Breughel, Oudry, Chardin, and Corot.

In the Hôtel Guénégaud, 60 rue des Archives, 3rd arr. ✆ **01-53-01-92-40.** Admission 30F (4.55€, $4.35) adults, 15F (2.30€, $2.20) students/seniors, 5F (.75€, 75¢) ages 5–16, children 4 and under free. Tues–Sun 11am–6pm. Métro: Rambuteau or Hôtel de Ville.

Musée de l'Erotisme   A tribute to the primal appeal of human sexuality, this art gallery/museum opened in 1997 in a 19th-century town house that had been a raunchy cabaret. It presents a tasteful but appealingly risqué collection of art and artifacts, with six floors boasting an oft-changing array of exhibits like erotic sculptures and drawings. The oldest object is a palm-size ancient Roman *tintinabulum* (bell), a phallus-shaped animal with the likeness of a nude woman riding astride it. Modern objects include resin, wood, and plaster sculptures by French artist Alain Rose and works by American, Dutch, German, and French artists, including the free-form works of Robert Combas. Also look for everyday items with erotic themes from South America (terra-cotta pipes shaped like phalluses) and the States (a 1920s belt buckle that resembles a praying nun when it's fastened and a nude woman when it's open). The gift shop sells Asian amulets, African bronzes, and terra-cotta figurines from South America. There's also an art gallery where serious works of art are sold.

72 bd. de Clichy, 18th arr. ✆ **01-42-58-28-73.** Admission 40F (6.10€, $5.80) adults, children under 17 not permitted. Daily 10am–2am. Métro: Blanche.

Musée du Parfum (Perfume Museum)   This museum is in an overhauled 19th-century theater on one of Paris's busiest thoroughfares. As you enter the lobby through a quiet courtyard, the lightly scented air will remind you why you're there—to appreciate perfume enough to buy a bottle in the ground-floor shop. But first, a short visit upstairs introduces you to the rudiments of perfume history. The copper containers with spouts and tubes were used in the distillation of perfume oils, and the exquisite collection of perfume bottles from the 17th to the 20th century is impressive. Even if perfume bores you, the air-conditioning is a welcome relief in summer, and the rest rooms are spotless and free.

39 bd. des Capucines, 1e. ✆ **01-42-60-37-14.** Free admission. Mon–Sat 9am–6pm. Métro: Opéra.

Musée du Vin (Wine Museum)   This museum is in an ancient stone-and-clay quarry used by 15th-century monks as a wine cellar. It provides a good introduction to the art of wine making, displaying various tools, beakers, cauldrons, and bottles in a series of exhibits. The quarry is right below Balzac's house (see below), and the ceiling contains a trap door he used to escape from his creditors.

5 rue des Eaux, 16th arr. ✆ **01-45-25-63-26.** Admission 39F (5.95€, $5.65) adults, 34F (5.15€, $4.95) students, 32F (4.85€, $4.65) over age 60. Tues–Sun 10am–6pm. Métro: Passy.

6 The Important Churches

Turn to "The Top Attractions," earlier in this chapter, for a full look at the **Cathédrale de Notre-Dame, Basilique du Sacré-Coeur,** and **Sainte-Chapelle.**

American Cathedral of the Holy Trinity   This cathedral is one of Europe's finest examples of Gothic Revival architecture and a growing center for music and art. Consecrated in 1886, it was created by George Edmund Street, best known for the London Law Courts. Aside from the great architecture, you'll find remarkable pre-Raphaelite stained-glass windows illustrating the *Te Deum,* an early-15th-century triptych by the Roussillon Master, an anonymous painter, probably a monk; a needlepoint collection including kneelers depicting the 50 state flowers; and the 50 state flags in the nave. A **Memorial Cloister** commemorates Americans who died in Europe in World War I and all the victims of World War II. Documentation in several languages explains these and other highlights. The cathedral is also a center of worship and community outreach, with a schedule of Sunday and weekday services in English. Les Arts George V, a cultural organization, presents reasonably priced choral concerts, lectures, and art shows.

23 av. George V, 8th Arr. ✆ **01-53-23-84-00.** Free admission. Daily 9am–5pm. Sun Holy Eucharist 9am and 11am. Métro: Alma-Marceau or George V.

Basilique St-Denis ★★   In the 12th century, Abbot Suger placed an inscription on the bronze doors here: "Marvel not at the gold and expense, but at the craftsmanship of the work." France's first Gothic building that can be dated precisely, St-Denis was the "spiritual defender of the State" during the reign of Louis VI ("The Fat"). The massive facade has a rose window and a crenellated parapet on the top similar to the fortifications of a castle. The stained-glass windows—in stunning mauve, purple, blue, and rose—were restored in the 19th century.

The first bishop of Paris, St. Denis became the patron saint of the monarchy, and royal burials began here in the 6th century and continued until the Revolution. The sculpture designed for the **tombs**—some two stories high—span French artistic development from the Middle Ages to the Renaissance. (There are guided tours of the crypt, but in French only.) François I was entombed at St-Denis, and his funeral statue is nude, though he demurely covers himself with his hand. Other kings and queens here include Louis XII and Anne de Bretagne, as well as Henri II and Catherine de Médicis. Revolutionaries stormed through the basilica during the Terror, smashing many marble faces and dumping royal remains in a lime-filled ditch in the garden. (These remains were reburied under the main altar during the 19th century.) Free organ concerts are given Sundays at 11:15am.

Place de l'Hôtel-de-Ville, 2 rue de Strasbourg, St-Denis. © 01-48-09-83-54. Admission 32F (4.85€, $4.65) adults, 21F (3.20€, $3.05) seniors/students, age 11 and under free. Apr–Sept Mon–Sat 10am–7:30pm, Sun noon–6:30pm; Oct–Mar Mon–Sat 10am–5pm, Sun noon–5pm. Métro: St-Denis.

La Madeleine ★★ La Madeleine is one of Paris's minor landmarks, dominating short rue Royale, which culminates in place de la Concorde. Though construction began in 1806, it wasn't consecrated as a church until 1842. Resembling a Roman temple, the building was intended as a monument to the glory of the Grande Armée (Napoléon's idea, of course). Later, several alternative uses were considered: the National Assembly, the Bourse, and the National Library. Climb the 28 steps to the facade and look back: You'll be able to see rue Royale, place de la Concorde and its obelisk, and (across the Seine) the dome of the Hôtel des Invalides. Don't miss Rude's *Le Baptême du Christ,* to the left as you enter.

Place de la Madeleine, 8th arr. © 01-44-51-69-00. Free admission. Daily 7:30am–7pm. Métro: Madeleine.

Mosquée de Paris ★ This beautiful pink marble mosque was built in 1922 to honor the North African countries that had given aid to France during World War I. Today, North Africans living in Paris gather on Friday, the Muslim holy day, and during Ramadan to pray to Allah. Short tours are given of the building, its central courtyard, and its Moorish garden; guides present a brief history of the Islamic faith. However, you may want just to wander around on your own, then join the students from nearby universities for couscous and sweet mint tea at the Muslim **Restaurant de la Mosquée de Paris** (© 01-43-31-18-14), adjoining the grounds, open daily from noon to 3pm and 7 to 10:30pm.

Place du Puits-de-l'Ermite, 5th Arr. © 01-45-35-97-33. Admission 15F (2.30€, $2.20) adults, 10F (1.50€, $1.45) students/children. Sat–Thurs 9:30am–5pm. Métro: Monge.

St-Germain-des-Prés ★★ Outside, it's a handsome early-17th-century town house. Inside, it's one of Paris's oldest churches, from the 6th century, when a Benedictine abbey was founded here by Childebert, son of Clovis. Alas, the marble columns in the triforium are all that remain from then. The Normans nearly destroyed the abbey at least four times. The present building has a Romanesque nave and a Gothic choir with fine capitals. At one time, the abbey was a pantheon for Merovingian kings. Restoration of the site of their tombs, **Chapelle de St-Symphorien,** began in 1981, and unknown Romanesque paintings were discovered on the triumphal arch. Among the others interred here are Descartes (his heart at least) and Jean-Casimir, the king of Poland who abdicated his throne. The Romanesque tower, topped by a 19th-century spire, is the most enduring landmark in St-Germain-des-Prés. Its church bells, however, are hardly noticed by the patrons of Les Deux Magots across the way.

When you leave the church, turn right on rue de l'Abbaye and have a look at the 17th-century pink **Palais Abbatial.**

3 place St-Germain-des-Prés, 6th Arr. © 01-43-25-41-71. Free admission. Daily 8am–8pm. Métro: St-Germain-des-Prés.

⌒ *Moments* **Gregorians Unplugged**

St-Germain-des-Prés stages the most wonderful concerts on the Left Bank; it boasts fantastic acoustics and a marvelous medieval atmosphere. The church was built to accommodate an age without microphones, and the sound effects will thrill you. For more information, call ℂ **01-43-25-41-71.** Arrive about 45 minutes before the performance if you'd like a front-row seat. Tickets are 120 to 250F (18.25 to 38€, $17.40 to $36.25).

St-Sulpice ☆☆   Pause first outside St-Sulpice. The 1844 fountain by Visconti displays the sculpted likenesses of four bishops of the Louis XIV era: Fenelon, Massillon, Bossuet, and Flechier. Work on the church, at one time Paris's largest, began in 1646 as part of France's Catholic revival. Though laborers built the body by 1745, work on the bell towers continued until 1780, when one was finished and the other incomplete. One of the priceless treasures inside is Servandoni's rococo **Chapelle de la Madone (Chapel of the Madonna),** with a Pigalle statue of the Virgin. The church has one of the world's largest organs, comprising 6,700 pipes; it has been played by musicians like Charles-Mari Widor and Marcel Dupré.

The real reason to come here is to see the Delacroix frescoes in the **Chapelle des Anges (Chapel of the Angels),** the first on your right as you enter. Seek out his muscular Jacob wrestling (or dancing?) with an effete angel. On the ceiling, St. Michael is having some troubles with the Devil, and yet another mural depicts Heliodorus being driven from the temple. Painted in Delacroix's final years, the frescoes were a high point in his baffling career. If these impress you, pay the painter tribute by visiting the Musée Delacroix (see "The Major Museums").

Rue St-Sulpice, 6th arr. ℂ **01-46-33-21-78.** Free admission. Daily 7:30am–7:30pm. Métro: St-Sulpice.

St-Etienne-du-Mont ☆☆   Once there was an abbey here, founded by Clovis and later dedicated to St. Geneviève, the patroness of Paris. Such was the fame of this popular saint that the abbey proved too small to accommodate the pilgrimage crowds. Now part of the Lycée Henri IV, the Tour de Clovis (Tower of Clovis) is all that remains of the ancient abbey—you can see the tower from rue Clovis. Today the task of keeping St. Geneviève's cult alive has fallen on this church, practically adjoining the Panthéon. The interior is Gothic, an unusual style for a 16th-century church. Building began in 1492 and was plagued by delays until the church was finally finished in 1626.

Besides the patroness of Paris, such men as Pascal and Racine were entombed here. Though St. Geneviève's tomb was destroyed during the Revolution, the stone on which her coffin rested was discovered later, and her relics were gathered for a place of honor at St-Etienne. The church possesses a remarkable early–16th century **rood screen:** Crossing the nave, it's unique in Paris—called spurious by some and a masterpiece by others. Another treasure is a woodcarved **pulpit,** held up by Samson, clutching a bone in one hand, with a slain lion at his feet. The fourth chapel on the right when you enter contains impressive 16th-century stained glass.

Place Ste-Geneviève, 5th arr. ℂ **01-43-54-11-79.** Free admission. Sept–June Mon–Sat 8:30am–noon and 2–7pm, Sun 8:30am–noon and 3–7:30pm; July–Aug Tues–Sun 10am–noon and 4–7pm. Métro: Cardinal Lemoine or Luxembourg.

St-Eustache 🏛🏛 This mixed Gothic and Renaissance church completed in 1637 is rivaled only by Notre-Dame. Madame de Pompadour and Richelieu were baptized here, and Molière's funeral was held here in 1673. The church has been known for organ recitals ever since Liszt played here in 1866. Inside rests the **black-marble tomb** of Jean-Baptiste Colbert, the minister of state under Louis XIV; atop the tomb is his marble effigy flanked by statues of *Abundance* by Coysevox and *Fidelity* by Tuby. The church's most famous painting is Rembrandt's *The Pilgrimage to Emmaus.* There's a side entrance on rue Rambuteau.

2 rue du Jour, 1st Arr. 🕐 **01-42-36-31-05.** www.st-eustache.org. Free admission. Apr–Sept daily 9am–8pm; Oct–Mar daily 9am–7pm. Sun mass 9:30am, 11am, and 6pm; Sun organ recitals 5:30pm. Métro: Les Halles.

St-Germain l'Auxerrois 🏛🏛 Once it was the church for the Palais du Louvre, drawing an assortment of royalty, courtesans, men of art and law, and even local artisans. Sharing place du Louvre with Perrault's colonnade, the church contains only the foundation stones of its original 11th-century belfry. The primitive chapel that had stood here was greatly enlarged in the 14th century by the addition of side aisles and became a beautiful church, with 260 feet of stained glass, including some rose windows from the Renaissance. The intricately carved **church-wardens' pews** are outstanding, based on 17th-century Le Brun designs. Behind them is a **15th-century triptych** and **Flemish retable,** so badly lit you can hardly appreciate it. The organ was ordered by Louis XVI for Sainte-Chapelle. Many famous men were entombed here, including the sculptor Coysevox and the architect Le Vau. Around the chancel is an intricate **18th-century grille.**

The saddest moment in the church's history was on August 24, 1572, the evening of the St. Bartholomew Massacre. The tower bells rang, signaling the supporters of Catherine de Médicis, Marguerite de Guise, Charles IX, and the future Henri III to launch a slaughter of thousands of Huguenots, who'd been invited to celebrate the marriage of Henri de Navarre to his cousin, Marguerite de Valois.

2 place du Louvre, 1st arr. 🕐 **01-42-60-13-96.** Free admission. Daily 8am–8pm. Métro: Louvre-Rivoli.

Val-de-Grâce 🏛🏛 According to an old proverb, to understand the French you must like Camembert cheese, the pont Neuf, and the dome of Val-de-Grâce. Its origins go back to 1050, when a Benedictine monastery was built here. In 1619, Louis XIII appointed as abbess Marguerite Veni d'Arbouze, who asked Louis's wife, Anne of Austria, for a new monastery because the original was decaying. After 23 years of a childless marriage, Anne gave birth to a boy who went on to be known as the Sun King. To express his gratitude, Louis XIII approved the rebuilding of the church, and at the age of 7, on April 1, 1645, the future Louis XIV laid Val-de-Grâce's first stone. Mansart was the main architect, and to him we owe the facade in the Jesuit style. Le Duc, however, designed the dome, and Mignard added the frescoes. Le Mercier and Le Muet also had a hand in the church's fashioning. The church was turned into a military hospital in 1793 and an army school in 1850.

1 place Alphonse-Laveran, 5th arr. 🕐 **01-40-51-51-92.** Admission 30F (4.55€, $4.35) adults, under 6 free. Tues–Wed noon–5pm, Sat 1–5pm, Sun 1–5pm (5pm is last entrance). Métro: Port Royal.

7 Architectural & Historic Highlights

Arènes de Lutéce Discovered and partially destroyed in 1869, this amphitheater is Paris's second most important Roman ruin after the baths in the Musée de Cluny (see "The Major Museums"). Today the site is home to a small arena, not as grand as the original, and pleasant gardens. You may feel as if you've discovered a private spot in the heart of the city, but don't be fooled. Your solitude is sure to be interrupted, if not by groups of students playing soccer then at least by parents pushing strollers down the walking paths. This is an ideal spot for a picnic—bring a bottle of wine and fresh baguettes to enjoy in this vestige of the ancient city of Lutétia.

At rues Monge and Navarre, 5th Arr. No phone. Free admission. May–Sept daily 10am–10pm; Oct–Apr daily 10am–5:30pm. Métro: Jussieu.

Bibliothèque Nationale de France, Site Tolbiac/François Mitterrand (French National Library)

Opened in 1996 with a dramatic futuristic design by Dominique Perrault (a quartet of 24-story towers evoking the look of open books), this is the last of the *grand projets* of the late François Mitterrand. It boasts the same grandiose scale as the Cité de la Musique (see "Specialty Museums" for its museum) and houses the nation's literary and historic archives; it's regarded as a repository of the French soul, replacing outmoded facilities on rue des Archives. The library incorporates space for 3,600 readers at a time, many of whom enjoy views over two levels of a garden-style courtyard that seems far removed from the urban congestion of Paris.

This is one of Europe's most user-friendly academic facilities, emphasizing computerized documentation and microfiche—a role model that'll set academic and literary priorities well into the future. The public has access to as many as 750,000 books and periodicals, with an additional 10 million historic (including medieval) documents shown only to qualified experts. Though the appeal of this place extends mainly to serious scholars researching French history and culture, there's a handful of special exhibits that might interest you, as well as concerts and lectures. Concert tickets rarely exceed 100F (15.20€, $14.50) adults and 65F (9.90€, $9.45) students, seniors, and children; a schedule is available at the library.

Quai François-Mauriac, 13th Arr. ✆ 01-53-79-59-59. Admission 20F (3.05€, $2.90). No one under 16 admitted Tues–Sat 10am–8pm, Sun noon–7pm. Métro: Bibliothèque François-Mitterrand.

Conciergerie ★★

London has its Bloody Tower and Paris has its Conciergerie. Even though the Conciergerie had a long regal history before the Revolution, it was forever stained by the Reign of Terror and lives as an infamous symbol of the time when carts pulled up constantly to haul off fresh supplies of victims for Dr. Guillotin's wonderful little invention.

Much of the Conciergerie was built in the 14th century as an extension of the Capetian royal Palais de la Cité. You approach through its landmark twin towers, the **Tour d'Argent** (where the crown jewels were stored at one time) and **Tour de César,** but the vaulted **Salle des Gardes (Guard Room)** is the actual entrance. Even more interesting is the vast, dark, and foreboding Gothic **Salle des Gens d'Armes (Room of People at Arms),** utterly changed from the days when the king used it as a banquet hall. However, architecture plays a secondary role to the list of prisoners who spent their last miserable days here. Few in its history endured tortures as severe as those imposed on Ravaillac, who assassinated Henry IV in 1610. In the Tour de César, he received pincers in the flesh and had hot lead and boiling oil poured on him like bath water before being executed (see the Hôtel de Ville entry below). During the Revolution, the Conciergerie became a symbol of terror to the nobility and enemies of the State. A short walk away, the Revolutionary Tribunal dispensed a skewed, hurried justice—if it's any consolation, the jurists didn't believe in torturing their victims, only in decapitating them.

After being seized by a crowd of peasants who stormed Versailles, Louis XVI and Marie Antoinette were brought here to await their trials. In failing health and shocked beyond grief, *l'Autrichienne* ("the Austrian," as she was called with malice) had only a small screen (sometimes not even that) to protect her modesty from the gaze of guards stationed in her cell. By accounts of the day, she was shy and stupid though the evidence is that on her death she displayed the nobility of a true queen. (What's more, the famous "Let them eat cake" she supposedly uttered when told the peasants had no bread, is probably apocryphal—besides, at the time, cake flour was less expensive than bread flour, so even if she said this it wasn't meant coldbloodedly.) It was shortly before noon on the morning of October 16, 1793, when her executioners came for her, grabbing her and cutting her hair, as was the custom for victims marked for the guillotine.

Later, the Conciergerie housed other noted prisoners, including Mme Elisabeth; Mme du Barry, mistress of Louis XV; Mme Roland ("O Liberty! Liberty! What crimes are committed in thy name!"); and Charlotte Corday, who killed Marat with a kitchen knife while he was taking a sulphur bath. In time, the Revolution consumed its own leaders, such as Danton and Robespierre. Finally, even one of Paris's most hated men, public prosecutor Fouquier-Tinville, faced the guillotine to which he'd sent so many others. Among the few interned here who lived to tell the tale was America's Thomas Paine, who reminisced about his chats in English with Danton.

1 quai de l'Horloge, 4th Arr. ☎ **01-53-73-78-50**. www.paris.org/Monuments/Conciergerie. Admission 35F (5.30€, $5.10) adults, 23F (3.50€, $3.35) ages 18–25/over 60, children under 12 free. Apr–Sept daily 9:30am–6:30pm; Oct–Mar daily 10am–5pm. Métro: Cité, Châtelet, or St-Michel. RER: St-Michel.

Hôtel de Ville ✸ On a large square with fountains and early-1900s lampposts, the 19th-century Hôtel de Ville isn't a hotel but Paris's grandiose City Hall. The medieval structure it replaced had witnessed countless municipally ordered executions. Henry IV's assassin, Ravaillac, was quartered alive on the square in 1610, his body tied to four horses that bolted in opposite directions. On May 24, 1871, the communards doused the City Hall with petrol, creating a blaze that lasted for 8 days. The Third Republic ordered the structure rebuilt, with many changes, even creating a Hall of Mirrors evocative of that at Versailles. For security reasons, the major splendor of this building is closed to the public. However, the information center sponsors exhibits on Paris in the main lobby.

29 rue de Rivoli, 4th Arr. ☎ **01-42-76-43-43**. Free admission. Information center, Mon–Sat 9am–6:30pm. Métro: Hôtel de Ville.

Institut de France ✸ Designed by Louis Le Vau, this dramatic baroque building with an enormous cupola is the seat of all five Academies that dominate France's intellectual life—Française, Sciences, Inscriptions et Belles Lettres, Beaux-Arts, and Sciences Morales et Politiques. The members of the Academie Française (limited to 40), guardians of the French language referred to as "the immortals," gather here. Many are unfamiliar figures (though Jacques Cousteau and Marshall Pétain were members), and the Academy is remarkable for the great writers and philosophers who have *not* been invited to join—Balzac, Baudelaire, Diderot, Flaubert, Descartes, Proust, Molière, Pascal, Rousseau, and Zola, to name only a few. The cenotaph was designed by Coysevox for Mazarin.

23 quai de Conti, 6th Arr. ℂ **01-44-41-44-41.** Free admission (guests can walk into courtyard only). Métro: Pont Neuf or Odéon.

La Grande Arche de La Défense ✿   Designed as the architectural center-piece of the sprawling satellite suburb of La Défense, this massive steel-and-masonry arch rises 35 stories. It was built with the blessing of the late François Mitterrand and extends the magnificently engineered straight line linking the Louvre, Arc du Triomphe du Carrousel, Champs-Elysées, Arc de Triomphe, avenue de la Grande Armée, and place du Porte Maillot. The arch is ringed with a circular avenue patterned after the one winding around the Arc de Triomphe. The monument is tall enough to shelter Notre-Dame beneath its heavily trussed canopy. An elevator carries you up to an observation platform, where you get a view of the carefully planned geometry of the surrounding streets.

You'll notice nets rigged along the Grande Arche. When pieces of Mitterrand's *grand projet* started falling to the ground, a mesh was erected to catch fragments before they hit people on the head. If only such protection existed from all politicians' follies.

1 place du parvis de La Défense, Puteaux, 15th arr. ℂ **01-49-07-27-57.** Admission 46F (7€, $6.65) adults, 35F (5.30€, $5.10) ages 15–17, 30F (4.55€, $4.35) ages 6–14, ages 5 and under free. Daily Apr–Oct 10am–7pm; off-season 10am–8pm. RER: La Défense.

Palais Bourbon/Assemblée Nationale ✿   The French parliament's lower house, the Chamber of Deputies, meets at this 1722 mansion built by the duchesse de Bourbon, a daughter of Louis XIV. You can make reservations for one of two types of visits as early as 6 months in advance. Tours on art, archi-tecture, and basic French government processes are given Monday, Friday, and Saturday. They're in French (in English with advance booking). You may also observe sessions of the National Assembly, held Tuesday afternoon and all day Wednesday and Thursday beginning at 9:30am. Do remember this is a working government building, and all visitors are subject to rigorous security checks.

33 quai d'Orsay, 7th arr. ℂ **01-40-63-64-08.** Free admission. Hours vary, so call ahead. Métro: Assemblée Nationale.

Palais Royal ✿✿   The Palais Royal was originally known as the Palais Cardi-nal, for it was the residence of Cardinal Richelieu, Louis XIII's prime minister. Richelieu had it built, and after his death it was inherited by the king, who died soon after. Louis XIV spent part of his childhood here with his mother, Anne of Austria, but later resided at the Louvre and Versailles. The palace was later owned by the duc de Chartres et Orléans (see the entry for Parc Monceau under "Parks & Gardens"), who encouraged the opening of cafes, gambling dens, and other public entertainments. Though government offices occupy the Palais Royal and are not open to the public, do visit the **Jardin du Palais Royal,** an enclosure bordered by arcades. Don't miss the main courtyard, with the contro-versial 1986 Buren sculpture—280 prison-striped columns, oddly placed.

Rue St-Honoré, 1st arr. No phone. Free admission. Daily 8am–7pm. Métro: Palais Royal–Musée du Louvre.

Panthéon ✿✿   Some of the most famous men in French history (Victor Hugo, for one) are buried here in austere grandeur, on the crest of the mount of St. Geneviève. In 1744, Louis XV vowed that if he recovered from a mysterious illness, he'd build a church to replace the decayed Abbaye de Ste-Geneviève. He recovered but took his time in fulfilling his promise. It wasn't until 1764 that

Mme de Pompadour's brother hired Soufflot to design a church in the form of a Greek cross with a dome reminiscent of St. Paul's in London. When Soufflot died, his pupil Rondelet carried out the work, completing the structure 9 years after his master's death.

After the Revolution, the church was converted into a "Temple of Fame" and became a pantheon for the great men of France. Mirabeau was buried here, though his remains were later removed. Likewise, Marat was only a temporary tenant. Voltaire's body was exhumed and placed here—and allowed to remain. In the 19th century, the building changed roles so many times—a church, a pantheon, a church—that it was hard to keep its function straight. After Hugo was buried here, it became a pantheon once again. Other notable men entombed within are Rousseau, Soufflot, Zola, and Braille. Only one woman has so far been deemed worthy of placement here, Marie Curie, who joined her husband, Pierre. Most recently, the ashes of André Malraux were transferred to the Panthéon because, according to President Jacques Chirac, he "lived [his] dreams and made them live in us." As Charles de Gaulle's culture minister, Malraux decreed the arts should be part of the lives of all French people, not just Paris's elite.

Before entering the crypt, note the striking frescoes: On the right wall are scenes from Geneviève's life and on the left are the saint with a white-draped head looking out over medieval Paris, the city whose patron she became, as well as Geneviève relieving victims of famine with supplies.

Place du Panthéon, 5th arr. ☎ **01-44-32-18-00.** Admission 42F (6.40€, $6.10) adults, 23F (3.50€, $3.35) ages 18–25, age 11 and under free. Apr–Sept daily 9:30am–6:30pm; Oct–Mar daily 10am–6:15pm (last entrance 45 min. before closing). Métro: Cardinal Lemoine or Maubert-Mutualité.

8 Literary Landmarks

If there's a literary bone in your body, you'll feel a vicarious thrill on discovering the haunts of the famous writers and artists who've lived, worked, and played in Paris.

Take the Métro to place St-Michel to begin your tour. As you wander away from the Seine, you'll encounter **rue de la Huchette,** one of the Left Bank's most famous streets. Its inhabitants were immortalized in Eliot Paul's *The Last Time I Saw Paris.* Continuing on, you'll enter the territory of the Beat Generation, home to the **Café Gentilhomme** (no longer there) described by Jack Kerouac in *Satori in Paris.* Allen Ginsberg's favorite, the **Hôtel du Vieux-Paris,** 9 rue Gît-le-Coeur, still attracts those in search of the Beats.

Stroll down **rue Monsieur-le-Prince,** the "Yankee alleyway," where Richard Wright, James McNeill Whistler, Henry Wadsworth Longfellow, and Oliver Wendell Holmes all lived at one time or another. During a famous visit in 1959, Martin Luther King Jr. came to call on Richard Wright, the Mississippi-born African-American novelist famous for *Native Son.* King climbed to the third-floor apartment at **no. 14,** only to find that Wright's opinions on the civil rights movement conflicted with his own. Whistler rented a studio at **no. 22,** and, in 1826, Longfellow lived for a short time at **no. 49.** Oliver Wendell Holmes Sr. lived at **no. 55.** After strolling along this street, you can dine at the former haunts of Kerouac and Hemingway. (See our recommendation of **Crémerie-Restaurant Polidor,** 41 rue Monsieur-le-Prince, 6th arr., in chapter 5.) Or cross back over to the Right Bank for a drink at the famed **Hôtel de Crillon,** 10 place de la Concorde, 8th arr. (see chapter 5), where heroine Brett Ashley broke her promise to rendezvous with Jake Barnes in Hemingway's *The Sun Also Rises.* Zelda and F. Scott Fitzgerald lifted their glasses here as well.

For details on **Harry's New York Bar,** 5 rue Daunou, 2nd arr., see "Literary Haunts" in chapter 10. For a description of **Les Deux Magots, Le Procope,** and **La Rotonde,** see "The Top Cafes" in chapter 6. And for coverage of the bookstore **Shakespeare and Company,** see chapter 9.

Here are two great museums for hardcore literary fans:

Maison de Balzac   In the residential district of Passy, near the Bois de Boulogne, sits this modest house on the slope of a hill, with a small courtyard and garden. The great Honoré de Balzac fled to this house in 1840 after his possessions and furnishings were seized, and he lived here for 7 years (to see him you had to know a password). If a creditor knocked on the rue Raynouard door, Balzac was able to escape through the rue Berton exit. The museum's most notable memento is Balzac's "screech-owl" (his nickname for his tea kettle), which he kept hot throughout the night as he wrote *La Comédie humaine.* Also enshrined here are Balzac's writing desk and chair and a library of special interest to scholars. The little house is filled with reproduced caricatures of Balzac. A biographer once wrote: "With his bulky baboon silhouette, his blue suit with gold buttons, his famous cane like a golden crowbar, and his abundant, disheveled hair, Balzac was a sight for caricature."

47 rue Raynouard, 16th arr. ☎ **01-55-74-41-80.** www.paris-france.org/musees. Admission 30F (4.55€, $4.35) adults, 20F (3.05€, $2.90) ages 26 and under/over age 60. Tues–Sun 10am–5:40pm. Métro: Passy or La Muette.

Maison de Victor Hugo ⭐   Today, theatergoers who've seen *Les Misérables,* even those who haven't read anything by Paris's great 19th-century novelist, come to place des Vosges to see where Victor Hugo lived and wrote. Some thought Hugo a genius, but Cocteau called him a madman, and an American composer discovered that in his old age he was carving furniture with his teeth! From 1832 to 1848, the novelist/poet lived on the second floor of the old Hôtel Rohan Guéménée, built in 1610 on what was then place Royale. The museum owns some of Hugo's furniture as well as pieces that once belonged to Juliette Drouet, the mistress with whom he lived in exile on Guernsey, one of the Channel Islands.

Worth the visit are Hugo's drawings, more than 450, illustrating scenes from his own works. Mementos of the great writer abound, including samples of his handwriting, his inkwell, and first editions of his works. A painting of Hugo's 1885 funeral procession at the Arc de Triomphe is on display, as are plentiful portraits and souvenirs of his family. Of the furnishings, a chinoiserie salon stands out. The collection even contains Daumier caricatures and a bust of Hugo by David d'Angers, which, compared to Rodin's, looks saccharine.

6 place des Vosges, 4th Arr. ☎ **01-42-72-10-16.** Admission 22F (3.35€, $3.20) adults, age 26 and under free. Tues–Sun 10am–5:40pm. Closed national holidays. Métro: St-Paul, Bastille, or Chemin-Vert.

9 Parks & Gardens

JARDIN DES TUILERIES

The spectacular statue-studded **Jardin des Tuileries** ⭐⭐, bordering place de la Concorde, 1st arrondissement (☎ **01-44-50-75-01;** Métro: Tuileries OR Concorde), are as much a part of Paris as the Seine. They were designed by Le Nôtre, Louis XIV's gardener and planner of the Versailles grounds. About 100 years

Fun Fact **Did You Know?**

The odd name of the Jardins des Tuileries comes from the clay earth of the land here, once used to make roof tiles called *tuiles.*

Seemingly, half of Paris can be found in the Tuileries on a warm spring day, listening to the chirping birds and admiring the daffodils and tulips. As you walk toward the Louvre, you'll enter the **Jardin du Carrousel,** dominated by the **Arc de Triomphe du Carrousel,** at the Cour du Carrousel. Pierced with three walkways and supported by marble columns, the monument honors Napoléon's Grande Armée, celebrating its victory at Austerlitz on December 5, 1805. The arch is surmounted by statuary, a chariot, and four bronze horses.

before that, Catherine de Médicis ordered a palace built here, the **Palais des Tuileries,** connected to the Louvre; other occupants have included Louis XVI (after he left Versailles) and Napoléon. Twice attacked by enraged Parisians, it was finally burned to the ground in 1871 and never rebuilt. The gardens, however, remain. In orderly French manner, the trees are arranged according to designs and even the paths are arrow-straight. Breaking the sense of order and formality are bubbling fountains.

JARDIN DU LUXEMBOURG

Hemingway once told a friend that the **Jardin du Luxembourg** ✹✹ in the 6th arrondissement (Métro: Odéon; RER: Luxembourg) "kept us from starvation." He related that in his poverty-stricken days in Paris, he wheeled a baby carriage (the vehicle was considered luxurious) through the garden because it was known "for the classiness of its pigeons." When the gendarme went across the street for a glass of wine, the writer would eye his victim, preferably a plump one, then lure him with corn and "snatch him, wring his neck," and hide him under the blanket. "We got a little tired of pigeon that year," he confessed, "but they filled many a void."

The Luxembourg has always been associated with artists, though children, Sorbonne students, and tourists predominate nowadays. Watteau came this way, as did Verlaine. Balzac, however, didn't like the gardens at all. In 1905, Gertrude Stein would cross them to catch the Batignolles/Clichy/Odéon omnibus, pulled by three gray mares, to meet Picasso in his studio at Montmartre, where he painted her portrait.

Marie de Médicis, the neglected wife of the roving Henri IV, ordered the **Palais du Luxembourg** built on this site in 1612, shortly after she was widowed. A Florentine by birth, the regent wanted to create another Pitti Palace, where she could live with her "witch" friend, Leonora Galigal. Architect Salomon de Brossee wasn't entirely successful, though the overall effect is Italianate. Alas, the queen didn't get to enjoy the palace, as she was forced into exile by her son, Louis XIII, when he discovered she was plotting to overthrow him. She died in poverty in Cologne. For her palace, she'd commissioned from Rubens 21 paintings that glorified her life, but they're now in the Louvre. You can visit the palace only the first Sunday of each month at 10:30am, for 50F (7.60€, $7.25) adults or 40F (6.10€, $5.80) 25 years or under. However, you must call ✆ **01-44-61-21-66** to make a reservation.

However, you don't come to the Luxembourg to visit the palace—not really. The gardens are the attraction. For the most part, they're in the classic French tradition: well-groomed and formally laid out, the trees planted in patterns. A large central water basin is encircled by urns and statuary on pedestals, one honoring Paris's patroness, St. Geneviève, with pigtails reaching to her thighs. Another memorial is dedicated to Stendhal. It's a good place for kids: They can sail a toy boat, ride a pony, or attend an occasional Grand Guignol puppet show. And you can play *boules* with a group of elderly men who aren't ashamed to wear black berets and have Gauloises dangling from their mouths.

BOIS DE BOULOGNE

One of the most spectacular parks in Europe is the **Bois de Boulogne** ⋪⋪, Porte Dauphine, 16th arrondissement (✆ **01-40-67-90-82;** Métro: Les Sablons, Porte Maillot, or Porte Dauphine), often called the "main lung" of Paris. Horse-drawn carriages traverse it, but you can also drive through. Its hidden pathways, however, can be discovered only by walking. You could spend days in the Bois de Boulogne and still not see everything.

Porte Dauphine is the main entrance, though you can take the Métro to Porte Maillot as well. West of Paris, the park was once a forest kept for royal hunts. It was in vogue in the late 19th century: Along avenue Foch, carriages with elegantly attired and coiffured Parisian damsels would rumble along with their foppish escorts. Nowadays, it's more likely to attract run-of-the-mill picnickers. (And at night, hookers and muggers are prominent, so be duly warned.)

When Napoléon III gave the grounds to the city in 1852, they were developed by Baron Haussmann. Separating Lac Inférieur from Lac Supérieur is the **Carrefour des Cascades** ⋪ (you can stroll under its waterfall). The Lower Lake contains two islands connected by a footbridge. From the east bank, you can take a boat to these idyllically situated grounds, perhaps stopping off at the cafe/restaurant on one of them.

Restaurants in the bois are numerous, elegant, and expensive. The **Pré Catelan** ⋪ contains a deluxe restaurant of the same name (✆ **01-44-14-41-14**) occupying a gem of a Napoléon III–style château and a Shakespearean theater in a garden planted with trees mentioned in the bard's plays. Nearby is **La Grande Cascade** (✆ **01-45-27-33-51**), once a hunting lodge for Napoléon III.

Jardin d'Acclimatation, at the northern edge of the park, is for children, with a small zoo, an amusement park, and a narrow-gauge railway (see "Especially for Kids" for more details). Two racetracks, the **Hippodrome de Longchamp** ⋪⋪⋪ and the **Hippodrome d'Auteuil,** are in the park (see "A Day at the Races"). The Grand Prix is run in June at Longchamp (the site of a medieval abbey). Fashionable Parisians always turn out for this, the women in their finest haute couture. To the north of Longchamp is the **Grand Cascade,** an artificial waterfall.

In the western section of the bois, the 60-acre **Parc de Bagatelle** ⋪ owes its existence to a bet between the comte d'Artois (later Charles X) and Marie Antoinette, his sister-in-law. The comte wagered he could erect a small palace in less than 3 months, so he hired nearly 1,000 craftsmen (cabinetmakers, painters, Scottish landscape architect Thomas Blaikie, and more) and irritated the locals by requisitioning all shipments of stone and plaster arriving through Paris's west gates. He won his bet. If you're here in late April, it's worth visiting the Bagatelle just for the tulips. In late May, one of the finest rose collections in Europe is in full bloom. For some reason, as the head gardener confides to us, "This is the

Map labels: Jardin d'Acclimatation, bd. Maurice Barrès, Palais des Congrès, place de la Porte Maillot, Musée National des Arts et Traditions Populaires, allée du Bord de l'Eau, Ile de Puteaux, Bagatelle, av. Foch, Musée Arménien, Musée d'Ennery, allée de Longchamps, pont de Suresnes, Musée de Contrefaire, av. Victor Hugo, rte. de Serres à Neuilly, Pré Catelan, Lac Inférieur, rte. de la Grande Cascade, Grande Cascade, allée de Reine Marguerite, rte. de l'Hippodrome, Jardin Ranelagh, Musée Marmottan, allée des Fortifications, Hippodrome de Longchamp, Lac Supérieur, Seine, Hippodrome d'Auteuil, Fondation Le Corbusier, Roland Garros Stadium, Seine

major rendezvous point in Paris for illicit couples." In September, the light is less harsh than in summer or even in February; when stripped of much of its greenery, the park's true shape can be seen.

PARC MONCEAU

Much of **Parc Monceau** ⚐, 8th arrondissement (ⓒ **01-42-27-39-56**; Métro: Monceau or Villiers), is ringed with 18th- and 19th-century mansions, some evoking Proust's *Remembrance of Things Past*. Carmontelle designed it in 1778 for the duc d'Orléans (who came to be known as Philippe-Egalité), at the time the richest man in France. The duke was noted for his debauchery and pursuit of pleasure, so no ordinary park would do. It was opened to the public in the days of Napoléon III's Second Empire.

Monceau was laid out with an Egyptian-style obelisk, a medieval dungeon, a thatched farmhouse, a Chinese pagoda, a Roman temple, an enchanted grotto, various chinoiseries, and a waterfall. These fairy-tale touches have largely disappeared, except for a pyramid and an oval naumachia fringed by a colonnade. Now the park is filled with solid statuary and monuments, one honoring Chopin. In spring, the red tulips and magnolias are worth the air ticket to Paris.

10 Cemeteries

Sightseers often view Paris's cemeteries as being somewhat like parks, suitable places for strolling. The graves of celebrities past are also a major lure. Père-Lachaise, for example, is a major sightseeing goal; the other cemeteries are of lesser interest.

Impressions

Mrs. Allongby: They say, Lady Hunstanton, that when good Americans die they go to Paris.

Lady Hunstanton: Indeed? And when bad Americans die, where do they go?

Lord Illingworth: Oh, they go to America.
— Oscar Wilde, A Woman of No Importance (1893)

Cimetière de Montmartre ⭐ This cemetery, from 1795, lies west of Montmartre and north of boulevard de Clichy. Russian dancer **Vaslav Nijinsky,** novelist **Alexandre Dumas** *fils,* impressionist **Edgar Degas,** and composers **Hector Berlioz** and **Jacques Offenbach** are interred here, along with **Stendhal** and lesser literary lights like **Edmond** and **Jules de Goncourt** and **Heinrich Heine.** A more recent tombstone honors **François Truffaut,** film director of the *nouvelle vague.* We like to pay our respects at the tomb of **Alphonsine Plessis,** heroine of *La Dame aux camélias,* and **Mme Récamier,** who taught the world how to lounge. **Emile Zola** was buried here, but his corpse was exhumed and promoted to the Panthéon in 1908. In tragic 1871, the cemetery was used for mass burials of victims of the Siege and the Commune.

20 av. Rachel, 18th arr. ✆ **01-43-87-64-24.** Free admission. Mon–Fri 8am–6pm, Sat 8:30am–6pm, Sun 9am–6pm (to 5:30pm in winter). Métro: Blanche or Place Clichy.

Cimetière de Passy This cemetery runs along Paris's old northern walls, south and southwest of Trocadéro. It's a small graveyard, sheltered by chestnut trees, but it contains many gravesites of the famous—a concierge at the gate can guide you. Painters **Edouard Manet** and **Romaine Brooks** and composer **Claude Debussy** are tenants. Many great literary figures since 1850 were interred here, including **Tristan Bernard, Jean Giraudoux,** and **François de Croisset.** Also present are composer **Gabriel Fauré,** aviator **Henry Farman,** actor **Fernandel,** and high priestess of the city's most famous literary salon, **Natalie Barney,** along with **Renée Vivien,** one of her many lovers.

2 rue du Comandant-Schloesing, 16th arr. ✆ **01-47-27-51-42.** Free admission. Mar–Nov daily 8:30am–5:45pm; Dec–Feb daily 8:30am–5:15pm. Métro: Trocadéro.

Cimetière du Montparnasse ⭐ In the shadow of the Tour Montparnasse, this debris-littered cemetery is a burial ground of yesterday's celebrities. A map available to the left of the main gateway will direct you to the shared gravesite of its most famous couple, **Simone de Beauvoir** and **Jean-Paul Sartre.** Others resting here include **Samuel Beckett, Guy de Maupassant,** editor **Pierre Larousse** (famous for his dictionary), **Capt. Alfred Dreyfus,** auto tycoon **André Citroën,** sculptors **Ossip Zadkine** and **Constantin Brancusi,** actress **Jean Seberg,** composer **Camille Saint-Saëns,** photographer **Man Ray,** and **Charles Baudelaire,** who'd already written about "plunging into the abyss, Heaven or Hell."

3 bd. Edgar-Quinet, 14th Arr. ✆ **01-44-10-86-50.** Free admission. Mon–Fri 8am–6pm, Sat 8:30am–6pm, Sun 9am–6pm (to 5:15pm Nov–Mar). Métro: Edgar Quinet.

Cimetière du Père-Lachaise ⭐⭐⭐ When it comes to name dropping, this cemetery knows no peer; it has been called the "grandest address in Paris." A free map of Père-Lachaise is available at the newsstand across from the main entrance (also see the map on p. 218–219).

Père-Lachaise Cemetery

Abélard & Héloïse **37**
Guillaume Apollinaire **5**
Pierre-Auguste
  Beaumarchais **30**
Hans Bellmer **24**
Sarah Bernhardt **9**
Georges Bizet **17**
Maria Callas **3**

Frédéric Chopin **36**
Colette **23**
Auguste Comte **34**
Jean Baptiste Camille
  Corot **11**
Honoré Daumier **10**
Jaques-Louis David **19**
Honoré de Balzac **16**

Eugène Delacroix **15**
Gustave Doré **14**
Isadora Duncan **6**
Paul Eluard **26**
Max Ernst **2**
Théodore Géricault **20**
Jean-Auguste-Dominique
  Ingres **13**

avenue Circulaire

Mur des Fédérés

25

26

97

27

94

avenue Transversale No. 3

28

avenue Greffulhe

avenue Pacthod

96

92

95

avenue Transversale No. 2

35

76

avenue Circulaire

41

34

42

40

33

43

29

38

25

33 32

31

28

30

36

26

27

37

29

avenue des Acacias

19

chemin du Dragon

30

31

75

18

34

17

32

Carrefour du Grand-Rond

16

15

35

13

14

74

36

avenue Casimir-Perrier

6

5

8

73

37

Ancienne Séperation du Cimetière Israélite

39

38

7

Jean La Fontaine **33**
René Lalique **12**
Lefebvre Masséna **29**
Amedeo Modigliani **28**
Molière **32**
Jim Morrison **35**
Alfred de Musset **21**
Edith Piaf **27**

Camille Pissarro **38**
Marcel Proust **4**
Gioacchio Antonio Rossini **22**
Rothschild family plot **39**
Henri de Saint-Simon **31**

Georges Seurat **18**
Simone Signoret & Yves Montand **8**
Gertrude Stein & Alice B. Toklas **25**
Oscar Wilde **1**
Richard Wright **7**

Everybody from Sarah Bernhardt to Oscar Wilde to Richard Wright is here, along with Honoré de Balzac, Jacques-Louis David, Eugène Delacroix, Maria Callas, Max Ernst, and Georges Bizet. Colette was taken here in 1954; her black granite slab always sports flowers, and legend has it that cats replenish the roses. In time, the little sparrow, Edith Piaf, followed. The lover of George Sand, poet Alfred de Musset, was buried under a weeping willow. Napoléon's marshals, Ney and Masséna, lie here, as do Frédéric Chopin and Molière. Marcel Proust's black tombstone rarely lacks a tiny bunch of violets (he wanted to be buried beside his friend/lover, composer Maurice Ravel, but their families wouldn't allow it).

Some tombs are sentimental favorites: Love-torn graffiti radiates half a mile from the tomb of Doors singer **Jim Morrison.** The great dancer **Isadora Duncan** came to rest in the Columbarium, where bodies have been cremated and "filed" away. If you search hard enough, you can find the tombs of that star-crossed pair **Abélard** and **Héloïse,** the ill-fated lovers of the 12th century—at Père-Lachaise they've found peace at last. Other famous lovers also rest here: A stone is marked **"Alice B. Toklas"** on one side and **"Gertrude Stein"** on the other, and eventually France's First Couple of film were reunited when **Yves Montand** joined his wife, **Simone Signoret.** (Montand's gravesite attracted much attention in 1998: His corpse was exhumed in the middle of the night for DNA testing in a paternity lawsuit—he wasn't the father.)

Covering more than 110 acres, Père-Lachaise was acquired by the city in 1804. Nineteenth-century sculpture abounds, as each family tried to outdo the other in ornamentation and cherubic ostentation. Frenchmen who died in the Resistance or in Nazi concentration camps are also honored by monuments. Some French Socialists still pay tribute at the **Mur des Fédérés,** the anonymous gravesite of the Communards who were executed in the cemetery on May 28, 1871. When these last-ditch fighters of the Commune, the world's first anarchist republic, made their final desperate stand against the troops of the French government, they were overwhelmed, lined up against the wall, and shot in groups. A handful survived and lived hidden in the cemetery for years like wild animals, venturing into Paris at night to forage for food.

16 rue du Repos, 20th arr. ☎ **01-43-70-70-33.** Free admission. Mon–Fri 8am–6pm, Sat 8:30am–6pm, Sun 9am–6pm (to 5:30pm early Nov–early Mar). Métro: Père-Lachaise.

Cimetière St-Vincent   Because of the artists and writers who have their resting place in the modest burial ground of St-Vincent, with a view of Sacré-Coeur on the hill, it's sometimes called "the most intellectual cemetery in Paris"—but that epithet seems more apt for other graveyards. Artists **Maurice Utrillo** and **Théopile-Alexandre Steinien** were buried here, as was musician **Arthur Honegger** and writer **Marcel Aymé.** In theory, the cemetery is open all day, but if you disturb the caretaker's lunch—any time from noon to 2pm—you'll regret it.

6 rue Lucien-Gaulard, 18th Arr. ☎ **01-46-06-29-78.** Free admission. Mar 16–Nov 5 Mon–Fri 8am–6pm, Sat 8:30am–6pm, Sun 9am–6pm; Nov 6–Mar 15 Mon–Fri 8am–5:30pm, Sat 8:30am–5pm, Sun 9am–5pm. Métro: Lamarck-Caulaincourt.

11 Paris Underground

Les Catacombes ✿   Every year an estimated 50,000 visitors explore some 1,000 yards of tunnel in these dank catacombs to look at 6 million ghoulishly arranged skull-and-crossbones skeletons. First opened to the public in 1810, this "empire of the dead" is now illuminated with overhead electric lights over its entire length. In the Middle Ages, the catacombs were quarries, but by the end of the 18th century, overcrowded cemeteries were becoming a menace to the public health. City officials decided to use the catacombs as a burial ground, and the bones of several million persons were transferred here. In 1830, the prefect of Paris closed the catacombs to the public, considering them obscene and indecent. During World War II, the catacombs were the headquarters of the French Resistance.

1 place Denfert-Rochereau, 14th arr. ℂ 01-43-22-47-63. www.multimania.com/houze. Admission 33F (5€, $4.80) adults, 23F (3.50€, $3.35) seniors, 17F (2.60€, $2.45) ages 7–25/students, age 6 and under free. Tues–Fri 2–4pm, Sat–Sun 9–11am and 2–4pm. Métro: Denfert-Rochereau.

Les Egouts (Sewers of Paris) ⭐   Some sociologists assert that the sophistication of a society can be judged by the way it disposes of waste. If so, Paris receives good marks for its mostly invisible sewer network. Victor Hugo is credited with making them famous in *Les Misérables:* Jean Valjean takes flight through them, "all dripping with slime, his soul filled with a strange light." Hugo also wrote, "Paris has beneath it another Paris, a Paris of sewers, which has its own streets, squares, lanes, arteries, and circulation."

In the early Middle Ages, drinking water was taken directly from the Seine and wastewater poured onto fields or thrown onto the then-unpaved streets, transforming the urban landscape into a sea of rather smelly mud. Around 1200, the streets were paved with cobblestones, and open sewers ran down the center of each. These open sewers helped spread the Black Death, which devastated the city. In 1370, a vaulted sewer was built on rue Montmartre, draining effluents into a Seine tributary. During Louis XIV's reign, improvements were made, but the state of waste disposal in Paris remained deplorable.

During Napoléon's reign, 18½ miles of sewer were constructed beneath the Parisian landscape. By 1850, as the Industrial Revolution made the manufacture of iron pipe and steam-digging equipment more practical, Baron Haussmann developed a system that used separate underground channels for drinking water and sewage. By 1878, it was 360 miles long. Beginning in 1894, the network was enlarged, and new laws required that discharge of all waste and storm-water runoff be funneled into the sewers. Between 1914 and 1977, an additional 600 miles were added beneath the pavements of a burgeoning Paris. Today, the network of sewers is 1,300 miles long. It contains freshwater mains, compressed air pipes, telephone cables, and pneumatic tubes. Every day, 1.2 million cubic meters of wastewater are collected and processed by a plant in the suburb of Achères. One of the largest in Europe, it's capable of treating more than 2 million cubic meters of sewage per day.

The city's *égouts* are constructed around four principal tunnels, one 18 feet wide and 15 feet high. As Hugo observed, it's like an underground city, with the street names clearly labeled. Further, each branch pipe bears the number of the building to which it's connected. These underground passages are truly mammoth. Sewer tours begin at pont de l'Alma on the Left Bank, where a stairway leads into the city's bowels. However, you often have to wait in line as much as half an hour. Visiting times might change during bad weather, as a storm can make the sewers dangerous. The tour consists of a film on sewer history, a small museum visit, and then a short trip through the maze. *Be warned:* The smell is pretty bad, especially in summer.

Pont de l'Alma, 7th arr. ℂ 01-53-68-27-81. Admission 25F (3.80€, $3.65) adults, 20F (3.05€, $2.90) students/seniors/children 5–12, under 5 free. May–Oct Sat–Wed 11am–5pm; Nov–Apr Sat–Wed 11am–4pm. Closed 3 weeks in Jan. Métro: Alma-Marceau. RER: Pont de l'Alma.

12 A Day at the Races

Paris boasts an army of avid horse-racing fans who get to the city's eight race-tracks whenever possible. Information on current races is available in newspapers and magazines like *Tierce, Paris-Turf, France-Soir,* and *L'Equipe,* all sold at kiosks throughout the city.

The epicenter of Paris horse racing is the **Hippodrome de Longchamp** ★★★, in the Bois de Boulogne (© **01-44-30-75-00;** Métro: Auteuil, then a shuttle bus). Established in 1855, during the autocratic but pleasure-loving reign of Napoléon III, it's the most prestigious, boasts the greatest number of promising thoroughbreds, and awards the largest purse in France. The most important events at Longchamp are the **Grand Prix de Paris** in late June and the **Prix de l'Arc de Triomphe** in early October.

Another horse-racing venue is the **Hippodrome d'Auteuil,** also in the Bois de Boulogne (© **01-40-71-47-47;** Métro: Auteuil, then a shuttle bus). Known for its steeplechases and obstacle courses, it sometimes attracts more than 50,000 Parisians at a time. Spectators appreciate the park's open-air promenades as much as they do the equestrian events. Opened in 1870, the racetrack is scattered over a sprawling 30 acres of parkland. It's designed to show, to maximum advantage, the skill and agility of both horses and riders. Races are conducted early March to late December.

13 Neighborhood Highlights

Paris's neighborhoods often turn out to be attractions unto themselves. The 1st arrondissement, for example, probably has a higher concentration of attractions per block than anywhere else. Though all Paris's neighborhoods are worth wandering, some are more interesting than others. This is especially true of Montmartre, the Latin Quarter, and the Marais, so we've featured them as walking tours in chapter 8. Our other favorites follow here.

For other strolls in the City of Light, see *Frommer's Memorable Walks in Paris.*

ISLANDS IN THE STREAM: ILE DE LA CITÉ & ILE ST-LOUIS

ILE DE LA CITÉ: WHERE PARIS WAS BORN ★★★   Medieval Paris, that blend of grotesquerie and Gothic beauty, bloomed on this island in the Seine (Métro: Cité). Ile de la Cité, which the Seine protects like a surrounding moat, has been known as "the cradle" of Paris ever since. As Sauval once observed, "The Island of the City is shaped like a great ship, sunk in the mud, lengthwise in the stream, in about the middle of the Seine."

Few have written more movingly about its heyday than Victor Hugo, who invited the reader "to observe the fantastic display of lights against the darkness of that gloomy labyrinth of buildings; cast upon it a ray of moonlight, showing the city in glimmering vagueness, with its towers lifting their great heads from that foggy sea." Medieval Paris was a city not only of legends and lovers but also of blood-curdling tortures and brutalities. No story illustrates this better than the affair of Abélard and his charge Héloïse, whose jealous and unsettled uncle hired ruffians to castrate her lover. (The attack predictably quelled their ardor, and he became a monk, she an abbess.) You can see their graves at Père-Lachaise (see "Cemeteries").

Because you'll want to see all the attractions on Ile de la Cité, here is the most logical way to proceed. Begin, of course, at the cathedral of Notre-Dame.

Ile de la Cité & Ile St-Louis

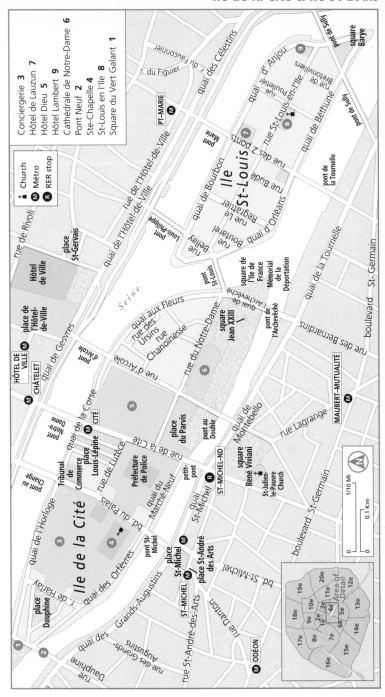

Conciergerie **3**
Hôtel de Lauzun **7**
Hôtel Dieu **5**
Hôtel Lambert **9**
Cathédrale de Notre-Dame **6**
Pont Neuf **2**
Ste-Chapelle **4**
St-Louis en l'Ile **8**
Square du Vert Galant **1**

✝ Church
Ⓜ Métro
Ⓡ RER stop

Proceed next to the Ste-Chapelle moving west. After a visit there, you can head northeast to the Conciergerie. To cap your visit, and for the best scenic view, walk to the northwestern end of the island for a view of the bridge, pont Neuf, seen from Square du Vert Galant.

The island's undisputed stars, as mentioned, are **Notre-Dame, Sainte-Chapelle,** and the **Conciergerie**—all described earlier in this chapter. Across from Notre-Dame is the **Hôtel Dieu,** built from 1866 to 1878 in neo-Florentine style. This is central Paris's main hospital, replacing the 12th-century hospital that ran the island's entire width. Go in the main entrance and take a break in the spacious neoclassical courtyard whose small garden and fountain make a quiet oasis.

Don't miss the ironically named **pont Neuf** ("New Bridge") at the tip of the island opposite from Notre-Dame. The span isn't new—it's actually Paris's oldest bridge, begun in 1578 and finished in 1604. In its day it had two unique features: It was paved and it wasn't flanked with houses and shops. Actually, with 12 arches, it's not one bridge but two (they don't quite line up)—one from the Right Bank to the island and the other from the Left Bank to the island. At the **Musée Carnavalet** (see "The Major Museums"), a painting called *The Spectacle of Buffoons* shows what the bridge was like between 1665 and 1669. Duels were fought on it; the nobility's great coaches crossed it; peddlers sold their wares on it; and entertainers like Tabarin went there to seek a few coins from the gawkers. As public facilities were lacking, the bridge also served as a de facto outhouse.

Just past pont Neuf is the "prow" of the island, the **square du Vert Galant.** Pause to look at the equestrian statue of the beloved Henri IV, who was assassinated by Ravaillac (see the entry for the Conciergerie). A true king of his people, Henri was also (to judge from accounts) regal in the boudoir—hence the nickname "Vert Galant" (Old Spark). Gabrielle d'Estrées and Henriette d'Entragues were his best-known mistresses, but they had to share him with countless others, some of whom would casually catch his eye as he was riding along the streets. In fond memory of the king, the little triangular park continues to attract lovers. If at first it appears to be a sunken garden, that's because it remains at its natural level; the rest of the Cité has been built up during the centuries.

ILE ST-LOUIS ★★ Cross pont St-Louis, the iron footbridge behind Notre-Dame, to Ile St-Louis, and you'll find a world of tree-shaded quays, aristocratic town houses with courtyards, restaurants, and antiques shops. (You can also take the Métro to Sully-Morland or Pont Marie and cross the bridge.) The fraternal twin of Ile de la Cité, Ile St-Louis is primarily residential; nearly all the houses were built from 1618 to 1660, lending the island a remarkable architectural unity. Plaques on the facades identify the former residences of the famous. **Marie Curie** lived at 36 quai de Béthune, near pont de la Tournelle, and sculptor **Camille Claudel** (Rodin's mistress) lived and worked in the Hôtel de Jassaud, 19 quai de Bourbon.

The most exciting mansion—though perhaps also the one with the saddest history—is the 1656–57 **Hôtel de Lauzun,** 17 quai d'Anjou, built for Charles Gruyn des Bordes. He married Geneviève de Mouy and had her initials engraved on much of the interior decor; their happiness was short-lived, however, because he was convicted of embezzlement and sent to prison in 1662. The next occupant was the duc de Lauzun, who resided there for only 3 years. He had been a favorite of Louis XIV until he asked for the hand of the king's first cousin, the duchesse de Montpensier. Louis refused and had Lauzun tossed into the Bastille. Eventually the duchesse pestered Louis into releasing her beloved, and they married secretly and moved here in 1682, but domestic bliss eluded them—they fought often and separated in 1684. Lauzun then sold the house to the grand-nephew of Cardinal Richelieu and his wife, the grand-niece of Cardinal Mazarin, who had such a grand time throwing parties they went bankrupt and separated. Baron Pichon bought it in 1842 and rented it out to a hashish club. Tenants Baudelaire and Gaultier regularly held hashish soirées in which Baudelaire did research for his *Les Paradis artificiels* and Gaultier for his *Le Club hes hachichins.* Now the mansion belongs to the city and is used to house official guests. The interior is sometimes open for temporary exhibits, so call the tourist office.

The **Hôtel Lambert,** 2 quai d'Anjou, was built in 1645 for Nicholas Lambert de Thorigny. The portal on rue St-Louis-en-l'Ile gives some idea of the splendor within, but the house's most startling element is the oval gallery extending into the garden. Designed to feature a library or an art collection, it's best viewed from the beginning of quai d'Anjou. Voltaire and his mistress, Emilie de Breteuil, lived here at one time—their raucous quarrels were legendary. The mansion also housed the

> ### Ice Cream
> If you need a refreshment break on Ile St-Louis, head for ice cream at **Berthillon,** 31 rue St-Louis-l'Ile.

Polish royal family, the Czartoryskis, for over a century, before becoming the residence of actress Michèle Morgan. It now belongs to the Rothschild family and isn't open to the public.

Numbers 9, 11, 13, and 15 quai d'Anjou also belonged to the Lambert family. At **no. 9** stands the house where painter/sculptor/lithographer Honoré Daumier lived from 1846 to 1863, producing hundreds of caricatures satirizing the bourgeoisie and attacking government corruption. He was imprisoned for 6 months because of his 1832 cartoon of Louis-Philippe swallowing bags of gold that had been extracted from the people.

Near the Hôtel de Lauzun is the church of **St-Louis-en-l'Ile,** no. 19 bis rue St-Louis-en-l'Ile. Despite a dour exterior, the ornate interior is one of the finest examples of Jesuit Baroque. Built between 1664 and 1726, this church has been and still is the site of many weddings—with all the white stone and gilt, you'll feel as if you're inside a wedding cake. Look for the 1926 plaque reading "In grateful memory of St. Louis in whose honor the city of St. Louis, Missouri, USA, is named."

RIGHT BANK HIGHLIGHTS

LES HALLES ⭐ For 8 centuries, **Les Halles** (Métro: Les Halles; RER: Châtelet–Les Halles) was the city's major wholesale fruit, meat, and vegetable market. In the 19th century, Zola called it "the underbelly of Paris." The smock-clad vendors, beef carcasses, and baskets of vegetables all belong to the past, for the original market, with zinc-roofed Second Empire "iron umbrellas," has been torn down. Today the action has moved to a steel-and-glass edifice at Rungis, a suburb near Orly. In 1979, the area saw the opening of the **Forum des Halles,** 1–7 rue Pierre-Lescot, 1st arrondissement. This large complex, much of it underground, contains shops, restaurants, and movie theaters. Many of the shops are unattractive, but others contain a wide display of merchandise that has made the mall popular with both residents and visitors.

For many visitors, a night on the town still ends in the wee hours with a bowl of onion soup at Les Halles, usually at **Au Pied de Cochon (The Pig's Foot),** 6 rue Coquillière, 1st (see chapter 6), or at **Au Chien Qui Fume (The Smoking Dog),** 33 rue du Pont-Neuf (📞 **01-42-36-07-42).** One of the most classic scenes of old Paris was elegantly dressed Parisians (many fresh from Maxim's) standing at a bar drinking cognac with blood-smeared butchers. Some writers have suggested that 19th-century poet Gérard de Nerval introduced the custom of frequenting Les Halles at such an unearthly hour. (His life was considered "irregular," and he hanged himself in 1855.)

A newspaper correspondent described today's scene this way: "Les Halles is trying to stay alive as one of the few places in Paris where one can eat at any hour of the night."

LEFT BANK HIGHLIGHTS

ST-GERMAIN-DES-PRÉS ★★ This neighborhood in the 6th arrondissement (Métro: St-Germain-des-Prés) was the postwar home of existentialism, associated with Sartre, de Beauvoir, Camus, and an intellectual bohemian crowd that gathered at **Café de Flore, Brasserie Lipp,** and **Les Deux Magots** (see chapter 6). Among them, black-clad poet and singer Juliette Greco was known as *la muse de St-Germain-des-Prés,* and to Sartre she was the woman who had "millions of poems in her throat." Her long hair, black slacks, black sweater, and black sandals launched a fashion trend adopted by young women everywhere. In the 1950s, new names appeared, like Françoise Sagan, Gore Vidal, and James Baldwin, but by the 1960s, tourists became firmly entrenched.

St-Germain-des-Prés still retains an intellectually stimulating bohemian street life, full of many interesting bookshops, art galleries, *cave* (basement) clubs, bistros, and coffeehouses. But the stars of the area are two churches, **St-Germain-des-Prés,** 3 place St-Germain-des-Prés, 6th, and **St-Sulpice,** rue St-Sulpice, 6th (for both, see "The Important Churches"), and the **Musée National Eugène Delacroix,** 6 place de Furstemburg, 6th (see "The Major Museums"). Nearby, **rue Visconti** was designed for pushcarts and is worth visiting today. At **nos. 20–24** is the residence where dramatist Jean-Baptiste Racine died in 1699. And at **no. 17** is the house where Balzac established his printing press in 1825. (The venture ended in bankruptcy, forcing the author back to his writing desk.) Such celebrated actresses as Champmeslé and Clairon also lived here.

MONTPARNASSE ★★ For the "lost generation," life centered around the literary cafes of Montparnasse, at the border of the 6th and 14th arrondissements (Métro: Montparnasse-Bienvenue). Hangouts like the **Dôme, Coupole, Rotonde,** and **Sélect** became legendary, as artists—especially American expatriates—turned their backs on Montmartre, dismissing it as too touristy. Picasso, Modigliani, and Man Ray came this way, and Hemingway was also a popular figure. So was Fitzgerald when he was poor (when he wasn't, you'd find him at the Ritz). Faulkner, MacLeish, Duncan, Miró, Joyce, Ford Madox Ford, and even Trotsky spent time here.

The most notable exception was Gertrude Stein, who never frequented the cafes. To see her, you had to wait for an invitation to her salon at **27 rue de Fleurus.** She bestowed this favor on Sherwood Anderson, Elliot Paul, Ezra Pound, and, for a time, Hemingway. When Pound launched himself into a beloved chair and broke it, he incurred Stein's wrath, and Hemingway decided there wasn't "much future in men being friends with great women" (for more on Gertrude, see the box "The Mother of the Lost Generation").

American expatriate writer Natalie Barney, who moved to Paris as a student in 1909 and stayed for over 60 years, held her grand salons at **20 rue Jacob**

The Mother of the Lost Generation

"So Paris was the place that suited those of us that were to create the twentieth century art and literature, naturally enough." Gertrude Stein, who made this pronouncement, wasn't known for her modesty.

In the 1920s, she and her lover, Alice B. Toklas, became the most famous expats in Paris. To get an invitation to call on Lovey and Pussy (nicknames for Gertrude and Alice) at **27 rue de Fleurus,** in the heart of Montparnasse, was to be invited into the innermost circle of expatriate Paris. Though their former residence is in private hands and you can't go inside, literary fans flock to this fabled address to stare at the facade.

Though Gertrude didn't achieve popular success until the 1933 publication of her *Autobiography of Alice B. Toklas,* she was adored by many members of the Lost Generation—all except Ernest Hemingway, who tarred her in his posthumous memoir, *A Moveable Feast.* But to many sensitive young men (often gay) arriving from America in the 1920s, La Stein was "The Mother of Us All." These young fans hung onto her every word, while Alice baked her notorious hash brownies in the kitchen.

At rue de Fleurus, Gertrude and Alice surrounded themselves with modern paintings, including pieces by Vallotton, Toulouse-Lautrec, Picasso, Gauguin, and Matisse. Gertrude paid $1,000 for her first Matisse and $30 for her first Picasso. In fact, the two artists met here. The Saturday-night soirées became a Montparnasse legend, and one writer said her salon was engaged in an international conspiracy to promote modern art. Not all visitors came to worship, however. Gertrude was denounced by many, including avant-garde magazines of the time, which called her a "fraud, egomaniac, and publicity seeking." Braque called her claim to influence art in Paris "nonsense."

In spite of the attacks, jokes, and lurid speculation, Stein, at least in public, kept her ego intact. Bernard Fay once told her he'd met three people in his life who ranked as geniuses: Gide, Picasso, and herself. "Why include Gide?" Stein asked.

(actually in St-Germain-des-Prés). Every Friday, her salon attracted the literati of her day, like Gertrude Stein, Djuna Barnes, Colette, Sherwood Anderson, T. S. Eliot, Janet Flanner, James Joyce, Sylvia Beach, Marcel Proust, and William Carlos Williams. The group met on and off for half a century, interrupted only by two world wars. Near place de Furstemburg, Barney's former residence is landmarked but not open to the public. In the garden you can see a small Doric temple bearing the inscription *A l'Amitié,* "to friendship."

Aside from the literary legends, one of the most notable characters of the sector was **Kiki de Montparnasse** (actually named Alice Prin, born illegitimate). She was raised by her grandmother in Burgundy until her mother called her to Paris to work in a series of shops. When a sculptor discovered her, she became an artist's model and adopted her new name; soon she became a prostitute as well, and would bare her breasts to anyone who'd pay her 3F. She sang at

Le Jockey, 127 bd. du Montparnasse, which no longer exists: In her black hose and garters, she captivated dozens of men, among them Frederick Kohner, who went so far as to entitle his memoirs *Kiki of Montparnasse.* Kiki later wrote her own memoirs, with an introduction by Hemingway. Papa called her "a Queen," noting that was "very different from being a lady."

Completed in 1973 and rising 688 feet above the skyline, the **Tour Montparnasse** (© **01-45-38-52-56**) was denounced by some critics as "bringing Manhattan to Paris." The city soon passed an ordinance outlawing any further structures of this size in the heart of Paris. Today, the modern tower houses a mammoth underground shopping mall as well as much of the infrastructure for the Gare de Montparnasse rail station. You can ride an elevator up to the 56th floor (where you'll find a bar and restaurant), then climb three flights to the roof terrace. The view includes virtually every important Paris monument, including Sacré-Coeur, Notre-Dame, and La Défense. Admission to the tower is 46F (7€, $6.65) adults, 38F (5.80€, $5.50) seniors, 35F (5.30€, $5.10) students, and 30F (4.55€, $4.35) children 5 to 14 (children 4 and under enter free). April to September, it's open daily 9:30am to 11:30pm; October to March, hours are Sunday to Thursday 9:30am to 10:30pm and Friday to Saturday 9:20am to 11:00pm.

The life of Montparnasse still centers around its cafes and exotic nightclubs, many only a shadow of what they used to be. Its heart is at the crossroads of **boulevard Raspail** and **boulevard du Montparnasse,** one of the settings of *The Sun Also Rises.* Hemingway wrote that "boulevard Raspail always made dull riding." Rodin's controversial statue of Balzac swathed in a large cape stands guard over the prostitutes who cluster around the pedestal. Balzac seems to be the only one in Montparnasse who doesn't feel the weight of time.

14 Especially for Kids

If you're staying on the Right Bank, take the children for a stroll through the **Jardin des Tuileries** (see "Parks & Gardens"), where there are donkey rides, ice-cream stands, and a marionette show; at the circular pond, you can rent a toy sailboat. On the Left Bank, similar delights exist in the **Jardin du Luxembourg** (see "Parks & Gardens"). After a visit to the Eiffel Tower, you can take the kids for a donkey ride in the nearby **Champ de Mars** (see the "Time Out at the Tower" box in this chapter).

A great Paris tradition, **puppet shows** are worth seeing for their enthusiastic colorful productions—they're a genuine French child's experience. At the Jardin du Luxembourg, puppets reenact sinister plots set in Gothic castles and Oriental palaces; many young critics say the best puppet shows are held in the Champ de Mars.

On Sunday afternoon, French families head up to the **Butte Montmartre** to bask in the fiesta atmosphere. You can join in the fun: Take the Métro to Anvers and walk to the *funiculaire* (the silver cable car that carries you up to Sacré-Coeur). Once up top, follow the crowds to place du Tertre, where a Sergeant Pepper–style band will usually be blasting off-key and you can have the kids' pictures sketched by local artists. You can take in the views of Paris from the various vantage points and treat your children to ice cream. For a walking tour of Montmartre, see chapter 8.

Of course, your kids will likely want to check out the Gallic versions of Mickey Mouse and his pals, so see chapter 11 for details on **Disneyland Paris.**

MUSEUMS

Cité des Sciences et de l'Industrie ⭐⭐   A city of science and industry has risen here from the most unlikely ashes. When a slaughterhouse was built on the site in the 1960s, it was touted as the most modern of its kind. It was abandoned as a failure in 1974, and the location on the city's northern edge presented the government with a problem. What could be built in such an unlikely place? In 1986, the converted premises opened as the world's most expensive ($642 million) science complex, designed to "modernize mentalities" in the service of modernizing society.

The place is so vast, with so many exhibits, that a single visit gives only an idea of the scope of the Cité. Busts of Plato, Hippocrates, and a double-faced Janus gaze silently at a tube-filled riot of high-tech girders, glass, and lights. The sheer dimensions pose a challenge to the curators of its constantly changing exhibits. Some exhibits are couched in Gallic humor—imagine using the comic-strip adventures of a jungle explorer to explain seismographic activity. **Explora,** a permanent exhibit, occupies the three upper levels of the building and examines four themes: the universe, life, matter, and communication. The Cité also has a **multimedia library,** a **planetarium,** and an **"inventorium"** for kids. The silver-skinned geodesic dome called **La Géode**—a 112-foot-high sphere with a 370-seat theater—projects the closest thing to a 3-D cinema in Europe and has several surprising additions, including a real submarine.

The Cité is in the **Parc de La Villette,** an ultramodern science park surrounding some of Paris's newest housing developments. This is Paris's largest park, with 136 acres of greenery—twice the size of the Tuileries. The playgrounds, fountains, and sculptures are all innovative creations. Here you'll find a belvedere, a video workshop for children, and information about exhibits and events, along with a cafe and restaurant.

In the Parc de La Villette, 30 av. Corentine-Cariou, La Villette, 19th arr. ℂ **01-40-05-80-00.** www.cite-sciences.fr. Cité Pass (entrance to all exhibits) 50F (7.60€, $7.25) adults, age 7 and under free. Géode 57F (8.65€, $8.25). Tues–Sat 10am–6pm, Sun 10am–7pm. Métro: Porte de La Villette.

Musée de la Marine ⭐⭐   If your children have saltwater in their veins, you may want to take them to this museum. Old ship models abound, like the big galley *La Réale,* the *Royal-Louis,* the rich ivory *Ville de Dieppe,* the gorgeous *Valmy,* and a **barge** built in 1811 for Napoléon I, which was used to carry Napoléon III and Empress Eugénie on their visit to Brest in 1858. You'll find some souvenirs of explorer Laperouse's wreck on Vanikoro Island in 1788 as well as many documents and artifacts concerning merchant fishing and pleasure fleets, oceanography, and hydrography, with films illustrating the subjects. Thematic exhibits explain ancient wooden shipbuilding and the development of scientific instruments.

In the Palais de Chaillot, place du Trocadéro, 16th Arr. ℂ **01-53-65-69-69.** Admission 39F (5.95€, $5.65) adults, 26F (3.95€, $3.75) ages 8–25/over 65, age 7 and under free. Wed–Mon 10am–5:30pm. Métro: Trocadéro.

Musée Grévin ⭐   The Grévin is Paris's number-one waxworks. Comparisons to Madame Tussaud's are almost irresistible, but it isn't all blood and gore and doesn't shock as much as Tussaud's. It presents French history in a series of tableaux. Depicted are the 1429 consecration of Charles VII in the Cathédrale de Reims (armored Joan of Arc, carrying her standard, stands behind the king); Marguerite de Valois, first wife of Henri IV, meeting on a secret stairway with La Molle, who was soon to be decapitated; Catherine de Médicis with

Florentine alchemist David Ruggieri; Louis XV and Mozart at the home of the marquise de Pompadour; and Napoléon on a rock at St. Helena, reviewing his victories and defeats. There are also displays of contemporary sports and political figures, as well as 50 of the world's best-loved film stars.

Two shows are staged frequently throughout the day. The first, called the **"Palais des Mirages,"** starts off as a sort of Temple of Brahma and, through magically distorting mirrors, changes into an enchanted forest, then a fête at the Alhambra in Granada. A magician is the star of the second show, **"Le Cabinet Fantastique;"** he entertains children of all ages.

10 bd. Montmartre, 9th arr. ✆ **01-47-70-85-05.** Admission 60F (9.10€, $8.70) adults, 40F (6.10€, $5.80) children 14 and under. Apr–Aug daily 1–7pm; Sept–Mar daily 1–6:30pm; school holidays daily 10am–7pm. Ticket office closes 1 hour before museum. Métro: Grands Boulevards.

Musée National d'Histoire Naturelle (Museum of Natural History)
This museum in the Jardin des Plantes, founded in 1635 as a scientific research center by Guy de la Brosse, physician to Louis XIII, has a wide range of science and nature exhibits. The museum's **Grande Gallery of Evolution** recently received a $90-million restoration. At the entrance, an 85-foot skeleton of a whale greets you. One display containing the skeletons of dinosaurs and mastodons is dedicated to endangered and vanished species, and there are galleries specializing in paleontology, anatomy, mineralogy, and botany. Within the museum's grounds are **tropical hothouses** containing thousands of species of unusual plant life and a **menagerie** with small animal life in simulated natural habitats.

57 rue Cuvier, 5th arr. ✆ **01-40-79-30-00.** Admission 10–40F (1.50–6.10€, $1.45–$5.80) adults, age 3 and under free. Apr–Sept Wed–Mon 10am–6pm; Oct–Mar Wed–Mon 10am–5pm. Métro: Jussieu or Gare d'Austerlitz.

AN AMUSEMENT PARK
Jardin d'Acclimatation ★ Paris's definitive children's park is the 25-acre Jardin d'Acclimation in the northern part of the Bois de Boulogne. This is the kind of place that satisfies tykes and adults alike but not teenagers. The visit starts with a ride on a green-and-yellow narrow-gauge train from Porte Maillot to the Jardin entrance, through a stretch of wooded park. The train operates Wednesday, Saturday, and Sunday from 1:30pm until the park closes; one-way fare is 6F (.90€, 85¢). En route you'll find a **house of mirrors,** an **archery range,** a **miniature-golf course, zoo animals,** a **bowling alley,** a **puppet theater** (performances Thursday, Saturday, Sunday, and holidays), a **playground,** a **hurdle-racing course, junior**-scale **rides, shooting galleries,** and **waffle stalls.** You can trot the kids off on a **pony** or join them in a **boat** on a mill-stirred lagoon. **La Prévention Routière** is a miniature roadway operated by the Paris police: Youngsters drive through in small cars equipped to start and stop, and are required by two genuine Parisian gendarmes to obey all street signs and light changes. Inside the gate is an easy-to-follow map. The park is circular—follow the road in either direction, and it'll take you all the way around and bring you back to the train at the end.

In the Bois de Boulogne, 16th arr. ✆ **01-40-67-90-82.** Admission 13F (2€, $1.90), age 3 and under free. June–Sept daily 10am–7pm; Oct–May daily 10am–6pm. Métro: Sablons.

A ZOO
Parc Zoologique de Paris There's a modest zoo in the Jardin des Plantes, but without a doubt, the best zoo is here on the southeastern outskirts of Paris,

quickly reachable by Métro. Many of this modern zoo's animals, who seem happy and are playful, live in settings similar to their natural habitat, hemmed in by rock barriers, not bars or cages. You'll never see an animal in a cage too small for it. The lion has an entire veldt to himself, and you can lock eyes comfortably across a deep protective moat. On a cement mountain like Disneyland's Matterhorn, exotic breeds of mountain goats and sheep leap from ledge to ledge or pose gracefully for hours watching the penguins in their pools at the mountain's foot. Keep well back from the bear pools or you might get wet.

In the Bois de Vincennes, 53 av. de St-Maurice, 12th arr. ✆ **01-44-75-20-10**. Admission 40F (6.10€, $5.80) adults, 30F (4.55€, $4.35) children 4–15/students 16–25/over 60, age 3 and under free. Daily 9am–6pm (to 5pm Dec–Mar). Métro: Porte Dorée.

15 Organized Tours

BY BUS

Tours are offered by **Cityrama,** 147–149 rue St-Honoré, 1st (✆ **01-44-55-61-00;** Métro: Palais Royal or Musée du Louvre), which operates double-decker red-and-yellow buses with oversize windows and multilingual recorded commentaries giving an overview of Paris's history and monuments.

By far the most popular tour is a 2-hour bus ride, with recorded commentary in your choice of 13 languages, through Paris' monumental heart. Departing from place des Pyramides, adjacent to rue de Rivoli, it's offered seven times a day between May and October, and four times a day between November and April. Cost for this is 150F (22.80€, $21.75) per person, free for children under 12. Other, more specialized (and detailed) tours include a 3½-hour "Artistic Tour" that encompasses the interiors of Notre Dame and the Louvre (every day except Tuesday and Sunday, and departing at 9:45am), priced at 310F (47.10€, $44.95). Tours to the mammoth royal palace at Versailles depart twice a day (at 9:30am and 2:45pm) year-round for a price of 330F (50.15€, $47.85) per person. And 5-hour jaunts to the majestic gothic cathedral at Chartres depart every Tuesday, Thursday, and Saturday at 1:45pm for a per person price of 300F (45.60€, $43.50). Tours of Paris by night depart at 10pm for a price of 150F (22.80€, $21.75) per person. Any of these night tours can be supplemented—for an additional fee—with optional add-ons that include river cruises on the Seine and attendance at selected cabaret shows.

CRUISES ON THE SEINE

A Seine boat tour provides sweeping vistas of the riverbanks and some of the best views of Notre-Dame. Many of the boats have open sundecks, bars, and restaurants. **Bateaux-Mouche** cruises (✆ **01-42-25-96-10** for reservations, 01-40-76-99-99 for schedules; Métro: Alma-Marceau) depart from the Right Bank, next to pont de l'Alma, and last about 75 minutes, costing 45F (6.85€, $6.55) adults and 20F (3.05€, $2.90) children 4 to 12. May to October, tours leave daily at 30-minute intervals, beginning at 11am and ending at 11pm; November to April, there are at least nine departures daily from 11am to 9pm, with a schedule that changes according to demand and the weather. Three-hour dinner cruises depart daily at 8:30pm and cost 500 to 800F (76 to 121.60€, $72.50 to $116), depending on which fixed-price menu you order; jackets and ties are required for men. Less formal lunch cruises, departing every day at 1pm and returning about 2 hours later, cost 300F (45.60€, $43.50) per person.

Some people prefer longer excursions on the Seine and its network of canals. The 3-hour **Seine et le Canal St-Martin** tour, offered by **Paris Canal**

(℃ **01-42-40-96-97**), requires advance reservations. The tour begins at 9:30am on the quays in front of the Musée d'Orsay (Métro: Solférino) and at 2:30pm in front of the Cité des Sciences et de l'Industrie at Parc de La Villette (Métro: Porte de La Villette). Excursions negotiate the waterways and canals of Paris, including the Seine, an underground tunnel below place de la Bastille, and the Canal St-Martin. Tours are offered twice daily from mid-March to mid-November; the rest of the year, tours are only on Sunday. The cost is 100F (15.20€, $14.50) adults and children under 4 free. With the exception of trips on Sundays and holidays, prices are usually reduced to 75F (11.40€, $10.90) for passengers 12 to 25 and over 60, and to 55F (8.35€, $8) for children 4 to 11.

BIKE TOURS

The best are offered by **Bullfrog Bike Tours** (℃ **06-09-98-08-60**), departing from avenue Gustave-Eiffel near the tower (look for a large green flag advertising the tours). From May to September 15, tours leave daily at 11am and 3:30pm, costing 125F (19€, $18.15). Night tours are at 9pm Monday and Thursday. You get an English-speaking look at Paris almost entirely on sidewalks, in parks, and along the Seine, taking in the most famous landmarks, like the Louvre and Notre-Dame.

Strolling Around Paris

The best way to discover Paris is on foot, using your own shoe leather. Our favorite walks are along the banks of the Seine and down the Champs-Elysées from the Arc de Triomphe to the Louvre, but in this chapter we highlight the attractions of the Montmartre, the Latin Quarter, and the Marais.

For a greater selection of walking tours in the City of Light, see *Frommer's Memorable Walks in Paris*.

WALKING TOUR 1   MONTMARTRE

Start:	Place Pigalle (Métro: Pigalle).
Finish:	Place Pigalle.
Time:	5 hours—more if you break for lunch. It's a 3-mile trek.
Best Time:	Any day it isn't raining. Set out by 10am at the latest.
Worst Time:	After dark.

Soft white three-story houses and slender barren trees sticking up from the ground like giant toothpicks—that's how Utrillo, befogged by absinthe, saw Montmartre. Toulouse-Lautrec brush-stroked it into a district of cabarets, circus freaks, and prostitutes. Today Montmartre remains truer to the dwarfish Toulouse-Lautrec's conception than it does to Utrillo's.

Before all this, Montmartre was a sleepy farming community with windmills dotting the landscape. The name has always been the subject of disagreement, some maintaining it originated from the "mount of Mars," a Roman temple that crowned the hill, others asserting it means "mount of martyrs," a reference to the martyrdom of St. Denis, who was beheaded on the mountain along with fellow saints Rusticus and Eleutherius.

Turn right after leaving the Métro station and proceed down boulevard de Clichy, turn left at the Cirque Medrano, and begin the climb up rue des Martyrs. On reaching rue des Abbesses, turn left and walk along this street, crossing place des Abbesses. Go uphill along rue Ravignan, which leads directly to tree-studded place Emile-Goudeau, in the middle of rue Ravignan. At no. 13, across from the Timhôtel, is the

❶ Bateau-Lavoir
(Boat Washhouse)
Though gutted by fire in 1970, this building, known as the cradle of cubism, has been reconstructed by the city. While Picasso lived here

(1904–12), he painted one of the world's most famous portraits, *The Third Rose* (of Gertrude Stein), as well as *Les Demoiselles d'Avignon*. Other residents were van Dongen, Jacob, and Gris, and Modigliani, Rousseau, and Braque had studios nearby.

Rue Ravignan ends at place Jean-Baptiste-Clément. Go to the end of the street and cross onto rue Norvins (on your right). Here rues Norvins, St-Rustique, and des Saules collide a few steps from rue Poulbot, a scene captured in a famous Utrillo painting. Turn right and head down rue Poulbot. At no. 11, you'll come to

❷ Espace Montmartre Dalí

This phantasmagorical world of Espace Montmartre Dalí (✆ **01-42-64-40-10**) features 300 original Dalí works, including his famous 1956 lithograph of Don Quixote.

Rue Poulbot crosses tiny

❸ Place du Calvaire

Here you find a panoramic view of Paris. On this square once lived artist/painter/lithographer Maurice Neumont (a plaque marks the house).

From place du Calvaire, head east along rue Gabrielle, taking the first left north along the tiny street rue du Calvaire, which leads to

❹ Place du Tertre

This old town square is now tourist central. All around the square run terrace restaurants with dance floors and colored lights while Sacré-Coeur gleams white through the trees. Here the cafes overflow with people, as do the indoor and outdoor art galleries. Some of the "artists" still wear berets (you'll be asked countless times if you want your portrait sketched in charcoal). So loaded with local color, applied as heavily as bad makeup, the square can seem somewhat gaudy and inauthentic.

TAKE A BREAK

Many restaurants in Montmartre, especially those around place du Tertre, are unabashed tourist traps. An exception is **La Crémaillère 1900**, 15 place du Tertre, 18 arr. (✆ **01-46-06-58-59**). As its name suggests, this is a Belle-Époque dining room, retaining much of its original look, including many paintings. You can sit on the terrace opening onto the square or retreat to the internal courtyard garden. A full menu is served throughout the day, including a standard array of French classics. Go any time daily from noon to 12:30am.

Right off the square fronting rue du Mont-Cenis is

❺ St-Pierre

Originally a Benedictine abbey, this church has played many roles—a Temple of Reason during the Revolution, a food depot, a clothing store, and even a munitions factory. These days, one of Paris's oldest churches is back to being a church.

Facing St-Pierre, turn right and follow rue Azais to

❻ Sacré-Coeur

The basilica's Byzantine domes and bell tower loom above Paris and present a wide vista on sunny days (see "The Top Attractions" in chapter 7). Behind the church and clinging to the hillside are steep and crooked little streets that have survived the relentless march of progress.

Facing the basilica, take the street on the left (rue du Cardinal-Guibert), then go left onto rue du Chevalier-de-la-Barre and right onto rue du Mont-Cenis. Continue on this street to rue Cortot, then turn left. At no. 12 is the

❼ Musée de Vieux Montmartre

Musée de Vieux Montmartre (✆ **01-46-06-61-11**) presents a wide collection of mementos of the neighborhood. Luminaries like Dufy, van Gogh, Renoir, and Suzanne Valadon and her son, Utrillo, occupied this famous 17th-century house, and it was here that Renoir put the final touches on his *Moulin de la Galette* (see below).

From the museum, turn right, heading up rue des Saules past a winery, a reminder of the days when Montmartre was a farming village on the outskirts of Paris. A grape-harvesting festival is held here every October. The intersection of rue des Saules and rue St-Vincent is one of the most visited and photographed corners of the Butte. Here, on one corner, sits what was the famous old

❽ Cabaret des Assassins

This was long ago renamed **Au Lapin Agile** (see *"Chansonniers"* in chapter

Walking Tour 1: Montmartre

Area of Detail

17e, 18e, 19e, 20e, 9e, 10e, 8e, 2e, 3e, 11e, 12e, 1e, 4e, 7e, 6e, 5e, 16e, 15e, 14e, 13e

1 Bateau-Lavoir
   (Boat Washhouse)
2 Espace Montmartre Dalí
3 Place du Calvaire
4 Place du Tertre
5 St-Pierre
6 Sacré-Coeur
7 Musée de Vieux
   Montmartre
8 Cabaret des Assassins
9 Moulin de la Galette
10 Cimetière de
   Montmartre
11 Moulin Rouge
12 Boulevard de Clichy
13 Place Pigalle

✝ ■ Church
Ⓜ Métro
Ⓣ "Take a Break"

> **Tips** **Another Way to See Montmartre**
>
> Those finding the uphill climb to Paris's highest elevation too arduous can take the diesel-powered Le Petit Train de Montmartre, which rolls along the steep streets on a 35-minute guided tour (for details, see "Neighborhood Highlights" in chapter 7).

---

10). Picasso and Utrillo once frequented this little cottage, which numerous artists have patronized and painted. On any given afternoon, French folk tunes, love ballads, army songs, sea chanteys, and music-hall ditties stream out of the cafe and onto the street.

Turn left on rue St-Vincent, passing the Cimetière St-Vincent on your right (see "Cemeteries" in chapter 7). Take a left onto rue Girardon and climb the stairs. In a minute or two, you'll spot on your right two of the windmills *(moulins)* that used to dot the Butte. One of these, at no. 75, is the

⑨ Moulin de la Galette

This windmill (entrance at 1 av. Junot) was built in 1622 and was immortalized in oil by Renoir (see the painting in the Musée d'Orsay). When it was turned into a dance hall in the 1860s, it was named for the *galettes* (cakes made with flour ground inside the mills) that were sold here. Later, the dance hall was populated by Toulouse-Lautrec, van Gogh, and Utrillo. A few steps away at the angle of rue Lepic and rue Girardon is the second windmill, the Moulin Radet, now part of a restaurant.

Turn right onto rue Lepic and walk past no. 54. In 1886, van Gogh lived here with his brother Guillaumin. Take a right turn onto rue Joseph-de-Maistre, then left again on rue Caulaincourt until you reach the

⑩ Cimetière de Montmartre

This final resting place is second in fame only to Père-Lachaise and is the haunt of Nijinsky, Dumas *fils,* Stendhal, Degas, and Truffaut, among others (see "Cemeteries" in chapter 7).

From the cemetery, take avenue Rachel, turn left onto boulevard de Clichy, and go to place Blanche, where stands a windmill even better known than the one in Renoir's painting, the

⑪ Moulin Rouge

One of the world's most talked about nightclubs, the Moulin Rouge was immortalized by Toulouse-Lautrec. The windmill is still here and so is the cancan, but the rest has become an outrageously expensive, super-slick variety show with a heavy emphasis on undraped females (see "Nightclubs & Cabarets" in chapter 10).

From place Blanche, you can begin a descent on

⑫ Boulevard de Clichy

En route, you'll have to fight off the pornographers and hustlers trying to lure you into tawdry sex joints. With some rare exceptions, notably the citadels of the *chansonniers* (songwriters), boulevard de Clichy is one gigantic tourist trap. But everyone who comes to Paris invariably winds up here.

The boulevard strips and peels its way down to where you started:

⑬ Place Pigalle

The center of nudity in Paris was named after a French sculptor, Pigalle, whose closest brush with nudity was a depiction of Voltaire in the buff. Toulouse-Lautrec had his studio right off the square at 5 av. Frochot. Of course, place Pigalle was the notorious "Pig Alley" of World War II. When Edith Piaf was lonely and hungry, she sang in the alleyways, hoping to earn a few francs for the night.

THE LATIN QUARTER

Start: Place St-Michel (Métro: St-Michel).
Finish: The Panthéon.
Time: 3 hours, not counting stops.
Best Time: Any weekday, Monday to Friday from 9am to 4pm.
Worst Time: Sunday morning, when everybody is asleep.

This is the precinct of the Université de Paris (known for its most famous branch, the Sorbonne), where students meet and fall in love over *café crème* and croissants. Rabelais named it the Quartier Latin after the students and the professors who spoke Latin in the classroom and on the streets. The sector teems with belly dancers, exotic restaurants, sidewalk cafes, bookstalls, *caveaux* (basement nightclubs), *clochards* (bums), *chiffonniers* (ragpickers), and *gamins* (boys and girls).

A good starting point for your tour is
❶ Place St-Michel
Balzac used to draw water from the fountain (Davioud's 1860 sculpture of St. Michel slaying the dragon) when he was a youth. This was the scene of frequent skirmishes between the Germans and the Resistance in the summer of 1944, and the names of those who died here are engraved on plaques around the square.

TAKE A BREAK
Open 24 hours, **Café le Départ St-Michel,** 1 place St-Michel (✆ **01-43-54-24-55),** lies on the banks of the Seine. The decor is warmly modern, with etched mirrors reflecting the faces of a diversified crowd. If you want to fortify yourself for your walk, opt for one of the warm or cold snacks, including sandwiches.

To the south, you find
❷ Boulevard St-Michel
A.k.a. **Boul' Mich,** this is virtually the main street of the Latin Quarter as it heads south. This is a major tourist artery and won't give you a great insight into local life. For that, you can branch off onto virtually any of the streets that feed into the boulevard and find cafes, bars, Greek gyro

counters, ice cream stands, crêpe stands, and bistros like those pictured in movies set in Paris in the 1950s. The Paris Commune began here in 1871 as did the student uprisings of 1968.

From place St-Michel, with your back to the Seine, turn left down
❸ Rue de la Huchette
This typical street was the setting of Elliot Paul's *The Last Time I Saw Paris* (1942). Paul first wandered here "on a soft summer evening, and entirely by chance," in 1923 and then moved into no. 28, the **Hôtel Mont-Blanc.** Though much has changed since, some of the buildings are so old they have to be propped up by timbers. Paul captured the spirit of the street more evocatively than anyone, writing of "the delivery wagons, makeshift vehicles propelled by pedaling boys, pushcarts of itinerant vendors, knife-grinders, umbrella menders, a herd of milk goats, and the neighborhood pedestrians." (The local bordello has closed, however.) Today you see lots of Greek restaurants.

Branching off from this street to your left is
❹ Rue du Chat-qui-Pêche
This is said to be the shortest, narrowest street in the world, containing not one door and only a handful of

windows. It's usually filled with garbage or lovers or both. (Before the quay was built, the Seine sometimes rose above its banks, flooding the cellars of the houses here, and legend has it that an enterprising cat took advantage of its good fortune and went fishing in the confines of the cellars—hence the street's name, which means "Street of the Cat Who Fishes.")

Now retrace your steps toward place St-Michel and turn left at the intersection with rue de la Harpe, which leads to rue St-Séverin. At the intersection, take a left to see

❺ St-Séverin

A flamboyant Gothic church named for a 6th-century recluse, St-Séverin was built from 1210 to 1230 and was reconstructed in 1458, over the years adopting many of the features of Notre-Dame, across the river. The tower was completed in 1487 and the chapels from 1498 to 1520; Hardouin-Mansart designed the Chapelle de la Communion in 1673 when he was 27 years old, and it contains some beautiful Roualt etchings from the 1920s. Before entering, walk around the church to examine the gargoyles, birds of prey, and reptilian monsters projecting from its roof. To the right, facing the church, is the 15th-century "garden of ossuaries." The stained glass inside St-Séverin, behind the altar, is a stunning adornment using great swaths of color to depict the Seven Sacraments.

After visiting the church, go back to rue St-Séverin and follow it to rue Galande, then continue on until you reach

❻ St-Julien-le-Pauvre

This church is located on the south side of lovely **square René-Viviani.** First stand at the gateway and look at the beginning of rue Galande, especially the old houses with the steeples of St-Séverin rising across the way—one of the most frequently painted scenes on the Left Bank. Enter the courtyard and you'll be in medieval Paris. The garden to the left of the entrance offers the best view of Notre-Dame. Everyone from Rabelais to Thomas Aquinas has passed through the doors of this church. Before the 6th century, a chapel stood on this spot. The present church goes back to the Longpont monks, who began work on it in 1170 (making it the oldest existing church in Paris). In 1655, it was given to the Hôtel Dieu and in time became a small warehouse for salt. In 1889, it was presented to the followers of the Melchite Greek rite, a branch of the Byzantine church.

Return to rue Galande and turn left at the intersection with rue St-Séverin. Continue on until you reach rue St-Jacques, turn left, and turn right when you reach boulevard St-Germain. Follow this boulevard to rue de Cluny, turn left, and head toward the entrance to the

❼ Musée de Cluny

Even if you're rushed, take time out to see *The Lady and the Unicorn* tapestry and the remains of the Roman baths. (See "The Major Museums" in chapter 7.)

After your visit to the Cluny, exit onto boulevard St-Michel, but instead of heading back to place St-Michel, turn left and walk to place de la Sorbonne and the

❽ Sorbonne

One of the most famous academic institutions in the world, the Sorbonne was founded in the 13th century by Robert de Sorbon, St. Louis's confessor, for poor students who wished to pursue theological studies. By the next century it had become the most prestigious university in the West, attracting such professors as Thomas Aquinas and Roger Bacon and such students as Dante, Calvin, and Longfellow. Napoléon reorganized it in 1806. The courtyard and galleries are open to the public when the university is in session. In the Cour d'Honneur are statues of Hugo and Pasteur.

Walking Tour 2: The Latin Quarter

1 Place St-Michel
2 Boulevard St-Michel
3 Rue de la Huchette
4 Rue du Chat-qui-Pêche
5 St-Séverin
6 St-Julien-le-Pauvre
7 Musée de Cluny
8 Sorbonne
9 Eglise de la Sorbonne
10 Panthéon

At first glance from place de la Sorbonne, the Sorbonne seems architecturally undistinguished. In truth, it was rather indiscriminately reconstructed in the early 1900s. A better fate lay in store for the

9 Eglise de la Sorbonne
Built in 1635 by Le Mercier, this church contains the marble tomb of Cardinal Richelieu, a work by Girardon based on a design by Le Brun. At his feet is the remarkable statue *Learning in Tears.*

From the church, go south on rue Victor-Cousin and turn left at rue Soufflot. At street's end lies place du Panthéon and the

10 Panthéon
Sitting atop Mont Ste-Geneviève, this non-religious temple is the final resting place of such distinguished figures as Hugo, Zola, Rousseau, Voltaire, and Curie. (See "Architectural & Historic Highlights" in chapter 7.)

WALKING TOUR 3 THE MARAIS

Start:	Place de la Bastille (Métro: Bastille).
Finish:	Place de la Bastille.
Time:	4¹⁄₂ hours, with only cursory stops en route. The distance is about 2³⁄₄ miles.
Best Time:	Monday to Saturday, when more buildings and shops are open. If interiors are open, often you can walk into courtyards.
Worst Time:	Toward dusk, when shops and museums are closed, and it's too dark to admire the architectural details.

When Paris began to overflow the confines of Ile de la Cité in the 13th century, the citizenry began to settle in Le Marais, a marsh that used to be flooded regularly by the high-rising Seine. By the 17th century, the Marais had become the center of aristocratic Paris and some of its great mansions *(hôtels particuliers)*, many now restored or still being spruced up, were built by the finest craftsmen in France. In the 18th and 19th centuries, fashion deserted the Marais for the expanding Faubourg St-Germain and Faubourg St-Honoré. Industry soon took over, and once-elegant *hôtels* deteriorated into tenements. There was talk of demolishing the blighted neighborhood, but in 1962 an alarmed community group banded together and saved the historic district.

Today, the 17th-century mansions are fashionable once again. The *International Herald Tribune* called this area the latest refuge for the Paris artisan fleeing the tourist-trampled St-Germain-des-Prés. (However, that doesn't mean the area doesn't get its share of tourist traffic—quite the contrary.) The "marsh" sprawls across the 3rd and 4th arrondissements bounded by the Grands Boulevards, rue du Temple, place des Vosges, and the Seine. It has become Paris's center of gay/lesbian life, particularly on rues St-Croix-de-la-Bretonnerie, des Archives, and Vieille-du-Temple, and is a great place for window-shopping in trendy boutiques, up-and-coming galleries, and more.

Begin your tour at the site that spawned one of the most celebrated and abhorred revolutions in human history:

❶ Place de la Bastille

On July 14, 1789, a mob attacked the Bastille prison located here, igniting the French Revolution. Now nothing of this symbol of despotism remains. Built in 1369, its eight 100-foot towers once loomed over Paris. Within them, many prisoners, some sentenced by Louis XIV for "witchcraft," were kept, the best known being the "Man in the Iron Mask." And yet when the revolutionary mob stormed the fortress, only seven prisoners were discovered. (The Marquis de Sade had been shipped to the madhouse 10 days earlier.) The authorities had discussed razing it anyway, so the attack really meant little. But what it symbolized and what it unleashed will never be undone, and each July 14 the entire country celebrates Bastille Day with great festivity. Since the late 1980s, what had been scorned as a dull and grimy-looking traffic circle has become an artistic focal point, thanks to the construction of the Opéra Bastille on its eastern edge (see "The Performing Arts" in chapter 10).

It was probably easier to storm the Bastille in 1789 than it is now to cross over to the center of the square for a close-up view of the

❷ Colonne de Juillet

The July Column doesn't commemorate the Revolution but honors the victims of the July Revolution of 1830, which put Louis-Philippe on the throne after the heady but wrenching victories and defeats of Napoléon Bonaparte. The tower is crowned by the winged *God of Liberty,* whose forehead bears an emerging star.

From place de la Bastille, walk west along rue St-Antoine for about a block. Turn right and walk north along rue des Tournelles, noting the

❸ Statue of Beaumarchais

Erected in 1895, it honors the 18th-century author of *The Barber of Seville* and *The Marriage of Figaro,* which Rossini and Mozart brilliantly set to music.

Continue north for a long block along rue des Tournelles, then turn left at medieval-looking rue Pas-de-la-Mule (Footsteps of the Mule), which will open suddenly onto the northeastern corner of enchanting

❹ Place des Vosges

This is Paris's oldest square and once its most fashionable, boasting 36

Key:
- † Church
- Ⓜ Metro Stop
- ☕ "Take a Break"

1 Place de la Bastille
2 Colonne de Juillet
3 Statue of Beaumarchais
4 Place des Vosges
5 Deborah Chock
6 Maison de Victor Hugo
7 Musée Carnavalet
8 Hôtel Le Peletier de St-Fargeau
9 Musée Picasso
10 Yvon Lambert
11 Les Iles Grecques
12 Hier, Aujourd'hui, et Demain
13 Dominique Picquier
14 Passage de Retz
15 Hôtel de Rohan
16 Hôtel des Ambassadeurs de Hollande
17 Rue des Rosiers
18 Hôtel de Beauvais
19 Hôtel de Sens
20 Hôtel de Bethune-Sully

brick-and-stone pavilions rising from covered arcades that allowed people to shop at all times no matter what the weather. The buildings were constructed according to a strict plan—the height of the facades is equal to their width and the height of the triangular roofs is half the height of the facades. It was begun on Henri IV's orders and called place Royal; the king intended the square to be the scene of businesses and social festivities and even planned to live there, but Ravaillac had other plans and assassinated Henri 2 years before its completion. In 1559, Henri II was killed while jousting on the square, in the shadow of the Hôtel des Tournelles; his widow, Catherine de Médicis, had the place torn down. By the 17th century, the square was the home of many aristocrats. During the Revolution, it was renamed place de l'Invisibilité, and its statue of Louis XIII was stolen (probably melted down). A replacement statue now stands in its place.

In 1800, the square was renamed place des Vosges because the Vosges *département* was the first in France to pay its taxes to Napoléon. The addition of chestnut trees sparked a controversy—critics say they spoil the perspective. Even though its fortunes waned when the Marais went out of fashion, place des Vosges is now back big time. Over the years, the famous often took up residence: Descartes, Pascal, Cardinal Richelieu, courtesan Marion Delorme, Gautier, Daudet, and Mme de Sévigné all lived here. But its best-known occupant was Victor Hugo (his home, now a museum, is the only house you can visit without a private invitation—see below).

Place des Vosges is the centerpiece of many unusual, charming, and/or funky shops. At 24 place des Vosges is one of the best of these,

5 Deborah Chock

Deborah Chock ((*C* **01-48-04-86-86**) sells a constantly changing roster of

avant-garde and contemporary paintings. Use it as a debut before you explore the many other art galleries in the neighborhood. The staff is English-speaking and well-versed in the currents of the Paris art scene.

TAKE A BREAK
Two cafes hold court from opposite sides of place des Vosges, both serving *café au lait*, glasses of wine, and *eaux de vie*, sandwiches, pastries, and afternoon tea: **Ma Bourgogne** at no. 19 ((*C* **01-42-78-44-64**), on the western edge, and **La Chope des Vosges** at no. 22 ((*C* **01-42-72-64-04**).

Near the square's southeastern corner at 6 place des Vosges, commemorating the life and times of a writer whose works were read with passion in the 19th century, is the

6 Maison de Victor Hugo

Hugo's former home is now a museum ((*C* **01-42-72-10-16**) and literary shrine you can visit (see "Literary Landmarks" in chapter 7). Hugo lived there from 1832 to 1848, when he went into voluntary exile on the Channel Islands after the rise of the despotic Napoléon III.

Exit from place des Vosges from its north-western corner (directly opposite the Maison de Victor Hugo) and walk west along rue des Francs-Bourgeois until you reach the inter-section with rue de Sévigné, then make a right. At no. 23 is the

7 Musée Carnavalet

This16th-century mansion is now a museum ((*C* **01-42-72-21-13**) devoted to the history of Paris and the French Revolution (see "The Major Museums" in chapter 7).

Continue to a point near the northern terminus of rue de Sévigné, noting no. 29 (now part of the Carnavalet). This is the

8 Hôtel le Peletier de St-Fargeau

The structure bears the name of its former occupant, who was considered responsible for the death sentence of Louis XVI. It's used as offices and can't be visited.

At the end of the street, make a left onto lovely rue du Parc-Royal, lined with 17th-century mansions. It leads to place de Thorigny, where at no. 5 you'll find the

⑨ Musée Picasso

The museum occupies the Hôtel Salé, built by a salt-tax collector (see "The Major Museums" in chapter 7). You can visit the museum either now or come back at the end of the tour.

Walk northeast along rue Thorigny and turn left onto rue Debelleyme. After a block, near the corner of rue Vieille-du-Temple, at 108 rue Vieille-du-Temple, is a worthwhile art gallery among the dozens in this neighborhood:

⑩ Yvon Lambert

This gallery (② **01-42-71-09-33**) specializes in contemporary and some-times radically avant-garde art from international artists. The art is dis-played in a cavernous main show-room, spilling over into an "annex" room. An excellent primer for the local arts scene, it makes a nice con-trast to the 17th-century trappings all around you.

Continue north for 2 short blocks along rue Debelleyme until you reach rue de Bretagne. Anyone who appreciates a really good deli will want to stop at 14 rue de Bretagne,

⑪ Les Iles Grecques

This deli (② **01-42-71-00-56**) is the most popular of the area's ethnic take-out restaurants, a perfect place to gather picnic supplies before heading to nearby square du Temple (up rue de Bretagne) or place des Vosges. You'll find flavorful Greek cuisine like mous-saka, stuffed eggplant, stuffed vine leaves, olives, tarama (a savory paste made from fish roe), and both meat-balls and vegetarian balls. It's open Monday from 3:30 to 8pm and Tues-day to Sunday from 10am to 2pm and 3:30 to 8pm.

After you fill up on great food, note that at the same address is

⑫ Hier, Aujourd'hui, et Demain

At this shop (② **01-42-77-69-02**) you can appreciate France's love affair with 1930s Art Deco. Michel, the owner, provides a tempting array of bibelots and art objects, with one of the widest arrays of colored glass in town. Works by late-19th-century glassmakers such as Daum, Gallé, and Legras are avidly collected. Some items require special packing and great care in transport; others (many amusing) can be carted home as a souvenir.

Now walk southeast along rue Charlot to no. 10 at the corner of rue Pastourelle, where you'll be tempted by the fabrics of

⑬ Dominique Picquier

Looking to redo your favorite settee? This stylish shop (② **01-42-72-39-14**) sells a wide roster of fabric (50 percent cotton, 50 percent linen) that stands up to rugged use. Most patterns are based on some botanical inspiration, like ginko leaves, vanilla pods and vines, and magnolia branches. Every-thing costs 390F (59.30€, $56.55) per meter or 346F (52.60€, $50.15) per yard—proof that the good life has returned to the Marais.

Nearby, at 9 rue Charlot, adjacent to the cor-ner of rue Charlot and rue du Perche, is the Marais's largest and most experimental art gallery, the

⑭ Passage de Retz

Opened in 1994, this avant-garde gallery (② **01-48-04-37-99**) has about 2,100 square feet of space to show off its highly amusing exhibits. It has shown Japanese textiles, Ameri-can Abstract Expressionist paintings, modern Venetian glass, contemporary Haitian paintings, and selections from affiliated art galleries in Québec.

Walk 1 block farther along rue Charlot, turn left for a block onto rue des 4 Fils, then go right on rue Vieille-du-Temple to no. 87, where you'll come across Delamair's

⑮ Hôtel de Rohan

This was once occupied by the fourth Cardinal Rohan, the larcenous cardinal of the "diamond necklace scandal" that led to a flood of destructive publicity for Marie Antoinette. The first occupant of the hotel was reputed to be the son of Louis XVI. The interior is usually closed to the public, except during an occasional exhibit—if it's open, check out the amusing Salon des Singes (Monkey Room). Sometimes you can visit the courtyard, which boasts one of the finest sculptures of 18th-century France, *The Watering of the Horses of the Sun*, with a nude Apollo and four horses against a background of exploding sunbursts. (If you want to see another Delamair work, detour to 60 rue des Francs-Bourgeois to see the extraordinary **Hôtel de Soubise,** now housing the Musée de l'Histoire de France—see "Specialty Museums" in chapter 7.)

Along the same street at no. 47 is the

⑯ Hôtel des Ambassadeurs de Hollande

Here, Beaumarchais wrote *The Marriage of Figaro.* It's one of the most splendid mansions in the Marais and despite its name was never actually occupied by the Dutch embassy.

Continue walking south along rue Vieille-du-Temple until you reach:

⑰ Rue des Rosiers

Rue des Rosiers (Street of the Rosebushes) is one of the most colorful and typical streets remaining from Paris's old Jewish quarter, and you'll find an intriguing blend of living memorials to Ashkenazi and Sephardic traditions. The Star of David shines from some of the shop windows; Hebrew letters appear, sometimes in neon; couscous is sold from shops run by Moroccan, Tunisian, or Algerian Jews; restaurants serve strictly kosher food; and signs appeal for Jewish liberation. You'll come across many delicacies you might've read about but never seen, such as savory sausage stuffed in a gooseneck, roots of black horseradish, and pickled lemons.

TAKE A BREAK
The street offers a cornucopia of ethnic eateries that remain steadfast to their central European, Ashkenazi origins. **Chez Jo Goldenberg,** 7 rue des Rosiers (✆ 01-48-87-20-16), has plenty of room to sit down and eat (see chapter 6 for more details).

Take a left onto rue des Rosiers and head down to rue Pavée, which gets its name from the fact that it was the first street in Paris, sometime during the 1300s, to have cobblestones placed over what had been an open sewer. At this "Paved Street," turn right and walk south until you reach the St-Paul Métro stop. Make a right along rue François-Miron and check out no. 68, the 17th-century

⑱ Hôtel de Beauvais

Though the facade was badly damaged in the Revolution, it remains one of Paris's most charming *hôtels.* A plaque announces that Mozart lived there in 1763 and played at the court of Versailles. (He was all of 7 at the time.) Louis XIV presented the mansion to Catherine Bellier, wife of Pierre de Beauvais and lady-in-waiting to Anne of Austria; she reportedly had the honor of introducing Louis, then 16, to the facts of life. To visit the interior, apply any afternoon to the **Association du Paris Historique** on the ground floor.

Continue your walk along rue François-Miron until you come to a crossroads, where you take a sharp left along rue de Jouy, cross rue Fourcy, and turn onto rue du Figuier, where at no. 1 you'll see the

⑲ Hôtel de Sens

The structure was built between the 1470s and 1519 for the archbishops of Sens. Along with the Cluny on the Left Bank, it's the only domestic architecture remaining from the 15th century. Long after the archbishops had departed in 1605, the wife of Henri IV, scandalous Queen Margot, lived here. Her new lover, "younger and more virile," slew her old lover as she looked on in great amusement. Today, the *hôtel* houses the **Bibliothèque Forney** (© **01-42-78-14-60**). Leaded windows and turrets characterize the facade; you can go into the courtyard to see more of the ornate stone decoration—the gate is open Tuesday to Friday from 1:30 to 8:30pm and Saturday from 10am to 8:30pm.

Retrace your steps to rue de Fourcy, turn right, and walk up the street until you reach the St-Paul Métro stop again. Turn right onto rue St-Antoine and continue to no. 62,

⑳ Hôtel de Bethune-Sully

Work began on this mansion in 1625, on the order of Jean Androuet de Cerceau. In 1634, it was acquired by the duc de Sully, once Henri IV's minister of finance. After a straitlaced life as the "accountant of France," Sully broke loose in his declining years, adorning himself with diamonds and garish rings and a young bride, who's said to have had a thing for very young men. The *hôtel* was acquired by the government just after World War II and is now the seat of the National Office of Historical Monuments and Sites, with an info center and a bookshop inside. Recently restored, the relief-studded facade is especially appealing. You can visit the interior with a guide on Saturday or Sunday at 3pm and can visit the courtyard and the garden any day; chamber music concerts are frequently staged here.

9

Shopping

Shopping is a favorite pastime of Parisians; some would even say it reflects the City of Light's soul. This is one of the rare places in the world where you don't have to go to any special area to shop—shopping opportunities surround you wherever you may be. Each walk you take will immerse you in uniquely French styles. The windows, stores, and people (even their dogs) brim with energy,

creativity, and a sense of visual expression found in few other cities.

You don't have to buy anything to appreciate shopping in Paris—just soak up the art form the French have made of rampant consumerism. Peer in the *vitrines* (display windows), absorb cutting-edge ideas, witness new trends, and take home with you a whole new education in style.

1 The Shopping Scene

BEST BUYS

PERFUMES, MAKEUP & BEAUTY TREATMENTS A discount of 20% to 30% makes these items a great buy; qualify for a VAT refund (see below) and you'll save 40% to 45% off the Paris retail price, allowing you to bring home goods at half the U.S. price. Duty-free shops abound in Paris and are always less expensive than the ones at the airports.

For bargain cosmetics, try out French dime store and drugstore brands like **Bourjois** (made in the Chanel factories), **Lierac,** and **Galenic. Vichy,** famous for its water, has a complete skin care and makeup line. The newest retail trend in Paris is the *parapharmacie,* a type of discount drugstore loaded with inexpensive brands, health cures, beauty regimes, and diet plans. These usually offer a 20% discount.

FOODSTUFFS Nothing makes a better souvenir than a product of France brought home to savor later. Supermarkets are located in prime tourist neighborhoods; stock up on coffee, designer chocolates, mustards (try Maille or Meaux brand), and perhaps American products in French packages for the kids. However, to be sure you don't try to bring home a foodstuff that's prohibited, see "Entry Requirements & Customs Regulations" in chapter 3.

FUN FASHION Sure you can spend and spend on couture or *prêt-à-porter,* but French teens and trendsetters have their own stores where the latest looks are affordable. Even the dime stores in Paris sell designer copies and hotshot styles. In the stalls in front of the department stores on boulevard Haussmann, you'll find some of the latest accessories, guaranteed for a week's worth of small talk once you get home.

GETTING A VAT REFUND

In April 2000, the French **value-added tax (VAT—TVA** in French) came down from 20.6% to 19.6%, but you can get most of that back if you spend 1,200F

> *Tips* **Shopping Etiquette**
>
> When you walk into a French store, it's traditional to greet the owner or sales clerk with a direct address, not a fey smile or even a weak *bonjour.* Only a clear and pleasant *"Bonjour, madame/monsieur"* will do.
>
> And if you plan to enter the rarefied atmospheres of the top designer boutiques (to check out the pricey merchandise if not to buy anything), be sure to dress the part. You don't need to wear couture, but do leave the sneakers and sweatsuit back at your hôtel. The sales staff will be much more accommodating if you look as if you belong there.

(182.40€, $174) or more in any store that participates in the VAT refund program. Most stores participate.

Once you meet your required minimum purchase amount, you qualify for a tax refund. The amount of the refund varies with the way the refund is handled and the fee some stores charge you for processing it. So the refund at a department store may be 13%, whereas at a small shop it may be 15% or even 18%.

You'll receive **VAT refund papers** in the shop; some stores, like Hermès, have their own; others provide a government form. Fill in the forms before you arrive at the airport and expect to stand in line at the Customs desk for as long as half an hour. You're required by law to show the goods at the airport, so have them on you or visit the Customs office before you check your luggage. Once the papers have been mailed to the authorities, a credit will appear, often months later, on your credit-card bill. All refunds are processed at the final point of departure from the **European Union (EU),** so if you're going to another EU country, don't apply for the refund in France.

Be sure to mark the paperwork to request that your refund be applied to your credit card so you aren't stuck with a check in francs that's hard to cash. This also ensures the best rate of exchange. In some airports, you're offered the opportunity to get your refund back in cash, which is tempting. But if you accept cash in any currency other than francs, you'll be losing money on the conversion rate.

To avoid VAT refund hassles, ask for a Global refund form ("Shopping Checque") at a store where you make a purchase. When leaving an EU country, have it stamped by customs, after which you take it to the Global Refund counter at more than 700 airports and border crossings in Europe. Your money is refunded on the spot. For information, contact **Global Refund,** 707 Summer St., Stamford, CT 06901 (*©* **800/566-9828;** www.globalrefund.com).

DUTY-FREE BOUTIQUES

The advantage of duty-free shops is that you never have to pay the VAT, so you avoid the red tape of getting a refund. Both Charles de Gaulle and Orly airports have shopping galore (de Gaulle has a virtual shopping mall with crystal, cutlery, chocolates, luggage, wine, pipes and lighters, lingerie, silk scarves, perfume, knitwear, jewelry, cameras and equipment, cheeses, and even antiques). You'll find lots of duty-free shops on the avenues branching out from the Opéra Garnier, in the 1st arrondissement. Sometimes there are bargains here, but most often not. Usually these stores jack prices up, so even though there's no duty, you'll find no bargain on most goods. In general, these duty-free shops are best left for last-minute buys or the impulsive shopper who feels he or she is leaving Paris without having bought enough.

BUSINESS HOURS

Usual shop hours are Monday to Saturday from 10am to 7pm, but the hours vary greatly, and Monday mornings in Paris don't run at full throttle. Small shops sometimes close for a 2-hour lunch break and may not even open until after lunch on Monday. Thursday is the best day for late-night shopping, with stores open to 9 or 10pm.

Sunday shopping is currently limited to tourist areas and flea markets, though there's growing demand for full-scale Sunday hours. The big department stores are now open on the five Sundays before Christmas. The **Carrousel du Louvre,** a mall adjacent to the Louvre, is open and hopping on Sunday, but closed on Monday. The tourist shops lining rue de Rivoli across from the Louvre are all open on Sunday, as are the antiques villages, assorted flea markets, and specialty events. There are several good food markets in the streets on Sunday. For our favorites, see the box "Food Markets" (p. 259). The **Virgin Megastore** on the Champs-Elysées, a big teen hangout, pays a fine to stay open on Sunday.

SHIPPING IT HOME

Shipping charges will possibly double your cost on goods, and you may have to pay duties on the items (see above). The good news: The VAT refund is automatically applied to all shipped items, so there's no need to worry about the 1,200F (182.40€, $174) minimum. Some stores do have a $100 minimum for shipping, though. You can also walk into any post office and mail home a jiffy bag or small box of goodies. French do-it-yourself boxes can't be reopened once closed, so pack carefully. The clerk at the post office will help you assemble the box (it's tricky), seal it, and send it off.

GREAT SHOPPING NEIGHBORHOODS

Here are the best of the shopping arrondissements:

1ST & 8TH ARRONDISSEMENTS   These two *quartiers* adjoin each other (invisibly) and form the heart of Paris's best Right Bank shopping strip—they're one big hunting ground. This area includes the famed **rue du faubourg St-Honoré,** where the big designer houses are, and the **Champs-Elysées,** where the mass market and teen scene are hot. At one end of the 1st is the **Palais Royal,** one of the best shopping secrets in Paris, where an arcade of boutiques flanks each side of the garden of the former palace.

Also here is **avenue Montaigne,** Paris's most glamorous shopping street, boasting 2 blocks of ultrafancy shops, where you simply float from big name to big name and in a few hours can see everything from Dior to Caron. Avenue Montaigne is also the address of **Joseph,** a British design firm, and **Porthault,** makers of the poshest sheets in the world.

2ND ARRONDISSEMENT   Right behind the Palais Royal is the **Garment District** (Sentier), as well as a few sophisticated shopping secrets, such as **place des Victoires.**

In the 19th century, this area became known for its *passages,* literally glass-enclosed shopping streets—in fact, the world's first shopping malls. They were also the city's first buildings to be illuminated by gaslight. Many have been torn down, but, amazingly, a dozen or so have survived. Of them all, we prefer *Passage den Grand Cerf,* between 145 rue St-Denis and 10 rue Dussoubs, 2nd (Métro: Bourse), lying a few blocks from the Beaubourg. It's a place of wonder, filled with everything from retro-chic boutiques and (increasingly) Asian-themed shops. What's exciting is to come upon a discovery, perhaps a postage stamp shop with some special jeweler who creates unique products such as jewel-toned safety pins.

3RD & 4TH ARRONDISSEMENTS The border between these two arrondissements gets fuzzy, especially around **place des Vosges,** center stage of the Marais. No matter. The districts offer several dramatically different shopping experiences.

On the surface, the shopping includes the "real people stretch" (where all the non-millionaires shop) of **rue de Rivoli** and **rue St-Antoine,** featuring every-thing from GAP and a branch of Marks & Spencer, to local discount stores and mass merchants. Two "real people" department stores are in this area, **Samari-taine** and **BHV;** there's also **Les Halles** and the **Beaubourg** neighborhood, which is anchored by the Centre Pompidou.

Meanwhile, hidden in the Marais is a medieval warren of tiny twisting streets chockablock with cutting-edge designers and up-to-the-minute fashions and trends. Start by walking around place des Vosges for art galleries, designer shops, and special little finds, then dive in and lose yourself in the area leading to the Musée Picasso.

Finally, the 4th is also the home of the **Bastille,** an up-and-coming area for artists and galleries where you'll find the newest entry on the retail scene, the **Viaduc des Arts** (which actually stretches into the 12th). It's a collection of about 30 stores occupying a series of narrow vaulted niches under what used to be railroad tracks. They run parallel to avenue Daumesnil, centered around boulevard Diderot.

6TH & 7TH ARRONDISSEMENTS Though the 6th is one of the most famous shopping districts in Paris—it's the soul of the Left Bank—a lot of the really good stuff is hidden in the zone that turns into the wealthy residential dis-trict of the 7th. **Rue du Bac,** stretching from the 6th to the 7th in a few blocks, stands for all that wealth and glamour can buy.

9TH ARRONDISSEMENT To add to the fun of shopping the Right Bank, the 9th sneaks in behind the 1st, so if you choose not to walk toward the Champs-Elysées and the 8th, you can head to the city's big department stores, all built in a row along **boulevard Haussmann** in the 9th. Department stores include not only the two big French icons, **Au Printemps** and **Galeries Lafayette,** but also a large branch of Britain's **Marks & Spencer** and a branch of the Dutch answer to Kmart, low-priced **C&A.**

2 Shopping A to Z
ANTIQUES

Argenterie de Turenne *(Finds* Inside, you'll find old-fashioned gentility and masses of silver, both sterling and plated, much of which was made in France dur-ing the 19th and early 20th centuries. The array of trays, water pitchers, napkin rings, tumblers, and punchbowls is staggering, but what many visitors find amaz-ing is that congenially battered silverplated forks and spoons are sold by weight, at the rate of 400F (60.80€, $58) per kilo. The store lies within the Marais, a short walk from the Place des Vosges, on a block that's lined with purveyors of other old-fashioned grace notes that include antique glassware and porcelain. 19 rue de Turenne, 4th arr. (01-42-72-04-00. Tues–Sat 10:30am–7pm. Métro: St-Paul.

Le Louvre des Antiquaires Across from the Louvre, Le Louvre des Anti-quaires offers three levels of fancy knickknacks and 250 vendors. It's just the place if you're looking for 30 matching Baccarat crystal champagne flutes from the 1930s, a Sèvres tea service dated 1773, or a small signed Jean Fouquet gold-and-diamond pin. Too stuffy? No problem. There's always the 1940 Rolex with the aubergine crocodile strap. Prices can be high, but a few reasonable items are hidden here. What's more, the Sunday scene is fabulous, and there's a cafe with a variety of lunch menus beginning around 100F (15.20€, $14.50). Pick up a free map and brochure of the premises from the information desk. 2 place du Palais-Royal, 1st arr. ⓒ **01-42-97-00-14.** Tues–Sun 11am–7pm. Closed Sun July–Aug. Métro: Palais Royal.

Mlinaric, Henry, and Zervudachi   David Mlinaric is the British interior designer who redecorated Spencer House (the late Princess Diana's ancestral home in London) as well as all of Lord Rothschild's private residences. Tino Zervudachi is one of the hot young turks of Paris design. Hugh Henry, like Mlinaric, is English. Together, these three musketeers are the chicest antiques dealers on the Right Bank, specializing in museum-quality 18th-century items. 54 Galerie de Montpensier, Palais-Royal, 1st arr. ⓒ **01-42-96-08-62.** Mon–Fri 9:30am–1pm and 2–6:30pm (Fri to 5:30pm). Métro: Palais Royal.

Village St-Paul   This isn't an antiques center but a cluster of dealers in their own hole-in-the-wall hideout. It really hops on Sunday. Bring your camera, because inside the courtyards and alleys is a dream vision of hidden Paris: dealers in a courtyard selling furniture and other decorative items in French country and formal styles. The rest of the street, stretching from the river to the Marais, is also lined with dealers. 23–27 rue St-Paul, 4th arr. No phone. Thurs–Mon 11am–7pm. Métro: St-Paul.

ART

Artcurial   This is the best, most famous, and most prestigious place in Paris for contemporary art. Many art forms are displayed here, from jewelry and design to sculpture and tapestries. Centre d'Art Contemporain, 61 ave. Montaigne, 8th arr. ⓒ **01-42-99-16-16.** Métro: Franklin D. Roosevelt.

Galerie 27   This tiny closet of a store sells lithographs by some of the most famous artists of the early 20th century, including Picasso, Coll, Miró, and Léger. 27 rue de Seine, 6th arr. ⓒ **01-43-54-78-54.** Tues–Sat 10am–1pm and 2:30–7pm. Métro: St-Germain-des-Prés or Odéon.

Galerie Adrien Maeght   This art house is among the most famous names in galleries, selling contemporary art on a very fancy Left Bank street that's far more chic and fashionable than the bohemian Left Bank that Picasso knew. 42 rue du Bac, 7th arr. ⓒ **01-45-48-45-15.** Mon 10am–6pm, Tues–Sat 9:30am–7pm. Métro: Rue du Bac.

Librarie Elbe   The souvenir stands are filled with copies of Toulouse-Lautrec posters, but if you want something original, this shop sells early-1900s advertising and railroad posters, as well as etchings and cartoons, at very reasonable prices. 213 bis bd. St-Germain, 7th arr. ⓒ **01-45-48-77-97.** Tues–Sat 10am–1pm and 2–6:30pm. Closed Aug. Métro: Rue du Bac.

Viaduc des Arts   This renovated place occupies a long 2-block stretch from the Opéra Bastille to Gare de Lyon and features art galleries and artisans in individual boutiques created within the arches of an old train viaduct. It's nothing spectacular, but makes for interesting shopping. 9–147 av. Daumesnil, 12th arr. ⓒ **01-44-75-80-66.** Mon–Sat 11am–7pm. Métro: Bastille, Ledru-Rollin, Reuilly-Diderot, or Gare de Lyon.

Finds **An Open-Air Canvas Gallery**

The **Paris Art Market** is "the place to go" on a Sunday. Located at the foot of Montparnasse Tower, this market is like an open-air gallery and has done much to restore the reputation of Montparnasse (14th) as a *quartier* for artists. Some 100 artists participate, including painters, sculptors, and photographers, even jewelers and hat-makers. Head for the mall along the boulevard Edgar Quinet for the best work. Go any time on Sunday between 10am and 7:30pm (Métro: Montparnasse).

BOOKS

If you like the rare and unusual in books, patronize one of the *banquinistes*, the owners of those army-green stalls that line the Seine. Perhaps you'll get lucky and find a copy of an original edition of Henry Miller's *Tropic of Cancer*, banned for decades in the United States. This is where tourists in the 20s and 30s went to buy "dirty" French postcards. Occasionally you'll come across some treasured book edition. We like to start with the guy who sells travel posters, perhaps of old Pan Am Jets, lying right off the pont des Arts and work our way toward all the rest. Some of the *banquinistes* are noted for giving the Parisians a reputation for rudeness. But don't let them intimidate you, although they'll often try.

See also the **Marché aux Livres** under "Markets" and **FNAC** and **Virgin Megastore** under "Music."

Brentano's A block from the Opéra Garnier, Brentano's is a large English-language bookstore selling guides, maps, novels, and non-fiction as well as greeting cards, postcards, holiday items, and gifts. 37 av. de l'Opéra, 2nd arr. ✆ **01-42-61-52-50**. Mon–Sat 10am–7:30pm. Métro: Opéra or Pyramide.

Galignani Sprawling over a large street level and supplemented by a mezzanine, this venerable wood-paneled bookstore has thrived here since it opened in 1810. Enormous numbers of books are available in both French and English, with a special emphasis on French classics, modern fiction, sociology, and fine arts. Looking for English-language translations of works by Balzac, Flaubert, Zola, or Colette? Most of them are here; if not, they can be ordered. 224 rue de Rivoli, 1st arr. ✆ **01-42-60-76-07**. Mon–Sat 10am–7pm. Métro: Tuileries.

Les Mots à la Bouche This is Paris's largest and best-stocked gay bookstore, where you can find French- and English-language books as well as gay info magazines like *Illico*, *e.m@le*, and *Lesbia*. You'll also find lots of free pamphlets advertising gay/lesbian venues and events. 6 rue Ste-Croix-la-Bretonnerie, 4th arr. ✆ **01-42-78-88-30**. Mon–Sat 11am–11pm, Sun 3–8pm. Métro: Hôtel de Ville.

Librairie la Bail-Weissert Paris is filled with rare bookshops, but this one has the best collection of atlases, rare maps, and engravings from the 15th to the 19th century. The shop sells original topographical maps of European and world cities, along with various regions of Europe. There's also a superb collection of architectural engravings. 5 rue Lagrange, 5th arr. ✆ **01-43-29-72-59**. Mon–Fri 10am–12:30pm and 2–7pm. Sat only by appointment. Métro: Maubert-Mutualité or St-Michel.

Shakespeare and Company The most famous bookstore on the Left Bank was Shakespeare and Company, on rue de l'Odéon, home to the legendary Sylvia Beach, "mother confessor to the Lost Generation." Hemingway, Fitzgerald, and Stein were frequent patrons, as was Anaïs Nin, the diarist noted for her description of struggling American artists in 1930s Paris. Nin helped her companion, Henry Miller, publish *Tropic of Cancer,* a book so notorious in its day that returning Americans trying to slip copies through Customs often had them confiscated as pornography. (When times were hard, Nin herself wrote pornography for a dollar a page.) Long ago, the shop moved to rue de la Bûcherie, a musty old place where expatriates still swap books and literary gossip and foreign students work in exchange for modest lodgings. Check out the lending library upstairs. 37 rue de la Bûcherie, 5th arr. No phone. Daily 11am– midnight. Métro: St-Michel.

Tea and Tattered Pages   At this largely English-language paperback bookshop, you can take a break from browsing to have tea at a little table. Though it's slightly out of the way, an extra dose of charm makes it worth the trip. 24 rue Mayet, 6th arr. © 01-40-65-94-35. Daily 10am–10pm. Métro: Duroc.

Village Voice Bookshop   This favorite of expatriate Yankees is on a side street in the heart of the best Left Bank shopping district, near some of the gathering places described in Gertrude Stein's *The Autobiography of Alice B. Toklas.* Opened in 1981, the shop is a hangout for the literati. Its name has nothing to do with the counterculture New York newspaper. 6 rue Princesse, 6th arr. © 01-46-33-36-47. Mon 2–8pm, Tues–Sat 10am–8pm, Sun 2–7pm. Métro: Mabillon.

W. H. Smith   This store provides books, magazines, and newspapers published in English (most titles are from Britain). You can get the *Times* of London, of course, and the Sunday *New York Times* is available every Monday. There's a fine selection of maps and travel guides, plus a special children's section that includes comics. 248 rue de Rivoli, 1st arr. © 01-44-77-88-99. Mon–Sat 9am–7:30pm, Sun 1–7:30pm. Métro: Concorde.

CERAMICS, CHINA & PORCELAIN

La Maison Ivre   This charming shop is perfect for country-style ceramics that add authenticity to French-country decor. It carries an excellent selection of handmade pottery from all over France, with an emphasis on Provençal and southern French ceramics, including ovenware, bowls, platters, plates, pitchers, mugs, and vases. 38 rue Jacob, 6th arr. © 01-42-60-01-85. Mon 2–7pm, Tues–Sat 10:30am–7pm. Métro: St-Germain-des-Prés.

Limoges-Unic/Madronet   Housed in two shops of more or less equal size on the same street, this store is crammed with crystals like Daum, Baccarat, Lalique, Haviland, and Bernardaud. You'll also find other table items: glass and crystal, silver, whatever your heart desires. They'll ship your purchases, and English is widely spoken. 34 and 58 rue de Paradis, 10th arr. © 01-47-70-54-49 or 01-47-70-61-49. Mon–Sat 10am–6:30pm. Métro: Gare de l'Est.

Manufacture Nationale de Sèvres   This is one of only two official outlets in Paris for the production of Sèvres porcelain. The other is in the western suburb of Sèvres, near the Musée National de Céramique de Sèvres (see chapter 7). Because only about 5,000 pieces of the stuff are made every year, the porcelain is prized as one of the most celebrated names in French industry. 4 place André-Malraux, 1st arr. © 01-47-03-40-20. Mon–Fri 11am–6pm. Métro: Palais Royal.

CHILDREN: FASHION & TOYS

Au Nain Bleu   This is the largest, oldest, and most centrally located toy store in Paris. More important, it's probably the fanciest toy store in the world. But don't panic—in addition to the expensive stuff, you'll find rows of cheaper items (like penny candy) in jars on the first floor. 406 rue St-Honoré, 8th arr. ℭ **01-42-60-39-01**. Mon–Sat 9:45am–6:30pm. Métro: Concorde or Madeleine.

Bonpoint   Grandparent alert! Bonpoint is part of a well-known almost-haute-couture chain specializing in clothing for children and adolescents ages 1 week to 16 years. The clothing is well-tailored, traditional, and extremely expensive. Drool over formal party and confirmation dresses and long baptismal robes, embroidered in France and edged in lace. 15 rue Royale, 8th arr. ℭ **01-47-42-52-63**. Mon–Sat 10am–7pm. Métro: Concorde.

Dipaki *Finds*   If you prefer clothes that have hip, hot style, and color but are wearable, washable, and affordable, forget Bonpoint and try this small shop—it's a representative of a truly sensational French line of clothes for toddlers. And it's only a block from place de la Madeleine. 18 rue Vignon, 9th arr. ℭ **01-42-66-24-74**. Mon–Sat 10am–7pm. Métro: Madeleine.

Natalys   Part of a French chain with a dozen stores in Paris and many else-where, Natalys sells upscale versions of children's (6 and under) and maternity wear. It has just enough French panache without going over the top in design or price. 92 av. des Champs-Elysées, 8th arr. ℭ **01-43-59-17-65**. Mon–Sat 10am–7:30pm. Métro: F. D. Roosevelt.

CRYSTAL

Baccarat   Opened in 1764, Baccarat is one of Europe's leading purveyors of full-lead crystal. You won't be able to comparison-shop Baccarat crystal at its various branches—a central organization sets rigid prices. But if you're hunting for bargains, head for the rue de Paradis outlet and check out special sales or promotions on discontinued items. These sales are the biggest during 2 weeks in mid-January. Baccarat's more prestigious outlet is on place de la Madeleine, but the rue de Paradis one is larger and contains the **Musée de Baccarat** (see chapter 7). (1) 11 place de la Madeleine, 8th arr. ℭ **01-42-65-36-26**. Tues–Fri 10am–7pm, Mon and Sat 10am–7:30pm. Métro: Madeleine. (2) 30 bis rue de Paradis, 10th arr. ℭ **01-47-70-64-30**. Mon–Fri 10am–6:30pm, Sat 10am–noon and 2–5:30pm. Métro: Gare de l'Est.

Lalique   Lalique is known around the world for its smoky frosted glass sculpture, Art-Deco crystal, and unique perfume bottles. The shop sells a wide range of merchandise, including leather belts with Lalique buckles and top-quality silk scarves at about 1,000F (152€, $145), designed to compete directly with those sold by Hermès. 11 rue Royale, 8th arr. ℭ **01-53-05-12-12**. Mon 10am–6:30pm, Tues–Fri 9:30am–6:30pm, Sat 9:30am–7pm. Métro: Concorde or Madeleine.

DEPARTMENT STORES

In addition to the stores below, **La Samaritaine,** 19 rue de la Monnaie, 1st arr. (ℭ **01-40-41-20-20;** Métro: Pont Neuf or Châtelet–Les Halles), and **BHV,** 52 rue de Rivoli, 4th arr. (ℭ **01-42-74-90-00;** Métro: Hôtel de Ville), offer the department store experience at slightly lower prices. La Samaritaine has a fine inexpensive restaurant with a panoramic view on the top floor.

Au Bon Marché   Don't be fooled by the name ("low-budget" or "cheap") of this two-part Left Bank department store—for about 20 years, it has worked hard to position itself in the luxury market, selling fashion for men, women, and children; furniture; upscale gifts; and housewares. Some visitors compare it to Bloomingdale's with a French accent. This is the oldest department store in Paris dating from 1852. Of course, it can't compete with the grand magasins like Galeries Lafayette, except in one category. Au Bon Marché has a superior rug department, which it has fine-tuned as its specialty since 1871. It also has one of the largest food halls in Paris. 22 rue de Sèvres, 7th arr. ℰ 01-44-39-80-00. Mon–Fri 9:30am–7pm, Sat 9:30am–8pm. Métro: Sèvres-Babylone.

Au Printemps   Take a look at the facade of this megastore for a reminder of the gilded age. Inside, the merchandise is divided into housewares (**Printemps Maison**), women's fashion (**Printemps de la Mode**), and men's clothes (**Brummel**). This is better for women's and children's fashion than Galeries Lafayette. As for perfume, it's in a dead-head race with Galeries Lafayette, with all the top names in fragrances. Although visitors feel more pampered in Galeries Lafayette, Au Printemps also dazzles with its customer services, putting all major department stores in London to shame. Check out the magnificent stained-glass dome, through which turquoise light cascades into the sixth-floor **Café Flo,** where you can have a coffee or a full meal. Interpreters at the Welcome Service in Printemps de la Mode will help you find what you're looking for, claim your VAT refund, and so on. Au Printemps also has a tourist discount card, offering a flat 10% discount. Behind the store is a branch of the discount clothing/grocery store **Monoprix.** 64 bd. Haussmann, 9th arr. ℰ 01-42-82-50-00. Mon–Wed and Fri–Sat 9:35am–7pm, Thurs 9:35am–10pm. Métro: Havre-Caumartin. RER: Auber or Haussmann St-Lazare.

Colette   Named after the still controversial great French writer, Colette is a swank citadel for *à la mode* fashion. It buzzes with excitement, displaying fashions by some of the city's most promising young talents, including Marni and Lucien Pellat-Finet. This is for the sophisticated, upmarket shopper who'd never be caught dead shopping the Galeries Lafayette and the like. Not to be overlooked are home furnishings by designers like Tom Dixon and even zany Japanese accessories. Even if you don't plan to buy anything from the department store, patronize the tea salon, with its fresh quiches, salads, and cakes, plus three-dozen brands of bottled water. 213 rue St-Honoré, 1st arr. ℰ 01-55-35-33-90. Mon–Sat 10:30am–7:30pm. Métro: Tuileries or Pyramide.

Galeries Lafayette   Opened in 1896, with a lobby capped by an early-1900s stained glass cupola classified as a historic monument, Galeries Lafayette is Europe's largest department store. If you have time for only one Paris department store, make it this one. This store could practically provision a small city with everything from perfume to fashion. It is more user-friendly than even Au Printemps, and in fashion it places more emphasis on young and upcoming designers. It also concentrates on an upscale roster of everything you'd need to furnish and maintain a home; thousands of racks of clothing for men, women, and children; and a staggering array of cosmetics, makeup products, and perfumes. Menswear is concentrated in a section called **Lafayette Hommes;** also in the complex is **Lafayette Gourmet,** one of the fanciest grocery stores in Paris, selling culinary exotica at prices usually lower than those at Fauchon (see "Food"). A floor above street level is a concentration of high-end semi-independent boutiques, including Cartier, Vuitton, and Prada Sport. A fashion show is held at least once daily, usually in the grand **Salon Opéra.** At the street-level **Welcome Desk,** you can be told in many languages where you can find this or that in the store, where you can get a taxi back to your hotel, and so on. 40 bd. Haussmann, 9th arr. ℰ 01-42-82-34-56. Mon–Wed and Fri–Sat 9:30am–6:45pm, Thurs 9:30am–9pm. Métro: Chaussée d'Antin. RER: Auber.

FABRICS

Souleiado   This is the only Paris branch of one of Provence's most successful purveyors of the bright fabrics and thick pottery of France's southern tier.

Fabrics are carefully measured out here by scissors-wielding saleswomen, then sold by the meter for seamstresses to whip into curtains, tablecloths, or whatever. There's also rack after rack of *prêt-à-poser* ("ready-to-hang") curtains, tablecloths, and bedcovers, each based on historically accurate reproductions of 18th-century prints as discovered in such cities as Avignon, Arles, and Marseille. In a separate shop just around the corner, at 78 rue de Seine (same phone), there are displays of table settings, housewares, and gift items, each reflecting the bright sunshine and colors (usually ochre, cerulean blue, and a strong medium green) of the *Midi*. 3 rue Lobineau, 6th arr. ℂ 01-43-54-62-25. Mon–Sat 10am–6pm. Métro: Odéon or Mabillon.

FASHION
CUTTING-EDGE CHIC

Azzedine Alaïa   Alaia, who became the darling of French fashion in the 1970s, is the man who put body consciousness back into Paris chic. If you can't afford the current collection, try the **stock shop** around the corner at 18 rue de Verrerie (ℂ **01-40-27-85-58**), where last year's leftovers are sold at serious discounts. Both outlets sell leather trench coats, knit dresses, pleated skirts, cigarette pants, belts, purses, and fashion accessories. 7 rue de Moussy, 4th arr. ℂ **01-42-72-19-19**. Mon–Sat 10am–7pm. Métro: Hôtel de Ville.

Courrèges   Don't look now: André Courrèges is hot again. Even those little white vinyl go-go boots and disco purses in silver metallic cloth are back. Courrèges's brings a humorous touch to 1970s retro, with bold color, plastic, and fun. There's another branch of his store in the **Carrousel du Louvre** mall (ℂ **01-40-15-05-85**). 40 rue François-Ier, 8th arr. ℂ **01-53-67-30-00**. Mon–Sat 10am–7pm. Métro: F. D. Roosevelt.

Hervé Leger   This creator of the Band Aid Dress *(La Robe à bandes)*, a tightly wrapped concoction of stretch materials and color, has opened his own shop for those with curves to flaunt and cash to burn. 29 rue du faubourg St-Honoré, 8th arr. ℂ **01-40-20-16-50**. Mon–Sat 10am–7pm. Métro: Concorde or Madeleine.

Jean-Charles de Castelbajac   Castelbajac is the bad boy of French fashion, known for flamboyant and amusing gear in primary colors, often with cryptic but evocative inscriptions. Examples are excerpts from novels and poems by Proust and Mallarmé and autobiographical snippets ("in 1968, I created my first overcoat, using a fabric similar to this one you see here"). His store is in a cluster of designer shops that's great for gawking. 26 rue Madame, 6th arr. ℂ **01-45-48-40-55**. Mon–Sat 10am–7pm. Métro: St-Sulpice.

Jean Paul Gaultier   Tucked in one of Paris's most famous passageways, this large boutique features the typical fare of this master punk turned tailor: street fashion made high fashion for men and women. A slightly newer branch of the store, featuring exactly the same inventory, is at 30 rue du faubourg St-Antoine, 12th arr. (ℂ **01-44-68-84-84;** Métro: Bastille). 6 rue Vivienne, 2nd arr. ℂ **01-42-86-05-05**. Mon–Fri 10am–7pm, Sat 11am–7pm. Métro: Bourse.

Lolita Lempicka   Lolita, formerly of the hidden Marais and the underground fashion scene, has gone mainstream with her own shop, tiny but quite visible, on this street of streets. The women's clothes continue to be inventive and creative and usually very sexy. 18 rue du faubourg St-Honoré, 8th arr. ℂ 01-45-02-14-46. Mon–Sat 10:30am–7pm. Métro: Concorde or Madeleine.

DESIGNER BOUTIQUES & FASHION FLAGSHIPS

There are two primary fields of dreams in Paris when it comes to showcasing the international big names: rue du faubourg St-Honoré and avenue Montaigne. Though the Left Bank is gaining in designer status with recent additions like Dior, Armani, and Vuitton, the heart of the international designer parade is on the Right Bank.

Rue du faubourg St-Honoré is so famously fancy it's simply known as "the Faubourg." It was the traditional miracle mile until recent years, when the really exclusive shops shunned it for the wider and even more deluxe avenue Montaigne at the other end of the arrondissement. (It's a long but pleasant walk from one fashion strip to the other.) **Avenue Montaigne** is filled with almost unspeakably fancy shops, but a few of them have affordable cafes (try Joseph at no. 14) and all have sales help that's almost always cordial to the well dressed.

The mix is quite international—from British (**Joseph**), to German (**Jil Sander**), to Italian (**Krizia**). **Chanel, Lacroix, Porthault, Ricci, Dior,** and **Ungaro** are a few of the big French names. Also check out some of the lesser-known creative powers that be. And don't miss a visit to **Caron.** Most of the designer shops sell men's and women's clothing. The Faubourg hosts other traditional favorites: **Hermès, Lanvin, Jaeger, Rykiel,** and the upstart **Façonnable,** which sells preppy men's clothing in the United States through a business deal with Nordstroms. Note that Lanvin has its own men's shop (**Lanvin Homme),** which has a cafe that's perfect for a light (and affordable) lunch.

Alain Figaret   Alain Figaret is one of France's foremost designers of men's shirts and women's blouses. Though this store has a broad range of fabrics, 100 percent cotton is its specialty. Also check out the silk neckties in distinctively designed prints and the silk scarves for women. If you're comparison shopping, Figaret and Charvet (below) are half a block apart. 21 rue de la Paix, 2nd arr. ℭ **01-42-65-04-99.** Mon–Sat 10am–7:30pm. Métro: Opéra.

Chanel   If you can't have the sun, the moon, and the stars, at least buy something with Coco Chanel's initials on it, either a serious fashion statement (drop-dead chic) or something fun and playful (tongue in chic). Karl Lagerfeld's designs come in all different flavors and have added a subtle twist to Chanel's classicism. This store is adjacent to the Chanel couture house and behind the Ritz, where Mlle Chanel once lived. Check out the beautiful staircase of the maison before you shop the two-floor boutique—it's well worth a peek. 31 rue Cambon, 1st arr. ℭ **01-42-86-28-00.** Mon–Sat 10am–7pm. Métro: Concorde or Madeleine.

Charvet   The duke of Windsor made Charvet famous, but Frenchmen of distinction have been buying their shirts here for years. The store offers ties, pocket squares, underwear, and pajamas as well, plus women's shirts, all custom-tailored or straight off the peg. 28 place Vendôme, 1st arr. ℭ **01-42-60-30-70.** Mon–Sat 9:45am–6:30pm. Métro: Opéra.

Christian Dior   This fashion house is set up like a small department store, selling men's, women's, and children's clothing, as well as affordable gift items, makeup, and perfume on the street level. For several years, cutting-edge Brit designer John Galliano has been in charge of the collections. Unlike some of the other big-name fashion houses, Dior is very approachable. 30–32 av. Montaigne, 8th arr. ℭ **01-40-73-54-44.** Mon–Sat 10am–7pm. Métro: F. D. Roosevelt.

Favourbrook   English taste and conservative style are the hallmarks of this upscale woodsy-looking store resembling a men's club. You'll find vests, dinner jackets, ascots, neckties, shirts, cummerbunds, and the kind of items that make super wedding gifts. Fashion accessories for women are available at its sibling store, **Violet,** also in Le Village Royal. Le Village Royal, 25 rue Royale, 8th arr. ✆ 01-40-17-06-72. Mon–Sat 10am–7pm. Métro: Concorde or Madeleine.

Givenchy   Opened in 1962 and noted for high-profile good taste often mentioned in annual lists of best-dressed women (particularly the late Audrey Hepburn), Givenchy still maintains a shop that makes couture clothes to order, and if that's what you're looking for, head a floor above street level. Otherwise, look for ready-to-wear clothing and accessories for men and women on the street level. (1) 3 av. George V, 8th arr. ✆ 01-44-31-50-00. Métro: Alma-Marceau. (2) 28 rue du faubourg St-Honoré, 8th arr. ✆ 01-42-65-54-54. Métro: F. D. Roosevelt. (3) 6 rue du Cherche-Midi, 6th arr. ✆ 01-42-65-03-37. Métro: Odéon. All three locations open Mon–Sat 10am–7pm.

Hermès   France's single most important status item is a scarf or tie from Hermès. Patterns on these illustrious scarves, retailing for about 1,500F (228€, $217.50), have recently included the galaxies, Africa, the sea, the sun, and horse racing and breeding. But the choices don't stop there—this large flagship store has beach towels and accessories, dinner plates, clothing for men and women, a large collection of Hermès fragrances, and even a saddle shop; a package of postcards is the least expensive item sold. Ask to see the private museum upstairs. Outside, note the horseman on the roof with his scarf-flag flying. 24 rue du faubourg St-Honoré, 8th arr. ✆ 01-40-17-47-17. Tues–Sat 10am–6:30pm, Mon 10am–1pm and 2:30–6:30pm. Métro: Concorde.

Louis Vuitton   This Left Bank store is so gorgeous, the famed merchandise becomes secondary. Not content to cover the world's luggage with his initials, Vuitton has branched into assorted colored leather goods, writing instruments, travel products, and even publishing. Look for the traditional collection of leather, including Vuitton's monogrammed brown-on-brown bags in printed canvas, on the street level. The mezzanine showcases upscale pens, writing supplies, and stationery. And the top floor carries the company's newest line of goods—women's shoes and bags. (1) 101 av. des Champs-Elysées, 8th arr. ✆ 01-53-57-24-00. Mon–Sat 10am–7pm. Métro: Georges V. (2) 6 place St-Germain-des-Prés, 6th arr. ✆ 01-45-49-62-32. Mon–Sat 10am–7pm. Métro: St-Germain-des-Prés.

Yves Saint Laurent Rive Gauche   The rue du faubourg St-Honoré branch sells the most upscale of the women's ready-to-wear clothing by the folk at Saint Laurent. Every season, the entire line is available for viewing here, and sales tend to be brisk. The two other outlets are somewhat smaller but still stocked with choice merchandise. If you're looking for menswear, head to **Yves Saint Laurent Rive Gauche Hommes,** 9 place St-Sulpice, 6th arr. (✆ 01-43-46-84-40; Métro: St-Sulpice). **Yves St-Laurent Haute Couture** is at 5 av. Marceau, 16th arr. (✆ 01-44-31-64-00; Métro: Alma-Marceau). (1) 38 rue du faubourg St-Honoré, 8th arr. ✆ 01-42-65-74-59. Métro: Concorde. (2) 6 place St-Sulpice, 6th arr. ✆ 01-43-29-43-00. Métro: St-Sulpice. (3) 19–21 av. Victor-Hugo, 16th arr. ✆ 01-45-00-64-64. Métro: Etoile or Victor Hugo. Hours at all stores are Mon 11am–7pm, Tues–Sat 10:30am–7pm.

VINTAGE COUTURE

Didier Ludot   Fashion historians salivate when they're confronted with an inventory of the *haute couture* of yesteryear. In this frenetically stylish shop, albeit at prices that rival what you'd expect to pay for a serious antique, you'll find a selection of gowns and dresses created between 1900 and 1980 for designing women who looked *faaabulous* at Maxim's, at chic cocktail parties on the

Avenue Foch, in Deauville, or wherever. Maintaining the same hours, and just across the courtyard enclosed by the Palais-Royal, is **Didier Ludot's Little Black Dress Shop,** where only cocktail dresses (specifically, *prêt-à-porter* black dresses, with their accessories) provide the kind of garment that might make any woman feel like Catherine Deneuve at her most alluring. Didier Ludot, 24 Galerie de Montpensier, in the arcades surrounding the courtyard of the Palais-Royal. 1st arr. ℰ 01-42-96-06-56. Didier Ludot's Little Black Dress Shop, 125 Galerie de Valois, across the courtyard, (ℰ 01-40-15-01-04). Hours at both stores: Mon–Sat 11am–7pm. Métro: Palais-Royal.

DISCOUNT & RESALE

Anna Lowe   This is one of the premier boutiques for the discriminating woman who wishes to purchase a little Chanel or Versace at a discount. Many clothes are runway samples; some have been gently worn. 104 rue du faubourg St-Honoré, 8th arr. ℰ 01-42-66-11-32. Mon–Sat 10am–7pm. Métro: Miromesnil.

Défilé des Marques   French TV stars often shop here, picking up St. Laurent, Dior, Lacroix, Prada, Hermès, and others at a fraction of the price, often half off. Yes, they sell discounted Hermès scarves as well. 171 rue de Grenelles, 7th arr. ℰ 01-45-55-63-47. Tues–Sat 10:30am–7pm. Métro: Latour-Maubourg.

L'Annex des Créateurs *Value*   This is the place where you go to stock up on last year's luxurious brands from the collection of Versace, Gabbana, Fred Sathal, Sophie Sitbon, and the like. All merchandise is discounted from 40% to 70%. 19 rue Godot de Mauroy, 9th arr. ℰ 01-42-65-43-40. Mon–Sat 10:30am–7pm. Métro: Madeleine or Aubert.

L'Une et L'Autre *Finds*   Hidden away in an apartment on the second floor of a building, this shop offers very luxurious clothing. You get the big brand names that sell in super-expensive 16th arrondissement boutiques at amazing discounts. For example, an item that might sell for 3,500F (532€, $507.50) in a boutique is sold here for 1,500F (228€, $217.50). We first accompanied a chic Parisian woman here who purchased a cashmere coat at one half its retail price. 24 rue Feydeau, 2nd arr. ℰ 01-44-76-03-03. Mon–Fri and first Sat of the month 11am–6pm. Métro: Saint-Paul.

Réciproque   Forget about serious bargains here but celebrate what could be your only opportunity to own designer clothing of this caliber—every major name is carried, along with shoes, accessories, menswear, and wedding gifts. Everything has been worn, but some items only on fashion runways or during photo shoots. 88–123 rue de la Pompe, 16th arr. ℰ 01-47-04-30-28. Tues–Fri 11am–7:30pm, Sat 10:30am–7:30pm. Métro: Rue de la Pompe.

SR Store   This is where great designer Sonia Rykiel dumps all that good stuff she didn't move in main-line boutiques. Everything is half price. You get some really good deals here. 64 rue Alésia, 14th arr. ℰ 01-43-95-06-13. Tues 11am–7pm, Wed–Sat 10:30am–7pm. Metro: Alésia.

Tati   Some of its fans define this place as a low-end version of Galeries Lafayettes, with lower prices and a lot less class. What you'll find is crowded display racks, indifferent service, and absolutely no emphasis on architectural finesse. Despite that, the place does a roaring business in, among others, sales of wedding dresses that range from bouffant to sleek. The displays sprawl over several floors of jumbled-up housewares, clothing, sportswear and sporting-goods equipment, and kitchenware. Genuine bargains can sometimes be culled from the maze. There are three locations: (1) 140 rue de Rennes, 6th arr. ℰ 01-45-48-68-31.

Food Markets

Outdoor food markets are plentiful in Paris. Some of the better-known ones are the **Marché Buci** (see "Markets"); the **rue Mouffetard market,** open Tuesday to Saturday from 9:30am to 1pm and 4 to 7pm and Sunday from 9:30am to 1pm (6th arr.; Métro: Monge or Censier-Daubenton); and the **rue Montorgueil market,** just behind the St-Eustache church, open Monday to Saturday from 9am to 7pm (1st arr.; Métro: Les Halles). The trendiest of the food markets is **Marché Biologique** along Boulevard Raspail, a tree-lined stretch lying between rue de Rennes and rue du Cherche-Midi, 6th arr. (Métro: Montparnasse). Even Parisian celebrities can be spotted shopping under brightly colored awnings among the stacks of organic dairy products, fish, seafood, and fresh fruits and vegetables sold by butchers, bakers, winemakers, and green grocers. You can also eat here, perhaps lured to a vendor from Brittany making whole-grain crêpes or one selling algae bread. Non-food items are also for sale. Do you own a doormat made from recycled tires? You can if you shop here.

Métro: Rennes. (2) 13 place de la République, 3rd arr. ✆ **01-48-87-72-81.** Métro: République. (3) 4 bd. Rochechouart, 18th arr. ✆ **01-55-29-50-00.** Métro: Barbés. Hours for all stores are Mon–Sat 10am–7:15pm.

FOOD: CHOCOLATE, HONEY, PÂTÉS & MORE

Albert Ménès   One of Paris's most prestigious small-scale purveyors of food-stuffs prides itself on selling only goods that have been picked, processed, and packaged by hand. The 45 producers represented supply sugared almonds, sardines, exotic honeys, terrines and pâtes, baked goods, and more. It's all esoteric, even by French standards. Ménès prides itself, strangely enough, on being the first food store in France to import both Heinz Ketchup and Kellogg's Corn Flakes, both of which appeared on shelves for the first time here in the 1920s. 41 bd. Malesherbes, 8th arr. ✆ **01-42-66-95-63.** Mon 2–7pm, Tues–Sat 10am–7pm. Métro: St-Augustin or Madeleine.

Christian Constant   Opened in 1970, Christian Constant sells some of Paris's most delectable chocolates at 490F (74.50€, $71.05) per kilo. Each is a blend of raw ingredients from Ecuador, Colombia, or Venezuela, usually mingled with scents of spices and flowers like orange blossoms, jasmine, the Asian blossom ylang, and vetiver and verveine (herbs usually made to brew tea). 37 rue d'Assas, 6th arr. ✆ **01-53-63-15-15.** Mon–Fri 8:30am–9pm, Sat–Sun 8am–8:30pm. Métro: St-Placide or Rennes.

Fauchon   At place de la Madeleine stands one of the city's most popular sights—not the church, but Fauchon, now a three-part shop crammed with gastronomical goodies perfect for picnics in your hotel room or *en plein air.* One shop sells dry goods; one sells candy, pastry, and bread; and one sells fresh fruits and veggies. A cafeteria and a coffee bar called Brasserie Fauchon are in the basement of one shop. Even though the prices are steep, it's easier than ever to pay for your goods: You're given an electronic card when you enter, and the value of each purchase is electronically encoded on it. When you finish shopping, head for the *caisse* (register), surrender the card, and pay the tally, then return to the counters to pick up your groceries.

Fauchon also offers a new tea salon, which showcases the talents of the great pâtissier Sébastien Gaudard. You'll fall in love with his looks and his *Paris-Brest,* a ring in the shape of a bicycle wheel loaded with pastery cream, almond praline, buttercream, and hazelnut paste capped with almond shards. 26–30 place de la Madeleine, 8th arr. (✆ **01-47-42-60-11.** Mon–Sat 9:30am–7pm. Métro: Madeleine or Auber.

Hédiard This 1850 temple of *haute gastronomie* has recently been completely renovated, perhaps to woo tourists away from nearby Fauchon. The decor is now a series of salons filled with almost Disneyesque displays meant to give the store the look of an early-1900s spice emporium. Upstairs, you can eat at the Restaurant de l'Epicerie. 21 place de la Madeleine, 8th arr. (✆ **01-43-12-88-77.** Mon–Sat 9am–11pm. Métro: Madeleine or Auber.

Jadis et Gourmande This small chain of Parisian chocolatiers has a less lofty rep than Christian Constant and much more reasonable prices. They're best known for their alphabetical chocolate blocks, which allow you to spell out any message you want (well . . . almost), in any language. *"Merci"* comes prepackaged. 27 rue Boissy d'Anglas, 8th arr. (✆ **01-42-65-23-23.** Mon 1–7pm, Tues–Fri 9:30am–7pm, Sat 10:30am–7pm. Métro: Madeleine.

Les Abeilles *(Finds* This store inventories a greater supply of French-derived honey than we've ever seen compiled into one boutique. Test your understanding of France's diverse geography by asking for honey that's culled from flowers in whatever region of the country you specify. And for a scented reminder of your trip to the City of Light, ask for "urban honey" that's derived from beehives within Paris and its suburbs. For a variety of reasons, this honey may be among the most desirable of all. Jean-Jacques Schakmundes is the storeowner and beekeeper. 21 rue de la Butte-aux-Cailles, 13th arr. (✆ **01-45-81-43-48.** Tues–Sat 11am–7pm. Métro: Porte d'Italie or Corvisart.

Maison de la Truffe This tiny shop resembles a New York deli more than a Parisian boutique. It's your source not only for truffles but also foie gras, caviar, and other gourmet foodstuffs. Gift food baskets are a house specialty. There are also a few tables and chairs so you can grab a quick bite. 19 place de la Madeleine, 8th arr. (✆ **01-42-65-53-22.** Tues–Sat 9am–9pm, Mon 9am–8pm. Métro: Madeleine or Auber.

Maison du Chocolat At its five Paris locations, this shop offers racks and racks of marvelous chocolates priced individually or by the kilo, at near or over 500F (76€, $72.50) per kilo. These stores offer a variety of chocolate-based products, including chocolate pastries, usually more affordable than the candy, and even chocolate milk! (1) 225 rue du faubourg St-Honoré, 8th arr. (✆ **01-42-27-39-44.** Métro: Ternes. (2) 52 rue François-Ier, 8th arr. (✆ **01-47-23-38-25.** Métro Alma-Marceau. (3) 8 bd. de la Madeleine, 8th arr. (✆ **01-47-42-86-52.** Métro: Madeleine. (4) 19 rue de Sèvres, 6th arr. (✆ **01-45-44-20-40.** Métro: Rue de Sèvres. (5) 89 av. Raymond-Poincaré, 16th arr. (✆ **01-40-67-77-83.** Métro: Victor Hugo. All locations open Feb–Apr Mon–Sat 10am–7:30pm; May–Oct Mon–Sat 10am–7pm; Nov–Jan Mon–Sat 9:30am–7:30pm.

Maison du Miel "The House of Honey" has been a family tradition since before World War I. The entire store is devoted to products made from honey: honey oil, honey soap, and various honeys to eat, including one made from heather. This store owes a tremendous debt to the busy bee. 24 rue Vignon, 9th arr. (✆ **01-47-42-26-70.** Tues–Sat 10am–7pm. Métro: Madeleine.

Marks & Spencer   Okay, so it's a British department store specializing in clothing for men, women, and children. But the entire ground floor is a giant supermarket devoted to the St. Michael's brand of English foodstuff and includes prepared foods for picnics. (1) 35 bd. Haussmann, 9th arr. ☎ 01-47-42-42-91. Mon, Wed, and Fri–Sat 9am–8pm; Tues 9:30am–8pm; Thurs 9am–9pm. Métro: Chausée d'Antin. (2) 88 rue de Rivoli, 4th arr. ☎ 01-44-61-08-00. Mon–Sat 10am–8pm. Métro: Hôtel de Ville.

Poilâne   One of Paris's best-loved bakeries, Poilâne hasn't changed much since it opened in 1932. Come here to taste and admire the beautiful loaves of bread decorated with simple designs of leaves and flowers that'll make you yearn for an all-but-disappeared Paris. Specialties include apple tarts, butter cookies, and a chewy sourdough loaf cooked in a wood-burning oven. Breads can be specially wrapped to stay fresh during your journey home. Cash only. (1) 8 rue du Cherche-Midi, 6th arr. ☎ 01-45-48-42-59. Mon–Sat 7:15am–8:15pm. Métro: St-Sulpice. (2) 49 bd. de Grenelle, 15th arr. ☎ 01-45-79-11-49. Tues–Sun 7:15am–8:15pm. Métro: Dupleix.

JEWELRY

Bijoux Burma   If you're feeling crestfallen because you can't afford any of the spectacular and spectacularly expensive bijoux at the city's world-famous jewelers, come here to console yourself with some of the best fakes anywhere. This quality costume jewelry is the secret weapon of many a Parisian woman. 50 rue François-ler, 8th arr. ☎ 01-47-23-70-93. Mon–Sat 10am–6:30pm. Métro: F. D. Roosevelt.

Cartier   One of the most famous jewelers in the world, Cartier has prohibitive prices to match its glamorous image. Go to gawk, and if your pockets are deep enough, pick up an expensive trinket. 7 place Vendôme, 1st arr. ☎ 01-44-55-32-50. Mon–Sat 10:30am–7pm. Métro: Opéra or Tuileries.

Van Cleef & Arpels   Years ago, Van Cleef's designers came up with an intricate technique that remains a vital part of its allure—the invisible setting, wherein a band of sparkling gemstones, each cut to interlock with its neighbor, creates an uninterrupted flash of brilliance. Come browse with the rich and famous. 22 place Vendôme, 1st arr. ☎ 01-53-45-45-45. Mon–Sat 10am–6:30pm. Métro: Opéra or Tuileries.

KITCHENWARE

A. Simon   This large kitchenware shop supplies restaurants and professional kitchens. But it will also cover your table with everything from menu cards and wine tags to knives, copper pots, and pans—not to mention white paper doilies and those funny little paper things they put on top of the tablecloth at bistros. 48 rue Montmartre, 2nd arr. ☎ 01-42-33-71-65. Tues–Sat 9am–6:30pm; Mon 1:30–6:30pm. Métro: Les Halles.

Dehillerin   Dehillerin is Paris's most famous cookware shop, located in the "kitchen corridor," alongside A. Simon (above) and several other kitchenware stores. The shop has more of a professional feel to it than beginner-friendly A. Simon, but don't be intimidated. Equipped with the right tools from Dehillerin, you too can learn to cook like a master chef. 18 rue Coquillière, 1st arr. ☎ 01-42-36-53-13. Tues–Sat 9am–6pm, Mon 8am–12:30pm and 2–6pm. Métro: Les Halles.

LEATHER GOODS

Lamarthe   A cult hero in France yet virtually unknown elsewhere, this designer is famous for his handbags and small leather goods in funky fashion shades like melon and mint. Sure, he does more conservative colors like navy and black, but if you want the world to know you've been to Paris and you're totally *branché* (plugged in), spring for a risqué shade. 219 rue St-Honoré, 1st arr. ℂ **01-42-96-09-90.** Mon–Sat 10am–7pm. Métro: Tuileries.

Longchamp Longchamp is a French brand known for high-quality leather and strong everyday durables that come in basic as well as fashion shades. Check out its pale-pink or steel-colored patent leather for a touch of Paris. The best bet is a series of nylon handbags attached to leather handles that fold for storage or travel and unfold for shopping. Items are priced according to size but begin at around 483F (73€, $70). 404 rue St-Honoré, 1st arr. ℂ **01-43-16-00-12.** Mon–Sat 10am–7pm. Métro: Concorde or Madeleine.

Morabito While Hermès has the international rep, Morabito is the secret insider's source for chicer-than-thou handbags that begin at a bare minimum of 2,000F (304€, $290) and quickly climb to 35,000F (5,320€, $5,075) and more. 55 rue François-Ier, 8th arr. ℂ **01-53-23-90-40.** Mon–Sat 10am–7pm. Métro: F. D. Roosevelt or George V.

LINGERIE

Cadolle Herminie Cadolle invented the brassiere in 1889. Today the store she founded is managed by her family, and they still make the specialty brassieres for the Crazy Horse Saloon. This is the place to go if you want made-to-order items or are hard to fit. 14 rue Cambon, 1st arr. ℂ **01-42-60-38-37.** Mon–Sat 9:30am–1pm and 2–6:30pm. Métro: Concorde.

Marie-Claude Fremau The French are big on shops that sell towels and bathrobes as well as underwear. Naturally, French bathroom wear has flair and style—we're talking about a yellow silk bathrobe with a ruffled collar for about 2,069F (314F, $300). (1) 9 rue Broca, 5th arr. ℂ **01-43-37-85-70.** Mon–Sat 10am–7pm. Métro: Opéra. (2) 104 rue de Rennes, 6th arr. ℂ **01-45-48-82-76.** Mon–Fri 10am–7pm, Sat 10:30am–7:30pm. Métro: Rennes.

Nikita This is the discount sales outlet for all the big names in lingerie, including Bolero, Lise Charmel, Lejaby, Simone Pérèle, and Aubade. Most of the lingerie sold here is half the price of its counterparts in Right Bank boutiques. 22 rue Levis, 7th arr. ℂ **01-42-12-01-30.** Mon–Sat 9:30am–2pm. Métro: Villiers.

Sabbia Rosa Everything here is filmy, flimsy, silky, and sexy. Look for undergarments (slips, brassieres, and panties) and the kind of négligées that might've been favored by Brigitte Bardot in *And God Created Woman*. Madonna has been spotted here shopping for panties that can go as high as $400. 73 rue des Sts-Pères, 6th arr. ℂ **01-45-48-88-37.** Mon–Sat 10am–7pm. Métro: Sèvres-Babylone or St-Germain.

MALLS

Carrousel du Louvre If you want to combine an accessible location, a fun food court, handy boutiques, and plenty of museum gift shops with a touch of culture, don't miss the Carrousel. Always mobbed, this is one of the few venues allowed to open on Sunday. There's a Virgin Megastore, a branch of The Body Shop, and several other emporiums for conspicuous consumption. Check out Diane Claire for the fanciest souvenirs of Paris you've ever seen. 99 rue de Rivoli, 1st arr. No phone. Tues–Sun 10am–8pm. Métro: Palais Royal or Musée du Louvre.

Forum des Halles Once the site of Paris's great produce market, Les Halles is now a vast crater of modern metal with layers of boutiques built around a courtyard. There's one of everything here, but the feel is very sterile, without a hint of the famous French *joie de vivre*. 1–7 rue Pierre-Lescot, 1st arr. No phone. Mon–Sat 10am–7:30pm. Métro: Etienne-Marcel or Châtelet–Les Halles.

Les Trois Quartiers   Named after the junction of the three neighborhoods (Madeleine, Opéra, and Concorde) where it sits, this is a mall of at least 15 upscale boutiques specializing in clothing, perfume, and cosmetics for men and women. The largest is Madelios, a menswear store that stocks Yves Saint Laurent, Ralph Lauren, and Hugo Boss, among others. 23 bd. de la Madeleine, 1st arr. ℂ 01-42-97-80-06. Mon–Sat 10am–7pm. Métro: Madeleine.

Marché St-Germain   The Marché St-Germain used to be an open-air food market until it was transformed into a modern shopping mall. Now only a few food and vegetable stalls remain in one corner—the rest of the market is dominated by low ceilings, neon lights, and mostly American and British chain stores like Kitchen Bazaar and Kenzo. 14 rue Lobineau, 6th arr. No phone. Mon–Sat 11am–7pm. Métro: Odéon.

Montparnasse Shopping Centre   This shopping center is sort of a quick fix minimall in a business center and hotel (Le Meredien) complex, with a small branch of Galeries Lafayette and some inexpensive boutiques. Visiting it is really worthwhile only if you also take a trip across the street to Inno, with its deluxe supermarket in the basement. Between rue de l'Arrivée and 22 rue du Départ, 14th arr. No phone. Mon–Sat 8:30am–10pm. Métro: Montparnasse-Bienvenue.

Palais des Congrès de Paris Boutiques   A shopping center for convention-goers inside the Palais des Congrès, this mall offers some 50 shops, including branch stores of many French big names. You'll also find a Japanese department store and hairdresser. Its anonymity and distance from most of touristy Paris has taken its toll on some of the shops, but if you happen to be in the neighborhood, it might be useful. 2 place de la Porte-Maillot, 17th arr. No phone. Mon–Sat 10am–7pm. Métro: Porte Maillot.

MARKETS

Marché aux Fleurs   Artists and photographers love to capture the Flower Market on canvas or film. The stalls are ablaze with color, and each is a showcase of flowers, most of which escaped the perfume factories of Grasse on the French Riviera. The Flower Market is along the Seine, behind the Tribunal de Commerce. On Sunday it becomes the **Marché aux Oiseaux** (Bird Market). Place Louis-Lépine, Ile de la Cité, 4th arr. No phone. Daily 8:30am–4pm. Métro: Cité.

Marché aux Livres   This charming two-building market for used books, old books, rare books, and some ephemera is slightly in the middle of nowhere but nonetheless thronged by serious collectors. The market is covered, but open, and doesn't close on a rainy day—the really valuable texts are draped in plastic. (For more books, don't forget the *bouquinistes* along the left bank of the Seine, on quai de Montebello.) Square Georges-Brancion, 15th arr. No phone. Sat–Sun 10am–4pm in winter, 10am–6pm in summer. Métro: Porte de Vanves.

Marché aux Puces de la Porte de Vanves   This weekend event sprawls along two streets and is actually the best flea market in Paris—dealers swear by it. There's little in terms of formal antiques and few large pieces of furniture. You'll do better if you collect old linens, used Hermès scarves, toys, ephemera, costume jewelry, perfume bottles, and bad art. Asking prices tend to be high, as dealers prefer to sell to nontourists. On Sunday, there's a food market one street over. Av. Georges-Lafenestre, 14th arr. No phone. Sat–Mon 6:30am–4:30pm. Métro: Porte de Vanves.

Marché aux Puces St-Ouen de Clignancourt   Paris's most famous flea market is actually a grouping of more than a dozen flea markets—a complex of

2,500 to 3,000 open stalls and shops on the northern fringe of the city, selling everything from antiques to junk, from new to vintage clothing. The market begins with stalls of cheap clothing along avenue de la Porte de Clignancourt. As you proceed, various streets will tempt you. Hold on until you get to rue des Rosiers, then turn left. Vendors start bringing out their offerings around 9am and start taking them in around 6pm. Hours are a tad flexible depending on weather and crowds. Monday is traditionally the best day for bargain seekers, because the market is more sparsely attended, and the merchants are more eager to sell.

First-timers always want to know two things: "Will I get any real bargains?" and "Will I get fleeced?" Actually, it's all relative. Obviously, the best buys have been skimmed by dealers (who often have a prearrangement to have items held for them). And it's true that the same merchandise displayed here will sell for less in the provinces. But from the point of view of the visitor who has only a few days to spend in Paris—and only half a day for shopping—the flea market is worth the experience. Vintage French postcards, old buttons, and bistro ware are quite affordable; each market has its own personality and an aura of Parisian glamour you can't find elsewhere.

Dress casually and show your knowledge if you're a collector. Most dealers are serious and get into the spirit of things only if you speak French or make it clear you know what you're doing. The longer you stay, the more you chat, the more you show your respect for the goods, the more room you'll have for negotiating the price. Most of the markets have rest-room facilities; some have central offices to arrange shipping. Cafes, pizza joints, and even a few real restaurants are scattered around. Beware of pickpockets and teenage troublemakers. Av. de la Porte de Clignancourt, 18th arr. No phone. Sat–Mon 9am–7pm. Métro: Porte de Clignancourt (turn left and cross bd. Ney, then walk north on av. de la Porte Montmartre). Bus: 56, 85, 155, or 166.

Marché aux Timbres   This is where Audrey Hepburn figured it out in *Charade*, remember? At this stamp collector's paradise, nearly two-dozen stalls are set up on a permanent basis under shady trees on the eastern edge of the Rond-Point. The variety of stamps is almost unlimited—some common, some quite rare. Av. Matignon, off the Champs-Elysées at Rond-Point, 8th arr. No phone. Generally Thurs–Sun 10am–7pm. Métro: F. D. Roosevelt or Champs-Elysées–Clemenceau.

Marché Buci   This traditional French food market is held at the intersection of two streets and is only a block long, but what a block it is! Seasonal fruits and vegetables dance across tabletops as chickens spin on the rotisserie. One stall is entirely devoted to big bouquets of fresh flowers. Monday mornings are light. Rue de Buci, 6th arr. No phone. Daily 9am–7pm. Métro: St-Germain-des-Prés.

MUSEUM SHOPS

La Boutique de la Comédie Française   This is the official gift/souvenir shop of France's most historic and prestigious theater. The plays commemorated inside have elicited in the French as much emotion and loyalty as Shakespeare has in the British. Look for plates and cups depicting 18th-century misers, maidens, and faithful servants, as well as scarves, pens, drinking glasses, and napkins honoring the French theater. You might appreciate the beer mugs *(les chopes)* emblazoned with the frontispiece of Molière's original folio for *Le Bourgeois Gentilhomme*. The gift shop remains open in August, when the theater is closed. 2 rue de Richelieu, 1st arr. ✆ 01-44-58-14-30. Daily 11am–8:30pm. Métro: Palais Royal.

La Boutique du Musée de la Monnaie   Jewelry made from coins and/or semiprecious stones, reproductions of antique coins, and medallions of every imaginable sort are sold here. If your tastes and interests involve small, cunning, and valuable objects, this might be the place for you. 11 quai de Conti (entrance at 2 rue Guénégaud), 6th arr. (C) 01-40-46-55-35. Tues–Fri 11am–5:30pm, Sat noon–5:30pm. Métro: Pont Neuf or Odéon.

La Boutique du Musée des Arts Décoratifs   This two-part boutique is divided by the entryway to the museum. On the right is a fabulous bookstore. On the left is a boutique selling reproductions of museum items: gifts, knickknacks, and even a custom-made Hermès scarf. In the Palais du Louvre, 105 rue de Rivoli, 1st arr. (C) 01-42-61-04-02. Thurs–Tues 10am–7pm, Wed 10am–9pm. Métro: Palais Royal or Tuileries.

Musée et Compagnie   This shop contains a selection of reproductions of originals contained in France's 20 *Musées Nationaux,* including the Louvre, the Musée d'Orsay, the Grand Palais, and the Musée Picasso. Prices range from 100F (15.20€, $14.50) for a pair of ear clips to as much as 3,000F (456€, $435) for a reproduction of an object from Greek, Assyrian, or Roman antiquity. It's useful to check out the larger inventories of roughly equivalent merchandise at the sibling shop, the **Musée Halles,** Forum des Halles, Porte-Berger Niveau-2, 2nd arr. ((C) **01-40-39-92-21;** Métro: Halles), open Monday to Saturday from 10:30am to 7:30pm. 49 rue Etienne-Marcel, 1st arr. (C) 01-40-13-49-13. Mon–Sat 10am–6:30pm. Métro: Etienne-Marcel.

Printemps Design   This shop's designers liken its merchandise to what's in the MOMA gift shop in New York City. Loosely associated with Le Printemps department store (but without the clothing), it features a frequently changing roster of stylish art objects and gift items. Many of the pieces are the work of well-known masters of their craft, like Phillippe Starck, Ron Arad, and the four-woman French design team known as Tse-Tse. In the Centre Pompidou, 19 rue Beaubourg, 4th arr. (C) 01-44-78-15-78. Sat–Thurs 11am–10pm. Métro: Hôtel de Ville.

MUSIC

FNAC   This is a large chain of music and bookstores known for its wide selection and discounted prices. There are eight branches in Paris, with the largest being at 136 rue de Rennes, Montparnasse. (1) 136 rue de Rennes, 6th arr. (C) 01-49-54-30-00. Mon–Sat 10am–7:30pm. Métro: St-Placide. (2) 109 rue St-Lazare, 9th arr. (C) 01-55-31-20-00. Same hours as first location. Métro: St-Lazare. (3) 74 av. des Champs-Elysées, 8th arr. (C) 01-53-53-64-64. Daily noon–midnight. Métro: St-Lazare. (4) Forum des Halles, 1–7 rue Pierre-Lescot, 1st arr. (C) 01-40-41-40-00. Mon–Sat 10am–7:30pm. Métro: Châtelet–Les Halles.

Virgin Megastore   Paris has three branches of Europe's biggest and most widely publicized tape, CD, and record store. The Champs-Elysées branch is the city's largest music store; a bookstore and cafe are downstairs. The store's opening in a landmark building helped rejuvenate the avenue. You'll also find a Virgin Megastore at each airport. (1) 52–60 av. des Champs-Elysées, 8th arr. (C) 01-49-53-50-00. Mon–Sat 10am–midnight, Sun noon–midnight. Métro: F. D. Roosevelt. (2) Carrousel du Louvre, 99 rue de Rivoli, 1st arr. No phone. Tues–Sun 10am–8pm. Métro: Palais Royal or Musée du Louvre. (3) Gare Montparnasse, Level A, bd. de la Montparnasse, 6th arr. (C) 01-45-38-06-06. Mon–Thurs 7am–8:30pm, Fri 7am–9pm, Sat 7am–8pm. Métro: Montparnasse.

PERFUME & MAKEUP (DISCOUNT)

Catherine (Value)   This family-owned shop sells an impressive stock of all the big-name perfumes and cosmetics at discounts of 20% to 25%. In addition, its paperwork is usually extremely well-organized, allowing refunds of the value-added tax (VAT) to be cleared quickly through Customs. Many of the staff speak

The Scent of a Parisian

If there's one thing international shoppers come to Paris for, it's cosmetics—after all, the City of Light is the world capital of fragrances and beauty supplies. These are a few of our favorite perfume and makeup shops:

While you can buy **Parfums Caron** scents in any duty-free or discount *parfumerie,* it's worth visiting the source of some of the world's most famous perfumes. The tiny shop is at 34 av. Montaigne, 8th arr. (© **01-47-23-40-82;** Métro: F. D. Roosevelt), boasting old-fashioned glass beakers filled with fragrances and a hint of yesteryear. Fleur de Rocaille, a Caron scent, was the featured perfume in the movie *Scent of a Woman.* Store hours are Monday to Saturday from 10am to 6:30pm.

While there are other branches and you can test Goutal bathroom amenities at many upscale hotels, the sidewalk mosaic tile and the unique scents make the **Annick Goutal,** at 14 rue Castiglione, 1st arr. (© **01-42-60-52-82;** Métro: Concorde), worth stopping by. Try Eau d'Hadrien for a unisex splash of citrus and summer. Store hours are Monday to Saturday from 10am to 7pm.

Off a small courtyard halfway between place de la Madeleine and the Champs-Elysées, **Makeup Forever,** 5 rue de la Boetie, 8th arr. (© **01-42-66-01-60;** Métro: St-Augustin), is where French models and actors go for their makeup. They also have fashion sunglasses at reasonable prices. The outlet was created by French stylist/entrepreneur Dany Sanz in 1984 and now maintains branches in New York and throughout the world. Check out the accessories, like suitcases, purses, and small travel kits ranging from 100 to 3,000F (15.20 to 456€, $14.50 to $435). Store hours are Monday to Saturday from 10am to 7pm.

If you think you've heard of every perfume and aromatherapy gimmick out there, this one will still impress you: At the very new-age **Octée,** 18 rue des Quatre-Vents, 6th arr. (© **01-46-33-18-77;** Métro: Odéon), the collection of fragrances is color-coded to match your personality, skin type, and mood. There are perfumes, sprays, soaps, and body lotions, and you test everything on colored ribbons. Store hours are Tuesday to Saturday from 11am to 7pm.

Shiseido, the world's fourth-largest maker of cosmetics and skincare goods, has become more prominent thanks to the merchandising efforts of the beautiful **Salons du Palais Royal Shiseido,** 142 Galerie de Valois, Palais Royal, 1 arr. (© **01-49-27-09-09;** Métro: Palais Royal). In addition to an awesome array of skin-care products and makeup, it stocks over two-dozen exclusive fragrances created by the company's artistic director, Serge Lutens. Don't be afraid to wander in and ask for some scent strips.

English. 7 rue Castiglione, 1st arr. © **01-42-61-02-89.** Tues–Sat 9am–7pm; Mon 10:30am–7pm. Métro: Concorde or Tuileries.

Freddy Parfums   The discounts here are fabulous: up to 40% on perfumes, handbags, cosmetics, silk scarves, and neckties. Freddy of Paris is near American

Express and the Opéra. 3 rue Scribe, 9th arr. ☎ **01-47-42-63-41**. Mon–Fri 9am–7pm, Sat 9:30am–6pm. Métro: Opéra.

Maki   You get some of the best deals in cosmetics and makeup here. In fact, it's the place where French actors and many models come for quality makeup products at discounted prices. The shop lies in the middle of a theater area. The staff will often give you advice about makeup. 9 rue Mansart, 9th arr. ☎ **01-42-81-33-76**. Tues–Sat 11am–1pm and 2:30–6:30pm. Metro: Blanche.

Parfumerie du Havre   This shop offers good discounts, depending on the brand (10% on Chanel, 30% on Sisley). There are tons of fragrances and a few designer accessories in this bright, modern, chic shop. Discounts are included in the prices as marked. 15 place du Havre, 8th arr. ☎ **01-43-87-35-15**. Mon–Sat 10:30am–7:30pm. Métro: St-Lazare.

SOUVENIRS & GIFTS

Au Nom de la Rose   Everything sold here is coming up roses. Inventories include home accessories, fashion accessories, perfumes, scented candles and soaps, and gift items that re-create the spirit of Valentine's Day year-round. Attached to the shop is a florist open Monday to Saturday from 9am to 9pm and Sunday from 9am to 2pm. 46 rue du Bac, 7th arr. ☎ **01-42-22-22-12**. Mon–Sat 10am–7:30pm. Métro: Rue du Bac.

Axis   If you're looking for a set of dinner plates imprinted with the cartoon character TinTin or a Philippe Starck chrome spider lemon press, head here to check out the wonderfully offbeat assortment of contemporary gifts. The stock is generally both cheap and very original. (1) 14 rue Lobineau, Marché St-Germain, 6th arr. ☎ 01-43-29-66-23. Mon–Sat 10am–8pm. Métro: Mabillon. (2) 13 rue de Charonne, 11th arr. ☎ 01-48-06-79-10. Tues–Sat noon–8pm. Métro: Bastille.

Galerie Architecture Miniature Gault   This store features Lilliputian town models complete with houses, stores, and fountains—miniature versions of French country villages and Parisian neighborhoods, all built to scale. A hand-painted ceramic depiction of a house or French national monument ranges from 65 to 4,000F (9.90 to 608€, $9.45 to $580), depending on its size and intricacy. 206 rue de Rivoli, 1st arr. ☎ 01-42-60-51-17. Mon–Sat 10am–7pm, Sun 11am–7pm. Métro: Tuileries.

La Tuile à Loup   This emporium has been selling authentic examples of all-French handcrafts since around 1975, making a name for itself through its concentration of authentic hand-produced woven baskets, cutlery, and wood-carvings. Especially appealing are the hand-painted crockery and charming stoneware from traditional manufacturers like Quimper and Lunéville and from small-scale producers in the Savoie Alps and Alsace. 35 rue Daubenton, 5th arr. ☎ 01-47-07-28-90. Mon 1–7pm, Tues–Sat 10:30am–7:30pm. Métro: Censier-Daubenton.

STATIONERY

Cassegrain   Nothing says elegance more than thick French stationery and note cards. Cassegrain offers beautifully engraved stationery, most often in traditional patterns, and business cards engraved to order. Several other items for the desk, many suitable for gifts, are for sale as well; there are even affordable pencils and small desktop accessories. 422 rue St-Honoré, 8th arr. ☎ 01-42-60-20-08. Mon–Sat 10am–7pm. Métro: Concorde.

TABLEWARE

Conran Shop   This shop might remind you of an outpost of the British Empire, valiantly imposing Brit aesthetics and standards on the French-speaking world. Inside, you'll find articles for the kitchen and dining room, glass and crystal vases, fountain pens and stationery, reading material and postcards, and even a selection of chocolates, teas, and coffees to help warm up a foggy English day. (1) 117 rue du Bac, 7th arr. ℭ **01-42-84-10-01.** Mon–Fri 10am–7pm, Sat 10am–8pm. Métro: Sèvres-Babylone. (2) 30 bd. des Capucines, 9th arr. ℭ **01-53-43-29-00.** Mon–Sat 10am–7:30pm. Métro: Madeleine.

Geneviève Lethu   This Provençal designer has shops all over France, with 19 others in and around Paris, all selling her clever and colorful Pottery-Barn-meets-French-Mediterranean tableware. The rue de Rennes branch is the largest, with the rue de Vaugirard branch runner-up. Newer designs stress influences from India, South America, and Africa as well. Energy, style, and verve are rampant here. The prices are moderate. 95 rue de Rennes, 6th arr. ℭ **01-45-44-40-35.** Mon–Sat 10am–7pm. Métro: St-Sulpice. (2) 317 rue de Vaugirard, 15th arr. ℭ **01-45-31-77-84.** Mon–Sat 10:15am–7pm. Métro: Convention.

WINES

Les Caves Taillevent   This is a temple to the art of making fine French wine. Associated with one of Paris's grandest restaurants, nearby Taillevent, it occupies the street level and cellar of an antique building. Stored here are more than half a million bottles of wine, ranging from 26F (3.95€, $3.75) to exceptionally rare vintages like a 1995 Romani-Conti Burgundy (Côtes de Nuit) at 22,000F (3,344€, $3,190). 199 rue du faubourg St-Honoré, 8th arr. ℭ **01-45-61-14-09.** Mon 2–8pm, Tues–Fri 9am–8pm, Sat 9am–7:30pm. Métro: Charles de Gaulle–Etoile or Ternes.

Nicholas *Value*   The flagship store of this boutique chain, with more than 110 branches in and around Paris, offers very fair prices for bottles you might not be able to find in the States. Aside from the usual Bordeaux and Burgundies, look at some of the rarer regional wines, like Gewürztraminer from Alsace, Collioure from Languedoc-Rousillon, and the pricey but sublime Côte Rotie from the Côtes du Rhône outside Lyon. 31 place de la Madeleine, 8th arr. ℭ **01-42-68-00-16.** Métro: Madeleine.

10

Paris After Dark

When darkness falls, the City of Light certainly lives up to its name—all the monuments and bridges are illuminated, and the glow of old-fashioned and modern street lamps, the blaze of sidewalk cafe windows, and the glare of huge neon signs flood the avenues and boulevards. Parisians start the serious part of their evenings just as Anglos stretch, yawn, and announce it's time for bed. Once a Paris workday is over, most people go straight to a cafe to meet with friends over a drink and perhaps a meal (see "The Top Cafes" in chapter 6); then they may head home or proceed to a restaurant or the theater; and much later they may grace a nightclub, a bar, or a disco.

In this chapter, we describe Paris's many after-dark diversions—from attending a Molière play at the Comédie-Française to catching a can-can show at the Moulin Rouge to sipping a sidecar at Harry's New York Bar to partying at Le Queen with all the boys.

1 The Performing Arts

LISTINGS   Announcements of shows, concerts, and operas are plastered on kiosks all over town. You'll find listings in the weekly *Pariscope,* an entertainment guide with a section in English, or the English-language bimonthly *Boulevard.* Performances start later in Paris than in London or New York—from 8 to 9pm—and Parisians tend to dine after the theater. You may not want to do the same, because many of the less-expensive restaurants close as early as 9pm.

TICKETS   There are many ticket agencies in Paris, most of them near the Right Bank hotels. *Avoid them if possible.* You can buy the cheapest tickets at the box office of the theater itself or at discount ticket agencies that sell tickets for cultural events and plays at discounts of up to 50%. One is the **Kiosque Théâtre,** 15 place de la Madeleine, 8th arr. (no phone; Métro: Madeleine), offering leftover tickets for about half price on the performance day. Tickets for evening shows are sold Tuesday to Friday from 12:30 to 8pm and Saturday from 2 to 8pm. Tickets for matinees are sold Saturday from 12:30 to 2pm and Sunday from 12:30 to 4pm. Other branches are in the basement of the Châtelet–Les Halles Métro station and in front of Gare Montparnasse.

Students with ID can often get last-minute tickets by applying at the box office an hour before curtain time.

Of course, the most effortless way to get tickets, especially if you're staying in a first-class or deluxe hotel, is to ask your concierge to arrange them. This is also the most expensive way and a service fee is added, but it's a heck of a lot easier if you don't want to waste precious hours in Paris trying to secure tickets, often hard-to-get ones.

Tips **A Stateside Ticket Agency**

Selling tickets to just about any Paris show, **Globaltickets** has an office in the States at 1270 Ave. of the Americas, Suite 2414, New York, NY 10020 (℃ **800/223-6108** or 914/328-2150; www.globaltickets.com). The Paris office is at 19 rue des Mathurins, 9th arr. (℃ **01-42-65-39-21;** Métro: Havre-Caumartin). A personal visit isn't necessary. The company will mail tickets to your home, fax you a confirmation, or leave tickets at the box office in Paris. There's a markup of 10% to 20% (excluding opera and ballet) over box-office prices, plus a U.S. handling charge of $8. Hotel-and-theater packages are also available.

For easy availability of tickets for festivals, concerts, and the theater, try one of these locations of the **FNAC** record store chain: 136 rue de Rennes, 6th arr. (℃ **01-49-54-30-00;** Métro: Montparnasse-Bienvenue), or in the Forum des Halles, 1–7 rue Pierre-Lescot, 1st arr. (℃ **01-40-41-40-00;** Métro: Châtelet–Les Halles).

THEATER

Comédie-Française Those with even a modest understanding of French can still delight in a sparkling production of Molière at this national theater, established to keep the classics alive and promote the most important contemporary authors. Nowhere else will you see the works of Molière and Racine so beautifully staged. The box office is open daily from 11am to 6pm, but the hall is dark mid-July to early September. In 1993, a Left Bank annex was launched, the **Comédie Française–Théâtre du Vieux-Colombier,** 21 rue du Vieux-Colombier, 4th arr. (℃ **01-44-39-87-00**). Though its repertoire varies, it's known for presenting some of the most serious French dramas in town. Tickets are 160F (24.30€, $23.20) or 65F (9.90€, $9.45) age 26 and under. Discounts are available if you reserve in advance. 2 rue de Richelieu, 1st arr. ℃ **01-44-58-15-15.** Tickets 70–190F (10.65–28.90€, $10.15–$27.55). Métro: Palais Royal or Musée du Louvre.

OPERA, DANCE & CLASSICAL CONCERTS

Cité de la Musique This testimony to the power of music has been the most widely applauded, the least criticized, and the most innovative of late François Mitterrand's half-dozen *grands projets*. At the city's northeastern edge in what used to be a run-down and depressing neighborhood, this $120-million stone-and-glass structure incorporates a network of concert halls, a library and research center for the study of all kinds of music, and a museum (see "Specialty Museums" in chapter 7). The complex hosts a rich variety of concerts, ranging from Renaissance music through 19th- and 20th-century works, including jazz and traditional music from nations around the world. 221 av. Jean-Jaurès, 19th arr. ℃ **01-44-84-45-00,** or 01-44-84-44-84) for tickets. Tickets 80–200F (12.15–30.40€, $11.60–$29) for 4:30 and 8pm concerts.

Musée de Radio France This is the site of many of the performances of the **Orchestre Philharmonique de Radio France** and the somewhat more conservative **Orchestre National de France.** The concert hall's box office is open Monday to Saturday from 11am to 6pm. 116 av. Président-Kennedy, 16th arr. ℃ **01-56-49-21-80.** Tickets 25F (3.80€, $3.65). Métro: Passy-Ranelagh.

Opéra Bastille   This controversial building—it has been called a "beached whale"—was designed by Canadian architect Carlos Ott, with curtains by Japanese designer Issey Miyake. Since the house's grand opening in July 1989 for the French Revolution's bicentennial, the Opera National de Paris has presented works like Mozart's *Marriage of Figaro* and Tchaikovsky's *Queen of Spades*. The main hall is the largest of any French opera house, with 2,700 seats, but music critics have lambasted the acoustics. The building contains two other concert halls, including an intimate 250-seat room that usually hosts chamber music. Both traditional opera performances and symphony concerts are presented here, as well as both classical and modern dance. Several concerts are given for free in honor of certain French holidays. Write ahead for tickets. Place de la Bastille, 120 rue de Lyon. © **01-43-43-96-96.** Tickets 60–670F (9.10–101.85€, $8.70–$97.15) opera, 60–660F (9.10–100.30€, $8.70–$95.70) dance. Métro: Bastille.

Opéra Comique   This is a particularly charming venue for light opera, on a smaller scale than Paris's major opera houses. Built in the late 1890s in an ornate style that might remind you of the Opéra Garnier, it's the site of small productions of operas like *Carmen, Don Giovanni, Tosca,* and *Palleas & Melisande.* There are no performances from mid-July to late August. The box office, however, is open year-round Monday to Saturday from 11am to 7pm. 5 rue Favart, 2nd arr. © **01-42-44-45-45.** Tickets 50–610F (7.60–92.70€, $7.25–$88.45). Métro: Richelieu-Drouot.

Opéra Garnier   The Opéra Garnier, once the haunt of the ill-fated Phantom, is the premier stage for dance and once again for opera. This 1875 rococo wonder was designed as a contest entry by architect Charles Garnier during the heyday of the French Empire; the facade is adorned with marble and sculpture, including *The Dance* by Carpeaux. Following a year-long renovation, during which the famous Chagall ceiling was cleaned and air-conditioning was added, the facade is gleaming as it did for its patron, Napoléon III. You can actually see the original gilded busts and statues, the rainbow-hued marble pillars, and the delicate mosaics. The Opéra Garnier combines ballet and opera, and still offers one of the most elegant evenings you can spend in the City of Light. Because of the competition from the Bastille, the Garnier has made great efforts to present more up-to-date dance works, like choreography by Jerome Robbins, Twyla Tharp, Agnes de Mille, and George Balanchine. The box office is open Monday to Saturday from 11am to 6:30pm. Place de l'Opéra, 9th arr. © **01-40-01-17-89.** Tickets 60–670F (9.10–101.85€, $8.70–$97.15) opera, 30–420F (4.55–63.85€, $4.35–$60.90) dance. Métro: Opéra.

Théâtre des Champs-Elysées   This Art-Deco theater, attracting the haute couture crowd, hosts both national and international orchestras (perhaps the Vienna Philharmonic) as well as opera and ballet. The box office is open Monday to Saturday from 11am to 7pm. There are no performances in August. 15 av. Montaigne, 8th arr. (© **01-49-52-50-50** or 01-49-52-07-41) for box office. Tickets 60–750F (9.10–114€, $8.70–$108.75). Métro: Alma-Marceau.

Théâtre National de Chaillot   Part of the architectural complex facing the Eiffel Tower, this is one of the city's largest concert halls, hosting a variety of cultural events that are announced on billboards in front. Sometimes (rarely) dance is staged here, or you might see a brilliantly performed play by Marguerite Duras. The box office is open Monday to Saturday from 11am to 7pm and Sunday from 11am to 5pm. 1 place du Trocadéro, 16th arr. © **01-53-65-30-00.** Tickets 160F (24.30€, $23.20) adults, 120F (18.25€, $17.40) over 60, 80F (12.15€, $11.60) under age 25. Métro: Trocadéro.

2 The Club & Music Scene

Paris is still a late-night mecca, though some of the once-unique attractions now glut the market. The fame of Parisian nights was established in those distant days when the British and Americans still gasped at the sight of a bare bosom in a chorus line. The fact is that contemporary Paris boasts less vice than London, Hamburg, or San Francisco.

Nevertheless, both the quantity and the variety of Paris nightlife still exceed that of other cities. Nowhere else will you find such a huge and mixed array of nightclubs, bars, dance clubs, cabarets, jazz dives, music halls, and honky-tonks.

A MUSIC HALL

Olympia   Charles Aznavour and other big names frequently appear in this cavernous hall. The late Yves Montand appeared once, and the performance was sold out 4 months in advance (nowadays he performs at Père-Lachaise cemetery). Today you're more likely to catch Gloria Estefan. A typical lineup might include an English rock group, showy Italian acrobats, a well-known French singer, a dance troupe, juggling American comedians (doing much of their work in English), and the featured star. A witty MC and an on-stage band provide a smooth transition. Performances usually begin at 8:30pm Tuesday to Sunday, with Saturday matinees at 5pm. 28 bd. des Capucines, 9th arr. © **01-47-42-25-49.** Tickets 150–300F (22.80–45.60€, $21.75–$43.50). Métro: Opéra or Madeleine.

CHANSONNIERS

Chansonniers (literally "songwriters") provide a bombastic musical satire of the day's events. This combination of parody and burlesque is a time-honored Gallic amusement and a Parisian institution. Songs are often created on the spot, inspired by the "disaster of the day."

Au Caveau de la Bolée   To enter this bawdy *boîte,* you descend into the catacombs of the early14th-century Abbaye de St-André, once a famous cafe that attracted Verlaine and Oscar Wilde, who slowly snuffed out his life in absinthe here. The singing is loud and smutty, just the way the predominantly student audience likes it. Occasionally, the audience sings along. You'll enjoy this place

---

Moments **The Music of Angels**

If you're so inclined, some of the most moving music in Paris echoes through the drafty corridors of churches, some of the sounds taking you back to the Middle Ages. At **Eglise de St-Eustache,** rue Rambuteau (© **01-42-36-31-05;** Métro: Les Halles), in the former market district of Maris, High Mass with organ playing and choir singing is presented at 11am on Sunday. In summer, concerts are played on the organ, marking the church's role in holding the premiere of Berlioz's *Te Deum* and Liszt's *Messiah* in 1886. Tickets to these special concerts sell for 80 to 150F (12.15 to 22.80€, $11.60 to $21.75).

The American Church in Paris, 65 quai d'Orsay, 7th arr. (© **01-40-62-05-00;** Métro: Invalides or Alma Marceau), sponsors free concerts from September to June on Sunday at 6pm. You can also attend free concerts at **Eglise St-Merri,** 78 rue St-Martin, 4th arr. (© **01-42-71-40-75;** Métro: Hotel-de-Ville). These performances are staged September to July on Saturday at 9pm and again on Sunday at 4pm.

a lot more if you can follow the thread of the French-language jokes and satire, but even if you can't, there are enough visuals (magic acts and performances by singers) to amuse. The fixed-price dinner is followed by a series of at least four entertainers, usually comedians. In lieu of paying admission for the cabaret, you can order dinner. If you've already had dinner, you can order just a drink. 25 rue de l'Hirondelle, 6th arr. ℭ **01-43-54-62-20.** Fixed-price dinner 300F (45.60€, $43.50) Mon–Fri, 300F (45.60€, $43.50) Sat. Cover 150F (22.80€, $21.75) Mon–Sat if you don't order dinner. Dinner Mon–Sat 8:30pm; cabaret 10:30pm. Métro: St-Michel.

Au Lapin Agile   Picasso and Utrillo patronized this little cottage near the top of Montmartre, then known as the Cabaret des Assassins, and it has been painted by many artists, including Utrillo. You'll sit at carved wooden tables in a dimly lit room with walls covered by bohemian memorabilia and listen to French folk tunes, love ballads, army songs, sea chanteys, and music-hall ditties. You're encouraged to sing along, even if it's only the "*oui, oui, oui—non, non, non*" refrain of "Les Chevaliers de la Table Ronde." The best sing-alongs are on weeknights after tourist season ends. 22 rue des Saules, 18th arr. ℭ **01-46-06-85-87.** Cover (including 1st drink) 130F (19.75€, $18.85). Tues–Sun 9pm–2am. Métro: Lamarck.

Théâtre des Deux Anes   Since around 1920, this theater has staged humorous satires of the foibles, excesses, and stupidities of various French governments. Favorite targets are President Jacques Chirac and other mandarins and kingmakers of the *héxagone française*. Cultural icons, French and foreign, receive a grilling that's very funny and sometimes harshly caustic. The place considers itself more of a theater than a cabaret and doesn't serve drinks or refreshments. The 2½-hour show is conducted entirely in rapid-fire French slang, so if your syntax isn't up to par, you won't appreciate its charms. 100 bd. de Clichy, 18th arr. ℭ **01-46-06-10-26.** Tickets 205–225F (31.15–34.20€, $29.75–$32.65). Performances Tues–Sat at 9pm, Sun matinee 3:30pm. Closed July–Sept. Métro: Blanche.

NIGHTCLUBS & CABARETS

Decidedly expensive, these places give you your money's worth by providing some of the most lavishly spectacular floor shows anywhere. With the exception of Café Concert Ailleurs, they generally attract an older crowd in their 40s or 50s. They are definitely not youth-oriented.

Café Concert Ailleurs   The young Juliette Greco or Simone de Beauvoir of today gravitates to this cafe/cabaret operated by a group of artists. Some of the latest and most experimental music is performed here nightly over dinner. You can also show up for the 9pm show if you don't plan on dining here. Surprisingly, the cover charge is what you tell them you can pay. 13 rue Jean-de-Beausire, 4th arr. ℭ **01-44-59-82-82.** Cover 30F (4.55€, $4.35), 50F (7.60€, $7.25), or 80F (12.15€, $11.60). Dinner nightly at 8pm. Métro: Bastille.

Chez Michou   The setting is blue, the MC wears blue, and the spotlights bathe performers in yet another shade of blue. The creative force behind the color coordination and a hearty dollop of cross-genderism is Michou, veteran impresario whose 20-odd cross-dressing belles bear names like Hortensia and DuDuche; they lip-synch in costumes from haute couture to haute concierge, paying tribute to Americans like Whitney Houston, Diana Ross, and Tina Turner, and French stars like Mireille Mathieu, Sylvie Vartan, "Dorothée," and Brigitte Bardot. If you don't want dinner, you'll have to stand at the bar, paying a compulsory 220F (33.45€, $31.90) for the first drink. 80 rue des Martyrs, 18th arr. ℭ **01-46-06-16-04.** Cover (including dinner, aperitif, wine, coffee, and show) 600F (91.20€, $87). Dinner nightly at 8:30pm (reservations required); show begins nightly at 10:30pm. Métro: Pigalle.

Crazy Horse Saloon   Since it opened in 1951, this sophisticated strip joint has thrived thanks to good choreography and a sly, coquettish celebration of the female form. The theme binding each of the 5-minute numbers (featuring gorgeous dancers in erotic costumes) is La Femme in her various emotional states: temperamental, sad, dancing/bouncy, or joyful. Dance numbers that endure season after season include "The Itch" and "The Erotic Lesson." Dinner is a tasteful event served at Chez Francis, a restaurant under separate management a few steps from the cabaret. Shows last just under 2 hours. 12 av. George V, 8th arr. ☎ 01-47-23-32-32. Reservations recommended. Cover 450–560F (68.40–85.10€, $65.25–$81.20) including 2 drinks at a table; 290F (44.10 €, $42.05) including 2 drinks at the bar; dinner spectacle 660F (100.30€, $95.70). Shows Sun–Fri 8:30 and 11pm; Sat 7:30, 9:45, and 11:50pm. Métro: George V or Alma-Marceau.

Folies-Bergère   The Folies-Bergère has been an institution for foreigners since 1886. Josephine Baker, the African-American singer who danced in a banana skirt and threw bananas into the audience, became "the toast of Paris" here. According to legend, the first GI to reach Paris at the 1944 Liberation asked for directions to the club. Don't expect the naughty and slyly permissive skin-and-glitter revues of the past. In 1993, all that ended with a radical restoration and reopening under new management. Today, it's a conventional 1,600-seat theater featuring musical revues with a sense of nostalgia for old Paris. You're likely to see an intriguing, often charming, but not exactly erotic repertoire of mostly French songs, interspersed with the banter of an MC. A restaurant serves fixed-price dinners in an anteroom. 32 rue Saulnier, 9th arr. ☎ 01-44-79-98-98. Cover 150–350F (22.80–53.20€, $21.75–$50.75); dinner and show 370–550F (56.25–83.60€, $53.65–$79.75). Tues–Sat at 9pm, Sun at 3pm. Métro: Rue Montmartre or Cadet.

L'Ane Rouge   This red-and-black minitheater has been a showcase for French satire and humor since it opened shortly after World War II. You'll enjoy a well-flavored dinner of conservative French specialties, followed by a 2-hour medley of French-language standup comedy, ribald stories, and politicized jokes. If your knowledge of French is zero, you won't enjoy this place, and if you hate being singled out by a comedian in front of a crowd, stay away. 3 rue Laugier, 17th arr. ☎ 01-43-80-79-97. Reservations recommended. Dinner and show 300–500F (45.60–76€, $43.50–$72.50). Dinner at 8pm; show from 10pm–midnight. Métro: Ternes.

Le Canotier du Pied de la Butte   The worst thing you can say about this place is that it's touristy, but the visitors who show up share a genuine appreciation of the nuances, lyricism, and poetry of popular French songs. Each performance includes appearances by two men and two women, who interact with their own versions of the hits made famous by Piaf, Montand, Brel, and Chevalier. The byword is nostalgia, unleashed by the bucketful in a cozy red, black, and white theater with room for no more than 70. 62 bd. Rochechouart, 18th arr. ☎ 01-46- 06-02-86. Reservations required. Cover 210F (31.90€, $30.45) including 1st drink. Performances daily 7:30–10:30pm. Métro: Anvers.

Le Paradis Latin   Built in 1889 by Alexandre-Gustave Eiffel, with the same metallic skeleton as the famous tower, Le Paradis Latin represents the architect's only venture into theater design. The place is credited with introducing vaudeville and musical theater to Paris. In 1903, the building was a warehouse, but in the 1970s it was transformed into a successful cabaret whose singers, dancers, and special effects extol the fun, frivolity, and permissiveness of the City of Light. The MC speaks in French and English. 28 rue Cardinal-Lemoine, 5th arr. ☎ 01-43-25-28-28. Cover 465F (70€, $67.45) including half bottle of champagne; dinner and show

680–1,250F (103.35–190€, $98.60–$181.25). Dinner Wed–Mon 8pm, revue at 9:30pm. Métro: Jussieu or Cardinal Lemoine.

Lido de Paris   The Lido's $15-million current production, *C'est Magique,* is a dramatic reworking of the classic Parisian cabaret show, with eye-popping special effects and bold new themes, both nostalgic and contemporary, including aerial and aquatic ballets using more than 60,000 gallons of water per minute. The show, the most expensive ever produced in Europe, uses 80 performers, $4 million in costumes, and a $2-million lighting design with lasers. There's even an ice rink and a pool that magically appear and disappear. The legendary Bluebell Girls are still here, however. Now that celebrated chef Paul Bocuse is a consultant, the cuisine is better than ever. 116 bis av. des Champs-Elysées, 8th arr. ℂ 800/227-4884 or 01-40-76-56-10. Cover for 10pm or midnight show 460–560F (69.90–85.10€, $66.70–$81.20) including half bottle of champagne; 8pm dinner dance, including half bottle of champagne, and 10pm show 815–1,015F (123.95–154.35€, $118.25–$147.25). Métro: George V.

Moulin Rouge   This is a camp classic. Toulouse-Lautrec immortalized the Moulin Rouge and its habitués in his works, but he'd probably have a hard time recognizing it today. Colette created a scandal here by giving an on-stage kiss to Mme de Morny, but it's harder to shock today's audiences. Try to get a table, as the view is much better on the main floor than from the bar. The emphasis on the strip routines and saucy sexiness of the Belle Époque and of promiscuous Paris between the world wars keeps drawing the crowds. Handsome men and women, virtually all topless, contribute to the appeal. The finale usually includes two dozen of the belles ripping loose with a topless cancan in a style that might've been appreciated by Gigi herself. Place Blanche, 18th arr. ℂ 01-53-09-82-82. Cover 520–580F (79.05–88.15€, $75.40–$84.10) including champagne; dinner and show from 790F (120.10€, $114.55). Seats at the bar, cover 370F (56.25€, $53.65) includes 2 drinks. Dinner nightly at 7pm; shows nightly at 9 and 11pm. Métro: Blanche.

Villa d'Este   In the past, this club booked Amalia Rodrigues, Portugal's leading *fadista,* and French chanteuse Juliette Greco. Today you're more likely to hear French singer François de Guelte or other top talent from Europe and America. Villa d'Este has been around for a long time, and the quality of its offerings remains high. You'll probably hear some of the greatest hits of beloved French performers like Piaf, Aznavour, Brassens, and Brel. 4 rue Arsène-Houssaye, 8th arr. ℂ 01-42-56-14-65. Cover 190F (28.95€, $27.55) including 1st drink; dinner (including wine) and show 340–750F (51.70–114€, $49.30–$108.75). Daily, doors open at 8pm, the orchestra plays from 8:30pm, the show begins at 9:45pm, and dancing after the show lasts until 2am. Métro: Charles de Gaulle–Etoile.

JAZZ, SALSA, ROCK & MORE

The great jazz revival that long ago swept America is still going strong here, with Dixieland or Chicago rhythms being pounded out in dozens of jazz cellars, mostly called *caveaux.* Most clubs are between rue Bonaparte and rue St-Jacques on the Left Bank. The crowds attending clubs to hear rock, salsa, and the like are definitely young, often in their late teens, 20s, or early 30s. The exception to that is in the clubs offering jazz nights. Lovers of jazz span across all ages.

Au Duc des Lombards   Comfortable and appealing, this jazz club replaced an earlier club 9 years ago and has thrived in a low-key way ever since. Artists begin playing at 9pm and continue (with breaks) for 5 hours, touching on everything from "free jazz" to more traditional forms like "hard bop." Unlike at many of its competitors, tables can be reserved here and will usually be held until

10:30pm. 42 rue des Lombards, 1st arr. ℂ **01-42-33-22-88.** Cover 100–120F (15.22–18.25€, $14.51–$17.40). Daily 9pm–3am. Métro: Châtelet.

Baiser Salé This musically varied cellar club is lined with jazz-related paintings and has a large central bar and an ongoing roster of videos showing great jazz moments from the past. There's no food or even any particular glamour—everything is very mellow and laid-back. Genres featured include Afro-Caribbean, Afro-Latino, salsa, merengue, R&B, and sometimes fusion. 58 rue des Lombards, 1st arr. ℂ **01-42-33-37-71.** Cover 50–100F (7.60–15.20€, $7.25–$14.50) Wed–Sun. Daily 6pm–6am, music daily 10pm–3am. Métro: Châtelet.

Bus Palladium In a single room with a very long bar, this rock temple has varnished hardwoods and fabric-covered walls that barely absorb the reverberations of non-stop recorded music. You won't find techno, punk rock, jazz, blues, or soul. It's rock for hard-core, mostly heterosexual, rock wannabes ages 25 to 35. 6 rue Fontaine, 9th arr. ℂ **01-53-21-07-33.** Cover 100F (15.20€, $14.50) Fri–Sat. Tues–Sat 11pm–6am. Métro: Blanche or Pigalle.

Caveau de la Huchette This celebrated jazz *caveaux*, reached by a winding staircase, draws a young crowd, mostly students, who dance to the music of well-known jazz combos. In pre-jazz days, Robespierre and Marat frequented the place. 5 rue de la Huchette, 5th arr. ℂ **01-43-26-65-05.** Cover 60F (9.10€, $8.70) Sun–Thurs, 75F (11.40€, $10.95) Fri–Sat; students 55F (8.35€, $8.05) Sun–Thurs, 75F (11.40€, $10.95) Fri–Sat. Sun–Thurs 9:30pm–2:30am, Fri–Sat and holidays 9:30pm–4am. Métro/RER: St-Michel.

La Chapelle des Lombards *Finds* The club's proximity to the Opéra Bastille seems incongruous, considering the radically experimental African/Caribbean jazz and Brazilian salsa that's the norm. It's a magnet for South American and African expatriates, and the rhythms and fire of the music propel everyone onto the dance floor. 19 rue de Lappe, 11th arr. ℂ **01-43-57-24-24.** Cover 100–120F (15.20–18.25€, $14.50–$17.40) including 1st drink. Women free Thurs before midnight. Thurs–Sat 10:30pm–dawn. Métro: Bastille.

L'Arbuci The artists who perform here are likely to be lesser-known players, sometimes from Southeast Asia, Madagascar, or the Philippines. The venue is subterranean, smoky, and intimate, and the music and ambience are often more appealing than the entrance suggests. If you don't want dinner, you're charged 70 to 100F (10.65–15.20€, $10.15–$14.50) per drink. The bar is open to 3am. 25–27 rue de Buci, 6th arr. ℂ **01-44-32-16-00.** No cover. Dinner 200–250F (30.40–38€, $29–$36.25). Tues–Sat dinner services at 7:30 and 10:30pm; live music begins at 10pm. Métro: Mabillon or St-Germain-des-Prés.

Le Bilboquet/Club St-Germain This restaurant/jazz club/piano bar, where the film *Paris Blues* was shot, offers some of the best music in Paris. Jazz is played on the upper level in the restaurant, **Le Bilboquet,** a wood-paneled room with a copper ceiling, brass-trimmed sunken bar, and Victorian candelabra. The menu is limited but classic French, specializing in lamb, fish, and beef. Dinner is 180 to 300F (27.35–45.60€, $26.10–$43.50). Under separate management is the downstairs **Club St-Germain** disco, where entrance is free, but drinks cost 100F (15.20€, $14.50). You can walk from one club to the other but must buy a new drink each time you change venues. 13 rue St-Benoît, 6th arr. ℂ **01-45-48-81-84.** No cover. Le Bilboquet nightly 8pm–2:45am; jazz music 10:30pm–2:45am. Club St-Germain Tues–Sun 11pm–5am. Métro: St-Germain-des-Prés.

Le Petit Opportun *Finds* Cramped and convivial, with a lingering sense of the 13th-century masons who built the cellar, this is a jazz club seating no more than 45 patrons, many of whom are regulars. Its specialty is the traditional back-to-basics "hard bop" that avoids the dissonance and irregular rhythms of "free jazz." Artists come from Europe and North America and perform for 3-hour sessions. The rest of the time, the place is an arts-conscious cafe/pub. 15 rue des Lavandières Ste-Opportune, 1st arr. ✆ **01-42-36-01-36.** Cover 80–100F (12.15–15.20€, $11.60–$14.50). Tues–Sat 9pm–5am; live music 10:30pm–2:30am. Métro: Châtelet.

Le Sunset   Since 1976, this club has flourished in a setting that includes a street-level restaurant, where set menus are 82F (12.45€, $11.94). In the smoky cellar, gloss-white tiles emulate a workaday Métro station. A roster of Italian, French, and American jazz artists—including names like Roy Haynes, Also Romano, and Richard Galliano—play in sets until 2am. 60 rue des Lombards, 1st arr. ✆ **01-40-26-46-60.** Cover 50–120F (7.60–18.25€, $7.25–$17.40). Daily 7:30pm–3am; music 8:30pm–2am. Métro: Châtelet.

Les Etoiles   Since 1856, this red-swabbed music hall has shaken with the sound of performers at work and patrons at play. Its newest incarnation is as a restaurant discothèque where the music is exclusively salsa and the food Cubano. Expect hearty portions of fried fish, shredded pork or beef, white rice, beans, and flan as bands from Venezuela play to a crowd which dances to the rhythms. 61 rue du Château d'Eau, 10e. ✆ **01-47-70-60-56.** Cover 120F (18.25€, $17.40) including 1st drink. Métro: Château d'Eau.

New Morning   Jazz maniacs come to drink, talk, and dance at this long-enduring club. It remains on the see-and-be-seen circuit, so you might see Spike Lee or Prince. The high-ceilinged loft was turned into a nightclub in 1981. Many styles of music are played and performed, and the club is especially popular with jazz groups from Central and South Africa. A phone call will let you know what's going on the night you plan to visit. Sometimes it's open on Sunday. 7–9 rue des Petites-Ecuries, 10th arr. ✆ **01-45-23-51-41.** Cover 100–180F (15.20–27.35€, $14.50–$26.10). Call ahead, but hours are generally Mon–Sat 8pm–1:30am. Métro: Château d'Eau.

Slow Club   One of the most famous jazz cellars in Europe, capped with medieval ceiling vaults that have been praised for their acoustic intimacy, this presents a revolving set of artists who tend to focus on New Orleans jazz. Patrons, mostly in their 30s and early 40s, appreciate the music's cross-cultural diversity. 130 rue de Rivoli, 1st arr. ✆ **01-42-33-84-30.** Cover 80–100F (12.15–15.20€, $11.60–$14.50). Tues–Thurs 10pm–3am, Fri–Sat 10pm–4am. Métro: Châtelet.

DANCE CLUBS

The nightspots below are among hundreds of places where young people in their 20s or early 30s go chiefly to dance—distinct from others where the main attraction is the music. The area around the church of **St-Germain-des-Prés** is full of dance clubs, but they come and go so quickly you could arrive to find a hardware store in the place of last year's white-hot disco—but, like all things in nature, the new spring up to take the place of the old. Check in *Time Out: Paris* or *Pariscope* to get a sense of the current trends. Most of these clubs don't really get going until after 10pm.

Batofar   The hippest after-dark dive in town is actually on a barge in the Seine. This boat was once a lighthouse, and from its innards a cavernous night club has been carved, including a spacious dance floor packed with a gyrating crowd mostly in their 20s. House, garage, techno, and "blue note groove" live jazz round out the bill. This music is spun by the city's best DJs. Tapes can be

A Bar Crawl in Trendy Ménilmontant

If **rue Oberkampf** (11th arr.) were any hotter, it would melt off the map. How did it all happen so fast? Longtime residents shake their heads in disbelief and worry that the quirky authenticity of the neighborhood may disappear under the swarms of night crawlers who've migrated north en masse from the Bastille. "Too many *banlieusards* go to the Bastille," the owner of Café Cannibale told us, referring to the well-known reluctance of trendy Parisians to socialize with the suburban crowd.

The success of ultrahip **Café Charbon**, 109 rue Oberkampf (✆ **01-43-57-55-13**), open daily from 9am to 2am, encouraged entrepreneurs to renovate abandoned factories and seedy bars for the artists who were flowing into the neighborhood and for the restless crowd that was already tiring of the Bastille. Some of the new spots are intentionally dilapidated, while others evoke the elegance of 19th-century watering holes. The walls often exhibit the work of local artists, the music is kept fairly low-key, and the drinks are reasonably priced (a glass of mint tea makes a refreshing alternative to alcohol). You can have a salad, snack, or hot *plat du jour,* but the food is secondary to the ambience.

Start from the Ménilmontant Métro stop and head down rue Oberkampf. Your first stop should be the divey **Le Scherkhan** at no. 144 (✆ **01-43-57-29-34**), where you can sink into an easy chair under the fangs of a stuffed tiger, inhale the incense, and dream of equatorial Africa. It's open daily from 5pm to 2am. Stop in at the live-music club **Le Cithéa** at no. 114 (✆ **01-40-21-70-95**). Here you get a show ranging from funk reggae to jazz fusion and electronic house. Later continue on to

ordered costing 20F (3.05€, $2.90) each. Facing 11 Quai Francois Mauriuac, 13th arr. ✆ **01-56-29-10-33**. Summers only, Tues–Sun 6pm–am (no set time). Cover 100F (15.20€, $14.50). Métro: Quai de la Gare.

Club Zed *(Finds)* This popular nightspot in a former bakery with a vaulted masonry ceiling may surprise you with its mix of musical offerings, including samba, rock, 1960s pop, and jazz. 2 rue des Anglais, 5th arr. ✆ **01-43-54-93-78**. Cover 50–100F (7.60–15.20€, $7.25–$14.50), including 1st drink. Wed–Thurs 10:30pm–3am, Fri–Sat 11pm–5:30am. Métro: Maubert-Mutualité.

La Balajo Opened in 1936, this dance club is best remembered as the venue where Edith Piaf first won the hearts of thousands of Parisians. Today, Le Balajo is hardly as fashionable, though it continues its big-band tradition on Sunday afternoons, when patrons 45 and up dance to swing and bebop. Thursday to Saturday nights, they bring out the disco ball or play reggae, salsa, rock, and rap. 9 rue de Lappe, 11th arr. ✆ **01-47-00-07-87**. Cover 50F (7.60€, $7.25) including 1st drink on Sun afternoon, 100F (15.20€, $14.50) evenings. Thurs–Sat 11:30pm–5am, Sun 1–11pm. Métro: Bastille.

La Coupole This landmark cafe has a basement ballroom that's a popular place to waltz and tango to orchestra music as well as bump and grind to "disco retro" (the best tunes of the 1960s, 1970s, and 1980s). The upstairs cafe is covered in "The Top Cafes," in chapter 6. 102 bd. Montparnasse, 14th arr. ✆ **01-43-**

Café **Mercerie** at no. 98 (℃ **01-43-38-81-30**), open Monday to Friday from 5pm to 2am and Saturday and Sunday from 3pm to 2am. At the end of the fashionably grungy bar is a tiny back room lined with long sofas. Across the street at no. 109 is **Café Charbon,** set in an early-1900s dance hall with a stunning Art-Nouveau interior; it makes a relaxed place to hang out during the day and a crowded hotspot at night. Farther down on the same side of the street at no. 99 is the plush **Mecano Bar** (℃ **01-40-21-35-28**), open daily from noon to 2am. Mysterious old implements on the wall are left over from its days as a tool factory. The spacious back room has a palm tree, a skylight, and murals of seminude ladies lounging about in fin-de-siècle naughtiness. Backtrack a few steps and turn left onto rue St-Maur to nos. 111–113, the **Blue Billard** (℃ **01- 43-55-87-21**), open daily from 11am to 2am. This camera factory turned into an upscale bar/pool hall has 22 blue tables under a mezzanine and skylight. A few steps farther on at no. 117 is a local favorite, **Les Couleurs** (℃ **01-43-57-95-61**), open daily from noon to 2am. It's outfitted with tacky posters, chrome-and-plastic chairs, and kitschy rec-room lamps. Live bands regularly play "free jazz," alternative rock, and anything experimental. Turn right at rue Jean-Pierre-Timbaud and at no. 93 you'll find **Café Cannibale** (℃ **01-49-29-95-59**), open daily from 8am to 2am. This softly lit beauty shimmers with candles, mirrors, and chandeliers. The menu includes a good-value Sunday brunch for 80F (12.15€, $11.60).

20-14-20. Ballroom cover 100F (15.20€, $14.50) for evening sessions, 40–80F (6.10–12.15€, $5.80–$11.60) for Sat and Sun matinees. Tues 9:30pm–4am, Fri–Sat 3–7pm and 9:30pm–4am, Sun 3–9pm. Métro: Vavin.

La Flèche d'Or *Value*   Part of the chic swing to East Paris, this is a particularly lively counterculture cafe/club. After you've visited Jim Morrison at Père-Lachaise, you can enjoy live concerts here on Friday and Saturday, everything from Jamaican reggae to Celtic rock. Salsa or swing music from a live dance band enlivens Sundays at 5pm. Anything might be happening—art shows, political debates, video nights, whatever. 102 bis rue de Bagnolet, 20th arr. ℃ **01-43-72-06-87.** Cover free to 50F (7.60€, $7.25). Tues–Sun 10–2am. Métro: Alexandre Dumas.

La Java   This dance hall used to be one of the most frequented in Paris, and the great Piaf and Chevalier made their names here. Today, you can still dance the waltz and perhaps even tango on a Sunday afternoon. Brazilian and Latin themes predominate on some nights. 105 rue du faubourg du Temple, 10th arr. ℃ **01-42-02-20-52.** Cover 80F (12.15€, $11.60) Thurs, 100F (15.20€, $14.50) Fri–Sat, 40F (6.130€, $5.80) Sun. Thurs–Sat 11pm–5am, Sun 8pm–2am. Métro: Belleville.

Le Riverside   If thoughts of Woodstock fill you with nostalgia and you want to meet Parisians between 25 and 40 who feel the same, this is the place for you. The battered Left Bank cellar club attracts droves of people who appreciate the indestructible premises and nostalgic music. You'll hear a range of 1970s

More After-Dark Diversions

On a Paris night, the cheapest entertainment, especially if you're young, is **"the show"** staged at the southeasterly tip of Ile de la Cité, behind Notre-Dame. A sort of Gallic version of the Sundowner Festival in Key West, Florida, it spontaneously attracts just about everyone who ever wanted to try their hand at performance art. The entertainment is strictly spontaneous and usually includes magicians, fire eaters, jugglers, mimes, and music makers from all over, performing against the backdrop of the illuminated cathedral. This is one of the greatest places in Paris to meet other young people in a sometimes moderately euphoric setting.

Also popular is a **stroll along the Seine** after 10pm. Take a graveled pathway down to the river from the Left Bank side of pont de Sully, close to the Institut du Monde Arabe, and walk to the right, away from Notre-Dame. This walk, which comes to an end near place Valhubert, is the best place to see spontaneous Paris in action at night. Joggers and saxophone players come here, and many Parisians show up to take part in impromptu dance parties.

To quench your thirst, wander onto Ile St-Louis and head for the **Café-Brasserie St-Regis**, 6 rue Jean-du-Bellay, 4th arr., across from pont St-Louis (✆ **01-43-54-59-41**; Métro: Musée du Louvre). If you want to linger inside, you can order a *plat du jour* or a coffee at the bar. But try doing as the Parisians do and order a 13F (2.05€, $1.95) beer to go (*une bière àà emporter*) in a plastic cup and take it with you on a stroll around the island. The little cafe is open daily from 7am to 2am.

If you're caught waiting for the Métro to start running again at 5am, try the **Sous-Bock Tavern**, 49 rue St-Honoré, 1st arr. (✆ **01-40-26-46-61**; Métro: Pont Neuf), open daily from 11am to 5am. Young drinkers gather here to sample some 400 varieties of beer. If you want a shot of whiskey to accompany your brew, you face a choice of 150 varieties. The dish to order is a platter of mussels—curried, with white wine, or with cream sauce; they go well with the brasserie-style fries.

If you're looking for the most flamboyant drag in Paris, head to **Madame Arthur**, 75 bis rue des Martyrs, 18th arr. (✆ **01-42-54-40-21**; Métro: Abbesses or Pigalle). It's the longest-running transvestite show in

electronic rock and pop, especially The Doors. 7 rue Grégoire-de-Tours, 6th arr. ✆ **01-43-54-46-33**. Cover for men 90F (13.70€, $13.05) including 1st drink, but women pay cover only after midnight Fri–Sat. Daily 11pm–6am. Métro: St-Michel or Odéon.

Le Saint   Occupying three medieval cellars deep in Paris's university area, this place lures 20- and 30-somethings who dance and drink and generally feel happy to be in a Left Bank student dive. The music melds New York, Los Angeles, and Europe and often leads to episodes of "Young Love Beside the Seine." 7 rue St-Severin, 5th arr. ✆ **01-43-25-50-04**. Cover 60–90F (9.10–13.70€, $8.70–$13.05) including 1st drink. Daily 11pm–6am. Métro: St-Michel.

Les Bains   This chic enclave has been pronounced "in" and "out," but lately it's very "in," attracting more model types and gays, especially on Monday night.

town, attracting both straights and gays. The creative force behind the affair is Mme Arthur, who's no lady and whose stage name during her shticks as MC is Chantaline. The performances include 9 to 11 artists with names like Vungala, Lady Lune, and Miss Badabou. You can visit just to drink or you can dine from a fixed-price menu (reservations required). The club is open daily from 9 to 10:30pm for dinner, with the show beginning at 10:30pm. Additional shows, according to demand, are Friday and Saturday at 7pm, with dinner beginning at 6pm. After the last show, around 12:30am, the place becomes a disco. Cover (including the first drink) is 165F (25.10€, $23.95); dinner and the show is 295F (44.85€, $42.85) Sunday to Thursday and 395F (60.05€, $57.35) Friday and Saturday.

If drag shows aren't your cup of tea, how about *The Last Tango in Paris*? At **Le Tango,** 13 rue au Maire, 3rd arr. (© **01-42-72-17-78;** Métro: Arts et Métiers), memories of Evita and Argentina live on. This dive with a bordello decor features zouk music from the French Caribbean and Africa, as well as house, garage, and virtually every form of high-energy dance music known in New York and Los Angeles. Most patrons are gay and lesbian and in their 20s and 30s. The cover is 40F (6.10€, $5.80). It's open Friday and Saturday from midnight to 5am.

Another fun and trendy dance place is **La Guinguette Pirate,** Quai de la Gare, 13th arr. (© **01-44-24-89-89;** Métro: Quai de la Gare), a Chinese junk moored off the banks of the Seine. This is the latest version of the fabled *guinguette* (river cafe), offering great jazz, zouk, and live salsa. Cover is 50F (7.60€, $7.25).

If you're looking for a sophisticated, laid-back venue without the high-energy exhibitionism of nightclubs, consider a drink at the **Sanz-Sans,** 49 rue du faubourg St-Antoine, 4th arr. (© **01-44-75-78-78;** Métro: Bastille). Testifying to the unifying power of jazz, it's a multiethnic playground where the children of prominent Parisians mingle. In this red-velvet duplex, the most important conversations seem to occur over margaritas on the stairway or the back-room couches. The later it gets, the sexier the scene becomes. There's no cover.

Everyone dresses more for show than for comfort. The name Les Bains comes from the place's old function as a Turkish bath attracting gays, none more notable than Marcel Proust. It may be hard to get in if the bouncer doesn't like your looks. A restaurant has been added. 7 rue du Bourg-l'Abbé, 3rd arr. © **01-48-87-01-80.** Cover 120F (18.25€, $17.40) including 1st drink. Daily 11:30pm–6am. Métro: Réaumur.

Les Coulisses/La Bohème   Its premises combine a cellar-level disco with a street-level restaurant that bears two names. During the day, from 7:30am to around 8pm, it's known as La Bohème; from 8pm to 5:30am, it becomes a bit more formal and is called Les Coulisses. The food remains the same, with a set-price menu at 160F (24.30€, $23.20) and platters at 70 to 100F (10.65–15.20€, $10.15–$14.50). Most nighttime patrons eventually filter down to the disco, where the decor is a cross between a feudal château and a scene from the

Italian *Commedia dell'Arte*. The crowd ranges in age from 20 to around 45. 5 rue Ste. Rustique, 18th arr. ✆ **01-42-62-89-99.** Cover 160F (24.30€, $23.20) Fri–Sat, but free for patrons of either restaurant. Restaurants daily 8pm–5am; disco 11pm–5am. Métro: Abbesses or Funiculaire.

Theatre Rex Club   This echoing blue-and-orange space emulates the techno-grunge clubs of London, complete with an international mood-altered crowd enjoying the kind of music only someone 18 to 28 could love. A revolving host of DJs is on hand, including regular appearances from a local techno-circuit celeb, Laurent Garnier. 5 bd. Poissonière, 2nd arr. ✆ **01-42-36-83-98.** Cover 50–80F (7.60–12.15€, $7.25–$11.60) including 1st drink. Wed–Sat 11:30pm–6am. Métro: Bonne Nouvelle.

3 Bars, Pubs & Clubs

WINE BARS

Many Parisians now prefer the wine bar to the traditional cafe or bistro. The food is often better and the ambience more inviting. For cafes, see "The Top Cafes" in chapter 6.

Au Sauvignon   This tiny place, with old ceramic tiles and frescoes done by Left Bank artists, has tables overflowing onto a covered terrace where wines range from the cheapest Beaujolais to the most expensive St-Emilion Grand Cru. A glass of wine is 22 to 32F (3.35 to 4.85€, $3.25 to $4.65), and it costs an extra 2F (.30€, 34¢) to consume it at a table. To accompany your wine, choose an Auvergne specialty, like goat cheese or a terrine. The fresh Poilâne bread is ideal with ham, pâté, or goat cheese. 80 rue des Sts-Pères, 7th arr. ✆ **01-45-48-49-02.** Mon–Sat 8:30am–10:30pm. Métro: Sèvres-Babylone.

Aux Négociants   Ten minutes downhill from the north facade of Sacré-Coeur, this *bistro à vins* has flourished since 1980 as an outlet for wines produced in the Loire Valley. Artists, street vendors, and office workers come here, linked only by an appreciation of wine costing 16 to 28F (2.45 to 4.25€, $2.30 to $4.05) per glass and the allure of the hearty *plats du jour* costing 60 to 70F (9.10 to 10.65€, $8.70 to $10.15). 27 rue Lambert, 18th arr. ✆ **01-46-06-15-11.** Mon and Fri noon–8pm, Tues–Thurs noon–10:30pm. Métro: Lamarck-Caulincourt or Château Rouge.

Juveniles   This is a British-owned spin-off of one of Paris's most successful wine bars, nearby Willi's. Louder, less formal, less restrained, and (at least to wine lovers) more daring than its older sibling, it prides itself on experimenting with a wide roster of wines from "everywhere." High-quality but lesser-known wines from Spain, France, California, and Australia decant for 18 to 48F (2.75 to 7.30€, $2.60 to $6.95) per glass. Anything you like, including the "wine of the week," can be hauled away uncorked from the wine boutique here. There's also an assortment of tapas-inspired platters for 35 to 65F (5.30 to 9.95€, $5.15 to $9.45). 47 rue de Richelieu, 1st arr. ✆ **01-42-97-46-49.** Bar Mon–Sat noon–1am; restaurant Mon–Sat noon–11pm. Métro: Palais Royal.

La Tartine   Mirrors, brass detail, and frosted-globe chandeliers make La Tartine look like a movie set of old Paris. At least 60 wines are offered at reasonable prices, including 7 kinds of Beaujolais and a large selection of Bordeaux by the glass. Glasses of wine are 10 to 18F (1.50 to 2.75€, $1.45 to $2.60), and the charcuterie platter is 45F (6.85€, $6.55). We recommend the light Sancerre wine and goat cheese from the Loire Valley. 24 rue de Rivoli, 4th arr. ✆ **01-42-72-76-85.** Thurs–Mon 8:30am–10pm and Wed noon–10pm. Métro: St-Paul.

Le Sancerre Produced in the Loire Valley in red, rosé, and especially white, Sancerre wine is known for its not-too-dry fruity aroma and legions of fans who believe it should be more celebrated than it is. That's all you'll find here, where the wine comes from several producers in the Sancerre district and is 14 to 26F (2.15 to 3.95€, $2.05 to $3.75) per glass. Simple platters of food cost 45 to 75F (6.85 to 11.40€, $6.55 to $10.95). 22 av. Rapp, 7th arr. ☎ **01-45-51-75-91.** Mon–Sat 8am–10pm. Métro: Alma-Marceau.

Les Bacchantes Les Bacchantes prides itself on offering more wines by the glass (at least 50) than any other wine bar in Paris and also does a hefty restaurant trade serving well-prepared *cuisine bourgeoise.* Amid massive exposed beams, Belle-Époque posters, and old-fashioned paneling, chalkboards announce a great list of vintages and platters. The wines, at 14 to 30F (2.15 to 4.55€, $2.05 to $4.35) per glass, are mainly French. Platters of food cost 62 to 100F (9.40 to 15.20€, $9.05 to $14.50). 21 rue Caumartin, 9th arr. ☎ **01-42-65-25-35.** Mon–Sat noon–midnight. Métro: Opéra or Madeleine.

Willi's Wine Bar Journalists and stockbrokers patronize this increasingly popular wine bar in the center of the financial district, run by Englishman Mark Williamson. About 250 kinds of wine are offered, including a dozen wine specials you can taste by the glass for 22 to 82F (3.35 to 12.45€, $3.25 to $11.95). Lunch is the busiest time—on quiet evenings you can better enjoy the warm ambience and 16th-century beams. Daily specials are likely to include lamb brochette with cumin and Lyonnaise sausage in truffled vinaigrette, plus spectacular desserts like chocolate terrine. 13 rue des Petits-Champs, 1st arr. ☎ **01-42-61-05-09.** Mon–Sat noon–11pm. Métro: Bourse, Pyramide, or Palais Royal.

BARS & PUBS

These "imported" places try to imitate American cocktail bars or masquerade as British pubs—most strike an alien chord. But that doesn't prevent fashionable Parisians from bar hopping (not to be confused with cafe sitting). Many bars in Paris are youth-oriented. But if you're an older traveler who prefers to take your expensive drink in one of the grand *luxe* bars of the world, Paris has that waiting for you, too. The bars at the Plaza Athénée, Crillon, and Ritz, for example, are among the grandest in the world and form an experience uniquely Parisian for those who want to don their finest apparel and take along a gold-plated credit card. In general, bars and pubs are open daily from 11am to 1:30am.

Académie de la Bière *(Value)* The decor is paneled and rustic, an appropriate foil for an "academy" whose curriculum includes more than 150 kinds of beer from microbreweries. Stella Artois, Belgium's best-selling beer, isn't available, though more than half of the dozen on tap are from small-scale breweries in Belgium that deserve to be better known. Snack-style food is available,

---

Tips **What's in a Name?**

Paris's bar scene is hopping, though bars here aren't as clearly defined as in other cities—they can be cafes, and cafes can be bars, restaurants can be bars, and bars can also be clubs. It can get confusing. The best way to think about it is not to let the name give you any preconceived notion of what the place might be like. (Café Marly, for example, is much more than just a cafe, and Buddha Bar is known more for its food than its cocktails. See chapter 6 for descriptions of these two places.)

including platters of mussels, assorted cheeses, and sausages with mustard. 88 bis bd. du Port-Royal, 5th arr. ℂ **01-43-54-66-65**. Daily 11am–2:30am. Métro: Port Royal.

The Bar at the Plaza Athénée   Residents of the surrounding neighborhood have always enjoyed dropping into this hotel for a drink in cosseted, well-upholstered comfort. The drinking venue has now moved from the Bar Anglais, on the lower level, to one of the street-level salons. A pianist and singer usually perform between 10:30pm and 1:30am. In the Hôtel Plaza Athénée, 25 av. Montaigne, 8th arr. ℂ **01-53-67-66-65**. Daily 5:30pm–1:30am. Métro: Alma-Marceau.

Bar du Crillon   Though some visitors consider the Bar du Crillon too stiff and elegant to ever allow anyone to have a good time, its social and literary history is remarkable. Hemingway set a climactic scene of *The Sun Also Rises* here, and over the years it has attracted practically every upper-level staff member of the nearby American embassy, as well as heiresses, stars, starlets, and wannabes. Under its new owner, the Concorde Group, the bar has been redecorated by designer Sonia Rykiel. Down the hall is the Edwardian **Jardin d'Hiver,** where, amid potted palms and upscale accessories, you can order tea, cocktails, or coffee; it's open daily from noon to 9pm. In the Hôtel du Crillon, 10 place de la Concorde, 8th arr. ℂ **01-44-71-15-00**. Daily 11am–2am. Métro: Concorde.

Bar Hemingway/Bar Vendôme   In 1944, during Paris's liberation, Ernest Hemingway and a group of Allied soldiers made history by "freeing" the Ritz from the Nazis and ordering a round of martinis at the bar (see the "A Hotel Tale" box in chapter 5). The Ritz commemorates this event in the **Bar Hemingway** with bookish memorabilia, rows of newspapers, and stiff drinks served in a woodsy English club setting. Look for its entrance, and homage to other writers, close to the hotel's rue Cambon entrance. If you get thirsty during the daytime, when the bar isn't open, head for the **Bar Vendôme,** near the main (place Vendôme) entrance; it's equally cozy, albeit a bit grander. Between 5:30 and 8:30pm, it's wise to reserve a table. In the Hôtel Ritz, 15 place Vendôme, 1st arr. ℂ **01-43-16-30-30**. Bar Hemingway daily 6pm–2am; Bar Vendôme daily 10am–2am. Métro: Opéra.

Barrio Latino   It would be easy to spend an entire evening at this multistoried emporium of good times, Gallic flair, and Latino charm. You won't be finished with this place until you've done a bit of exploring, so here's what you can expect: Tapas bars and dance floors on the street level (*rez-de-chausée*) and 3rd floor (*2eme étage*); a Latino restaurant on the 2nd floor (*1er étage*); and a private club on the top floor. Staff members roll glass-covered carts, loaded with tapas, around the floors, selling them like hotdogs at an American baseball game. The restaurant (open daily from noon to 3pm and 7:30pm to 1am) specializes in food that jaded French palates sometimes find refreshing. Main courses range from 80 to 110F (12.15–16.70€, $11.60–$15.95) and include Argentinian steaks, Brazilian *fejoiada,* and Mexican *chili con carne,* all of which taste wonderful with beer, *caipirinhas,* Cuba Libres, and/or rum punches. Everywhere, you'll be surrounded in a recorded cocoon of marvelous Latino music. Clientele is very mixed, mostly straight, partly gay, and 100-percent blasé about matters such as an individual's sexuality. 46 rue du Faubourg St-Antoine, 4th arr. ℂ **01-55-78-84-75**. Cover 50F (7.60€, $7.25) but only for non-diners, non-VIPs, and only on Fri–Sat after 9pm. Daily 11am–2 am. Métro: Bastille.

China Club   Designed to recall France's 19th-century colonies in Asia or a bordello in 1930s Shanghai (on the ground floor) and England's empire-building zeal in India (upstairs), the China Club will allow you to chitchat or flirt with the singles who crowd into the street-level bar, then escape to calmer, more contemplative climes upstairs. You'll see regulars from the worlds of fashion and the arts, along with a pack of postshow celebrants from the nearby Opéra Bastille. A street-level Chinese restaurant serves dinner daily from 7pm to 12:30am, and in the more animated (and occasionally raucous) cellar bar, live music is presented every Friday and Saturday from 10pm to 3am. 50 rue de Charenton, 12th arr. ℂ 01-43-43-82-02. Daily 7pm–2am. Métro: Bastille or Ledru Rollin.

Le Bar de L'Hôtel This is the hyper-artsy and theatrically overdecorated bar of a hotel that has wooed film-industry types who want to avoid the more mainstream luxury of Paris's palatial hotels. The rose-filter cheeriness is deceptive: This is the hotel where Oscar Wilde died, disgraced and impoverished. The staff is conscientiously straitlaced, but you'd expect a musical comedy to break out at any moment. In L'Hôtel, 13 rue des Beaux-Arts, 6th arr. ℂ 01-44-41-99-00. Daily 7pm–1am. Métro: St-Germain-des-Prés.

Le Forum Its patrons, who include frequent business travelers, compare this place to a private club in London. Part of that comes from the carefully polished oak paneling and ornate stucco and part from its store of single-malt whiskeys. You can also try 150 cocktails, including many that haven't been popular since the jazz age. Champagne by the glass is common, as is that high-octane social lubricant, the martini. 4 bd. Malesherbes, 8th arr. ℂ 01-42-65-37-86. Daily 2pm–midnight. Métro: Madeleine.

Le Fumoir At Le Fumoir, the well-traveled crowd that lives or works in the district provides a kind of classy raucousness. The decor is a lot like that of an English library, with about 6,000 books providing an aesthetic backdrop to the schmoozing. A Danish chef prepares an international menu featuring meal-size salads (the one with scallops and lobster is great), roasted codfish with zucchini, and roasted beef in red-wine sauce. More popular are the stiff mixed drinks, the wines and beers, and the dozen or so types of cigars for sale. 6 rue de l'Amiral-de-Coligny, 1st arr. ℂ 01-42-92-00-24. Daily 11am–2am. Métro: Louvre-Rivoli.

Le Web Bar Occupying a three-story space at the eastern edge of the Marais, Le Web Bar echoes with the sound of people schmoozing with one another and with silent computer partners thousands of miles away. On the street level is a restaurant, on the second floor is a battery of at least 25 computers you can use for free, and on the top floor is an art gallery. To keep things perking, there's daily entertainment beginning around 7pm. Menu items stress comfort food like *boeuf bourguignonne*. 32 rue de Picardie, 3rd arr. ℂ 01-42-72-66-55. www.webbar.fr. Mon–Fri 8:30am–2am, Sat–Sun 11am–2am. Métro: République or Temple.

Maito Habana The macho brown-and-green decor evokes a private men's club. You can drink Cuba libres, cognac, or coffee or eat platters of food. You can also puff away at any of the cigars stocked for the pleasure of the patrons (regulars sometimes store their cigars in a safe originally designed as a safety-deposit vault). 19 rue de Presbourg, 16th arr. ℂ 01-45-00-60-63. Cafe and cigar service Mon–Sat 10:30am–2am; meals Mon–Sat noon–2pm and 8–11:15pm. Métro: Etoile.

Man Ray This chic rendezvous off the Champs-Elysées is dedicated to Man Ray, the famous photographer and American Dadaist, who usually felt more comfortable roaming Montparnasse than the 8th. Many of Man Ray's photos decorate the club. The entry is discreet through large wrought-iron doors and virtually no sign. In the basement is a bustling brasserie presided over by two winged Oriental goddesses. The bar upstairs is big and bustling, and jazz is often presented there. 34 rue Marbeuf, 8th arr. ℂ **01-56-88-36-36.** Brasserie Mon–Fri noon–2:30pm, daily 6pm–2am; bar Sun–Thurs 6pm–2am, Fri–Sat 7pm–2am. Métro: F. D. Roosevelt.

Pub St-Germain-des-Prés   With 9 rooms and 650 seats, this is France's largest pub, offering 450 brands of beer, 26 on draft. The deliberately tacky decor consists of leather booths, faded gilt-framed mirrors, hanging lamps, and a stuffed parrot in a gilded cage. The atmosphere is usually quiet, relaxed, and posh. Featured beers change frequently but usually include Amstel, various Belgian brews, Whitbread, and Pimm's No. 1. If frat houses turn you on, it gets really fun from 10:30pm to 4am. 17 rue de l'Ancienne-Comédie, 6th arr. ℂ **01-43-29-38-70.** Daily 24 hours. Métro: Odéon.

4 Gay & Lesbian Bars & Clubs

Gay life is centered around **Les Halles** and **Le Marais,** with the greatest concentration of gay/lesbian clubs, restaurants, bars, and shops between the Hôtel de Ville and Rambuteau Métro stops. Gay dance clubs come and go so fast that even the magazines devoted to them—*e.m@ale* and *Illico,* both distributed free in the gay bars and bookstores—have a hard time keeping up. For lesbians, the guide *Exes Femmes* publishes a free seasonal listing of bars and clubs. Also look for Gai Pied's *Guide Gai* and *Pariscope's* regularly featured English-language section, "A Week of Gay Outings."

For all you need to know about Paris's gay and lesbian scene, buy *Frommer's Gay & Lesbian Europe.*

Café Cox, 15 rue des Archives, 4th arr. (ℂ **01-42-72-08-00**), gets so busy in the early evening the crowd stands on the sidewalk. This is where you'll find the most mixed gay crowd in Paris—from hunky American tourists to sexy Parisian men. A new hot place in Les Halles is **Le Tropic Café,** 66 rue des Lombards, 1st arr. (ℂ **01-40-13-92-62**; Métro: Châtelet–Les Halles), where the trendy good-looking crowd parties until dawn. **Le Gibus,** 18 rue du faubourg du Temple, 11th arr. (ℂ **01-47-00-78-88**; Métro: République), rocks on Fridays and Saturdays with guest DJs. Some of the most drop-dead gorgeous men in Paris show up here, often to be entertained by drag shows.

A restaurant with a bar popular with women is **Okawa,** 40 rue Vieille-du-Temple, 4th arr. (ℂ **01-48-04-30-69**; Métro: Hôtel de Ville), where trendy lesbians (and some gay boys) sip drinks at happy hour. **Les Scandaleuses,** 26 rue des Ecouffes, 3rd arr. (ℂ **01-48-87-39-26**; Métro: St-Paul), continues to be one of the city's most popular rendezvous spots for lesbians. Acquired by a beautiful young woman, **L'Entr'acte,** 25 bd. Poissonnière, 2nd arr. (ℂ **01-40-26-01-93**; Métro: Montmartre), attracts a crowd much like the owner. More butch, **L'Enfer,** 34 rue du Départ, 15th arr.(ℂ **01-42-79-94-94**; Métro: Montparnasse), rocks with a crowd of trendy lesbians on Friday and Saturday; Thursday is more mixed, with gay men welcome.

Amnesia Café   The Amnesia's function and crowd may change during the day, but you'll always find a cadre of local gays. This cafe/tearoom/bistro/bar includes two bar and dining areas, a mezzanine, and a cellar bar open in the evening. The drinks of choice are beer, cocktails, and *café amnesia,* a specialty coffee with cognac and Chantilly cream. Deep armchairs, soft pillows, and 1930s accents create an ambience conducive to talk and laughter—it's not as sexually charged as nearby bars. *Plats du jour* include favorites like Basque chicken and *boeuf bourguignonne.* 42 rue Vieille-du-Temple, 4th arr. ℂ **01-42-72-16-94.** Daily 10am–2am. Métro: Hôtel de Ville.

Banana Café   This popular bar is a usual stop for gays visiting or doing business in Paris. Occupying two floors of a 19th-century building, it has walls the color of an overripe banana, dim lighting, and a policy of raising the drink prices after 10pm, when things become really interesting. There's a street-level bar and a cellar dance floor that features a live pianist and recorded music—sometimes with dancing. On many nights, go-go dancers perform from spotlit platforms in the cellar. 13 rue de la Ferronnerie, 1st arr. ℂ **01-42-33-35-31**. Daily 5pm–between 4 and 5am. Métro: Châtelet–Les Halles.

La Champmeslé   La Champmeslé—with dim lighting, background music, and comfortable banquettes—is a great cozy meeting place for lesbians (and even for "well-behaved" gay men). It's housed in a 300-year-old building with exposed stone and ceiling beams and 1950s-style furnishings. On Thursdays, one of the premier lesbian events of Paris, a cabaret, begins at 10pm; every month there's a well-attended exhibit of paintings by mostly lesbian artists. The bar honors a celebrated 17th-century actress, La Champmeslé, who was instrumental in interpreting the fledgling dramatic efforts of celebrated playwright Racine. 4 rue Chabanais, 2nd arr. ℂ **01-42-96-85-20**. Mon–Wed 5pm–2am, Thurs–Sat 5pm–5am. Métro: Pyramides or Bourse.

Le Bar   Covering the street level and cellar of a sprawling building in an area long known for an availability of commercial sex, this is the largest gay bar in Paris. You'll find three bars on the premises, a mostly blue decor incorporating lots of sinuous lines, and an ambience that's more sexually charged and explicit in the cellar than on the street level. The average age is early 30s. 5 rue de la Ferronerie, 1st arr. ℂ **01-40-41-00-10**. Daily 5pm–between 4 and 5am. Métro: Châtelet.

Le Central   Le Central is one of the oldest bars for men in the Hôtel de Ville area. It's tacky and a bit drab but still gets its share of visitors and regulars. A small hotel is upstairs (see "Gay-Friendly Hotels" in chapter 5). Both the bar and its hotel are in a 300-year-old building in the heart of the Marais. 33 rue Vieille-du-Temple, 4th arr. ℂ **01-48-87-99-33**. Mon–Fri 4pm–2am, Sat–Sun 2pm–2am. Métro: Hôtel de Ville.

Le Pulp   This is one of the most popular lesbian discos, looking like a burgundy-colored 19th-century French music hall. It's best to show up before midnight. The venue, as the French like to say, is *trés cool*, with cutting-edge music played in a setting that just happens to discourage the presence of men. 25 bd. Poissonnière, 2nd arr. ℂ **01-40-26-01-93**. Cover 50F (7.60€, $7.25). Fri–Sat 5pm–4am. Métro: Rue Montmartre.

Le Queen   Should you miss gay life à la New York, follow the flashing purple sign on the "main street" of Paris, near the corner of avenue George V. The place is often mobbed, primarily with gay men and (to a lesser degree) models, actresses, and the like. Look for go-go boys, drag shows, muscle shows, and everything from 1970s-style disco nights (Monday) to Tuesday-night foam parties (only in summer), when cascades of mousse descend onto the dance floor. Go very, very late. 102 av. des Champs-Elysées, 8th arr. ℂ **01-53-89-08-90**. Cover 50F (7.60€, $7.25) Sun–Mon, 100F (15.20€, $14.50) Fri–Sat, 30F (4.55€, $4.35) Wed. Daily 11pm–between 4 and 5am. Métro: F. D. Roosevelt.

5 Literary Haunts

Closerie des Lilas   Hemingway, Picasso, Gershwin, and Modigliani all loved the Closerie, and ever since, Parisians and foreigners, literary or not, have flocked here. Even though the lilacs that gave the place its name bloom only in spring, the management strews bouquets of them throughout the bar all year long. Don't expect a reverent hush—on some nights the place is as energetic as a New York singles bar. Look for the brass nameplate of your favorite Lost Generation artist along the banquettes or at the bar. See chapter 6 for a dining review. 171 bd. du Montparnasse, 6th arr. ℂ **01-40-51-34-50.** Daily 11am–2am. Métro: Port Royal.

Harry's New York Bar   The ads tell you to instruct your cab driver, "Sank roo doe Noo." Opened on Thanksgiving Day in 1911 by a bearded Hemingway precursor by the name of MacElhone, it's sacred to Papa disciples as the spot where members of the ambulance corps drank themselves silly during World War I. White lady and sidecar cocktails were invented here in 1919 and 1931, respectively, and it's the alleged birthplace of the bloody Mary and the head-quarters of a fraternity of drinkers known as the International Bar Flies (IBF). In the street-level bar, daytime crowds draw from the area's insurance, banking, and travel industries; evening crowds include pre- and post-theater groupies and night owls. In the cellar, a pianist plays daily from 10pm to 2am. 5 rue Daunou, 2nd arr. ℂ **01-42-61-71-14.** Daily 10:30–4am. Métro: Opéra or Pyramides.

Rosebud   The popularity of this place, known for a bemused and indulgent attitude toward anyone looking for a drink and some talk, hasn't diminished since the 1950s, when it attained its fame. The name refers to the beloved sled of Orson Welles's great *Citizen Kane*. Around the corner from Montparnasse's famous cafes, and thick in associations with Sartre and de Beauvoir, Ionesco, and Duras, Rosebud draws a crowd aged 35 to 65, though the staff has recently remarked on the appearance of students. Drop in at night for a glass of wine, a shot of whiskey, or a hamburger or chili con carne. 11 bis rue Delambre, 14th arr. ℂ **01-43-35-38-54.** Daily 7pm–2am. Métro: Vavin.

11

Side Trips from Paris

Paris, the city that began on an island, is itself the center of a curious land-locked island known as the **Ile de France.** Shaped roughly like a saucer, it's encircled by a thin ribbon of rivers: the **Epte, Aisne, Marne,** and **Yonne.** Fringing these rivers are mighty forests with famous names—**Rambouillet, St-Germain, Compiègne,** and **Fontainebleau.** These forests are said to be responsible for Paris's clear gentle air and the unusual length of its spring and fall. This may be debatable, but there's no argument they provide

the capital with a fine series of day trips, all within easy reach.

The forests surrounding Paris once were the domain of royalty and the aristocracy, and they're still sprinkled with the magnificent châteaux of their former masters. Together with ancient villages, glorious cathedrals, and cozy country inns, they make the Ile de France irresistible. In this chapter, we offer only a handful of the possibilities for day jaunts. For a more extensive list, see *Frommer's France 2002.*

1 Versailles

13 miles SW of Paris, 44 miles NE of Chartres

For centuries, the name of the Parisian suburb of Versailles resounded through the consciousness of every aristocratic family in Europe. The palace here out-dazzled every other kingly residence in Europe—it was a horrendously expensive scandal and a symbol to later generations of a regime obsessed with prestige above all else.

Back in the *grand siècle,* all you needed was a sword, a hat, and a bribe for the guard at the gate. Providing you didn't look as if you had smallpox, you'd be admitted to the Château de Versailles, where you could stroll through salon after glittering salon—watching the Sun King rise and dress and dine and do even more intimate things while you gossiped, danced, plotted, flirted, and trysted.

Today, Versailles needs the return of Louis XIV and his fat treasury. You wouldn't believe it when looking at the glittering Hall of Mirrors, but Versailles is down-at-the-heels. It suffers from a lack of funds, which translates into a shortage of security forces; this budget crunch was made even worse on Christmas Day in 1999, when a horrendous windstorm wreaked havoc here (see "Your Own Tree at Versailles," below).

You get to see only half of the palace's treasures; the rest are closed to the public. Some 3.2 million visitors arrive annually, and on average they spend 2 hours.

ESSENTIALS
GETTING THERE To get to Versailles, 13 miles southwest of Paris, catch the **RER** line C at the Gare d'Austerlitz, St-Michel, Musée d'Orsay, Invalides, Ponte de l'Alma, Champ de Mars, or Javel stop and take it to the Versailles Rive

Gauche station, from which there's a shuttle bus to the château. The 35F (5.30€, $5.15) trip takes 35 to 40 minutes; Eurailpass holders travel free on the train but pay 20F (3.05€, $2.90) for a ride on the shuttle bus. Regular **SNCF trains** make the run from central Paris to Versailles: One train departs from Gare St-Lazare for the Versailles Rive Droite RER station, a 15-minute walk from the château. If you can't or don't want to walk, you can take bus B from Versailles Chantiers to the château for 8F (1.20€, $1.15) each way.

As a last resort, you can use a combination of **Métro and city bus.** Travel to the Pont de Sèvres stop by Métro, then transfer to bus 171 for a westward trek that'll take 20 to 45 minutes, depending on traffic. The bus will cost you three Métro tickets and deposit you near the château gates. If you have a **car,** take N-10, following the signs to Versailles, and then proceed along avenue de Général-Leclerc. Park on place d'Armes in front of the château.

VISITOR INFORMATION Three main avenues radiate from place d'Armes in front of the palace. The **tourist office** is at 7 rue des Réservoirs (© **01-39-24-88-88**).

TOURING VERSAILLES

Château de Versailles ★★★ Within 50 years, this residence was transformed from Louis XIII's simple hunting lodge into an extravagant palace. Begun in 1661, the construction of the château involved 32,000 to 45,000 workmen, some of whom had to drain marshes—often at the cost of their lives—and move forests. Louis XIV set out to build a palace that would be the envy of all Europe, and he created a symbol of pomp and opulence that was to be copied, yet never quite duplicated, all over Europe and even in America.

So he could keep an eye on the nobles of France (and with good reason), Louis XIV summoned them to live at his court. Here he amused them with constant entertainment and lavish banquets and balls, and amused himself with a roster of mistresses, the most important of which was Mme de Maintenon (he secretly married her after his queen, Marie-Thérèse of Spain, died). To some he awarded such vital tasks as holding the hem of his ermine-lined robe. While the aristocrats frivolously played away their lives, often in silly intrigues and games, the peasants on the estates, angered by their absentee landlords, sowed the seeds of the Revolution.

When Louis XIV died in 1715, he was succeeded by his great-grandson, Louis XV, who continued the outrageous pomp, though he's said to have predicted the outcome: *"Après mois le déluge"* (After me, the deluge). His wife, Marie Leszcynska of Poland, was shocked by the court's blatant immorality. When her husband tired of her, she lived as a nun, and the king's attention turned to Mme de Pompadour, who was accused of running up a debt far beyond that of a full-scale war. Mme de Pompadour handpicked her successor, Mme du Barry, who was just about as foolhardy with the nation's treasury.

Louis XVI found his grandfather's and father's behavior scandalous—in fact, on gaining the throne in 1774 he ordered the "stairway of indiscretion" (secret stairs leading up to the king's bedchamber) be removed. This dull, weak king (who was virtuous and did have good intentions) and his Austrian-born queen, Marie Antoinette, were well-liked at first, but the queen's excessive frivolity and wild spending soon led to her downfall. Louis and Marie Antoinette were at Versailles on October 6, 1789, when they were notified that mobs were marching on the palace. As predicted, *le déluge* had arrived.

Napoléon stayed at Versailles but never seemed fond of it. Louis-Philippe prevented the destruction of the palace by converting it into a museum dedicated to the glory of France. To do that, he had to surrender some of his own not-so-hard-earned currency. Many years later, John D. Rockefeller contributed heavily toward the restoration of Versailles and work continues to this day.

The six magnificent **Grands Appartements** ✿✿✿ are in the Louis XIV style, each named after the allegorical painting on the room's ceiling. The best known and largest is the **Hercules Salon,** with a ceiling painted by François Lemoine, depicting the Apotheosis of Hercules. In the **Mercury Salon** (with a ceiling by Jean-Baptiste Champaigne), the body of Louis XIV was put on display in 1715; his 72-year reign was one of the longest in history.

The most famous room at Versailles is the 236-foot-long **Hall of Mirrors** ✿✿✿, built to link the north and south apartments. Begun in 1678 by Mansart in the Louis XIV style, it was decorated by Le Brun and his team with

A Weekend in London

Of course, Paris offers a seemingly endless list of wonderful things to see and do, but now that transit between the French capital and the British capital is easier than ever, why not take a weekend jaunt to London?

The **Eurostar** train roars through the **Channel Tunnel (Chunnel),** reducing the travel time between Paris's Gare du Nord and London's Waterloo Station to a mere 3 hours. With some restrictions, fares between London and Paris begin at $139 for one-way transport (and at $158 for round-trip transport), in second class. First-class transit begins at $219 one-way and $248 round-trip, per person. Additional discounts, in many cases, are offered to holders of valid Eurail and Britrail passes, youths under 26, students, and persons over 60. And for passengers looking for additional perks to first-class transport, packages can be bought beginning at $369 per person each way, that allow access to first-class waiting lounges in both Paris and London, enhanced cuisine on board, and taxi service between the railway station of your final destination and your hotel. If you need a hotel in either London or Paris, the staff at Eurostar can set up a rail/hotel package at a highly discounted rate. For round-trip transport plus a night in a hotel in either London or Paris, plus a sightseeing package, rates begin at $595 per person in first class and $435 per person in second class. If, during your dialogues with Eurostar, you ask about special promotions, you may discover some surprising discounts. Examples include a departure from and a return to either city on the same day, at round-trip rates that can be about the same as a conventional one-way ticket.

From North America, call the **Eurostar** division of RailEurope at ✆ **800/EUROSTAR.** For details about hotel packages, contact **Euro-Vacations** at ✆ **888/281-EURO.** If you're already in Paris, contact any travel agency, talk to your concierge, or check www.raileurope.com.

17 large arched windows matched by corresponding beveled mirrors in simulated arcades, plus amazing chandeliers and gilded lamp bearers. The vaulted ceiling is covered with paintings in classic allegorical style depicting the story of Louis XIV. On June 28, 1919, the treaty ending World War I was signed in this corridor. Ironically, the German Empire was also proclaimed here in 1871.

The royal apartments were for show, but Louis XV and Louis XVI retired to the **Petits Appartements** ★★ to escape the demands of court etiquette. Louis XV died in his bedchamber in 1774, a victim of smallpox. In the second-floor **King's Apartments,** which you can visit only with a guide, he stashed away first Mme de Pompadour and then Mme du Barry. Attempts have been made to return the **Queen's Apartments** to their appearance in the days of Marie Antoinette, when she played her harpsichord in front of specially invited guests.

Her king, Louis XVI, had an impressive **Library,** designed by Gabriel, which was sumptuous. Its panels are delicately carved, and the room has been restored and refurnished. The **Clock Room** contains Passement's astronomical clock, encased in gilded bronze. Twenty years in the making, it was completed in 1753 and is supposed to keep time until the year 9999. At the age of 7, Mozart played for the court in this room.

Gabriel designed the **Opéra** ✶✶ for Louis XV in 1748, though it wasn't completed until 1770. In its heyday, it took 3,000 candles to light the place. With gold-and-white harmony, Hardouin-Mansart built the **Royal Chapel** ✶✶✶ in 1699, dying before its completion. Louis XVI, when still the dauphin (crown prince), married Marie Antoinette here in 1770. Both the bride and the groom in this arranged marriage were teenagers.

After having been closed for years, the **Musée de France** (✆ **01-39-67-07-73**), has now reopened and is accessible via Porte D (Door D) in the château. The museum traces the history of the parliamentary process in France following the collapse of the monarchy in 1789, with exhibits describing the processes whereby laws and the democratic process are made and enforced. Admission is 20F (3.05€, $2.90) adults and half-price for children under 18, and rental of a prerecorded audio guide (English or French) is 25F (3.80€, $3.65). It's open Tuesday to Saturday 9am to 5:30pm.

Place d'Armes. ✆ **01-30-83-78-00**. Admission to the château 46F (7€, $6.65) adults, 35F (5.30€, $5.10) ages 18–25; under age 18/over 60 free. Reduced rates for adults after 3:30pm. May 2–Sept 30 Tues–Sun 9am–6:30pm (to 5pm the rest of the year).

Gardens of Versailles ✶✶✶   Spread across 250 acres, the Gardens of Versailles were laid out by the great landscape artist Le Nôtre, who created a Garden of Eden using ornamental lakes and canals, geometrically designed flower beds, and avenues bordered with statuary. At the peak of their glory, 1,400 fountains spewed forth. *The Buffet* is an exceptional one, having been designed by Mansart. One fountain depicts Apollo in his chariot pulled by four horses, surrounded by tritons emerging from the water to light the world. On the mile-long Grand Canal, Louis XV—imagining he was in Venice—used to take gondola rides with his favorite of the moment.

On Christmas Day 1999, the most violent windstorm in France's history thundered through Paris, causing extensive damage to parks and gardens in the Ile de France. At Versailles, the wind toppled 10,000 trees and blew out some windows at the magnificent château. The palace has now reopened, but the difficult task of replanting the thousands of trees will take some time, and it'll be years before they return to their lush grandeur. Nonetheless, there is still much that remains to enchant, and the gardens get better and better every month.

Fun Fact **Your Own Tree at Versailles**

The gardeners of Versailles claim (in French, of course) that it's an ill wind that doesn't blow someone some good. Before that crippling storm at Christmas in 1999, many of their trees were too tall, weak, aged, and diseased. The storms took care of that, uprooting such classics as Marie Antoinette's much-loved Virginia tulip tree planted in 1783. With $40 million in funds allocated, the park is being restored to the way it was in the heyday of Louis XIV, the Sun King. When the work is completed, the grounds of Versailles will look more spectacular than ever. For a donation of $155, you, too, can sponsor a new tree for the park. For more details on this, hook into www.chateauversailles.fr.

Place d'Armes (behind the Palace of Versailles). ℭ **01-30-83-78-00.** Free admission. Daily 7am–dusk (between 5:30 and 9:30pm).

The Trianons & The Hamlet   A long walk across the park will take you to the Grand Trianon 🏵🏵, in pink-and-white marble. Le Vau built a Porcelain Trianon here in 1670, covered with blue and white china tiles, but it was fragile and soon fell into ruin. So, in 1687, Louis XIV commissioned Hardouin-Mansart to build the Grand Trianon. Traditionally, it has been a place where France has lodged important guests, though de Gaulle wanted to turn it into a weekend retreat. Nixon once slept here in the room where Mme de Pompadour died. Mme de Maintenon also slept here, as did Napoléon. The original furnishings are gone, of course, with mostly Empire pieces there today.

Gabriel, the designer of place de la Concorde in Paris, built the **Petit Trianon** 🏵🏵 in 1768 for Louis XV. Louis used it for his trysts with Mme du Barry. When he died, Louis XVI presented it to his wife, and Marie Antoinette adopted it as her favorite residence, a place to escape the rigid life at the main palace. Many of the current furnishings, including a few in her rather modest bedchamber, belonged to the ill-fated queen.

Rousseau's theories about recapturing the natural beauty of life were much in favor in the late 18th century, and they prompted Marie Antoinette to have Mique build her a 12-house **Hamlet** on the banks of the Grand Trianon Lake in 1783. She wanted a chance to experience the simplicity of peasant life—or at least peasant life as seen through the eyes of a frivolous queen. Dressed as a shepherdess, she would come here to watch sheep being tended and cows being milked, men fishing and washerwomen beating their laundry in the lake, and donkey carts bringing corn to be ground at the mill.

Place d'Armes (to the immediate right after entering the Palace of Versailles). ℭ **01-30-83-78-00.** Grand Trianon 25F (3.80€, $3.65) adults, 15F (2.35€, $2.25) ages 18–25, under age 18 free. Petit Trianon 15F (2.35€, $2.25) adults, 10F (1.50€, $1.45) ages 18–25, under age 18 free. Both Trianons 30F (4.55€, $4.35) adults, 20F (3.05€, $2.90) ages 18–25, under age 18 free. Reduced rates for adults after 3:30pm. May 2–Sept 30 Tues–Sun 10am–6:30pm (to 5pm the rest of the year). Hamlet free; daily 7am–dusk (between 5:30 and 9:30pm).

SEASONAL EVENTS

SUMMER EVENING SPECTACLES   The **Fêtes de Nuit de Versailles (Rêve de Roi)** is a government-sponsored summer program of evening fireworks and illuminated fountains. These always capture the heightened sense of the glory of France's *ancien régime*. At various dates throughout summer, 200 actors in period costume portray Louis XVI and members of his court. April to June

---

Impressions

When Louis XIV had finished the Grand Trianon, he told [Mme de] Maintenon he had created a paradise for her, and asked if she could think of anything now to wish for. . . . She said she could think of but one thing—it was summer, and it was balmy France—yet she would like well to sleigh ride in the leafy avenues of Versailles! The next morning found miles and miles of grassy avenues spread thick with snowy salt and sugar, and a procession of those quaint sleighs waiting to receive the chief concubine of the gaiest and most unprincipled court that France has ever seen!

—Mark Twain, *The Innocents Abroad* (1869)

and October shows begin at 10:30pm; 9:30pm in August and September. You sit on bleachers clustered at the château's boulevard de la Reine entrance, adjacent to the Fountain (Bassin) of Neptune. The most desirable seats are 250F (38€, $36.25), with standing room at 70F (10.65€, $10.15). Gates that admit you into the bleacher area open 90 minutes before show time, and the show itself lasts 90 minutes.

You can buy tickets in advance at the **tourist office** in Versailles—inquire by phone, fax, or mail—or in central Paris at any of the **FNAC** stores (see chapter 9). You can also take your chances and buy tickets an hour prior to the event from a kiosk adjacent to the boulevard de la Reine entrance. Call ℂ **01-30-83-78-88** for general info about any of the nighttime or afternoon spectacles on the grounds.

AFTERNOON PROMENADES IN THE PARK _Moments_ Every Sunday early April to mid-October and every Saturday early July to late August, between 11am and noon and between 3:30 and 5:30pm, classical music is broadcast throughout the park and every fountain is turned on. The effect of these **Grandes Eaux Musicales** is to duplicate the landscaping vision of the 18th-century architects who designed Versailles. They even allow you to walk freely around the park, enjoying the juxtapositions of grand architecture and lavish waterworks. The cost of admission to the park during these events is 25F (3.80€, $3.65) per person.

WHERE TO DINE

Le Potager du Roy ⭐ FRENCH   Philippe Letourneur cooks from the heart, specializing in a simple cuisine with robust flavors. His attractive restaurant occupies an 18th-century building in a neighborhood known during the days of the French monarchs as the Parc des Cerfs ("Stag Park," where courtiers could find paid companionship with B- and C-list courtesans). The skillfully prepared menu is reinvented with the seasons and may include foie gras with vegetable-flavored vinaigrette; roasted duck with a navarin of vegetables; macaroni ragout with a persillade of snails; and roasted codfish with roasted peppers in the style of Provence. For something unusual, order the fondant of pork jowls with a confit of fresh vegetables. Try to save room for the chocolate cake, flavored with orange and served with coconut ice cream.

1 rue du Maréchal-Joffre. ☎ **01-39-50-35-34.** Reservations required. Fixed-price menu 145F (22.05€, $21.05) at lunch, 189–285F (28.75–43.30€, $27.40–$41.35) at dinner. AE, V. Tues–Fri noon–2:30pm and 7–10:30pm, Sat 7–10:30pm.

Le Quai No. 1 *Value* FRENCH/SEAFOOD   This informal bistro occupies an 18th-century building overlooking the château's western facade. Lithographs and wood paneling spangle the dining room, and outside is a terrace. Though the cuisine isn't as opulent or expensive as what's served in chef Gérard Vié's grander Les Trois Marches (below), it's charming and dependable in presentation. The fixed-price menus make Le Quai a bargain. Specialties are seafood sauerkraut, seafood paella, bouillabaisse, home-smoked salmon, and an upscale version of North American surf and turf, with grilled lobster and sizzling sirloin. Care and imagination go into the food, and the service is professional and polite.

1 av. de St-Cloud. ☎ **01-39-50-42-26.** Reservations required. Main courses 90F (13.70€, $13.05); fixed-price menu 120F (18.25€, $17.40) at lunch, 150–190F (22.80–28.90€, $21.75–$27.55) at dinner. MC, V. Tues–Sat noon–2:30pm and 7:30–11pm, Sun noon–2:30pm.

Les Trois Marches ⭐⭐⭐ FRENCH   This is one of the best restaurants not only in Versailles but in the Ile de France. The Hôtel Trianon Palace became famous in 1919 when it served as headquarters for signatories to the Treaty of Versailles, and the dining room retains an old-world splendor. Gérard Vié is the most talented and creative chef in town, attracting a discerning crowd that doesn't mind paying the high prices. His *cuisine moderne* is subtle, often daring, and the service is smooth. Begin with the lobster salad with fresh herbs, served with onion soufflé; the galette of potatoes with bacon, chardonnay, and sevruga caviar; or the citrus-flavored scallop bisque. Stars among the main courses are the pigeon roasted and flavored with rosé and accompanied by celeriac and truffles, and the celeriac fashioned into ravioli, filled with foie gras, and topped by a thick slice of black truffle. If you arrive in late autumn, you might find penne-like pasta, tossed with morels, mushrooms, and Parmesan and blended in a butter sauce with white Alba truffles. For dessert, opt for the signature assortment.

In the Hôtel Trianon Palace, 1 bd. de la Reine. © **01-39-50-13-21.** Reservations required far in advance. Fixed-price menu 350F (53.20€, $50.75) at lunch Mon–Fri, 650–850F (98.80–129.20€, $94.25–$123.25) at lunch Sat–Sun and at dinner. AE, DC, MC, V. Daily noon–2pm and 7:30–10pm. Closed Aug.

2 The Forest & Château of Rambouillet

34 miles SW of Paris, 26 miles NE of Chartres

Once known as La Forêt d'Yveline, the **Forest of Rambouillet** ⚹ is one of the loveliest woods in France. More than 47,000 acres of greenery stretch from the valley of the Eure to the high valley of Chevreuse, the latter rich in medieval and royal abbeys. Lakes, copses of hiding deer, and even wild boar are some of the attractions of this "green lung." Most people, however, come here to see the château, which you can visit when it's not in use as a "Camp David" for French presidents.

ESSENTIALS

GETTING THERE   It takes 2 hours to see the château at Rambouillet. **Trains** depart from Paris's Gare Montparnasse every 30 minutes throughout the day. One-way passage costs 42F (6.45€, $6.15) for about a 35-minute ride. Information and train schedules can be obtained by contacting **La Gare de Rambouillet,** place Prud'homme (© **01-53-90-20-20**). By **car,** take N-10 southwest from Paris, passing Versailles along the way.

VISITOR INFORMATION   The **tourist office** is at the Hôtel de Ville, place de la Libération (© **01-34-83-21-21**).

SEEING THE CHATEAU

Château de Rambouillet ★   Dating from 1375, the château is surrounded by a park in one of the most famous forests in France. Superb woodwork is used throughout, and the walls are adorned with tapestries, many from the era of Louis XV. Before it became a royal residence, the marquise de Rambouillet kept a house here; it's said she taught Paris's cultured ladies and gentlemen how to talk, introducing them to a long string of poets and painters. François I, the Chevalier king, died of a fever here in 1547 at age 52. When the château was later occupied by the comte de Toulouse, Rambouillet was often visited by Louis XV, who was amused (in more ways than one) by the comte's high-spirited wife. Louis XVI eventually acquired the château, but Marie Antoinette found it boring and called it "the toad." In his surprisingly modest boudoir are four panels representing the continents.

In 1814, Napoléon's second wife, Marie-Louise (daughter of Francis II, emperor of Austria), met at Rambouillet with her father, who convinced her to abandon Napoléon and France itself after her husband's humiliating defeats at Moscow and Leipzig. Afterward, she fled to her original home, the royal court in Vienna, with Napoléon's 3-year-old son, François-Charles-Joseph Bonaparte (also known as l'Aiglon, the young eagle, and, at least in title, the king of Rome). Before his death in Vienna at age 21, his claim on the Napoleonic legacy was rejected by France's enemies, despite the fact that his father had had a special annex to the château at Rambouillet built especially for his use. A year later, before his final exile to the remote island of St. Helena, Napoléon insisted on spending a final night at Rambouillet, where he secluded himself with his meditations and memories.

In 1830, the elderly Charles X, Louis XVI's brother, abdicated the throne at Rambouillet as a Parisian mob marched on the château and his troops began to

Moments Through an Enchanted Forest

Rambouillet and its forests provide a verdant interlude within a day that might otherwise be filled with forest views from the inside of a car. If you've exhausted the idea of a ramble through the gardens that surround the château of Rambouillet (or if they're closed because of the security issue associated with a visit from the President of France), consider a visit to the **Rochers d'Angennes,** rocky hillocks that remain as leftovers from the Ice Age. To reach them, park your car on the D107, about 3 miles north of the hamlet of Épernon. At the site where you'll see a sign pointing to the **Rochers et Étang d'Angennes,** you can park your car and walk along a clearly marked trail, through a pine forest, before you eventually reach a rocky plateau overlooking the hills and a pond *(l'Étang d'Angennes)* nestled into the surrounding countryside. Round-trip, from the site of your parked car to the plateau and back, your promenade should take between 30 and 45 minutes.

An alternative escapade involves parking your car in the hamlet of St-Hubert, which lies beside the N191 about 5 miles SW of the larger village of Montfort-l'Amaury. Within a 10-minute walk south of St-Hubert, along footpaths pointing to *l'Étang de St-Hubert,* you'll reach the waters of one of a series of serpentine-shaped ponds that were dug out, and dammed, on orders of Louis XIV in the 18th century, as part of a series of irrigation and flood-control measures. There was an elaborate hunting lodge built by Louis XV that once stood near this village, but it was destroyed during the Revolution. The promenade, about 15 minutes from your parked car to the lake and back, encompasses views of massive colonies of water lilies, part of the horticultural legacy of gardeners at the time who tried to beautify the lake for the French kings.

desert him. From Rambouillet, he embarked for a safe but controversial haven in England. Afterward, Rambouillet fell into private hands. At one time it was a fashionable restaurant attracting Parisians by offering gondola rides. Napoléon III, however, returned it to the Crown. In 1897, it was designated a residence for the presidents of the Republic. And in 1944, Charles de Gaulle lived here briefly before giving the order for what was left of the French army to join the Americans in liberating Paris.

Parc du Château. ✆ **01-34-94-28-00.** Admission 32F (4.85€, $4.65) adults, 21F (3.20€, $3.05) students 12–25, children 11 and under free. Wed–Mon 10–11:30am and 2–4:30pm (to 3:30pm Oct–Mar).

WHERE TO DINE

La Poste FRENCH (TRADITIONAL)   On a street corner in the town's historic center, this restaurant dates from the mid-19th century, when it provided meals and shelter for the region's mail carriers. The two dining rooms have rustic beams and old-fashioned accents that complement the flavorful old-fashioned food. Good-tasting menu items include homemade terrines of foie gras and freshly made pastries. A particularly flavorful dish is beef filet served with a Perigueux sauce of Madeira wine and foie gras.

101 rue du Général-de-Gaulle. ⓒ **01-34-83-03-01.** Reservations recommended Sat–Sun. Main courses 120–156F (18.25–23.70€, $17.40–$22.60); fixed-price menu 120–190F (18.25–28.90€, $17.40–$27.55). AE, MC, V. Tues–Sun noon–2pm; Tues–Wed and Fri–Sat 7–10pm.

3 The Cathedral at Chartres

60 miles SW of Paris, 47 miles NW of Orléans

Many observers feel the architectural aspirations of the Middle Ages reached their highest expression in the glorious Cathédrale de Chartres. Come to see its soaring architecture, highly wrought sculpture, and, above all, its stained glass, which gave the world a new color, Chartres blue.

ESSENTIALS

GETTING THERE   It takes a full day to see Chartres. From Paris's Gare Montparnasse, **trains** run directly to Chartres, taking less than an hour and passing through a sea of wheat fields. **By car,** take A10/A11 southwest from the *périphérique* and follow the signs to Le Mans and Chartres (the Chartres exit is clearly marked).

VISITOR INFORMATION   The **tourist office** is on place de la Cathédrale (ⓒ **02-37-18-26-26**).

SEEING THE CATHEDRAL

Cathédrale Notre-Dame de Chartres ✦✦✦   Reportedly, Rodin once sat for hours on the edge of the sidewalk, admiring this cathedral's Romanesque sculpture. His opinion: Chartres is the French Acropolis. When it began to rain, a kind soul offered him an umbrella, which he declined, so transfixed was he by the magic of this place.

The cathedral's origins are uncertain; some have suggested it grew up over an ancient Druid site that had later become a Roman temple. It is known that as early as the 4th century there was a Christian basilica here. An 1194 fire destroyed most of what had then become a Romanesque cathedral but spared the western facade and crypt. The cathedral you see today dates principally from the 13th century, when it was rebuilt with the efforts and contributions of kings, princes, churchmen, and pilgrims from all over Europe. One of the world's greatest high Gothic cathedrals, it was the first to use flying buttresses to support the soaring dimensions within.

French sculpture in the 12th century broke into full bloom when the **Royal Portal** ✦✦✦ was added. A landmark in Romanesque art, the sculptured bodies are elongated, often stylized, in their long flowing robes. But the faces are amazingly (for the time) life-like, occasionally winking or smiling. In the central tympanum, Christ is shown at the Second Coming, with his descent depicted on the right, his ascent on the left. Before entering, walk around to both the **North Portal** and the **South Portal,** each from the 13th century. They depict such biblical scenes as the expulsion of Adam and Eve from the Garden of Eden.

Inside is a celebrated **choir screen;** work on it began in the 16th century and lasted until 1714. The niches, 40 in all, contain statues illustrating scenes from the life of the Madonna and Christ—everything from the *Massacre of the Innocents* to the *Coronation of the Virgin.*

But few rushed visitors ever notice the screen: They're too transfixed by the light from the **stained glass** ✦✦✦. Covering an expanse of more than 3,000 square yards, the glass is truly mystical, unlike anything else in the world. The stained glass, most of which dates from the 12th and 13th centuries, was spared

Moments **Music of the Spheres**

If you're visiting Chartres on a Sunday afternoon, the cathedral features a free 1-hour organ concert beginning at 4:45pm, when the filtered light of the Ile de France sunset makes the western windows come thrillingly alive.

in both world wars by painstakingly removing it piece by piece. See the windows in the morning, at noon, in the afternoon, at sunset—as often as you can. Like the petals of a kaleidoscope, they constantly change. It's difficult to single out one panel or window above the others, but an exceptional one is the 12th-century *Vierge de la belle verrière* (**Our Lady of the Beautiful Window**) on the south side. Of course, there are three fiery rose windows, but you couldn't miss those if you tried.

The **nave,** the widest in France, still contains its ancient floor labyrinth, which formed a mobile channel of contemplation for monks. The wooden *Notre-Dame du piller* (**Virgin of the Pillar**), to the left of the choir, dates from the 14th century. The crypt was built over 2 centuries, beginning in the 9th. Enshrined within is *Our Lady of the Crypt,* a 1976 Madonna that replaced one destroyed during the Revolution.

Try to take a tour conducted by **Malcolm Miller** (© **02-37-28-15-58;** fax 02-37-28-33-03), an Englishman who has spent 3 decades studying the cathedral and giving tours in English with a rare blend of scholarship, enthusiasm, and humor. He usually conducts 75-minute tours at noon and 2:45pm Monday to Saturday for 40F (6.10€, $5.80). Tours are canceled in the event of pilgrimages, religious celebrations, and large funerals. French-language tours at 35F (5.30€, $5.15) are conducted by other guides Easter to late October at 10:30am and 3pm and the rest of the year at 2:30pm.

If you feel fit enough, don't miss the opportunity, especially in summer, to climb to the top of the **New Bell Tower.** Open the same hours as the cathedral, except for a closing between noon and 2pm, it costs 25F (3.80€, $3.65) for adults and 15F (2.35€, $2.25) for students. The **crypt,** gloomy and somber but rich with a sense of medieval history, can be visited only as part of a French-speaking tour conducted whenever there's enough demand. The cost is 11F (1.65€, $1.60).

After your visit, stroll through the **Episcopal Gardens** and enjoy yet another view of this remarkable cathedral.

16 Cloître Notre-Dame. © 02-37-21-56-33. Admission free. Mon–Sat 7:30am–7pm, Sun 8:30am–7pm.

EXPLORING THE OLD TOWN

If time remains, you may want to explore the medieval cobbled streets of the **Vieux Quartier** ✦ (Old Town). At the foot of the cathedral are lanes containing gabled houses and humped bridges spanning the Eure River. From the pont de Bouju, you can see the lofty spires in the background. Try to find **rue Chantault,** which boasts houses with colorful facades, one 8 centuries old.

A highlight of your visit will be **Musée des Beaux-Arts de Chartres,** ✦ 29 Cloître Notre-Dame (© **02-37-36-41-39**), next door to the cathedral. A former episcopal palace, the building at times competes with its exhibitions—one part dates from the 15th century and encompasses a courtyard. This museum of fine arts boasts a permanent painting collection covering the 16th to the 20th century, including the work of masters like Zurbarán, Watteau, and Brosamer. Of particular interest is David Ténier's *Le Concert.* Special exhibits are often mounted. October 31 to May 2, it's open Wednesday to Monday from 10am to noon and 2 to 5pm; the rest of the year, hours are Wednesday to Monday from 10am to noon and 2 to 6pm. Admission is 15F (2.35€, $2.25) adults and 7.50F (1.15€, $1.15) children.

WHERE TO STAY

Hotel Châtelet   This relatively modern hotel has many traditional touches. The rustic guest rooms are inviting, with reproductions of Louis XV and Louis XVI furniture. The larger, more expensive rooms face a garden and avoid street noise. Many windows along the front (street) side of the hotel open onto a view of the cathedral. The baths are boxy, without a lot of shelf space. In chilly weather, there's a log-burning fire in one of the salons. Breakfast is the only meal served, but there are numerous restaurants close by.

6–8 av. Jehan-de-Beauce, 28000 Chartres. ✆ **02-37-21-78-00.** Fax 02-37-36-23-01. 48 units. 395–510F (60.05–77.50€, $57.30–$73.95) double. 3rd person 60F (9.10€, $8.70) extra. AE, DC, MC, V. Free parking. **In-room amenities:** TV, minibar, hair dryer.

Le Grand Monarque Best Western Chartres's leading hotel occupies a mid–19th century building enclosing a courtyard. It attracts people who enjoy its old-world charm, with its Art-Nouveau stained glass and Louis XV chairs in the dining room. The guest rooms are decorated with reproductions of antiques, and most have sitting areas. The baths are motel standard. The hotel also has an anachronistic restaurant (a local critic found the kitchen trapped in an "ancien régime time warp").

22 place des Epars, 28005 Chartres. ✆ **800/528-1234** in the U.S., or 02-37-21-00-72. Fax 02-37-36-34-18. www.bw-grand-monarque.com. 54 units. 615–740F (93.55–112.55€, $89.25–$107.30) double, 1,230F (186.95€, $178.35) suite. AE, DC, MC, V. Parking 50F (7.60€, $7.25). **Amenities:** Restaurant; bar; room service; laundry/dry cleaning. *In room:* TV, minibar.

WHERE TO DINE

La Truie qui File (Choukroune) ★★★ FRENCH (MODERN) At last Chartres offers a restaurant worthy of some of the more stellar choices in Paris. The blue-and-yellow decor of this place includes modern furniture and art that's set beneath the venerable ceiling beams of a building erected in the 15th century. The interior, coupled with the savory cuisine of Gilles and Geneviève Choukroune, creates a combination that usually bustles with good cheer and repeat visitors. The only option on the menu is a fixed-price menu with five choices for the starter, main course, and dessert. The pleasing menu items change with the season, but are likely to include foie gras with spice bread, a combination of crayfish and snails in a blanquette, oxtail stewed in Loire valley wine, and roasted scallops with coriander oil. The signature dessert combines fresh clementines with cumin. Cooking times are unerringly accurate, and there is a certain charm and fragrance to every dish.

Place Poissonnerie. ✆ **02-37-21-53-90.** Reservations required. Fixed-price menu 230F (34.95€, $33.35). Tues–Sun noon–2pm; Tues–Sat 7:30–9:30pm. Closed Aug.

Le Buisson Ardent *(Value)* FRENCH (TRADITIONAL) Housed in a charming 300-year-old house in the most historic section of town, this restaurant is one floor above street level in the shadow of the cathedral. The composition of the fixed-price menus changes with the seasons. The least expensive one is known for offering one of the town's best luncheon values, of special interest to day-trippers. Everything is made with fresh meats, produce, and fish. The most popular dishes are escalope of warm foie gras with apples and Calvados and émincée of roasted pigeon with sweetbreads and honey sauce. Other dishes are simpler, the kind you might've noticed in bistros, like codfish flavored with coriander and served with parsley flan. A dessert specialty is crispy hot pineapples with orange and passion fruit salad.

10 rue au Lait. ✆ **02-37-34-04-66.** Reservations recommended. Main courses 90–142F (13.75–21.65€, $13.05–$20.65); fixed-price menu 145–250F (22.05–38€, $21.05–$36.25). MC, V. Thurs–Tues noon–2pm and 7:30–9:30pm.

4 Giverny

50 miles NW of Paris

On the border between Normandy and the Ile de France, **Giverny** is home to the Claude Monet Foundation, in the house where the Impressionist painter lived for 43 years. The restored house and its gardens are open to the public.

ESSENTIALS

GETTING THERE   It takes a full morning to get to Giverny and to see its sights. Take the Paris-Rouen **train** from Paris's Gare St-Lazare to the Vernon station, where a taxi can take you the 3 miles to Giverny. Perhaps the easiest way to enjoy Giverny is on a full-day **bus tour** whose focal point is Monet's house and garden. In summer you can arrange this through **Cityrama,** 2 rue des Pyramides, 1st arr. (© **01-44-55-61-00;** Métro: Palais Royal), or year-round by contacting **American Express,** 11 rue Scribe, 9th arr. (© **01-42-27-58-80;** Métro: Opéra).

By **car,** take the Autoroute de l'Ouest (Port de St-Cloud) toward Rouen. Leave the autoroute at Bonnières, then cross the Seine on the pont de Bonnières. From here, a direct road with signs will bring you to Giverny. Expect about an hour of driving; try to avoid weekends. Another way to get to Giverny is to leave the highway at the Bonnières exit and go toward Vernon. Once in Vernon, cross the bridge over the Seine and follow the signs to Giverny or Gasny (Giverny is before Gasny). This is easier than going through Bonnières, where there aren't many signs.

SEEING MONET'S HOUSE & GARDEN

Claude Monet Foundation ★★★   French painter Claude Monet was a spiritualist of light, brilliantly translating its effects at different times of the day. In fact, some critics claim he "invented light." His series of paintings of the Rouen Cathedral and of the water lilies, which one critic called "vertical interpretations of horizontal lines," are just a few of his masterpieces.

Monet came to Giverny in 1883, at age 43. While taking a small railway linking Vetheuil to Vernon, he discovered the village at a point where the Epte stream joined the Seine. Many of his friends used to visit him here at Le Pressoir, including Clemenceau, Cézanne, Rodin, Renoir, Degas, and Sisley. When Monet died in 1926, his son, Michel, inherited the house but left it abandoned until it decayed into ruins. The gardens became almost a jungle, inhabited by river rats. In 1966, Michel died and left the house to the Académie des Beaux-Arts. It wasn't until 1977 that Gerald van der Kemp, who restored Versailles, decided to work on Giverny. A large part of it was restored with gifts from American benefactors, especially the late Lila Acheson Wallace, former head of *Reader's Digest.*

You can stroll through the garden and view the thousands of flowers, including the famous *nymphéas* (water lilies). The Japanese bridge, hung with wisteria, leads to a dreamy setting of weeping willows and rhododendrons. Monet's studio barge was installed on the pond.

Rue Claude-Monet Parc Gasny. © **02-32-51-28-21.** Admission 35F (5.30€, $5.15) adults, 20F (3.05€, $2.90) ages 7–18, under 7 free. Apr–Oct Tues–Sun 10am–6pm.

WHERE TO DINE

Auberge du Vieux Moulin FRENCH (TRADITIONAL)   This stone-sided restaurant is a convenient lunch stop where the Boudeau family maintains a series of cozy dining rooms filled with original Impressionist paintings. Because you can walk here from the museum in about 5 minutes, leave your car in the museum lot. Specialties include appetizers like snails in puff pastry with garlic-flavored butter sauce, guinea fowl braised in cider, chicken with shrimp, and escalope of salmon with sorrel sauce. Dessert might be a *tarte Normande* prepared with apple slices and Calvados. The kitchen doesn't pretend the food is any more than it is: hearty country fare with panache. The charm of the staff helps a lot, too.

21 rue de la Falaise. ℐ **02-32-51-46-15.** Main courses 74–98F (11.25–14.90€, $10.75–$14.20); fixed-price menu 135–155F (20.50–23.55€, $19.65–$22.55). MC, V. Tues–Sun noon–3pm and 7:30–10pm. Closed Jan.

5 Disneyland Paris

20 miles E of Paris

After provoking some of the most controversial reactions in recent French history, the multimillion-dollar Euro Disney Resort opened in 1992 as one of the world's most lavish theme parks, situated on a 5,000-acre site (about one-fifth the size of Paris) in the suburb of Marne-la-Vallée. In 1994, it unofficially changed its name to Disneyland Paris. The early days of this megascale project weren't particularly happy: European journalists delighted in belittling it and accusing it of everything from cultural imperialism to the death knell of French culture. But after financial jitters and goodly amounts of public relations and financial juggling, the resort is on track.

In fact, it's now the number-one attraction in France, with 50 million annual visitors. MONSIEUR MICKEY TRIUMPHS! the French press headlined. Disney surpasses the Eiffel Tower and the Louvre in numbers of visitors and accounts for 4% of the tourism industry's foreign currency sales. Disneyland Paris looks, tastes, and feels like its parents in California and Florida—except for the European flair (the use of pastel colors rather than primary colors) and the $10 cheeseburgers *"avec pommes frites."* Allow a full day to see the park.

ESSENTIALS
GETTING THERE   The resort is linked to the **RER** commuter express rail network (Line A), which maintains a stop within walking distance of the park. Board the RER at such Paris stops as Charles de Gaulle–Etoile, Châtelet–Les Halles, or Nation. Get off at Line A's last stop, Marne-la-Vallée/Chessy, 45 minutes from central Paris. The round-trip fare from central Paris is 80F (12.15€, $11.60). Trains run every 10 to 20 minutes, depending on the time of day.

Each of the hotels in the resort connects by **shuttle bus** to both Orly and Charles de Gaulle. Buses depart from both airports at intervals of 45 minutes. One-way transportation to the park from either airport costs 85F (12.90€, $12.35).

If you're coming by **car,** take A-4 east from Paris, getting off at exit 14, marked PARC EURO DISNEYLAND. Guest parking at any of the thousands of parking spaces is 40F (6.10€, $5.80) per day. An interconnected series of moving sidewalks speeds up pedestrian transit from the parking areas to the theme park's entrance. Parking for guests at any of the resort's hotels is free.

SPENDING THE DAY AT DISNEY
Disneyland Paris ✫✫✫   The resort was designed as a total vacation package: Included within one enormous unit are the Disneyland Park with its five entertainment "lands," six large hotels, a campground, an entertainment center (Village Disney), a 27-hole golf course, and dozens of restaurants, shows, and shops. Peak season is mid-June to mid-September, as well as Christmas and Easter weeks. Entrance to Village Disney is free, though there's usually a cover charge for the dance clubs.

One of the attractions, **Main Street, U.S.A.,** features horse-drawn carriages and street-corner barbershop quartets. From the "Main Street Station," steam-powered railway cars leave for a trip through a Grand Canyon Diorama to

Sizing Up Monsieur Mickey

In terms of how Disneyland Paris compares to Disney's parks in the United States, the French park definitely lies in the middle, with top honors going to Florida's Walt Disney World and California's Disneyland running a distant third. The layout of Disneyland Paris resembles Walt Disney World's Magic Kingdom; however, the French property is smaller and has fewer attractions and rides. Disneyland Paris will be expanded in 2002 with the addition of Walt Disney Studios, which will focus on the role of movies in popular culture.

Frontierland, with paddle-wheel steamers reminiscent of the Mississippi Valley described by Mark Twain. The park's steam trains chug past **Adventureland**— with swashbuckling 18th-century pirates, the tree house of the Swiss Family Robinson, and a roller coaster, Indiana Jones and the Temple of Peril . . . Backwards!, that travels in reverse—to **Fantasyland.** Here you can see the symbol of the theme park, the Sleeping Beauty Castle *(Le Château de la belle au bois dormant),* whose soaring pinnacles and turrets are a spectacular idealized interpretation of the châteaux of France.

Visions of the future are displayed at **Discoveryland,** whose tributes to human invention and imagination are drawn from the works of Leonardo da Vinci, Jules Verne, H. G. Wells, the modern masters of science fiction, and the *Star Wars* series. Discoveryland has proven among the most popular of all the areas and is one of the few that was enlarged (in 1995) after the park's inauguration. A noteworthy addition was a new roller coaster called **Space Mountain,** which emulates an earth-to-moon transit as conceived by Jules Verne. Another popular attraction here is an in-theater experience, **Honey, I Shrunk the Kids,** where 3-D and animation gives the illusion that the audience has been shrunk.

As Disney continues to churn out animated blockbusters, look for its newest stars to appear in the theme park. The fact that the characters from such films as *Aladdin, The Lion King,* and *Pocahontas* are actually made of celluloid hasn't kept them out of the Ice Capades, and it certainly won't keep them out of Disneyland Paris.

Disney also maintains an entertainment center, **Village Disney,** whose indoor/outdoor layout is a cross between a California mall and the Coney Island boardwalk. Scattered on either side of a pedestrian walkway, illuminated by overhead spotlights, it's just outside the boundaries of the fenced-in acreage containing the bulk of Disneyland's attractions. The complex accommodates dance clubs, snack bars, restaurants, souvenir shops, and bars for adults who want to escape from the children for a while. Unlike the rest of the park, admission to **Village Disney** is free, so it attracts night owls from Paris and its suburbs who wouldn't otherwise be particularly interested in the park itself.

Disneyland Paris recognizes that long lines tend to frustrate families. In 2000, the park inaugurated the **Fast Pass** system, whereby participants show up at the various rides, and receive a reservation for a 1-hour time block within which they should return. Within that 1-hour period, waiting times are usually no more than 8 minutes. This system is presently used for five of the most popular rides: Space Mountain (Discoveryland); Indiana Jones and the Temple of

Disneyland Paris

Pirates
of the
Caribbean

Adventureland

Adventure
Isle

Peter Pan's
Flight

Indiana Jones
et le
Temple du Péril

La Cabane
des Robinson

Le Passage
d'Aladdin

Critter
Corral

Disneyland Railroad
Frontierland Depot

Frontierland

Legends
of the
Wild West

The
Chaparral
Stage

River Rogue
Koolboats

Shootin'
Gallery

Big Thunder
Mountain

Riverboat
Landing

Phantom
Manor

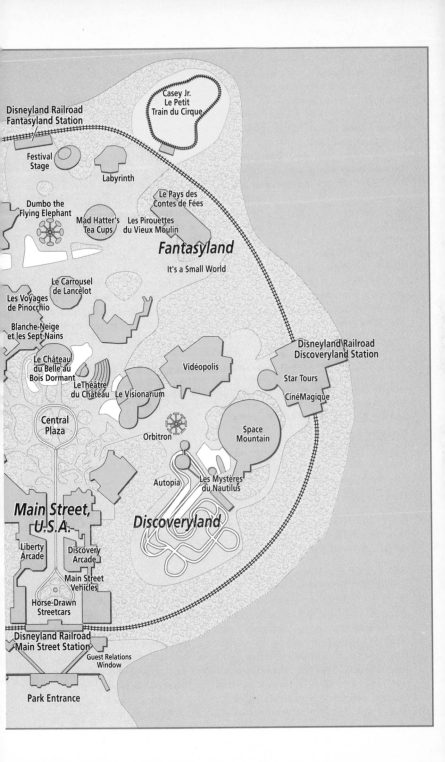

Casey Jr.
Le Petit
Train du Cirque

Disneyland Railroad
Fantasyland Station

Festival
Stage

Labyrinth

Le Pays des
Contes de Fées

Dumbo the
Flying Elephant

Mad Hatter's
Tea Cups

Les Pirouettes
du Vieux Moulin

Fantasyland

It's a Small World

Le Carrousel
de Lancelot

Les Voyages
de Pinocchio

Blanche-Neige
et les Sept Nains

Disneyland Railroad
Discoveryland Station

Le Château
du Belle au
Bois Dormant

Vidéopolis

Star Tours

LeThéatre
du Château

Le Visionarium

CinéMagique

Central
Plaza

Orbitron

Space
Mountain

Autopia

Les Mystères
du Nautilus

**Main Street,
U.S.A.**

Discoveryland

Liberty
Arcade

Discovery
Arcade

Main Street
Vehicles

Horse-Drawn
Streetcars

Disneyland Railroad
Main Street Station

Guest Relations
Window

Park Entrance

Peril . . . Backwards! (Adventureland); Big Thunder Mountain (Frontierland); Star Tours (Discoveryland); and Peter Pan's Flight (Fantasyland).

The park places height restrictions on only three rides, each of which involves some kind of scary roller-coaster experience. Riders of **Big Thunder Mountain** roller coaster must be at least 1 meter (3 feet, 3 inches) tall; and riders of both **Space Mountain** and **Indiana Jones and the Temple of Peril . . . Backwards!** must be at least 1 meter 40 centimeters (4 feet, 7 inches) tall.

Other than that, age suggestions for individual rides become meaningless, because many adults seem to adore rides that are safe for even the youngest children. Examples include **Peter Pan's Flight** and **Snow White's Ride.** The official guide to the park, distributed free at the resort's hotels and at City Hall on Main Street USA, gives subtle suggestions, but it's anything but dictatorial (in fact, it's deliberately vague) about delineating what rides are suitable for what age groups.

Guided 3½-hour tours for 20 or more people can be arranged for 50F (7.60€, $7.25) for adults and 35F (5.30€, $5.15) for children 3 to 11. In view of the well-marked paths leading through the park and the availability of ample printed information in any language, the guided tours aren't really necessary. You can rent coin-operated lockers for 10F (1.50€, $1.45) and can store larger bags for 15F (2.30€, $2.20) per day. Children's strollers and wheelchairs rent for 30F (4.55€, $4.35) per day, with a 20F (3.05€, $2.90) deposit. Baby-sitting is available at any of the hotels if 24-hour advance notice is given.

Marne-la-Vallée. (C) **01-60-30-60-53** (Disneyland Paris Guest Relations office, in City Hall on Main Street, U.S.A.). www.disneylandparis.com. Admission to park for 1 day, depending on season, 170–220F (25.85–33.45€, $24.65–$31.90) adults, 140–175F (21.35–26.60€, $20.30–$25.45) children 3–12, children 2 and under always admitted free. July–Aug daily 9am–11pm; Sept–June Mon–Fri 10am–6pm, Sat–Sun 9am–8pm. Hours vary with the weather and the season.

WHERE TO STAY

The only reason it's necessary to spend the night here is if you didn't get enough of Mickey Mouse the first day and want to hang out for another Disney adventure the following morning. Otherwise, you can easily make Disney a day trip from Paris because the transportation links are excellent.

The resort's six theme hotels share a reservation service. In North America, call (C) **407/W-DISNEY.** In France, contact the **Central Reservations Office,** Euro Disney Resort, S.C.A., B.P. 105, F-77777 Marne-la-Vallée Cedex 4 ((C) **01-60-30-60-30**).

VERY EXPENSIVE

Disneyland Hotel ★★   Mouseketeers who have rich daddies and mommies check in here at Disney's poshest resort charging Paris Ritz tariffs. At the park entrance, this flagship four-story hotel is Victorian, with red-tile turrets and jutting balconies. The spacious guest rooms are plushly furnished but evoke the image of Disney, with cartoon depictions and a candy-stripe decor. The beds are king, double, or twin; in some rooms armchairs convert to day beds. Paneled closets, large mirrors, and safes are found in some units. Accommodations in the rear overlook Sleeping Beauty's Castle and Big Thunder Mountain. Some less desirable units open onto a parking lot. The luxurious combination baths have marble vanities and twin basins. On the Castle Club floor, you get free newspapers, all-day beverages, and access to a well-equipped private lounge.

Disneyland Paris, B.P. 105, F-77777 Marne-la-Vallée Cedex 4. (C) **01-60-45-65-00.** Fax 01-60-45-65-33. www.disneylandparis.com. 496 units. 2,260–3,320F (343.50–504.65€, $327.70–$481.40) double; from

4,950F (752.40€, $717.75) suite. Rates include 2-day pass and breakfast. AE, DC, DISC, MC, V. **Amenities:** 2 restaurants; 2 bars; health club with indoor/outdoor pool; whirlpool; sauna; room service; baby-sitting; laundry/dry cleaning. *In room:* A/C, TV, minibar, hair dryer.

EXPENSIVE

Hotel New York ✦   Picture an Art-Deco New York of the '30s. Inspired by the Big Apple, this hotel is designed around a nine-story central "skyscraper" flanked by the Gramercy Park Wing and the Brownstones Wing. (The exteriors of both wings resemble row houses.) More interested in convention bookings, this hotel is less family-friendly than the others previously recommended. Guest rooms are comfortable, with Art-Deco accessories, New York–inspired memorabilia, and roomy combination baths with twin basins. The most desirable units are called Castle Club and lie on the upper floors. Try for one of the units fronting Lake Buena Vista instead of those opening onto the parking lot.

Disneyland Paris, B.P. 100, F-77777 Marne-la-Vallée Cedex 4. ✆ **01-60-45-73-00.** Fax 01-60-45-73-33. www.disneylandparis.com. 563 units. 1,650–2,420F (250.80–367.85€, $239.25–$350.90) double; from 3,350F (509.20€, $485.75) suite. Rates include 2-day pass and breakfast. AE, DC, DISC, MC, V. **Amenities:** 2 restaurants; bar; pool; exercise room; sauna; room service; baby-sitting. *In room:* A/C, TV, minibar, hair dryer, safe.

Newport Bay Club ✦✦   You expect to see the reincarnation of old Joe Kennedy walking along the large veranda with its slated roofs, awnings, and pergolas. It's very Hyannis Port here. It's also the biggest hotel in France. This hotel is designed with a central cupola, jutting balconies, and a blue-and-cream color scheme, reminiscent of a harborfront New England hotel around 1900. The layout is irregular, with nautically decorated guest rooms in various shapes and sizes. The most spacious rooms are the corner units. The combination baths are roomy, with deluxe toiletries. The upscale Yacht Club and the less formal Cape Cod are the dining choices.

Disneyland Paris, B.P. 105, F-77777 Marne-la-Vallée Cedex 4. ✆ **01-60-45-55-00.** Fax 01-60-45-55-33. www.disneylandparis.com. 1,098 units. 1,520–2,160F (231.05–328.30€, $220.40–$313.20) double; from 2,970F (451.45€, $430.65) suite. Rates include 2-day pass and breakfast. AE, DC, DISC, MC, V. **Amenities:** 2 restaurants; bar; indoor and outdoor pool; health club; sauna. *In room:* A/C, TV, minibar, hair dryer.

Sequoia Lodge   Built of gray stone and roughly textured planking and capped by a gently sloping green copper roof, this hotel resembles a lodge in a remote section of the Rockies. The design, with parquet floors and giant chimneys, evokes the Prairie Houses of architect Frank Lloyd Wright. The hotel consists of a large central building with five chalets nearby, each housing 100 rooms. The guest rooms are comfortably rustic, with tiled baths (hair dryers are available on request). The Hunter's Grill serves spit-roasted meats carved on your plate. Less formal is the Beaver Creek Tavern.

Disneyland Paris, B.P. 114, F-77777 Marne-la-Vallée Cedex 4. ✆ **01-60-45-51-00.** Fax 01-60-45-51-33. www.disneylandparis.com. 1,011 units. 1,410–2,060F (214.30–313.10€, $204.45–$298.70) double; from 2,630F (399.75€, $381.35) suite. Rates include 2-day pass and breakfast. AE, DC, DISC, MC, V. **Amenities:** 2 restaurants; bar; indoor/outdoor pool; health club; Jacuzzi. *In room:* A/C, TV, minibar.

MODERATE

Hotel Cheyenne/Hotel Santa Fe *Kids*   Next door to each other near a recreation of Texas's Rio Grande and evoking the Old West, these are the resort's least expensive hotels. The Cheyenne accommodates visitors in 14 two-story buildings along Desperado Street; the Santa Fe, sporting a desert theme, encompasses four "nature trails" winding among 42 adobe-style pueblos. The Cheyenne is a particular favorite among families, offering a double bed and bunk beds. An array of activities are offered for children, including a play area in a log cabin with a lookout tower and a section where you can explore the "ruins" of an ancient Anasazi village. There's a mariachi atmosphere in the Rio Grande Bar, and country music in the Red Garter Saloon Bar. The only disadvantage, according to some parents with children, is the absence of a pool. Tex-Mex specialties are offered at La Cantina (Santa Fe), and barbecue and smokehouse specialties predominate at the Chuck Wagon Cafe (Cheyenne).

Disneyland Paris, B.P. 115, F-77777 Marne-la-Vallée Cedex 4. ✆ **01-60-45-62-00** (Cheyenne) or 01-60-45-78-00 (Santa Fe). Fax 01-60-45-62-33 (Cheyenne) or 01-60-45-78-33 (Santa Fe). 2,000 units. Hotel Cheyenne 1,200–1,850F (182.40–281.20€, $174–$268.25) double; Hotel Santa Fe 1,100–1,760F (167.20–267.50€, $159.50–$255.20) double. Rates include 2-day pass and breakfast. AE, DC, DISC, MC, V. **Amenities:** 2 restaurants; bar; indoor/outdoor pool; 2 tennis courts; health club; sauna; hammock; ice-skating rink in winter; room service; massage; baby-sitting. *In room:* A/C, TV, minibar, hair dryer, safe.

WHERE TO DINE

Disneyland Paris offers a gamut of cuisine served from no less than 45 restaurants and snack bars. You can live on burgers and fries for weeks at this place, or you can experiment with vaunted cuisine that's best appreciated at the following upscale restaurants.

Auberge de Cendrillon FRENCH (TRADITIONAL)   This is a fairy-tale version of Cinderella's sumptuous country inn, with a glass couch in the center. A master of ceremonies, in a plumed tricorner hat, wearing an embroidered tunic and lace ruffles, welcomes you. There are corny elements here, but the chefs do go out of their way to make a big deal out of French cuisine. For the most part, they succeed admirably. The tone is set by the appetizers. Our favorites are their warm-goat cheese salad with lardons or else their smoked salmon platter. Either choice will put you in the mood for some of the classics of the French table, especially loin of lamb roasted under a zesty mustard coating or tender sautéed veal medallions that are like nuggets of flavor. An aromatic chicken is also perfectly roasted in puff pastry. Because the restaurant follows the park's seasonal schedules, lunches are usually easier to arrange than dinners.

In Fantasyland. ✆ **01-64-74-24-02.** Reservations recommended. Main courses 110–140F (16.70–21.30€, $15.95–$20.30); fixed-price menu 175F (26.60€, $25.40). AE, DC, DISC, MC, V. Daily 11:30am–90 min. before park closing.

California Grill 🎖🎖🎖 CALIFORNIAN/FRENCH   This is the showcase restaurant of this vast Disney world. At the California Grill, chef Eric Leaty, a well-known cookbook author, prepares food that's the equivalent of a one-Michelin-star restaurant. Focusing on the lighter specialties for which the Golden State is famous, with many concessions to French palates, this elegant restaurant manages to accommodate both adults and children gracefully. Even French food critics are impressed with the chef's oysters prepared with leeks and salmon. We also embrace the appetizer of foie gras with roasted red peppers, and rate as "Simply fabulous" the entree of roasted pigeon with braised Chinese cabbage and black-rice vinegar. Another winning selection is fresh salmon roasted over beechwood and served with a sprinkling of walnut oil, sage sauce, asparagus, and fricassée of forest mushrooms. Many items, such as "Mickie's pizzas," spaghetti Bolognese, and grilled ham with fries, are specifically for children. If you want a quiet, mostly adult venue, go here as late as your hunger pangs will allow.

In the Disneyland Hotel. ✆ **01-60-45-65-00.** Reservations required. Main courses 55–205F (8.35–31.15€, $8–$29.75); children's menu 85F (12.90€, $12.35). AE, DC, MC, V. Sun–Fri 7–11pm, Sat 6–11pm.

Inventions *Value* INTERNATIONAL   This might be the only buffet restaurant in Europe where animated characters from the Disney films (including Mickey and Minnie) go table-hopping, in a way you'd expect from a family-friendly restaurant in Los Angeles. With views over a park, the restaurant contains both smoking and non-smoking sections, and four enormous buffet tables devoted, respectively, to starters, shellfish, main courses, and desserts. Selections are wide, portions can be copious, and absolutely no one leaves this place hungry. Don't expect *grande cuisine*—that's the domain of the more upscale (also-recommended) California Grill, within the same hotel. What you'll get is a sense of American bounty and culinary generosity, with ample doses of cartoon fantasy thrown in for seasoning.

In the Disneyland Hotel. (✆ **01-60-45-65-83.** Reservations not necessary. Lunch buffet 180F (27.35€, $26.10) adults; 110F (16.70€, $15.95) children 7–11; 95F (14.45€, $13.83) children 3–6; dinner buffet 250F (38€, $36.25) adults; 140F (21.30€, $20.30) children 7–11; 95F (14.45€, $13.85) children 6 and under. AE, DC, MC, V. Daily noon–3pm and 6–10:30pm.

DISNEYLAND AFTER DARK

The premier theatrical venue of Disneyland Paris is **Le Legende de Buffalo Bill** in the Disney Village (✆ **01-60-45-71-00**). This twice-per-night stampede of entertainment recalls the show that once traveled the West with Buffalo Bill and Annie Oakley. You'll dine at tables arranged amphitheater-style around a rink where sharpshooters, runaway stagecoaches, and dozens of horses and Indians ride fast and perform alarmingly realistic acrobatics. A Texas-style barbecue, served assembly line by waiters in 10-gallon hats, is part of the experience. Despite its corny elements, it's not without its charm and an almost mournful nostalgia for a way of life of another continent and another century. Wild Bill himself is dignified and the Indians suitably brave. Two shows are staged at 6:30 and 9:30pm costing (with dinner included) 325F (49.40€, $47.15) for adults or 195F (29.65€, $28.35) ages 3 to 11.

6 Fontainebleau

37 miles S of Paris, 46 miles NE of Orléans

Within the vestiges of a forest that bears its name (the Forêt de Fontainebleau), this suburb of Paris has offered refuge to French monarchs throughout the country's history. Kings from the Renaissance valued it because of its nearness to rich hunting grounds and its distance from the slums and smells of the city. Napoléon referred to the Palais de Fontainebleau, which he reembellished with his distinctive monogram and decorative style, as "the house of the centuries." Many pivotal and decisive events have occurred inside, perhaps none more memorable than when Napoléon stood on the horseshoe-shaped exterior stairway and bade farewell to his shattered army before departing for Elba.

After the glories of Versailles, a visit to Fontainebleau can be a bit of a letdown, especially if followed immediately on the day after you saw Versailles. Fontainebleau, although a grand château, actually looks like a place a king could live, whereas Versailles is more of a production.

ESSENTIALS

GETTING THERE   If you stay for lunch, a trip to Fontainebleau should last a half-day. **Trains** depart from Paris's Gare de Lyon. The trip takes between 45 and 60 minutes each way and costs 94F (14.30€, $13.65) round-trip. Fontainebleau's rail station is 3 miles from the château, in the suburb of Avon.

A local bus (it's marked simply *château*) makes the trip to the château at 15-minute intervals every Monday to Saturday, and at 30-minute intervals every Sunday, for 10F (1.50€, $1.45) each way. By **car,** take A-6 south from Paris, exit onto N-191, and follow the signs.

VISITOR INFORMATION   The main squares are place du Général-de-Gaulle and place d'Armes. The **tourist office** is at 4 rue Royale (€ **01-60-74-99-99**).

SEEING THE PALACE

Palais de Fontainebleau ★★★   Napoléon's affection for this palace was understandable. He was following the pattern of a succession of French kings in the pre-Versailles days who used Fontainebleau as a resort and hunted in its magnificent forests. François I, who tried to turn the hunting lodge into a royal palace in the Italian Renaissance style, brought along several artists, including Benvenuto Cellini, to work for him. Under this patronage, the School of Fontainebleau gained prestige, led by painters Rosso Fiorentino and Primaticcio. The artists adorned the 210-foot-long **Gallery of François I** ★★★, where stucco-framed panels depict such scenes as *The Rape of Europa* and the monarch holding a pomegranate, a symbol of unity. The salamander, the symbol of the Chevalier king, is everywhere.

Sometimes called the Gallery of Henri II, the **Ballroom** ★★★ displays the interlaced initials "H&D," referring to Henri and his mistress, Diane de Poitiers. Competing with this illicit tandem are the initials "H&C," symbolizing Henri and his ho-hum wife, Catherine de Médicis. At one end of the room is a monumental fireplace supported by two bronze satyrs, made in 1966 (the originals were melted down during the Revolution). At the other side is the balcony of the musicians, with sculptured garlands. The ceiling displays octagonal coffering adorned with rosettes. Above the wainscoting is a series of frescoes, painted between 1550 and 1558, which depict mythological subjects such as *The Feast of Bacchus.* An architectural curiosity is the richly adorned **Louis XV Staircase** ★★. The room above it was originally decorated by Primaticcio for the bedroom of the duchesse d'Etampes, but when an architect was designing the stairway, he simply ripped out her floor. Of the Italian frescoes that were preserved, one depicts the queen of the Amazons climbing into Alexander the Great's bed.

When Louis XIV ascended to the throne, he neglected Fontainebleau because of his preoccupation with Versailles. However, he wasn't opposed to using the palace for houseguests, specifically such unwanted ones as Queen Christina, who had abdicated the throne of Sweden in a fit of religious fervor. Under the assumption that she still had "divine right," she ordered the brutal murder of her companion Monaldeschi, who had ceased to please her. Though Louis XV and then Marie Antoinette took an interest in Fontainebleau, the château found its renewed glory under Napoléon. You can wander around much of the palace on your own, visiting sites evoking the Corsican's 19th-century imperial heyday. They include the **throne room** where he abdicated his rulership of France, his **offices,** his monumental **bedroom,** and his **bathroom.** Some of the smaller Napoleonic Rooms contain his personal mementos and artifacts.

After your long trek through the palace, visit the **gardens** and, especially, the **carp pond;** the gardens, however, are only a prelude to the Forest of Fontainebleau.

In the Forêt de Fontainebleau. € **01-60-71-50-70.** Combination ticket for *grands appartements* 35F (5.30€, $5.15) adults, 23F (3.50€, $3.35) students 18–25, under age 18 free. Ticket to *petits appartements*

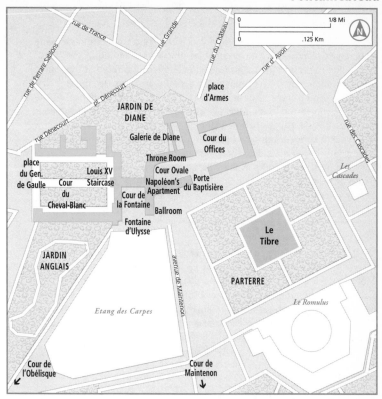

and Napoleonic Rooms 16F (2.45€, $2.30) adults, 12F (1.80€, $1.75) students 18–25, under age 18 free. June–Sept Wed–Mon 9:30am–6pm; Oct–May Wed–Mon 9:30am–5pm.

WHERE TO STAY

Hotel de l'Aigle-Noir (The Black Eagle) ⭐ Once the home of Cardinal de Retz, this mansion stands opposite the château. It was built with a formal court-yard entrance, using a high iron grille and pillars crowned by black eagles. It was converted into a hotel in 1720 and has recently been remodeled, making it the finest lodgings in town. The guest rooms are decorated with Louis XVI, Empire, or Restoration antiques or reproductions with plush mattresses and elegant bathroom amenities. All but four units have a complete tub-shower combination. Have a drink in the Napoléon III–style piano bar before dinner. Later, you can dine on elegant French cuisine with formalized service in the grand dining room of the hotel, Le Beauharnais.

27 place Napoléon-Bonaparte, 77300 Fontainebleau. ✆ **01-60-74-60-00.** Fax 01-64-23-42-22. www. hotellaiglenoir.fr. 56 units. 1,210–1,420F (183.90–215.85€, $175.45–$205.90) double; from 2,400F (364.80€, $348) suite. AE, DC, MC, V. Parking 55F (8.35€, $8.05). **Amenities:** Restaurant; bar; indoor pool; exercise room; sauna; room service; baby-sitting; laundry/dry cleaning. *In room:* A/C, minibar, coffeemaker, hair dryer.

WHERE TO DINE

Le Caveau des Ducs FRENCH (TRADITIONAL) Beneath a series of 17th-century stone vaults, this restaurant occupies what was once a storage cellar

---

Moments **Hiking Along Trails Left by French Kings**

The Forest of Fontainebleau is riddled with hiking trails originally made by French kings and their encoutages who went hunting in the forest. A guide to these trails, called *Guide des Sentiers,* is offered at the tourist information center (see above). Bike paths are also cut through the forest. You can rent bikes at the Fontainebleau-Avon rail depot. At the station, go to the kiosk, **MBK** (*(C)* **01-64-22-36-14**). The cost of a bike is 60F (9.10€, $8.70) per half day, going up to 120F (18.25€, $17.40) for a regular bike for a full day. Open Monday to Friday from 10am to 6pm and Saturday and Sunday from 10am to 7pm.

The most scenic route in our view is to take the trail on the map leading to Tour Denecourt, lying 3 miles northeast of the château. Along the way you can take in good views of the beeches, birches, and pines, a truly idyllic setting.

---

for the château. Wood and flickering candles preserve the illusion. In terms of grandeur, it's not in the same league as Le Beauharnais, the dining room of the Hôtel de l'Aigle Noir, but it offers simpler food in a dramatic antique setting. Each dish could stand in a museum of 1950s French food: snails in garlic butter, roast leg of lamb with garlic-and-rosemary sauce, and virtually everything that can be done with a duck. The rump steak filet is quite tasty, served in Brie sauce, as is the platter of sole, crayfish tails, and salmon served on a bed of pasta.

24 rue de Ferrare. *(C)* **01-64-22-05-05**. Reservations recommended. Main courses 85–130F (12.90–19.75€, $12.35–$18.85); fixed-price menu 135–250F (20.50–38€, $19.60–$36.25). AE, MC, V. Daily noon–2pm and 7–10pm.

Le François-Ier *(★)* FRENCH (TRADITIONAL)   The premier dining choice attracts with a Louis XIII decor, winemaking memorabilia, and walls the owners think are about 200 years old. If weather permits, sit on the terrace overlooking the château and the Cour des Adieux. In game season, the menu includes hare, roebuck, duck liver, and partridge. Other choices may be cold salmon with *cèpes* (flap mushrooms), *rognon de veau* (veal kidneys) with mustard sauce, and a salad of baby scallops with crayfish. The cuisine is meticulous, with an undeniable flair. The *magrêt de canard* (duck) flavored with cassis is delicious.

3 rue Royale. *(C)* **01-64-22-24-68**. Reservations required. Main courses 80–135F (12.15–20.50€, $11.60–$19.60); fixed-price menus 160–250F (24.30–38€, $23.20–$36.25). AE, DC, MC, V. Mon–Sat noon–2:30pm and 7:30–10pm, Sun noon–2:30pm.

Appendix A:
Paris History 101

IN THE BEGINNING

Paris emerged at the crossroads of three major traffic arteries on the muddy island in the Seine that today is known as Ile de la Cité.

By around 2000 B.C., the island served as the fortified headquarters of the Parisii tribe, who called it Lutétia. The two crude wooden bridges connecting the island to the river's left and right banks were among the region's most strategically important, and the settlement attracted the attention of the Roman Empire. In his *Commentaries,* Julius Caesar described his conquest of Lutétia, recounting how its bridges were burned during the Gallic War of 52 B.C. and how the town on the island was pillaged, sacked, and transformed into a Roman-controlled stronghold.

Within a century, Lutétia became a full-fledged Roman town, and some of the inhabitants abandoned the frequently flooded island in favor of higher ground on what is today the Left Bank. By A.D. 200, barbarian invasions increasingly threatened the stability of Roman Gaul, and the populace from the surrounding hills flocked to the island's fortified safety. Over the next 50 years, a Christian community gained a tenuous foothold there. According to legend, St. Denis served as the city's first bishop (beginning around 250). Though by this time the Roman Empire's political power had begun to wane in the region, the cultural and religious attachment of the community to the Christian bishops of Rome grew even stronger.

During the 400s, with the great decline of the Roman armies, Germanic tribes from the east (the Salian Franks) were able to invade the island successfully, founding a Frankish dynasty and prompting a Frankish-Latin cultural fusion in the burgeoning town. The first of these Frankish kings, Clovis (466–511), founder of the Merovingian dynasty, embraced Christianity as his tribe's official religion and spearheaded an explicit rejection of Roman cultural imperialism by encouraging the adoption of Parisii place names like "Paris," which came into common usage during this time.

The Merovingians were replaced by the Carolingians, whose heyday began with Charlemagne's coronation in 800. The Carolingian Empire sprawled over western Germany and eastern France, but Paris was never its capital. The city remained a commercial and religious center, sacred to the memory of St. Geneviève, who reputedly protected Paris when it was attacked again and again by the Huns in the final days of the Roman Empire. The Carolingians came to an end in 987, when the empire fragmented because of the growing regional, political, and linguistic divisions between what would become modern France and modern Germany. Paris became the seat of a new dynasty, the Capetians, whose kings ruled France throughout the Middle Ages. Hugh Capet (ca. 938–996), the first of this line, ruled as comte de Paris and duc de France from 987 to 996.

THE MIDDLE AGES

Around 1100, Paris began to emerge as a great city, boasting on its Left Bank a university that attracted scholars from all over Europe. Meanwhile, kings and bishops began building the towering Gothic cathedrals of France, one of the greatest of which became Paris's Notre-Dame, a monument rising from the beating heart of the city. Paris's population increased greatly, as did the city's mercantile activity. During the 1200s, a frenzy of building transformed the skyline with convents and churches (including the jewel-like Sainte-Chapelle, completed in 1249 after just 2 years). During the next century, the increasingly powerful French kings added dozens of monuments of their own.

As time passed, Paris's fortunes became closely linked to the power struggles between the French monarchs in Paris and the various highly competitive feudal lords of the provinces. Because of this tug-of-war, Paris was dogged by civil unrest, takeovers by one warring faction after another, and a dangerous alliance between the English and the powerful rulers of Burgundy during the Hundred Years' War. Around the same time, the city suffered a series of plagues, including the Black Death. To the humiliation of the French monarchs, the English army invaded the city in 1422. Joan of Arc (ca. 1412–31) tried unsuccessfully to reconquer Paris in 1429, and 2 years later the English, supported by a tribunal of French ecclesiastics, burned her at the stake in Rouen. Paris was reduced to poverty and economic stagnation, and its embittered and greatly reduced population turned to banditry and street crime to survive.

Despite Joan's ignominious end, the revolution she inspired continued in protracted form until Paris was finally taken from the English armies in 1436. During the following several decades,

Dateline

- **2000 B.C.** Ancient Lutétia (Paris) thrives along a strategic crossing of the Seine, the fortified headquarters of the Parisii tribe.
- **52 B.C.** Julius Caesar conquers Lutétia during the Gallic Wars.
- **A.D. 150** Lutétia flourishes as a Roman colony, expanding to the Left Bank.
- **200** Barbarian Gauls force the Romans to retreat to the fortifications on Ile de la Cité.
- **300** Lutétia is officially renamed Paris; Roman power weakens in northern France.
- **350** Paris's Christianization begins.
- **400s** The Franks invade Paris, with social transformation from the Roman to the Gallo-Roman culture.
- **466** Clovis, founder of the Merovingian dynasty and first non-Roman ruler of Paris since the Parisi, is born.
- **800** Charlemagne, founder of the Carolingian dynasty and first Holy Roman Emperor, is coronated and rules from Aachen in modern Germany.
- **987** Hugh Capet, founder of France's foremost early medieval dynasty, rises to power; he and his heirs rule from Paris.
- **1100** The Université de Paris attracts scholars from throughout Europe.
- **1200s** Paris's population and power grow, though the city is frequently unsettled by plagues and feudal battles.
- **1422** England invades Paris during the Hundred Years' War.
- **1429** Joan of Arc tries unsuccessfully to regain Paris for the French; the Burgundians later capture and sell her to the English, who burn her at the stake in Rouen.
- **1500s** François I, first of the French Renaissance kings, embellishes Paris but chooses to maintain his court in the Loire Valley.
- **1549** Henri II rules France from Paris; the construction of public and private residences begins, many in the Marais.
- **1564** Construction begins on Catherine de Médicis's Palais des Tuileries; building facades in Paris move from

continues

the English retreated to the port of Calais, abandoning their once-mighty French territories. France, under the leadership of Louis XI (1423–83), witnessed an accelerating rate of change that included the transformation of a feudal and medieval social system into the nascent beginnings of a modern state.

THE RENAISSANCE & THE REFORMATION

The first of the Renaissance monarchs, François I (1494–1547), began an extensive enlargement of Paris's Louvre (which had begun as a warehouse storing the archives of Philippe Auguste before being transformed into a Gothic fortress by Louis IX in the 1100s) to make it suitable as a royal residence. Despite the building's embellishment and the continued designation of Paris as the French capital, he spent much of his time at other châteaux amid the fertile hunting grounds of the Loire Valley. Many later monarchs came to share his opinion that Paris's narrow streets and teeming commercialism were unhealthy and upsetting, and chose to reside elsewhere.

In 1549, however, Henri II (1519–59) triumphantly established his court in Paris and successfully ruled France from within its borders, solidifying the city's role as the nation's undisputed capital. Following their ruler's lead, fashionable aristocrats quickly began to build private residences (*hôtels particuliers*) on the Right Bank, in a marshy low-lying area known as Le Marais (the swamp).

It was during this period that Paris, as the world knows it today, came into existence. The expansion of the Louvre continued, and Catherine de Médicis (1518–89) began building her Palais des Tuileries in 1564. From the shelter of dozens of elegant urban residences, France's aristocracy imbued Paris with its sense of architectural and social style, as well as the Renaissance's mores

half-timbered to more durable chiseled stonework.

- 1572 The Wars of Religion reach their climax with the massacre of Protestants on St. Bartholomew's Day.
- 1598 Henri IV, the most eccentric and enlightened monarch of his era, endorses the Edict of Nantes, granting tolerance to Protestants; because of this, a crazed monk fatally stabs him 12 years later.
- 1615 Construction begins on the Palais du Luxembourg for Henri IV's widow, Marie de Médicis.
- 1636 The Palais Royal is launched by Cardinal Richelieu; soon thereafter, two marshy islands in the Seine are interconnected and filled in to create Ile St-Louis.
- 1643 Louis XIV, the "Sun King" and the most powerful ruler since the Caesars, rises to power; he moves his court to the newly built Versailles.
- 1776 The American Declaration of Independence strikes a revolutionary chord in France.
- 1789 The French Revolution breaks out.
- 1793 Louis XVI and his Austrian-born queen, Marie Antoinette, are publicly guillotined.
- 1799 Napoléon Bonaparte crowns himself Master of France and embellishes Paris further with neoclassical splendor.
- 1803 Napoléon abandons French overseas expansion and sells Louisiana to America.
- 1812 Napoléon is defeated in the Russian winter campaign.
- 1814 Aided by a military coalition of France's enemies, especially England, the Bourbon monarchy under Louis XVIII is restored.
- 1821 Napoléon Bonaparte dies.
- 1824 Louis XVIII dies and Charles X accedes.
- 1830 Charles X is deposed and the more liberal Louis-Philippe is elected king; Paris prospers as it industrializes.
- 1848 A violent working-class revolution deposes Louis-Philippe, who's replaced by autocratic Napoléon III.
- 1853–70 On Napoléon III's orders, Baron Haussmann forcibly redesigns

continues

and manners. Stone quays were added to the Seine's banks, defining their limits and preventing future flood damage, and royal decrees established a series of building codes. To an increasing degree, Paris adopted the planned perspectives and visual grace worthy of the residence of a monarch.

During the late 1500s and 1600s, Protestants were brutally persecuted by the French kings. The bloodletting reached a high point under Henri III (1551–89) during the St. Bartholomew's Day massacre of 1572. Henri III's tragic and eccentric successor, Henri IV (1553–1610), ended the Wars of Religion in 1598 by endorsing the Edict of Nantes, offering religious freedom to the Protestants of France. Henry IV also laid out the lines for one of Paris's memorable squares: place des Vosges. As a reward for his leniency, he was stabbed in 1610 by a deranged monk infuriated by the king's support of religious tolerance.

After Henri IV's death, his second wife, Marie de Médicis (1573–1642), acting as regent, planned the Palais du Luxembourg (1615), whose gardens have functioned ever since as a rendezvous for Parisians. In 1636, Cardinal Richelieu (1585–1642), who virtually ruled France during the minority of Louis XIII (the period in which the boy king was still too young to rule), built the sprawling premises of the Palais Royal. Under Louis XIII (1601–43), two uninhabited islands in the Seine were joined together with landfill, connected to Ile de la Cité and to the mainland with bridges, and renamed Ile St-Louis. Also laid out were the Jardin des Plantes, whose flowers and medicinal herbs were arranged according to their scientific and medical category.

THE SUN KING & THE FRENCH REVOLUTION

Louis XIV (1638–1715) was crowned king of France when he was only

Paris's landscapes and creates the grand boulevards.

- **1860s** The impressionist style emerges.
- **1870** The Franco-Prussian War ends in the defeat of France; Paris is threatened with bombardment by Prussian cannons placed on the outskirts; a revolution in the aftermath of this defeat destroys the Palais des Tuileries and overthrows the government; the Third Republic rises with its elected president, Marshal MacMahon.
- **1878–1937** A series of international expositions adds many enduring monuments to the Paris skyline, including the Tour Eiffel and Sacré-Coeur.
- **1914–18** World War I rips apart Europe.
- **1940** German troops invade Paris; the official French government, under Marshal Pétain, evacuates to Vichy, while the French Resistance under Gen. Charles de Gaulle maintains symbolic headquarters in London.
- **1944** U.S. troops liberate Paris; de Gaulle returns from London in triumph.
- **1948** The revolt in the French colony of Madagascar costs 80,000 French lives; France's empire continues to collapse in Southeast Asia and equatorial Africa.
- **1954–62** War begins in Algeria and is eventually lost; refugees flood Paris, and the nation becomes bitterly divided over its North African policies.
- **1958** France's Fourth Republic collapses; General de Gaulle is called out of retirement to head the Fifth Republic.
- **1968** Paris's students and factory workers engage in a general revolt; the French government is overhauled in the aftermath.
- **1981** François Mitterrand is elected France's first socialist president since the 1940s; he's reelected in 1988.
- **1989** Paris celebrates the bicentennial of the French Revolution.
- **1992** Euro Disney opens on the outskirts of Paris.
- **1994** François Mitterrand and Queen Elizabeth II take a ride together under the English Channel in the new Chunnel.

continues

9 years old. Cardinal Mazarin (1602–61), Louis's Sicilian-born chief minister, dominated the government in Paris during the Sun King's minority. This era marked the emergence of the French kings as absolute monarchs. As if to concretize their power, they embellished Paris with many of the monuments that still serve as symbols of the city. These included new alterations to the Louvre and the construction of the pont Royal, quai Peletier, place des Victoires, place Vendôme, Champs-Elysées, and Hôtel des Invalides. Meanwhile, Louis XIV absented himself from the city, constructing, at a staggering expense, the Château de Versailles, 13 miles southwest. Today, the palace stands as the single most visible monument to the most flamboyant era of French history.

- 1995 Mitterrand dies and Jacques Chirac is elected; Paris is crippled by a general strike; terrorists bomb the subway.
- 1997 Authorities enforce strict immigration laws, causing strife for African and Arab immigrants and dividing the country; French voters rebuff Chirac, electing Socialist Lionel Jospin as his new prime minister.
- 1998 Socialists triumph in local elections across France.
- 1999 The euro is introduced; on Christmas Day a violent storm assaults Paris and the Ile de France, damaging several buildings and toppling thousands of trees.
- 2000 Paris welcomes the new millennium.
- 2001 France buries its national currency, the French franc, and switches to the euro, the equivalent of a European dollar.

Meanwhile, the rising power of England, particularly its navy, represented a serious threat to France, which was otherwise the world's most powerful nation. One of the many theaters of the Anglo-French conflict was the American Revolution, during which the French kings supported the Americans in their struggle against the Crown. Ironically, within 15 years, the fervor the monarchs had nurtured crossed the Atlantic and destroyed them. The spark that kindled the fire came from Paris itself. For years before the outbreak of hostilities between the Americans and the British, the Enlightenment and its philosophers had fostered a new generation of thinkers who opposed absolutism, religious fanaticism, and superstition. Revolution had been brewing for almost 50 years, and after the French Revolution's explosive events, Europe was completely changed.

Though it began with moderate aims, the Revolution had soon turned the radical Jacobins into overlords, led by Robespierre (1758–94). On August 10, 1792, troops from Marseilles, aided by a Parisian mob, threw Louis XVI (1754–93) and his Austrian-born queen, Marie Antoinette (1755–93), into prison. Several months later, after countless humiliations and a bogus trial, they were guillotined at place de la Révolution (later renamed place de la Concorde) on January 21, 1793. The Reign of Terror continued for another 18 months, with Parisians of all political persuasions fearing for their lives.

THE RISE OF NAPOLÉON

It required the militaristic fervor of Napoléon Bonaparte (1769–1821) to unite France once again. Considered then and today a strategic genius with almost limitless ambition, he restored to Paris and to France a national pride that had been diminished during the Revolution's horror. After many impressive political and military victories, he entered Paris in 1799, at the age of 30, and crowned himself "First Consul and Master of France."

A brilliant politician, Napoléon moderated the atheistic rigidity of the early adherents of the Revolution by establishing peace with the Vatican. Soon thereafter, the legendary love of Parisians for their amusements began to revive;

boulevard des Italiens became the rendezvous point of the fashionable, while boulevard du Temple, which housed many of the capital's vaudeville and cabaret theaters, became the favorite watering hole of the working class. In his self-appointed role as a French Caesar, Napoléon continued to alter Paris's face with the construction of the neoclassical arcades of rue de Rivoli (1801), the triumphal arches of the Arc du Carrousel and Arc du Triomphe, and the neoclassical grandeur of La Madeleine. On a less grandiose scale, the city's slaughterhouses and cemeteries were sanitized and moved away from the center of town, and new industries began to crowd workers from the countryside into the cramped slums of a newly industrialized Paris.

Napoléon's victories had made him the envy of Europe, but his infamous retreat from Moscow during the winter of 1812 reduced his formerly invincible army to tatters as 400,000 Frenchmen lost their lives. After a complicated series of events that included his return from exile, Napoleon was defeated at Waterloo by the armies of the English, the Dutch, and the Prussians. Exiled to the British-held island of St. Helena in the remote South Atlantic, he died in 1821, possibly the victim of an unknown poisoner. Some time later, his body was returned to Paris and interred in a massive porphyry sarcophagus in the Hôtel des Invalides, Louis XIV's monument to the ailing and fallen warriors of France.

In the power vacuum that followed Napoléon's expulsion and death, Paris became the scene of intense lobbying over the future fate of France. The Bourbon monarchy was soon reestablished, but with reduced powers. In 1830, the regime was overthrown. Louis-Philippe (1773–1850), duc d'Orléans and the son of a duke who had voted in 1793 for the death of Louis XVI, was elected king under a liberalized constitution. His prosperous reign lasted for 18 years, during which England and France more or less collaborated on matters of foreign policy.

Paris reveled in its new prosperity, grateful for the money and glamour that had elevated it to one of the world's top cultural and commercial centers. Moving into the modern age, Paris received its first railway line in 1837 (running from the center of town to a suburb near St-Germain) and its first gas-fed streetlights shortly thereafter. It was a time of wealth, grace, culture, and expansion for some people, though the industrialization of certain working-class districts of Paris produced horrible poverty. The era also witnessed the development of French cuisine to the high form that still prevails, while a newly empowered bourgeoisie reveled in its attempts to create the good life.

THE SECOND EMPIRE

In 1848, a series of revolutions spread from one European capital to the next. The violent upheaval in Paris revealed the increasing dissatisfaction of many members of the working class. Fueled by a financial crash and scandals in the government, the revolt forced Louis-Philippe out of office. That year, on the dawn of the Second Republic, Emperor Napoléon's nephew, Napoléon III (1808–73), was elected president by moderate and conservative elements. Appealing to the property-owning instinct of a nation that hadn't forgotten the violent revolution of less than a century before, he established a right-wing government and assumed complete power as emperor in 1851.

In 1853, Napoléon III undertook Europe's largest urban redevelopment project by commissioning Baron Eugène-Georges Haussmann (1809–91) to redesign Paris. Haussmann created a vast network of boulevards interconnected with a series of squares that cut across old neighborhoods. While this reorganization gave the capital the look for which it's now famous, screams of outrage sounded

Impressions

The French will only be united under the threat of danger. Nobody can simply bring together a country that has 265 kinds of cheese.

—Charles de Gaulle

throughout the neighborhoods that the construction split apart. By 1866, the entrepreneurs of an increasingly industrialized Paris began to regard the Second Empire as a hindrance. In 1870, during the Franco-Prussian War, the Prussians defeated Napoléon III at Sedan and held him prisoner along with 100,000 of his soldiers. Paris was threatened with bombardments from German cannons, by far the most advanced of their age, set up on the city's eastern periphery.

Although agitated diplomacy encouraged a Prussian withdrawal, international humiliation and perceived military incompetence sparked a revolt in Paris. One of the immediate effects of the revolt was the burning of one of Paris's historic landmarks, the Palais des Tuileries. Today, only the sprawling gardens of this once-great palace remain. The tumultuous events of 1870 ushered in the Third Republic and its elected president, Marshal Marie Edme Patrice Maurice de MacMahon (1808–93), in 1873.

Under the Third Republic, peace and prosperity gradually returned, and Paris regained its glamour. Universal Expositions held in 1878, 1889, 1900, and 1937 were the catalyst for the construction of such enduring Paris monuments as the Trocadéro, the Palais de Chaillot, the Tour Eiffel, the Grand Palais and the Petit Palais, and the neo-Byzantine Sacré-Coeur. Simultaneously, the *réseau métropolitain* (the Métro) was constructed, providing a model for subsequent subway systems throughout Europe.

WORLD WAR I

International rivalries and conflicting alliances led to World War I, which, after decisive German victories for 2 years, degenerated into the mud-slogged horror of trench warfare. Industrialization during and after the war transformed Paris and its environs into a vast interconnected whole, by now one of the largest metropolitan areas in Europe and undisputed ever since as the center of France's intellectual and commercial life.

Immediately after the Allied victory, grave economic problems, coupled with a populace demoralized from years of fighting, encouraged the rise of Socialism and the formation of a Communist party, both movements centered in Paris. Also from Paris, the French government, led by the vindictive Georges Clemenceau (1841–1929), occupied Germany's Ruhr Valley, then and now one of that country's most profitable and industrialized regions, and demanded every centime of reparations it could wring from its humiliated neighbor, a policy that contributed to the outbreak of World War II.

THE 1920S—AMERICANS IN PARIS

The so-called Lost Generation, led by American expatriates Gertrude Stein and Alice B. Toklas, led the list of celebrities who "occupied" Paris after World War I, ushering in one of its most glamorous eras. The living was cheap in Paris. Two people could manage for about a year on a $1,000 scholarship, providing they could scrape up another $500 or so in extra earnings. Paris attracted the littérateur, bon viveur, and drifter, and writers like Henry Miller, Ernest Hemingway, and F. Scott Fitzgerald all lived here. Even Cole Porter came, living first at the Ritz, then at 13 rue de Monsieur. James Joyce, half blind and led around by

Ezra Pound, arrived in Paris and went to the salon of Natalie Barney, a leading exponent of Amazon Love. She became famous for pulling off stunts like inviting Mata Hari to perform a Javanese dance, completely nude, at one of her parties, labeled "for women only, a lesbian orgy." Colette was barred, though she begged her husband to let her go.

With the collapse of Wall Street, many Americans returned home, except hard-core artists like Henry Miller, who wandered around smoking Gauloise cigarettes and generating several pages a day of *Tropic of Cancer,* which was banned in America for decades. "I have no money, no resources, no hopes. I am the happiest man alive," Miller said. Eventually, he met the narcissistic diary writer, Anaïs Nin, and they began to live a life that gave both of them material for their prose. But even such diehards as Miller and Nin eventually realized 1930s Paris was collapsing as war clouds loomed. Gertrude and Alice remained in France, as other American expats fled to safer shores.

THE WINDS OF WAR

Thanks to an array of alliances, when Germany invaded Poland in 1939, France had no choice but to declare war. Within only a few months, on June 14, 1940, Nazi armies marched arrogantly down the Champs-Elysées and passed beneath the Arc de Triomphe. Newsreel cameras recorded the French openly weeping at the sight. The city suffered little from the war materially, but for 4 years it survived in a kind of half life, cold, dull, and drab, fostering scattered pockets of fighters who resisted sometimes passively and sometimes with active sabotage.

During the Nazi occupation of Paris, the French government, under Marshal Henri Pétain (1856–1951), moved to the quiet and isolated resort of Vichy and cooperated (or actually collaborated, depending on your point of view) with the Nazis. Tremendous internal dissension, the memory of which still simmers today, pitted many factions against one another. The Free French Resistance fled for its own safety to London, where it was headed by Charles de Gaulle (1880–1970), who became president of France's Fourth Republic after the war.

POSTWAR PARIS

Despite its gains in prestige and prosperity after the end of World War II, Paris was rocked many times by internal dissent as domestic and international events embroiled the government in dozens of controversies. In 1951, Paris forgot its cares by celebrating the 2,000th anniversary of the city's founding and poured much of its energy into rebuilding its image as a center of fashion, lifestyle, and glamour. Paris became internationally recognized as both a staple in the travel diets of many North Americans and as a beacon for art and artists.

The War of Algerian Independence (1954–58), in which Algeria sought to go from being a French *département* (an integral extension of the French nation) to an independent country, was an anguishing event, more devastating than the earlier loss of France's colonies. The population of France (Paris in particular) ballooned immediately as French citizens fled Algeria and returned home with few possessions and much bitterness. In 1958, as a result of the enormous loss of lives, money, and prestige in the Algerian affair, France's Fourth Republic collapsed, and de Gaulle was called out of retirement to form a new government: the Fifth Republic. In 1962, the Algerian war ended with victory for Algeria, as France's colonies in central and equatorial Africa became independent one by one. The sun had finally set on the French Empire.

In 1968, a general revolt by Parisian students, whose activism mirrored that of their counterparts in the United States, turned the capital into an armed camp, causing a near-collapse of the national government and the very real possibility of total civil war. Though the crisis was averted, for several weeks it seemed as if French society was on the brink of anarchy.

CONTEMPORARY PARIS

In 1981, François Mitterrand (1916–96) was elected the first Socialist president of France since World War II by a very close vote of 51%. Massive amounts of capital were taken out of the country, and though the drain slowed somewhat after initial jitters, many wealthy Parisians still prefer to invest their money elsewhere.

Paris today still struggles with social unrest in Corsica and from Muslim fundamentalists both inside and outside of France. In the mid-1990s, racial tensions continued to nag at France, as the debate over immigration raged. Many right-wing political parties have created a racial backlash against North Africans and against "corruptive foreign influences" in general.

On his third try, Jacques Chirac (b. 1932), survivor of many terms as mayor of Paris, won the presidency of France in 1995 with 52% of the vote. Mitterrand turned over the reigns on May 17 and died shortly thereafter. France embarked on a new era, but Chirac's popularity soon faded in the wake of unrest caused by an 11.5% unemployment rate. In the spring of 1998, France ousted its Conservative parties in a powerful endorsement of Prime Minister Lionel Jospin (b. 1937) and his Socialist-led government. The triumph of Jospin and his Communist and Green Party allies represented a fresh disavowal of the center-right Conservatives. This was a stunning blow to Chirac's Neo-Gaullists and the center-right parties led by François Leotard, and certainly to Jean-Marie Le Pen's often fanatical National Front.

By putting the Left back in charge, the French had voted against all the new ideas proposed to them for pushing their country into competitiveness and out of its economic doldrums. In spite of this resistance to change, Jospin is still ever so gently moving France into the new millennium. Without breaking the budget or losing public favor, the prime minister has picked his way through the minefields of French politics—militant unions, a public wedded to generous benefits, and widespread resistance to change. Jospin refers to his path as "leftist realism."

In 1999, France joined with 10 other European Union countries in adopting the euro as its standard of currency, though the French franc will still be in circulation until 2002. The new currency will accelerate the creation of a single economy, comprising nearly 300 million Europeans, with a combined gross national product approaching, by some estimates, $9 trillion, larger than that of the United States.

On Christmas night in 1999, one of the worst storms in recorded history ravaged the north of France. Wind gusts of 100 m.p.h. caused massive damage to buildings, homes, monuments, and gardens. One of the hardest hit was the Château de Versailles, which lost 10,000 trees planted during the 18th and 19th centuries; the loss included two trees planted for Marie Antoinette. Even though it will take quite a long time for the replacement trees to mature, the damage to buildings was repaired.

One of the most enduring symbols of France, its French franc, was assigned to the dustbin of history in 2001, as the country joined other European Union nations such as Spain and Germany in a switch to the euro, which stands now as a virtual European dollar.

Appendix B:
Useful Terms & Phrases

1 Glossary of French-Language Terms

A well-known character is the American or lapsed Canadian who returns from a trip to Paris and denounces the ever-so-rude French. "I asked for directions, and he glowered at me, muttered inaudibly, and turned his back." "She threw her baguette at me!" While Parisians often seem to carry upon their backs a burden of misery that they famously dole out to immigrants and foreigners, it's often amazing how a word or two of halting French will change their dispositions, and if not bring out the sun, at least put an end to the Gallic thunder and rain. At the very least, try to learn a few numbers, basic greetings, and—above all—the life-raft, *"Parlez-vous anglais?"* As it turns out, many Parisians do speak passable English and will use it liberally if you demonstrate the basic courtesy of greeting them in their language. Go out, try our glossary on, and don't be bashful. *Bonne chance!*

BASICS

English	French	Pronunciation
Yes/No	**Oui/Non**	wee/nohn
Okay	**D'accord**	dah-*core*
Please	**S'il vous plaît**	seel voo *play*
Thank you	**Merci**	mair-*see*
You're welcome	**De rien**	duh ree-*ehn*
Hello (during daylight hours)	**Bonjour**	bohn-*jhoor*
Good evening	**Bonsoir**	bohn-*swahr*
Good-bye	**Au revoir**	o ruh-*vwahr*
What's your name?	**Comment vous appellez-vous?**	ko-mahn voo za-pell-ay-*voo*?
My name is . . .	**Je m'appelle . . .**	jhuh ma-*pell* . . .
Happy to meet you	**Enchanté(e)**	ohn-shahn-tay
Miss	**Mademoiselle**	mad-mwa-*zel*
Mr.	**Monsieur**	muh-*syuh*
Mrs.	**Madame**	ma-*dam*
How are you?	**Comment allez-vous?**	kuh-mahn tahl-ay-*voo*?
Fine, thank you, and you?	**Très bien, merci, et vous?**	tray bee-ehn, mare-ci, ay *voo*?
Very well, thank you	**Très bien, merci**	tray bee-ehn, mair-*see*
So-so	**Comme ci, comme ça**	kum-*see*, kum-*sah*
I'm sorry/excuse me	**Pardon**	pahr-*dohn*
I'm so very sorry	**Désolé(e)**	day-zoh-*lay*
That's all right	**Il n'y a pas de quoi**	eel nee ah pah duh kwah

GETTING AROUND/STREET SMARTS

English	French	Pronunciation
Do you speak English?	**Parlez-vous anglais?**	par-lay-voo ahn-*glay*?
I don't speak French	**Je ne parle pas français**	jhuh ne parl pah frahn-*say*
I don't understand	**Je ne comprends pas**	jhuh ne kohm-*prahn* pas
Could you speak more loudly/more slowly?	**Pouvez-vous parler un peu plus fort/plus lentement?**	poo-vay-voo par-lay un puh ploo for/ploo lan-te-*ment*?
Could you repeat that?	**Répetez, s'il vous plaît?**	ray-pay-*tay*, seel voo *play*
What is it?	**Qu'est-ce que c'est?**	kess kuh *say*?
What time is it?	**Qu'elle heure est-il?**	kel uhr eh-*teel*?
What?	**Quoi?**	kwah?
How? or What did you say?	**Comment?**	ko-*mahn*?
When?	**Quand?**	kahn?
Where is . . . ?	**Où est . . . ?**	ooh eh . . . ?
Who?	**Qui?**	kee?
Why?	**Pourquoi?**	poor-*kwah*?
Here/there	**ici/là**	ee-*see*/lah
Left/right	**à gauche/à droite**	a goash/a drwaht
Straight ahead	**tout droit**	too drwah
I'm American/ Canadian/British	**Je suis américain(e)/ canadien(e)/anglais(e)**	jhe sweez a-may-ree-*kehn*/can-ah-dee-*en*/ahn-glay (*glaise*)
Fill the tank (of a car), please	**Le plein, s'il vous plaît**	luh plan, seel voo *play*
I'm going to . . .	**Je vais à . . .**	jhe vay ah . . .
I want to get off at . . .	**Je voudrais descendre à . . .**	jhe voo-*dray* day-son-drah ah
I'm sick	**Je suis malade**	jhuh swee mal-*ahd*
airport	**l'aéroport**	lair-o-*por*
bank	**la banque**	lah bahnk
bridge	**pont**	pohn
bus station	**la gare routière**	lah gar roo-tee-*air*
bus stop	**l'arrêt de bus**	lah-*ray* duh boohss
by means of a bicycle	**en vélo/par bicyclette**	uh *vay*-low/par bee-see-*clet*
by means of a car	**en voiture**	ahn vwa-*toor*
cashier	**la caisse**	lah *kess*
cathedral	**cathédral**	ka-tay-*dral*
church	**église**	ay-*gleez*
dead end	**une impasse**	ewn am-*pass*
driver's license	**permis de conduire**	per-mee duh con-*dweer*
elevator	**l'ascenseur**	lah-sahn-*seuhr*
entrance (to a building or a city)	**une porte**	ewn port
exit (from a building or a freeway)	**une sortie**	ewn sor-*tee*
fortified castle or palace	**château**	sha-*tow*
garden	**jardin**	jhar-dehn

gasoline	du pétrol/de l'essence	duh pay-*troll*/de lay-*sahns*
ground floor	rez-de-chausée	ray-de-show-*say*
highway to . . .	la route pour	la root por
hospital	l'hôpital	low-pee-*tahl*
insurance	les assurances	lez ah-sur-*ahns*
luggage storage	consigne	kohn-*seen*-yuh
museum	le musée	luh mew-*zay*
no entry	sens interdit	sehns ahn-ter-*dee*
no smoking	défense de fumer	day-*fahns* de fu-may
on foot	à pied	ah pee-*ay*
one-day pass	ticket journalier	tee-kay jhoor-nall-ee-*ay*
one-way ticket	aller simple	ah-*lay sam*-pluh
police	la police	lah po-*lees*
rented car	voiture de location	vwa-*toor* de low-ka-see-on
round-trip ticket	aller-retour	ah-*lay*-re-*toor*
second floor	premier étage	prem-ee-*ehr* ay-*taj*
slow down	ralentir	rah-lahn-*teer*
store	magasin	luh ma-ga-*zehn*
street	rue	roo
suburb	banlieu/environs	bahn-*liew*/en-veer-*ohns*
subway	le Métro	le *may*-tro
telephone	le téléphone	luh tay-lay-*phone*
ticket	un billet	uh *bee*-yay
ticket office	vente de billets	vahnt duh bee-*yay*
toilets	les toilettes/les WC	lay twa-*lets*/les vay-*say*
tower	tour	toor

NECESSITIES

English	French	Pronunciation
I'd like . . .	Je voudrais . . .	jhe voo-*dray* . . .
a room	une chambre	ewn *shahm*-bruh
the key	la clé (la clef)	la *clay*
I'd like to buy . . .	Je voudrais acheter . . .	jhe voo-dray ahsh-*tay* . . .
aspirin	des aspirines/des aspros	deyz ahs-peer-*eens*/ deyz ahs-*prohs*
cigarettes	des cigarettes	ay see-ga-*ret*
condoms	des préservatifs	ay pray-ser-va-*teefs*
dictionary	un dictionnaire	uh deek-see-oh-*nare*
dress	une robe	ewn robe
envelopes	des envelopes	days ahn-veh-*lope*
gift (for someone)	un cadeau	uh kah-*doe*
handbag	un sac	uh sahk
hat	un chapeau	uh shah-*poh*
magazine	une revue	ewn reh-*vu*
map of the city	un plan de ville	unh plahn de *veel*
matches	des allumettes	dayz a-loo-*met*
necktie	une cravate	uh cra-*vaht*
newspaper	un journal	uh zhoor-*nahl*
phone card	une carte téléphonique	uh cart tay-lay-fone-*eek*
postcard	une carte postale	ewn carte pos-*tahl*

road map	une carte routière	ewn cart roo-tee-*air*
shirt	une chemise	ewn che-*meez*
shoes	des chaussures	day show-*suhr*
skirt	une jupe	ewn jhoop
soap	du savon	dew sah-*vohn*
socks	des chaussettes	day show-*set*
stamp	un timbre	uh *tam*-bruh
trousers	un pantalon	uh pan-tah-*lohn*
writing paper	du papier à lettres	dew pap-pee-*ay a let*-ruh
How much does it cost?	C'est combien?/ ça coûte combien?	say comb-bee-*ehn*?/ sah coot comb-bee-*ehn*?
That's expensive	C'est cher/chère	say share
That's inexpensive	C'est raisonnable/ C'est bon marché	say ray-son-*ahb*-bluh/ say bohn mar-*shay*
Do you take credit cards?	Est-ce que vous acceptez les cartes de credit?	es-kuh voo zaksep-*tay* lay kart duh creh-*dee*?

IN YOUR HOTEL

English	French	Pronunciation
Are taxes included?	Est-ce que les taxes sont comprises?	ess-keh lay taks son com-*preez*?
balcony	un balcon	uh bahl-cohn
bathtub	une baignoire	ewn bayn-*nwar*
bedroom	une chambre	ewn *shawm*-bruh
for two occupants	pour deux personnes	poor duh pair-sunn
hot and cold water	l'eau chaude et froide	low showed ay fwad
Is breakfast included?	Petit dé jeuner inclus?	peh-*tee* day-jheun-*ay* ehn-*klu*?
room	une chambre	ewn *shawm*-bruh
shower	une douche	ewn dooch
sink	un lavabo	uh la-va-*bow*
suite	une suite	ewn sweet
We're staying for . . .	On reste pour . . .	ohn rest poor . . .
days	jours	jhoor
with	avec	ah-*vek*
with air-conditioning	avec climatisation	ah-*vek* clee-mah-tee-zah-sion
without	sans	sahn
youth hostel	une auberge de jeunesse	oon oh-bayrge duh jhe-ness

IN THE RESTAURANT

English	French	Pronunciation
I would like . . .	Je voudrais	jhe voo-*dray*
to eat	manger	mahn-*jhay*
to order	commander	ko-mahn-*day*
Please give me . . .	Donnez-moi, s'il vous plaît . . .	doe-nay-*mwah*, seel voo play . . .
a bottle of . . .	une bouteille de . . .	ewn boo-*tay* duh . . .

English	French	Pronunciation
a cup of . . .	une tasse de . . .	ewn tass duh . . .
a glass of . . .	un verre de . . .	uh vair duh . . .
a plate of . . .	une assiette de . . .	ewn ass-ee-*et* duh . . .
an ashtray	un cendrier	uh sahn-dree-*ay*
bread	du pain	dew pan
breakfast	le petit déjeuner	luh puh-*tee* day-zhuh-*nay*
butter	du beurre	dew burr
check/bill	l'addition/la note	la-dee-see-*ohn*/la noat
Cheers!	à votre santé	*ah* vo-truh sahn-*tay*
Can I buy you a drink?	Puis-je vous payer un verre?	*pwee*-jhe voo pay-ay uh *vaihr*?
cocktail	un apéritif	uh ah-pay-ree-*teef*
coffee	du café	dew ka-*fay*
coffee—black	un café noir	uh ka-*fay* nwahr
coffee—with cream	un café crème	uh ka-*fay* krem
coffee—with milk	un café au lait	uh ka-*fay* o *lay*
coffee—decaf	un café décaféiné	uh ka-*fay* day-kah-fay-*nay*
coffee—espresso	un café express	uh ka-fay ek-*sprehss*
dinner	le dîner	luh dee-*nay*
fixed-price menu	un menu	uh may-new
fork	une fourchette	ewn four-*shet*
Is the tip/service included?	Est-ce que le service est compris?	ess-ke luh ser-vees eh com-*pree*?
knife	un couteau	uh koo-*toe*
napkin	une serviette	ewn sair-vee-*et*
pepper	du poivre	dew *pwah*-vruh
platter of the day	un plat du jour	uh plah dew jhoor
salt	du sel	dew sell
soup	une soupe/un potage	ewn soop/uh poh-*tahj*
spoon	une cuillère	ewn kwee-*air*
sugar	du sucre	dew *sook*-ruh
tea	un thé	uh tay
tea—with lemon	un thé au citron	uh tay o see-*tron*
tea—herbal	une tisane	ewn tee-*zahn*
Waiter!/Waitress!	Monsieur!/ Mademoiselle!	mun-*syuh*/mad-mwa-*zel*
wine list	une carte des vins	ewn cart day *van*
appetizer	une entrée	ewn en-*tray*
main course	un plat principal	uh plah pran-see-*pahl*
tip included	service compris	sehr-*vees* cohm-*preez*
wide-range sample of the chef's best efforts	menu dégustation	may-new *day*-gus-ta-see-on
drinks not included	boissons non comprises	bwa-*sons* no com-*preez*
cheese tray	plâteau de fromage	plah-*tow* duh fro-*mahj*

SHOPPING

English	French	Pronunciation
antiques store	un magasin d'antiquités	uh maga-*zan* don-tee-kee-*tay*
bakery	une boulangerie	ewn boo-lon-zhur-*ree*
bank	une banque	ewn bonk

bookstore	une librairie	ewn lee-brehr-*ree*
butcher	une boucherie	ewn boo-shehr-*ree*
cheese shop	une fromagerie	ewn fro-mazh-*ree*
dairy shop	une crémerie	ewn krem-*ree*
delicatessen	une charcuterie	ewn shar-koot-*ree*
department store	un grand magasin	uh grah maga-*zan*
drugstore	une pharmacie	ewn far-mah-*see*
fishmonger shop	une poissonerie	ewn pwas-son-*ree*
gift shop	un magasin de cadeaux	uh maga-*zan* duh ka-*doh*
greengrocer	un marchand de légumes	uh mar-*shon* duh lay-*goom*
hairdresser	un coiffeur	uh kwa-*fuhr*
market	un marché	uh mar-*shay*
pastry shop	une pâtisserie	ewn pa-tee-*sree*
supermarket	un supermarché	uh soo-pehr-mar-*shay*
tobacconist	un tabac	uh ta-*bah*
travel agency	une agence de voyages	ewn azh-ahns duh vwa-*yazh*

COLORS, SHAPES, SIZES, ATTRIBUTES

English	French	Pronunciation
black	noir	nwahr
blue	bleu	bleuh
brown	marron/brun	mar-*rohn*/bruhn
green	vert	vaihr
orange	orange	o-*rahnj*
pink	rose	rose
purple	violet	vee-o-*lay*
red	rouge	rooj
white	blanc	blahnk
yellow	jaune	jhone
bad	mauvais(e)	moh-*veh*
big	grand(e)	gron/gronde
closed	fermé(e)	fer-*meh*
down	en bas	on *bah*
early	de bonne heure	duh bon *urr*
enough	assez	as-*say*
far	loin	lwan
free, unoccupied	libre	*lee*-bruh
free, without charge	gratuit(e)	grah-*twee*/grah-*tweet*
good	bon/bonne	bon/bun
hot	chaud(e)	show/shoad
near	près	preh
open (as in "museum")	ouvert(e)	oo-*ver*/oo-*vert*
small	petit(e)	puh-*teel*/puh-*teet*
up	en haut	on *oh*
well	bien	byehn

NUMBERS & ORDINALS

English	French	Pronunciation
zero	zéro	zare-*oh*
one	un	uh

two	**deux**	duh
three	**trois**	twah
four	**quatre**	*kaht*-ruh
five	**cinq**	sank
six	**six**	seess
seven	**sept**	set
eight	**huit**	wheat
nine	**neuf**	nuf
ten	**dix**	deess
eleven	**onze**	ohnz
twelve	**douze**	dooz
thirteen	**treize**	trehz
fourteen	**quatorze**	kah-*torz*
fifteen	**quinze**	kanz
sixteen	**seize**	sez
seventeen	**dix-sept**	deez-*set*
eighteen	**dix-huit**	deez-*wheat*
nineteen	**dix-neuf**	deez-*nuf*
twenty	**vingt**	vehn
twenty-one	**vingt-et-un**	vehnt-ay-*uh*
twenty-two	**vingt-deux**	vehnt-*duh*
thirty	**trente**	trahnt
forty	**quarante**	ka-*rahnt*
fifty	**cinquante**	sang-*kahnt*
sixty	**soixante**	swa-*sahnt*
sixty-one	**soixante-et-un**	swa-*sahnt*-et-*uh*
seventy	**soixante-dix**	swa-sahnt-*deess*
seventy-one	**soixante-et-onze**	swa-sahnt-et-*ohnze*
eighty	**quatre-vingts**	kaht-ruh-*vehn*
eighty-one	**quatre-vingt-un**	kaht-ruh-vehn-*uh*
ninety	**quatre-vingt-dix**	kaht-ruh-venh-*deess*
ninety-one	**quatre-vingt-onze**	kaht-ruh-venh-*ohnze*
one hundred	**cent**	sahn
one thousand	**mille**	meel
one hundred thousand	**cent mille**	sahn meel
first	**premier**	*preh*-mee-ay
second	**deuxième**	*duhz*-zee-em
third	**troisième**	*twa*-zee-em
fourth	**quatrième**	kaht-ree-em
fifth	**cinquième**	*sank*-ee-em
sixth	**sixième**	*sees*-ee-em
seventh	**septième**	*set*-ee-em
eighth	**huitième**	*wheat*-ee-em
ninth	**neuvième**	*neuv*-ee-em
tenth	**dixième**	*dees*-ee-em
eleventh	**onzième**	*ohnz*-ee-em
twelfth	**douzième**	*dooz*-ee-em
thirteenth	**treizième**	*trehz*-ee-em
fourteenth	**quatorzième**	kah-*torz*-ee-em
twentieth	**vingtième**	*vehnt*-ee-em

thirtieth	**trentième**	*trahnt*-ee-em
one-hundredth	**centième**	*sant*-ee-em

THE CALENDAR

English	French	Pronunciation
January	**janvier**	*jhan*-vee-ay
February	**février**	*feh*-vree-ay
March	**mars**	marce
April	**avril**	a-*vreel*
May	**mai**	meh
June	**juin**	jhwehn
July	**juillet**	*jhwee*-ay
August	**août**	oot
September	**septembre**	sep-*tahm*-bruh
October	**octobre**	ok-*toh*-bruh
November	**novembre**	no-*vahm*-bruh
December	**decembre**	day-*sahm*-bruh
Sunday	**dimanche**	dee-*mahnsh*
Monday	**lundi**	*luhn*-dee
Tuesday	**mardi**	*mahr*-dee
Wednesday	**mercredi**	*mair*-kruh-dee
Thursday	**jeudi**	*jheu*-dee
Friday	**vendredi**	*vawn*-druh-dee
Saturday	**samedi**	*sahm*-dee
yesterday	**hier**	ee-*air*
today	**aujourd'hui**	o-jhord-*dwee*
this morning/ this afternoon	**ce matin/cet après-midi**	suh ma-*tan*/set ah-preh-mee-*dee*
tonight	**ce soir**	suh *swahr*
tomorrow	**demain**	de-*man*

2 Glossary of Basic Menu Terms

Note: To order any of these items from a waiter, simply preface the French-language name with the phrase *"Je voudrais"* (jhe voo-dray), which means, "I would like . . ." Also see the "In the Restaurant" entries above. *Bon appétit!*

MEATS

English	French	Pronunciation
beef stew	**du pot au feu**	dew poht o *fhe*
marinated beef braised with red wine and served with vegetables	**du boeuf à la mode**	dew bewf ah lah *mhowd*
brains	**de la cervelle**	duh lah ser-*vel*
chicken	**du poulet**	*dew poo*-lay
rolls of pounded and baked chicken, veal, or fish, often pike, usually served warm	**des quenelles**	day ke-*nelle*
chicken, stewed with mushrooms and wine	**du coq au vin**	dew cock o vhin

chicken wings	des ailes de poulet	dayz ehl duh poo-lay
frogs' legs	des cuisses de grenouilles	day cweess duh gre-*noo*-yuh
ham	du jambon	dew jham-bohn
haunch or leg of an animal, especially that of a lamb or sheep	du gigot	dew *jhi*-goh
kidneys	des rognons	day *row*-nyon
lamb	de l'agneau	duh lahn-*nyo*
lamb chop	une cotelette de l'agneau	ewn koh-te-lette duh lahn-*nyo*
rabbit	du lapin	dew lah-pan
sirloin	de l'aloyau	duh lahl-why-*yo*
steak	du bifteck	dew beef-*tek*
filet steak, embedded with fresh green or black peppercorns, flambéed and served with a cognac sauce	un steak au poivre	uh stake o *pwah*-vruh
double tenderloin, a long muscle from which filet steaks are cut	du chateaubriand	dew *sha*-tow-bree-ahn
stewed meat with white sauce, enriched with cream and eggs	de la blanquette	duh lah blon-*kette*
sweetbreads	des ris de veau	day *ree* duh voh
veal	du veau	dew *voh*

FISH

English	French	Pronunciation
fish (freshwater)	du poisson de rivière, or du poisson d'eau douce	dew pwah-sson duh ree-vee-*aire*, dew pwah-sson d'o *dooss*
fish (saltwater)	du poisson de mer	dew pwah-sson duh *mehr*
mediterranean fish soup or stew made with tomatoes, garlic, saffron, and olive oil	de la bouillabaisse	duh lah booh-ya-*besse*
eel	de l'anguille	duh lahn-*ghee*-uh
herring	du hareng	dew ahr-*rahn*
lobster	du homard	dew oh-*mahr*
mussels	des moules	day *moohl*
mussels in herb-flavored white wine with shallots	des moules marinières	day moohl mar-ee-nee-*air*
oysters	des huîtres	dayz hoo-*ee*-truhs
pike	du brochet	dew broh-*chay*

shrimp	des crevettes	day kreh-*vette*
smoked salmon	du saumon fumé	dew sow-mohn fu-*may*
tuna	du thon	dew tohn
trout	de la truite	duh lah tru-*eet*
wolffish, a Mediterranean sea bass	du loup de mer	dew loo duh *mehr*

SIDES/APPETIZERS

English	French	Pronunciation
butter	du beurre	dew bhuhr
bread	du pain	dew pan
goose liver	du foie gras	dew fwah grah
liver	du foie	dew fwah
potted and minced pork and pork by-products, prepared as a roughly chopped pâté	des rillettes	day ree-*yett*
rice	du riz	dew ree
snails	des escargots	dayz ess-car-*goh*

FRUITS/VEGETABLES

English	French	Pronunciation
cabbage	du choux	dew *shoe*
eggplant	de l'aubergine	duh loh-ber-*jheen*
grapefruit	un pamplemousse	uh *pahm*-pluh-moose
grapes	du raisin	dew ray-*zhan*
green beans	des haricots verts	day ahr-ee-coh *vaire*
green peas	des petits pois	day puh-tee *pwah*
lemon/lime	du citron/ du citron vert	dew cee-*tron*/dew cee-tron *vaire*
orange	une orange	ewn o-*rahnj*
pineapple	de l'ananas	duh lah-na-*nas*
potatoes	des pommes de terre	day puhm duh *tehr*
potatoes au gratin	des pommes de terre dauphinois	day puhm duh tehr doh-feen-wah
french fried potatoes	des pommes frites	day puhm *freet*
spinach	des épinards	dayz ay-pin-*ards*
strawberries	des fraises	day *frez*

SOUPS/SALADS

English	French	Pronunciation
cucumber salad	une salade de concombres	ewn sah-lahd duh con-*con*-bruh
fruit salad	une salade de fruit/ une macédoine de fruits	ewn sah-lahd duh *fwee*/ewn mah-say-doine duh fwee
green salad	une salade verte	ewn sah-lahd *vairt*
lettuce salad	une salade de laitue	ewn sah-lahd duh lay-tew
onion soup	de la soupe à l'oignon	duh lah soop ah low-*nyon*

salad, native to Nice, composed of lettuce, tuna, anchovies, capers, tomatoes, olives, olive oil, wine vinegar, and herbs	**une salade niçoise**	ewn sah-lahd nee-*swaz*
sauerkraut	**de la choucroute**	duh lah chew-*kroot*
vegetable soup with basil	**de la soupe au pistou**	duh lah soop oh pees-tou

BEVERAGES

English	French	Pronunciation
beer	**de la bière**	duh lah bee-*aire*
milk	**du lait**	dew *lay*
orange juice	**du jus d'orange**	dew joo d'or-*ahn*-jhe
water	**de l'eau**	duh lo
red wine	**du vin rouge**	dew vhin *rooj*
white wine	**du vin blanc**	dew vhin *blahn*
coffee	**un café**	uh ka-*fay*
coffee (black)	**un café noir**	uh ka-fay *nwahr*
coffee (with cream)	**un café crème**	uh ka-fay *krem*
coffee (with milk)	**un café au lait**	uh ka-fay o *lay*
coffee (decaf)	**un café décaféiné** (slang: **un déca**)	un ka-fay day-kah-fay-*nay* (uh *day*-kah)
coffee (espresso)	**un café espresso** (**un express**)	uh ka-fay e-*sprehss-o* (un ek-*sprehss*)
tea	**du thé**	dew *tay*
herbal tea	**une tisane**	ewn tee-*zahn*
drinks not included	**boissons non compris**	bwa-sons nohn com-*pree*

DESSERTS

English	French	Pronunciation
cake	**du gâteau**	dew gha-tow
cheese	**du fromage**	dew fro-*mahj*
thick custard dessert with a caramelized topping	**de la crème brulée**	duh lah krem bruh-*lay*
caramelized upside-down apple pie	**une tarte tatin**	ewn tart tah-*tihn*
tart	**une tarte**	ewn tart
vanilla ice cream	**de la glace à la vanille**	duh lah glass a lah vah-*nee*-yuh
fruit, especially cherries, cooked in batter	**du clafoutis**	dew kla-foo-*tee*

SPICES/CONDIMENTS

English	French	Pronunciation
mustard	**de la moutarde**	duh lah moo-*tard*-uh
pepper	**du poivre**	dew *pwah*-vruh
salt	**du sel**	dew *sel*
sour heavy cream	**de la crème fraîche**	duh lah krem *fresh*
sugar	**du sucre**	dew *sooh*-kruh

COOKING METHODS

English	French	Pronunciation
cooked in parchment paper	en papillotte	ehn pah-pee-*yott*
cooked over a wood fire minced and potted meat, seasoned and molded into a crock	cuit au feu de bois une terrine	kwee oh fhe duh *bwoi* ewn tair-*een*
puff pastry shell	vol-au-vent	vhol-o-*vhen*
a method of food preparation native to Lyon and its region that usually includes wine sauce accented with shredded and sautéed onions	à la lyonnaise	ah lah lee-ohn-*nehz*
in the style of Burgundy, usually with red wine, mushrooms, bacon, and onions	bourgignon/à la bourguignonne	boor-geehn-*nyon*/a lah boor-geeh-ny-*uhn*
method of cooking whereby anything (including fish, meat, fruits, or vegetables) is simmered in a reduction of its own fat or juices	un confit	uh khon-*feeh*

MISCELLANEOUS

English	French	Pronunciation
I'm a vegetarian	Je suis végétarien/ Je suis végétarienne	Jhe swee vay-jhay-tar-e-en/ Jhe swee vay-jhay-tar-e-*enne*
a fixed-price, pre-composed meal, usually offering a limited choice of the specific dishes that comprise it	le menu/le prix fixe/ la formule/la table d'hôte	le meh-noo/le pree-feex/ lah for-*muhl*/lah tah-bluh *doht*
tasting menu	le menu gastronomique/ le menu dégustation	le meh-noo gah-stroh-noh-meek/le meh-noo *day*-goo-stah-see-on

Index

See also Accommodations and Restaurant indexes, below.

RESTAURANTS

FROMMER'S® COMPLETE TRAVEL GUIDES

Alaska
Amsterdam
Argentina & Chile
Arizona
Atlanta
Australia
Austria
Bahamas
Barcelona, Madrid & Seville
Beijing
Belgium, Holland &
  Luxembourg
Bermuda
Boston
British Columbia & the
  Canadian Rockies
Budapest & the Best of Hungary
California
Canada
Cancún, Cozumel & the
  Yucatán
Cape Cod, Nantucket &
  Martha's Vineyard
Caribbean
Caribbean Cruises & Ports
  of Call
Caribbean Ports of Call
Carolinas & Georgia
Chicago
China
Colorado
Costa Rica
Denmark
Denver, Boulder & Colorado
  Springs
England
Europe

European Cruises & Ports of Call
Florida
France
Germany
Greece
Greek Islands
Hawaii
Hong Kong
Honolulu, Waikiki & Oahu
Ireland
Israel
Italy
Jamaica
Japan
Las Vegas
London
Los Angeles
Maryland & Delaware
Maui
Mexico
Montana & Wyoming
Montréal & Québec City
Munich & the Bavarian Alps
Nashville & Memphis
Nepal
New England
New Mexico
New Orleans
New York City
New Zealand
Nova Scotia, New Brunswick &
  Prince Edward Island
Oregon
Paris
Philadelphia & the Amish
  Country
Portugal

Prague & the Best of the Czech
  Republic
Provence & the Riviera
Puerto Rico
Rome
San Antonio & Austin
San Diego
San Francisco
Santa Fe, Taos & Albuquerque
Scandinavia
Scotland
Seattle & Portland
Shanghai
Singapore & Malaysia
South Africa
Southeast Asia
South Florida
South Pacific
Spain
Sweden
Switzerland
Texas
Thailand
Tokyo
Toronto
Tuscany & Umbria
USA
Utah
Vancouver & Victoria
Vermont, New Hampshire
  & Maine
Vienna & the Danube Valley
Virgin Islands
Virginia
Walt Disney World & Orlando
Washington, D.C.
Washington State

FROMMER'S® DOLLAR-A-DAY GUIDES

Australia from $50 a Day
California from $70 a Day
Caribbean from $70 a Day
England from $70 a Day
Europe from $70 a Day

Florida from $70 a Day
Hawaii from $70 a Day
Ireland from $60 a Day
Italy from $70 a Day
London from $85 a Day

New York from $80 a Day
Paris from $80 a Day
San Francisco from $60 a Day
Washington, D.C.,
  from $70 a Day

FROMMER'S® PORTABLE GUIDES

Acapulco, Ixtapa &
  Zihuatanejo
Alaska Cruises & Ports
  of Call
Amsterdam
Australia's Great Barrier Reef
Bahamas
Baja & Los Cabos
Berlin
Boston
California Wine Country
Charleston & Savannah
Chicago

Dublin
Hawaii: The Big Island
Hong Kong
Houston
Las Vegas
London
Los Angeles
Maine Coast
Maui
Miami
New Orleans
New York City
Paris

Phoenix & Scottsdale
Portland
Puerto Rico
Puerto Vallarta, Manzanillo &
  Guadalajara
San Diego
San Francisco
Seattle
Sydney
Tampa & St. Petersburg
Vancouver
Venice
Washington, D.C.

FROMMER'S® NATIONAL PARK GUIDES

Family Vacations in the
  National Parks
Grand Canyon

National Parks of the American
  West
Rocky Mountain
Yellowstone & Grand Teton

Yosemite & Sequoia/
  Kings Canyon
Zion & Bryce Canyon

FROMMER'S® MEMORABLE WALKS

Chicago
London

New York
Paris

San Francisco
Washington, D.C.

FROMMER'S® GREAT OUTDOOR GUIDES

Arizona & New Mexico
New England

Northern California
Southern California & Baja

Southern New England
Vermont & New Hampshire

FROMMER'S® BORN TO SHOP GUIDES

Born to Shop: France
Born to Shop: Hong Kong,
   Shanghai & Beijing

Born to Shop: Italy
Born to Shop: London

Born to Shop: New York
Born to Shop: Paris

FROMMER'S® IRREVERENT GUIDES

Amsterdam
Boston
Chicago
Las Vegas
London

Los Angeles
Manhattan
New Orleans
Paris
San Francisco

Seattle & Portland
Vancouver
Walt Disney World
Washington, D.C.

FROMMER'S® BEST-LOVED DRIVING TOURS

America
Britain
California
Florida

France
Germany
Ireland
Italy

New England
Scotland
Spain
Western Europe

THE UNOFFICIAL GUIDES®

Bed & Breakfasts in California
Bed & Breakfasts in
   New England
Bed & Breakfasts in the
   Northwest
Bed & Breakfasts in Southeast
Beyond Disney
Branson, Missouri
California with Kids
Chicago
Cruises
Disneyland
Florida with Kids

Golf Vacations in the
   Eastern U.S.
The Great Smoky &
   Blue Ridge Mountains
Inside Disney
Hawaii
Las Vegas
London
Mid-Atlantic with Kids
Mini Las Vegas
Mini-Mickey
New England with Kids

New Orleans
New York City
Paris
San Francisco
Skiing in the West
Southeast with Kids
Walt Disney World
Walt Disney World for
   Grown-ups
Walt Disney World for Kids
Washington, D.C.
World's Best Diving Vacations

SPECIAL-INTEREST TITLES

Frommer's Britain's Best Bed & Breakfasts and
   Country Inns
Frommer's France's Best Bed & Breakfasts and
   Country Inns
Frommer's Italy's Best Bed & Breakfasts and
   Country Inns
Frommer's Caribbean Hideaways
Frommer's Adventure Guide to Australia &
   New Zealand
Frommer's Adventure Guide to Central America
Frommer's Adventure Guide to India & Pakistan
Frommer's Adventure Guide to South America
Frommer's Adventure Guide to Southeast Asia
Frommer's Adventure Guide to Southern Africa
Frommer's Gay & Lesbian Europe
Frommer's Exploring America by RV
Hanging Out in England

Hanging Out in Europe
Hanging Out in France
Hanging Out in Ireland
Hanging Out in Italy
Hanging Out in Spain
Israel Past & Present
Frommer's The Moon
Frommer's New York City with Kids
The New York Times' Guide to Unforgettable
   Weekends
Places Rated Almanac
Retirement Places Rated
Frommer's Road Atlas Britain
Frommer's Road Atlas Europe
Frommer's Washington, D.C., with Kids
Frommer's What the Airlines Never Tell You